GREAT EVENTS FROM HISTORY

Great Events from History

82,977

Ancient and Medieval Series

Volume 1
4000 - 1 B.C.

Edited by
FRANK N. MAGILL

Associate Editor
E. G. Weltin

SALEM PRESS, Incorporated
Englewood Cliffs, New Jersey

LIBRARY OF CONGRESS CATALOG CARD NUMBER:
72-86347

FIRST EDITION
Third Printing

Library of Congress Cataloging in Publication Data

Magill, Frank Northen, 1907-
　Great events from history: Ancient and medieval
series. Edited by Frank N. Magill. Associate editor:
E. G. Weltin. Englewood Cliffs, N.J., Salem Press
[1972]
　　3v. 24 cm.

　Includes bibliographies.
　CONTENTS: v. 1. 4000-1 B.C.—v. 2. A.D. 1-
950.—v. 3. 951-1500.
　1. History, Ancient. 2. Middle Ages—History.
I. Title　　　REF

D59.M26　　909'.09'812　　72-86347
　　　　　　　　　　　　　　MARC

PRINTED IN THE UNITED STATES OF AMERICA

PREFACE

The thread of civilization is slender and unsubstantial. Man's destiny is neither unalterably bound in with his previous experience nor necessarily controlled by the momentum of his past. On the contrary, the direction of his forward progress may be altered by a single event, such as a battle (Waterloo, Gettysburg), a political occurrence (election of Hitler as German Chancellor), a technical application (development of the steam engine), an intellectual happening (publication of a book such as ON THE ORIGIN OF SPECIES), or even a cultural thrust (influence of the Puritan ethic in Colonial America).

Indeed, change is man's renewal within himself, his growth process, and it is through our study of the past and how men and events have altered it that we come to a recognition of history as a logical continuum. The past has been a slave to no pattern but, rather, has responded to those internal stresses and external forces that have resulted from the strivings, the achievements, the clashing of wills among human beings throughout time. Examination of the cumulative results is a pleasure and satisfaction that need not be limited to the scholar or the professional historian.

GREAT EVENTS FROM HISTORY comprises a nine-volume set dealing with more than one thousand events from history. The articles are presented in three groups: Ancient and Medieval events, three volumes; Modern European events, three volumes; and events from American history, three volumes. Each article consists of four sections: (1) Quick reference material at the beginning showing type of event, time, locale, and principal personages involved if applicable; (2) Summary of Event, a "journalistic" account of the occurrence describing the basic facts of what took place and some of the causes and effects. (3) Pertinent Literature, wherein two original essay-reviews of scholarly works written about the event are presented. The works reviewed are usually books though sometimes scholarly articles are reported on instead. An effort has been made to select for review works of divergent viewpoints, especially if the event under consideration is controversial; and (4) Additional Recommended Reading, which lists and annotates several other works that the student or researcher might profitably examine if he is interested in an in-depth study of the event. The critical evaluations presented in Items (2) and (3) provide a review of the immediate and long-range effects of an occurrence and should enable the reader to view objectively the forces that sparked the event.

The primary objective of the editors has been to present an individual discussion and analysis of more than one thousand significant happenings whose consequences have changed the course of history in the Western world. Events considered in addition to the conventional political and military groups include those dealing with intellectual, scientific, literary, sociological, and cultural achievements as well as various other civilizing forces. A major purpose also has been to make available, along with the narrative summaries of the occurrences themselves, scholarly evaluations of representative literature dealing with the events.

The report of an event itself, usually about eight hundred words in length, uses the historical techniques of tracing cause and effect, of evaluating and interpreting facts as the summary unfolds. The contributing professors and scholars have brought their special knowledge and skill to the task of writing the capsule summaries of events and the six-hundred-word individual evaluations of the two thousand appropriate works that are reviewed. Each contributor has made his articles accurate in reporting facts and ideas, scholarly but not dull, clear and not technical without cause, explanatory as an account of the event covered and as a presentation of the central ideas of the books being reviewed.

Events are presented in chronological order and this particular series, the Ancient and Medieval section containing 336 events, could have begun at any number of beginnings. It actually starts about 4000 B.C. with the domestication of the horse, an occurrence that removed certain physical burdens from the back of man and gave him time to begin the slow process of philosophical self-examination, with a critical look at the world and his relationship thereto. The origin of writing is another early event of singular importance, for it eliminated time and proximity as major factors in communication. The invention of bronze heralded the end of the Stone Age and enabled man to develop tools of some sophistication which could be used to improve his lot economically and, alas, to fight battles more efficiently. Notice is also taken of an early literary innovation, for in examining the Gilgamesh Epic one is reminded that Gilgamesh was the first literary hero in Western history.

Man realized early that his community would operate more efficiently if certain restraints were imposed on the behavior of individuals for the benefit of all. Thus Hammurabi's Babylonian legal code came into being as an early attempt to codify standards of behavior and establish punishments for deviations therefrom.

Bronze was expensive because its ingredients were not plentiful. When men discovered how to use iron, which was plentiful, in ways similar to the rarer metals, a new "industrial" age began which meant plentiful agricultural implements and a consequent rise in the standard of living for those who wished to work.

About 1250 B.C., Israel's covenant with Yahweh through Moses solidified the ethnic and religious unity of a people, resulting in the wellspring from which most Western religious, moral, and cultural tenets have been derived.

Through the ILIAD the enigmatic figure of "Homer" stands astride the literary path leading from oral tradition to moving epic poetry set down and repeated to the accompaniment of drum and lyre. To Homer and Hesiod the West is indebted for much of its early poetic inspiration.

About the same time, a more mundane affair evolved which greatly stimulated trade and demolished forever the clumsy concept of barter as the only means of exchanging goods. The invention of coinage was among the most important events in early trade and communication because it gave the trader confidence that he could dispose of his goods in foreign markets at some specific value whereas previously he had been at the mercy of those who, for example, might want his grain but had only lumber to barter.

After several millenniums the "philosophical self-examination" mentioned above began to bear fruit in the early stirrings of the discipline that was to become philosophy. Thales of Miletus is traditionally credited with being the first to promulgate a nonmythological approach to the origin and nature of our corner of the universe. The idea of such study flourished in his students and those who followed them so that within two centuries the concept had flowered into the lofty level of thought represented in the ideas advanced by Socrates, Plato, Aristotle, and others. The fact that abstract thought which, unlike a battle or the Olympic Games, doesn't *do* anything, could attract the full attention of the finest minds of the time, is a great tribute to the species.

Many other instances of events that exerted enormous influence on the progress of civilization could be cited from the Ancient and Medieval Series. One such event would be the passage of the Canuleian Law which rescinded the ban on intermarriage between patrician and plebeian, an act highly gratifying to the Roman lower classes. Other events with a high level of historical interest are the victorious campaigns of Alexander the Great, whose short life is unmatched in military achievements; or the composition of the AENEID, a majestic literary work that inspired an entire race of people to excel; or the absolutely immeasurable impact of the legacy of Jesus Christ, implemented by the conversion of Constantine in 312 and the later building of cathedrals and monasteries all over Europe; or the establishment of Alcuin's palace school which attracted the greatest scholars of the day to the Court of Charlemagne; or the thirteenth century developments in navigation which led to continental discoveries and world-wide trade; or the invention of movable type printing which put a healthy end to the withholding of knowledge from the masses and for the first time in history made the wide dissemination of information relatively easy; or the magnificent example of the nobility of the human spirit exhibited by Constantine XI as he doffed his royal robes and joined his lowly foot soldiers in the hopeless defense to the death of his thousand-year-old city against the overwhelming assault of the Turks; or hundreds of other striking examples of man's nobility, his brutality, his curiosity about the unknown, his inventiveness, his greed, his suspicions, his loyalty to his friends, and above all his scorn for the *status quo*. To many readers the collective story is irresistible.

The preparation of this nine-volume work has required the active assistance of some one hundred fifty history professors and scholars from more than fifty campuses throughout the United States. The names and academic affiliations of the sixty who contributed to the Ancient and Medieval Series appear elsewhere in this volume. To these dedicated individuals I express my sincere thanks. Similar sentiments are due the associate editors and researchers whose assistance in bringing this work to completion was invaluable. I wish especially to thank Mr. David W. Fox for his two years of tireless contribution to this aspect of the work.

I am certain that all staff members share my hope that this work will prove useful and rewarding to students, teachers, librarians, researchers, and those resolute readers who long ago decided that "the collective story is irresistible."

FRANK N. MAGILL

INTRODUCTION

The term "great" by necessity involves one in all sorts of value judgments bound to be colored by one's peculiar philosophy of history. While an event may be considered "great" in its own splendid isolation, such an evaluation rests ultimately on such a highly subjective individualistic commitment that it is not likely to be of much value to general readers. More safely, and more usefully, an event may be termed "great" if the general concensus of later history tends to view it as influential or important in an extended context. Whether history makes itself or whether historians make history is a question, however, best left to philosophers at this point. Considering the purpose of these volumes and their intended audiences, the term "great" is taken to mean important in the development of Western values, their preservation and propagation.

Any attempt to extract some three-hundred fifty events as "great" and representative from the wide fields of ancient and medieval history is a task inviting controversy. In a case such as this, one is asked to evaluate all kinds of facts: political, technological, theological, sociological, philosophical, and economic, all of which are woven inextricably into the complicated pattern of unconscionably long eras. Under the circumstances, many readers are bound to decry the omission or inclusion of certain historical happenings about which they entertain definite views. For this reason, it seems judicious to state at the outset that events of "Oriental" ancient history which have no clear or heavy bearing on Western history are purposely omitted.

One of the unique difficulties involved in choosing significant events from ancient history, and to a large extent from medieval, stems from the fact that often, it appears, the ancient historian, more than his colleagues dealing with later periods, is impelled toward a pursuit of intellectual history. Apart from archaeological remains, ideas constitute the greatest part of the legacy from ancient times, ideas which are expressed in still extant writings from that period. Consequently there appears by necessity in these volumes what might seem to historians of later periods to be an excessive amount of literary compositions. Incidents usually termed "great" in relation to the founding of viable institutions are, for example, relatively scarce in ancient history in comparison to the medieval age, which was more prolific in the establishment of permanent institutions basic to the Western world. Most of the direct, concrete, institutional modern links with the ancient world, it appears, are found in the Jewish and Christian orbit.

In part, the choice of events has been dictated by the conviction that the ancient historian generally has been too prone to emphasize his period as an isolated era that comes to some mysterious ideological close with Constantine or to some sudden political end with the mythical "fall of Rome" in 476. These indefensible positions, arising from overspecialization or overdedication, slight an appreciation of the Christian contribution which, historically, probably should be viewed as the most significant legacy of Hellenistic and Roman history. It is hoped that the inclusion in these volumes of a generous amount of religious events, both Jewish and Christian, will help make this series more than usual an accurate and useful reflection of the composite Western tradition which rests so squarely on both a Greco-Roman and a Judeo-Christian foundation. If this view is correct, the development of Papal decretals is more important than the enunciation of Pericles' Funeral Oration, however cherished conventional periodization of history has made that masterpiece.

Assuming that Western history is a continuity from ancient times through the catalyst of Christianity with its Jewish background, the Middle Ages, far from being disparaged, must be considered an imposing period of inventive history when the West constructed its basic institutions to enshrine its newly-distilled soul. Just as medieval banking presumes a far more sophisticated knowledge and creativity than the primitive economic exchange of the ancient world so, too, the Gothic cathedral is a daring architectural experiment compared to the static post-and-lintel structure of Greek temples, however magnificent the Parthenon may be in conception and execution.

The arrangement of the events has been made purposely chronological rather than alphabetical so that these volumes will serve as something more than an encyclopedic reference. The chronological juxtaposition of events quite often proves surprisingly enlightening as one discovers on proximate pages that isolated happenings are associated in time. In this way, a religious affair may be thrown, for example, in relief against a contemporary scientific development, or an event in Greek history set in chronological contrast with a Jewish episode.

Some defense should be made for what must appear to many as totally arbitrary dates assigned to the events. "Events" in ancient history are often more "topics" than isolated happenings; they tend to be developments often extending over hundreds or even thousands of years. To establish some workable chronology, a certain stage or distinct facet of a development often had to be chosen as a point around which the major "event" itself could be fixed and described. Arbitrariness is inevitable. Finally, it appears useful to remind ourselves that dates in ancient history are often quite controversial and in a state of flux perpetuated by the positions of different scholarly authorities.

It is axiomatic throughout that the nature and arrangement of these volumes imposes, by design, an artificial, disjunctive, isolated character on the course of history, making it impossible to deal in a sustained developmental way with any event, to relate it ideologically to any large extent with associated events, or to assess the importance of any happening in relation to others.

The matter of the interpretations appended to each event deserves some comment. In order to throw an event into high relief, efforts were made to obtain different, and preferably contrasting, interpretations to be found in the scholarly literature built up around the happening under consideration. Unfortunately, many matters in ancient history probably do not stand in as sharp a contrast as do those of "modern times," where relevancy supposedly is more readily apparent and biases definitely more virulent. One might say that only much of what was "best" or most useful in ancient times has been preserved over the years and is, therefore, not likely to be viewed in extremes. Moreover, the format of these volumes, limiting the interpretations to those available in English, has considerably curtailed the scope of interpretative material, much of which, in the fields of ancient and medieval history, is available only in foreign languages, generally German or French. The short bibliographies at the conclusion of each contribution also have been restricted to literature in English.

The editor wishes to thank the contributors to these volumes, writers all too few, especially in the field of ancient history, both secular and religious. Appreciation should also be expressed to Mr. James Turner, a graduate student of Washington University's history department, whose time and suggestions proved valuable in the preparation of these volumes.

E. G. WELTIN
Professor of History
Washington University

LIST OF EVENTS IN VOLUME ONE
Ancient and Medieval Series

MEMBERS OF THE WRITING STAFF
Ancient and Medieval Series

	GRADUATE SCHOOL	ACADEMIC AFFILIATION
Martin J. Baron M.A.	Columbia University	Columbia University
Ludovico Borgo Ph. D.	Harvard University	Brandeis University
Mortimer Chambers Ph. D.	Harvard University	University of California at Los Angeles
Patricia G. Chandler Ph. D.	Louisiana State University	State University of New York at Plattsburg
Carl W. Conrad Ph. D.	Harvard University	Washington University
M. Joseph Costelloe Ph. D.	The Johns Hopkins University	Creighton University
Gary A. Crump Ph. D.	University of Illinois	Louisiana State University
John Francis Daly M.S.	Saint Louis University	Saint Louis University
Lowrie John Daly Ph. D.	University of Toronto	Saint Louis University

Phillip H. De Lacy Ph. D.	Princeton University	University of Pennsylvania
Samuel K. Eddy Ph. D.	University of Michigan	Syracuse University
Sarah M. Farley Ph. D.	University of Edinburgh	Southwest Missouri State College
Everett Ferguson Ph. D.	Harvard University	Abilene Christian College
Chauncey E. Finch Ph. D.	University of Illinois	Saint Louis University
James H. Forse Ph. D.	University of Illinois	Bowling Green State University
William G. Haag Ph. D.	University of Michigan	Louisiana State University
Willine S. Hardy Ph. D.	Louisiana State University	University of Illinois
John J. Healy M.A.	Indiana University	Saint Joseph Seminary
Richard H. Helmholz Ph. D.	University of California at Berkeley	Washington University
Kevin Herbert Ph. D.	Harvard University	Washington University
Paul J. Hopper Ph. D.	University of Texas	Washington University
Robert Jaques Ph. D.	University of Toronto	Emory and Henry College

Mary Evelyn Jegen Ph. D.	Saint Louis University	University of Dayton
G. Burke Johnston Ph. D.	Columbia University	Virginia Polytechnic Institute and State University
Edward P. Keleher Ph. D.	Saint Louis University	Purdue University at Calumet
Dorothy Kinsella Ph. D.	Saint Louis University	College of Saint Francis
Fred B. Kniffen Ph. D.	University of California at Berkeley	Louisiana State University
Edgar M. Krenz Ph. D.	Washington University	Concordia Seminary
Frances R. Lipp Ph. D.	Yale University	Washington University
Elizabeth J. Lipscomb Ph. D.	Harvard University	Virginia Highlands Community College
Joseph A. McCallin Ph. D.	Saint Louis University	Saint Louis University
Daniel D. McGarry Ph. D.	University of California at Berkeley	Saint Louis University
John F. McGovern Ph. D.	University of Wisconsin at Milwaukee	University of Wisconsin at Milwaukee
James P. McNab Ph. D.	Duke University	Virginia Polytechnic Institute and State University
Roger B. McShane Ph. D.	University of Illinois	Trinity University

Abraham J. Malherbe Ph. D.	Harvard University	Abilene Christian College
Lynewood F. Martin Ph. D.	Saint Louis University	Lindenwood College
George E. O'Keefe M.A.	Saint Louis University	Saint Louis University
Zola M. Packman Ph. D.	Yale University	Washington University
George M. Pepe Ph. D.	Princeton University	Washington University
M. Anne Pernoud Ph. D.	Saint Louis University	Meramee Community College
R. M. Rentner M.A.	Saint Louis University	Saint Louis University
Robert Clive Roach Ph. D.	Saint Louis University	Saint Louis University
Carl F. Rohne Ph. D.	University of Southern California	Southern Methodist University
Joseph J. Romano Ph. D.	Bryn Mawr College	Cabrini College
Joseph R. Rosenbloom D.H.L.	Hebrew Union College	Washington University
John S. Scarborough Ph. D.	University of Illinois	University of Kentucky
Raymond H. Schmandt Ph. D.	University of Michigan	Saint Joseph College
David Sider Ph. D.	Columbia University	University of North Carolina

David Charles Smith Ph. D.	Yale University	Bates College
Norris K. Smith Ph. D.	Columbia University	Washington University
C. Leo Sweeney Ph. D.	University of Toronto	Creighton University
Mitchell H. Taibleson Ph. D.	University of Chicago	Washington University
James A. Turner M.A.	Washington University	Washington University
Joseph M. Victor Ph. D.	Columbia University	Syracuse University
Carl A. Volz Ph. D.	Fordham University	Concordia Seminary
J. A. Wahl Ph. D.	Saint Louis University	Saint Jerome's College
E. G. Weltin Ph. D.	University of Illinois	Washington University
Richard J. Wurtz M.A.	University of Kansas	Southern Illinois University
Lowell H. Zuck Ph. D.	Yale University	Eden Seminary

INITIALS IDENTIFYING CONTRIBUTORS
OF SIGNED ARTICLES

A.J.M.	Abraham J. Malherbe	*J.P.M.*	James P. McNab
C.A.V.	Carl A. Volz	*J.R.R.*	Joseph R. Rosenbloom
C.E.F.	Chauncey E. Finch	*J.S.S.*	John S. Scarborough
C.F.R	Carl F. Rohne	*K.H.*	Kevin Herbert
C.L.S.	C. Leo Sweeney	*L.B.*	Ludovico Borgo
C.W.C.	Carl W. Conrad	*L.F.M.*	Lynewood F. Martin
D.C.S.	David Charles Smith	*L.H.Z.*	Lowell H. Zuck
D.D.M.	Daniel D. McGarry	*L.J.D.*	Lowrie John Daly
D.K.	Dorothy Kinsella	*M.A.P.*	M. Anne Pernoud
D.S.	David Sider	*M.C.*	Mortimer Chambers
E.F.	Everett Ferguson	*M.E.J.*	Mary Evelyn Jegen
E.G.W.	E. G. Weltin	*M.H.T.*	Mitchell H. Taibleson
E.J.L.	Elizabeth J. Lipscomb	*M.J.B.*	Martin J. Baron
E.M.K.	Edgar M. Krenz	*M.J.C.*	M. Joseph Costelloe
E.P.K.	Edward P. Keleher	*N.K.S.*	Norris K. Smith
F.B.K.	Fred B. Kniffen	*P.G.C.*	Patricia G. Chandler
F.R.L.	Frances R. Lipp	*P.H.D.*	Phillip H. De Lacy
G.A.C.	Gary A. Crump	*P.J.H.*	Paul J. Hopper
G.B.J.	G. Burke Johnston	*R.B.M.*	Roger B. McShane
G.E.O.	George E. O'Keefe	*R.C.R.*	Robert Clive Roach
G.M.P.	George M. Pepe	*R.H.H.*	Richard H. Helmholz
J.A.M.	Joseph A. McCallin	*R.H.S.*	Raymond H. Schmandt
J.A.T.	James A. Turner	*R.J.*	Robert Jaques
J.A.W.	J. A. Wahl	*R.J.W.*	Richard J. Wurtz
J.F.D.	John Francis Daly	*R.M.R.*	R. M. Rentner
J.F.M.	John F. McGovern	*S.K.E.*	Samuel K. Eddy
J.H.F.	James H. Forse	*S.M.F.*	Sarah M. Farley
J.J.H.	John J. Healy	*W.G.H.*	William G. Haag
J.J.R.	Joseph J. Romano	*W.S.H.*	Willine S. Hardy
J.M.V.	Joseph M. Victor	*Z.M.P.*	Zola M. Packman

GREAT EVENTS FROM HISTORY

DOMESTICATION OF THE HORSE

Type of event: Sociological: advance in transportation
Time: c. 4000 B.C.
Locale: West-central Asia

Summary of Event

Strangely enough, the horse was among the last important animals to be tamed. While it is not now possible to pinpoint the time when horses were first domesticated, a reasonably close estimate can be made. As long ago as the Solutrean period of the Old Stone Age, perhaps nearly twenty thousand years ago, European wild horses were hunted so eagerly as big game that they were apparently brought to extinction in parts of Europe. There is no evidence that any efforts were then made to tame these animals despite their appearance in primitive statuary and cave paintings.

For tens of thousands of years the homeland of the true horse was the north European plains and the western Asiatic steppes. Other forms of equids were distributed throughout the grasslands of Asia and Africa, but since there was no significant overlapping of their ranges, distinct species evolved; the hemionids, such as the onager, inhabited southwest Asia, the true asses lived in north Africa, and the zebras claimed east and south Africa.

Two types of wild horses survived in the Old World. One of these, known as Przewalski's horse, evolved in Mongolia (where wild survivors may

still exist) but spread into southwest Asia and eastern European grasslands after the retreat of the last of the Pleistocene ice. Specimens may still be seen in modern zoölogical gardens in Europe and America. Przewalski's horse is a heavily built animal with sturdy short legs; its head is large and mulish in appearance, and it stands about thirteen hands high.

The other type of horse is called the "tarpan." It evolved in south Russia, although it was known archaeologically and historically to central Sweden and the North Sea coast. It survived in the Ukraine until the mid-nineteenth century. Generally smaller than the Mongolian wild horse, the tarpan had a stiff upright mane and a dark stripe extending from mane to tail on its mouse-gray body. It was systematically hunted to extinction by Ukrainians because wild stallions enticed domesticated mares away from the farms.

Present-day evidence strongly suggests that tarpan stock was the principal contributor to the modern domesticated horse, although some authorities consider that Przewalski's horse is the dominant strain. Since these two horse ranges overlapped in eastern Europe and Turkestan, it is possible that the modern horse is de-

1

scended from a mixture of the two races. Recent genetic studies, however, have established that Przewalski's horse has a different chromosome number $(2n = 66)$ from all races of modern horses $(2n = 64)$. This fact strengthens the claim for the tarpan contribution being the greater of the two. It is not now possible of course to resolve this question by checking the chromosome number of the extinct tarpan. All present-day Mongolian ponies have come from the West. There is still debate whether the heavy Western European draft horse was derived from tarpan stock or from some yet undiscovered large race. A heavy-boned Pleistocene horse has been found in glacial deposits in Western Europe, but it is known neither archaeologically nor historically. Horse bones do not show any singular osteological changes concomitant with domestication as do the horns of sheep, goats, and cattle.

Although the first historical writings which mention horses as being usefully employed by men date from about 2000 B.C., it seems safe to infer that the horse had already been domesticated for at least two millenia by that time. After 2000 B.C., there are numerous literary references to the horse in addition to various representations in statuary and paintings. An educated guess for the beginnings of horse domestication is a date about 4000 B.C.

On the basis of the distribution of the true horse six thousand years ago, it appears that the area where domestication was first tried was Turkestan in central Asia. Perhaps around 3000 B.C. small numbers of domesticated horses diffused to eastern and north-central Europe. About the same time

the same type of horse appeared in the Iranian plateau, and it appeared a little later in Bronze Age cultures of the Near East.

The first application of the horse as an aid to mankind was in the dubious role of chariot-puller. The chariot, developed from the two-wheeled cart originally drawn by cattle, had obvious strategic value in giving greater mobility to a single warrior. When this vehicle was introduced into Egypt by the Hyksos in 1788 B.C., the accompanying horses were almost certainly of Asian origin but of tarpan ancestry. They were rather large in size but delicate in head and body-build and bay or black in color. These animals were the progenitors of the Nubian horse, the strain from which the Barb of Morocco was derived and whose genes may still be viable in some modern thoroughbreds, hunters, remounts, and plow horses. The chariot was in use in Greece in 1000 B.C. but survived in Caesar's Rome mainly for ceremonial occasions and for races.

Riding astride the horse may have begun in Turkestan before 3000 B.C. Cavalry, an integral part of the Greek fighting force by 800 B.C., became the dominating part of the Roman fighting machine. Continuing through feudal times in Europe until the beginning of World War II, the development of several new breeds of horses was influenced by military needs.

The horse that has served man economically in so many fundamental ways began its career as a luxury item drawing chariots for heroes. It seems destined to draw to an end its services to mankind by surviving again as a luxury item for the affluent.

Domestication of the Horse

Pertinent Literature

Zeuner, Frederick D. *A History of Domesticated Animals.* London: Hutchinson and Co., Ltd. 1963.

Basic literature about the domestication of animals is invariably in German, and this book by Zeuner contains the only good text of the subject in English. It is comprehensive and represents the accumulated information on domestication that Zeuner has been amassing for years. The chapters on the origins and evolution of domestication are the first definitive statements on the subject since Eduard Hahn's *Die Haustiere,* which appeared in 1896. Zeuner devotes a chapter to the horse in a section appropriately entitled "mammals domesticated primarily for transport and labour by secondary nomads." The onager, ass, and mule are treated in separate chapters.

Zeuner discusses the distribution of the wild horse over the open lands of the Old World during the closing stages of the Pleistocene or Ice Age. Zeuner does not concern himself with the early history of the horse, for this paleontological story is more than adequately covered by Simpson's work described below. Zeuner does show that the geographic location of the surviving horses in Europe and Asia can be informative in deciding which wild horses gave rise to modern domesticates.

Zeuner properly ventilates the moot question of the existence of a Western European wild heavy horse, a race that may have given rise to the modern Clydesdales, Shires, and their kin. Although bones of Ice Age wild heavy horses have been found in Western Europe there are no connections between these and the draft animals used several thousand years later. Apparently, there is nothing beyond circumstantial evidence to suggest a connection.

Zeuner chooses to consider the domesticated horse to be almost entirely derived from tarpan stock. He believes that this domesticated animal eventually displaced or absorbed Przewalski's horse even in Inner Mongolia. When horses began to be diffused throughout the Old World, it was tarpan stock that formed the foundation for all breeding stocks in the various areas, except, perhaps, in China where Przewalski's horse was domesticated locally under stimulus from the West.

The concluding sections of this chapter give detailed analyses of the history of the later horse domestication, dispersal, and employment in the Middle East, Europe, north Africa, India, and China.

Simpson, George Gaylord. *Horses: The Story of the Horse Family in the Modern World and Through Sixty Million Years of History.* New York: Oxford University Press, 1951.

The horse family has been of interest to mankind for several centuries. Man's most revered friend after the dog, the horse has inspired some of the world's greatest literature and has brought about great events in history through its presence. To write a definitive history of the subject is impossible, although many excellent specialized treatises are available. The author of this relatively small volume has been associated for several decades with recent developments in the fossil story of the horse and in changes in the role of the horse in modern culture. After twenty years his study is still the authoritative comprehensive treatise.

The book is divided into three main sections: Living Horses; the Lineage of the Horse; and Horses and Evolution. Since Simpson is primarily a vertebrate paleontologist, the last two parts bear the stamp of authority, but the book is written more for the interested layman than the technically critical expert. The first section includes discussion of the wild equids and the horse in history.

Regarding modern domesticates, Simpson supports the view that several wild races gave rise to local domesticated forms in separate areas. He considers that domestication of the horse was relatively easy once the idea was grasped. Even the onager was domesticated or tamed in Mesopotamia before the true horse displaced it, and after a few domesticated breeds were developed in parts of Europe and southwest Asia, they interbred so freely that a fairly uniform type emerged. This development precludes the tracing of modern breeds to the original wild races.

Simpson departs from Zeuner in suggesting that domestication of the horse did not take place earlier than 2500 B.C. Since the earliest historical accounts in Mesopotamia and China date from about 2000 B.C., Simpson concludes that development was rapid before that time, although other authorities using the same evidence argue for a long slow development before 2000 B.C.

Simpson believes, along with most scholars, that the horse's greatest influence on history has been in warfare. Classic events such as the Battle of Poitiers in A.D. 732 when Charles Martel defeated the Saracen invaders, and the siege of Tenochtitlan by the Spaniards in 1521, may well have been changed by the presence of horses. But Simpson displays his comprehensive knowledge more by discussion of various breeds, and the range and influence of ancient and recent imports into America. — *F.B.K.*

Additional Recommended Reading

Lydekker, R. *The Horse and Its Relatives.* London: George Allen and Company, 1898. Although surpassed by modern studies of the horse's history, this book still has valuable descriptions of various members of the horse family.

Ridgeway, W. *The Origin and Influence of the Thoroughbred Horse.* Cambridge: The University Press, 1905. An old work but still one of the most quoted on the thoroughbred and the horse in general.

Vesey-Fitzgerald, B. *The Book of the Horse.* London and Brussels: Nicholson and Watson, 1946. A well-illustrated, popular work.

INTRODUCTION OF THE WHEEL

Type of event: Technological: application of a power-producing principle
Time: c.3500 B.C.
Locale: Mesopotamia

Summary of Event

The wheel is probably the most significant mechanical principle discovered and applied by man. Evidence points to the first use of the wheel in Mesopotamia slightly before the appearance of bronze. Eventually, it came to be used widely throughout the world, although Negro Africa, the simpler Asiatic peoples, and Oceania never adopted it, and it was essentially unknown in pre-Columbian America.

The wheel is one of many mechanical applications involving rotary motion. Some devices, such as the spindle, the fire drill, and the rotary quern (invented later for grinding grain) apparently show no evolutionary relationship; on the other hand, the potter's wheel, the vehicular wheel, the water mill, the spinning wheel, and the windmill appear to represent a related sequence of applications using a common principle.

The true wheel rotates completely, and as an applied mechanical device it is fixed on an axle or pivot; as a toy, a wheel or hoop is not so controlled. The making of a true wheel requires the ability to trace a circle on wood or other material and to cut it out. The use of fibers to draw a circle was undoubtedly within the range of accomplishment of Bronze Age people.

It is not certain whether the potter's wheel preceded the wheeled vehicle, but in any event, both appeared in Mesopotamia some five or six thousand years ago and both involved complete rotation with the wheel fixed by axle or spindle. It has often been suggested that the vehicular wheel was derived from rollers used in moving heavy objects, but the Maya used rollers to smooth their roads and yet did not devise a wheeled vehicle. Moreover, the first wheels appear to have been tripartite discs, three pieces of wood held together with cross braces; had rollers inspired this development, one would have expected each wheel to consist of a solid piece of wood sawed off a log.

The one-wheeled wheelbarrow did not appear in Europe until the twelfth century A.D., though it was in use in China in the first century. Two-wheeled carts and four-wheeled wagons appeared about the same time, and so apparently did wheels rotating on both fixed and rotating axles. The bodies of the first carts consisted of the older sledges, and the vehicle was drawn by a paired draught, a team of oxen yoked to a tongue as in an earlier invention, the plow. Probably the best proof of the single origin and diffusion of the wheeled vehicle is to be found in this almost universal association of tripartite wheel and paired draught, a conclusion borne out by the simultaneous appearance of both in areas remote from Mesopotamia. The tripartite wheel was not displaced until about 2000 B.C. when the heat

5

treatment of wood for bending gave rise to the spoked wheel.

Wheeled vehicles were first used primarily as hearses for the great and as military adjuncts until they gradually came to be used more for carriers of goods. Even during the Classical Age in Greece, chariots were declining in importance for warfare, and they were finally used only for sport. In early times carts with shafts for single animals were preferred in outlying countries where roads were poor, but with improvement in roads came heavy wagons and the use of several animals for power.

Further exploitation of the wheel had to await the utilization of power other than human or animal. Pulleys were known among the ancients, and cogwheels and gears were described by Archimedes. When the use of water for power became common in the third century B.C., the water mill was utilized by the Greeks as it had been earlier in China and India. The first water wheels were mounted horizontally so that power could be applied directly to stones for grinding grain. The vertical wheel involved gearing and the earliest mention is by Vitruvius in the first century B.C.

The windmill was unknown both to Greeks and Romans. It first appeared in Persia in the seventh century A.D., possibly being derived from prayer wheels. It appeared in China in the twelfth century, and Western Europe in the thirteenth. There it reached maximum development, performing a variety of tasks ranging from milling grain to pumping water.

It was not really until the Renaissance that a further step forward was made when Leonardo da Vinci (1452-1519) and Galileo (1564-1642) applied the wheel to more advanced inventions which ultimately became basis for the Industrial Revolution. The steam engine fathered the paddle-wheel steamship and the railroad of the nineteenth century. Modern developments in machinery and transportation are still largely dependent upon use of the wheel which originated in ancient Mesopotamia.

Pertinent Literature

Childe, V. Gordon. "Rotary Motion," in *A History of Technology*. Vol. I, pp. 187-215. Oxford: The University Press, 1954.

The definitive treatment of rotary motion and its place in the complex of material culture was written by the late V. Gordon Childe, one of the most respected of British prehistorians, who dealt with the whole sweep of European and Middle Eastern early cultural history.

Rotary motion as we know it in machines and vehicles came comparatively late in the broad span of human time. The potter's wheel and the wheeled vehicle are only some six thousand years old, while the spindle is only two thousand years older. However, tools involving rotary or partially rotary motion appeared long before. As Childe points out, for true rotary motions the revolving part of the instrument must be free to turn in the same direction indefinitely, while in partially rotary motion the revolving object may frequently reverse directions, or actually never

6

complete a single cycle.

Partially rotary motion is found in such a simple implement as a bone awl when it is twisted first one way and then the other to perforate leather. More direct in its function was the hand drill, consisting of a solid or hollow shaft and in some cases tipped with stone. Twirled back and forth between the palms of the hands, such implements could make fire or could even drill through stone. Improvement was introduced when a strap turned about the shaft and pulled back and forth to impart partially rotary motion more easily. A further advance came with the use of a bow to transmit motion to the drill. The bow drill was widely distributed and continued to be used in Europe for most drilling operations until the introduction of the brace in the Middle Ages.

A final step in hand drills was attained with the pump drill which did not appear before Roman times. This evolved instrument in its perfected form has a flywheel and a cross piece that steadies the shaft. The distribution of the pump drill was more limited than that of its predecessors, an expected result considering its late development. A different and ancient implement is the spindle, a straight shaft steadied and given momentum by an attached flywheel or whorl. The spindle was twirled repeatedly between thumb and finger to constitute true rotary motion.

"All effective industrial applications of rotary motion have developed from some sort of wheel, ideally a disk equipped with bearings to allow it to spin freely." Such a true wheel was in use in the form of a potter's wheel and a cart or wagon wheel in the fourth millennium B.C. Since both kinds of wheels were made of wood, evidence of their existence must come indirectly from artifacts less prone to complete destruction. Since potsherds are practically indestructible, they reveal much about the development of the wheel. Oldest evidence of vehicular wheels is found in inscriptions on stone or vases and in toy models in clay. Also, early wheeled vehicles were prestige items and as such were occasionally preserved in tombs or as votive offerings in bogs.

The original solid disc wheel soon gave way to the crossbar spoked wheel, subsequently to the true spoked wheel, and finally to the dished wheel. In the last form, spokes and hub form a flattened cone rather than a plane with the rim. Its effectiveness in fostering greater maneuverability and strength is still debated. Though an expression of the wheel principle, the spoked wheel is regarded as a new invention rather than a modification of the disc wheel.

Another application of true rotary motion came with the windlass about 1000 B.C. Not until the Classical Age were the olive press, the quern, the donkey mill, the waterwheel, the capstan, and the screw invented.

Forbes, R. J. "Power," in *A History of Technology*. Vol. II, pp. 589-622. Oxford: The University Press, 1956.

At each stage in technological evolution craftsmen command certain tools and machines for the purpose of converting raw materials into finished products. Some of the simpler machines, such as the hammer, the chisel, and the rotary quern, are known as "direct actors" since they complete the task directly. More sophisticated are the "prime-movers," machines which produce power to operate other tools; they convert sources of energy (animal, wind, falling water, or fuels) into applicable power.

In the simplest stage, man alone provided the power, whatever the task. Domesticated-animal power appeared during the Neolithic period. The third stage was initiated by the appearance of the water mill during Roman Imperial times. The first water mill was the so-called "Norse" or "Greek" mill, which probably originated in the upland regions of the Near East. It diffused westward and eastward, reaching both Ireland and China by the third and fourth centuries A.D.

The Norse mill had a horizontal wheel which called for small volumes of water moving at high velocity. These conditions were met only in hilly areas, directly in streams or by means of aqueducts. Horizontal mills did not spread to Egypt and Mesopotamia, probably because of the great seasonal fluctuation of water volume and the normal low velocity of the streams. Inefficient as it is, the horizontal wheel remains in use today and was the precursor of the modern water turbine.

The deficiencies of the horizontal mill may have inspired the Roman engineer Vitruvius to design a vertical wheel in the first century B.C. His was a more complicated operation because the horizontal shaft of the vertical wheel had to be geared in order to transmit power to the vertical shaft of the flat-lying millstones. The gear ratio was such that the millstones turned a number of times for each revolution of the waterwheel. The first vertical water mill had an undershot wheel, the moving water hitting the paddles below the axle. Undershot wheels work best in swift streams with constant volumes of water, often without dam, pond, or millrace. If velocity and volume were not favorable, an aqueduct might be constructed to induce favorable conditions. Dams and ponding became common only in the thirteenth century.

An advancement in mechanical efficiency came with the appearance of the overshot wheel, which requires a properly directed and regulated water supply. Dams or aqueducts make it possible to utilize sluggish streams of variable volume since they raise the level of the stream, thus providing the necessary fall and constant volume. This efficient type of mill seems to have been in existence during the time of Vitruvius in the first century B.C. For reasons not entirely clear, the superior overshot wheel and even the more primitive mills were adopted slowly, and their use was restricted almost entirely to the grinding of grain. Man and animal power, often transmitted through treadmills, was used extensively throughout the Roman Empire long after the water mill had been perfected. Forbes believes that the inadequacies of the Mediterranean climate, or a lack of stimulus, left Roman technology practically stagnant. Only in the fourth century A.D. did an acute shortage of labor favor utilization of the water mill, but it took a change in social values concerning

8

the degrading character of manual labor and the stimulus of barbarian tribes receptive to technical change to realize fully the mechanical potential of water power.

Two interesting sidelights concerning the waterwheel occurred in the fourth and fifth centuries A.D. About 370 an unknown Roman apparently designed a paddle-wheel boat, obtaining power by having oxen walk around a capstan. Later, when the Goths besieged Rome in 537, they attempted to starve out the inhabitants by cutting the aqueducts which powered the grain mills; Roman engineers responded by devising the floating mill, a waterwheel mounted between rafts and anchored in the Tiber. — *F.B.K.*

Additional Recommended Reading

Childe, V. Gordon. "Wheeled Vehicles," in *A History of Technology*. Vol. I, pp. 716-729. Oxford: The University Press, 1954. An excellent summary of the earliest use of wheeled vehicles.

Ekholm, Gordon F. "Transpacific Contacts," in *Prehistoric Man in the New World*. Pp. 489-510. Chicago: University of Chicago Press, 1964. An account of the wheeled clay toys and ceremonial objects of Mexico.

Forbes, R. J. "Hydraulic Engineering and Sanitation," in *A History of Technology*. Vol. II, pp. 663-694. Oxford: The University Press, 1956. Contains accounts of early applications of the wheel to hydraulic engineering.

Jope, E. M. "Vehicles and Harness," in *A History of Technology*. Vol. II, pp. 537-562. Oxford: The University Press, 1956. An excellent description of wheeled vehicles through the Middle Ages.

Krober, A. L. *Anthropology*. New York: Harcourt, Brace & World, Inc., 1948. A general work which includes an assessment of the place of the wheel in cultural development.

Wailes, Rex. "Windmills," in *A History of Technology*. Vol. III, pp. 89-109. Oxford: The University Press, 1957. A thorough treatment of windmills from the Renaissance to the Industrial Revolution.

ORIGIN OF WRITING

Type of event: Cultural: development of visual communication
Time: c.3500 B.C.
Locale: Egypt and Sumer

Summary of Event

The value of writing is incalculable; Breasted called it "the greatest influence in uplifting the human race." Its definition, however, is difficult, involving sophisticated theories which conflict with one another. It may suffice to state that essentially writing is a means of communication between humans through conventional visible marks. As such, writing spans the entire history of visual communication from early pictographic beginnings to alphabetical writing, the latter being a technological system developed between 1800 and 1000 B.C.

The most primitive nonverbal means of communication used objects: a pile of stones marked a grave, or a group of sticks kept a tally of things. Advanced mnemonic use of objects involving color can be found in the wampum belts of northeastern American Indians in which strings of interwoven white and purple shell beads record tribal agreements.

Writing properly so called began when marks were made on objects, marks which were drawn, painted, scratched, or incised as the etymology of the word "writing" reveals in various languages. Picture writing was the most primitive of these visual communications, as shown for example in the cave paintings of the Upper Paleolithic era. The oldest picture writing identified in Mesopotamia was made about 3500 B.C. at Kish, a Sumerian town. A dozen or so pictures inscribed on both sides of a limestone tablet a few inches square clearly aim to record an event rather than present a graphic representation. Picture representation as primitive writing is independent of speech since it is not interested in or capable of reproducing sounds.

Picture writing advanced when it conveyed a thought through a sequence of pictures; it became more sophisticated when the picture began to stand for something other than itself. Originally the drawing of an eye meant an eye, a tooth meant a tooth, and a circle meant the sun. A subtle change developed in Mesopotamia when the drawing of an eye began to stand for seeing, a tooth signified eating, and a circle stood for daytime. The idea associated with the picture became important. Moreover when one picture began to stand for two or more things which had names that sounded alike, picture writing became still more versatile, especially in languages that possessed many homonyms. Thus, taking English examples, the picture of a fly might stand for the activity rather than the insect, an ant might stand for a relative, and so on. This "rebus writing" was the first major step toward true writing. It may have taken place almost simultaneously in Sumer and in Egypt, although in Egypt it first appears so well developed that the

10

idea may have been diffused there from Sumer.

Rebus writing was an advance because it made it possible to write about ideas; a "bee" plus a "leaf" could convey the idea of "belief." Nonetheless it still dealt with material objects; the sign for "bee" had not yet become the sign for a sound. That momentous achievement was accomplished in Mesopotamia about 1800 B.C.

Syllabic writing was probably the next step in the final development of the alphabet. The language spoken by Sumerians during the third millennium was characterized by single-syllable words, although bisyllabic and trisyllabic words were made by compounding roots. These roots consisted of a consonant and its associated vowel sounds such as ti, mu, po, and so forth. The Sumerians were the first people to begin to give a sound value to a syllabic sign. This syllabary began with thousands of signs, but by 2000 B.C. these signs had been greatly reduced in number. The idea was again further exploited by the Egyptians, although they frequently used syllables of two or more consonants, the associated vowels of which had to be inferred. When the Babylonians conquered the

Sumerians they took over and perfected the syllabary. By 1800 B.C. they had reduced the number of sound-signs to a few. It is believed by some scholars that it was Semitic speakers somewhere in Palestine or Syria who took Egyptian word-signs and used the first sound of the pronunciation of the word for true alphabetic writing containing definite vowels, which by 1000 B.C. became widespread.

The earliest writing began with the Sumerians who scratched pictures on clay tablets before the beginning of the third millennium. When it became evident that figures could be pressed into moist clay more easily than they could be drawn, a sharpened, wedge-shaped, cane stylus became the conventional writing tool, and the wedge-shaped writing itself came to be called cuneiform from the Latin *cuneus* or wedge. Each symbol or sign represented a syllable which was often a whole word. First written in columns beginning at the upper right downward, it shifted to a horizontal left-to-right system about 2600 B.C.

In Egypt sacred formulas were carved on stone, but paper made from reed pith was developed at an early date. Egyptians invented ink about 3200 B.C.

Pertinent Literature

Gelb, I. J. *A Study of Writing.* Chicago: University of Chicago Press, 1952.

Many good books about various phases of the origin of writing have a sameness about their strictly historical treatment. Gelb's work, on the other hand, attempts to lay a foundation for a full science of writing, yet to be written, which one might call "gram-matology," involving an establishment of the principles of writing that will assure a more scientific treatment of the subject than the purely historical or geographical approaches. As the Frank P. Hixon Distinguished Service Professor of Assyriology at the Oriental Institute of the University of Chicago, the author shows himself to be eminently qualified to launch such a lucid, coherent, and authoritative work. There is, in fact, little doubt that Professor Gelb is one of the major theoreticians among linguists.

In an essentially evolutionary commitment, he takes issue with those who define writing in too static a manner. There are those who oversimplify by declaring it to be a "device for recording speech by means of visible marks," which ignores the developmental aspects of early forms of writing. Others believe that even after phonetization, writing was still used to record or transmit both ideas and sounds. This school of thought errs in failing to understand that eventually writing "lost its independent character and became a written substitute for its spoken counterpart." Conscious of the evolutionary character of writing, the author describes stages in its growth. The earliest and most widespread is labelled "semasiographic," which indicates the expression of meaning largely through pictures and is not associated with speech. This stage includes primitive drawings, petroglyphs, and Gelb's own identifying-mnemonic devices. Many peoples never outgrew this stage. Gelb sees it, however, as the basis for the later development of true writing which he divides into three further stages of development as it becomes more and more phonographic, or capable of expressing speech.

The first of these true writing levels is called "logosyllabic" because it utilizes a combination of logographic and syllabary signs; signs standing for whole words are used in conjunction with signs representing syllables. The author believes that "seven original and fully developed systems of writing" appeared apparently independently of one another: Sumerian about 3100 B.C., Proto-Elamite about 3000 B.C., Proto-Indic about 2200 B.C., Chinese about 1300 B.C., Egyptian about 3000 B.C., Cretan about 2000 B.C., and Hittite about 1500 B.C. Only Sumerian, Egyptian, Hittite, and Chinese have been deciphered. In the second stage of development, "logographic," the logograms completely displace the syllabic elements. The third stage of true writing is "alphabetic," in which a sign normally stands for one or more single sounds of a language.

The author agrees with a majority of linguists in defining writing as "a system of intercommunication by means of conventional visible marks." However, his definition of alphabetic writing as a "system of signs expressing single sounds of speech" is not universally held. Gelb believes that the first alphabet which can be justifiably so called is that of the Greeks. The Greeks fully accepted "the forms of the West Semitic syllabary [and] evolved a system of vowels, which attached to the syllabic signs reduced the value of these syllables to simple consonantal signs." The creation of vowels thus produced for the first time a fully alphabetic system. Gelb believes that this development occurred in the ninth century B.C., but most students of writing would argue that true alphabetic writing appeared as early as 1800 B.C.

Our own English alphabet is virtually unchanged from the Latin. It in turn was developed from the Greek alphabet which was an adaptation of writing by Semites in Syria about 1500 B.C. The Semite in principle resembles the Egyptian syllabary.

The Egyptian belongs to the family of ancient Oriental writings of which the Sumerian may be the original.

Gleason, H. A. *An Introduction to Descriptive Linguistics.* New York: Holt, Rinehart and Winston, 1965.

Controversy over the origin of writing has led to such specialized scholarly investigation that the study of linguistics has become a complex science with vocabulary and concepts beyond the understanding of nonspecialists. One of the most straightforward studies is that by Gleason, a work intended as a textbook for college students in this rapidly growing field.

In chapter twenty-six the author discusses "written languages," or the application of writing to language. After saying that a "written language is basically a representation of a spoken language," the author reminds his readers that such a representation is never complete or exact. It is well to remember also that early writing had little or no connection with phonology.

There are obvious differences between writing and speaking languages. Dialects of a particular language differ considerably when they are spoken, whereas dialectic variations in writing are minimal. Sometimes phonetic differences may be so extreme in dialects that they are unintelligible to two peoples even when they read the same written language. In German, for instance, the difference between the official *Schriftdeutsch,* or written literary German, and a native dialect may be great enough to constitute almost a different language altogether. Sometimes a "dialect" such as Dutch develops its own written form in competition with a more universal written

system such as *Schriftdeutsch,* and it may be so different that it can aid in dilineating the political boundaries of an independent national state.

The origins of written languages are varied. Sometimes the written form of one dialect dominates others. In the case of Italian, the original dialect of Tuscany spread until it modified and was modified by other dialects and finally the written Italian became a "sort of average of all the local dialects." On occasion an artificial written language is contrived, such as the "union Shona" of Africa which provides a common medium for five different spoken languages.

Other features besides dialects illustrate differences between written and spoken languages. In English for instance, the system of punctuation is utilized for clarification. While communication in spoken language is made through intonation of the voice, there is "only more-or-less incidental correlation between punctuation marks and different intonation contours." Punctuation marks indicate logical units of thought expressed as dependent clauses or phrases, but they are not really features of speech and as such they are not universal but associated with various syntaxes.

Finally the written language may not reproduce the phonetic language because it tends to lag behind the spoken word which changes through constant use. Moreover spelling does not accord with pronunciation. The written language tends to preserve the identity of such homophonous words as "sight" and "site" in English because in writing they are easily understandable. The written language in such cases may be forced to use circumlocutions or restatements. Sometimes the reverse is true. For example, one sometimes finds it impossible to write accurately what may be correctly stated orally, as in this case: "There are three *to's* in the English language."

Furthermore, written and spoken languages have different vocabularies. Colloquialisms are not generally used in writing, nor are technical terms used in daily communication. Synonyms tend to take the place in written language of "intonation and other qualities of voice associated with emotion," which are part of spoken language.

Sometimes two competing written languages are associated with the same spoken dialect, as is the case with Urdu and Hindi in northern India; the first uses the Persian form of the Arabic alphabet while the other employs a variant of a Sanskrit script.

Finally, a well-established written language tends to create a "speech form" which approximates an oral rendition of the literary language." Latin and Greek plurals found in written language, for instance, are incorporated into spoken language. — *P.G.C. and W.G.H.*

Additional Recommended Reading

Diringer, David. *The Alphabet: A Key to the History of Mankind*. London: Hutchinson & Co., 1968. A recognized authority on the subject.

Chiera, W. *They Wrote on Clay*. Chicago: University of Chicago Press, 1938. A book for the nonspecialist that explores the origin of cuneiform.

Cleator, P. E. *Lost Languages*. New York: John Day, 1961. An excellent treatment of the decipherment of cuneiform and hieroglyphic writing together with descriptions of other systems such as the Mycenaean syllabary, Linear B, and scripts from the Indus, the Maya, and Easter Island.

Diringer, D. *Writing*. New York: Frederick A. Praeger, 1962. Perhaps one of the best volumes to cover the whole topic of writing from primitive means of communication to the origin and diffusion of the alphabet.

Doblhofer, E. *Voice in Stone: The Decipherment of Ancient Scripts and Writings*. New York: The Viking Press, 1961. A comprehensive history of the deciphering of many examples of ancient writings.

Friedrich, J. *Extinct Languages*. New York: Philosophical Library, 1957. Primarily concerned with three scripts: Egyptian hieroglyphic, cuneiform, and that associated with Hittite inscriptions.

Irwin, K. G. *The Romance of Writing*. New York: The Viking Press, 1967. A nontechnical work directed at the origins of the modern alphabet, including the use of clay tablets, papyrus, and paper.

Mason, W. A. *A History of the Art of Writing*. New York: The Macmillan Company, 1928. An older work which traces writing from earliest to modern times.

Moorhouse, A. C. *The Triumph of the Alphabet.* New York: Henry Schuman, 1953. An account of the development of writing.

Ogg, Oscar. *The 26 Letters.* New York: Thomas Y. Crowell, 1961. A simple and informal introduction to the alphabet.

Moran, H. A., and D. H. Kelley. *The Alphabet and the Ancient Calendar Signs.* 2nd ed. Foreword by David Diringer. Palo Alto, California: Daily Press, 1969. The first article attributes the alphabet to northwestern Semites rather than to peoples dwelling within the Phoenician-Egyptian axis; the second article, *American Parallels,* argues that Mayan and Aztec writing received direct influences from Asia about 200 B.C.

INVENTION OF BRONZE

Type of event: Technological: advance which brought an end to the Neolithic Age
Time: c.330 B.C.
Locale: Probably northeast Persia

Summary of Event

Bronze is an alloy of approximately nine parts of copper to one part of tin. In the ancient Near East and in prehistoric Europe, copper was also alloyed with lead, antimony, arsenic, and zinc, but the copper-tin alloy was the one generally used. Golden brown in color, bronze had considerable hardness, tensile strength, and density.

The Neolithic Age slowly came to an end as various cultures in Eurasia that had depended on wood, stone, and bone for tools began to develop the techniques of metallurgy. For centuries man had used native metals such as gold, silver, and copper for jewelry and small objects, but the true transition from stone and other materials to metal could not take place until man had learned to smelt or extract metals from ores and work them by heating and casting. Native copper began to be used about 5000 B.C., and it was being annealed or tempered about 4200 B.C. Sometime in the fourth millenium, techniques for the reduction of oxide and carbonate ores of copper were discovered, and the metal was being melted and cast. Such knowledge diffused slowly from the region of its origin, probably in northeast Persia, eastward into the Indus River valley and westward into the headwaters area of the Tigris-Euphrates system, to western Anatolia, to Cyprus, and up the Danube valley; thence it spread radially to the eastern Baltic region, Scandinavia, Britain, southern France, and northern Italy. It must, however, be recognized that this diffusion took from 3500 to 2000 B.C., so that the Bronze Age began at a later date in each successive region.

The discovery of the casting of copper appears to belong to the Ubaid-Uruk period in Mesopotamia about 3300 B.C., when small flat objects such as axheads, arrowheads, and spearheads were made from open molds. For casting in the round, molds of two or more parts were used. The cutting edges of copper tools or weapons were hardened by cold-hammering, a treatment which gave them the hardness, though not the tensile strength, of mild steel. Soon after the introduction of copper metallurgy, copper alloys began to be used, the most common of which was the bronze alloy of copper and tin. In fact it now appears from recent archaeological discoveries that no true age of copper preceded the Bronze Age anywhere except in Egypt, where the use of bronze did not become widespread until about 2000 B.C. because tin ore does not occur in Egypt.

The superior physical characteristics of bronze and the ease with which it could be cast makes its discovery second in importance only to the dis-

16

covery of the means of smelting copper. Apart from the open and closed methods of casting already described, there was a third: *cire perdue,* from the French for "lost wax." Especially suited to the making of ornaments and art work, it remains in use with few changes today. It is a process of hollow casting in which a core of clay or plaster is covered with wax modeled to the extent required in the finished work. Over this surface is shaped a clay or plaster coating thin enough to find its way into details of the wax model but thick enough to form a mold. The structure is supported by metal rods which pass through the wax to the core. When heat is applied, the wax melts and runs out through holes left for this purpose. In this way a negative image of the model is left on the inside of the mold. Molten bronze is then poured into the space between the mold and the core; after a period of cooling the mold is broken away, the supporting rods are removed, and the inner core is scraped out. The result is a hollow bronze figure. In the casting process it was necessary to make crucibles in which to melt the metal. At first these crucibles were shallow terracotta bowls, but later a deep cylindrical form was favored in order to hold more molten metal and expose less surface to the air.

With the coming of bronze there was a great increase in the quantity and quality of tools of every kind. Stone implements by their very nature were crude and limited in their application, but cast bronze offered hardness and a refinement of form for many tasks. The hammer, man's oldest tool, the celt or axhead, the chisel, the drill, the saw, and the file all were made of bronze in a variety of shapes. Weapons such as daggers and swords, spearheads, arrowheads, and battle axes were also produced. The development of the bronze sword illustrates the use of the new techniques. It began as an outgrowth of the dagger by lengthening the blade, which was then strengthened with ribs along its flat sides. When it was observed that a riveted hilt was a source of weakness, hilt and blade were cast in one piece. In time, thin-bladed rapiers for thrusting and heavy-bladed sabers for slashing were produced.

With the introduction of iron for implements and weapons the Bronze Age came to an end. The Iron Age also started in one region and slowly spread to other areas. Iron metallurgy appeared for the first time in Anatolia in the fourteenth century B.C., and by the tenth century B.C. it was known to the Hallstatt culture of central Europe. The cheapness and the efficiency with which it could be worked were the chief factors that caused iron to supersede bronze as the favored utilitarian metal.

Pertinent Literature

Bromhead, C. N., R. J. Forbes, H. H. Coghlan, Herbert Maryon, and H. J. Plenderleith, in Charles Singer *et al.,* eds. *A History of Technology.* Vol. I: *From Early Times to the Fall of the Ancient Empires.* Pp. 558-662. Oxford: The Clarendon Press, 1955.

This volume and those following it form an indispensable reference work on the history of technology. Volume I contains 803 pages of detailed and fascinating information, 570 figures illustrating the text, and thirty-six plates. References and a bibliography are appended to each chapter, and there is a series of chronological tables and maps.

Gold, copper, and tin were sought by man at a very early period in the alluvial deposits of rivers and streams. But the advance from the washings of alluvium to the working of ore lodes in underground mines took a long time. The Sumerians in the second half of the fourth millennium B.C. received copper shipments from Anatolia, Armenia, and Elam. Assyrian traders dealt in copper ingots cast in the shape of oxhides from about 2000 B.C. onwards. Smelting of copper ore was known in Egypt in predynastic times, and beginning with Dynasty III about 2600 B.C. the mining of copper in various parts of the kingdom became a state industry. The main location was in the Sinai peninsula where ancient mining camps have been discovered consisting of miners' and soldiers' huts, temples, and fortified compounds built for protection against desert tribesmen. Shafts were extended horizontally into the rock almost two hundred feet in search of ore lodes, with most of the work, ironically enough, being performed with stone tools. Smelting was done at these camps, but the ingots were brought back to Egypt to be refined. It has been estimated that down to about 1200 B.C., when the Sinai mines were abandoned and copper began to be imported from Cyprus and Armenia, Egypt had produced some ten thousand tons of the metal.

East of the Sinai peninsula in the Wadi Arabah, the kings of Israel, especially Solomon, worked copper mines to supply their needs, and a superb description of Bronze Age mining techniques appears in Job 28:1-11. The actual description is incidental, as the passage is intended to teach the inadequacy of human technology in the face of divine knowledge or "wisdom." Cyprus was another copper-producing region, supplying Egypt during Dynasty XVIII and later, but its chief reputation rests upon the fact that it supplied Crete, Troy, and the mainland of Greece with the metal during the heroic age and later.

Some of the greatest pieces of ancient art, in all sizes from the colossal to miniature, were executed in bronze. A superb head of Sargon the Great, King of Akkad about 2250 B.C., was found at Ninevah and is now in the Iraq Museum, Baghdad. It is the earliest known portrait head in cast bronze, and the patterned treatment of the beard and hair is remarkable in so early a piece. Though the use of bronze for weapons and tools was superseded with the coming of the Iron Age, bronze remained a favorite with artists and craftsmen throughout antiquity; some of the greatest works of Greek sculpture, such as the Poseidon from Artemision and the Charioteer at Delphi, are in bronze.

Invention of Bronze

Forbes, R. J. *Studies in Ancient Technology.* Vol. IX. Leiden: E. J. Brill, 1964.

Forbes, a recognized expert in the field of ancient technology, presents chapters on copper, tin, and bronze; antimony and arsenic; and the early story of iron. In his treatment of the origin of bronze, he presents the following sequence for the Near East: (1) Cassiterite, a tin oxide found as vein ore and stream tin, was discovered in alluvial sands and clays. (2) This stream tin was then reduced by metallurgists who already knew how to work gold, copper, and lead; the resulting product was believed to be lead, since the ancients could not then distinguish between tin, lead, and antimony. (3) Either this tin was then added to copper, or perhaps at some earlier date stream tin was mixed with copper ores before smelting, to produce bronze. The earliest known bronzes often contain lead or antimony, but tin replaced other ores when it was seen to produce better bronze. (4) About 2500 B.C. stream tin was reduced with charcoal and smelted crude copper. (5) Meanwhile, in the working of certain mixed ores a so-called natural bronze was produced, since these raw mixtures sometimes contained as much as two percent of tin. In fact, in the oldest Mesopotamian bronzes the tin content was as high as four percent.

Forbes suggests that 2500 B.C. was the earliest date when it can be said that bronze with a tin content suitable for the intended object was being manufactured. By 2000 B.C. Sumerian smiths were using a controlled tin content of between six and ten percent, and the same percentages have been found in contemporary objects from Crete and Troy.

No sooner had the metallurgical problem been solved than the stream deposits of tin began to give out as a result of growing demands for the ore. Axes of unalloyed copper from the Sargonid period are inferior to the splendid bronzes of early Dynastic Ur. This depletion of raw materials and the resulting technical difficulties caused serious problems. When the known deposits became depleted, prospectors and traders began to move westward across Anatolia, the Black Sea, the Aegean Sea, and up the Danube River into Bohemia and Saxony, where new supplies of tin were eventually discovered. Finally in the period between 1800 and 1500 B.C., a technical improvement occurred when the cassiterite was reduced separately so that metallic tin could be mixed directly with the copper. This advance permitted better control of the tin content so that in succeeding centuries smiths were able to produce alloys adapted to specific purposes such as weapons, utensils, statues, mirrors, or bells. — *K.H.*

Additional Recommended Reading

Forbes, R. J. *Metallurgy in Antiquity.* Leiden: E. J. Brill, 1950. An excellent work which is devoted exclusively to ancient metalworking.

Lucas, A. *Ancient Egyptian Materials and Industries.* 3rd ed. London: E. J. Arnold, 1962. A mine of information on ancient Egyptian crafts and technology.

Schaeffer, C. F. A., "The Appearance and Spread of Metal," in *Larousse Encyclopedia of Prehistoric and Ancient Art.* Pp. 176-180. New York: Prometheus Press, 1966. A short but useful summary.

CREATION OF THE SEXAGESIMAL SYSTEM

Type of event: Intellectual: development of a numerical notation
Time: c.2700 B.C.
Locale: Mesopotamia

Summary of Event

The civilization of the fourth millennium existing in Mesopotamia, the valley region between the Tigris and Euphrates rivers, is commonly known as Sumerian. Despite an early origin, its achievements were outstanding. Its "empire," while extensive and homogeneous, remained basically a realm of local city-states whose individual "patesi" might at different times lord it over other cities as a preëminent "lugal," or king.

The culture of the Sumerians was sophisticated: their ziggurats were decorated with refined geometrical patterns, their notable metal work involved complicated casting and a knowledge of alloys, and their concern for irrigation caused them to develop an advanced engineering technology. Their wedge-shaped cuneiform writing, possibly predating Egyptian hieroglyphics, was made by pressing symbols with a stylus on clay tablets which were later baked.

On a substantial number of tablets extant from a period in the early part of the third millennium, more than two thousand separate symbols are found. A group among them reveals a well-developed system of numeration. The Sumerians clearly had separate symbols for: (1) one unit, made by pressing a small cylindrical stylus at an angle into the clay to make a wedge-shaped mark; (2) ten units, made by pressing the small cylinder vertically into the clay to make a circular mark; (3) sixty units, a wedge mark made by a large cylinder; and (4) 3600, or 60 x 60, units, a circular mark made by pressing the larger cylinder vertically into the clay. These symbols were combined to represent intermediate numbers as well as larger ones. Using both ten and sixty as bases, the system is somewhat refined but not uncommon among primitive civilizations. An analogy may help to clarify how this system differs from a place-value system such as is used today. In a basic system, 11 would represent 1 plus 1, or two; not 10 plus 1, or eleven. There are certain similarities between the former system and the Roman numeration method, although the Roman numerals II and I are separate symbols for two and one respectively, so that II is not a short means of expressing I plus I.

About 2250 B.C. the Akkadians under the leadership of Sargon I conquered the Sumerians and adapted cuneiform writing to their own language. This task was simplified because by the time of the Akkadian conquest the numerous separate symbols of Sumerian writing had been reduced to a few hundred. The system of numeration was further refined but remained a primitive mixed-base arrangement.

Other information about Mesopotamian numeration is derived from the tablets of two periods separated by more than a thousand years: the Old Babylonian age in the early part of the second millennium, and the Seleucid period in the last part of the first millennium.

The mathematics of the Mesopotamian civilizations became fully developed in the Old Babylonian age after the time of Hammurabi. For example, it became possible to solve by essentially modern methods a variety of algebraic equations including quadratic equations with real roots. Using what was later to be known as the Pythagorean theorem, it became possible to compute the length of the diagonal of a square accurate in decimal notation to six significant figures. A new numeration scheme was developed using a place-value system, a system in which the value of a digit depended not only on its literal representation but also on its position relative to other digits.

The Old Babylonian era retained the sexagesimal system based on the number sixty as compared to the modern decimal system which is based on the number ten. The digits from one to fifty-nine were written out in a primitive decimal representation, and these were used as digits in the sexagesimal system. Thus, the symbol for one could represent 1, 60, 3600, or 1/60; and the value of any number could represent any product of that number times a power of sixty in the same way that using the modern decimal system, 7 can represent 7/100, 7/10, 7, 70, or 700. This method simplifies computation since the multiplication and addition of whole numbers is reduced to addition and multiplication of the numbers from one to fifty-nine, in the same way that the decimal system uses the numerals from one to nine, and an electronic computer using a base of two needs only two numerals.

It is significant that this number system was used only for computational purposes; no other known application was made of it during the Old Babylonian age. A date indicated on a tablet generally appears in a decimal form using number words for powers of ten just as modern scientific notation expresses the mean distance of the sum as 9.3×10^7 miles. No means of signifying the "sexagesimal point" was ever developed, creating a situation similar to a present condition which would allow no distinction between 2.1, 21, or 210. This lack of a "point" was not a critical problem since multiplication of any "pointed" number by any other was accomplished in exactly the same way as numbers without a point; moreover, the magnitude of the number could usually be determined from context. More serious is the fact that the ancients had no symbol for zero except, on occasion, a well-indicated space between digits. This deficiency was remedied during the Seleucid period. Starting about 300 B.C., two short, slanted wedge marks were used to indicate the absence of a digit at a given place. This was the first occurrence of a zero symbol as a place holder, so that it was possible to distinguish between numbers such as 21, 201, and 2001. This zero symbol, however, was never used at the beginning or end of digital representation as in modern mathematics to distinguish, say, between .02, 2, and 20. That refinement is credited to later Greek

22

thought since it was first introduced by Ptolemy, the astronomer, who adopted the old Sumerian sexagesimal system and used it extensively in his computations.

Strangely enough, the fifteen hundred years from the Old Babylonian age to that the Seleucids show no great advancement in mathematics itself, but it was a period of great scientific progress, and the sexagesimal system in its improved form came to be used extensively in astronomy.

Pertinent Literature

Neugebauer, O. *The Exact Sciences in Antiquity*. Providence: Brown University Press, 1957.

This study of the sources of Greek science discusses Mesopotamian mathematics, astronomy, and numeration, and it provides illustrations of original cuneiform documents.

The notion of number as used in ancient science includes a thorough discussion of the variety of ways in which numbers can be represented, not merely a presentation of various representation schemata. This section is well illustrated with details of Mesopotamian, Greek, Egyptian and Roman systems as well as many others. Of particular interest is the application of Mesopotamian computation to problems involving the calendar and astronomy. There is a further analysis of the manner in which Mesopotamian culture combined base sixty and base ten, and of the variety of schemes that were used at different times and for various purposes. Analogies are drawn from modern mixed base systems such as: twelve inches to the foot, and three feet to the yard; or two pints to the quart, and four quarts to the gallon. Computations are performed using Egyptian and Mesopotamian notation.

An account is given of Babylonian astronomy, of Egyptian mathematics and astronomy, and of Hellenistic science in general, showing how Mesopotamian mathematics affected Hellenistic science and how the Greeks in turn influenced modern science and mathematics.

Van Der Waerden, B. L. *Science Awakening*. Croningen, Holland: P. Noordhoff Ltd., 1954, and New York: Oxford University Press, 1961.

Professor Van Der Waerden is an accomplished mathematician with a professional interest in the history of mathematics. He deals with the Egyptians and the Babylonians as mathematicians, and with number systems, digits, and the art of computing. The entire work is a masterful analysis of ancient mathematics; the first part should be required reading for anyone with more than a passing interest in the subject.

Van Der Waerden raises the intriguing question: how did the sexagesimal system originate? Answers range from logical arguments, through consideration of the weights, measures, and monetary systems in use in the Mesopotamian world, to considerations of properties of sixty that make

23

computations with many common fractions simple with this base. 2, 3, 4, 5, 6, 10, 12, 15, 20, and 30, are all factors of sixty. The author believes that the introduction of the fraction 1/60 led to the development of the Babylonian number system. Examples of computation using the sexagesimal system are given, and there is information on the origin of the zero symbol and its later use by Greeks and Hindus. Because both the Greeks and the Hindus used the symbol 0 for zero many scholars suppose that it was the result of close contact between the two civilizations. — *M.H.T.*

Additional Recommended Reading

Conant, Levi. *The Number Concept. Its Origin and Development.* New York: The Macmillan Company, 1923. An excellent account of the way number concepts and systems developed.

Neugebauer, O., and A. Sachs. *Mathematical Cuneiform Texts.* New Haven: Yale University Press, 1945. A work for those who wish to study cuneiform writing.

Boyer, Carl B. *A History of Mathematics.* New York: John Wiley and Sons, Inc., 1968. A good text with a short treatment of Mesopotamian mathematics and the sexagesimal notation.

Smith, David Eugene. *History of Mathematics.* New York: Dover Publications, Inc., 1958. A work similar to Boyer's.

BUILDING OF THE GREAT PYRAMID

Type of event: Technological: building of one of the wonders of the ancient world
Time: c.2550-2530 B.C.
Locale: Giza, Egypt

Principal personage:
   CHEOPS, Pharaoh of Egypt c.2560-2530, builder of the
   Great Pyramid

Summary of Event

The three great pyramids at Giza in Egypt are undoubtedly the most celebrated group of monuments in the world, and because of their sepulchral purpose and their survival over a span of four and a half millennia, they at once sum up for the modern mind the dominant religious concept and the enduring architectural achievements of the ancient Egyptians. Although some eighty of these great tombs erected over the long span of Egyptian antiquity are now known to archaeologists, the specific period known as the Age of the Pyramids covers Dynasties III through VI (c.2700-2180 B.C.), and the greatest of all these works is that of the Pharaoh Cheops, who ruled about 2560-2530 B.C. in Dynasty IV. His monument and those of two later kings of the same dynasty, Chephren and Mycerinus, compose the great triad of monuments on the plateau at Giza, at the edge of the Western Desert south of the modern city of Cairo.

The pyramid of Cheops, still the largest stone structure in the world, is preëminent both for size and quality of workmanship. The Greek historian Herodotus, after visiting the site in 449 B.C., stated that the construction required the efforts of a hundred thousand men for a period of twenty years, and these are the figures most often repeated in the later literature. It is now believed, however, that only between two thousand and four thousand construction workers were actually employed on the working face at any one time, with perhaps four times that number engaged in transport work and in the quarries at the site, in the Mukattam Hills on the east side of the Nile, and at Aswan, some five hundred miles upstream. No exact estimate of the amount of hewn stone used is possible because the core of the Great Pyramid consists of a nucleus of living rock, but a likely conjecture is that the completed structure contained some 2,300,000 separate blocks of stone weighing an average of two and a half tons each and reaching an individual maximum of fifteen tons. The base of each of the four sides measures approximately 755 feet and exhibits an almost true north-south or east-west orientation, so that the four corners are almost perfect right angles. Rising at an incline of 51° 52′ the sides originally reached a height of 481½ feet, but the top thirty-one feet are now lost. The total area covered by the base measures 13.1 acres. By comparison, the dome of St. Peter's in Rome is 404 feet above the ground, while

25

the Washington Monument stands 555 feet 5 inches high.

Seen from a distance, the Great Pyramid appears to be well-preserved, but closer observation shows that it has suffered severe damage over the centuries. Apart from the loss of some twelve courses and the capstone at the top, the entire outer facing of Tura limestone, once about seventeen feet in thickness, has been lost. In its original condition this gleaming white stone, fitted to the closest possible tolerances, presented a smooth and shining surface on all sides which must have dazzled the onlooker. Today, a surviving portion of this facing atop the neighboring Pyramid of Chephren gives the spectator some inkling of the grandeur of these monuments at the time of their completion.

The interior passageways of the Great Pyramid, the plans of which were changed three times during the course of construction, are now open at the upper levels to the visitor. As in all pyramids the entrance is on the north side, in this case forty-nine feet above ground level. At first the corridor slopes downward for sixty-two feet, then ascends at a point where the passage was blocked with granite to guard against tomb robbers. Here the passage rises for a distance of about sixty feet to reach the great chamber, which measures 153 feet in length, thirty feet in height, but only seven feet three inches in width. At its upper end one passes through an antechamber into the royal funerary room, 137 feet above ground level, in which the granite sarcophagus of Cheops stands at the western end. This huge coffin measures a few inches more in width than the passageway and therefore had to be in

place when construction reached this level, not after completion of the entire monument.

The Great Pyramid was built mainly of limestone from the quarries nearby and across the Nile, but granite for the columns, architraves, door-jambs, lintels, and other parts of the sepulchral complex comprising the valley temple, covered causeway, funerary temple, and the pyramid itself came from Aswan, far up the Nile. As early as Dynasty I the Egyptians had copper saws and chisels capable of cutting any kind of limestone, but special dolorite hammers were required to chip rough slots into the quarry walls of the very hard granite. After wooden wedges were pounded into the slots they were soaked in water, and the resulting expansion split off chunks of the stone. The finished blocks in all the quarries were moved by work gangs of about eighteen to twenty men using hawsers, levers, log rollers, and sledges. Heavy barges carried the blocks during the journey down the river.

Preparation of the site and construction methods remain to be considered. A rocky knoll at the desert's edge was selected as the substructure to support the great weight of more than five-and-a-half million tons of the monument. Terraces to serve as the foundations had to be cut into the irregular sides of the hill at an absolute level if the structure was to be true, and to accomplish this the architects designed a system of water-filled trenches about the base. Then, with the water level as a standard, areas between two trenches were leveled by measurements made from a string stretched between sticks of equal length, each of which was held at the surface of the water. This horizontal string-line provided a perfect level for the work of flattening the terraces. The basic construction technique for moving the huge blocks up to the ever higher courses, on the other hand, remains a matter of dispute. One theory holds that four mud-brick ramps were built, one starting at each corner, against the outer surface of the casing stones. As each course added to the height these ramps were extended, with the stones being dragged up three of them by sledge and with the fourth reserved for the descending work gangs. Elegant though it appears at first sight, this theory has serious flaws; I. E. S. Edwards in *The Pyramids of Egypt* describes an alternate and perhaps more probable method.

Pertinent Literature

Edwards, I. E. S. *The Pyramids of Egypt.* 2nd ed. Baltimore, Maryland: Penguin Books, 1961.

This book provides the best survey on the entire subject of the pyramids in any language. After an introduction which gives the historical background and a brief summary of the religious beliefs which led to the building of the pyramids, there follows a treatment in chronological sequence of early burial customs and the mastaba tombs, the step pyramids, the transition to the true pyramid and the Giza group, pyramids of Dynasties V, VI, and the later periods, and lastly, a study of construction methods and the purpose of pyramids. There is also a table of the major pyramids of the Old and Middle Kingdoms, with over ninety plates and drawings to illustrate the subject.

The attraction of the ancient Egyptians toward the world of the dead is dramatized by their greatest architectural achievement, the Great Pyramid, which exacted an unimaginable cost in human and material resources as a tomb for the Pharaoh Cheops. But this is only the supreme example among countless lesser ones. In fact, by far the major portion of Egyptian antiquities come from the tombs, whereas the private and public buildings in which the people lived and worked, as well as the great capital cities of Memphis and Thebes, have all disappeared almost without a trace. The physical explanation for this strange imbalance of surviving objects is an obvious one: Egyptian tombs after the earliest period were all built of stone or hewn out of rock, while the houses and palaces in which the populace resided consisted of mud-brick, wood, and gesso. To the Egyptian the house in which he lived was finite and replaceable, but the tomb in which he would rest unendingly had to last forever. This attitude derived from his belief that bliss after death could be achieved only upon the fulfillment of two essential conditions: his body must be preserved and the physical needs of his *ka,* or spirit, must be supplied. Though the form of the final resting place varied many times during the long course of history, the essential purpose of this eternal and enduring last domicile remained unchanged.

One of the most interesting chapters of the book is devoted to construction and purpose of the pyramids. Among other matters, the author here discusses the problem of the ramps whereby the blocks of stone were dragged to the required level, and he rejects the view that one ramp began at each corner of the pyramid and continued in an upward, corkscrew manner around the four faces. Archaeology and engineering both tend to disprove this ingenious but overly complex theory. Such ramps would depend for their support beyond the first stage on the casing-blocks, which it is held were laid in a fairly well-cut, step-like progression. But no evidence of such ramps has been found at any pyramid site; undressed casing-blocks that lie at the base of the Pyramid of Mycerinus are not step-like and would not have supported such a ramp; and it is questionable whether the widest possible step would have provided sufficient room for blocks of the size used at Giza to be unloaded and fixed in place. Instead, it is far more likely that a single supply ramp was built to cover the whole of one side of the pyramid. As the building progressed upwards the ramp would not only increase in height but also in length in order to maintain an unchanging gradient for the work gangs dragging the great blocks up the ramp.

Lange, K. and M. Hirmer. *Egypt. Architecture, Sculpture, Painting in Three Thousand Years*. London: Phaidon Press, 1961.

The plan of this book is to present the reader with 260 large and excellent plates, the results of Hirmer's photography, and to follow this section with detailed commentary on the various periods of ancient Egypt and on the individual works presented in the plates. This latter section is enhanced by forty figures, most of which are plans or sections of the structures studied. Plates 26-47 and the accompanying text treat the pyramids and the adjacent areas at Giza.

Though the conventional photographs of the Giza pyramids invariably show them standing against the stark desert background and a clear sky, the implication that these monuments stand alone and isolated is a false one. Each pyramid complex consisted of four structures: the gate or valley temple; the covered causeway running westward toward the pyramid; the funerary temple in front of the great tomb; and the pyramid itself as the climax of this succession of monuments. The best preserved of these groups belongs to the Pyramid of Chephren, not that of Cheops, the auxiliary structures of which have to a large degree been destroyed. To the north of the beginning of the causeway of the valley temple to Chephren's pyramid lies the great Sphinx in the form of a colossal, couchant lion with human head. This famous figure measures sixty-five feet in height and 238 feet in length, and was carved out of the remains of a limestone quarry from which the blocks for the Pyramid of Cheops were cut. In Egyptian mythology the lion is often the guardian of holy places, and incorporated into the majestic figure of the Great Sphinx at Giza, where it is combined with human facial features depicting the Sun-god Ra, it represents Chephren acting as divine guardian of the great necropolis. In the vicinity of each of the three pyramids stand smaller ones for members of the royal family and scores of mastaba tombs for members of the royal household and court. The valley temple or gateway for each of the three pyramids at Giza lay on a branch of the Nile. In the surviving valley temple of Chephren, the simplicity, proportions, and materials make it a structure of great beauty. Sphinxes flanked each of its two entrances on the eastern side. The main halls consist of an inverted T-plan with monolithic granite pillars thirteen and a half feet high. Against the walls there once stood twenty-three statues of Chephren, the best surviving of which can now been seen in the Cairo Museum. From an oblique side corridor the five-hundred-yard covered causeway led to the funerary temple standing before the east side of the pyramid itself. This structure was built of local limestone faced with granite and consists of three successive entry halls, the last of which leads into the great court where sacrifices on

behalf of the dead King were offered. Adjoining this court on the West were five chapels, with a statue of the Pharaoh in each for worship under one of his five names.

When the King died, his body was borne across the Nile to the great necropolis on the west side. In the valley temple the corpse was prepared for burial by the process of mummification. On the day of interment the mummy was hauled up the great causeway in a ritual barge to the funerary temple, where the last rites were performed. Then it was taken up into the great chamber of his pyramid, in which his loyal subjects confidently believed his body would remain for all time.

This book by Lange and Hirmer combines superb photography with an accurate and enlightening text, and by a judicious selection of topics it properly places the pyramids within the context of Egyptian civilization and art over the course of three millennia.
— *K.H.*

Additional Recommended Reading

Smith, W. Stevenson. *The Art and Architecture of Ancient Egypt. Pelican History of Art.* Baltimore: Penguin Books, 1958. A sober and scholarly presentation of the major topics, including the pyramids.

Aldred, Cyril. *Egypt to the End of the Old Kingdom.* New York: McGraw-Hill Book Co., 1965. A paperback with concise text and excellent illustrations, many in color. The second half of the book covers the Age of the Pyramids.

Woldering, Irmgard. *The Art of Egypt. The Time of the Pharaohs.* New York: Greystone Press, 1963. A well-illustrated book covering the prehistoric to the Greco-Roman periods.

DOMESTICATION OF THE CAMEL

Type of event: Sociological: advance in transportation
Time: c.2500 B.C.
Locale: Arabia

Summary of Event

The camel, even though one of the later animal domesticates, has been of great economic importance in Asia for more than three thousand years. Since neither of the two species, *Camelus dromedarius*, and *Camelus bactrianus* the two hump or "true" camel, is gifted with sufficient intelligence even to "identify" with its owner or to be particularly protective toward its young, the assets which predisposed the animal to domestication were doubtless physical. However, its passive, dull, "fatalistic" temperament, making it largely indifferent to friendly, gentle treatment probably recommended it as a rough beast of burden. It was even occasionally trained to fight.

Physically the camel is peculiarly adapted to an arid habitat rather than a hot climate, since the bactrian prefers a cold desert environment even though the dromedary is a hot desert animal. Special muscles conveniently enable the camel to close its nostrils against blowing sands, and its large shapeless feet, heavily padded, spread readily when set down, a definite asset when walking on loose sand. Furthermore, it is capable of surviving on plant foods utterly useless to other ruminants. It seems to need halophytes in its diet and will thrive on salt plants wholly rejected by other animals. Far from being a storage place for water, the camel's hump is a soft mass of fat, a reservoir of calories to be drawn upon as needed. Since the hump stands erect when the animal is well fed, a camel driver can readily tell the condition of his animal. Nor does the beast's three-chambered ruminating stomach store water as such. The camel may need as much as fifty quarts of water at a single drinking, though fortunately it can use brackish or even salty water. While it has been lauded for its speed and tirelessness, the animal's maximum gait is about ten miles per hour; its cruising speed is about three or four, the rate of a walking man. It may cover as much as fifty miles a day, although the average is less. It is a good swimmer, has keen eyesight and hearing, and possesses a particularly sharp sense of smell.

Even though these peculiar qualities suitable to the demands of the desert recommended the animal for early domestication as a beast of burden, its history as a tame and docile cud-chewer may not go back much further than 2000 B.C. The donkey, *Equus asinus,* may well have preceded it as a beast of burden around oases. Most paleontologists and archaeologists are agreed that the fossil *Camelus sivalensis* of early Pleistocene times found in northern India must have been the ancestor of both species of modern camels. These primeval animals had a long time to spread through southeast Asia, where they were doubtless hunted by Paleolithic man. Both Harappa and Mohenjo-Daro, archaeological sites in the Indus Valley, have yielded dromedary bones, but no evidence at all reveals that domesticated camels existed in prehistoric Asia. At a number of sites in Egypt, figurines and pottery effigies of camels tend to place domestication of the dromedary as far back as the third millenium B.C. Even so, the animal would scarcely be known in Egypt until late predynastic times; in fact, it probably did not become a common domesticated animal there until the sixth century B.C. In Mesopotamia the camel began to be an important domesticate perhaps about 1000 B.C., although it was known in several places a thousand or so years earlier. References to the camel in Genesis and Exodus suggest that the beast was known to Abraham about 1800 B.C., but these later-written sources may well contain anachronistic material. The camel was unknown in Carthage before the downfall of that city, and it did not appear in West Africa until several centuries after the

beginning of the Christian era. The bactrian or "true" camel was introduced to the north shore of the Black Sea by Goths only in the third or fourth century A.D. Even though evidence now available indicates that the dromedary has been economically important in Arabia and its environs for about three thousand years and that the bactrian may have been in use longer in Syria and the East, it would appear to be reasonable to date the general domestication of the camel around 2000 B.C. or slightly earlier. Since the question whether any wild camels still exist is as yet unanswered, no untrained strains are available to throw light on the instinctive character of the species or the procedures used to tame it. The methods and people involved in ancient times are not known.

The camel's future is less in doubt than its past, with the introduction of the truck and the preservation of the horse as a prestige animal in the East.

Pertinent Literature

Leonard, A. G. *The Camel: Its Uses and Management*. New York: Longman's Green and Co., 1894.

This interesting old book, largely a veterinarian and field guide for the care of the camel, was written by an army major well acquainted with the beast as a military pack animal in the far-flung British Empire.

Much of the author's information, especially in the field of domestication was antiquated and naïve even for the 1890's. His dependence on the Bible as a prime source for historical information should not be indicted however, since the Old Testament is still well regarded by respected authorities

on the camel. Rather naïvely, he believes that the Flood probably restricted the habitat of the camel but that strays might have walked to Greece from Arabia when Africa and Europe were joined. The number of camels must have been great in Biblical times considering the report that the tribes of Reuben and Manasseh took away fifty thousand of the animals from the defeated Hagarites. Leonard could find no hieroglyphic references to camels in Egypt. This observation is not wholly true, although it is correct to say that camels arrived much later in the Nile and the Sudan than in southwestern Asia.

In his book Leonard delivers a eulogy on the camel. He states that early civilizations were more dependent upon the beast than Laplanders are on the reindeer. Camels can be ridden, driven, and used as pack animals. They are natural pacers, providing "a jolting swinging motion . . . something like that of a ship rolling and pitching at sea." They can carry great loads, up to fifteen hundred pounds for a few miles, although three to five hundred pounds is the average. In addition, the 1000- to 1150-pound camel furnishes a great deal of food. The milk is especially nourishing. When sour it may be mixed with flour or when sweet boiled with rice and flour. Indeed, in Nubia and the Sudan many Arabs exist principally on cereal grains and camel's milk. Both butter and cheese can be manufactured from the milk. Eating the flesh is prohibited by Jews although the Arabs value the fatty hump especially of young animals as a delicacy. Harness and shoes are made from camel hide; toothbrushes and fine paint brushes are products of camel hair, which is very durable when woven with wool or cotton. Even the dried dung of the animal is useful for fuel especially in desert regions where wood is nonexistent or scarce.

Leonard well understood that among all other domesticated animals the camel has few friends. Herodotus reported that horses could not endure the sight or smell of the animal, and he attributed the defeat of Croesus by the Persians under Cyrus in 557 B.C. in part to the panic that was created in the Lydian cavalry when Persian camels appeared. Fortunately for Leonard, camels by 1890 were no longer used for cavalry by the British but were restricted to hauling guns and equipment.

In discussing the breeding of the shorter but heavier and more muscular bactrian with the dromedary, Leonard reports that crosses of male bactrians and female dromedaries produce a single-hump hybrid, tough and hardy, able to withstand intense cold and exposure. Products of male dromedaries and female bactrians he labels as useless, vicious, and refractory. All crossbred hybrids are infertile, a fact that has led modern students to conclude that the two forms of the camel are distinct although their main physical difference is the number of humps. The feet and teeth formations of the camel seem to show distant kinship with the elephant.

After devoting more than three hundred pages to the camel and its assets, Leonard concludes that the mule is the more useful of the two.

Fowler, H. D. *Camels to California.* Stanford: Stanford University Press, 1950.

Prospects for the camel once looked bright in America. In the nineteenth century Jefferson Davis when Secretary of War was the principal proponent of a project to establish the camel in the southwest desert regions of the United States as part of his efforts to open up the West. Most observers scorned the idea as coming from an impractical mind, and Congress considered that $30,000 was an extravagant sum to risk on such a venture, but Davis was persuasive. Having digested every report or treatise he could find on the use of camels, he was particularly impressed with a report of Major Henry Wayne in 1853 entitled "General Remarks on the Use of Camels and Dromedaries for Transportation and Military Purposes other than those of Burden—as for Expresses, the Pursuit of Marauders, etc." Davis envisioned the swift pursuit of raiding Apache Indians by a Camel Corps of the U.S. Cavalry. When the discovery of gold in California in 1848 increased eastern interest in the West, a group of New York capitalists formed a corporation, The American Camel Company, to import camels for trade and travel in the West. Under pressure, Congress supported the project in 1855.

Chosen to purchase camels in the Near East was a forty-two-year-old lieutenant, David Dixon Porter, a veteran of several navy campaigns in the tropics. Porter was to take a navy storeship, the *Supply,* to the Levant and bring back a shipload of camels. Major Wayne, author of the tract which had impressed Davis and himself a camel enthusiast, was sent to London to observe a few camels in the gardens of the Zoölogical Society. He also went to Paris where he found only one specimen to study. When he joined Porter on the *Supply* in Italy, the shopping spree for camels began in earnest.

Purchasing camels was not a simple matter. In countries where the exportation of the animals was prohibited, U.S. consuls had to exert influence. Eventually *Supply* headed for Texas with a full load of thirty-three fine animals. Porter subsequently brought in forty-one more.

The task of transferring these animals to California was not to be hurried. A newly established military post at Camp Verde, sixty-five miles north of San Antonio, became the training ground for the beasts for almost a year. In mid-1857 the herd was placed under the direction of Edward Fitzgerald Beale, a former navy lieutenant and an experienced western traveler, who finally transported the animals fifteen hundred miles to Fort Tejon, California, where they were quartered for several years. They justified all expectations and performed well as pack animals.

Despite the good record of the camels' performance and the repeated requests of Secretary of War Floyd in 1858, 1859, and 1860 that more camels be purchased, the Civil War was the last straw that broke the camel's back. In 1864, the government auctioned off the surviving thirty-seven animals and thus brought to a close a promising military logistic experiment. It is interesting to speculate on what the outcome of these endeavors might have been.

The camels imported by the War Department were not the only ones to be found in Texas and the southwest. After the Civil War scattered specimens appeared in local circuses and a few were actually used as pack animals by prospectors and miners. As late as the first decade of the twentieth century there were authentic reports of the survival of offspring of these animals and for years afterward the sightings of "phantom ships of the desert" appeared as news items in the southwest. After these exploits, the camel was left to work out his future in the Near East from which he originally came. — *W.G.H.*

Additional Recommended Reading

Zeuner, Frederick E. *A History of Domesticated Animals.* Ch. 13. London: Hutchinson & Co., 1963. A historical sketch of camel origins and utilization.

COMPOSITION OF EGYPTIAN WISDOM LITERATURE

Type of event: Literary: dissemination of teachings on ethics and social conduct
Time: After c.2400 B.C.
Locale: Egypt

Summary of Event

Wisdom literature is a genre common to all the civilizations of the ancient Near East. The Egyptian wisdom texts are among the most valuable sources for reaching an understanding of the cultural life of Egypt, particularly that of the ordinary Egyptian, who, like the common man of any civilization, has been slighted in historical literature until fairly recent times. The body of writings called wisdom literature comprises texts covering more than two thousand years of Egyptian history. The oldest and best known is the advice of the vizier Ptahhotep, which is supposed to have been written in Dynasty V about 2400 B.C., while the latest was written about 500 B.C.

In form, the wisdom texts consist of easily memorized aphoristic statements. The sayings are put in the mouth of a father or superior speaking to a son or to some other young man. Clearly reflective of the intrinsic ultra-conservatism of Egyptian culture, the texts are founded on the assumption that the young person will achieve maturity by absolute acceptance of the advice of his elders. These purely didactic texts were aimed at helping the Egyptian to live according to standards of justice and honesty. They deal indiscriminately with moral standards and norms of behavior, including such matters as rules of etiquette in dealing with superiors, conduct in law courts, and relations between husband and

wife. The copies that have been preserved were used as texts for schoolboys. This fact is significant in that it tells us not only something of the value system of the Egyptians but also one important way in which values were transmitted.

Wisdom literature is the closest approach to philosophy in ancient Egypt, though it grapples not with ontological, epistemological, or cosmological problems, but rather with ethics, and even then only in a limited sense. The Egyptians never seem to have achieved a systematic philosophy; at no time in Egypt's long history was there a set of working principles commanding consensus or demanding criticism.

The earliest texts, emphasizing worldly success, reflect the optimism of the old kingdom, Egypt's most creative period. The *Instruction of Ptahhotep,* for example, reflects an individualism and a strong sense of personal initiative, and it breathes a feeling of great self-assurance, though it counsels modest and deferential behavior. The young man for whom the *Instruction of Ptahhotep* was written is advised to beware of covetousness, because it is an incurable sickness; to guard against arrogance merely because he has knowledge; to take counsel with the ignorant as well as with the wise, since no one has a monopoly on knowledge or skill.

There is keen psychology in the advice to be a ready listener. The instruc-

35

tor tells his pupil to hear anyone to the end, because a person with an anxiety or a request will get more satisfaction from the experience of being heard to the end than he would if his request were granted. No one, the passage continues, expects to get everything he asks for, but if he receives a considerate hearing, at least he will come away with a soothed heart. Another passage makes a distinction between listening and actually hearing, and plays on the idea that maturity comes to the man who really hears, that is, gives actual assent to his father's words. This ability to hear is a sign of God's favor. It is God who touches the heart and makes it docile and capable of comprehending. Here there is a wedding of Egyptian conservatism and religious idealism.

Inasmuch as Egypt found its focus in religion, a question arises about the relationship of the wisdom texts to Egyptian religious literature. From one point of view, wisdom literature is secular in form and content. It bears close resemblance to the advice of Polonius to his son in Shakespeare's *Hamlet*, or, as the noted Egyptologist John Wilson observes, to Lord Chesterfield's *Letters to His Son* and to *Poor*

Richard's Almanac. On the other hand, there is in the Egyptian wisdom literature a concept of God which, to some students, closely approximates monotheism, though monotheistic tendencies revealed in such texts never developed into a lasting cult.

Ever since the early eighteenth century there has been a growing awareness that Near Eastern and Egyptian literature in the form of creation myths, epics, laws, historical texts, rituals, hymns, prayers, and wisdom literature should be studied closely for a better understanding of the Old Testament. Consequently the question arises whether there is a relationship between Egyptian wisdom literature and similar Hebrew writings, especially Proverbs. All scholars do not agree on this question, but they do take note of intriguing similarities such as the following:

Make no friendship
  with a man given to anger,
nor go with a wrathful man.
  (Proverbs 22:24)

Join thyself not
  to the passionate man,
and approach him not for conversation.
(Instruction of Amenemope 11(13-14)

Pertinent Literature

Erman, Adolf. *The Ancient Egyptians: A Sourcebook of Their Writings.* Translated by Aylward M. Blackman. New York: Harper & Row Publishers Incorporated, 1966.

This book is a reprint of a work first published in German in 1923 and in English in 1927. It remains the best and most easily accessible anthology of Egyptian writings. The introduction to the present edition, by William Kelly Simpson offers a critique of the orig-

inal work, a selective bibliography of more recent editions and translations of individual pieces in the collection, citations of related articles and books, and notes on the present translation.

Simpson points out that the year after Erman published his collection, the *Instruction of Amenemope* was published. Simpson considers this important addition to the corpus of wisdom literature as the culmination of the genre. He quotes selections from Amenemope, one of which will remind the reader acquainted with the Bible of familiar images.

> Do not ridicule a blind man nor taunt a dwarf, and do not interfere with the business of a lame man.
> Do not taunt a man who is in the hand of God, and do not be frightening when he goes astray.
> As for man, he is clay and straw and God is his potter . . . .

Another recent addition to Egyptian wisdom literature which Simpson mentions is a short series of "prohibitions" translated into English in 1957. He also includes an account of, and examples from, late Egyptian wisdom literature of the fifth and fourth centuries B.C. The close resemblance to early texts demonstrates the strong tradition in Egyptian culture of these moralizing commonplaces.

Erman's selections from Egyptian wisdom literature include passages from the *Instruction of Ptahhotep,* the *Instruction for Kagemni,* the *Instruction of Duauf,* the *Instruction of King Amenemhet,* the *Instruction of King Merikere,* and the *Instruction of Sehetepibre.*

The *Instruction of Ptahhotep,* according to Erman, had a twofold object. Not only did it give lessons in good conduct; it was also intended as a sort of model of rhetoric. Simpson calls attention to the practical nature of the advice in this instruction, in contrast to the more ethical and religious

tone in later examples of the same kind of writing.

The *Instruction of Duauf* is distinctive as a piece of propaganda extolling schools and education. This particular piece became a favorite textbook. It satirizes various professions, and praises scribes, describing their lot as particularly favorable. "Would that I might make thee love books more than thy mother," the father tells his son, so that he could as a scribe avoid the crocodile-skinned fingers of the smith and the broken back of the mason.

Erman points out the elevated religious conceptions in the *Instruction of King Merikere,* and Simpson adds that the piece has been analyzed as a true literary production and not merely a piece of propaganda. In this work, God's providence is extolled in a psalm-like passage: "Well tended are men, the cattle of God. He made heaven and earth according to their desire. He allayed the thirst for water. He made the air that their nostrils may live. They are his images, that have proceeded from His limbs. . . ."

In the section of Erman's anthology given to works of the New Kingdom (c.1540-1058 B.C.) is a selection, *The Wisdom of Ani,* which is a late imitation of the earlier books of wisdom. This selection is perhaps the best example of an Egyptian code of ethics. It urges prudence, piety, temperance, and honesty, even advising the reader to be mindful of death. Particularly graphic is a passage exhorting a young man to be grateful to his mother, who is described as patient and self-sacrificing. The passage is eloquent testimony to the Egyptian attitude towards women, at least on its idealistic side.

Frankfort, H. "The Egyptian Way of Life," in *Ancient Egyptian Religion: An Interpretation.* Ch. 3. New York: Harper & Row Publishers Incorporated. 1948.

In this philosophical analysis of the wisdom texts in the context of Egyptian religion, the author observes that there is no need to rely on inference when trying to understand the Egyptian idea of the good life, since the Egyptians were explicit in the matter. Frankfort does not see the Egyptian philosophy as evolving, and here he differs in his approach from James Breasted. Impressed by the sameness of ethical ideals throughout Egyptian history, he believes that it is possible to generalize about the Egyptian way of life using the wisdom texts of any period.

The fact that wisdom literature was so popular is itself significant because it shows that the Egyptians believed the good life could be taught. This optimistic view shows, says Frankfort, high estimate of man's ability to understand and reflects the peculiar Egyptian "feeling of security, of being in a world which is neither hostile nor, in the last analysis, problematical." This serene world view is contrasted with that of the peoples of Mesopotamia and also with the Hebrews. In Mesopotamia, the gods were unpredictable, and men always felt uncertain about them; while the Hebrews were anxious because they were never unmindful of the gravity of God's commands and their own propensity to break them. Frankfort suggests that it may be the serenity of the Egyptian wisdom literature which has led to its classification as secular writing. He thinks this is an error, and that the "teachings," as he prefers to call the wisdom literature, are accurately understood only as religious writings.

He explains that it is not easy to penetrate to the deeper levels of the teachings largely because of their haphazard arrangement, in which rules of etiquette and profound moral principle follow one upon the other with no apparent logic. The integrating factor in these passages is found in the concept *Maat,* an untranslatable term which, for the Egyptians, referred to the divine order established at the time of creation, to which man somehow became assimilated. It shows itself especially in the normal rhythms of nature, in which apparent opposites contain each other in equilibrium. Since man is part of nature, he too reflects *Maat* and in a way participates in it by aligning himself with nature's rhythms. Such a value system canonized custom almost absolutely, since custom was, in human behavior, the closest thing to a natural and predictable rhythm. Consequently Egyptian moral philosophy placed a premium on anything with a semblance of permanence, and it excluded ideas of progress, utopias, and revolutions.

Within this frame of reference, it becomes clear that the observance of a code of conduct was not merely a legalistic procedure, but rather a mode of behaviour having deep religious significance on both the private subjective experiences and the outward acts of the practitioner.

There is a strong element of predestination in Egyptian religious and philosophical thought, but it does not exclude the element of struggle. The wisdom literature shows that ignorance and passion are obstacles which man must overcome in order to attain the

38

good life. Only the self-disciplined, passionless man is master of himself and in tune with the existing order of the universe.

In the Egyptian ethical ideal of the wisdom literature, Frankfort sees the Greco-Roman concept of the golden mean and the Greek humanistic notion of pride. To the Egyptian pride meant the loss of a sense of proportion, which led to disaster. The consequences of pride, however, were not the same. Through pride, the Egyptian lost his place in society and his integration with nature; the proud Greek, however, incurred the resentment of the gods.

Such an ethic would seem to be necessarily fatalistic and capable of limitless rationalization over the suf- fering of others. Frankfort points out that the Egyptian did, however, have a sense of social concern or compassion. The *Instruction of Amenemope* encourages its reader to be generous to the poor if he would sleep easily and awaken with a feeling of satisfaction deriving from being in harmony with *Maat*.

Frankfort concludes his exploration of wisdom literature with a discussion of the effect of political catastrophe on the Egyptian view of the good life. He thinks that the disintegration of the central government in the third millennium left the Egyptians disorientated and unable to cope with a universe which had somehow gone awry. — *M.E.J.*

Additional Recommended Reading

Breasted, James Henry. *Development of Religion and Thought in Ancient Egypt.* New York: Harper & Row Publishers Incorporated, 1912; reprinted 1959. This reprinted edition of an old work is still valuable and gives considerable attention to Ptahhotep.

Wilson, John A. "Egypt: The Values of Life," in A. and H. A. Frankfort, John A. Wilson, and others. *The Intellectual Adventure of Ancient Man.* Chicago: University of Chicago Press, 1946. A perceptive analysis of the religion of ancient Egypt.

Gardiner, Sir Alan. *Egypt of the Pharaohs.* Oxford: The Clarendon Press, 1961. The wisdom literature is not treated at length in this standard history, but there is some discussion of the *Instruction of King Merikere*.

Pritchard, James B., ed. *Ancient Near Eastern Texts Relating to the Old Testament.* Pt. VI. Princeton: Princeton University Press, 1950. Texts from Egyptian wisdom literature are included along with selections from Akkadia.

Wilson, John A. *The Culture of Ancient Egypt.* Chicago: University of Chicago Press, 1951. The wisdom literature is given considerable attention in this well-written book.

Barton, G. A. *Archaeology and the Bible.* 7th ed. Philadelphia, Pennsylvania: American Sunday School Union, 1937. Translations of Near Eastern texts call attention to Biblical parallels.

APPEARANCE OF THE GILGAMESH EPIC

Type of event: Literary: creation of a myth
Time: c.2000 B.C.
Locale: Sumer

Principal personage:

ASHURBANIPAL, King of Assyria 669-c.626 B.C., preserver of the epic

Summary of Event

The Gilgamesh Epic is the oldest extant epic poem, and Gilgamesh, legendary King of Uruk, the first literary hero in history. Apart from the similarity of the flood episode to the account given in Genesis 7, Gilgamesh is worthy of study because he reveals the typical pessimism and insecurity felt by man more than twelve hundred years before the time of Homer.

It has been proved by quotations discovered on early Sumerian tablets of the third millenium that parts of the epic existed then, but the main portion was probably composed around 2000 B.C. Episodes are written on a large number of cuneiform clay tablets of varying dates unearthed at various places in the Near East, but an almost complete version, consisting of twelve tablets of about three hundred lines each, comes from the library of Ashurbanipal, King of Assyria from 669 to c.626 B.C. The simplicity and clarity of the tale indicates that it was probably designed for recitation rather than reading, and the Semitic parallelism of phrases is characteristic of the ancient epic style.

The main plot describes how the people of Uruk beg the gods to relieve them of oppression by their autocratic ruler Gilgamesh. Their prayer is answered when Enkidu, the counter-hero, enters the city and wrestles with Gilgamesh. Though Gilgamesh proves his physical superiority over Enkidu, the two become firm friends and inseparable companions. They set out to overcome the giant Humbaba, who has been appointed by the god Enlil to guard the cedar forest. Together Gilgamesh and Enkidu succeed in destroying Humbaba.

On their return to Uruk, the goddess Ishtar tries to win Gilgamesh as her lover, but is spurned. In revenge, she prevails upon Anu, father of the gods, to send upon Gilgamesh the Bull of Heaven, which represents seven years of drought. Gilgamesh is thus responsible for bringing destruction upon many of his own people. Eventually, Gilgamesh kills the bull, but that same night he learns in a dream that the gods have decreed that one of the two heroes, Gilgamesh or Enkidu, must lose his life for having slain Humbaba and the bull. The penalty falls on Enkidu, and Gilgamesh thus loses his inseparable companion. Grieving, he sets out to find Utnapishtim, the only human being who survived the Great Flood. Gilgamesh begs Utnapishtim to share with him the secret of immortality, and Utnapishtim gives him a branch from the plant of life. But on his way home, while Gilga-

40

mesh stops for a swim, a snake steals the precious branch. Gilgamesh faces the fact that death is his fate. This episode ends the epic, except for an epilogue in which Enkidu in the underworld tries to retrieve two lost objects of Gilgamesh.

This simple adventure tale both conceals and reveals a number of profound human problems and philosophical questions. It raises the question of the purpose of life, and comes to a conclusion characteristic of Mesopotamian culture in its pessimism. For though the Gilgamesh Epic does not see death as annihilation of the person, it views existence after death as essentially gloomy. After death, man dwells in a lower world described as a house of dust where he is a mere shadow of his former self. Thorkild Jacobsen remarks in *The Intellectual Adventure of Ancient Man* that the Gilgamesh Epic does not have a harmonious conclusion; its surging emotions are not alleviated; "nor is there, as in tragedy, any sense of catharsis, any fundamental acceptance of the inevitable." Its ending is unpleasant and disturbing. "An inner turmoil is left to rage on, a vital question finds no answer."

Another theme is the struggle of civilization against barbarism. Enkidu is tamed or "civilized" by succumbing to a woman sent to him for the specific purpose of overcoming him by her charms. The Humbaba episode can also be interpreted as representing the clash between civilization and barbarism, inasmuch as it shows the two heroes struggling against a creature who controls the forest essential to the economy of Uruk.

The Gilgamesh Epic had been forgotten during the Classical Age of Greece and Rome, and it was not brought into view again until the nineteenth century when the ruins of Nineveh were excavated.

The relationship of the Gilgamesh Epic to the Biblical account of the Flood in Genesis 7 has been carefully studied by scholars since the parallel was first revealed by George Smith, an English scholar, in 1872. There are striking similarities in the two accounts. Both tell of widespread destruction and the saving of a single man and his family: Utnapishtim in the Gilgamesh account, and Noah in the Bible. The differences, however, are more significant than the similarities in what they tell us about the two cultures. In the Biblical account, the Flood is a punishment for sin; in Gilgamesh, man is not guilty but rather the victim of the caprice of the gods. In Genesis, man is given an opportunity to repent in order to avert disaster; no such chance is offered in the Gilgamesh account. In the Mesopotamian version, the salvation of Utnapishtim is a purely personal boon, while in the case of Noah, the conclusion of the drama is a covenant between God and Noah as head of his descendants. The opinion widely held today is that the Hebrew and Babylonian versions may have had a common source, but the account in Genesis does not seem to have depended directly on the Gilgamesh Epic.

41

Appearance of the Gilgamesh Epic

Pertinent Literature

Sanders, N. K. *The Epic of Gilgamesh*. Baltimore, Maryland: Penguin Books Inc., 1960.

This translation of the Gilgamesh Epic into modern English prose is preceded by a felicitous introduction. N. K. Sanders writes of Gilgamesh as the first tragic hero of whom anything is known, a character typical of every man in his search for life and understanding.

In the section on the history of the epic, as well as in a later section on the epic's survival, there are informative accounts of King Ashurbanipal of Assyria and the political and cultural events of his reign which bear on the seventh century written form of the epic. It is a curious fact that after Ashurbanipal's capital, Nineveh, fell to the Medes and Persians in 612 B.C., the epic was all but forgotten except for the flood episode. Yet remnants remained in the memory of men, for there is unmistakable evidence of Gilgamesh elements throughout the Near East and parts of the area around the Aegean Sea. Sanders considers that any possible influence that Gilgamesh might have had on the Homeric heroes is unproven, and that any similarities are the results of "a similar atmosphere" rather than "prototypes and parentage."

The story of the discovery of the various tablets which form the basis of our present knowledge of the epic is told with sufficient detail to stir the admiration and fire the enthusiasm of any reader, even if he has only the most casual interest in the civilization of the ancient Near East. Appreciative credit is given to the archaeologists and scholars to whom our knowledge of the literature of Mesopotamia owes so much: Austen Layard, Henry Rawlinson, George Smith, and John Punnet Peters, as well as recent scholars such as Oliver Gurney, Samuel Noah Kramer, and E. A. Speiser.

In the shadowy political history of early Sumer, it is possible that the Gilgamesh of the epic had a human prototype in Gudea of Lagash. Whoever the prototype may have been, in the epic Gilgamesh is part god and part man, which is the source of his tragic dilemma. His mother is an obscure goddess, from whom he inherits his dynamic qualities of beauty, strength, and restlessness, while his father bequeaths to him mortality. Herein rests the tragedy of the conflict between the desires of the god and the destiny of the man. This theme, and the character of Gilgamesh who portrays it, are what give the work its spiritual unity over so many centuries during which it both grew and underwent revision. In a particularly poignant passage after Gilgamesh has told the wine goddess Siduri about his fear of death and his restless search for immortality, she warns him: "Gilgamesh, where are you hurrying to? You will never find that life for which you are looking. When the gods created man they alloted to him death, but life they retained in their own keeping. As for you, Gilgamesh, fill your belly with good things; day and night, night and day, dance and be merry, feast and rejoice." But Gilgamesh replies:

42

"How can I be silent, how can I rest, when Enkidu whom I love is dust, and I too shall die and be laid in the earth for ever?"

This fatalistic philosophy is the distinctive note of the Mesopotamian epic, and along with it goes a vivid conception of hell in striking contrast to the Egyptians' optimistic preoccupation with an afterlife akin to heaven. The malaise of Mesopotamian psychology lies in insecurity and the lack of a covenant such as the Hebrews had with Yahweh.

Sanders' analysis of the epic's content is perceptive. For example, she interprets the Enkidu forest episode on three levels: as a historical event showing Uruk's need for timber, as an adventure story, and finally as an allegory in which Humbaba represents evil. Ishtar is also discussed in depth; there is a particularly incisive treatment of the significance of Enkidu's death, an event which is Gilgamesh's undoing because it deprives him of an almost perfect friendship and he is unable to sustain the loss.

In the translation of the epic itself, Sanders omits apparatus showing alternative readings and lacunae. The result is an eminently readable translation.

Oppenheim, A. Leo. *Ancient Mesopotamia: Portrait of a Dead Civilization.* Chicago: The University of Chicago Press, 1964.

In the esoteric field of Assyriology, A. Leo Oppenheim is a competent scholar able to communicate both the significance and relevance of his subject.

He believes that the Gilgamesh Epic represents a type well suited for descriptions and orations, but not to the presentation of dramatic incidents. For this reason, much of the epic-type cuneiform literature is lifeless; it is an indication of the artistry of the author or authors of the late version of the Epic of Gilgamesh that the work rises above the limitations inherent in its literary form.

Oppenheim believes the epic provides a good example of Mesopotamian literary achievement at its best. It is a curious and thought-provoking fact that among the Babylonians themselves the work held no particular position of eminence in literary tradition, as few fragments have been found in Mesopotamia proper and there are few quotations from the epic in other works. Gilgamesh was more popular outside Mesopotamia.

Gilgamesh's drive for immortality is the main theme of the poem, according to Oppenheim. The sophistication of the structure of the poem is evident in the use of two parallel scenes, one at the beginning and the other near the end of the epic. In each case, the episode has to do with the walls which Gilgamesh built for his city; these walls alone guarantee the hero an immortal reputation. Oppenheim believes that the author of the poem did not have Gilgamesh seek immortality through his descendants because the epic may have been composed in the court of a childless ruler, who would be embarrassed by such a solution.

Oppenheim differs from the generally held view in his argument that the Epic of Gilgamesh was meant to be read rather than recited. He bases his conclusion on internal evidence, acknowledging at the same time that the early Akkadian versions of the epic suggest a background of popular verse. The episode of the slaying of Humbaba, the giant of the cedar forest, poses a problem for Oppenheim. As the text of this adventure is poorly preserved, adequate analysis is impossible, but the importance of the episode is evident from references to it earlier in the epic, and by frequent allusions to it elsewhere. Full understanding of the episode awaits the discovery of more tablets which may provide a fuller text. Meanwhile, it is clear that Enkidu represents the "noble savage" and that his death is the turning point of the epic. The human appeal comes from the combination of two themes: friendship and fear of death. After Enkidu's death, there is a change of mood; Gilgamesh no longer pursues fame, and his sole aim is to escape death.

The account of the flood takes up less than two hundred lines, and is given to Gilgamesh by Utnapishtim when they meet on the island of the blessed. Oppenheim joins with most scholars when he describes the episode as "a gem of Mesopotamian poetry."
— *M.E.J.*

Additional Recommended Reading

Covensky, Milton. *The Ancient Near Eastern Tradition.* New York: Harper and Row Publishers Incorporated, 1966. The chapter on archaic Mesopotamian civilization and the bibliography are useful for a general introduction to the subject.

Jacobsen, Thorkild. "The Good Life," in H. and H. A. Frankfort, John A. Wilson, and others. *The Intellectual Adventure of Ancient Man: An Essay on Speculative Thought in the Ancient Near East.* Ch. 7. Chicago: University of Chicago Press, 1946. An article discussing Gilgamesh and the problem of death.

Gaster, Theodor H., trans. *The Oldest Stories in the World.* Boston: Beacon Press, 1952. A study expounding literary forms and providing a modern prose version of portions of the Gilgamesh Epic.

Heidel, Alexander. *The Gilgamesh Epic and Old Testament Parallels.* Chicago: University of Chicago Press, 1949. This translation is considered among the best in English.

Kramer, Samuel Noah. *History Begins at Sumer.* 2nd ed. London: Thames and Hudson, 1961. A discussion of the earliest versions of several episodes from the Gilgamesh Epic.

Kramer, Samuel Noah. *Sumerian Mythology: A Study of Spiritual and Literary Achievements in the Third Millennium B.C.* 2nd ed. New York: Harper & Row Publishers Incorporated, 1961. Interpretations of earliest versions of the Gilgamesh story.

PROMULGATION OF HAMMURABI'S CODE

Type of event: Legal: promulgation of amendments to current law
Time: c.1750 B.C.
Locale: Babylon

Principal personage:
HAMMURABI, ruler of Mesopotamia c.1790-1750

Summary of Event

That Hammurabi's laws are neither the oldest extant laws nor even a law code as popularly thought does not alter the fact that their promulgation and preservation constitute a landmark in history.

Hammurabi, who ruled from about 1790 to 1750 B.C., was the sixth Amorite king of a Semitic dynasty which had imposed its rule on the native Sumerian population of the territory within about a fifty-mile radius of Babylon some two hundred years earlier. Hammurabi himself, late in the course of a forty-three-year reign, extended his rule in the direction of Assyria and northern Syria. It was, at least in part, as a means of unifying this heterogeneous society that Hammurabi published what has come to be known as his code of laws.

An almost complete copy of the laws, engraved on a diorite column or stele about eight feet tall, was discovered in Susa in 1901. This stele is now in the Louvre, Paris. Apparently the laws were engraved on diorite, the most durable substance known to the Babylonians, so that a copy of the laws would stand as a public reference. Many fragments of other copies have been discovered and transcribed, and it is by comparing these that gaps in the Susa stele have been filled, providing a reasonably complete and accu-

rate version of the laws promulgated close to the end of Hammurabi's reign.

The laws are introduced by a prologue in which Hammurabi, in the first person singular, describes his efforts to make law prevail in his lands. He states that the gods Anim and Enlil had appointed him, as a god-fearing prince, to advance the welfare of the people by promoting justice. He was to destroy the wicked and curtail the oppression of the strong over the weak. This divine commission would cause him "to rise like the sun over the black-headed people, and to light up the land."

Following the prologue, 282 articles or laws treat personal property, real estate, business, trade, agriculture, marriage, inheritances, adoption, contracts, and leases. The law also details penalties for injuries both to person and property. Finally, an epilogue recounts in detail Hammurabi's achievements and concludes with a list of blessings for those who keep the laws, and for those who violate them a much longer and more elaborate set of curses.

The collection of laws is not a code, but a set of amendments of existing laws. In the prologue, Hammurabi never calls himself a codifier or legislator. Instead, his aim seems to be to promote public order by making easily available current interpretations and applications of the existing law. This becomes clear when his laws are compared with earlier laws in use in Mesopotamia. Of these there remain sizable fragments of at least three antecedents of Hammurabi's work. The threefold division into prologue, the laws themselves, and an epilogue glorifying the lawgiver, was a conventional form in Hammurabi's time.

Hammurabi's laws provide material for reconstructing the evidence of a remarkable civilization. What emerges is the picture of a society with a defined class system, well-developed agriculture, a viable economy based on foreign as well as internal trade, and a government with a strong judiciary.

At least three social classes are discernible in Babylonian society as reflected in the code: the highest class, including the king, civil and military officials, priests, landed proprietors, rich merchants, and manufacturers; a lower class comprising laborers and farmers, including many tenant farmers; and finally, a slave class made up of those captured in war, together with men who had lost their freedom through debt. Here it should be noted that in Babylon, as in Israel, a slave was not a mere chattel, as he became later in Roman law and practice. In the ancient Near East, there was little difference between the hired workman and the slave. Indeed, the Hebrew noun for "slave" means simply a "worker."

The role of women was significant in that the law accorded women marriage and property rights in advance of other societies of a considerably later time. Women could divorce,

transact business, and inherit or bequeath property. The law recognized a clear distinction between the legitimate wife and the concubine. "If a man take a wife and do not draw up a contract with her, that woman is not his wife." However, even the harlot was protected from wanton exploitation, as were slaves and children. If a man handed over his wife, his son, or his daughter to the service of another, they must work only three years in the house of their purchaser or master; in the fourth year they secured their freedom.

In many respects the laws of Hammurabi appear excessively harsh. Criminal law follows the *lex talionis,* the vengeful principle of an eye for an eye. "If a man destroy the eye of another man, they shall destroy his eye. If he break a man's bone, they shall break his bone."

Undergirding the individual laws was an exalted ideal of justice and concern for the vulnerable members of society who were referred to in ancient literature collectively as "the widow and the orphan." In the prologue of his laws, Hammurabi declared that he was the agent of the gods, appointed to protect the weak by enforcing just laws. Again in the epilogue he stated that his purpose was to hinder the strong from oppressing the weak, to protect widows and orphans from injustice, and to affirm every man's right to equitable treatment.

The laws of Babylonia are significant because of the light they throw on the ways of life of an ancient civilization. However, in the case of Hammurabi's redaction, the importance transcends the geographic and historical boundaries of the ancient Near

East. Hammurabi's laws coincide with the period which saw a considerable expansion of Babylonian civilization, though recent research shows that the influence was more by commerce than by conquest. Not only Egypt and the Eastern Mediterranean, but also the Aegean lands knew the influence of the Babylonian culture. A chief means of transmission of this culture was the law.

It was especially in the case of the Hebrews that this influence was felt, and it was primarily through the Hebrews that some of the political and legal concepts of Hammurabi's laws have become a fundamental part of the heritage of Western civilization and ultimately of the world. In some re-spects the Babylonian laws reveal a civilization in advance of that of the Hebrews; certainly this is true on the material and economic side. On the other hand, the Hebrew law implies a recognition of a fundamental human equality premised on a recognition of creation by one God, and from this developed a system of ethics far in advance of anything in the Babylonian law. Nevertheless, the historical connections between the two are direct and intimate, and Hammurabi's laws continue to be seen rightly as an early crystallization of some of man's deepest aspirations for social justice and public order, and ultimately for the good life, conceived in much more than economic or even legal terms.

Pertinent Literature

Driver, G. R. and John C. Miles, eds. *The Babylonian Laws.* Vol. I. Oxford: The Clarendon Press, 1952.

Driver and Miles' work on Hammurabi's laws can be considered the standard English commentary. The first volume, after a disappointingly thin sketch of the background and antecedents of Hammurabi's laws, gives a massive and detailed historical and legal commentary on the laws themselves.

The authors explain that the laws are in no sense a code, but a series of amendments and restatements of laws in force at Hammurabi's time. The evidence indicates that Hammurabi simply chose for publication those particular laws he thought needed re-emphasis by publication. In this respect, the laws are likened to the Anglo-Saxon *dooms* promulgated by rulers with the advice of their wise men. In neither case was there proba-bly any conscious aim of constructing a code of law; rather, both Hammurabi and the Anglo-Saxons two-and-a-half millenia later were intent on declaring old customs and making amendments in matters of practical detail. Or again, Hammurabi's laws can be likened to a collection of decisions based on isolated individual cases. In studying Hammurabi's law, one is faced with the difficulty of dealing with a large number of amendments without access to the main body of the laws to which the amendments are related.

When due allowance has been made for these qualifications, however, it is still true that Hammurabi's work is built on recognizable principles of logic. The 282 articles are so grouped that they treat in turn: (1) offenses against the administration of justice;

(2) offenses against property; (3) land and houses; (4) trade and commerce; (5) marriage, family, and property; (6) assaults and talion; (7) professional men; (8) agriculture; (9) wages and rates of hire; and (10) slaves. The largest number of articles, eighty-eight, deal with marriage, family, and property. Among the important topics not touched upon are attempted murder, parricide, theft of chattels, and encroaching on a neighbor's land.

It is not known to what extent Hammurabi was personally responsible for the laws which bear his name. On the basis of extant letters which show Hammurabi's concern for matters of law and justice, however, Driver and Miles assume that his personal role was considerable and comparable to Napoleon's role in constructing the French code. Whatever the extent of Hammurabi's personal contribution, the laws themselves are remarkable for clarity and precision. The authors describe the compilation as a work of art in drafting, a model in its choice of accurate terminology with a pithy clarity.

In an attempt to help readers see Hammurabi's laws in Babylonian terms, the authors of the commentary make some keen observations on those particular matters where the ancient approach to law differs radically from our basic assumptions. Three points are particularly deserving of attention. First, the laws were not enforced by the Babylonian courts; they were more like rules or norms in which the spirit is more important than the letter. This conclusion is based on the fact that there is no evidence of any kind of verbal interpretation of Ham-

murabi's laws, nor any references to the exact wording of the laws in other Babylonian writings. It follows that the "laws" were not imperative; that is, parties to a dispute were free to make any agreements outside the law in an attempt to settle their differences. Second, the Babylonian documents dealing with property matters should not be seen as contracts, but as memoranda of transactions. The statements in the contract-like documents were liable to modification by oral evidence. Third, Driver and Miles make a distinction between ancient and primitive laws. While there are primitive elements in Hammurabi's law, some savage punishments, for example, in other respects the laws are in no sense a reflection of a primitive society.

Throughout the legal commentary, there are frequent comparisons between Babylonian and Hebrew law, a fact which adds greatly to the value of this work for the student of history of ideas or comparative cultures. For example, there are parallels between Hebrew laws and the form of Hammurabi's epilogue, with its list of blessings and curses.

A most significant contrast is in the law regarding treatment of slaves. Hebrew law (Exodus 21:20-21, 26-27) punishes a master who injures his own slave. It is clear that the Hebrew saw the slave as having a value higher than a mere piece of property. Hebrew law was interested in the slave himself, not only in the master's economic interests.

Both laws recognized talion, but probably accepted a compensation in place of an eye for an eye or a tooth for a tooth. Hebrew law (Exodus 21: 15, 17) exacted a more severe penalty,

48

death, for striking or cursing a parent, where Babylonian law was satisfied by mutilation.

Finally, it is worth noting that Driver and Miles take issue with the general view that the sculpture of the diorite stele, chief source of our knowledge of the laws, supposedly depicts the god Shamash handing the laws to Hammurabi. That some kind of homage is represented is clear, but according to Driver and Miles, this is all that can be deduced from the sculpture itself. Hammurabi himself claims to be the author of the laws. While he may have claimed divine sanction, there is no evidence that he presented the laws as divine revelation.

Speiser, E. A. "Authority and Law in Mesopotamia," in *Journal of the American Oriental Society*. Supplement 17, 1954.

While Speiser's article is not concerned solely, or even specifically, with Hammurabi's laws, it places the laws in their political and social context. The author's thesis is that it is a people's concept of state and law, much more than other institutions, which enable one to understand the distinctive features of a civilization.

Essential to any kind of penetration of Babylonian law is a grasp of the institution of kingship. An outstanding feature of kingship in ancient Mesopotamia was the ruler's subservience to the gods, played out in an elaborate ritual of interpretation of omens. In practice, this meant that the temple exercised a check on the court.

Another qualifying factor of the king's power lay in the assembly. Speiser shows that ultimate authority resided not in an individual ruler, but in a corporate assembly. There is literary evidence that Babylonians saw the king and assembly as complementary and as marking an advance over an earlier barbarous stage when they had no consultative government.

The laws of Hammurabi and the three earlier "codes" or fragments known to Sumerologists are to be understood, then, not as decrees issued by an autocratic ruler, but as expressions of consensus in a society where royal authority was limited by religion and by some kind of assembly.

Early Sumerian political and religious thought, which became normative for subsequent peoples who invaded or conquered the area between the Tigris and Euphrates, did not make a clear distinction between divine and human societies. Among the gods, as among their human counterparts, the Sumerians pictured a divine assembly as the ultimate source of authority. This notion of a divine assembly added to the significance of the assembly on earth. In Sumerian mythology, the cosmic body alone was competent to name the head of the pantheon, regulate the lengths of reigns, and to grant immortality to humans.

The legal system of Babylonian society as we have evidence of it in Hammurabi's laws had a double function: it reflected the concept of government here described; it also implemented it. Unfortunately, there is little or no extant data about the legal theory that underlay the law. A good case can be made that this is not a lacuna attributable to a loss of materials, but rather to the fact that the Babylonians of the eighteenth century B.C. had not devised a body of legal theory. However, there is much data about legal practice, so that it is possible to reconstruct something of the court system both as to structure and procedure. Legal theory, Speiser explains, can be deduced or reconstructed at least partially on the basis of two key concepts: *kittum,* which can roughly be translated "truth," and *mesarum,* or "justice."

Mesarum is a process of applying the law equitably, and this is one of the ruler's principal duties. To fulfill his role adequately, the ruler must not only supervise the application of the laws, but must also adapt them to contingencies. We can see, then, the meaning of the lengthy account of his exploits which Hammurabi gives in the epilogue to his set of laws. It is less a eulogy than an account of the conditions which provide a rationale for his selection and amendments of older and well-known laws.

An analysis of the concept *kittum,* or truth, shows that the king was not the source of the law, but only its agent. Here the Babylonian notion is close to the medieval idea that law is something discovered rather than something contrived or constructed. In the Babylonian value system, the

cosmos is seen as founded on certain truths. The function of the law is to safeguard these truths, truths which bind the king as well as the lowliest slave. The ruler, therefore, is clearly under the law, not above it. Hammurabi himself succinctly expresses the meaning of *kittum* and *mesarum* when he speaks of himself as "the just king [*sar mesarum*], to whom Shamash [the sun-god] committed the truths."

The importance of statutes such as those known as Hammurabi's "code," a technical misnomer, now becomes clear. The collected statutes kept alive both the established traditions or customs, and also made possible the topical amendments to fit new circumstances.

Speiser concludes his treatment by reflecting that, together with the state, law was one of the unifying factors of Mesopotamian culture which influenced the Hittites, the Syrians, and ultimately many other peoples. On the negative side, he notes that the law was not conducive to ethical progress, and he attributes this to an underlying idea of the cosmos which saw ultimate authority, albeit collective, as arbitrary. — *M.E.J.*

Additional Recommended Reading

Frankfort, Henri. *The Intellectual Adventure of Ancient Man.* Chicago: University of Chicago Press, 1946. A perceptive discussion of the Mesopotamian view of the function of the state.

Gadd, C. J. *Hammurabi and the End of His Dynasty.* Cambridge: The University Press, 1965. A fascicle of the revised *Cambridge Ancient History* containing a helpful bibliography.

Gordon, Cyrus. *Hammurabi's Code: Quaint or Forward-Looking?* New York: Holt, Rinehart & Winston, Inc., 1957. A brief study with a careful summary of the laws and a clear introductory essay.

Kramer, Samuel Noah. *The Sumerians: Their History, Culture and Character.* Chicago: University of Chicago Press, 1963. A treatise by a foremost Sumerologist on the cultural background of Babylonian civilization.

Pritchard, James B., ed. *The Ancient Near East—An Anthology of Texts and Pictures.* Princeton: Princeton University Press, 1958. A well-known collection containing translated fragments from antecedents of Hammurabi's laws and the text of Hammurabi's Code.

Wooley, Sir Leonard. *The Beginnings of Civilization.* New York: Harper and Row Publishers Incorporated, 1963. A part of the UNESCO *History of Civilizations* project, this book incorporates much recent research.

DISSEMINATION OF THE *BOOK OF THE DEAD*

Type of event: Religious: popular use of magical-religious writings
Time: from c.1500 B.C.
Locale: Egypt

Summary of Event

The Egyptian *Book of the Dead* comprises lists of formulas and rubrics for the use of the soul in achieving a satisfactory state after separation from the body. The practice of reciting spells during the funeral ceremonies to safeguard the existence and welfare of the deceased dates from an early period in Egyptian history, though most of the texts known to Egyptologists were produced after 1550 B.C.

Many spells known from early pyramid texts were adopted for use by the common people over the years, and similar ones were added. These texts were not only recited during funerals but were also considered useful if placed close to the deceased where he could reach them if he had need. The texts were at one time inscribed on the walls of coffins; only later were they written on papyrus and buried with the dead. At this stage of usage such texts received the name *Book of the Dead,* or the *Book of Coming Forth by Day.* Such books or chapters are not systematic treatises about Egyptian beliefs regarding life after death, but a random collection of magical practices. These spells claim to give to the dead protection against hunger and thirst, the ability to assume various animal forms, and especially the power to come forth by day, that is to emerge at daylight from the tomb to partake of the funerary offerings.

Survival after death was a conviction firmly anchored in the minds of the Egyptians. Somehow, they conceived of death as separation of the spiritual and corporal elements of man; yet they believed that man's spirit continued to live close to the corpse and was in some way dependent upon it. The Egyptians' inability to abstract the survival of man's immortal parts from the continued existence of his body shows how they were bound to ideas of concrete, material reality. Though they admitted both death and survival, they could not imagine existence without a physical basis. The body was seen as the concrete substratum of man's individuality; the cell or tomb of the body, therefore, was looked upon as the eternal dwelling place of the soul. Life of the soul after death tended to be conceived of as gloomy, so that throughout Egyptian history there were efforts to provide a more pleasing substitute for this dismal existence.

At the beginning of Dynasty V, about 2500 B.C., believers in solar doctrine began to work out a place for the dead in their theology. The most well-developed of these paradises was that of Osiris, or "the West." "The West" was reserved for Osiris' believers, who became after death his subjects for all eternity. At first, the paradise of Osiris was reserved for the pharaoh, but gradually

52

it was, in a sort of democratic way, made accessible to more and more of the population. Entrance into paradise was a favor granted only on certain conditions. Among these was the ordeal of judgment.

One of the most popular religious texts of ancient Egypt was a section of the *Book of the Dead* known to scholars as Chapter Seventeen. This text, which seems to have been written during Dynasty IX, about 1200 B.C., opens with a monologue by the high god, and expresses a concept quite distinct from the rest of the composition. It indicates a belief, or at least the tendency toward a belief, in one supreme god who first existed as "word" and who manifested or created himself by pronouncing the names of his own limbs.

Chapter Thirty of the *Book of the Dead* provides an example of the attempt to use magical incantations to fulfill the ethical requirements of sinlessness in the judgment. This chapter is addressed to the heart, which the Egyptian held to be the most important agent whose favor had to be sought. It is remarkable that while magic had no official place in Egyptian worship of the gods as conducted in the temples, it was the basis of all funeral rites and worship of the dead. It was considered a science whereby through recited formulas and amulets protection was obtained against all evil spirits and from all kinds of danger. These formulas and amulets were widely used in all classes of society.

Chapter 125 in the *Book of the Dead* is probably the best known, and is sometimes taken as representa-tive of the whole. In its detailed description of the process of judgment it exemplifies both the highest ethical component and the most magical features of ancient Egyptian religion. The oldest copy of Chapter 125 dates from about 1550 B.C. An accompanying illustration shows the god Osiris seated at one end of a hall, and at the other end a dead man who has been brought in by Anubis, the soul leader. In the center of the hall is a set of scales with the heart of the dead man on one side, and the symbol of Maāt, the goddess of justice, on the other. Anubis supervises the weighing and records the results. The text of the judgment consists of a greeting to the god, and then successive declarations of innocence made by the dead man. The declarations are known as the "negative confessions." In these, the man declares he has not committed a whole series of faults which the Egyptian value system saw as immoral.

The negative confessions themselves reflect high moral concepts, as a few examples will illustrate. The dead man declares that he has not oppressed the members of his family, that he has not been domineering with his servants or filched the property of the lowly man. He further states that he has not inflicted pain, that he has not permitted any man to suffer hunger, that he has neither murdered nor given an order to cause murder, and that he has been just in commercial transactions.

Apparently, during most of the millennium or more the "negative confession" formula was in use; its very recital magically won paradise. One did not state the truth; rather,

one created it. This magico-supersti-
tious approach was offset in Egyptian
culture by a more rational ethic, as
exemplified in the wisdom literature,
which was also popular and flourished
throughout Egyptian civilization.

Pertinent Literature

Frankfort, H. *Ancient Egyptian Religion: An Interpretation.* New York: Harper
& Row Publishers Incorporated, 1948.

Henri Frankfort was research professor of Oriental Archaeology in
the University of Chicago, a leading
center for Egyptian studies, when he
wrote this book. In its present form,
the work is an expanded version of
lectures sponsored by the American
Council of Learned Societies, and is
recognized as a lucid and scholarly
work on an abstruse subject.

Frankfort's thesis is that just
as there was a unity of the Egyptian
people with respect to language,
material culture, and even physique,
there was a corresponding unity in
the domain of the spirit. He claims
that a certain coherence of Egyptian
doctrines is based on the fact that the
Egyptians were concerned that the
universe was essentially static. This
notion of the changeless world provides a useful key to enter the mind
of the Egyptians who compiled and
used the *Book of the Dead.*

In Frankfort's book, the main
references to the *Book of the Dead*
are found in Chapter Four, "The
Egyptian Hope." Here the author
demonstrates his thesis by attempting
to show that the Egyptians believed
that man could find immortality and
peace by becoming part of one of the
cycles of nature. This is the unifying
thread connecting so many different
religious ideas, customs, and symbols.
Frankfort here recognizes a paradox:
the Egyptians conceived of the world

as static, yet they thought of immortality as participation in perpetual
movement. Frankfort implies, however, that even this movement was in
some sense static, since it was part
of the changeless order of the world.
The Egyptians saw the world as an
equilibrium of opposites. Death appears to us as a singular event; to the
Egyptian it was at most an interrup-
tion in life.

This attitude is reflected in Egyptian art and writing regarding death,
an attitude confident in the ability
of men to continue interpersonal
relations with the dead. Frankfort
refers to texts which show the idea
of a reciprocal emotional involvement between dead persons and their
relatives. For example, a mother is
asked to arbitrate between her sons,
one of whom is dead and the other
alive; a dead man is urged to persuade
his ancestors to rescue his widow and
son from grasping relatives.

Yet Frankfort insists that the notion that the Egyptians imagined
life after death as a mere continuation of earthly life is only a partial
truth. While he agrees that the Egyptians could not conceive of a life
after death which did not depend on
material goods, he thinks that this led
the Egyptian "not to a materialistic
interpretation of life, but to a spiritual view of food." He draws this
conclusion in part from linguistic

evidence, pointing out that the same word, *Ka,* denotes both man's impalpable, vital force, and his sustenance.

This notion provides an easy transition to an understanding of such Egyptian practices as feast day celebrations, including a meal, at the tombs of the dead; and it clarifies much of the subject matter of the *Book of the Dead.*

On the one hand, the dead man was considered as having an animated existence. This is the meaning of the term *Ba,* which should not be translated as soul. *Ba* is not part of a living person, but the whole person as he appears after death. The Egyptian also regarded a dead person as *Akh* or transfigured spirit. As *Akh* a dead person had an exalted form of existence, and was seen at night as a star in the sky. Thus, the dead were thought to be incorporated in the cosmic order, and therefore eternal. Frankfort claims that this most profound conception of death is reflected in other writings as well as in the *Book of the Dead.*

Egyptian judgment after death, Frankfort holds, is not at all thought of in the Judaeo-Christian sense. For the Egyptian, the righteous man is in harmony with the divine order; therefore, all manifestations of concern with judgment are simply expressions of fear of the unknown. For Frankfort, Egyptian fear of death and belief in everlasting life are not incompatible. It is the belief in life which is dominant, while the "anxiety of the Egyptian in the face of death gives a rather striking foil to the serenity of his positive beliefs in a future life."

In concluding the chapter on "The Egyptian Hope," Frankfort reminds his readers that to attempt to understand the Egyptian view of death and life after death from isolated passages of the *Book of the Dead* and other funerary texts is like trying to understand the stars from newspaper horoscopes. An accurate understanding can only be gained from a comprehensive view, such as the one Frankfort cogently presents in his book. No one, he remarks, can penetrate the Egyptian mentality unless he appreciates the Egyptians' deep emotional involvement with the phenomena of nature and is able to accept the paradoxes of the complexity of the Egyptian view of death and afterlife.

Breasted, James Henry. *Development of Religion and Thought in Ancient Egypt.* New York: Harper Torchbooks, 1955.

This book, originally published in 1912, is in many ways supplanted by later works, though not entirely. James Henry Breasted (1865-1935) was the man who did most to introduce Egyptian studies in the United States. As founder of the Oriental Institute at the University of Chicago in 1919, he was responsible for establishing one of the leading centers of research into Egyptian culture. The present edition of Breasted's work is introduced by the eminent Egyptologist John Wilson, who says of the book that it is still a monument and a classic.

Breasted's point of view in this work is indicated in the title. He saw a developmental process in Egyptian religious thought, and he belongs to what we may call the "progress school" of historians. As result, he tends to interpret his data to support his view that the ancient Egyptian gradually moved to a rational system of religion and ethics. Along with this there is a pronounced element of moralizing in Breasted's book. He considers that ancient beliefs about God express the best thoughts and feelings of man personified in a supreme character of which he dreamed. The Egyptian succeeded in slowly "gaining his honest god." Ours came by the same process, beginning among the Hebrews, and Breasted is convinced that "religion is still in the making."

While Breasted's interpretation of the *Book of the Dead* is highly colored by his philosophy of religion and history, it nevertheless is valuable because he has the gift of sharing clearly his own ideas and his broad and deep acquaintance with Egyptian texts and related materials. He cites many examples to show the continuity of the *Book of the Dead* with the earlier pyramid and coffin texts, while at the same time demonstrating the distinctive characteristics of the *Book of the Dead*. These distinguishing characteristics include an emphasis on the myth of Osiris, and a large element of superstition, supported and promoted by the priests, a class for which Breasted has little sympathy.

In the growth of the Osiris cult, Breasted sees a triumph of folk religion as contrasted with the state cult. As folk religion the Osiris cult was highly superstitious, involving increased reliance on magic. Magic

tended to dominate every facet of life. The author illustrates his viewpoint with examples including a description of a mother's use of magic to ward off danger from her child, and many others taken directly from the *Book of the Dead*. To Breasted the *Book of the Dead* as a whole contains a far-reaching and complex illustration of the increasing dependence on magic in the hereafter. Priests, according to the author, took advantage of the opportunity offered them by the gullibility of simple people, and provided all sorts of charms for the journey to the hereafter. Some charms assured the user that he would reach his destination, while others guaranteed protection against specific injuries: loss of a limb, amnesia, and so on.

To this extent, the *Book of the Dead* represents a decline or corruption of the pure religion which Breasted sees as evolutionary. However, another aspect of the *Book of the Dead* which the author discusses in considerable detail is its "elaboration of the ancient idea of the moral judgment, and its evident appreciation of the burden of conscience." This ethical element is found in the passages of the *Book of the Dead* which consider judgment. The so-called negative confession in the judgment accounts is a misnomer, conducive to serious misunderstanding of Egyptian religious development, according to the author. He says that the confession is rather a declaration of innocence which illustrates the Egyptian's growing awareness of the supreme value of moral worthiness, of goodness for its own sake without reference to future reward or punishment. The superstitious element of the *Book of the Dead* retarded this development, because it became a magical means of effortless salvation. To this extent, Breasted sees such an element as a tendency toward evil. Nevertheless, the religious development, Breasted is convinced, is present and could not be destroyed. Breasted ends on a characteristically optimistic note, seeing in "the eyes of these early Nile-dwellers the vision of the world-god."

— *M.E.J.*

Additional Recommended Reading

Aldred, Cyril. *The Egyptians.* London: Thames and Hudson, 1961. A survey enhanced by excellent plates and line drawings.

Frankfort, H. and H. A., John A. Wilson, and others. *The Intellectual Adventure of Ancient Man.* Chicago: University of Chicago Press, 1946. Essays on the culture of Egypt, Mesopotamia, and the Hebrews, written by scholars for the educated layman.

Mercer, Samuel A. B. *The Religion of Ancient Egypt.* London: Luzac and Company, 1949. A description of the main characteristics of Egyptian religion based on extensive use of primary and secondary sources.

Mertz, Barbara. *Red Land, Black Land: The World of the Ancient Egyptians.* London: Hodder and Stoughton, 1967. An informal work, juvenile in style but containing substantial material.

Mertz, Barbara. *Temples, Tombs and Hieroglyphs.* London: Victor Gollancz, 1964. Perceptive comments on the element of magic in funeral texts, together with a useful annotated bibliography.

Wilson, John A. *The Culture of Ancient Egypt.* Chicago: University of Chicago Press, 1951. A stimulating interpretive essay on Egyptian history.

Zandee, J. *Death as an Enemy According to Ancient Egyptian Conceptions.* Leiden: E. J. Brill, 1960. Scientific study of pyramid and coffin texts and *Book of the Dead* as revealing Egyptian notions of death and afterlife.

"DISCOVERY" OF IRON

Type of event: Technological: utilization of a new metal
Time: c.1500 B.C.
Locale: Asia Minor

Summary of Event

In considering the discovery of iron as a historic event, two factors should be considered: first, the technological mastery of the processes by which iron was made functional; and second, the political, social, and economic context of the technological accomplishment.

With increasing frequency in the last decade, archaeologists have been insisting that the classic division of civilization into stone and metal ages, with the metals following in an orderly progression through copper, bronze, and iron, is not a realistic way to periodize cultures and civilizations. Although meteoric iron, a natural alloy of nickel and iron, was on occasion used for making beads in predynastic Egypt in the fourth millenium or earlier, the significance of the knowledge of iron in this form at this early date should not be overestimated.

For a long time after metals were known, little progress was made towards using them, simply because they were less functional for many purposes than stone. Metallurgy advanced very slowly; it took generations to develop the combination of skills necessary to produce bronze that surpassed flint or stone, and it was a matter of centuries before iron replaced bronze as the metal of major importance.

At first iron was used like stone. Among certain Latin American Indians such as the Aztecs of Mexico, the Mayas of Yucatan, and the Incas of Peru, the use of iron never advanced beyond this stage; such cultures cannot be said to have advanced to an iron age. Nor can it be assumed that once the first process of refining iron was mastered, one invention would necessarily lead to another. The Vikings learned to make iron anchors, but never learned to make steel swords with good cutting edges.

Wrought iron was discovered accidentally when smiths found that by hammering the small bead-like pieces of iron left as a residue after smelting copper they could form the iron particles into a mass. This kind of wrought iron, however, was good only for decorative purposes, and for more than a thousand years after 2500 B.C., iron remained a precious ornamental metal. Bronze, which was harder and capable of being sharpened to a fine cutting edge, continued to be the functional metal for tools and weapons.

The real advent of the Iron Age came not with the discovery of the metal, but with the invention of the process of casing or steeling it, probably about 1500 B.C. This happened when it was learned that by repeatedly reheating wrought iron in a charcoal fire and then hammering it, it not only became harder than bronze but also kept its hardness after long use. The

58

next technological improvement, which again meant a further hardening of the metal, was the process of quenching it, that is, a process of repeatedly plunging the hot iron into cold water. It was only after this series of discoveries and inventions that the significant impact of iron on culture and civilization was appreciably felt.

Bronze did not extend man's control over nature nearly so much as did iron because of the scarcity and consequent costliness of the earlier metal. For this reason, iron has been called, in contrast to bronze, the "democratic metal." Bronze could not furnish an important proportion of agricultural tools but was reserved largely for weapons. It remained for the most part a luxury item made for the wealthy by a small number of skilled craftsmen. In the Bronze Age, therefore, production remained basically neolithic. In contrast, widespread use of iron tools meant a general increase in living standards. For example, the use of iron axes brought about the clearing of forests, and much new land came under cultivation. Other significant developments included the application of iron tools to sheep-shearing and cloth-cutting, and the invention of the lathe, the most fundamental machine tool.

About 1500 B.C., the Hittites of Asia Minor enjoyed a monopoly in the manufacture of iron. For them it was a precious metal, worth five times the value of gold, and forty times the value of silver. Iron was used for ornaments; it seems likely that even when it began to be used for weapons, they were inferior to bronze and even to stone. On an industrial scale, iron was not smelted or worked anywhere before 1400 B.C. There are grounds for suspecting that the Hittites jealously guarded the secret of iron because they realized the advantages of iron weapons in war; on the other hand, there is evidence that they exported iron ornaments and daggers as gifts to foreign rulers. What is certain is that the change from a bronze to an iron technology meant a radical change in the manner of warfare. As long as bronze was the predominant metal, only a small number of men could be armed with metal weapons. The rank-and-file soldier was limited to stone clubs and stone-tipped arrows. When steeled or cased iron came to commonly used for weapons, the destructive potential of an army was immeasurably increased.

Concerning the process and channels of diffusion of iron technology, research does not yet provide certainty. Surely the breakup of the empire of the Hittites shortly after 1200 B.C. was a major factor in the rapid and widespread dissemination of iron technology. Iron-working was practiced in Palestine and in the area of the Aegean by 1000 B.C., but it was not adopted in the Nile valley for another four hundred years, when Egypt came under Greek influence. Before that time it did not answer a socially-approved need of Egyptian culture.

In continental Europe, iron was known in the ninth century B.C., but it was not used on a comparatively large scale until the seventh century. By the sixth century, iron-using cultures in Europe extended from

Yugoslavia and the eastern Alps to France, and extended north to the middle Rhine. The next major advance in iron technology, true crucible steel, probably of Indian origin, did not reach Europe until the eleventh century A.D. Meanwhile, iron tools greatly influenced carpentry and other crafts.

In Africa, Carthage was making general use of iron tools at a date traditionally set at the end of the ninth century B.C. Iron technology spread in parts of India in the fifth century B.C.

Pertinent Literature

Childe, Gordon. *What Happened in History*. Rev. ed. Baltimore: Penguin Books, 1954.

Childe's discussion of the discovery of iron complements well the treatment by Forbes discussed below. Childe, a foremost prehistorian, is a contributor to the multivolume Oxford *History of Technology*, as is Forbes; however, his perspective in *What Happened in History* is more that of a social and economic historian.

Avowedly influenced by the Marxist interpretation of history, Childe sees production relationships as the key to understanding the historical process. In this book, written in 1942, and revised and reprinted many times since, he surveys the broad sweep of history from paleolithic times to the decline of Rome in the West. Two chapters are devoted to the early Iron Age.

One of Childe's guiding principles is that each phase of a culture can be described in terms of new forces of production, and that the contradictions embedded in each new phase eventually compelled the emergence of new productive forces and a new cycle of social evolution. In the case of the emergence of iron technology, Childe claims that the use of iron was learned by the Egyptians and Hittites from mercenaries in their armies. Only temporarily did it serve the ends of the ruling class; soon it democratized warfare and also agriculture and industry. Throughout the discussion, Childe uses classic Marxist terminology, so that the reader must be wary and adjust such terms as "democracy," "masses," and "class struggle" to ancient civilization as this is known from other sources.

Because he sees the Iron Age chiefly in economic terms, Childe gives it a late beginning date, about 1000 B.C. With the effective use of maps, he shows that in the first five centuries of the Iron Age the area of civilization in the Near East and Europe increased more than in the fifteen hundred years of the preceding Bronze Age. By 500 B.C., the zone of literate societies extended from Spain to India. Together with iron, the alphabet and coined money are the other two inventions critical in the civilizing process, or what for Childe is the same, the progress of "democratization."

Two kinds of communities were in advantageous positions to exploit advances in the Iron Age: first, those that could readily engage in com-

60

merce because of closeness to waterways, and second, those not hampered by the cultural traditions of a prolonged bronze age. Only one people possessed both these advantages: the Greeks, who were therefore able to achieve their high civilization more readily than any of their contemporaries. Other peoples who benefited from one or the other of the two conditions Childe sets down were the Phoenicians, Etruscans, Hebrews, Romans, and Phrygians.

Among the political expressions of the economic changes of the Iron Age, Childe sees as most significant a class struggle in Greece leading to democracy, because in Greece, unlike Assyria, Babylonia, and Egypt, there was no strong heritage of monarchy. In the religious sphere, the social ferment of the Iron Age "began to dissolve established ideologies

that corporations of anonymous priests had wrought into dogmatic theologies in the Bronze Age." Thus, schools of philosophy and more rationalistic religion, such as the cosmologists in Greece, Lao-Tse and Confucius in China, Gautama Buddha in India, Zoroaster in Persia, and the prophetic movement among the Hebrews, all have their explanation in economic terms.

It is clearly evident that Childe's treatment has the strengths and weaknesses of a Marxist interpretation of history. Apart from this, the book contains many sweeping generalizations which the reader is expected to accept on the authority of the author's reputation rather than on evidence presented in the work itself. Some of the evidence is presented in other more specialized writings by Childe.

Forbes, R. J. *Studies in Ancient Technology.* Vols. VIII and IX. Leiden: E. J. Brill, 1964.

This is a historico-technical treatment containing a wealth of detail but written in a style intelligible to the nonspecialist. Though the work is a history of technology, Forbes is interested in the history of ideas, and is ever on the alert to show the relationship of technological advance to the cultural context in which it occurs.

Concerning the concept of stone and metal "ages," Forbes says that while these categories, which are as old as Hesiod's *Works and Days,* have their limitations, the sequence copper, bronze, and iron is nevertheless correct for Asia Minor and Eu-

rope. This is not true of Africa, where iron preceded the age of bronze, nor in some other parts of the world where there was no bronze age at all.

Metallurgy accompanied the rise of urban civilizations and the first empires in history. Metal made it possible for a conquering tribe to impose its rule on a neighboring peasant population many times its size. However, Forbes insists that metallurgy was not the prime factor in the rise of urban civilization, which was stimulated also by such inventions as the calendar, writing, and techniques of measurement.

Forbes sees a pattern in the evolution of metallurgy which is identical in the case of many metals. First, native metals such as copper, gold, silver, and meteoric iron are used as stones. In a second stage, the same four metals are hammered and cut. The third, or "ore stage," sees the development of metal alloys. Here composition is the primary factor, and the list of useful metals expands to include bronze. It is only in the fourth stage, when complex skills make processing the primary factor over composition, that iron became a functional metal.

Forbes' study probes beneath a surface description of processes to make some provocative generalizations on the subject of invention and discovery. He holds that "not need but prosperity is the mother of invention," and that the early metal worker did not consciously pursue a path of progress because he was not aware that there was such a path. He also disagrees with those who hold that since iron technology spread relatively more quickly than copper and bronze, the complex of operations was not diffused from one center but was discovered in many regions. Forbes' view is that the special set of techniques for producing durable iron, namely hammering, tempering, quenching, and annealing, and the knowledge of other techniques used in the production of other metals which iron-manufacturing requires, not only led to the conclusion that iron was of necessity a latecomer, but also argue for a single center of diffusion somewhere in the Hittite realm of Asia Minor. This view receives support from the

history of folklore and religion, which favors a late origin of the Iron Age.

Consonant with his interest in the interplay of technological advance and social and cultural values, Forbes' work includes many interesting examples of references to iron in ancient and classical literature. Thus, he quotes Pliny's observations on iron in the *Natural History,* "a metal which is at once the best and the worst servant of humanity, for to bring death more speedily to our fellowman, we have given wings to iron and taught it to fly." Forbes also notes another remark of Pliny that man, not nature, is to be blamed for such death. An even more telling passage is Pliny's account of an early Roman treaty which forbade the use of iron except for agriculture.

In explaining the series of discoveries and inventions which culminated in steel-cased iron, Forbes shows why the discovery of the separate processes extended over so many hundreds of years. The iron which was first produced as a waste product in the refining of copper was too soft, and the forging process, which demanded repeated heating to a temperature higher than that needed for copper, called for large quantities of fuel which were not easily obtainable. According to Forbes' chronology, only between 1200 and 1000 B.C. did the iron industry spread quickly in Iran, Transcaucasia, Syria, and Palestine. In another three hundred years, the transition from bronze to iron as the basic tool metal was complete.—*M.E.J.*

"Discovery" of Iron

Additional Recommended Reading

Aitchison, Leslie. *A History of Metals*. New York: Interscience Publishers, 1960. 2 vols. Iron is one of seven basic metals treated in Volume I. The work is well illustrated and has a bibliography.

Derry, T. K. and Trevor I. Williams. *A Short History of Technology from the Earliest Times to A.D. 1900*. New York: Oxford University Press, 1960. This is a topically arranged condensation of the five-volume *Oxford History of Technology*, containing good drawings and maps.

Forbes, Robert J. *Man the Maker: A History of Technology and Engineering*. New York: Henry Schuman, 1950. A study especially strong in the area of ancient technology.

Gurney, Oliver R. *The Hittites*. Revised ed. Baltimore: Penguin Books, 1961. An authoritative work on Hittite civilization.

Singer, Charles, E. J. Holmyard, and A. R. Hall, eds. *A History of Technology. Volume I—From Early Times to the Fall of Ancient Empires*. Oxford: The Clarendon Press, 1954. A series of essays on many aspects of ancient technology by various authorities.

63

FAILURE OF AKHENATEN'S CULTURAL REVIVAL

Type of event: Religious: attempt to introduce theological innovations
Time: c.1365 B.C.
Locale: Egypt

Principal personages:
AKHENATEN, formerly Amenhotep IV, tenth ruler of Dynasty XVIII, ruler of Egypt 1379-1365
NEFERTITI, Akhenaten's queen who supported the Aten cult
AMENHOTEP III, Akhenaten's father, pharaoh 1417-1379

Summary of Event

Akhenaten succeeded his father Amenhotep III in 1379 as Pharaoh of Dynasty XVIII of the New Kingdom of Egypt. Akhenaten began his reign as Amenhotep IV with his capital at Thebes. There is an apparently insoluble dispute about his age at the time he succeeded to the throne, a question of some importance in the light of the claims he made for his achievements.

The reign of Akhenaten's predecessor, Amenhotep III, had been a long and peaceful one of some forty years marked by military expeditions in the first decade and followed by three decades of affluent ease. During the latter period there was a remarkable outpouring of artistic talent issuing in splendid architectural achievements. Amenhotep III was influenced by his queen, Tiy, the daughter of a commoner who became the mother of Akhenaten. In the last decade of his reign Amenhotep was a sick man, unable to attend to affairs of government. Meanwhile Syria was restive, and Egypt was suffering from sporadic attacks by invaders. When the outlying districts sent pleas to the capital for military help, their requests were ignored. Conditions called for a vigorous new ruler. Instead, Egypt received a man who was, if not a religious extremist, certainly eccentric.

It is essential to have some grasp of traditional Egyptian religion in order to penetrate the meaning of the religious movement inaugurated by Akhenaten. Although Egyptian religion was polytheistic and allowed for the worship of distinctive local gods in various regions, Amen, the god of Thebes, had for all intents and purposes become the supreme god of the Egyptian pantheon. Amen, "the hidden one," was exemplified or manifest in the wind and also in breath, the life source of all living creatures.

Another god universally acknowledged among all Egyptians was Ra, the sun god. When Amen and Ra became conceptualized as a single god, Amen-Ra, combining the mysterious life-producing forces of air and the sun, Egypt had come close to the worship of a supreme and universal god. It was a worship built on a the-

64

ology which saw the gods as essentially immanent in nature, since knowledge was not yet sophisticated enough to permit the conception of the sun and wind as purely physical phenomena.

So there was at the time of Akhenaten's accession a growing unification in Egyptian worship, and along with this tendency the priesthood was becoming centralized. The priestly class had actually grown so much in wealth and concomitant political power that there was beginning a typical struggle between the ecclesiastical and the secular power blocs.

What Akhenaten attempted was a radical reform of the prevailing cult of Amen-Ra. The evidence, relatively abundant for so remote a period, is both archaeological and literary. Among the important documents are letters containing both sides of a diplomatic correspondence.

Akhenaten built an entire city for his god Aten at Akhetaten, midway between Thebes and Memphis. Here, monuments bear witness to a god represented as a disk or sun, with rays terminating in hands which sometimes hold to the noses of the King and members of the royal family the hieroglyphic sign for "life." Along with the missionary effort to propagate the new faith went a vigorous iconoclastic movement. Images of Amen, who was now seen as a rival to Aten, were ruthlessly destroyed, and the names of those who had promoted his cult, particularly that of Amenhotep III, were effaced from inscriptions. The change of the King's own title from Amenhotep IV to Akhenaten was a part of this movement.

How far the religious reform was accompanied by an effort to break the power of the priests of Amen is a matter of conjecture, with varying interpretations. The dogmatic ideas of the new religion are best expressed in the famous hymn to Aten, ascribed to Akhenaten himself. This psalm-like composition reflects a belief in a supreme provident god who resembles the God of the later Judeo-Christian tradition. These similarities led some historians of the late nineteenth and early twentieth centuries to see in Akhenaten's religion a monotheism which prefigured, if it did not actually influence, the Hebrew idea of one supreme, universal, and transcendent God. Apart from this problem, the hymn stands as a classic of ancient religious literature.

Actually, Akhenaten's religious movement was a failure in almost every respect. On the strictly religious side, it did not take hold of the people, who went on worshiping their old gods in familiar ways. Indeed, the cult of Aten seems to have been restricted almost completely to Akhenaten, his family, and the immediate entourage at Akhetaten, as the new capital at the site of modern Tell el-Amarna was called. The rigidly monotheistic religion of Akhenaten had little appeal to the ordinary Egyptian who saw manifestations, or even emanations, of the divine in all phenomena. The Aten cult ran counter to the popular polytheistic world view which seemed more tolerant of the complexities of observed realities.

Politically and militarily, Akhenaten's reign was devoid of any outstanding accomplishment, a fact which is generally attributed to his absorption in his attempted religious reform and his lethargy concerning matters of government. In the field of art, however, the era marked a decided turn to a more naturalistic style. Instead of the stylized figures which had become typical of Egyptian art for more than a thousand years, the sculptures depicting Akhenaten are characterized by a photographic realism. The King himself is depicted as a rather grotesque, ill-shapen man, his defects set off by the beauty of his wife, Nefertiti. There are extant a number of groups showing Akhenaten, Nefertiti, and several of their six daughters in domestic scenes which until that time were not considered

fit subjects for public art.

While the importance of the religious, political, and cultural aspects of Akhenaten's reform are considerable, it was in no sense typical of Egyptian civilization, and there is no evidence of the movement's lasting influence. A few years after his death, a deliberate and successful effort was made to obliterate traces of the cult of Aten. As Akhenaten had caused the very name of Amen-Ra to be erased from monuments—although it could not be eradicated from men's minds—so Akhenaten himself was subjected to the same treatment. Labeled the "heretic king," his very name was removed from the list of kings by his successor.

Pertinent Literature

Gardiner, Sir Alan. *Egypt of the Pharaohs*. Oxford: The Clarendon Press, 1961.

Sir Alan's book is a history of Egypt from the earliest times to the conquest of Alexander the Great in 332 B.C. It is written from a philological approach and is organized chronologically. The author devotes a chapter entitled "The Religious Revolution and After" to the Akhenaten story and its aftermath.

Gardiner himself says, by way of warning concerning the unevenness and scarcity of sources for European history: "What is proudly advertised as Egyptian history is merely a collection of rags and tatters." Nevertheless, he knows the difficult sources well and draws from them as much as can be expected from any Egyptologist. By the time his account reaches Akhenaten, the materials available to the historian are somewhat fuller, and this is immediately noticeable in

the author's more interpretative style. What is presented is much more than a strictly factual account.

Gardiner's enthusiasm centers on the earlier period of Egyptian history. He holds that the Old Kingdom "is the age in which the distinctive features of the Pharaonic civlization are seen at their purest and best." When he reaches Dynasty XVIII, which begins the New Kingdom, he is predisposed to see Akhenaten's movement in an unfavorable light. Indeed, it turns out, in Gardiner's view, to be an unmitigated disaster, a storm that broke over a land which had enjoyed a period of unparalleled prosperity under Akhenaten's immediate predecessor. On the other hand, the entire blame for the decline is not to be placed on Akhenaten himself, for Gardiner explains that the question needs to be reconsidered in the light of recent and continuing archaeological and philological study. Already it can safely be stated that the charges of pacifism, which amount to a claim that Akhenaten threw away an Egyptian empire in Palestine and Syria, are oversimplifications at best. Gardiner goes so far as to question the very existence of an Egyptian "empire." While it is true that Egypt exercised some kind of suzerainty over outlying areas, it is not certain how far this overlordship was effective, and the Tell el-Amarna letters show that already in the reign of Amenhotep III, appeals to Egypt for help went unanswered.

Basing his view on a letter to Queen Tiy and another to Akhenaten himself from the Hittite monarch Suppiluliumas, Gardiner asserts that Akhenaten never was coregent with his father and that he ruled independently from a conjectural 1367 to 1350. That the cult of Aten was not a completely original invention of Akhenaten, Gardiner shows from philological evidence, pointing out that inscriptions from the time of Amenhotep III show already a widespread use of the name "Aten," although not in the sharply defined context of the fully developed cult promoted later by Akhenaten. Gardiner agrees that the celebrated hymn to Aten is probably the work of Akhenaten himself, and calls attention to the striking resemblance of the hymn to Psalm 104. He observes that while the hymn embodies the new creed, almost everything in it had been said in earlier hymns to the sun god.

The new religion was, according to Gardiner, a genuine monotheism, and Akhenaten is given credit for moral courage in attempting to demythologize the traditional and inadequate Egyptian religion. Nonetheless, the other side of the Pharaoh's moral courage was the destructive zeal which displayed itself in trying to eliminate all traces of the traditional gods, destroying much of artistic and historical value in the process.

An important aspect of the Aten cult was its association with worship of the Pharaoh himself. Reliefs found on the site of Akhetaten, the city built for the god, show Akhenaten very much in the center of the picture, so that Gardiner suggests that the Pharaoh and the god were almost identical. A decided weakness of the Aten cult was its almost complete lack of an ethical component. This lack is attributed partly to the elimination of Osiris, the Egyptian god of the underworld before whom the dead gave an account of their lives. To the question whether Akhenaten attempted to found a universal religion, Gardiner suggests a negative answer, pointing out that this supposition has little support in the texts.

Gardiner's conclusion concerning Akhenaten's religious revolution is that even after a subsequent period of recovery, Egypt was "a changed world," with a "marked deterioration of the art, the literature, and indeed the general culture of the people." He notes a decline in language, and even in manuscript copying, pointing out that the tombs at Thebes no longer showed the bright, happy scenes of life that formerly characterized Dynasty XVIII. In short, whatever the extent of Akhenaten's personal role, Dynasty XVIII was dark.

White, Leslie A. *The Science of Culture: A Study of Man and Civilization.* New York: Grove Press, 1949.

White is an anthropologist, and the long chapter on Akhenaten, whom he calls "Ikhnaton," is valuable because it brings to bear on the same data available to the historian another set of principles, skills, and techniques. This approach can be of particular value in the early periods of history, where documentary evidence is exasperatingly meager.

White's clearly stated and oft-repeated thesis holds that the events of Akhenaten's reign are not novel, but simply part of a process centuries old by Akhenaten's time; namely, a philosophic trend towards monotheism and age-old rivalry between king and priests. Akhenaten's religious reform, which White prefers to call a philosophy, failed not for causes intrinsic to the movement itself but because the Pharaoh's party was inferior in political and economic power to that of the priesthood. White's basic argument, however, is that history cannot be explained by describing the deeds of outstanding personalities but is more meaningful in terms of cultural forces and processes: technologies, institutions, and philosophies.

White proceeds to examine the "great man" theory of history in the light of the available data concerning Akhenaten and finds abundant examples of fallacious reasoning, exaggerations, and downright distortion of the evidence. Having completed the negative task, he next turns to an examination of the development of culture in general, explaining that the evolution of society can be divided into two main stages: primitive or tribal, and civil or national. In the latter stage, differentiation of structure and specialization of function require an "integrative mechanism." Historically, according to White, this mechanism is the state-church, that is, "a mechanism having temporal and ecclesiastical aspects." Akhenaten's attempt to impose a new religion on his people is simply a play in the power struggle between church and state. The two are necessarily rivals wherever they are structurally distinct, observes White, adding that the reason is simply that both are engaged in the same tasks and both have the same functions in society: to integrate, to coördinate, and to regulate.

The historical records provide material to support this view, for it is true that during the reign of Akhenaten's father the priestly class had drawn immense power to itself. One of the two grand viziers of the kingdom was Ptahmose, a high priest of Amen, while another priest was chief treasurer. In view of such a situation, the religious aspects of Akhenaten's reform movement almost cease to exist for White, who sees only, or certainly primarily, a naked political struggle with high economic stakes.

The trend towards a monotheistic religion which would provide the vehicle for the struggle against priesthood likewise has its explanation in political-economic rather than in religious causes; it is the religious counterpart of Egyptian expansionism. White here cites with approval

68

the great Egyptologist James Breasted, who held that monotheism was simply imperialism in religion.

If one concurs in White's arguments, what was ostensibly a religious reform spearheaded by a zealous pharaoh was on the contrary actually a process that had little or nothing to do with religion and had everything to do with the dynamics of power and wealth. Even the artistic representations of Akhenaten can be used to bolster this view, for many reliefs show Akhenaten rewarding his faithful followers with gold and other gifts. In conclusion, Akhenaten is merely, for White, "the neurological locus of all that went on during his reign."

White's account has its obvious faults, some of which are the very ones for which he censures the "great man" historians. Not the least defect is the careless use of unwarranted generalizations. His somewhat belligerent style further detracts from the value of what he has to say, and he is given to a dogmatism which badly mars objectivity. Nevertheless, the account has real value, since it adds a dimension to the understanding of a complex historical phenomenon by showing something of the relationship between evolving social structures and the role of the individual. — *M.E.J.*

Additional Recommended Reading

Aldred, Cyril. *The Egyptians.* London: Thames and Hudson, 1961. A well-illustrated sociological approach to Egyptian civilization.

Frankfort, Henri. *Ancient Egyptian Religion, An Interpretation.* New York: Columbia University Press, 1948. A distinctive approach to the gods in Egypt.

Aldred, Cyril. *Kingship and Gods: A Study of Ancient Near Eastern Religion as the Integration of Society and Nature.* Chicago: University of Chicago Press, 1948. Two carefully documented studies using archaeological and anthropological data.

Murray, Margaret. *The Splendor That Was Egypt.* Rev. ed. New York: Hawthorn Books, 1963. An especially good interpretation of artifacts having to do with Egyptian kings.

Wilson, John A. *The Culture of Ancient Egypt.* Chicago: University of Chicago Press, 1951. A highly selective and well-illustrated study of Egyptian values.

Giles, Frederick J. *Ikhnaton: Legend and History.* Rutherford, New Jersey: Fairleigh Dickinson University Press, 1972.

BATTLE OF KADESH

Type of event: Military: employment of ancient strategy
Time: Spring of 1296 B.C.
Locale: Southern Syria, about eighty miles northeast of modern Beirut

Principal personages:
MUWATALLISH, Hittite King 1310-1294
RAMSES II, Pharaoh of Egypt c.1304-1237

Summary of Event

Carved on the walls and pylons of massive temples along the River Nile there remain pictorial and hieroglyphic reports of a military engagement between the Egyptians and the Hittites in 1296 B.C. which J. H. Breasted called "the earliest battle in history of which the strategy can be studied in detail."

Egypt had been intermittently at war with the Hittites in Syria for two hundred years, since Thutmose III in the early fifteenth century had extended his sway northward beyond the site of modern Lebanon. Later, however, Hittite kings had invaded Syria as far south as Kadesh, where the best routes inland from the Mediterranean Sea entered the valley of the Orontes River, chief passageway to the North and East. Thutmose III had once devoted an eight-year siege to conquer Kadesh, which now became the southern bastion of a widespread Hittite empire.

When Ramses II came to the throne about 1304 he desired to reassert Egyptian dominance in Syria. In the fourth year of his reign he sent troops north along the coast beyond modern Beirut to secure harbors, and then in his fifth year he personally led a large force through Palestine. His army was divided into four divisions named after the gods, Ra, Ptah, Amen, and Set, each division numbering about five thousand men. At the heart of this pharaonic army were professional charioteers, experts at using bows and spears.

Aware of the approach of Ramses, the Hittite King Muwatallish mustered a host of approximately equal size, between sixteen thousand and twenty thousand men, collected from vassal units of the Hittite empire, with at least half of his troops charioteers. Most Hittite chariots depicted in relief sculpture carried a driver along with two fighting men. With remarkable cunning Muwattalish concealed this large force from Egyptian scouts, and he sent several Bedouins to be captured by the Egyptians and to deceive Ramses about the location of the Hittites. Persuaded that the enemy was far to the north, Ramses allowed his army to straggle in their march with wide gaps between the divisions.

Only when the advance division, Amun, led by the Pharaoh himself, had crossed the Orontes River west of Kadesh did they discover, through the interrogation of new Hittite prisoners, that Muwattalish's main force was ominously near, just east of Kadesh. Alarmed, the Pharaoh hastily sent back a messenger and a staff officer to hurry forward the Ra division, next unit in line. But at this juncture Muwattalish, using the hill of Kadesh to screen his movement, launched his chariots in a surprise flank attack against the approaching Ra division. The Ra column was scattered in all directions.

Pursuing some Ra fugitives northwestward, Hittite chariots came upon the hill where Ramses with the Amen division was setting up camp; many of these Amen soldiers also broke and fled, leaving the Pharaoh with only a small bodyguard of chariots, encircled by the enemy. It was a perilous moment for the young Ramses. Nearly half his army had been slain or scattered, and the remaining units were far to his rear.

When the situation seemed desperate, according to eulogistic records carved later in Egypt, Ramses in his two-horse chariot charged into the midst of more than two thousand Hittite chariots and drove back the enemy. Emphasizing his personal heroism as divine, the sculptural accounts are vague about some timely aid which arrived in time to rescue Ramses. Modern historians generally credit these fresh troops, perhaps of the Ptah division, with rallying the scattered Egyptian forces, at a moment when Hittite charioteers were engaged in pillaging the Egyptian camp and chasing fugitives in several directions. The Hittites were driven back.

Muwattalish then brought into action another Hittite force of a thousand chariots and attempted six successive charges. However, these were driven off as additional Egyptian forces arrived on the battle scene, the Hittites suffering heavy losses. The next day Muwattalish may have agreed to a truce, once the entire Egyptian army had been assembled; the fresh division of Set had taken no part in the first day's battle. On the other hand Muwattalish had never used eight thousand foot soldiers stationed east of the river, perhaps because the swiftly changing strategy made less mobile infantry useless.

Even though Egyptian inscriptions claimed a triumph for Ramses, portraying the Kadesh plain as strewn with Hittite corpses, the Pharaoh's immediate retreat southward nevertheless evacuated the area as far as Damascus and left it in possession of the Hittites. More terse Hittite cuneiform inscriptions reveal that in their home cities the battle was reported as a crushing defeat for Egypt.

In following years there were minor Egyptian campaigns into Palestine, but archaeologists have discovered both Egyptian and Hittite copies of a peace treaty drawn up fifteen years after the Battle of Kadesh between these two powers. The peace was sealed by a marriage of Ramses II to a Hittite princess, and we know of no subsequent battles between Egyptians and Hittites which compare in significance to the conflict at Kadesh. C. S. Ceram in his *Secret of the Hittites* calls the Battle of Kadesh one of the world's most important engagements because it "decided the fate of Syria and Palestine," and fixed the balance of power between Egypt and Khatti. Kadesh actually represented a truce between the two powers; it appears to have had a debilitating effect on the

Hittites while it checked the rising glory of imperial Egypt. Both powers delineated their spheres of influence and became susceptible to the invading Sea Peoples shortly thereafter.

The Pharaoh's retreat from the area and his marriage with the Hittite house does not really suggest the overwhelming victory recorded on the Egyptian inscriptions.

Pertinent Literature

Breasted, J. H. *The Battle of Kadesh.* First series, Vol. 5 of Decennial Publications. Chicago: University of Chicago Press, 1904.

This volume was the first detailed study in English of the numerous Egyptian inscriptions describing the Battle of Kadesh, and it was supplemented three years later by a more popular account in Breasted's *Ancient Records of Egypt.* Points of departure among scholars do not concern so much the battle itself as the records describing it. Breasted divides the inscriptions into three categories. First, there is what he calls the "Poem," a text not actually in poetic form which survives in hieroglyphic copies on towers at Luxor, on the walls of the huge temple at Karnak, and at Abydos, as well as in one hieratic manuscript. It provides a valuable account of Ramses' march north to Kadesh but only a confusing synopsis of the battle, focused on personal exploits of the Pharaoh.

Second, Breasted bases his reconstruction of the battle chiefly on what he calls "the Record," an inscription preserved at three different temples which gives a more consecutive narration about the battle than the "Poem." Third, Breasted publishes full-page drawings of many of the sculptured reliefs engraved in seven different versions on temple walls, one as far south as the great cliff sanctuary at Abu Simbel.

Breasted includes a review of geographical data along with detailed maps showing five stages of troop dispositions before and during the conflict at Kadesh. Critically analyzing evidence on the size of earlier and later Egyptian armies, he arrives at estimates of the forces of Ramses II at Kadesh, estimates which have been generally accepted by later scholars. He then attempts to correlate literary and pictorial records so as to reconstruct the battle developments and strategies, offering hypotheses about obscure terms and sculptures.

While Breasted recognizes that the records leave vague the "recruits from Amor" who suddenly relieved Ramses in his most perilous moment, he theorizes that they were a regrouped section of the routed Amen division. He interprets the artistic representations to suggest that a high officer under Ramses hurried south to bring up the Ptah division, third force in the line of march, and it arrived in time to turn the tide of battle. Breasted also theorizes that Egyptian losses were heavier even than those of the Hittites. He attributes to "scribal flattery" the claim made in the "Poem" that Muwattalish humbly sought a truce on the morning after the battle.

Breasted's 1904 study remains a fundamental point of reference on this topic.

Gardiner, Alan H. *The Kadesh Inscriptions of Ramesses II.* Oxford: The University Press, for the Griffith Institute, 1960.

This publication by a distinguished Egyptologist offers a full translation of the various hieroglyphic records concerning Kadesh and a reassessment of their interdependence, considerably differing from the views of Breasted advanced more than fifty years earlier.

After a brief historical introduction, Gardiner arranges the translations in approximately the same order as Breasted. Following each translation is a line-by-line commentary, consisting mainly of philological notes for specialists. However, any serious student will find in Gardiner's translation and concluding discussions a valuable summary of a half century of scholarly publications in several languages, which have clarified obscurities in Breasted's texts and have added insights from new sources such as Hittite inscriptions.

Gardiner attempts to show coöperative authorship for all the inscriptions, arguing that the so-called "Poem" would better be called a "literary record" intended to supplement the "pictorial record" of sculptural reliefs. He proposes that only Ramses himself could have inspired the elaborated records in such numerous versions; hence Gardiner believes that a few sculptors and scribes worked in close collaboration, putting into verbal form only such elements as could not be portrayed graphically. Thus many battle incidents were presented only in pictures, with brief legends or titles to identify figures and explain the actions.

In parallel columns Gardiner illustrates how the diverse inscriptions dovetail into each other, without as much inconsistency as earlier scholars assumed had resulted from unrelated efforts by different scribes and sculptors. Neither hieroglyphics nor sculptures were ever intended to be complete in themselves, and the double record illuminates "emotional and conceptual" aspects of the battle in ways which neither words nor sculpture could convey by themselves.

Hence, Gardiner argues, Ramses and his advisers "invented an entirely new technique of narration, one that recalls Greek drama or a modern film except that these latter are audible and dynamic. . . ." The Kadesh records are almost unique in Egyptian literature, paralleled only by a few captioned scenes carved earlier by Hatshepsut and some later sculptures placed by Ramses III. Since the scribes of Ramses II lacked experience in this double-media historiography, Gardiner considers their product to be "slipshod and repetitious."

In his detailed conclusions about the battle, Gardiner accepts the proposals of Eduard Meyer and A. H. Burne in the *Journal of Egyptian Archaeology,* 7, 191ff. that the "recruits from Amor" were troops arriving opportunely from detached assignment in the land of Amor. — *R.B.M.*

73

Battle of Kadesh

Additional Recommended Reading

Richard, James B., ed. *Ancient Near Eastern Texts Relating to the Old Testament.* Princeton: Princeton University Press, 1955. A well-known work giving ancient texts in translation.

Breasted, J. H. *Ancient Records of Egypt.* New York: Russell and Russell, 1906, republished 1962. A study providing translations of Egyptian and Hittite records relating to the Battle of Kadesh.

Ceram, C. W. "The Battle of Kadesh," in *The Secret of the Hittites.* Ch. 9. New York: Alfred A. Knopf, Inc., 1963. A dramatic reconstruction of the event.

The Cambridge Ancient History. Revised ed. Vol. II. Cambridge: The University Press, 1965. R. O. Faulkner in chapter 23 gives the Egyptian viewpoint, while A. Goetze in chapter 24 offers the Hittite perspective and a survey of the cuneiform records relating to the Battle of Kadesh.

Breasted, J. H. "The Age of Ramses II," in *The Cambridge Ancient History.* Vol. II, ch. 7. Cambridge: The University Press, 1924. Another clear summary of Breasted's viewpoints.

Gardiner, Alan H. *Egypt of the Pharaohs.* Ch. 10. New York: Oxford University Press, 1966. A discussion of the Battle of Kadesh and related inscriptions is included in this work.

HEBREW EXODUS FROM EGYPT

Type of event: Religious and social: escape from bondage
Time: c.1250 B.C.
Locale: Egypt, and Sinai peninsula

Principal personages:
MOSES (fl.1250), charismatic leader of the escaping Hebrews
RAMSES II, Pharaoh of Dynasty XIX c.1290-c.1224, prob-
ably the "Pharaoh of the oppression"
MERNEPTAH, Pharaoh of Dynasty XIX c.1224-c.1211, vic-
tor over Israel in battle in Palestine c.1220

Summary of Event

A shared memory that they had once been slaves in Egypt but that they had been liberated by their god Yahweh and brought to dwell in the land promised to their nomadic ancestors, was one of the solemn ties binding together the Hebrew tribes. It is doubtful whether all the tribes had actually shared the experience, but it is clearly indicated that all looked back upon it as fundamentally formative in their national identity.

According to the Biblical account in Genesis and Exodus, the ancestors of the Hebrews had settled in the delta area of Egypt 430 years before the Exodus. A change of dynasty caused the Hebrews, because of their growing numbers, to be looked upon with hostility and then to be put to work as state serfs in the construction of the delta store-cities of Pithom and Ramses. There emerged at this time Moses, who was to be the agent of Yahweh's deliverance of his people. Moses was born, according to Exodus, of Levite parents and educated in the household of the Egyptian king. He had, upon reaching adulthood, identified himself with his own oppressed people and had gone into exile after killing an Egyptian task-master. In the wilderness of Sinai he had been commissioned by Yahweh to lead his people out of Egypt to freedom and into the Promised Land. The Biblical account tells of a series of confrontations of Moses with Pharaoh, who stubbornly refused, though faced with a succession of extraordinary divine signs and calamities, to permit the Hebrews to leave Egypt. Only after a final blow, the death of the first-born male of every household in Egypt, was the King prepared to permit the departure of the Hebrews. When they had gone a day's journey eastward, they were overtaken by a troop of Egyptian chariotry and their escape was now consummated by the last of Yahweh's mighty acts: the accounts are unclear as to where this event occurred, but the Hebrews saw the sea open up before them. While they passed through it on dry land, the pursuing Egyptians were swallowed up by the sea which closed again upon them.

There is no direct account of these events in Egyptian historical records, but evidence of several kinds corroborates the essential elements. Most significantly, the cities of Pithom and Ramses were constructed during the first half of the thirteenth century B.C. in the reign of Ramses II, and Egyptian records indicate that state serfs, including "Hebrews," worked in their construction. Hence it is reasonably certain that Ramses II, who reigned from about 1290 to about 1224, was the Biblical "Pharaoh of the oppression." Archaeological evidence in Palestine, moreover, reveals the conquest of a number of cities in the central hills and in the south in the latter part of the thirteenth century. Finally, a stele found at Thebes describes a victory by Merneptah, the son of Ramses II, which he won over Israel during the fifth year of his rule. The Exodus and the conquest of Palestine by the Hebrews may therefore be securely dated in the middle and last half of the thirteenth century B.C. The Biblical figure of 430 years for the Hebrew residence in Egypt would place Hebrew settlement in the Nile delta in the seventeenth century B.C., at which time the Hyksos, a partially Semitic nomadic people of upper Mesopotamian and Palestinian origins, were ruling Egypt from the delta city of Avaris from 1730 to 1570 B.C. It should however be added that Egyptian records also indicate the settlement of Semitic peoples, including "Hebrews," in the delta at several times during the period following the expulsion of the Hyksos from Egypt.

Some other evidence is at variance with the Biblical tradition. The "Tell el-Amarna letters," written by Palestinian governors to the Egyptian king in the early fourteenth century, indicate that central Palestine cities were then under attack by "Hebrews." The traditions of the book of Joshua seem to indicate that the tribal confederation established after the conquest included many tribes that had been settled in Palestine prior to and during the Exodus, and it is unlikely that the group led out of Egypt by Moses was as numerous as the Biblical tradition asserts. Nevertheless, by the time of the united kingdom of David and Solomon, when the settlement traditions of Israel were first consolidated in literary form, all the tribes were understood to have taken part in the great events of national history: the Exodus from Egypt, the Sinai covenant-making, and the conquest of Canaan.

The memory of enslavement in Egypt and subsequent liberation by Yahweh commemorated annually in the spring Passover festival, affected profoundly the Hebraic concept of Yahweh as a god of compassion who hated oppression, and this effect has found expression in the earliest Hebrew law code: "You shall not oppress a stranger; you know the heart of a stranger, for you were strangers in the land of Egypt," (Exodus 23:9). In the course of time, the Exodus became symbolic of departure from conditions unworthy of humanity to a promised land likewise symbolic of freedom and justice.

Hebrew Exodus from Egypt

Pertinent Literature

Rowley, H. H. *From Joseph to Joshua: Biblical Traditions in the Light of Archaeology*. London: Oxford University Press, 1950.

The historical questions surrounding the Exodus from Egypt are intimately related to the problems of the settlement of the tribes in Palestine. Even within the Biblical tradition there are indications of important distinctions between tribal groups that nominally traced their descent from the patriarch Jacob. There were six "Leah tribes" and three "Rachel tribes," Joseph being represented by Ephraim and Manasseh. There are two traditions of invasion and settlement: one of a long and slow penetration from the South, the other of a swift and decisive thrust into the central hills from east of the Jordan River. Archaeological evidence seems to bear out both traditions in part, and it is evident that several of the tribes which later formed Israel were already settled in Palestine at the time of the oppression in Egypt and Exodus. Several efforts have been made to harmonize the conflicting indications of archaeological evidence and the Biblical tradition. One of the more successful attempts at synthesis is that of H. H. Rowley in his Schweich lectures of 1948, *From Joseph to Joshua*.

Rowley postulates a primary migration of Hebrew tribes into southern Palestine in the mid-seventeenth century B.C. By the mid-fifteenth century a confederation of these tribes was formed at Kadesh with Yahweh as the covenant god. In the following century these tribes pushed northward and gradually established themselves successfully in the northern Galilee area and in the south, but the tribes of Levi and Simeon failed to secure a hold on the central hill country in the vicinity of Shechem. This northward thrust of the Kadesh tribes Rowley sees reflected in the Tell el-Amarna correspondence describing "Habiru" attacks on Canaanite cities about 1400 B.C.

An interesting feature of Rowley's hypothesis is his suggested solution of the question of which tribes actually shared in the Exodus and how the two distinct tribal groups are related to each other. Rowley grants a high degree of validity to the tradition of Joseph's rise to power in Egypt and the settlement of Joseph's kin in the delta area. He believes that this must have taken place during the period of the Tell el-Amarna letters, and that the Hebrews who settled in Egypt were members of the tribes of Simeon and Levi who had failed to occupy the central hills of Palestine. It was this group that was later set to work in the construction projects of Ramses II, was led out of captivity by Moses, and then quickly invaded the central hill country from east of the Jordan to settle as the tribes of Ephraim, Manasseh, and Benjamin.

Rowley's synthesis also incorporates the essentials of the "Kenite hypothesis" of the origins of Mosaic Yahwism. The Kenites were Yahweh-worshiping nomads who had been associated with the Kadesh confederacy. In his period of exile from Egypt Moses associated with a Kenite group in the Sinai peninsula, associ-

77

ated its god Yahweh with the god of his patriarchal ancestors, and conceived the notion of the theocratic covenant which he later mediated between Yahweh and the Exodus tribes, a covenant in which the Ethical Decalogue, or Ten Commandments, played a fundamental role. This theory helps to account for first, the tradition of the southern tribes that Yahweh had always been the god of the Hebrews; second, the tradition of the northern tribes that the name Yahweh was newly revealed to the Hebrews in the Exodus and covenant-making experience; and third, the greater strength of the Mosaic theocratic ideals among the peasantry of the central-hill tribes.

Noth, Martin. *Exodus: A Commentary.* Philadelphia: The Westminster Press, 1962.

A more skeptical view of the Biblical traditions based on a careful literary analysis of the book of Exodus is presented by Martin Noth in the course of a commentary on the book. Beginning with the documentary analysis of the Pentateuchal narrative as generally accepted in Biblical scholarship since Wellhausen, Noth first carefully distinguishes the portions of the narrative deriving from Yahwistic, Elohistic, and Priestly authors. He then seeks to distinguish the older elements of the tradition and to offer an account of its expansion into its final form.

Noth views the core of the tradition as the memory of enslavement in Egypt, of flight toward the Sinai wilderness, and of a miraculous divine deliverance of the fugitive Hebrews "at the sea" from pursuing Egyptian chariotry. The oldest form of the tradition is the simple liturgical formula found in Exodus 15:21. Noth does not doubt that a historical event underlies this tradition, but the three intertwined accounts of this event in chapter 14 differ radically from each other and only the late Priestly account offers a specific geographic locale: the Sirbonian lake off the Mediterranean coast east of the Nile delta. Only the Priestly account tells of a passage of the Hebrews through a dry channel in the midst of the "sea." The Yahwist account is conceived in terms of holy warfare; Yahweh gazed down at the Egyptian chariotry from a pillar of cloud and struck panic into them so that they were engulfed in the rushing waters of the sea.

The bulk of the Exodus narrative, chapters 7-13, is viewed by Noth as unhistorical, an expansion of legends which developed out of traditions associated with the spring Passover ritual. The ritual is surely much older than the Exodus. It seems originally to have been a springtime nomadic apotropaic rite performed on the eve of the herdsmen's departure from winter to summer pasturage. In order to protect the young of man and beast, and especially the first-born, an animal was sacrificed and its blood smeared on the tent posts to avert the attack of evil powers. The rite "then acquired a particular historical reference as a constantly repeated cultic representation of the one great 'departure,' namely the departure from Egypt, with the result that at the same time the account of the Exodus, as now handed down at the Passover sacrifice, was shaped along the lines of the Passover rite." The tradition of the slaughter of the first-born of Egypt as the culmination of Yahweh's act of deliverance of Israel from bondage thus developed from the Passover ritual. Noth believes that this tradition in turn may have led to the development of the narrative of plagues and divine signs.

The opening chapters of Exodus relate the birth and call of Moses. The oldest element of tradition here, in Noth's view, is that of a theophany of Yahweh to Moses on a mountain of God in Midian. Although this tradition is combined with the tradition of the Exodus from Egypt in the oldest literary formulations, Noth believes that it was originally distinct and belongs rather to a tradition of a covenant-making between Yahweh and Israel mediated by Moses which was only later incorporated into the basic framework of the narrative of the Exodus from Egypt and settlement in Palestine. The implication is that Moses and the covenant-making have no place in the actual history of the Exodus. It should be pointed out, however, that although the Exodus and the covenant-making traditions developed independently prior to their literary formulation, the covenant introduction itself in Exodus 20:2 identifies Yahweh as "your God, who brought you out of the land of Egypt, out of the house of bondage." — *C.W.C.*

Additional Recommended Reading

Bright, John. *A History of Israel.* Ch. 3. Philadelphia: Westminster Press, 1959. Offers a conservative but thorough and judicious evaluation of the Exodus, traditions and extra-Biblical evidence.

Buber, Martin. *Moses: the Revelation and the Covenant.* London: Horovitz Publishing Co. Ltd., 1946. Reprinted, New York: Harper & Row Publishers Incorporated, 1958. A commentary, historical and exegetical, on the salient episodes of the Exodus narrative.

Daube, David. *The Exodus Pattern in the Bible.* London: Faber & Faber, 1963. Examines the impact of the Exodus as a literary prototype in the Old Testament.

Gray, John. *Archaeology and the Old Testament World.* Chs. 3 & 4. London: Thomas Nelson and Sons Ltd., 1962. Reprinted. New York: Harper & Row Publishers Incorporated, 1965. Deals with archaeological evidence relevant to the Hebrew Exodus and settlement.

Meek, Theophile James. *Hebrew Origins.* 3rd ed. Ch. 1. New York: Harper & Row Publishers Incorporated, 1960. Discusses the Hebrew patriarchal, Exodus, and settlement traditions in the light of current historical knowledge.

TRANSMISSION OF THE ALPHABET

Type of event: Cultural: introduction of a system of writing
Time: c.1250 B.C.
Locale: Mediterranean world

Summary of Event

The earliest form of writing was the pictogram. Probably around the beginning of the second millenium B.C. the earliest form of the alphabet was developed by Semitic peoples of unknown identity.

A cuneiform alphabet of about thirty characters used in writing on clay tablets was discovered at Ras Shamra in 1928. Merchants of this city, across from Cyprus in northern Syria, traded widely but had close mercantile ties with nearby Phoenicia. According to the view accepted by most scholars, these early Semitic inventors had the idea of developing an alphabet through contact with Egyptian hieroglyphics. But although some of their symbols were Egyptian, the system of writing was distinctly their own, consisting of twenty-two characters representing consonants. In early Semitic writing the reader had to supply the vowels from his knowledge of the language without the aid of written directions. Symbols were selected on the acrophonic principle: key Semitic words were selected in such a way that each would begin with a different consonant. Then stylized pictures portraying the key words, generally nouns, were assigned the phonetic value of the initial sound of each word, thus demonstrating the gradual change from ideograms representing ideas to an alphabet representing sounds. In this manner the first character of the Semitic alphabet, *aleph*, originally meant and

was the symbol for an oxhead. The second, *beth*, meant "house" and various renderings of the symbol in early Phoenician writing reveal a shelter with a roof, which came to represent the consonantal sound "b." The third, *gimel*, was used for the initial sound of the word describing "camel," and all early signs reveal a clear hump. In the same way, *daleth* represented a stylized door, *he* to behold, *vau* a hook or nail, *zayin* a sickle or weapon, *cheth* a fence, and so on.

The Greeks adopted the Semitic alphabet rather than Egyptian hieroglyphics because it was easier for trading purposes. One Semitic group, the Phoenicians, brought the alphabet to Greece at a very early date, perhaps as early as the thirteenth century B.C. That the Greeks secured their alphabet from Semitic sources is indicated not only by the similarity in the forms of characters in the two systems, but also by the fact that the Greek names of the letters, which mean nothing in Greek, are obviously taken from the Semitic names, which are meaningful in that language. *Alpha, beta, gamma* and *delta* are clearly modifications of Semitic *aleph, beth, gimel,* and *daleth,* just as the Greek forms of these letters are clearly based on the corresponding Semitic characters. The Greeks, however, experienced difficulty in expressing the words of their language in written form without using characters for the vowels. Since the Greeks found

80

that they did not need some Semitic symbols to express consonants, they used them to take on the value of vowels, and this modification constitutes the greatest contribution of the Greeks to the development of the alphabet. The Semitic *aleph* became the Greek vowel *alpha, he* became *epsilon* (short "e"), *cheth* became *eta* (long "e"), *yod* became *iota,* and *ayin* became *omicron* (short "o").

In Greece the alphabet eventually developed two separate types: the East Greek and the West Greek, which differed in details. For example, the character which we know as *X* had the sound "kh" in East Greek and "ks" in West Greek. Although the West Greek alphabet eventually died out in Greece, it was used extensively in the Greek colonies in southern Italy and Sicily. From one of these, possibly Cumae, it was borrowed by the Etruscans about the eighth century B.C. Later the Romans also took over the West Greek alphabet, probably securing it directly from the Etruscans, though some argue that the Romans secured the alphabet independently from some Greek colony. The Romans made slight changes in the Greek alphabet in adapting it to their own purposes. Certain Greek characters not needed by the Romans as letters were used as numerals. *Theta,* for instance, gives rise to the *C* used for "hundred," *psi* to the *L* used for "fifty," and *phi* both to the *M* used for "thousand" and the *D* (half of *phi*) used for "five hundred." The Latin alphabet, as the West Greek version came to be called, was spread by the Romans throughout the civilized world, so that apart from a few European countries which use the Cyrillic or East Greek alphabet, the

entire Western hemisphere has adopted and adapted it.

In its completed form, the Latin alphabet had twenty-three characters, the remaining three now used being added in the Middle Ages when "I" was split into the vocalic "i" and the consonantal "j," "V" was split into the vocalic "u" and the consonantal "v", and "U" was doubled to produce the new character "W." Mixing of the separate traditions has led to confusion in spelling, because the Latins invariably corrupted "W" to "gu." This accounts for the Anglo-Saxon word *werre* meaning "war" becoming in French *guerre*; or the Old High German *Willihelm* turning up in French as *Guillaume* and in Spanish as *Guillermo.*

Whereas the German and Spanish languages have developed use of the alphabet phonetically, English has not; variations in spelling the same sound in different ways can be accounted for by trying to describe nearly a hundred sounds by twenty-six symbols. Various attempts have been made to introduce so-called "universal" phonetic alphabets (for instance, the efforts of the Frenchman Paul Passy and the International Phonetic Association in the late nineteenth century), but none has been successful.

The difficulty is enhanced in the modern world by different developments in the East. The Semitic alphabet gave rise to the Syriac from which grew the Arabic used throughout the Mohammedan world.

The East Greek was also the parent of several alphabets, including the Coptic which developed in Egypt in the fourth century and which incorporated some Egyptian characters. More im-

81

portantly, however, in the ninth century, Cyril, the Greek missionary who Christianized the Slavs, invented the Russian or Cyrillic alphabet from the East Greek, adding some twelve new characters for Slavonic sounds un-known to the Greeks.

Nowadays the Cyrillic alphabet is used in Russia, the Arabic is used in Mohammedan countries, and much of the rest of the world uses the Roman.

Pertinent Literature

Moorhouse, Alfred C. *The Triumph of the Alphabet.* New York: Henry Schuman, 1953.

This book was written, according to the author, "to show that the apparently simple act of writing, and especially of writing in an alphabetic manner, is one of the world's most original and important intellectual discoveries." Moorhouse shows the role played by the Semitic alphabet in bringing about the existence of the Greek, Etruscan, and Latin alphabets in antiquity as well as many of the modern alphabets, but he also deals with other types of writing and the problems involved in deciphering unknown languages. In this connection he provides extensive discussions of procedures which have been successfully used in the past by scholars for working with unknown tongues. His account of the work done by Grotefend and Rawlinson in the deciphering of Old Persian documents constitutes a fascinating part of his story. He likewise provides a very interesting account of the work done by Champollion in the interpretation of the Rosetta Stone and the significance of this event in the study of the Egyptian hieroglyphs. There is a thorough discussion of Hittite documents, both cuneiform and hieroglyphic. The author also deals at some length with the Cretan scripts, drawing attention to the distinction between Linear A and Linear B. This portion of the book, however, is somewhat out of date since it was produced before the decipherment of Linear B by Ventris in 1952 had become generally known. It is noteworthy that Moorhouse anticipates the possibility that some of the documents in Linear B might be Greek documents, as proved to be the case when Ventris revealed his discoveries.

This book is written in a popular, nontechnical style which makes it useful to the general reader with limited experience in dealing with foreign languages and systems of writing. It has an excellent bibliography for those who may desire to pursue the subject further.

Diringer, David. *The Alphabet.* 3rd ed. Revised by Reinhold Regensburger. New York: Funk and Wagnalls Co., 1968. 2 vols.

The first volume of this monumental work is made up of a series of discussions of the origins and development of a great number of different systems of writing, concluding with the story of the Greek and Latin alphabets. Covering much of the same material presented in the book of Moorhouse in greater detail, the information is more up-to-date. Diringer, for instance, includes the story of the decipherment of Linear B.

The second volume consists entirely of diagrams and photographs. There are 427 plates illustrating every kind of writing known to man, including both inscriptions and manuscripts. Unusually clear Greek inscriptions are shown, and there is a beautiful reproduction of part of the fourth century Codex Sinaiticus of the Bible. In the explanation beneath the photograph the author correctly states that the manuscript was purchased by the British Museum from the Soviet Government in 1933 for a hundred thousand pounds, but he is probably wrong when he states that this is perhaps the earliest Greek vellum codex extant. Many paleographers believe that Codex Vaticanus Graecus dates from a somewhat earlier part of the fourth century. Splendid examples of Greek minuscule manuscripts of the tenth century are to be found along with excellent examples of early Latin writing, including some of the fine examples of Rustic Capital manuscripts of Vergil from the fourth and fifth centuries and several instances of miniscule writing of later periods. By comparing these samples one can easily see how both Greek and Latin lower-case letters gradually developed out of the capitals which were used in the early periods. The quality of the photographs is extremely high in all cases. — *C.E.F.*

Additional Recommended Reading

Ullman, B. L. *Ancient Writing and Its Influence.* Ch. 2. New York: Cooper Square Publishers, 1963. This work includes a brief account of the development of the alphabet written by an outstanding scholar in this field; several plates provide excellent photographs of important Greek and Latin manuscripts.

Ogg, Oscar. *The 26 Letters.* New York: Thomas Y. Crowell Company, 1961. An account of the development of writing through the centuries, starting with the earliest cave drawings.

Doblhofer, Ernst. *Voices in Stone.* Translated from the German by Mervyn Savill. New York: Viking Press, Inc., 1961. An elucidation of the decipherment of ancient scripts and writings.

Driver, Godfrey R. *Semitic Writing.* Revised ed. Oxford: The University Press, 1954. A history of the development of writing from pictographs to the formation of the Semitic alphabet.

ESTABLISHMENT OF YAHWEH'S
COVENANT WITH ISRAEL

Type of event: Religious: development of a formal theocratic constitution
Time: c.1250 B.C.
Locale: Sinai peninsula and Palestine

Principal personages:
Moses (fl.1250), charismatic leader of the Hebrews and
mediator of the Sinai covenant between Yahweh and
Israel
Joshua, charismatic leader of the Hebrews in their conquest
of Canaan, successor to Moses, c.1200

Summary of Event

The most significant events in the history of Israel concern the transformations and conflicting interpretations of the "everlasting covenant" which, according to Hebrew tradition, was established on Mount Sinai between Yahweh and Israel immediately following the Exodus from Egypt and before the conquest of Canaan. While there can be no doubt about the historical foundation of the tradition, the Pentateuchal narrative containing it is complex and the elements entering into it involve numerous problems which admit few conclusions.

One problem is the location of Mount Sinai. Since the early Christian period it has traditionally been identified with Jebel Musa at the southern end of the Sinai peninsula, but the identification has been increasingly doubted. Martin Noth, on the basis of descriptive elements pointing to an active volcano in Exodus 19:18, suggests a site in western Arabia and argues that the tradition of Moses and the holy mountain was originally distinct from the Exodus tradition. A growing consensus in recent years favors the view that the basic covenant-making tradition belongs not to Mount Sinai at all but to the oasis of Kadesh-barnea in the northern Sinai peninsula.

A second problem concerns the provenance and nature of the Hebrew god Yahweh. Traditions of the southern Hebrew tribes speak of Yahweh as already revealing himself to Abraham, but Ephraimite traditions indicated in Exodus 3 present Yahweh as a god first revealing his full nature and name to Moses during the latter's exile in Midian and identifying himself with patriarchal gods known earlier by other names. A widely-accepted hypothesis holds that Moses first came into contact with Yahweh as a god of the Kenites, a nomadic people of the Negev probably akin to the earliest Hebrew elements entering Palestine. It is in the religious experience of Moses that Yahweh first acquires his fundamental character as a god of compassion and justice who binds himself to the historical life of a community which he himself has called into being.

Within the Pentateuchal narrative three distinct covenant-making traditions have been preserved. One in Exodus 24:9-11 tells simply of a sacrificial meal eaten atop the sacred mountain in the presence of Yahweh. The Yahwist tradition in Exodus 34 portrays Moses ascending the sacred mountain alone with two stone tablets, receiving from Yahweh the formal covenant stipulations which he then inscribes upon the tablets, and descending again to the host of Israel below. A third tradition in Exodus 24:3-8 describes a ritual performed at the foot of the mountain: Moses builds an altar, erects twelve pillars for the tribes of Israel, directs young men to slaughter sacrifical animals, and collects the blood of the animals in basins. After scattering half the blood upon the altar, he reads the stipulations of the covenant to the people and binds them to it by scattering the remainder of the blood upon them.

It has been established by recent form-critical research that the covenant-making traditions have been transmitted through a periodically repeated Covenant-renewal ceremony performed during the period of the tribal confederacy at Shechem, most likely at the Festival of Booths. The liturgical form of this ceremony, which has shaped the book of Deuteronomy especially but also the narrative of the events at Sinai, follows a sequence of rehearsal of the Sinai events, reading of the Law, sealing of the covenant, and recitation of blessings and curses attendant upon the keeping or breaking of the covenant law.

There are three bodies of covenant stipulations in the Exodus narrative. The Covenant Code, found in chapters 21-23, belongs to the period of the tribal confederacy and contains primarily casuistic formulations providing penalties for specific offenses. The "Ritual Decalogue" incorporated in the covenant-making narrative of chapter 34 is essentially a brief recapitulation of cultic obligations found in the Covenant Code. The "Ethical Decalogue" of chapter 20 is certainly the oldest set of covenant stipulations and is the core of Mosaic Yahwism, a skeletal constitution of a theocratic society. Yahweh declares his sole kingship over Israel by virtue of the deliverance from Egyptian bondage. He forbids allegiance to or worshipful dependence upon any other power in heaven or on earth, and he binds his covenant people to live justly and compassionately in mutual social responsibility.

The remarkable feature of this covenant is its nonreligious character. Since Israel's obligation to Yahweh is defined not in terms of cult but rather in terms of social morality, a basis is laid down at the outset of Israel's history for the tradition maintained by Old Testament prophets and by later Judaism of protest and rebellion against political absolutism and social oppression.

Pertinent Literature

Mendenhall, George E. *Law and Covenant in Israel and in the Ancient Near East.* Pittsburgh: The Biblical Coloquium, 1955. Originally published in *The Biblical Archaeologist* 17 (1954) 26-46, 50-76.

Recent scholarship in the field of Old Testament studies has come to appreciate in growing measure the formative significance of the institutions of the premonarchic tribal confederacy in Israel. In view of the strong probability that the tribes bound together in this confederacy were not kinship groups, George Mendenhall has argued that a covenant corresponding to international treaty forms of the period must have bound the tribes together. In the work here reviewed he examines in particular the form of Hittite state treaties of the period 1450-1200 B.C., and demonstrates striking parallels therein to the form of the Mosaic covenant.

Mendenhall concentrates especially on the "suzerainty treaty" drawn up between the Hittite king and a vassal ruler. In this form of treaty only the vassal is bound by an oath and obligated to abide by stipulations laid down by the great king. Yet the basis of the treaty is the vassal's trust in the king who has demonstrated by his acts his benevolence toward the vassal. The covenant is spoken of as "given" by the king to the vassal and the covenant stipulations are called the "words" of the king.

The suzerainty treaty has a fixed form with a sequence of regular elements including a preamble identifying the author of the covenant, a historical prologue relating the previous relations of the parties, a body of stipulations, a provision for deposit in the vassal's sanctuary and periodic public reading of the covenant, a list of gods witnessing the covenant, and a formula of curses and blessings. Among the stipulations are a prohibition of any relations with powers outside the Hittite empire, a ban on any enmity against peoples under the sovereignty of the king, and a provision that controversies between vassals be submitted to the king for judgment.

Most of the features of the suzerainty treaty are to be found in the Hebrew covenant tradition, either in the Ethical Decalogue itself or in Deuteronomy. Yahweh identifies himself in the first person, as is the pattern in the Hittite treaties, calls for trust and obedience in gratitude for his benevolent deliverance from Egyptian bondage, demands the exclusive loyalty of Israel to himself, and prohibits enmity between his subjects. The provision for deposit of the covenant document in the vassal's sanctuary may correspond to the Hebrew tradition that the tablets of the law were deposited in the Ark of the Covenant. The provision for periodic public readings is mirrored in the covenant renewal ceremony of the tribal confederacy, the formal structure of which is seen in Deuteronomy. The formula of blessings and curses is likewise seen in Deuteronomy and surely have been part of the covenant-renewal ceremony.

It is significant that this treaty form, which Mendenhall argues must have been common throughout the Middle East in the last half of the second millennium B.C., passed out of existence with the demise of the Hittite empire about 1200. Thus the form of the Hebraic covenant is shown to be coeval with the period of Moses and the establishment of the tribal confederacy. If the covenant is indeed this old, then the Hebraic sense of the unity of the historical and legal traditions of Israel is implicit in the constitution of the tribal confederacy itself. The political character of the covenant, its foundation upon the Kingship of God, also helps to explain the initial opposition to the establishment of the institution of monarchy in Israel and the repeated protests of the prophets against royal absolutism.

Buber, Martin. *Kingship of God.* 3rd ed. Translated from the third German edition, 1956. New York: Harper & Row Publishers Incorporated, 1967.

While Mendenhall's work has helped to clarify the external form of the covenant mediated by Moses between Yahweh and Israel, Martin Buber has written a complementary study analyzing the character of the premonarchic Israelite community as essentially political rather than religious in nature. In this period of direct theocracy, abiding authority lay exclusively with Yahweh the King, while only limited and temporary tasks were assigned to his agents, the charismatic leaders.

The type of deity known by Israel in its covenant relationship is identified by Buber with the West-Semitic *malk* whose function is distinctly social leadership, not land-ownership or unrelational divine potency. There is evidence within Israel's traditions that Yahweh was thus viewed. The title *Yahweh Zebaoth* or "Yahweh of hosts," originally referred to Yahweh's leadership of Israel's troops assembled for warfare. The Exodus traditions of Yahweh's presence with the marching nomads, astride his portable throne the Ark, and dwelling in his own tent outside the camp, bear witness to the same conception. Buber also brings to bear on this issue his "dialogical" conception of the faith of ancient Israel: this faith was not a creed but an ongoing intimate historical confrontation between a collectively singular Israel and a personal "Thou," Yahweh.

The formation of the Sinai covenant between Yahweh and the fugitives from Egyptian bondage was, in Buber's view, a "theo-political" act creating a political unity. The solemn sprinkling of sacrificial blood on the altar of Yahweh and on the people marked a reciprocal acceptance by the two parties of Yahweh as King and Israel as his people. Buber stresses the political content of the utterances of Yahweh in Exodus 19:3b-6, a passage now recognized as being of great antiquity. This statement brings together the concept of *berith* or "covenant" and the *melekh*-ship of Yahweh. Buber argues against the usual interpretation; Israel is to be a *goy qadosh,* not a "holy nation" but a nation "separate" or "withdrawn" from the rest.

87

It is also to be not a "kingdom of priests" (*mamlekheth kohanim*) but "direct servants of the King."

In this direct theocracy wherein all servants are equal, the only conceivable political office is charismatic, and it is characteristic of the charisma of Yahweh that it is always *labile* or "hovering," never a permanent endowment of any individual Israelite and never bestowed except for the performance of some specific task. Direct theocracy existed in Israel until the establishment of the monarchy, and its historical expression is especially the "holy war," the war of conquest fought by servant warriors led directly by Yahweh their King.

An interesting feature of Buber's discussion of covenant theocracy is his conception of the emergence of prophets and judges from a common cource in ecstatic circles of peasantry determined to keep alive the political character of the Yahweh confederacy. Joshua, says Buber, appointed no successor because, in the flush of initial victory of the tribes over the Canaanites, he assumed that the conquest was complete and therefore transformed the political community established by the Mosaic covenant into a religious community. Recurrent threats to Israel's hold on the land, however, both from within Palestine and from without, caused a reconstitution of the political community, at least for the temporary occasions of crisis, at the urging of circles which kept alive, in ecstatic liturgical celebrations, the traditions of the "kingly covenant." The Song of Deborah (Judges 5) and the tradition of Saul "among the prophets" point to the existence of such circles of expectant, dedicated Yahwists characterized by an attitude of uninhibited surrender to the spirit of Yahweh, empowering a charismatic leader, and summoning afresh the members of the King's army to do "holy war." Opposition to dynastic monarchy, especially among the northern tribes, would seem to be rooted in the same interpretation of the theocratic covenant. — *C.W.C.*

Additional Recommended Reading

Alt, Albrecht. "The Origins of Israelite Law," (1934) in *Essays on Old Testament History and Religion*. Oxford: Basil Blackwell, 1966. A study distinguishing between Israel's uniquely apodictic covenant law and the typically casuistic law of Israel's neighbours.

Buber, Martin. *Moses: the Revelation and the Covenant*. London: Horovitz Publishing Co., Ltd., 1946. Reprinted, New York: Harper & Row Publishers Incorporated, 1958. A commentary, historical and exegetical, on the salient episodes of the Exodus narrative.

Meek, Theophile James. "The Origins of Hebrew Law," in *Hebrew Origins*. 3rd ed. New York: Harper & Row Publishers Incorporated, 1956. An examination of the relationship between Hebrew Law and older Near Eastern legal traditions.

Noth, Martin. "The Laws in Pentateuch: Their Assumption and Meaning," (1940) in *The Laws of the Pentateuch and Other Studies.* Edinburgh and London: Oliver & Boyd, 1966. An investigation into the history of the Covenant concept and the legal tradition developing within it.

ESTABLISHMENT OF THE UNITED KINGDOM

Type of event: Political: transformation of a tribal confederacy into a monarchy
Time: c.1000 B.C.
Locale: Palestine

Principal personages:
SAMUEL, Hebrew visionary of Ramah appearing c.1070, sponsor of Saul
SAUL, Benjamite peasant, first King of Israel c.1020-c.1000
DAVID, Judean peasant, leader of mercenary troops, King first of Judah c.1000, and later of Israel also c.993-c.961
ABNER, military commander of Saul's troops
JOAB, military commander of David's troops
ISHBAAL, fourth son and successor of Saul as King over Israel c.1000-c.993

Summary of Event

The settlement of the Philistines along the southern coast of Palestine at the beginning of the eleventh century B.C. presented the Hebrew tribes occupying the central and southern hills with a challenge that could not be met through the military institutions of Israel's loose tribal confederacy. Coming from Crete, whence they had been displaced along with many other Aegean peoples in the turbulent era following the Dorian invasion, the Philistines brought with them the first iron tools and weapons known in Palestine. They organized themselves into five strong city-states and soon began to thrust inland into Hebrew territory. For two centuries the Hebrew tribes had successfully put together armies of peasantry led by temporary charismatic leaders, or "judges," to meet crises of invasion or threat from Canaanite city-states, but in a battle fought about 1050 B.C. the Hebrews were decisively defeated and the Ark of the Covenant itself was captured, after which the Philistines established garrisons in the central hill country.

With Israel pressed by the Philistines on the West, the Ammonites east of the Jordan seized the opportunity to regain territories previously lost to the Hebrew tribe of Gilead to their north and laid siege to the Gileadite city of Jabesh. At this point Saul emerged as a charismatic military leader of combined tribal forces that routed the Ammonites and relieved the siege of Jabesh. On their return across the Jordan, the Israelite militia elected Saul king, and for the next several years he maintained a standing army and engaged Philistine troops in battle with varying degrees of success.

The Hebrew tradition regarding the emergence of the monarchy in this crisis is contained in the first book of Samuel; it is a composite narrative woven together from two

90

sources, each of which has its own distinct and antithetical account of events and their evaluation. One source gives the account presented above, that Saul emerged as a political leader with a standing army following his successful leadership of the campaign against the Ammonites. The other source presents Saul as a figure subordinate to Samuel, who is portrayed as the last judge and the first prophet. Samuel, according to this account, commissioned Saul as a prince and annointed him as king over Israel after strongly protesting Israel's demand for a king in order to be "like the nations" and after warning of the dangers to be expected by Israel from the institution of dynastic monarchy. Upon Saul's failure to fulfill to the letter Samuel's instructions to conduct a holy war against the Amalekites in the south, Samuel proclaimed Saul's rejection by Yahweh and anointed David to be king in his stead. Saul did, however, continue in actuality to exercise rule over Israel in spite of the specific action of Saul in "deposing" him in favor of David.

The traditions regarding the emergence of Saul's successor, David, are partly legendary. As a young man he was a member of Saul's court, a close friend of Saul's son Jonathan, and was given Saul's daughter Michal as wife. His popularity aroused Saul's jealousy and eventually he fled to the south, where he organized a guerrilla band and ingratiated himself with Hebrew tribesmen of Judah by warring on Amalekites and other groups that had long harassed them. At the same time, he took service with the Philistine Achish, King of Gath, as a mercenary leader of his warrior band. The fortunes of Saul continued to fall as a consequence of his alienation of the priesthood of Yahweh and his own mentally disturbed condition. He was finally decisively defeated and met his death in battle with the Philistines at Mount Gilboa. Saul's surving son, Ishbaal, was taken by Abner, his commander, to Mahanaim, east of the Jordan, and nominally made king. David in the meantime was elected king of Judah by tribal elders at Hebron. In the ensuing period of intrigue, Abner and Ishbaal were both assassinated, and in a second assembly at Hebron elders of the northern tribes made David king over Israel. All the Hebrew tribes were thus now bound to David in a united monarchy over Israel and Judah.

David now consolidated his hold upon the kingdom by decisive victories over the Philistines, Ammonites, Aramaeans, Moabites, and Edomites; by bringing the Canaanite city-states of Palestine under his own power; and by conquering the centrally-situated Jebusite city of Jerusalem, which he made the capital of his kingdom. There he established a centralized political administration and gave his state a solid legitimacy by bringing the Ark of the Covenant to Jerusalem and establishing the cult of Yahweh as an official institution. The measure of his success in state-building is the oracle of Nathan the prophet, as recorded in II Samuel 7, wherein Yahweh guaranteed the perpetuity of David's dynasty. For the brief period of less than a century of rule by David and his son Solomon, Israel enjoyed political

91

unity, a considerable empire with international prestige, a flourishing economy, and a culture expressing the high spirits of successful nationalism.

Pertinent Literature

Alt, Albrecht. "The Formation of the Israelite State in Palestine," in *Essays on Old Testament History and Religion.* Pp.223-309. Garden City, New York: Doubleday & Company, Inc., 1967.

In this study of the constitutional development of the monarchies of Saul, David, and Solomon, Albrecht Alt concentrates on the impact of Philistine and Canaanite military institutions on the earlier charismatic military leadership of the Hebrew tribal confederacy. The Philistines, professional soldiers ruled by city-state kings grouped in a league situated on the southwestern Palestinian littoral, had succeeded by 1250 in establishing a feudal hegemony over central Palestine. Their intention was to dominate Palestine as a ruling military class exacting tribute from Hebrew and Canaanite farmers and herdsmen. The Hebrew tribes, widely dispersed throughout the mountainous hinterland, had no common political organization and were united only by common loyalty to Yahweh, but their military defensive operations were conducted independently of tribal political organization by charismatic leaders, each appointed by Yahweh as "judge" in time of crisis.

Saul's rise to power was based initially on this traditional charisma, by which he united tribal conscripts for a successful campaign against Ammon, but at Gilgal the assembled militia proclaimed him, probably in solemn covenant, as "king," granting him continuing military authority based on the need for recurrent mili-

tary conscription and continuity of command in the face of the magnitude of the Philistine crisis. Once established in this position, Saul relied not only on Israelite conscripts but also increasingly on a band of professional guerrilla-type warriors, a feature copied from Philistine military organization. No dynastic principle had been accepted by Israel, and the effort of Abner to secure the position of Saul's son, Ishbaal, to succeed his father after the disaster of Mount Gilboa, failed for want of Yahweh's charismatic designation of Ishbaal as judge and Ishbaal's failure to be accepted by the conscript army of Israel as king.

David's rise to power was set in the context of Saul's professional soldiery, clearly the most effective response to the Philistine challenge. Finally, there was a repetition by David of the pattern of Saul's ascendancy. Perhaps by a fiction, David was declared endowed with Yahweh's charisma, and his success in war brought him acclamation as commander by the tribal elders, first of Judah and later of Israel. But David's military success came not through leadership of conscripts but rather through his own force of professional soldiers personally loyal to him. After the break with Saul, David's rise to power proceeded outside the territory and political framework of the Israelite state. He was first a feudal prince over Ziklag as a vassal of the Philistine ruler of Gath, then acclaimed king over Judah at Hebron in solemn covenant. Judah was not a tribal state, Alt insists; it incorporated several distinct ethnic groups in southern Palestine.

The structure of David's regime was an amalgam of Hebraic and Canaanite types of monarchy bound together in the person of the king rather than organically. The covenant of Israel's elders with David was independent of the earlier covenant made by the elders of Judah. Jerusalem, a Canaanite city outside the Hebrew territories, was conquered and made a private royal domain of David as a king of a city-state. The Philistines were defeated but allowed to retain internal political control with their kings functioning as David's vassals. The Canaanite cities of the northwest plains were conquered and incorporated into the tribal territories of Israel on the basis of ancient territorial claims of the tribes, but they were not occupied by Hebrews, and provincial administrative boundaries were set to preserve the ethnic distinctions between Canaanite and Hebrew. Conquests east of the Jordan were made either vassal states subject to David on the pattern of the Philistine cities or else made royal domains of David on the pattern of Jerusalem.

Powerful tensions within David's empire were created by his unprecedented use of the conscript armies of Israel year after year for campaigns of conquest east of the Jordan River. In Israel's view, David exceeded his constitutional powers, and Alt believes that the internal crisis of the succession in David's reign was related to the burden of the military levy. The rebellion of Absalom was supported by Israel in the effort to replace David with a king more to Israel's liking, but it was put down by David's professional troops. The later rebellion of Sheba was an effort by Israel to withdraw from the personal union of the kingdom of Israel with that of Judah, and this effort was thwarted by the combined professional forces of David and the conscript army of Judah. Alt relates Solomon's avoidance of expansion of the empire to the idea of preventing further tension that might be created by use of the conscript armies for conquest. In the dynastic succession of Solomon to David's throne, the old concept of Yahweh's designation of commander by charisma is replaced by the new concept of Yahweh's covenant with the house of David, but this conception was accepted only by Judah, and at Solomon's death the whole imperial structure of Palestine, based as it was on the personal union of distinct political entities, fell apart and reverted to earlier conditions: the coëxistence of several ethnic polities in Palestine.

93

Establishment of the United Kingdom

Noth, Martin. *The History of Israel.* 2nd ed. New York: Harper & Row Publishers Incorporated, 1960.

Whereas Alt's account of the establishment of monarchy in Israel concentrates on development of constitutional forms, Noth focuses on the episodic and transitional character of Saul's rule and on the deliberately planned rise to power of David. Noting that monarchy came late in Israel's history in comparison with neighboring states, Noth argues that the anti-monarchic source in Samuel, though late in composition, must reflect the actual sentiments of many Israelites still loyal to the thought expressed by Gideon: Israel can have no king or dynasty because Yahweh alone rules over Israel. The conflict between the traditional concept of charismatic military leadership and continuous military and political authority is represented in both sources of Samuel by the conflict between Samuel and Saul. Samuel did encourage Saul to accept the charismatic role of judge in the crisis of the Ammonite siege of Jabesh but was unprepared for the acclamation of Saul as king by the militia at Gilgal, and he attempted to stop the development of Saul's power into a political role usurping religious functions. At any rate, Saul's success was short-lived. Two surprise victories over Philistine garrisons immediately following his acclamation as king did not establish the real authority of Israel over the Philistines, and in the decisive encounter at Mt. Gilboa the following spring, Saul and his army were disastrously overwhelmed by the Philistines. Noth thus accepts the indication of I Samuel 13:1 that

Saul reigned for two years only, a figure thought by most scholars to be based on a corrupt text at that point.

In dealing with David's rise to power, Noth emphasizes the deliberate plan by which the young man of extraordinary political acumen ingratiated himself with the elders of Judah as a condottiere of a troop of professional soldiers, instigated his acclamation as king over Judah at Hebron, sought to secure a dynastic right to succeed Saul by marrying his daughter Michal, and profited from the murders of Abner and Ishbaal when a deputation of elders of Israel came to Hebron and acclaimed him king over Israel. Noth does not hold David responsible for the two murders. Thus, where Alt sees David's rise as engineered by the historical logic of events, specifically his role as commander of the only kind of army capable of meeting the Philistine military challenge, Noth sees a more deliberate scheme of planning, waiting, and seizing of opportunities presented to David in their proper course.

The struggle for the succession among David's sons is not so closely related by Noth as by Alt, who stresses Israelite dissatisfaction with David's imperial policies and exploitation of the conscript militia for trans-Jordanian conquest, but Noth does note that there must have been concern among the tribes as to whether David's policies perhaps exceeded Israel's authentic history, since Israel was only a portion of David's essentially personal empire — *C.W.C.*

94

Establishment of the United Kingdom

Additional Recommended Reading

Hertzberg, Hans Wilhelm, *I & II Samuel: A Commentary*. Philadelphia: Westminster Press, 1965. A text and commentary dealing fully with source-analysis and historical evaluation of the chief historical document of the period.

Bright, John. "From Tribal Confederacy to Dynastic State," in *A History of Israel*. Ch. 5. Philadelphia: Westminster Press, 1959. A detailed treatment with careful analysis of the sources.

De Vaux, Roland. "The Israelite Concept of the State," in *Ancient Israel*. Vol. 1: *Social Institutions*. Pt. II, ch. 4. New York: McGraw-Hill Book Company, 1965. A systematic presentation of the form and development of the monarchy in Israel.

Ehrlich, Ernst Ludwig. *A Concise History of Israel*. Chs. 7 & 8. New York: Harper & Row Publishers Incorporated, 1965. A concise evaluation of the reigns of Saul and David.

COMPOSITION OF THE BOOK OF GENESIS

Type of event: Literary: formation of a Hebrew national epic
Time: c.950 B.C.
Locale: Jerusalem

Principal personages:

THE YAWIST (c.950 B.C.), principal compiler of Israel's sacral and folk tradition in the essential framework of the Pentateuch

THE ELOHIST (c.850 B.C.), principal compiler of the settlement and patriarchal traditions of the northern tribes of Israel

THE PRIESTLY WRITER (c.550 B.C.), principal compiler of Israel's priestly ritual traditions and theology of history

Summary of Event

The reign of Solomon was the culmination of two generations of an immense political and social transformation in Palestine. A weak and loosely organized confederation of Israelite tribes had been welded by the military and political astuteness of David into a powerful monarchy with a centralized national administration and religious cultus at Jerusalem. The Philistine harassment had been conclusively ended, the hitherto unconquered Canaanite cities had been absorbed into the new state, and the burgeoning Israelite empire had come to encompass the neighboring peoples of Aram, Ammon, Moab, and Edom. Under Solomon, trade flourished and wealth flowed into the new capital. Israel had become conscious of her national identity and now began to mold her ancient traditions, which had long been transmitted orally, into an epic of her national destiny.

It is one of the assured results of modern Biblical criticism that the essential pattern into which these ancient traditions were consolidated is the work of an anonymous tenth century writer whom scholars designate the "Yahwist" in recognition of the recurrent divine name Yahweh in those portions of the Pentateuch assigned by literary criticism to him. The fundamental framework of the epic was provided by the settlement traditions: the ancestors of the Israelites had been slaves in Egypt, whence their god Yahweh had called them forth into freedom and given them the land of Canaan in which to dwell. A second tradition, incorporated by the Yahwist into the framework of the settlement narrative, told of the solemn covenant made at the sacred mountain Sinai by Yahweh with Israel, and of Yahweh's covenant legislation by which Israel was bound. A third body of traditions concerning Israel's patriarchal ancestors, Abraham, Isaac, and Jacob, to whom that land had been promised by Yahweh as a habitation for their descendants and who had sojourned in it before the Egyptian enslavement, was prefixed to the settlement narrative. The

96

whole scheme, finally, was introduced by a fourth block of traditional materials dealing with the primeval history of mankind. Thus four groups of traditional material were incorporated into a single narrative tracing the divine providence of Yahweh by which the Israelite tribes had taken possession of Canaan in fulfillment of their national destiny.

The Yahwist not only molded the traditions together; he also infused the work as a whole with a theological perspective which makes the Hebrew epic more than a glorification of national success or a religious justification of Israel's claim to a conquered land. By means of the primeval history, which traces the progressive alienation of man from God from the time of his creation to the dispersal of peoples from Mesopotamia, the Yahwist sets Hebrew national history in the context of Yahweh's redemptive purposes for all mankind: the departure of Abraham toward the Promised Land is heralded with the promise that the nation to be formed by his descendants will be implicated in the blessing of all communities of men. By means of the patriarchal history, the Yahwist formulates the theological perspective on history which was to characterize the prophets of Israel: secular history, wherein men freely and responsibly interact to shape their own destinies, is the sphere in which Yahweh's historical purposes for Israel and all nations are worked out. Finally, through the incorporation of the Sinai tradition into the settlement account, the Yahwist enunciates another theological concept that was to be fundamental in the prophetic tra-

dition: Israel's tenure of the Promised Land and her very national identity is intimately bound up with her obedience to Yahweh, her sole legitimate sovereign, and to his covenant demand for justice and brotherhood in national corporate life.

Several additional blocks of material were incorporated into the Yahwist narrative before the Pentateuch assumed its authoritative form toward the end of the sixth century B.C. A second epic incorporating the settlement and patriarchal traditions of the northern tribes was composed in the ninth century by a second anonymous writer termed the "Elohist" by scholars, to distinguish him from the Yahwist, because of his characteristic use of the divine name Elohim in his narrative. In the course of the seventh century, materials from the premonarchic covenant-renewal ceremony of the tribes were edited into the core of the book of Deuteronomy. Finally, during and after the Exile in Babylon, the traditional ritual law and theology of history of the Jerusalem priesthood was formally written down as a framework binding together the whole complex of historical and cultic traditions of Israel into a literary whole. The resultant literary corpus is thus a complex document representing several distinct eras and theological perspectives, and reflecting the richness and diversity of Israel's national religious experience. Yet although the Priestly editors of the Pentateuch in its final form seem to have intended the document to serve as a constitutional foundation for the theocratic life of the second temple, the theological concepts of the Yahwist, most clearly evident in Genesis where his contributions bulk largest, mark the book as one of religious significance extending beyond Judaism to the Christian and Islamic traditions, and as a major constitutive element of Western European culture.

Pertinent Literature

Gunkel, Hermann. *The Legends of Genesis: The Biblical Saga and History* (1901). Reprinted New York: Schocken Books, 1964.

The literary analysis of the Pentateuch into its four primary documents, the Yahwist and Elohist epics, Deuteronomy, and the Priestly Code, was firmly established and stated in classic form in 1878 by Julius Wellhausen in his *Prolegomena to the History of Ancient Israel.* Scholarship in the intervening years since then has not fundamentally altered that analysis or the approximate dates of compilation of these documents. The documents themselves, however, have been reëvaluated radically, and a different view of the nature and historical significance of the documents prevails today because of new perspectives in crictical scholarship: archaeological, socio-anthropological, religio-historical, and perhaps more important, form-critical. Aware, as Wellhausen was not, that these Pentateuchal documents are not free compositions testifying simply to the religious, legal, and historical perspectives of the date of their emergence in literary form, but are rather compilations of traditions of perhaps equal antiquity that had long been transmitted orally, the form-critics have sought to ascertain the process by which the traditions themselves have developed and to answer questions about the meaning and form into which the traditions have finally been cast. The pioneer work in form-criticism was done by Hermann Gunkel. His classic study of the forms and development of the legendary material of the book of Genesis was originally published in 1901 as an introduction to his *Commentary on Genesis.* Although sections of this work, devoted to the later process of redaction of the Yahwist, Elohist, and Priestly documents, have been made obsolete by more recent study, the chapters dealing with the variety and literary form of the legends still provide one of the finest general treatments of this topic.

Gunkel begins by drawing a sharp distinction between history, a written account of great public events, and legend, traditional stories passed down orally over several generations dealing with more limited family and tribal memories. The materials comprised in Genesis are legendary rather than historical. Among them a further distinction must be made between the primeval history of the first eleven chapters, largely mythical with divinity the leading actor, and the patriarchal legends which make up the remainder of the book. The myths and legends may be classified according to the various functions which they serve. Some legends provide the aetiology of a cult practice such as circumcision (chapter 17) or the taboo on eating the thigh muscle (chapter 32). Others are foundation legends of sanctuaries (Beersheba: chapter 26; Bethel: chapter 28). Many are etymological and offer reasons for the naming of races, mountains, or wells. Several legends explain tribal migrations and interrelationships through the movements and deeds of eponymous ancestors, individuals who clearly serve in their narratives as representatives of whole tribal groups: such are Jacob the Hebrew, Esau the Edomite, Laban the Syrian, and Lot's children Moab and Ammon. Some legends have clearly been reinterpreted in a significance other than their original one: thus the legend of the attempted sacrifice of Isaac, originally an explanation of the prohibition against human sacrifice, has been transformed into a character portrait of Abraham.

The bulk of the patriarchal legends concerning Abraham, Isaac, and Jacob consists of loosely connected cycles of brief narrative units, the form of which, Gunkel's analysis indicates, were clearly suited to oral transmission. Each brief unit has a clear outline and structure, a minimum of characters (rarely more than two in a single scene), laconism of dialogue, a single emphasis and simplicity of character. There is no description of inner life and character is revealed in actions or in speech. These individual units have been linked to each other in smaller and then in greater cycles, but the links are clearly distinguishable. A common transitional device is a journey. The Joseph narrative is marked by features of greater literary sophistication indicating its later composition: here there is a genuine interest in the soul-life of characters, an expansive discursiveness in conversation and the deliberate suspenseful postponement of climax.

Von Rad, Gerhard. "The Form-Critical Problem of the Hexateuch" (1938), reprinted in *The Problem of the Hexateuch and Other Essays*. New York: McGraw-Hill Book Company, 1966.

While Gunkel's work exemplifies the concern of the earlier form-critics with the analytic units of the Biblical text, attention in recent years has been turned again to the question of the formal unity of composition in the texts that are clearly compilations. A most significant recent study of this nature is Gerhard von Rad's "The Form-Critical Problem of the Hexateuch." This term is used in preference to Pentateuch by many scholars since Wellhausen, in view of the fact that the narrative sources continue on through the book of Joshua. Von Rad views the formal unity of the Hexateuch as a "credal history of redemption," the outline of which is recognizable in several short confessional statements, perhaps the oldest of which is Deteronomy 26:5b-9. The same sequence of events in a number of liturgical confessions points to a cultic occasion at which the Exodus and conquest events were celebrated, and this occasion von Rad believes to have been the Feast of Weeks. Here at the annual harvest festival, the congregation of Israel acknowledged "the redemptive sovereignty of Yahweh, now seen as the giver of the cultivable land."

The remarkable fact about these liturgical formulas derived from the

Feast of Weeks is that, although other events of Israel's redemptive history were included in several of them, no mention of the Sinai covenant-making and legislation is found in any of them earlier than post-Exilic times. The reason for this, in von Rad's view, is that the Sinai tradition was celebrated at a distinct cultic occasion of its own, a covenant-renewal celebration held during the era of the tribal confederacy at Shechem. The liturgical pattern of this ceremony is reflected in the structure of Deuteronomy and in the sequence of events in the Sinai narrative in Exodus.

It is the Yahwist who has taken these cultic traditions and woven them into a unified narrative of Israel's redemptive history. Taking the settlement tradition as the foundation of his outline, he has incorporated the Sinai tradition into it and prefixed to it the already formulated patriarchal tradition of Abraham, Isaac, and Jacob, and the primeval history with its account of the growing power of sin in the world.

Apart from his tracing of the origins and growth of the traditional materials incorporated into his narrative scheme by the Yahwist, von Rad is concerned with what he calls the "theological problem of the Yahwist." The original cultic interest of the traditions has been transformed into a historical interest, yet the Yahwist is clearly concerned with presenting a theological perspective of significance for the people of his own era. Von Rad sees the essence of this theological perspective as the efficacy of Yahweh's providence in Israel's history outside the sacral institutions in secular events, and the major inspiration for this conception he views as the spectacular success of David and his consolidation of the age-old territorial claims of the tribes of Israel.
— *C.W.C.*

Additional Recommended Reading

Alt, Albrecht. "The God of the Fathers" (1929), in *Essays on Old Testament History and Religion*. Oxford: Basil Blackwell, 1966. Historical analysis of aspects of personal religion in the patriarchal narratives of Genesis.

Heidel, Alexander. *The Babylonian Genesis*. 2nd ed. Chicago: University of Chicago Press, 1951. A discussion of the relationship of the Genesis creation accounts with Babylonian creation poems.

Morgenstern, Julian. *The Book of Genesis, a Jewish Interpretation*. 2nd ed. New York: Schocken Books, 1965. A scholarly discussion of the major narrative units of Genesis with focus on literary and religious values.

Speiser, E. A. *The Anchor Bible: Genesis*. Garden City, New York: Doubleday & Company, Inc., 1964. The author's own translation and commentary with a full introduction.

Von Rad, Gerhard. *Genesis, a Commentary*. Philadelphia: The Westminster Press, 1961. The Revised Standard Version of the text of Genesis with commentary and an introduction.

Wellhausen, Julius. *Prolegomena to the History of Ancient Israel*. New York: Meridian Books, 1957. Originally published in German in 1878, this book did much to start modern textual criticism.

100

BUILDING OF THE TEMPLE

Type of event: Religious: construction of a sanctuary
Time: c.950 B.C.
Locale: Jerusalem

Principal personages:
DAVID, King of Israel c.1000-961
SOLOMON, King of Israel c.961-922
NATHAN, prophet at the royal court
HIRAM, King of Tyre

Summary of Event

Scripture records that David consulted the prophet Nathan about building a temple to Yahweh presumably as a thank offering for his successes and as an adornment for his new capital at Jerusalem. Whatever the initial inspiration Nathan encouraged David's project but a later vision revealed to the prophet that although David enjoyed God's favor, the building of the Temple would be reserved for a descendant of his house.

God's promise to David materialized under Solomon who, through a commercial alliance, employed architects from Tyre and imported the famous cedars of Lebanon for constructing the Temple. Scripture records the dedication ceremonies featuring special sacrifices and an address by Solomon. Thus the Temple arose, to play a dominant role in the religious and national life of Judaism, and to stand as an assurance of God's abiding presence among his Chosen People.

The site of the Temple was chosen by Solomon because it was the holy place of Zion, connected by tradition with the threshing floor of Araunah. The Temple itself was modest in size, being smaller than the palace Solomon built for himself; many consider it basically a royal chapel attached to the palace. Wrought exquisitely in traditional Phoenician architectural style, the new shrine was rectangular in shape, composed of three chambers, and faced over its entire width with a porch or vestibule. Temples of similar design have been unearthed in Syria and most recently at Hazor in Galilee. As with all ancient places of worship, the sanctuary provided no seats since there were no specified requirements for indoor worship. Although the courtyard was used for the celebration of great national festivals, the main function of the edifice was to provide a venerable place for the offering of sacrifice.

The erection of the Temple may be interpreted as part of Solomon's campaign to centralize his government and reinforce his larger program of administrative changes. He intended to establish new governmental districts cutting across old tribal boundaries, a plan designed to encourage centralization of power in the city of Jerusalem by breaking down tribal loyalties and other competing outlying vested centers of power. Building a central sanctuary in Jerusalem as early as Solomon

101

might facilitate such a program of organization, but it seems unlikely that it could be significant in this respect before the reign of Josiah in the seventh century. Its influence became so decisive, however, that foreign conquerors always regarded the Jewish polity as a temple-state.

The Deuteronomic authors who later centered about the Temple glorified Solomon retroactively for his role in constructing the shrine, although at the time it seems to have introduced no significant revolution in religious belief or practice. Syncretism was still much in evidence, and many local high places of foreign cult worship and sacrifice, such as those at Hebron and Bethel, continued to function during Solomon's reign. With the reforms of Josiah, the Temple at Jerusalem finally became the sole center of worship. As the edifice gradually grew in importance under the Deuteronomists, Solomon grew correspondingly famous as its

designer and builder, despite the idolatrous practices which he allowed to remain in vogue during his rule.

The major cultist innovation of the Deuteronomists was the centralization of worship at Jerusalem. They believed that the unity of God must be mirrored in unity of worship, that a multiplicity of sanctuaries corrupted the worship of God by associating it with a polytheistic paganism which worshiped in many temples nestled in high places. This centralizing reform around the Temple was, in turn, a direct steppingstone to the pure ethical monotheism of Second Isaiah, who enunciated clearly that there was only one God: Yahweh. Within the framework of his single Temple, his central sanctuary, Yahweh truly became one for Israel and the only One. His great new Temple became a concrete expression of his uniqueness and was to endure as such with replacements until A.D. 70.

Pertinent Literature

Clements, R. E. *God and Temple; the Presence of God in Israel's Worship.* Philadelphia: Fortress Press, 1965.

The author's purpose is to broaden the perspective in which the Temple is generally viewed. He puts it not only in the framework of a developing Jewish theology but also in the context of older religious forms in Canaan particularly at Jebus where the Temple was constructed. The work attempts to show that the notion of God living in one special place on earth is not as strange as it first appears and that it in no wise detracts from belief in a God who is the creator of the entire universe. Neither

Jerusalem nor Temple can hamper an unlimited conception of God nor diminish his lordship.

The Temple and its establishment should rather be envisaged as a segment of the historical development of the Judaism which began with the events of the Exodus and the conclusion of the covenant on Mount Sinai. Judaism, Clements reminds his readers, built on the foundations of earlier religious beliefs and practices. Even Mount Sinai itself, which was to play so important a role in the development of the Jewish faith, may have been a divine abode before the arrival of the Israelites. In the same way, the introduction of the worship of Yahweh into Jerusalem during David's reign and its subsequent localization there in the Temple establishes some continuity and recognition with the Canaanitic religious ideas associated with Mount Zion. The Temple stood as a symbol of the syncretism between two different religious traditions; the covenantal strain was commemorated by placing the Ark of the Covenant in the Holy of Holies, while the site of the Temple recalled the mythological ideas associated with mountain symbolism of the Jebusite religion practiced there when David conquered it. This dichotomy represented in the Temple, Clements asserts, reflects a tension between the Judean concept of Yahweh's transcendent freedom to enter freely into a covenant relationship with Israel, and the Canaanite immanent tradition of divinity's localized presence among a particular land and people.

However, according to Clements, the synthesis which the Temple represented did not herald any new development with Judaism since every state of Israel's history previously involved some sort of mixture of diverse elements. David's decision to bring the Ark to Jerusalem simply established the Yahwistic tradition in a central place; God's dwelling on foreign Mount Zion merely asserted his ownership of Canaan and furnished a testimonial to the legitimacy of the house of David. In this light the Temple of Solomon merely absorbed conceptions of divine presence which had already been developed.

Misgivings with this syncretism, indeed, were vented by the northern Israelites who saw their interests slighted as these religious developments took hold in Jerusalem and came to have political repercussions. Their prophets protested that Yahweh could not be bound to any place or people and warned that his presence could spell judgment as well as blessing. Such northern dissatisfaction eventually led them to form a separate kingdom rivaling that centered in Jerusalem.

Clements points out that the full import of the process begun by David with particular reference to Jerusalem and the Temple took centuries, until the reign of Josiah, to be fully realized. So important would the Temple become that its destruction in 586 brought the Davidic dynasty into eclipse and ruined the political and religious aspirations of Israel. The subsequent destruction of the second temple in A.D. 70 entailed a demoralization lasting virtually up to modern times.

Join-Lambert, Michel. *Jerusalem*. Translated by Charlotte Haldane. New York: G.P. Putnam's Sons, 1958.

This study is very different from Clements'. While Join-Lambert does mention the purpose of the Temple construction as an event calculated mainly to enhance the importance of Jerusalem, he is more concerned with the physical description of the building and its immediate purposes.

Utilizing a late Biblical source, the Books of Chronicles, the author recounts David's vision which led him to acquire the threshing floor of Ornan, or Araunah, overlooking the city as the site for the Temple structure. There he built an altar and offered sacrifices, while the actual construction of the Temple awaited his son and successor. David dreamed of the splendors of Jerusalem; Solomon executed them.

A period of peace, from approximately 970 to 930, assisted Solomon in his three great construction projects: the Temple, the royal palace, and the city's fortifications. Join-Lambert notes that the foundations of the Temple were laid during the fourth year of Solomon's reign and that the actual construction continued for seven years and five months, involving tens of thousands of workmen. While an abundance of stone for capitals and other monumental adornments was at hand, a shortage of suitable timber and precious stones, as well as skilled craftsmen and architects, forced Solomon to make a treaty of *commercium* with the Phoenicians. The building was rectangular, facing east and west, so designed as to receive the rays of the rising sun. It was not large, being approximately one hundred feet by thirty feet, and consisted of three sections: porch, hall, and Holy of Holies. Join-Lambert finds its exact duplication in Egypt, and he believes that Phoenician architects had employed this type of building plan for a long time before Solomon used their skill in Israel. There were apparently a number of small rooms surrounding the building. The Holy of Holies, containing nothing but the Ark of the Covenant, was entered only once a year on the Day of Atonement and then only by the High Priest. The interior was not designed as a place of prayer since the outside courtyard served this purpose. The Temple was in effect the divine residence and the site for the veneration of Yahweh. Blood sacrifices were performed only in the outer sanctuary where an altar of bronze was built. The Temple continued in existence for nearly four hundred years, gradually becoming not only the sole religious center of the people of Israel but more importantly the idealized spiritual focus of the entire Jewish people wherever they lived.
—*J.R.R.*

Additional Recommended Reading

Parrot, André. *The Temple of Jerusalem.* Translated by B. E. Hooke. London: Student Christian Movement Press, 1957. An interesting general survey of the Temple.

Brinker, R. *The Influence of Sanctuaries in Early Israel.* Manchester: Manchester University Press, 1946. An attempt to clarify the ideological background and function of sanctuaries in Israel.

Eversull, Harry K. *The Temples in Jerusalem.* Cincinnati, Ohio: Masonic Memorial Chapel Association, 1946. A collection of artists' representations of the Temple.

Johnson, Aubrey R. *Sacral Kingship in Ancient Israel.* Cardiff: University of Wales Press, 1955. An explanation of the cult of the Temple and the psalms used in the services.

Simons, J. *Jerusalem in the Old Testament.* Leiden: E. J. Brill, 1952. A scholarly account of the Temple, including its physical setting.

Brown, J. R. *Temple and Sacrifice in Rabbinic Judaism.* Evanston: Seabury-Western Theological Seminary, 1963. A study which describes the role of the Temple and sacrificial worship in Rabbinic Judaism at the time of the Christian era.

ESTABLISHMENT OF THE KINGDOM OF ISRAEL

Type of event: Religious: division of Hebrew polity
Time: 922 B.C.
Locale: Palestine

Principal personages:
SOLOMON, King of the united nation 961-922
REHOBOAM, King of Judah 922-915
JEROBOAM, first King of Israel 922-901
SHEBA, a Benjamite
AHIJAH, a prophet

Summary of Event

The pressing problem of the Hebrews was to forge a group of independent tribes into a strong functioning nation in order to conquer Canaan and subdue the Philistines and their allies. Although there had been some feeling of unity among the Hebrew tribes which settled in Canaan, it took approximately two hundred years for a unified state to evolve. Even when once organized, it apparently never overcame the vested interests of groups and individuals for it managed to survive for less than a century.

At first the tribes acted together occasionally under the temporary leadership of a hero called a "judge" in the Bible. By 1000, it became evident that a more stable unity under a permanent king was desirable, and Saul was called upon to rule. His death at the hands of the Philistines on Mt. Gilboa allowed David, who had to some extent already usurped power under Saul, to be declared next leader of the united tribes. Apparently he won confirmation as king through a covenant with the tribes which left them some autonomy as well as the right to confirm his suc-

cessors in office. Symptomatic of the lack of full acquiescence, especially on the part of the northern tribes, were the rebellions by David's son, Absalom, and by Sheba, a Benjamite. According to II Samuel 20:2 only "the men of Judah followed their king steadfastly."

Resentment against the monarchy increased, especially in the north during the reign of Solomon. Heavy exactions in money and men necessitated by his ambitious building programs became increasingly distasteful, as did his commercial alliance with Tyre involving repayment for supplies and services employed in the construction of the Temple. The tribal covenant entered into by David was virtually ignored; Judah was preferentially exempted from many of the onerous provisions demanded of the other tribes. More disturbing was Solomon's program of centralization which weakened the power of individual tribes by destroying their traditional boundaries through the creation of new administrative districts.

After Solomon's death, his son Rehoboam was immediately accepted as king by Judah. When Israel demurred, Rehoboam went to Shechem, the historic covenant center where Jacob had gone after his return from Haran and where the national assembly had been held in the time of Joshua. The assembled Israelites demanded that the oppressive rule imposed by Solomon be lightened, and they reminded Rehoboam that a king could not take the principle of hereditary monarchy for granted; nor did they intend to tolerate a second Solomon with a resplendent court resulting in extravagant demands for taxes and labor drafts.

When Rehoboam unfortunately heeded the advice of his luxury-minded young courtiers to ignore the demands of the northern Israelites, Jeroboam, a seditious leader of one of Solomon's labor battalions who had been forced to flee to Egypt for asylum, returned to take advantage of the new discontent. He was supported by the prophet Ahijah, who announced symbolically, by tearing a garment in ten pieces, that ten tribes would follow Jeroboam. Consequently, Jeroboam was proclaimed king at the Shechem assembly. He established his capital first at Shechem and then at Tirzah, placing sanctuaries at Dan and Bethel thus ending the united kingdom.

While the immediate cause of the breakup was the heavy-handed reign of the despotic Solomon which curtailed tribal freedoms and favored the south, the schism had deeper underlying causes. The hilly terrain encouraged sectional insularity. Each section had a different geography and therefore different economic orientation. The north, facing toward the plains, was agricultural and commercial; Judah, oriented toward the desert, was pastoral and nomadic. Moreover, the original separation of the northern or Jacob Hebrews and the southern or Abraham Hebrews was too deeply rooted to be wiped out in one or two generations. While Jeroboam and others had a personal interest in the breakup of the kingdom, the vital factor was the constant reassertion of tribal sympathies with all their religious implications. Whenever the northern Israelites established new religious centers, they implied the tacit rebellion of localism against the centralized regime in Jerusalem.

The northern branch of the Hebrew nation proved much stronger in population, economic resources, and cultural initiative. It possessed more fertile lands and its plain of Esdraelon controlled international highways. However, when great new empires arose in the vicinity, the more isolated and poorer Judah survived longer. Israel was destroyed by Assyria in 721, and became another "lost nation"; survival of Judaism was left to the weaker Judah.

Pertinent Literature

Lods, Adolphe. *Israel from Its Beginnings to the Middle of the Eighth Century.* Translated by S. H. Hooke. London: Routledge and Kegan Paul Ltd., 1932.

According to the Biblical account, the division of the Jewish nation involved a religious schism. It states that Jeroboam, fearing that the north would return to its allegiance to the "rightful" king, conceived the idea of making two golden calves, one at Bethel and the other at Dan, so that pilgrimages to Jerusalem would be unnecessary. Reputedly he also established other religious sanctuaries in high places, and appointed priests from outside the ranks of the Levites.

Lods shows that such an account is anachronistic. Jeroboam's supposed religious innovations would be disturbing only after the Josianic reforms in the late seventh century. Lods believes that passages in the Bible amply confirm the contention that the importations attributed to Jeroboam were actually old customs which had persisted in Israel after Judah had long abandoned or modified them. High sanctuaries devoted to local gods even in Judah were not condemned until the seventh century and non-Levite priests were still common in the time of David, since the priestly prerogatives of Levites were not established until the eighth century. The worship of golden calves was also well established in both south and north.

Any religious motivation to the split, Lods notes, would more likely have come from the desire to defend the traditional simplicity of Yahweh worship against the luxurious temple cult. The northerners were the religious conservatives; already the prophets Nathan and Ahijah were not enthusiastic about the Temple. The north rather than the south maintained itself as the true home of primitive Yahwism; the prophets Elijah, Elisha, Micaiah ben Imlah, Hosea, and even Amos, all came from Judah. Lods concludes that the split, then, was primarily political, with little if any of the religious motivation the Biblical account presents as primary.

Far from motivating the split, religion remained even after the schism a uniting force. Yahweh was still the one god of the two kingdoms; the Jews were still basically only one people, the people of Yahweh. Both parts, retaining the consciousness of belonging to a single religious nation, desired to reestablish unity but in different ways. The southern legitimists hoped for a return of the Israelite rebels to the authority of "David," while the northerners, and even some Judeans, felt that Judah should make the *rapprochement*.

Lods prefers to think that the difficulties stemmed from the persistent tribal consciousness which refused to be submerged in a larger state loyalty necessarily emerging out of the new conditions of a settled mode of life. Consolidation and centralization mitigated against ingrained ancient Bedouin individualism that was so strong in its opposition to a sophisticated commercial society.

Fleming, John Dick. *Israel's Golden Age: The Story of the United Kingdom.* Edinburgh: T. and T. Clark, 1907.

Fleming sees the period of the united Hebrew kingdom as the high point of ancient Jewish history, even though it soon decayed. During a single century the united kingdom solved many serious problems and precociously passed through all the successive stages of development:

youth, manhood, and declining old age. Saul awakened the nation to a consciousness of its strength. Under David it reached its zenith of power and entered upon a course of vigorous development. During the reign of Solomon the first signs of decadence appeared; advances in expansion of trade, increase in wealth and luxury, and other refinements of civilization were dimming the great goals of the nation. The unity imposed upon the Jews was purchased dearly at the price of absolute, disciplined tyranny. Pompous religious ceremonial betraying a secularizing spirit obscured Israel's distinctive, yet simple, spiritual mission and character.

Jeroboam adroitly marshaled the attitude of general disaffection with the monarchy. As an overseer of the work on the fortifications for Jerusalem he had a good opportunity to learn the temper of Solomon's subjects and apparently sympathized with their complaints, encouraging a spirit of sedition. His action forced him into exile in Egypt. After Solomon's death Jeroboam returned to lead the rebellion. The division of the kingdom, according to Fleming, was fatal to the nation's prosperity and disastrous in other respects. The elements of inner discord, which had been conciliated or suppressed while the kingdom was united, now revived and prevented further growth. The nation wore itself out in fifty years, never again to rise to its former glory. Religious life also suffered irreparably. Rather than advancing along the line David chartered for it, the state reverted to the conditions of previous anarchic periods. Contrary to the view of Lods, Fleming sees a revival of heathenism and an increase in idolatry, particularly in the north. — *J.R.R.*

Additional Recommended Reading

Robinson, Theodore H. *The Decline and Fall of the Hebrew Kingdoms.* Oxford: The University Press, 1926. A detailed account based directly on accounts of the Biblical prophets.

Bright, J. *Early Israel in Recent History Writing.* London: Student Christian Movement Press, 1956. A critical history in terms of modern scholarship.

Noth, Martin. *The History of Israel.* Translated by Stanley Goodman. New York: Harper & Row Publishers Incorporated, 1958. An excellent general history.

Albright, W. F. *The Biblical Period from Abraham to Ezra.* New York: Harper & Row Publishers Incorporated, 1963. A concise, detailed account of a controversial period of Jewish history.

Orlinsky, Harry. *Ancient Israel.* Ithaca: Cornell University Press, 1964. A brief history of the period.

Robinson, H. Wheeler. *The History of Israel.* London: Duckworth, 1957. A sound general account of Hebrew history.

HOMER'S COMPOSITION OF THE *ILIAD*

Type of event: Literary: creation of a major epic
Time: c.800 B.C.
Locale: Ionia, on the coast of Asia Minor

Summary of Event

The composition of the *Iliad* can be seen as both the beginning of Western literature as we know it and the culmination of a long tradition of oral epic poetry that may date from the height of Mycenaean civilization in the twelfth and thirteenth centuries B.C. Although verifiable facts about the identity of Homer and the time and place of the composition of the epic are almost nonexistent, the *Iliad* itself provides evidence for educated guesses. References to Homer's material in later writings suggest that the epic must have been widely circulated by 700 B.C., and descriptions of sculpture and certain types of shields that can be closely dated by archaeologists indicate that the final version of the *Iliad* is unlikely to have been composed much before 800 B.C.

Elements of the Aeolic and Ionic dialects in the poem make scholars confident that its author lived in one of the colonies on the coast of Asia Minor where Hellenes who had been powerful in Mycenaean days took refuge from Dorian invaders in the eleventh century B.C. Somehow the Ionian courts preserved for almost five hundred years, between the legendary fall of Troy and the writing of the *Iliad*, the names of Mycenaean heroes and cities powerful in the Aegean culture of the Bronze Age, as well as stories of events related to some conflict between Greeks and Trojans. The preservation of these elements of a dead civilization has been attributed to the existence of a strong oral tradition. In Books VIII and XXII the *Odyssey* describes court poets who entertained visitors with recitations of the deeds of heroes, and Homer's Demodocus and Phemius probably reflect his own role in Ionian society. Scholars have postulated the existence of poetic guilds that preserved and passed on with their own embellishments bodies of historical and legendary materials; modern research into oral transmission of folk epics in Yugoslavia and Finland proves what extraordinary amounts of material the human memory, properly trained, can retain.

These Ionian bards, like later ones who passed on the Germanic sagas, developed sophisticated techniques to assist them in their composition. At some point in the growth of the oral epic, dactylic hexameter became the accepted metrical form. It is a complex meter, not much more natural to the Greek language than to the English. The bards therefore developed formulas or groups of words that fitted metrically into various positions in the line and could be combined to form whole lines. Frequent use of the same epithets, such as "fleet-footed Achilles" or "Agamemnon, king of men," illustrates the technique; Hera is called "white-armed" or "Hera of the golden throne" according to whether she is mentioned at the beginning or end

110

of a line, not because of the context.

Learning hundreds of these formulas must have been part of the training of court poets, for the same phrases seem to have been handed down for generations. Once a satisfactory pattern had been established, it appears to have been preserved, even though its words might have vanished from ordinary speech. The use of formulas probably explains why, for example, there are contradictory descriptions of weapons in the *Iliad*. The swords and shields of Ajax, Agamemnon, and Hector sometimes resembled those which archaeologists have found among Mycenaean relics, sometimes those of eighth century Ionia.

In addition, whole passages, such as the catalogue of ships in Book II of the *Iliad*, seem to have been handed down almost intact. Many of the cities mentioned were centers in Mycenaean times but obliterated long before Homer lived. It is interesting to note that Homer considered the list of heroes important enough to preserve in his poem, even though many of the leaders mentioned play little or no part in the epic.

The nature of the *Iliad* makes it clear that the events surrounding the Trojan war were familiar to the poet's audience, for he begins *in medias res,* declaring his intention to sing of the wrath of Achilles; there is no need to discuss the causes of the war or its conclusion, and the characters need no introduction. The greatness of the poet was not his originality as a creator of plot, but his ability to bring a unified whole out of the masses of material at his disposal.

Controversy has raged for years over the authorship of the *Iliad*. Some see it as the work of one man, others as the work of several. The consensus at present seems to be that one controlling artistic imagination must have shaped the whole. The consistent characterizations, the epic similes with their sympathetic glimpses into the life of common people of Homer's day, and, above all, the unifying theme of the tragedy of Achilles can hardly have resulted from the work of a number of poets working separately.

It is equally clear, however, that the epic does contain inconsistencies. Some of these are related to the use of formulas and, probably, pieces of earlier epics. Others result, no doubt, from additions made by post-Homeric scribes and editors. It must also be remembered that the *Iliad* was composed for recitation over a period of days, not for reading. Both poet and hearers might reasonably be expected to forget or confuse certain details.

It is almost impossible to assess the enormous impact of the composition of the *Iliad* on Western civilization. It has been a part of the education of every cultivated man for nearly three thousand years, testifying to the significance of the Homeric understanding of the nature of man and his place in the world. In addition, the Homeric epic has fathered many of the great works of European literature, the *Aeneid* and the *Divine Comedy* among them.

Pertinent Literature

Bowra, C. M. *Tradition and Design in the Iliad.* Oxford: The Clarendon Press, 1950.

Writings on the Homeric epic could easily fill a library, and it is difficult to single out one or another as definitive. Bowra's book, however, must be ranked among the best analyses of the elements of tradition and individual genius that were combined to produce this epic.

On the question of authorship, Bowra insists that one must recognize the epic as the work of a single artistic imagination on traditional materials. He sees the story of Achilles as a moral tragedy, akin to the plays of Aeschylus and Sophocles. Achilles' wrath is related to dramatic *hubris*, or pride, which defies the laws of men and of gods, and brings about the fall of the hero and many others with him. Homer's equivalent of Aristotelian catharsis comes when Archilles finally conquers his anger and, moved by pity, allows Priam to take Hector's body back to Troy.

Bowra draws upon his encyclopedic knowledge of European epics to explain the use of traditional materials and also to underline the genius of Homer, whose work so far surpasses, for example, the *Song of Roland*. Bowra notes that while Homer's scale is "generous," he does not pad out his material as the French writer did.

Bowra presents a particularly interesting discussion of the historical background of the *Iliad*, again referring to later epics to show how poets often expanded and altered events for their purposes while preserving the kernels of truth. As Bowra notes, archaeologists have firmly established the exis-

tence of a historic Troy, a site where a number of civilizations flourished and fell. On the site of the sixth city, powerful in the thirteenth and twelfth centuries B.C., Mycenaean pottery has been found. Homer's descriptions of the city walls and the geographical landmarks agree for the most part with archaeological findings, although some geographical details are clearly incompatible with the facts. Whether this Trojan civilization ended after an attack by an Achaean confederation is a more difficult question to answer. Bowra establishes the possibility, if not the probability, that such an attack took place by referring to evidence in Egyptian and Hittite documents.

The Tell el Amarna letters, written about 1379 B.C., refer to a seafaring people from Asia Minor, who have been identified with the Lycians, and to the Danuna, probably Homer's Danaoi. Hittite records of about 1340 B.C. mention a king of Ahhiawa, a word linguists believe to be equivalent to Achaia. Around 1200 B.C., the legendary date of the Trojan war, northern invaders, possibly including the Achaeans, attacked Egypt and were finally defeated by the navy of Ramses III. The date is near that of the end of the Mycenaean culture, and it is not unlikely that the two events were related.

The position of Agamemnon as the military leader of a confederation of kings also has historical precedent in the alliances of states with and against the Hittites, whose great empire collapsed about the time of the Trojan war. Only by joining together in groups such as the one Homer portrays could small states have achieved the power that history attributes to the Hittites and to the Sea Raiders who invaded Egypt.

Bowra's book covers a number of other topics with equal thoroughness and erudition, among them Homer's language, his characters, his theology, and his concept of the heroic age. The entire volume merits the reader's time and attention.

Hadas, Moses. *A History of Greek Literature.* New York: Columbia University Press, 1950.

This book is especially valuable as a guide to Homer's place in the whole range of Greek literature. Its late author, a distinguished professor of classics at Columbia University for many years, had a rare gift of absorbing and synthesizing highly complex materials and presenting them in clear, elegant prose. Bowra's study is distinctly erudite, directed to the serious student of Greek; Hadas's can be recommended for the general reader.

In his introductory chapter on "The Nature of Greek Literature," Hadas points out several characteristics that all the great Greek writers shared: their preoccupation with man and his society; their concept of the poet as a professional, a public figure with responsibilities to the state; their preference for formalism in the structure of their works; and their "ebullience" of spirit. Greek literature was, suggests Hadas, adult, even in its beginnings, and that is why it speaks to modern readers with real meaning, not as a record of past intellectual currents but as an aid to living in the present.

Hadas begins his chapter on Homer with two revealing comments on the unique place of the poet in Western literature: "Poetic genius receives its ideal and complete meaning by reference to Homer" and "the only reasonable definition of 'epic' is a poem that somehow resembles the *Iliad.*" He points out the effectiveness of Homer's language, a tongue never spoken but created for epic by the anonymous bards who sang the early heroic poems.

Hadas comments on the interweaving of two separate themes in Homer's work; the "Achilleid" and the "Tale of Troy" enhance each other in much the same way that Shakespeare's plots and subplots intensify the meaning of his tragedies.

"Passion, made to conform to and serve civilization," is, in Hadas's view, the "keynote" of the epic. Homer's characters are men and women with deep feelings, their emotions are ours, raised to a higher degree, as is fitting for a nobler, more heroic age than ours. They live life intensely because they have pondered it and understand it. Their nobility comes from their ability to accept fully whatever life brings, be it feasting or death, and through them, suggests Hadas, the reader feels "vicarious pride in man's achievement."

Even Homer's gods are essentially human. They are immortal and eternally young, but they, too, are subject to the decrees of fate, and they squabble, love, and plot like human beings. In fact, Homer's treatment of them often borders on the comic. It is the men, more than the gods, who are

113

heroic.

Hadas points out the effectiveness of Homer's use of epic similes to provide brief respite from the intensity of the heroic age. These similes, he says, are the only medium through which the poet makes personal comment on the events of his poem. In addition, these passages are used as structural aids, breaking the monotony of a long battle scene, or marking the end of an episode or a lapse in time.

Hadas, like Bowra, was willing to accept inconsistencies and anachronisms as inevitable in an oral epic. He found the effort expended in debating the Homeric question "appalling," and he pointed out that while scholars have been willing to parcel out portions of the *Iliad*, poets are quick to recognize its artistic unity. This point brings out the keystone of Hadas's approach to the *Iliad:* it is, above all, poetry, and must be studied from that perspective. The epic must be valued for what it says about man, not for its possible historical evidence, its linguistic peculiarities, or its demonstration of the survival of folk myths. — *E.J.L.*

Additional Recommended Reading

Beye, Charles Rowan. *The Iliad, the Odyssey, and the Epic Tradition.* Garden City, New York: Anchor Books, Doubleday and Company, Inc., 1966. A helpful introduction to Homer with discussions of the oral tradition.

Carpenter, Rhys. *Folk Tale, Fiction, and Saga in the Homeric Epics.* Berkeley: University of California Press, 1956. A fascinating discussion of oral literature in which the author sometimes overstates his case in denying any historical foundation for the epics.

Lattimore, Richmond. *The Iliad of Homer.* Chicago: University of Chicago Press, 1951. A fine modern translation of the poem with introductory materials on plot, characterization, style, and historical background.

Lesky, Albin. *A History of Greek Literature.* Translated by James Willis and Cornelis de Heer. New York: Thomas Y. Crowell Company, 1966. A thorough, scholarly summary of the major aspects of Homer's work with some evaluation of recent studies.

Page, Denys L. *History and the Homeric Iliad.* Berkeley: University of California Press, 1966. An elaborate argument for the historicity of the *Iliad*, based on archaeological evidence and Hittite documents.

INAUGURATION OF THE OLYMPIC GAMES

Type of event: Religious: evolution of a festival
Time: 776 B.C.
Locale: Olympia, in the northwest of the Peloponnesus

Summary of Event

To contemporary thinking, the modern Olympic Games have political as well as athletic significance; held every four years since 1896 in imitation of the games of ancient Greece, they aim to channel aggressive national instincts into peaceful athletic competition. The competition has not always been so peaceful, for the number of gold medals has become a barometer of national pride and superiority; but the original Greek contest also transcended limits of athletic competition in its origin and importance.

In Greek tradition the Olympic Games began with the victory of Coroebus in a foot race in 776 B.C. This date is critical regardless of its historical accuracy because of the later Greek custom of dating subsequent events from it. Such a practice was a major advance in chronological bookkeeping since more Greek cities did not number their years in numerical sequence but preferred to distinguish individual years by reference to the name of a public official or high priest then reigning. Obviously this system could not correlate events in different cities. Such reckoning had to await the adoption of an internationally significant event as a fixed point in time from which all cities could date their history.

The year 776 B.C. probably marked the start of the international character of the Olympic Games rather than their inception, since before that time they were held as a local event for those living in the immediate vicinity of Olympia in the northwest corner of the Peloponnesus. The twenty-third book of the *Iliad,* recording the athletic games staged by Achilles in honor of his dead companion Patroclus, may suggest the way in which the Olympic Games probably evolved as a regular commemoration of the death of Pelops, the local hero and deity of the region around Olympia. However, the development of this purely local rite into a religious festival in honor of the father of the gods, Zeus, is untraceable. The dedication to Zeus nevertheless bestowed an international character on the contests, signalized by the first formal interstate competition in 776 B.C.

Apparently in its early years the agenda of the festival included only competition in foot racing and wrestling. From the list of Olympic victors kept by ancient historians it seems that Sparta dominated the games in the eighth century. Reorganization in the seventh century involving the addition of chariot racing and single-horse feats, together with the subsequent Spartan withdrawal from competition, indicate that control of the games had passed into new hands, possibly those of Pheidon, the energetic tyrant of Argos and a vigorous opponent of Spartan domination in the Peloponnesus. The fame of the expanded games attracted competitors from as far away as Sicily and southern Italy.

In 472 B.C., the program was further expanded. The length of time set aside for the games was extended to five days, the first being devoted to religious aspects of the festival: the formal sacrifices, and the solemn oath of contestants and judges to act fairly. The next day featured chariot and horse races, and the pentathlon (running, jumping, javelin and discus throwing, and wrestling). After contests for young boys on the third day, the program returned on the fourth day to men's competition in boxing, wrestling, running, jumping, and in a final race for men clad in full armor. The festival ended on the fifth day with sacrifices in the morning and a final banquet for the victors, who received wreaths of wild olive leaves as symbols of their success.

The site of Olympia itself was situated in a small but splendid valley between low hills flanking the River Alpheus. These physical endowments were enhanced by lavish architecture. The older temples, gradually eclipsed by new construction, gave way eventually to the magnificent temple of Zeus completed in 457 B.C. Competition in the games was open to all who spoke the Greek language, so that contestants and spectators came from all parts of the ancient world. To facilitate this traffic, a period of general truce was proclaimed guaranteeing all travelers safe passage, a

development of no small import in the refinement of interstate relationships. The Olympic Games eventually provided a natural political forum for the expression of new ideas. In 426 B.C., during the bitter war between Athens and Sparta, the orator Gorgias, for example, appeared at the Olympic Games to urge the end of such fratricidal conflicts and the undertaking of a united Greek expedition against the Persian empire. Presentation of the idea of a politically united Greece seemed appropriate in the setting of the Olympic Games, themselves a living expression of religious unity. Although the example of the games failed to induce the Greeks to overcome the divisive aspects of their political life, the Olympic Games continued to be celebrated as an expression of cultural and religious unity until their abolition by the Roman emperor Theodosius in A.D. 393.

The Olympic Games also served as a model for other festivals. In 582 B.C., the Pythian Games in honor of Apollo were inaugurated at Delphi; in 581 B.C., the Isthmian Games were established at Corinth in honor of Poseidon; finally, in 573 at Nemea, a city north of Argos, the first Nemean Games were held. None of these later imitations of the Olympic Games, however, acquired the renown or international importance as those first widely celebrated for Zeus in 776.

Pertinent Literature

Jaeger, Werner. "The Aristocracy: Conflict and Transformation," in *Paideia.* Vol. I, ch. 10. Oxford: Basil Blackwell, 1954.

The distinctive significance of the Olympic Games lies primarily in the

area of cultural traditions and values. That the games were much more than a series of sporting events no one has demonstrated more lucidly than Werner Jaeger. His *Paideia* is a monumental three-volume attempt to correlate the historical and intellectual processes that formed the Greek cultural experience. The first volume, *Archaic Greece and the Mind of Athens,* describes the earliest phases of this experience until the rise of Platonic philosophy. This period of approximately four hundred years witnessed the dominance of an aristocratic cultural unity that came under increasing attack, succumbing eventually to the cultural dynamism of fifth century Athens. Jaeger demonstrates convincingly that the Olympic Games formed an integral part of the older cultural values.

These values were essentially those of the dominant social class, the landed aristocracy. Succinctly put, these values required each aristocrat to strive continually for *arete* or "excellence": moral, physical, and material. In early Greek days there was a general absence of cultural conflict since there was a fairly unanimously acceptance of what constituted *arete*; with slight reservations, it was the code of action observed by the Homeric heroes. Such men revealed their *arete* not only as stalwart spearmen in war but as successful athletes in peace. Although it was natural for such a society to put a high premium on the physical prowess demanded by athletic competition, their commitment to athletics extended well beyond the benefits of keeping fit. Athletic excellence, typified by a victory in one of the funeral games, embodied the same ideal of *arete* that the warriors strove to display in war. The victo-

rious athlete and the victorious warrior were one and the same person. Success in either sphere represented the pinnacle of human accomplishment.

During the eight century this code had adjusted to new social conditions. Aristocrats now fought as citizen members of city-states, and as members of the same city-states they competed not in occasional funeral games but in the regular schedule of Olympic Games. The separate cities encouraged competition by their citizens and sought to establish their own games in imitation of the Olympic celebration, since it reflected the highest and most visible aspiration of their cultural ideals. For the spectators, the games provided not only a spectacle but more importantly an immediate experience of the values that regulated their society. For the contestants, the games made possible a justification and renewal of their claims to *arete*.

In fact, Jaeger views the games as the primary means of transmitting aristocratic ideals to succeeding generations. As the symbol *par excellence* of aristocratic culture, the games became a convenient target for the criticism of social reformers such as Xenophanes (fl.c.545-508), who claimed that greater benefit came to the city from intellectual pursuits than from the physical prowess of an Olympic victor. Against this challenge there arose one of the most ardent defenders of the aristocratic way of life, the Theban poet Pindar (518-438 B.C.).

Pindar's Epinician Odes sing the praises of victors at the four great Games: Olympian, Isthmean, Nemean, and Pythian. The use of the religious choral hymn, originally reserved for praise of a god, reflects Pindar's deep reverence for athletic victors. For him they had double claims on quasi-divinity. In the first place, only those with a divine ancestry could compete, and in the second place the victorious competitors uniquely approached a level of divinity since their victory manifested their *arete*, the highest perfection of humanity. To intensify his conviction of the supreme importance of the games, Pindar does not emphasize the physical details of the competition but rather its spiritual and cultural implications. After the fifth century, with the decline in aristocratic values, athletics became the occupation of professionals, and the games themselves retained only a dim trace of their former importance.

Harris, H. A. *Greek Athletes and Athletics.* London: Hutchinson & Co., Ltd., 1964.

Whereas Jaeger presents an abstract, analytic study of the cultural significance of the Olympic Games, Harris' work in a more modest way offers a straightforward, descriptive history of these athletic contests. This sober study should not be underrated, since neglect of the ordinary aspects of a cultural tradition often involves the danger of exaggerating and idealizing its spiritual values. For example, while award of the simple olive wreath to the Olympic victors indicated the spiritual significance attached to victory, substantial material awards were also at stake. Already Solon's legislation in Athens in 590 B.C. limited to five hundred drachmae the maximum amount that the city might bestow upon an Olympic victor. While this measure serves to reinforce Jaeger's contention that the entire city was intensely involved in the games, it also throws light on the material character of that involvement which tended to look upon the games as a status symbol rather than as an expression of ideal spiritual values.

An asset of Harris' book is his collection of most of the longer extant literary descriptions of ancient athletic contests. He ably shows that most of these excerpts are artificial and poor imitations of model passages in Homer such as the funeral games for Patroclus in the twenty-third book of the *Iliad* and the Phaeacian games in the *Odyssey*. While there were some ancient writers, notably the Roman poet Statius of the first century A.D., who describe athletic events as if they had actually seen them, the information to be gained from literary sources is meager. A detailed reconstruction is only possible through archaeological evidence.

Harris also provides useful information about the main events of the Olympic Games, the foot races and the pentathlon. Obviously the most popular event was the two-hundred-yard dash, as festivals were designated by the name of the victor in this particular race. It was run not on an oval track but on a sandy straight course so that contestants were forced to make an awkward 180° turn at the half-point marker. Though such a turn posed a hazard, the Greeks never thought of changing it. The pentathlon was also a strange anomaly since it combined five separate contests: long jumping,

118

wrestling, foot racing, and discus and javelin throwing, all calling on differing skills. Victory apparently went to the contestant who first won three of the five events. In the javelin throw, victory depended not on accuracy but on distance, a fact which deflates the theory that the games were originally a means of training skills required for war. Further refutation of this theory comes from the nonmilitary character of the discus throw. Both the shape of the discus itself and the centrifugal motion required to hurl it any significant distance made it ineffective as a weapon.

Although Harris provides insights into details concerning the administration of the games, the training of athletes, and the physical arrangements of the impressive buildings at Olympia, he does not do justice to the question of the nature and popularity of the games themselves. It is certainly fallacious to describe the games as a diversion in terms of the modern sports fan. On one level the games were a pleasant diversion, but they were also much more, and for this aspect the reader must turn to Jaeger. Harris satisfies a natural curiosity about the actual performance of the games, but Jaeger attempts through them to impart insight into a unique and important area of Greek culture. — *G.M.P.*

Additional Recommended. Reading

Robinson, R. S. *Sources for the History of Greek Athletics.* Urbana: University of Illinois Press, 1955. A valuable collection of ancient testimony on athletics.

Gardiner, E. Norman. *Greek Athletic Sports and Festival.* London: Macmillan and Company, 1910. A useful guide to the history of all major athletic games.

Gardiner, E. Norman. *Athletics of the Ancient World.* Oxford: The Clarendon Press, 1930. The definitive treatment of this topic.

Lattimore, Richmond. *The Odes of Pindar.* Chicago: University of Chicago Press, 1947. The best modern translation of Pindar's Victory Odes.

Gardiner, E. Norman. *History and Remains of Olympia.* Oxford: The Clarendon Press, 1925. An archaeological survey of the site and monuments of Olympia.

APOLLO'S REVELATIONS AT DELPHI

Type of event: Religious: emergence of a religious institution
Time: c.775 B.C.
Locale: Delphi on Mount Parnassus

Summary of Event

The temple and oracle of Apollo at Delphi, situated on the south slope of Mount Parnassus just north of the Gulf of Corinth, emerged into prominence as an institution of Panhellenic importance at about the same time that the poems of Homer appeared and the quadrennial athletic contests at Olympia first took place, at the beginning of the eighth century B.C. Tradition and archaeological evidence indicate that the site was sacred and oracular in Minoan times well before it was violently appropriated in the Mycenaean era by the eastern newcomer Apollo. The fact that Apollo's mouthpiece, the Pythia, was a woman and the legend of Apollo's slaying of a chthonic serpent, the Python, give substance to this view. The prominence of the oracle in the archaic period of Greek history is explained in part by the fact that the Delphic oracle gave responses to direct questions in contrast to the mere "yes" or "no" answers of other oracles, and in part by the fact that in a period of intense social unrest, the oracle's authority served to preserve traditional order, to provide divine sanction for changes in cult or polity, and to secure or restore the favor of heaven for cities and individuals under the stress of great anxieties.

Although the lot-oracle at Delphi seems to have functioned daily, the Pythia herself could be consulted only on one day of the month. Those wishing to consult the oracle first bathed in the spring of Caetalia and sacrificed to the god, then entered the temple and put their questions to the Pythia through the mediation of a priest. The Pythia, seated on a holy tripod, gave her answers in ecstatic utterances which were interpreted by the priest and usually put into verse form. The questions seem to have been formulated so as to learn whether a projected course of action was advisable or what course of action ought to be pursued in a public or private crisis. Extant oracular responses of the archaic period, many of them preserved in the historical narrative of Herodotus, are concerned more with political or private secular matters than with specifically religious matters. The riddling ambiguity of the responses was notorious; as Heraclitus said: "The lord whose oracle is that at Delphi neither speaks nor conceals, but indicates." A notable example is the case of Croesus of Lydia, who asked whether it was advisable for him to attack Cyrus of Persia; the response was that in so doing, he would destroy a mighty empire. The oracle was vindicated by the destruction of Croesus' own empire by Cyrus.

The oracle's predominant role was that of a mediator between men and the gods, especially in matters of cult. Portentous happenings and natural catastrophes were referred by individuals and states to the oracle for

120

interpretation and for directions on how to restore the divine favor. Changes in the cult of individual states or the institution of new rites were never undertaken without the oracle's sanction. A cultic matter affecting the inner peace of all cities was homicide, for which Apollo prescribed appropriate expiatory rites and regulated the participation of guilty parties in the cultic and public life of the community. The myths of Oedipus and Orestes especially bear witness to Apollo's role in this area.

During the archaic period of Greek history the oracle served an important function in the sending out of colonies by Greek cities throughout the Mediterranean world, but this role has often been misinterpreted. It was primarily through the oracle's function as a regulator and sanctioner of cultic practice, which was deemed intimately bound up with the establishment of new states and the promulgation of laws, that it made its influence felt. There is no sound evidence for the oracle's choice of sites for colonization or actual prescription of constitutional provisions. Rather, proposed plans of colonization and proposed constitutional changes were submitted to the oracle to determine whether they were in accord with the will of the gods.

In matters of morality, the Delphic oracle functioned not so much as a prophetic voice arousing consciences to purer practice but more as an expression of a spirit of legalism current in the minds of men in the archaic period. Some stories of oracular responses are indicative of a view that the gods disapprove not only of the evil deed, but also of the evil intention. Perhaps the most significant attitude fostered by the oracle was disapproval of human pride, an attitude finding expression in two proverbial imperatives associated with the oracle by the fifth century B.C.: "Nothing in excess" and "Know thyself." The latter enjoined the individual to recognize his mere humanity and shun a pride that would surely be offensive to the gods.

In international politics, the oracle tended to take a conservative stand. At the time of the Persian invasion, it counseled nonresistance, evidently on grounds that resistance would be futile. In the Peloponnesian War, the oracle supported the Spartan cause. In the course of the fifth century B.C. the oracle suffered a considerable loss of prestige and influence as a consequence of the growing secularization of life and the intellectual enlightenment of the period.

Pertinent Literature

Nilsson, Martin P. *A History of Greek Religion.* 2nd ed. Oxford: The Clarendon Press, 1952. Reprinted, New York: W. W. Norton & Company, Inc., 1964.

In the study of ancient religion, the scholarly authority of Martin Nilsson has been unequaled in our era. Although his massive, encyclopedic *Geschicte der griechischen Religion* is available only in a German edition, a shorter presentation of his views is accessible to the English-speaking public in *A History of Greek Religion.*

Nilsson's treatment of the nature and significance of the Delphic oracle of Apollo is to be found in his chapter entitled, "Legalism and Mysticism." Here the authority of the Delphic oracle in the Greek archaic period is the central focus of a discussion of the religious responses to men's yearnings for some authoritative direction and regulation of life and for appeasement of their troubled consciences during an era of political and social turmoil. Hesiod's *Works and Days* reveals these trends in its demand for justice in the city and in its rules for the direction of life throughout the farmer's year. The regulation of the calendar and the codification of civic law both take place during this era, and Delphic influence is evident in both. Finally, this era of ecstatic and missionary movements was evinced by Pythagoreanism, by the spreading institutionalization of the cult of Dionysos, and by the spread of Orphism.

The primary source of Delphic influence on Greek society is seen by Nilsson in Delphi's authority over the regulation of cultic practices. Whenever a community felt the need to reorganize a sector of its life involving the cult in any way, the divine sanction for a change was sought through Apollo's oracle at Delphi. Apollo's authority in the cities was represented by local exegetes, the more important of whom seem to have been selected by the Delphic priesthood. The principle of regulation employed by these exegetes was generally the reinforcement of ancestral custom, but in time of crisis when local tradition as interpreted by the exegetes failed to supply a solution, the oracle itself was consulted.

Nilsson devotes considerable attention to Apollo's role in the matter of expiation of bloodguilt. The older

tradition laid responsibility for avenging homicide upon the family of the man killed, but fear of the dead man's vengeance was strong, and in the course of the archaic era the states increasingly took the administration of justice into their own hands and punished or acquitted the guilty party on the basis of a judgment of his intention. Apollo aided the states in this process, but in addition, he insisted that even an involuntary homicide, though acquitted, must undergo a ritual of purification before he could again participate in the civic and cultic life of his community. The ritual gave a definite form to the fear of the dead man's vengeance, and while absolving the killer of his feelings of guilt, at the same time it helped to assure a greater respect for human life.

Nilsson sees the essential strength of the cult of Apollo at Delphi in its assumption of a role of central authority, imposing form on religious and secular life where disorganization was a serious threat. The weakness of Delphi was its very dependence on and dominant reinforcement of ancestral tradition. The authority of Apollo aided in the development of a higher morality in Greek life, but it did not take a leading role. Its influence was directed too much toward the external, ritual aspects of religious life, and partly for this reason Delphi could not create new religious values. To play such a role, Nilsson notes, Delphi would have needed a sacred book and an organized priesthood enforcing a single standard throughout Greece. These it lacked; Delphic authority reinforced local traditions rather than imposed national ones, and even the exegetes chosen by Apollo in local communities were primarily citizens of their own states, not members of an organized religious order of international stature.

Parke, H. W. and D. E. W. Wormell. *The Delphic Oracle.* Oxford: Basil Blackwell, 1956. 2 vols.

This work represents the sole extensive scholarly account of the nature and history of the Delphic oracle. The first volume discusses the origin and procedure of the oracle, and presents the history of the oracle in successive epochs of Greek and Roman history. The last section of the first volume discusses the role played by the oracle in Greek myths, in religious cults, in moral questions, and in private enquiry. The second volume contains the Greek text, a translation and a commentary on the extant oracles arranged, as far as possible, by historical periods.

In their chapter on the origins of the oracle, the authors discuss fully the literary sources for the legend of the oracle's foundation and correlate this tradition with archaeological evidence. Their conclusion is that the site of Delphi was originally devoted to the worship of Ge, Mother Earth, also known as Themis, and that the original oracle of Ge was appropriated by Apollo in the Mycenaean era.

Several theories of the source of inspiration of the Pythia are discussed. One theory, probably a rationalization developed in the fourth century B.C., held that vapors originating in the chasm below the tripod on which the priestess sat effected her intoxication. Geological examination of the site offers no confirmation of this theory. Nor is there any evidence for the notion that the chewing of laurel leaves or the waters of the Sacred Spring of Castalia produced inspiration. Few

critics ever thought the whole mantic operation was deception; even the early Christian apologists accepted the validity of the ecstatic revelation, explaining it, however, as the work of evil spirits. The authors of this study argue that the Pythia was under the spell of self-induced hypnosis. They hold, therefore, that the operation of the oracle was fully honest, but add that the adherence of the oracle to consistent policies throughout its history clearly indicates a role played by human intelligence.

The opportunism of the oracle in major political issues is seen by the authors as a consequence of the Delphic community's military weakness. Noting evidence from the early fourth century B.C. which shows that fewer than one thousand mature males were citizens of Delphi and that military help from the Amphictyony was unreliable, Parke and Wormell conclude that the Delphians were wise to steer a middle course in politics. Thus they supported tyrants in the age of tyranny and pursued a pro-Persian policy after the victory of Cyrus over Croesus of Lydia.

In general issues of politics, the oracle was much more impartial than is commonly recognized. Thus, despite its close affiliation with Dorian monarchies in the early period, it accepted the first tyrants; and while the Spartans received Delphic support for the restrictive amendment to the *Great Rhetra,* Cleisthenes also had support from Delphi for the extension of democracy in Athens. There are two instances of the advocacy of greater democracy in Megara and in Thebes. Thus the view that the oracle always supported the aristocracy is certainly false.

In religion, the oracle tended to support local traditions. The major innovations in cult for which Delphi seems to have been responsible were the spread of the religions of Dionysus and Asclepius. Even here, the oracle did not so much set a policy as formalize and regulate a popular movement.

In the area of morality, the oracle seems to have played a role in the elimination of human sacrifice through substitution of another rite. Certainly Apollo regulated blood guilt through a ritual of atonement already established in the early archaic period. A major handicap of the oracle, nevertheless, was its inability to initiate action in politics, morality, or religion: the priesthood had to await enquiry before it could express an influential opinion. — C.W.C.

Additional Recommended Reading

Dodds, E. R. "The Blessings of Madness," in *The Greeks and the Irrational*. Ch. III. Berkeley: University of California Press, 1951. A treatise on the nature of mantic and other types of ectasy.

Evelyn-White, H. G. *Hesiod, the Homeric Hymns and Homerica*. Pp.336-363. Cambridge: Harvard University Press, 1914. The text and translation of the *Hymn to Pythian Apollo*, the foundation legend of the temple and oracle at Delphi.

Farnell, L. R. *The Cults of the Greek States*. Vol. IV, pp.179-218. Oxford: The Clarendon Press, 1907. A treatment of the major features of the history, procedure, and influence of the Delphic oracle in the context of a fuller discussion of Apollo cults in Greece.

Nilsson, M. P. "Legalism and Superstition; Hell" and "Seers and Oracles," in *Greek Popular Religion*. New York: Columbia University Press, 1940. Republished, New York: Harper & Row Publishers Incorporated, 1961. Chapters deal extensively with the role of oracles in Greek life, especially with the influence of the Delphic oracle.

Pease, A. S. "Notes on the Delphic Oracle and the Greek Colonization," in *Classical Philology*. 12 (1917), 1ff. A discussion of the extent of Delphic influence on the colonizing movement.

THE TEACHING OF AMOS

Type of event: Religious: utterance of prophetic revelation
Time: 750 B.C.
Locale: Bethel, a national shrine in Israel

Principal personages:
AMOS, a herdsman of Judah who prophesied against Israel
JEROBOAM II, King of Israel c.785-744
AMAZIAH, priest at the national shrine of Bethel

Summary of Event

The eighth century B.C. brought to the Middle East the rising power of Assyria which swallowed up Israel and reduced Judah to vassalage. On this scene entered Amos to interpret the times in terms of the religion and destiny of Israel.

Probably of all ancient peoples, the Israelites alone enjoyed a dispensation from their God allowing inspired prophets to appear at crucial points in history to reveal the attitude of the deity. In Hebrew *navi*, one who speaks forth, in Greek *prophetes,* one who speaks for another, Biblical prophets were mouthpieces or spokesmen for the deity, not so much predicting coming social conditions as declaring, regardless of personal consequences, the will and judgment of God. More often than not, the long line of prophets from Elija (c.875) to Malachi (c.460) delivered a pessimistic message.

While Amos is the first of the canonical prophets, he was in a sense following in an old Hebrew tradition. Centuries earlier Nathan had arisen to rebuke David, and Elijah had challenged Ahab and Jezebel. But none of Amos' precursors had their statements recorded in books. Amos' message was directed primarily at Israel during

the reign of Jeroboam II. Even though the nation at this time was wealthy and expanding in size, beneath the surface there was much which the sensitive prophet detected as corrupt. With prosperity, social and economic inequality developed dramatically. While the upper urban class grew in wealth, the lower classes lost their independence in an inflationary economy, slipping first into debt and then into tenant farming. They had no legal redress in the corrupted court system or moral support in the current religiosity which had taken the place of true religion.

Little is known of Amos other than than he was from Tekoa, a small town south of Jerusalem. Tradition pictures him as a shepherd who trimmed sycamore trees during the harvest season. He probably became aware of the social conditions in the north while selling his wool in such trading centers as Bethel and Samaria where he could learn at first hand about the moral rot of the urban centers and also of the impending Assyrian menace. Not necessarily poor himself, his attacks on the rich were not against wealth *per se* but against the soft luxury and social abuse it entailed. His message at Bethel, a national shrine, won the rebuke of Amaziah, a priest of the

125

sanctuary, an episode repeated often in the age-long tension and conflict between priest and prophet.

The message of Amos was epochal in at least two respects. First, he indicated that true religion must serve as the conscience of an irresponsible social and religious order. The God of Amos was a fierce protector of what we would call "human rights." There was only one real test of faith in God: expression of brotherhood among all Israelites. Amos sought to have old moral ideals and aspirations continue to prevail in the new and more complex civilization the Jews were experiencing. His greatest fury was directed against the irreligion of the religious, those who paraded a faith vain and empty of any content, unproven by works.

Second, Amos was a spokesman for a mature and practical monotheism. Although going beyond the henotheism of Moses, which recognized that other national groups also had gods, he never reached the explicit monotheism of Second Isaiah, which denied categorically the existence of any other deities. Amos saw God as sovereign in all aspects of life, now even in Sheol and over all people, non-Israelites included.

Amos realized that Israel had to adjust mentally and theologically to the new era heralded by Assyrian imperialism. Although not a fertile innovator, he realized that Israel's election could no longer be interpreted to mean that it could expect an easier dispensation than other nations, who likewise were of concern to God. Israel had a special serious obligation as a partner to a sacred covenant relationship to do the justice which God required. While each nation would suffer for its iniquities, Israel would, because of its singular election, be more harshly judged. In Amos' thinking, addiction to the sacrificial cult often blinded people to their moral responsibilities. All in all, Amos was largely instrumental in setting the framework within which religion still functions today.

Pertinent Literature

Kapelrud, A. S. *Central Ideas in Amos.* Oslo: W. Nygaard, 1956.

Kapelrud, refusing to view Amos as a simple herdsman, maintains that he held a position of some prominence in the society of Judah, probably a person of high rank, perhaps responsible for part of the Temple herds. Possibly Amos failed to include himself among the prophets more out of contempt for his colleagues than any humility. From the style, form and content of his writings, it is apparent that Amos was well educated and well understood; in his preaching he forcefully used the religious traditions of his culture.

The author also concludes that the contemporary social conditions forced Amos to speak out of necessity. Even though the prophet accepted the religious tradition of his time, his association with the cult did not prejudice him in its favor. On the contrary, according to Kapelrud, Amos rejected the cult as irrelevant and preferred to center his thinking on the ethical element of religion. In fact the feature which Amos introduced into Judaism was his insistence that the whole relationship between Yahweh and his people and all other peoples depended upon moral conduct. Amos' idea of God, tending toward a clear universalism, was also not exactly compatible with that of his contemporaries. God was not bound to any cult sanctuary at Jerusalem because he was independent of all cults. Cultic sites were only important as they supported the ethical imperatives established by God, which were absolute and not national. He is, in fact, independent of Israel, which did not mean more to him than Philistia or Ethiopia.

In attempting to understand the background of Amos' universalism, Kapelrud recalls the distinction between Yahweh, the national God of the Israelites, and El, the older more general supreme deity of the entire region. Amos was merely featuring the universalistic characteristics of El which had been transferred to Yahweh so long ago that he was totally unconscious of any synthesis.

Kapelrud believes that the fact that Amos' time had not yet connected the name of Moses with the ancient law explains the prophet's silence in citing Moses as an authority. Amos' position as the first Old Testament prophet whose words have come down to posterity in a whole collection is explained on the basis that his intense stress on the impending doom of the Day of Yahweh probably gave his message currency in wide circles.

Morgenstern, Julian. *Amos Studies.* Leiden: E. J. Brill, 1951.

Morgenstern's study of Amos is placed in the context of the history not only of ancient Israel but also of the entire Middle East. Only after analyzing the social and economic history of the larger region, involving trade route disputes, the rural-urban conflicts between Jerusalem and the outlying regions of Judah, and the gradual destruction of the middle class, and then only after discussing the earlier preliterary prophets, does the author proceed to describe the immediate social and religious background and significance of Amos.

To Morgenstern, Amos was not a professional prophet but rather a highly skilled author and speaker who carefully composed and delivered his message for a distinct effect on a specific occasion. Modern criticism, Morgenstern believes, can isolate Amos' simple basic message from the accretions which time has added to the original text. The heart of his message, he thinks, was the concept of the *Yom Yahweh,* the Day of the Lord. According to him, Amos' address was thirty minutes in length and was delivered before a large crowd in the courtyard of the national sanctuary of the northern kingdom at Bethel near dawn on New Year's Day in 751, a day which would guarantee Amos a large and eager congregation. Morgenstern even tries to envisage the suspense Amos built up as he predicted the Day of the Lord, which his auditors believed would crown the military successes they were recently enjoying. Amos, however, declared that the Day of the Lord would not herald more and greater military successes but rather would be a day of judgment when Israel would be punished for its moral corruption, a judgment so severe that only an ineffective remnant would survive. Such a doom was indeed approximated a few years later, when in 722 Israel was destroyed and its population carried off into exile. Obviously Amos' concept of the *Yom Yahweh* is significant for subsequent development of the idea of Judgment Day. — *J.R.R.*

Additional Recommended Reading

Watts, J. D. W. *Vision and Prophecy in Amos.* Grand Rapids, Michigan: Eerdmans, 1958. A study which stresses the eschatology of Amos.

Robinson, T. H., ed. *The Book of Amos.* Naperville, Illinois: Alec R. Allenson, Inc., 1923, reprinted 1954. An excellent general discussion.

Honeycutt, Roy Lee. *Amos and His Message.* Nashville, Tennessee: Broadman Press, 1963. A recent and useful discussion of Amos, his background and message.

Harper, William R. *Amos and Hosea.* New York: Charles Scribner's Sons, 1915. An old but dependable line-by-line interpretation of the book of Amos, and an excellent background for understanding prophetism.

Wolfe, Rolland E. *Meet Amos and Hosea, the Prophets of Israel.* New York: Harper & Row Publishers Incorporated, 1945. A clear simple review of the messages of these prophets.

Ridge, F. Morgan. *The Prophet Amos.* London: Epworth Press, 1951. The author sees Amos as a prototype of the modern social reformer.

128

FOUNDING OF SYRACUSE

Type of event: Political: settlement of an overseas colony
Time: c.733 B.C.
Locale: Southeastern coast of Sicily

Principal personage:
ARCHIAS, Corinthian nobleman, founder of Syracuse

Summary of Event

Greece has always been a poor country economically. Deposits of minerals are not extensive, and the soil itself is thin and stony. Much of the land is mountainous, so that only a quarter of its surface has ever been arable. At the dawn of Greek history, Homer observed that Hellas was married to poverty. As time went on and the population of Greece grew, many states found themselves unable to support their citizens. The result was an acute need for more land, and since it could be found only by emigration overseas, colonization began around 750 B.C. and continued for approximately five centuries. Overpopulation was always a major cause.

One of the first states to send out colonies was Corinth, even though she was, by Greek standards, proverbially wealthy. Her position on the isthmus placed her astride both the land route between the Peloponnesus and central Greece, and the short overland connection between the Corinthian and Saronic Gulfs. She charged tolls on both routes, but the revenue received was insufficient to pay for imported food. Therefore, about 733 B.C., Corinth decided to dispatch two expeditions overseas. Archias, a member of the noble family of the Bacchiadae, was selected to be the founder of the colony which was to settle on the east coast of the fertile island of Sicily. If the Corinthians followed the procedure that we know was used later, they consulted the god Apollo at Delphi to receive his sanction for the venture and perhaps some useful advice.

Unfortunately, we know nothing of the story of the voyage to Sicily or of the early years of the new colony. We can say that the risks the Corinthians faced were about equal to those encountered by European settlers in America in the seventeenth century. While the Atlantic Ocean is more dangerous than the Mediterranean Sea, the Europeans had larger and stronger ships than the Greeks, compasses for steering, and fairly good ideas on how to navigate by sun and stars. They also had firearms to defend themselves against counterattacks by the original occupants of the land, while the Greeks had essentially the same weapons as the people they dispossessed. We do know, however, that Archias and his Corinthian force succeeded, and that within a generation or two Syracuse became a large and flourishing state. As a colony, it was not governed by Corinth, but was fully autonomous. Corinth and Syracuse always enjoyed the close and amicable relations typical of the relationship between a Greek metropolis and her offshoots, for war between colony and mother city was felt to be a particularly shameful thing. There were exceptions, of course, as in the case of Corcyra, also founded by Corinth about 733; we know of two wars fought between her and Corinth before the end of the fifth century, and there are indications that there may have been others.

Syracuse became so mighty and populous that it was forced to send out its own colonies to other parts of Sicily; and the mother city and her daughter states came to play an important role in the life and history of Sicily. At the beginning of the fourth century B.C., Syracuse was powerful enough under the tyrant Dionysius to attempt with temporary success to impose her hegemony on Sicily and southern Italy. The city became a brilliant center of Greek civilization and played a role of exceptional historical importance, for it was through it more than any other state that Hellenic culture was transmitted to Rome from Greece and from Hellenistic Alexandria.

After 650 B.C. a second motive for colonization supplemented the drive to acquire more land for agriculture; some colonies were founded for commercial reasons. For example, shortly before 600, Naucratis was established in Egypt by Miletus, Aegina, Samos, and some smaller states as depots for badly needed exports of grain from Egypt to Greece. In the west Massilia founded Emporium, whose name, "Trading Station," shows the intention of the founding city. Massilia, the modern Marseilles, also propagated Greek civilization up the valley of the Rhone into southern Gaul.

Corinth was not the only city to colonize extensively. Mention should also be made of Eretria, located on the island of Euboea, which settled many places on the northern coast of the Aegean, and of Miletus, an Ionian city with colonies especially numerous along the Black Sea coast. All this activity was of great significance, since Hellenism was spread from its original homeland into many parts of the Mediterranean. The Black Sea gradually became a Hellenic lake, and virtually all Sicily and the coastal regions of southern Italy were Hellenized by the descendents of the original Greek settlers of the western Mediterranean.

Pertinent Literature

Dunbabin, T. J. *The Western Greeks.* Oxford: The Clarendon Press, 1948.

One of the most fertile areas of Greek colonization was to the west of Hellas in Sicily and southern Italy. This region saw the establishment of many famous and powerful Greek states. Dunbabin's book covers the history of these western foundations from the time they were first sent out in the mid-eighth century, to 480 B.C. when Gelon of Syracuse defeated an attempt by the Carthaginians to extend their sway over the island and thus inaugurated the golden age of Hellenism in Sicily.

The early history of Greek Sicily is only partly known; literary evidence of the Greek invasion of the west is unfortunately scanty, so that one is forced to rely heavily upon the results of excavation. While pottery and other artifacts abound, their significance is difficult to establish. Sicily had been known to the inhabitants of Greece since early times, as is proved by finds of Mycenean pottery in the island. It is with the eighth century that extensive amounts of Hellenic pottery begin to be found there. These deposits show that the Greeks had taken increased interest in Sicily at least a generation before the first wave of settlers set out about 750. Dunbabin thinks that the Greeks desired trade with the West, and that this was from the beginning one of the powerful motives leading to the foundation of the western colonies, although he agrees that land hunger was also a driving force. In regard to Syracuse, he points out that the city was built on the finest harbor on the eastern coast, and from this undoubted fact he concludes that commercial motives must have lain behind the choice of site. This conclusion may be right, but reasons for the geographical situation of the city are open to more than this one interpretation. Syracuse was originally built on a small island, later connected to the mainland by a short causeway; the intention of Archias may actually have been to settle in a place which could easily be defended against the native population in the hinterland.

The pre-Hellenic inhabitants of Sicily were the Sicels, or Sicans. From the time of their first contact with the Greeks they began slowly to exchange their native ways for Greek, so that by about the mid-fifth century B.C., the Sicels were almost completely assimilated into Hellenic culture. Hellenization proceeded in a number of ways. As Greek power gradually penetrated inland, Sicel communities were sometimes enslaved wholesale, up-rooted, and forced to work in a Greek environment. Gentler means, however, were also used; some Greek states made alliances with the more primitive Sicels and a few even permitted intermarriage. In these circumstances, the Sicels slowly changed themselves into Greeks by adopting the language and culture of the superior invaders. The island came to be thoroughly Hellenized except for the western tip, which for a time was under Cathaginian influence. The Hellenization of southern Italy, however, proceeded much more slowly and less completely than that of Sicily, and although Greek civilization was known to mountain peoples such as the Samnites, they retained a good deal of their native Italian culture. Hellenism took hold best along the southern and western coasts at places like Taras (Tarentum) and Locri.

Colonies of the Dorian states of the Peloponnesus originally dominated the West, but later Ionian and Athenian influence began to be felt. This influence was all to the good for the development of the higher and finer aspects of Hellenism, for the level of civilization in the first colonies, as might be expected, lagged behind developments in Greece itself. While the western Greeks produced the remarkable law-givers Zaleucus of Locri and Charondas of Catana, it was not until the fifth century that Sicily and Italy came into their own and gave birth to such important figures as the philosopher Empedocles of Acragas and the rhetorician Gorgias of Leontini.

Founding of Syracuse

Graham, A. J. *Colony and Mother City in Ancient Greece*. Manchester: Manchester University Press, 1964.

One of the simple, old misconceptions of the status of colonial states in the Greek world was that each one became a completely free and sovereign new city. Graham's book shows that such independence was far from common and that any one of a number of different relationships between colony and metropolis might actually exist.

The foundation of a colony was almost always an official act of the founding state, and it sometimes occurred, therefore, that the mother city laid down conditions governing the life of the new colony. The metropolis provided the official Founder, *Oecist*, who was charged with the hazardous task of leading the settlers to the new site. The *Oecist* was usually accorded the honors due a hero, a sort of semi-divine being, and he was invariably worshiped after his death. The settlers took fire from the public hearth of the old city as a visible and material sign of the very definite religious links between the old city and the new. The colonists departed under the terms of an official act. Unfortunately, there are only a few examples of such foundation decrees extant, and all come from the fifth century or later, after the first great wave of colonists had emigrated. But these few surviving fragments help to illustrate some of the stipulations a metropolis might lay down.

Graham points out that the precise relations established depended upon a number of things. Primarily, there was the motive or temper of the founding city. Megara, for example, seems to have kept no control whatsoever over her colonies, and there is little evidence of her maintaining close relations with them. On the other hand, Miletus, a great trading state, founded many important colonies in the northern Aegean and Black Seas. She did not directly control them, but she did maintain close connections. Citizenship was mutual; that is, a Milesian who moved to Olbia could become legally a citizen of Olbia if he wished, and the Olbian a citizen of Miletus. Thasos, herself a colony of Paros, exercised real control over her foundations along the mineral-rich north shore of the Aegean. Here a second factor came into play: Thasos was quite close to her settlements, much closer than Miletus was to hers, so that the difficulties created by sheer distance were lacking.

Of all the important colonizing states of the early period, Corinth kept the closest control over her new colonies. She seems to have been determined to use them to help control the sea routes through the Gulf of Corinth in order to protect her imports of grain and other vital raw stuffs. The places settled by the Corinthian tyrants between 650 and 550, places such as Ambracia and Leucas, were subject to definite obligations. They were not only to perform certain religious duties and to use money nearly identical with that of the mother city, but they were also bound to have the same friends and enemies as Corinth and to be her allies in war. Graham, therefore, writes of Corinth and her colonial empire.

Athens did not take part in the early colonizing movement. By the fifth century, however, when she was faced with a rapidly expanding population, she sent out many settlements of a new kind. The old, independent colony of the archaic period, called *apoecia* in Greek, almost always had the status of a separate state, even if it was subject in one or more ways to the home government. The Athenians also developed a new legal concept which kept the settlers Athenian citizens still subject to the laws and the policies of the Assembly at Athens. It is likely that this kind of colony, called *cleruchy,* was intended to be an Athenian imperial outpost which might help the mother city to control the empire she had created in the Aegean. Since the colonists remained Athenians subject to Athens' will, the mother city was in no way deprived of military manpower or her ability to exercise her strength in strategic fashion. — *S.K.E.*

Additional Recommended Reading

Roebuck, Carl A. *Ionian Trade and Colonization.* New York: Archaeological Institute of America, 1959. A useful account of Ionian colonization and its relationship to trade.

Huxley, G. L. *The Early Ionians.* London: Faber and Faber, 1966. A description not only of the settlement of Ionian colonies but also of the contributions made by Ionians to Greek culture.

Rostovtzeff, M. I. *Iranians and Greeks in South Russia.* Oxford: The Clarendon Press, 1922. This classic work studies the contacts between Scyths and Greeks in the Black Sea region.

Hadas, Moses. *Hellenistic Culture: Fusion and Diffusion.* New York: Columbia University Press, 1957. A study of the interaction between Hellenism and native Oriental cultures in the Hellenistic period, the last great age of Greek colonization.

SPARTAN CONQUEST OF MESSENIA

Type of event: Military: war of expansion
Time: c.725 B.C.
Locale: Southwestern Peloponnesus

Principal personages:
THEOPOMPUS, Spartan king and commander in the First
Messenian War
TYRTAEUS, Spartan poet at the time of the Second Messenian War

Summary of Event

In the fifth and fourth centuries B.C., the institutions of the Pelopennesian city-state of Sparta, although imitated by no other states, were universally judged to be unique and were admired by many. In a Greek world increasingly dominated economically by commerce, Sparta remained exclusively agrarian. In a world in which other states had developed social diversity and rich cultural expression, Sparta retained a strict and simple social structure and a spiritual character rich in moral strength but almost totally wanting in creative artistic expression. Since archaeological and literary evidence indicates that Sparta was in the mainstream of Greek cultural development until the beginning of the seventh century B.C., the reason for Sparta's later uniqueness must be sought in a development of the seventh century. The likeliest explanation is to be found in the deliberate crystallization of permanent militarist institutions made necessary by Sparta's conquest of Messenia as a response to the problem of overpopulation in the eighth century.

The Dorian invaders of Laconia who settled in the valley of the Eurotas River in the course of the twelfth century

B.C. remained, throughout the following centuries, ethnically distinct from the residual non-Dorian inhabitants of the area whom they had conquered and over whom they exercised administrative jurisdiction. The distinction seems to have been preserved especially by maintenance of a social code retained from the period of the conquest and featuring strict separation of the sexes, military training for boys from an early age in kinship groups, and common daily messes of adult males, also in kinship groups.

In the course of the eighth century, most communities of the Greek world faced the problem of overpopulation and responded to the challenge by sending out colonies all over the Mediterranean world. Sparta stood aloof from this general movement of colonization and solved its problem of overpopulation by conquering its neighbors to the southwest in Messenia, one of the richest agricultural districts in Greece, which is generally rocky, mountainous, and infertile. The war extended over a twenty-year period at the end of the eighth century, approximately from 736 to 716 B.C. According to tradition, the Spartan army was led by Theopompus, one of

134

its two hereditary kings. There are abundant legends about the war, but little more can be firmly established other than the bare facts recounted above and the Spartan organization of the land and its people following the conquest. Since the war had been fought in response to the challenge of overpopulation, Messenian land was divided into estates distributed among the Spartan soldiery. The Messenians themselves continued to work the land as serfs and were obliged to pay one half of their produce to the new Spartan landowners. They were called "helots," a term which probably had the original meaning of "prisoners of war."

After several generations, the Messenians, probably encouraged by Sparta's involvement in local wars against Argos, Arcadia, and Elis in the mid-seventh century, attempted to throw off Spartan domination. The ensuing struggle was bitterly fought and seems to have engendered a constitutional crisis from which Sparta emerged as a permanently militarist society with a rigid social and political structure. Primary sources for events of this period are the poems of Tyrtaeus, exhortations of Spartan soldiery to resolution in the war with the Messenians, a paraphrase of an oracle of Delphi sanctioning the constitution which was either adopted or amended at this time, and the text (quoted by Plutarch in the *Life of Lycurgus*) of a document called the *Great Rhetra* which quotes provisions of this constitution in substantial agreement with Tyrtaeus.

A major factor in this political crisis was the change in military tactics from fighting based on spearmen and aristocratic cavalry to reliance upon the close-knit phalanx of heavily-armed foot soldiers called "hoplites." Throughout the Greek world, the shifting of the burden of community defense to the shoulders of the hoplite infantry was accompanied by a demand by these soldiers for greater political authority. In Sparta this demand also seems to have been made. The imperative economic necessity of the reconquest of Messenia brought aristocratic leaders to grant concessions formalized in the *Great Rhetra*; and a military organization based on local considerations rather than on claims of kinship was made the basis of the Spartan Assembly (*Apella*) of nine thousand warriors. According to the *Great Rhetra,* this assembly was to be sovereign in the state and hold final authority over the aristocratic council of thirty elders *(Gerousia).* Some adjustment of land distribution was evidently involved as well, for the nine thousand were henceforth called "equals" and were so content with their new lot that they did not resist the formulation of an amendment to the *Great Rhetra* granting the power of veto to the *Gerousia* over decision of the *Apella.*

The Messenian revolt was successfully suppressed, but Sparta, made aware through it that its economic security depended upon maintaining the subjection of a large population of serfs by a relatively small Spartan army, committed itself henceforth to a life of relentless military preparedness. This was maintained at the cost of cultural stagnation, a price which the Spartans themselves were willing to pay.

Pertinent Literature

Andrewes, A. *The Greek Tyrants.* First published in London in 1956. Reprinted, New York: Harper & Row Publishers Incorporated, 1963.

This book is a survey of the economic and social factors in various communities of the Greek world during the archaic era from 750 to 500 B.C. which led to the characteristic development of popular monarchies known as "tyrannies." A chapter entitled "The Spartan Alternative to Tyranny" appropriately places the period in Sparta with which this article is concerned in the context of comparable constitutional developments in other Greek communities, and explains Sparta's uniqueness largely in terms of the consequences of the conquest of Messenia.

Sources for Spartan social and political organization are, for the most part, late in date. A legend growing ever more elaborate from the fifth century B.C. onward attributed the total plan of organization of Spartan life to the legislation of Lycurgus, a shadowy figure placed by all sources early in Sparta's history. Andrewes proceeds in this chapter by first sketching briefly the several aspects of the "Lycurgan system" and then analytically examining the evidence for the development of each aspect. With regard to the social code of military training and common messes, Andrewes asserts that Sparta preserved, along with some Cretan communities, ancestral customs from the period of the Dorian invasions. Cultural development in Sparta seems to have proceeded on an equal level with other Greek communities into the sixth century. The tenure of land seems to have been regulated as a conse-

quence of the Messenian conquest. Since the soldier-citizen had to be economically independent and free to devote his time to military training, and since the formal qualification for citizenship was the ability to contribute one's share in kind to the common messes, the land was allotted to the citizenry on an equal basis. The military organization was changed at the beginning of the seventh century from a kinship division of three tribal regiments to a hoplite army of five locally based *lochoi.*

The Spartan political structure described in the *Great Rhetra* represents a characteristic seventh century constitution: a sovereign hoplite assembly with a probouleutic council whose function was to initiate proposals for assembly action. Oligarchic features of this constitution are the limitation of the assembly to nine thousand, the life-appointments of council memberships, and the hereditary office of the two kings. Yet the constitution shows signs of democratic features: the fact that the citizen-soldiers in the assembly were called "equals" seems to indicate an earlier inequality, probably by reason of land tenure.

Messenia was conquered at the end of the eighth century by an old-style army led by Theopompus. While Sparta was embroiled in local wars with neighbors in the mid-seventh century, the Messenians revolted. The hardships of the long struggle of reconquest seem to have led to agitation for land redistribution among the hoplite army, and the reforms of the

Great Rhetra were an answer to this agitation, Andrewes believes. The political structure was formally fixed and the assembly of hoplite "equals," secure in its privileged status of landlord over the rich land of Messenia, devoted itself with increasing steadfastness and austerity to the barracks life by which that status was retained. As Andrewes says, "the constitution which was liberal and progressive when it was defined in the Rhetra in the seventh century seemed archaic and reactionary to the democrats of the fifth."

With regard to Lycurgus, Andrewes suggests that the name of the lawgiver must already have been a part of Spartan tradition in the seventh century, and that the reforms of the *Great Rhetra* were carried through with the sanction of his name as a "restoration" of laws once promulgated by him.

Huxley, G. L. *Early Sparta.* Cambridge: Harvard University Press, 1962.

George Huxley's book on Sparta is unique in the bibliography of the city's history in that it offers a detailed chronological account of the evolution of Sparta's institutions by period. Most scholars, in view of overwhelming problems of Spartan chronology and conflicting evidence concerning the development of Spartan institutions, have chosen to examine critically the evidence for particular aspects of Spartan life and polity in separate investigations. Huxley does not really minimize the problems, but he does confidently assert the possibility of arriving at firm conclusions regarding the dates and course of consecutive developments of Spartan history, and thus he presents a continuous narrative with a much more detailed positive content than many scholars would be willing to credit.

The Spartan conquest of Messenia, says Huxley, surely took place in the last third of the eighth century B.C. The war lasted twenty years, as we know from Tyrtaeus; and since the last Messenian victory at the Olympic Games is listed at 736, Huxley suggests 736-716 B.C. as the period of the war, and relates its conflicts to the whole complex of late eighth century conflicts referred to by historians as the Lelantine War.

In the wake of the conquest and allotment of the conquered territory to the victorious warriors came political dissension at home. Younger men left out of the allotment attempted a coup against the aristocratic government, and after its failure these dissidents were led out as colonists to Tarentum in southern Italy in 706 B.C. Discontent was not sufficiently quelled by this measure, however, and Huxley gives credence to accounts that King Polydoros at this time increased the allotments of land in both Laconia and Messenia to a total of nine thousand. This reform is associated by Huxley with the whole complex of reforms attributed by tradition to Lycurgus. Huxley does not doubt the genuine historicity of Lycurgus and confidently dates him within this period. At a time when Cretan influence was strong in Sparta and at the Cretan-founded oracle of Apollo at Delphi, Lycurgus brought back from the oracle the constitution described in the *Great Rhetra* cited by Plutarch in chapter 6 of his *Life of Lycurgus.* Huxley be-

137

lieves that Plutarch's wording, with some minor emendations, is historically genuine. The new constitution, Huxley argues, was promulgated close to the time of Terpander's reformation of the Spartan festival of Apollo, the *Karneia*, in 676. This constitution was democratic, sanctioning election of a council of thirty elders by the populace: though this council was to propose legislation, the populace might make counterproposals and was in any case the final authority. As the new constitution was anathema to the Spartan aristocracy, a counterrevolution followed, during which King Polydoros was assassinated and Lycurgus fled into exile.

Soon after this constitutional crisis, a Spartan army was disastrously crushed by the Argives at Hysiae in 669 B.C. The Messenians seized the opportunity to revolt against their Spartan overlords and for several years a coalition of Messenians, Argives, Arcadians, and Eleans fought against Sparta in the Second Messenian War. In this critical situation the Spartans themselves found unity imperative, and an amendment to the *Great Rhetra* was adopted giving the power of veto to the council of elders over the actions of the popular assembly. The poet Tyrtaeus, who was active during the Second Messenian War, composed a paraphrase of the *Great Rhetra* incorporating the amendment and seeking to ground the amended constitution as a whole on the authority of Delphi. The effort was apparently successful, for further constitutional development toward democracy in Sparta was stifled. The coalition of allies against Sparta eventually fell apart, and by 659, most of Messenia had been reconquered. — *C.W.C.*

Additional Recommended Reading

Chrimes, K. M. T. *Ancient Sparta: A Reëxamination of the Evidence.* Manchester: Manchester University Press, 1949. Spartan institutions are examined carefully by working back from Hellenistic and Roman accounts.

Den Boer, W. *Laconian Studies.* Amsterdam: North-Holland Publishing Company, 1954. A discussion of problems of Spartan chronology, the *Great Rhetra*, marriage customs, and military training.

Michell, H. *Sparta.* Cambridge: The University Press, 1952. A discussion of several features of Spartan social, constitutional, and military organization.

HESIOD'S COMPOSITION OF THE *THEOGONY*

Type of event: Literary: statement of mythology
Time: c.720 B.C.
Locale: Chalcis, on the island of Euboea

Principal personage:
HESIOD (c.750-700 B.C.), Boeotian peasant and writer

Summary of Event

The *Theogony* of Hesiod may well be the earliest extant work of Greek literature. Although based on older oral traditions and on a mythological foundation that can be traced ultimately to Mesopotamia, it is stamped with the individuality of a single writer who names himself early in the work and declares it to be the expression of a personal revelation to him from the Muses. From a statement in his later poem, the *Works and Days,* it seems likely that the *Theogony* was originally composed for and recited at the funeral games of Amphidamas, a nobleman of Chalcis in Euboea who died fighting in the Lelantine War (730-700 B.C.).

The poem begins with a hymn to the Muses which includes the account of their theophany to him while he was pasturing his sheep in Boeotia at the foot of Mount Helicon. There follows an account of the origin of the world in the emergence of the first beings, Chaos (the murky abyss below the earth), Gaia (Earth), and Eros (the more-than-merely-sexual creative impulse of generation and maturation in the world-organism). Out of Chaos are generated Night, Darkness, and all that is mysterious and intangible including the abstractions of Death, Fate, Deceit, Strife, and the like. From Gaia are generated the visible and solid parts of the world and the familiar gods of cult and mythology. Hesiod then proceeds to name in genealogical order the three great generations of beings divine and less than divine who have played roles in shaping the cosmological and theological structures of human experience. The process of generation, often asexual in the earliest stages of creation, normally proceeds through the pairing of masculine and feminine deities to beget offspring. The genealogies are strikingly matrilinear throughout the greater part of the poem, and only in the later stages does the paternal parent clearly assume greater importance.

A major theme developed in the poem is that of usurpation of the power of the reigning deity: Ouranos (Sky), first ruler of the gods, by his son Kronos; and then of Kronos by his own son Zeus, who ultimately emerges as sole ruler without a successor to fear. Each stage in the succession is marked by intense hostility on the part of the fathers Ouranos and Kronos toward their children, whom they fear as potential threats to their authority. Ouranos refuses to allow his children by Gaia to be born; Kronos swallows his children by Rhea as soon as they are born. Each stage of the succession is also abetted by Gaia. Against

139

Ouranos she rouses her youngest son Kronos to lie in ambush and castrate his father with an adamantine sickle. Gaia later thwarts the intentions of Kronos by receiving his last-born son Zeus as soon as he is born and secreting him away in a cave in Crete, thus permitting Zeus to mature and ultimately to trick Kronos into disgorging the contents of his belly. Thereafter a ten-year war is waged between Kronos and his generation of Titans on the one hand, and Zeus and his Olympian brothers and sisters on the other. Zeus ultimately wins the war by liberating from their prison under the earth the fierce Hundred-handers Kottos, Gyges, and Briareos, and enlisting their aid against the Titans. Once defeated, the Titans are thrust below earth's surface into their everlasting murky prison-house in Tartaros. One final threat to the rule of Zeus, the raging monster of the tempest, Typhoios, is defeated and imprisoned below the earth. Only then can Zeus organize his realm and allot to the several deities their proper spheres of dominance in his world-order.

Three metaphors govern the course of Hesiod's narrative of the emergence of the generations of the gods and their successive rulers. One is the concept of organism: the world-order is conceived as a growing animate complex with an inner drive toward form and order. In this interpretation there is a germ of the Greek cosmological principle of *physis* and perhaps ultimately of Aristotle's conception of entelechic development. A second metaphor is the politicial: the world-order is a state which ultimately comes to be governed by a rational king, Zeus, who rules with political sagacity as well as by brute force. Here may be seen the germ of the cosmological concept of "laws" of nature as developed by Ionian philosophers and the Stoics. The third metaphor is that of moral maturation: the unruly, adolescent Titans led by the devious-minded Kronos are defeated by Zeus and his mature Olympians because the mind of Zeus has become master over his will and his passions. Greek anthropomorphism thus dominates the poem in that the world-order is represented as fundamentally akin to man in his physical nature, his political organizing ability, and his will to self-control.

Pertinent Literature

Hesiod. *Theogony*. Edited with *Prolegomena and Commentary* by M. L. West. Oxford: The Clarendon Press, 1966.

This new commentary on Hesiod's *Theogony* is a valuable new resource to students of Greek mythology thanks not only to its thorough discussion of the problems of textual criticism, interpretation, and relevant literature on every section of the work, but also to its expansive introductory "Prolegomena." Here West sets Hesiod's work in the context of world-wide theogonic literature, examines the near-Eastern sources of the Greek theogonic tradition, and offers an extensive treatment of textual transmission, style, vocabulary, dialect, and meter, in addition to providing a bibliography. Of particular interest is his discussion of the relation of the

140

succession-myth of the *Theogony* to the three most significant ancient near-Eastern parallel mythical texts from Mesopotamia, the Hurrian realm, and Phoenicia.

The Mesopotamian text, entitled *Enuma Elish,* dates from the first Babylonian dynasty (c.1895-1595 B.C.) and reflects the replacement of the city-god Enlil of Nippur by the city-god Marduk of Babylon. This myth presents the emergence of the divine order from a primeval pair, Apsu, the male sweet water, and Tiamat, the female sea water. Children are begotten by the pair and confined within Tiamat, children whom the father Apsu hates but Tiamat loves. At length the god Ea overpowers the oppressive Apsu with a trick and strips him of his symbols of strength. A war among the gods ensues wherein Marduk, the god of Babylon, becomes king and then organizes his realm by allotting their provinces to the several gods.

A second relevant parallel to Hesiod's succession-myth is found in Hittite texts which themselves date from the thirteenth century B.C. but are derived from Hurrian myths two or three centuries older. In this myth the first king in heaven is a relative nonentity Alalu, who is defeated in battle by his son Anu, the sky-god. After a reign of nine years, Anu is given battle by Kumarbi, who pursues Anu to the sky, biting off and swallowing his genitals. From the genitals within his belly emerge other gods, including his successor, the weather-god, who ultimately issues forth and is victorious over Kumarbi after a theomachy. After the weather-god's victory, he is confronted by a new threat in a monster, the prodigious stone-child Ullikummi, but over this challenge the weather-god also triumphs to secure his kingship. Here we have a parallel to Hesiod's succession-myth in the castration of the sky-god by a successor, the swallowing of the seed of his own successors and the theomachy followed by a further challenge of a great monster. The Hittite-Hurrian myth is clearly a derivative from Mesopotamia as can be seen in the appearance of the names of Babylonian deities in the myth.

The third document is a Greek translation by Herennius Philo of Byblos (A.D. 64-140) of a work entitled *Phoenician History* by one Sanchuniathon, claimed by Philo to have lived before the Trojan War. Though perhaps not that ancient, the myth does seem to reflect an early Phoenician form. Here, as in the Hittite-Hurrian myth, there are four generations; and here too the first king of heaven, Eliun-Hypsistos, is a relative nonentity succeeded by his children, Ge, (Earth), and Epigeios-Uranos, the sky-god who attempts to destroy his and Ge's children, but is ultimately ambushed and castrated by his son El-Kronos. El-Kronos ultimately yields his throne to Demarus-Zeus, who in this version is not his own son but rather another child of Ouranos.

The succession-myth of Hesiod is clearly derived from ancient near-Eastern theogonic traditions which much have come to Greece during the Minoan-Mycenean period, since it has agreements with *Enuma Elish* against the latter's Hurrian and Phoenician derivatives. Kumarbi and Kronos, the second generation rulers in the Hurrian and Greek versions, "owe their mythological thrones to Enlil"; they were never principal gods in their own area and may once have been local deities.

Sale, William. "The Dual Vision of the *Theogony*," in *Arion* (Winter, 1965), pp. 668-699.

The *Theogony*, it has usually been held, was composed with the purpose of organizing along genealogical lines the chaotic pantheon of Greek and older Minoan deities surviving into the Greek period. William Sale argues that the poem shows little evidence of such purpose: it concentrates on two or three of the great Olympian deities while paying the respect of brief mention to many others, and it allots considerable discussion to the numerous children of Ocean and Nereus and the monstrous offspring of Night. Nor is cosmology or cultural history of primary interest to Hesiod. What is fundamental to Hesiod is deity, and the poet is "a man with a religious vision to expound." This vision is expressed in two aspects, hierarchical and theogonical, and both voice a single truth: "In the heart of the world, a region to which our most intense religious exaltation lead us, there resides a transcendent God-head who is hardly more than human: he does transcend, because we know that he is utterly remote, but what we see is only that he lives forever, that he is more powerful, intelligent and just than we are, and that he knows a more complete joy."

Sale recognizes five "modes of religious reality" in Hesiod's hierarchical vision. Two of these, which he terms the upper and nether remote, are fully transcendent. The upper remote is the mode of transcendent brightness, clarity, beauty and joy; its symbols are Olympus and Heaven, and it is more a spiritual than a geographical realm. With this realm one experiences a sense of communion and transfiguration when engaged in activity appropriate to a particular deity of this mode: one communes with Aphrodite in the act of loving impregnation. The nether remote is the mode of transcendent darkness, murkiness, ugliness, and cruelty, and is symbolized usually by Tartarus, sometimes by Chaos or the far-western sunset region. The religious experience wherein a man apprehends this mode is that of utter horror, of helpless despair. As there is a polarity in the modes of upper and nether remote, so also there is one in the modes of the natural and the monstrous. When the phenomena of undying nature fills a man with awe, he experiences their divinity, but no self-transcending vision or communion is requisite for such an experience. The experience of the monstrous comes through dreams, but awe before the grotesque and unnatural is clearly distinct from the terror of a vision of the utter blackness of Tartarus. There is finally the human mode, about which there is nothing immortal or divine. Apprehended in it are chiefly the children of Night and Strife: death, sleep, woe, deceit, old age, quarrels, and the like—realities experienced in human life and marking its fundamental limitations and tragic imperfection. Sale argues that deity is a term that may properly be applied only to Hesiod's modes of the upper and nether remote and the natural, and he sees as the essence of deity for Hesiod the awe-inspiring sense of "the power beyond." The deity experienced by Hesiod is "hardly more than human," and there is nothing essentially nonhuman about it. The experience in which deity is apprehended is experience of the transcendent heights and depths of human existence itself.

In the theogonical vision Hesiod sees revealed the process of maturation of the godhead again in terms of the patterns of human existence. All the gods have been born in the orderly process of sexual union, conception, and successive generation. Sexual generation has violence as its natural consequence when older and younger generations confront each other. Intelligence enters in to regulate the problems brought on by sexual love and violence, first as adolescent cunning, finally as the mature ordering intelligence of Zeus, who is able to bring sex and violence under control. Thus in the two visions, hierarchical and theogonical, deity as experienced by Hesiod is shown by Sale to be defined by and within the limits of human existence. — *C.W.C.*

Additional Recommended Reading

Burn, A. R. *The World of Hesiod.* London: Trubner & Co., 1936. An examination of Hesiod's poems in the context of political, social, economic, and cultural conditions of his day.

Pritchard, J. B., ed. *Ancient Near Eastern Texts Relating to the Old Testament.* 2nd ed. Princeton: Princeton University Press, 1955. An anthology containing texts of Hittite and Babylonian myths related to Hesiod's *Theogony.*

Cornford, F. M. *Principium Sapientiae: The Origins of Greek Philosophical Thought.* Cambridge: The University Press, 1952. Discussion of the interrelation between ancient theogonic traditions, Hesiod, and Ionian cosmogony.

Solmsen, Friedrich. *Hesiod and Aeschylus.* Ithaca, New York: Cornell University Press, 1949. A study of the theology of Hesiod and the deliberate effort by Aeschylus to revise it.

INVENTION OF COINAGE

Type of event: Economic: development of a commonly accepted means of exchange
Time: c.650 B.C.
Locale: Western Asia Minor

Principal personages:
ALYATTES, King of Lydia c.610-560 B.C.
CROESUS, King of Lydia c.560-546 B.C.

Summary of Event

In very early times, commercial transactions were conducted by bartering goods; for example, wheat might be exchanged for copper. Occasionally, merchants traded goods for bullion, which took the form of silver or gold rings or bars. There were inconveniences in this primitive system. In the case of simple barter, the merchant who had wheat to trade might be offered only copper in return, and either he had to accept it, not knowing where he might dispose of it, or else he had to keep his wheat. If, on the other hand, he could get bullion, he could more easily dispose of it, because silver and gold were valuable everywhere. Even trading goods for bullion might itself be awkward, however, if the merchant did not know the purity of the metal. Governments also experienced inconveniences when wages were given in kind for the services of large gangs of workmen or bodies of mercenary troops. All these difficulties were eased by the invention of coinage, for coins were, at least in theory, identical small ingots of precious metal whose standard purity and weight were guaranteed by the issuing authority.

No one knows today exactly when or where coins were first minted. Greek literary tradition speaks of a number of widely separated times and places, which merely shows that by the fifth century B.C. memory of the event was already badly confused. All that we can say with certainty is that coinage was first struck somewhere in western Asia Minor around 650 B.C. Whether it was invented in one of the Greek states or by the Kings of Lydia is not known. Xenophanes of Colophon and Herodotus of Halicarnassus, natives of two cities of Asia Minor, give the credit to the Lydians. Their testimony together with the coins which have come down to us provide evidence in favor of Lydia, for Lydian coins are the earliest which can be identified and attributed to a specific state.

The first metals used for coinage were of silver and electrum, a natural alloy of silver and gold found in western Asia Minor. Gold was seldom used alone in the earliest centuries, and then only to meet a shortage of silver. But as time went on, gold was more frequently used, especially by Persia, the Hellenistic monarchies, and Rome. In the fourth century B.C., bronze replaced silver for fractional amounts of the large coins.

The ancients acquired great skill in the refinement of silver-bearing ores. At Athens, as we know from scientific analysis of its coinage, careful smelting consistently produced metal which was ninety-eight to ninety-nine percent pure. On the other hand, dilution of nearly pure silver with copper was a device sometimes resorted to by states to increase their supply of money.

Coins were made by striking, almost never by casting. The obverse, or top, die was placed in a closely fitting hole in an anvil. On this was placed a round blank of heated, carefully weighed metal. The reverse die was placed upon it and the whole was smartly struck with a hammer. The impressions made by these dies identified the issuing state. Athens used a head of Athena as obverse badge, an owl as reverse with the inscription AThE standing for "Athens." Corinth used a differently designed head of Athena or Aphrodite on the obverse and the winged horse Pegasus on the reverse with the letter Koppa standing for "Corinth." The coins of these two states were referred to as "owls" and "colts." Different states used coins of different standard weights, but this caused little difficulty since the standards were interchangeable. The Attic drachma weighed a little more than four grams, while that of the Corinthians weighed something over two, so that one Athenian drachma was equivalent to one Corinthian stater, or double-drachma piece.

Greek coiners lavished great care on the making of dies, partly for aesthetic reasons, partly to make the coins difficult to counterfeit. Some Greek coins are of great artistic merit, especially the fifth century coins of Elis with a majestic head of Zeus, and those of Syracuse showing a head of Arethusa surrounded by four graceful dolphins.

After the invention of coinage its use spread rapidly to all parts of the ancient world. By the end of the third century B.C., coins were being struck from the Indus valley to southern Britain. The effects of all this were important. Commerce was facilitated, since merchants could usually rely upon the purity and weight of precious metal received for goods, which were thus readily convertible into cash. The use of money also helped individual men to acquire great fortunes, sometimes through the manipulation of the value of agricultural products. Small farmers who borrowed cash to buy seed grain at planting time, when grain was scarce and its price high, had to sell grain to raise cash for repayment at harvest time, when grain was plentiful and cheap. The use of coinage also allowed military powers to accumulate large reserves of money for the payment of mercenary or other troops. This gave an advantage to states which possessed large amounts of silver ore. There can be no doubt that the strength of Athens, Macedonia, and Rome came, in part, from their having considerable deposits of silver within their territories.

Pertinent Literature

Head, Barclay V. *Historia Numorum*. 2nd ed. Oxford: The Clarendon Press, 1911.

Numismatics, the study of coinage, is one of the important auxiliary disciplines of ancient history. Its scientific basis was developed in the nineteenth century. One distinquished scholar contributing to the rise of this discipline was Barclay V. Head. The first edition of his book appeared in 1887, but the amount of work being done by other scholars at the same time forced the appearance of this second edition. Despite the title, which means "A History of Coins," the book is written in English; it is not really a history of all coinage but only of ancient Greek money.

The work of Head and his colleagues was by no means easy, since classical Greek coins seldom bear the date when they were struck, as modern coins do, and many of them have no inscription or mint mark to identify the place of origin. The task of the early numismatists was to assign to each type of unmarked coin a mint and date. In this book Head discusses the problems of attribution, and also the difficulty of discovering the place and date for the invention of coinage itself. He rejects the traditions in Greek literature that coins were first made by the semilegendary King Pheidon of Argos and that Athens' first money was issued by the legendary King Theseus. He also discusses the origins of Greek weight standards. Why did the Attic drachma weigh about 4.25 grams? It appears that this standard was ultimately derived from a Babylonian measure, the *mina* of the Old Testament, but even today we cannot explain this standard or show in what way it was transmitted to Greece. Greek traditions are of little help, because currency originated in the seventh century when few historical documents were kept, and later writers had no trustworthy records upon which to base their statements.

Head inevitably made mistakes which fifty years of subsequent study have partly rectified, so that his book is of somewhat limited value today. Especially important have been the studies made of the ever-increasing finds of buried hoards of ancient money. It is a truism that more coins of any given mint are usually found close to that mint than farther away, and study of the geographical distribution of unmarked coins often helps to attribute them to a mint. There are a few exceptions to the rule, as in the case of Corinth, more of whose silver coins have been found in Sicily and southern Italy than in the Corinthia itself. Furthermore, we now have more coin-types found in association with date-able pottery than existed in Head's day. Hence, it is now possible with the greater evidence at our disposal to be more accurate about matters of attribution and dating.

Head's book still has useful features. The currencies of the cities are arranged geographically, starting from the western Mediterranean and working eastward to Asia. A brief history of each mint city is given in chronological form and the actual products of the mint associated, where possible, with detailed events of that history. Head treats the bronze issues of Greek cities which continued into the Roman imperial age in addition to the autonomous silver issues of classical Greek times, and he includes information on the titles of magistrates in the Greek cities of the Roman era, a useful source of data on the form of organization and degree of autonomy of the local governments of that time. There is also a list of agonistic coins, that is, bronze currency struck in association with the great Panhellenic games such as the festival at Olympia. This information serves to widen our knowledge of Greek religion in the Christian era.

Kraay, C. M., and Max Hirmer. *Greek Coins.* London: Thames and Hudson, 1967.

This excellently produced and expensive volume is the most recent comprehensive handbook on the subject of Greek gold and silver money. It is the result of the joint labors of two distinguished European numismatists, Professor Max Hirmer and Dr. Colin M. Kraay.

The chief merit of the work lies in the more than eight hundred handsome photographs of the coins themselves, which Hirmer made over a period of ten years. He visited the most important public collections in Europe, such as those in the British Museum and the Cabinet des Medailles in Paris, in addition to the most significant private collections. Hence, a photograph of no important coin of the classical or Hellenistic periods is omitted. The pictures, of which twenty are in color, are well-produced enlargements of the coins to the second or even the fifth power, so that the intricate and beautiful craftsmanship of the greatest specimens of this minor Greek art can readily be studied in full detail. Here are the famous decadrachma pieces of Syracuse showing the nymph Arethusa wearing an elaborate coiffure and delicately made jewelry. Here, also, are the handsome, realistic portraits of the Seleucid kings.

The text which accompanies the plates is by C. M. Kraay of the Ashmolean Museum, Oxford. Kraay confines himself to a brief, well-executed essay on the invention of coinage, problems connected with the origins of weight standards, the importance of hoard evidence, and the like. The coinage of each of the principal Greek states is introduced by a page or two of comment on the origin of the city's currency, its subsequent development, and its most noteworthy features. Each article ends with a concise, up-to-date bibliography on the coinage of the state, and the volume ends with a general bibliography on the whole subject of Greek numismatics.

What gives this book its value is not only the magnificence of the plates but also Kraay's commentary, which is based on recent scholarship. The dating of the origin of coinage has been lowered by about a century from Head's day, and so have the dates of the earliest issues of the Greek states on the mainland. According to Kraay, who has written much on the subject elsewhere, the beginning of coinage at Athens, heretofore thought to have been in the late seventh century, is now placed at about 570 B.C. This thesis, which has not won universal acceptance, if correct, will have effects on our interpretation of the reforms of Solon. If coinage did not exist in his day, then the seasonal problems of indebted Athenian farmers would not have played a part in his scheme of reform, as many scholars have believed. In the West, the beautiful Syracusan decadrachma designed by Cimon, formerly believed to have been struck to commemorate the defeat of Athens in 413 B.C., is now thought to have been issued to celebrate a victory over Carthage in 405.

If this book has any shortcomings it is that it breaks off the history of Greek coinage in the first century B.C., whereas many Greek states continued to coin until the end of the ancient world and beyond. It is true, and perhaps a sufficient justification for the authors, that from the end of the first century B.C., the Greek world was in the grip of the Romans, and that their rights to issue silver coinage were severely restricted; usually the Greeks were permitted to strike bronze change only. There were, however, a few notable Greek silver coinages, such as those of Antioch and Alexandria, and they are omitted here.— *S.K.E.*

Additional Recommended Reading

Seltman, Charles. *Greek Coins.* 2nd ed. London: Methuen & Co., 1955. A standard work on the subject, superseded by Kraay and Hirmer on only a few points.

Mattingly, Harold B. *Roman Coins.* 2nd ed. London: Methuen & Co., 1960. A completely revised edition of the author's useful survey of Roman currency.

Kraay, Colin M., and Vera M. Emeleus. *The Composition of Greek Silver Coins.* Oxford: Ashmolean Museum, 1962. A study of the purity of the silver and of the various impurities in Greek coinage, with remarks on the sources of silver open to the various states.

Bolkenstein, H. *Economic Life in Greece's Golden Age.* Rev. ed. Leiden: E. J. Brill, 1958. A useful survey of the economic history of Classical Greece, with some remarks on the significance of coinage.

Michell, Humfrey. *The Economics of Ancient Greece.* Cambridge: The University Press, 1940. An older but still useful account of Greek economics and the impact of coinage upon the ancient economy.

THE REVELATION OF JEREMIAH

Type of event: Religious: prophetic utterance
Time: c.626-586 B.C.
Locale: Jerusalem

Principal personages:
JEREMIAH (c.645-580), a prophet
JOSIAH, King of Judah c.640-609
NECHO, Pharaoh of Egypt c.609-595
JEHOIAKIM, King of Judah 609-598
ZEDEKIAH, King of Judah 597-586
BARUCH, Jeremiah's secretary

Summary of Event

Some one hundred years before Jeremiah began to prophesy, the northern kingdom of Israel had been destroyed by Assyria. Most of its inhabitants were carried off into exile where they were assimilated: the Ten Lost Tribes. Jeremiah, apparently mindful of this catastrophe, was concerned over the destiny of the remnant of God's people in the southern kingdom of Judah, already faced with the new empire of Babylonia rising out of a renewed power struggle in the ancient East. The hopes of a revitalized Egypt to fill the power vacuum created by the fall of Assyrian Nineveh in 612 at the hands of the Medes and Chaldeans, was doomed when the Pharaoh Necho was defeated by the Babylonians at Carchemish in 605. Judah had great difficulty threading its tiny way through this maze of giant international rivalries. Some Jews were pro-Egyptian, some pro-Babylonian. Nebuchadrezzar, King of the new Chaldean empire, ended the perplexity by entering Jerusalem in 597 and again in 586, deporting Jews on each occasion to Babylonia. On his last raid he destroyed Jerusalem entirely and abolished the monarchy.

It was against this challenging and exciting background that Jeremiah lived and spoke. Much is known of him, his social insights, and his own personal characteristics. A man of integrity, motivated by devotion to his country but with a statesmanlike appreciation of practicality, he chose to see hope in the future. The new exile would not be a repetition of the northern kingdom's destruction by the Assyrians in 722 at the time of King Hoshea; rather, the Babylonian exile would be a source of renewal. It is a mistake to read into Jeremiah only a spirit of lamentation and miss his invincible optimism growing out of his faith in God. Rising above the narrow chauvinism of his time, he surrendered neither to the pessimism of the masses nor to the defeatism of the zealots.

Many scholars maintain that while much of what Jeremiah said was recorded at the time, more material was added by his secretary, Baruch, who may have gone into exile in Egypt with him after 586. The crux of Jeremiah's memoirs deals with the clash between his prophetic covenantal reading of history and the narrow politico-military outlook of the leaders of the time, such as the tyrannical Jehoiakim who cut up and burned the prophet's scrolls, and the vacillating Zedekiah. So unpopular was Jeremiah's message that he was thoroughly rejected, his writings were destroyed, and his own life was threatened. His personal anguish found vent in his "Confessions" in which he cursed the day of his birth and called upon God to visit vengeance on his adversaries.

Jeremiah equally rejected trust in either Egypt or Babylonia as allies. He denied the feasibility of national pretensions or any resistance. Under the circumstances, only Yahweh could be depended upon. In a letter he advised those carried off into exile in Babylon in 598 to live full lives, to rear families, and to keep the faith until return to Palestine was possible. God still intended the Jews to have a future, and faithfulness to God was not contingent upon locale. He hoped that the stark events would bring about the necessary repentance even of a few. To show evidence of his trust and hope that normal times would again prevail he even purchased a field in his home town of Anathoth during the final siege of Jerusalem in 586.

Jeremiah looked forward to a new covenant. Since the Hebrew nation with whom God made his original covenant had now ceased to exist, a new relationship had to be worked out between Yahweh and his people.

The new covenant must obviously be between God and individuals, an idea that arose partly from Jeremiah's own agonizing soul-searching. Yahweh will write his law in the hearts of Judeans and Israelites so that all will know God. Having thus made religion an individual affair, Jeremiah's immediate followers drew the conclusion that all men, even non-Jews, could enter into the new covenant. As an apostle of universalism, Jeremiah was greatly esteemed by the Christian Fathers who saw themselves and their fellow Christians beneficiaries of the new covenant. Many saw parallels between Jesus and Jeremiah because of their mutual involvement with their people both in castigating them and also in weeping and suffering for them. Among the Jews Jeremiah's ideas somewhat anticipated the Suffering Servant concept of Second Isaiah, and he remained a symbol of individual faithfulness to God under all circumstances. Jeremiah, concentrating on the themes of personal sin, responsibility, and faith, called for repentance and self-reformation rather than addiction to cult ritual. His disparagement of sacrificial worship was not new and stemmed partly from the fact that temple worship was suspended, and that a new substitute had to be found. He preferred an intimate inwardness of faith and the desire for a new heart that trusted in divine mercy. "Can vows and sacrificial flesh avert your doom?"

150

The Revelation of Jeremiah

Pertinent Literature

Hyatt, J. Philip. *Jeremiah: Prophet of Courage and Hope*. Nashville, Tennessee: Abingdon Press, 1957.

Since Hyatt wishes to point out that prophets were not puppets in the hand of an arbitrary deity but real men speaking to real people about real problems, he is interested in presenting in his book a vivid picture of the life and times of Jeremiah.

In the first place he offers a novel dating for the beginning of Jeremiah's prophecy which is usually set in 626 B.C. He prefers the date 609, late in the reign of Josiah. The year 626 he regards as the date of Jeremiah's birth believing that Jeremiah thought of himself as operating as a prophet from the time of his conception rather than at the beginning of his actual ministry. The active ministerial phase of Jeremiah's life is put late in the reign of Josiah or early in that of Jehoiakim.

The author envisages Jeremiah as neither a systematic nor an original thinker but rather a man who learned from his own religious experiences that the nature of true religion must be personal, internal, and spiritual. Hyatt rightly considers Jeremiah basically a realist rather than a pessimist in interpreting human nature and in understanding man's lack of gratitude and stubbornness of heart. His realism also permitted Jeremiah to be a man of hope. In the end the purposes of God would not be frustrated or defeated because as both sovereign Power and forgiving Love he exerted decisive direction in history and nature. Moreover, Jeremiah knew that men would change from sin through repentance, for God wished their salvation and would help to effect it.

Hyatt summarizes Jeremiah's chief convictions in concise form: The true prophet of God is not perfect but is a real man strenuously devoted to God; true prayer is a dialogue with God, involving a sharing of all thoughts and attitudes, desperately honest and serious; true religion is inward and personal, a spiritual fellowship with God resulting in social justice. As such it depends on neither Temple and sacrifices, nor ritual and location.

Blank, Sheldon H. *Jeremiah, Man and Prophet*. Cincinnati: Hebrew Union College Press, 1961.

While not an original treatment of Jeremiah, this study provides an excellent appraisal of the prophet by an outstanding scholar. Blank is particularly interested in trying to understand the character of a society which would tolerate a man like Jeremiah in its midst. No society particularly favors those rare and robust individuals who challenge it accurately and thoroughly. While Jeremiah suffered for his criticism, he was not executed, neither did he lose his wealth or his position in the community. Regardless of the efforts of his adversaries he continued to function and speak out in Jerusalem. Indeed, King Zedekiah continued to consult the prophet long after his challenging reputation was established. Jeremiah's experience indicates to Blank that the Jewish society had built into it some effective internal safety valve.

Blank concludes that while Jeremiah was well aware of the social and political dislocations in Judah and the ancient East with all their dire consequences, he could be optimistic by taking a long-range view. Admittedly, Jeremiah saw that his own time was beyond repair: constancy to God was lacking and he found himself addressing vainly men of "uncircumcised hearts." Even disciplinary acts by God were lost on his generation since the people had closed their minds and were determined that nothing would disturb their composure. Only after great disasters had chastened the people could Jeremiah envisage a hopeful future. This discernment made the fall of Jerusalem, the destruction of the Temple, and the Exile purposeful and inevitable. For God to show that he was greater than his people knew, the very ramparts of Jerusalem and even his own divine presence in the Temple would have to be jeopardized. The Jews would have to learn that the future would be based on an entirely different foundation from that of the past. The responsibility of maturity must be accepted; the comforts and confidence of easy religion must be surrendered; parochialism and the view of God as a local deity would have to be abandoned along with Jerusalem. Without such vision and perspective the people would die; only a broad perspective would save them. — *J.R.R.*

Additional Recommended Reading

Welch, A. C. *Jeremiah.* Oxford: Basil Blackwell, 1955. Welch is concerned with the authenticity of various passages of Jeremiah and believes that much of the book reflects the views of returned exiles rather than Jeremiah himself.

Driver, S. R. *The Book of the Prophet Jeremiah.* New York: Hodder and Stoughton, 1906. A treatment of the book of Jeremiah which sets his message in chronological order and indicates the historical setting.

Leslie, Elmer A. *Jeremiah.* Nashville, Tennessee: Abingdon Press, 1954. An attempt to make Jeremiah's statements understandable in terms of the events of the time and Jeremiah's psychology.

Bright, John. *Jeremiah.* Garden City, New York: Doubleday and Company, Inc., 1965. Bright provides a new, readable translation, and traces the development of prophecy in Israel.

Werfel, Franz. *Hearken Unto the Voice.* London: Jarrolds, 1938. A perceptive and popular account of Jeremiah as a human being.

ISSUANCE OF DRACO'S CODE

Type of event: Legal: enactment of a general code of laws
Time: 621/620 B.C.
Locale: Athens

Principal personages:
DRACO (fl.621/620), semimythical lawgiver
XENOPHANES (or Athenophanes, fl.409/408), who had
Draco's homicide law written on a stele in front of the
Royal Portico

Summary of Event

According to ancient traditions, Draco was a Greek legislator who drew up the first code of law for the Athenians during the archonship of Aristaechmus in 621/620 B.C. Though Draco and his laws are mentioned over fifty times in various sources, the evidence is so conflicting that it is difficult to determine the nature and extent of his legislation. It has even been denied by such competent scholars as Beloch, De Sanctis, and Aymard that there ever was a human lawgiver with this name, the Greek *drakon* referring instead to a "serpent god" that the Athenians credited with drawing up their first legal code. However, Draco was also a common personal name. Prodicus was aware of the difficulty surrounding the word *drakon,* and his famous pun reported in Aristotle's *Rhetoric* scarcely makes sense if the Athenians believed that their lawgiver was a snake: "They are not the laws of a man but of a 'snake,' so severe are they."

Other scholars have maintained that much of the evidence regarding Draco's legislation is the product of fourth century research and merely proves, if anything, that he drew up some laws regarding homicide. Such narrow in-terpretation of his activities, however, does not really agree with all the evidence available. Aristotle obviously attributed laws other than those on homicide to Draco. He states in his *Constitution of Athens,* for instance, that after Solon had drawn up a constitution and enacted new laws, "the ordinances of Draco ceased to be used, with the exception of those pertaining to murder [i.e. homicide]." Writers as early as Xenophon and Lysias refer to Draconian laws which were no longer in force. In 403, Tisamenus enacted a decree providing for the enforcement of the laws of Solon and of Draco as in earlier times. Various sources indicate that the legislation of Draco appeared to cover, in addition to homicide, such crimes as theft, vagrancy, adultery, the corruption of youth, neglect of the gods, and violation of the oath taken by jurors. Like other early lawgivers, Draco probably did not so much initiate new legislation as reduce customary law to an orderly and usable form in writing. He may also have drawn upon the decisions of earlier magistrates as recorded by the thesmothetes, or judges. According to Aristotle's *Politics,* there was nothing unusual enough to mention

153

about Draco's laws "except the greatness and severity of their penalties." Indeed, the severity of these laws had become legendary; Plutarch in his life of Solon reports that Draco's laws, except those relating to homicide, were repealed by Solon because they prescribed punishments regarded as too severe. Idleness or stealing a cabbage or an apple were capital offenses as serious as sacrilege or murder, and it was held that his laws were written not in ink but in blood. When Draco was asked why he assigned the death penalty for most offenses, he is reputed to have replied: "Small ones deserve that, and I have no higher for the greater crimes."

Such severity should not cause surprise. Most early codes of law were harsh in assigning severe penalties for petty crimes, as attested by early Hebrew law, Zaleucus' code, and the Twelve Tables of Rome. Not until the time of the Enlightenment was there concern to make the punishment fit the crime, and in England some severe and unreasonable penalties prescribed in Elizabethan times remained in force through the nineteenth century. Consequently, Draco's harshness, considering the times, can be overexaggerated. Death was not the only penalty inflicted on violators, lesser infringements drawing fines, disfranchisement, or exile. In the case of homicide, his legislation appears enlightened in that it drew careful distinction between willful murder and accidental or justifiable manslaughter. Evidence for such a view comes not only from the legal procedures which were established in his day but also from a copy of his homicide law which was erected in front of the Royal Portico in 409/408

by a decree of the Council and People initiated by Xenophanes or Athenophanes.

Moreover, Draco's laws marked definite advances. By designating crimes, fixing penalties, and establishing rules of procedure, he made it easier for the poor and the weak to obtain justice. His laws on homicide so effectively put an end to the blood feuds which had plagued Athens that other primitive communities adopted Athenian laws generally.

In this context it is well to recall Fustel de Coulanges' *Ancient City* which grew up gradually out of fused independent tribes that, in turn, had grown out of phratral or combinations of related families. The ancient city developed out of a gradual federation of groups, and it never was an "assembly of individuals." Draco's code represents the time when the coalescing city was forced to curtail the sovereignty of the tribe and family and to interfere first of all, for the sake of peace, in its prerogative of the blood feud. In the case of intentional homicide old tribal rights were still honored, but in the case of self-defense the new city saw a reasonable place to begin its encroachments on tribal rights. In the case of involuntary homicide, probably often occurring between persons of different groups and unknown to each other, the city again saw wisdom in restricting old tribal blood feuds. Consequently, Draco's code should be interesting not only for a history of Athenian jurisprudence but also as an index of the growing jurisdiction of the city of Athens itself. That the "state" did not concern itself with murder in Homer's day is quite likely inasmuch as the "city" in that era had not developed out of tribal associations but still repre- sented the bailiwick of a noble family.

Pertinent Literature

Adcock, F. E. "Draco," in *The Cambridge Ancient History*. Vol. IV. New York: The Macmillan Company, 1930.

This classic article represents, more or less, the traditional view of the story of Draco. The issuance of the code is pictured as an attempt, in the confusion over the sacrilege of murdering Cylon's followers, to standardize the practice of judges.

Since Solon's legislation overshadowed Draco's it is difficult to disentangle the latter's contribution to the later code. However, Adcock rightly sees that Draco's legislation on homicide was prompted by the problem of the blood feud. This popular pastime was rooted in the conviction that a murdered man's spirit cried for revenge and adversely affected the fertility of the soil until it secured satisfaction. So vital was this revenge that along with his father's possessions a son also inherited the obligation to punish the murderers of his father.

Adcock states that in Homeric society the state had no direct interest in murder; it remained a "diplomatic incident between families." In Greece proper, however, he thinks that the Delphian shrine taught after the eighth century that a killing defiled not only the perpetrator but also his city as well until it was purified. The state had to anathematize even an unknown killer to clear the land of guilt, and eventually it had to take an interest in a man claiming innocence, because the killing of a guiltless man in a blood feud obviously left the guilty party still at large to blight the land. Thus the Areopagus provided a sanctuary where those claiming innocence could be heard.

Adcock believes that it was at this point, for some inexplicable reason, that a moral judgment was first made regarding murder. If a would-be killer were himself killed in the assault, he would be to all intents and purposes his own murderer so that his spirit could have no just claim for vengeance. So arose the moral concept of justifiable homicide which Draco's code respects. Draco, however, went on to designate unintentional homicide, which was judged at the sanctuary of Pallas. The kinsmen of the dead man were required to leave such a person alone to go into exile until he was pardoned by the family or the dead man's phratry. This arrangement, claims Adcock, represents a "compromise between the anger of the dead man, the guilt of blood, and moral ideas of a more enlightened time."

Draco allows the family to prosecute for homicide or in the absence of a relative, the phratry of the deceased. The board of fifty-one "jurors" mentioned in connection with the code seems, in Adcock's opinion, to constitute a new Draconian court. He believes that these "jurors", former priests of sanctuary tribunals, were secularized and even organized as itinerant justices to adjudicate the cases of suppliants.

In short, Draco's murder laws represent to Adcock a more enlightened morality on one hand and "a more active intervention by the state on the other." Draco's code became a permanent part of Athenian jurisprudence, and Plato in his *Laws* incorporated Draco's statues into his model state.

Hignett, C. *A History of the Athenian Constitution to the End of the Fifth.Century B.C.* Oxford: The Clarendon Press, 1952.

In an appendix to this history of the Athenian constitution, Hignett discusses Draco's code and the ephetai or "jurors," placing special emphasis on his law pertaining to homicide. He starts with the historical fact that in the fourth century there were five separate courts dealing with cases of homicide, one of a sacral and four of a civil character. These latter four dealt with different types of homicide. The Areopagus handled cases of deliberate murder; the Palladian court tried those accused of involuntary homicide; the Delphinion court had cognizance of those responsible for accidental or justifiable manslaughter; and, finally, the court at Phreatto passed judgment on those who had been exiled for involuntary homicide and were later accused of willful murder. In a trial at Phreatto the defendant had to make his defense from a boat moored near the land in the harbor of Piraeus since he could not set foot on Attic soil.

The fifty-one ephetai mentioned by Pollux and in the inscription of 409/408 containing a copy of Draco's homicide law are generally assumed to have been jurors in the last three courts. In order to determine who these people were, Hignett examines what is known of Draco and his legislation.

In trying to ascertain the originality of Draco's murder legislation, it is relevant to ask first whether he drew up a full code of laws. Ancient writers maintain that Draco did indeed draw up a comprehensive code, the whole of which was repealed by Solon with the exception of the laws on homicide. The decree of Tisamenos, for example, ordained that Athenians should continue to use the *thesmoi* or ordinances of Draco, and the *nomoi* or laws of Solon. Since the Athenians of the fourth century ascribed their homicide laws to Draco and their other early laws to Solon, it is obvious that at least the former went back to pre-Solonian times. There is therefore no reason for not admitting the tradition that the homicide regulations were drafted by Draco. According to Atthidographers he drew them up during the archonship of Aristaechumus (621/620 B.C.). It seems likely that he was not one of the thesmothetes that year but the recipient of special legislative powers.

This idea does not carry with it the conclusion that Draco drew up a general code of laws, an honor generally ascribed to Solon. Texts adduced to prove Draco's authorship of a general code are inconclusive: "The fourth-century tradition that Draco promulgated a general code of great severity" might simply reflect "a popular memory of the severe punishments inflicted by the magistrates in the pre-Solonian period."

Even though Draco is accepted as a historical figure who first codified the rules of procedure in cases of homicide, the question remains whether he drafted into his homicide laws elements from an earlier age. This incorporation would appear to be likely if one regards the ephetai as jurors in three of the criminal courts. They cannot be identified with the old council of the Areopagus which probably tried all homicide cases in an early stage of the aristocratic period. Since the ephetai tried cases of lesser importance than those still reserved for the Areopagus in later centuries, "it is possible that the ephetai were originally appointed to relieve the Areopagus, which as a council had other duties as well, of some of the burden of jurisdiction." Such delegation of authority probably took place before Draco formulated his homicide laws, since the copy made in 409/408 presupposes the existence of the ephetai and, apparently, the different sites of their courts. Upon such considerations the originality of Draco is diminished insofar as he is merely reorganizing existing discrimination in kinds of murders already attended to by different courts.

There remains the question how much Draco's provisions were modified after his lifetime. Buried in Solon's code as Draco's laws are, it is impossible to tell. — *M.J.C.*

Additional Recommended Reading

Bonner, Robert J., and Gertrude Smith. *The Administration of Justice from Homer to Aristotle.* Chicago: University of Chicago Press, 1930-1938. 2 vols. A comprehensive study of Greek courts, with frequent references to Draco's legislation.

Greenidge, A. H. J. *A Handbook of Greek Constitutional History.* New York: The Macmillan Company, 1896. A clear presentation of the many problems connected with Greek laws, including those of Draco, and constitutions.

Jones, J. Walter, *The Law and Legal Theory of the Greeks. An Introduction.* Oxford: The Clarendon Press, 1956. A study somewhat skeptical about the code of laws commonly ascribed to Draco.

Stroud, Ronald Sidney. *The Law of Drakon on Homicide.* University of California, Berkeley, PhD., 1965. Ann Arbor: University Microfilms, Inc. This doctoral dissertation favors the acceptance of much of the ancient data.

Tod, Marcus N. *A Selection of Greek Historical Inscriptions to the End of the Fifth Century B.C.* Oxford: The Clarendon Press, 1946. A reproduction of the Greek text of, and brief commentary on, the marble stele erected in 409/408 containing the text of Draco's law on homicide.

Linforth, Ivan M. *Solon the Athenian.* Berkeley: University of California Press, 1949. A study involving Draco in the background of the Solonian code.

CELEBRATION OF THE ELEUSINIAN MYSTERIES

Type of event: Religious: solemnification of fertility cult
Time: before 600 B.C.
Locale: Eleusis, a small town northwest of Athens

Principal personages:
DEMETER, Greek goddess and principal figure in the
Eleusinian myth
PERSEPHONE, her daughter
TRIPTOLEMUS, Greek prince to whom Demeter taught the
arts of agriculture
PISISTRATUS, tyrant of Athens 560-528
CIMON (fl.480-449), Athenian general
PERICLES (fl.460-429), Athenian statesman

Summary of Event

In classical antiquity there were many secret cults or "mysteries" each of which characteristically required initiatory rites before full knowledge of its beliefs and liturgy would be revealed. Demeter and Dionysos were the deities with whom the most famous ancient Greek mysteries were associated, and the Eleusinian Mysteries, celebrated in honor of Demeter and her daughter Persephone, were perhaps the most renowned of all. The name is derived from Eleusis, a town some fourteen miles northwest of Athens, its acropolis facing the Bay of Salamis and dominating the rich Thriasian plain. It is with this city that one of the principal myths of antiquity became associated some time in the latter half of the second millenium B.C.; as a result, Eleusis became famous and wealthy as the site of a major sanctuary.

According to the early Greek poets, the goddess Demeter was a daughter of Kronos and Rhea. Like many of the Hellenic female deities she was a fertility goddess, her province being the care of agriculture in general, specifically of grain. By Zeus she had a daughter Persephone, known in the earliest myths as Kore, the Greek word for "maiden." One day as the beautiful Persephone was picking flowers, according to one version, in the lush fields of Sicily, Hades, god of the underworld, violently carried her off to make her queen of his realm. Her mother searched for the maiden all over the world, even, in one version of the story, lighting torches by the fires of the volcano Etna in order to continue her quest by night. In her wanderings she eventually came to Eleusis where in her weariness she was received hospitably and was entrusted with the care of the prince's newborn son, whose name is given as Demophon in the Homeric hymn but alternately as Triptolemus. Demeter decided to reward the hospitality of her hosts by holding the infant in the hearth fire to make him immortal. However, she was interrupted in the process and forced to admit her divinity in explanation of this strange act. The

158

people of Eleusis were ordered to erect a temple in her honor.

Since the crops and fruits withered and the earth became barren because of Demeter's sorrow and neglect, Zeus ordered Hades to release his captive queen. Hades agreed, but before Persephone left he gave her some pomegranate seeds to eat. Unaware that they would make impossible her permanent return from the underworld, she ate them. Consequently while Persephone might spend eight months of each year with her mother, she had to pass the remaining four in the company of Hades. The restriction could not tarnish Demeter's joy at seeing her daughter once more; in celebration she rewarded the Eleusians by teaching them the rites by which she was to be worshiped thereafter. According to one version of the tale, she subsequently dispatched Triptolemus to go about the world teaching the arts of agriculture to mankind.

Upon Persephone's return to earth the barren fields had blossomed anew, and therefore the myth of Demeter and Persephone may be said to symbolize the annual turn of the seasons from spring growth to summer harvest, and thence to the sterile time of late fall and winter. More specifically it can refer to the fact that in Greece the seed grain was stored in the ground from the harvest in June until the sowing in October when it was brought forth for the festival of planting.

Originally the Eleusinian Mysteries were an agrarian cult celebrated in the fall at the time of sowing. After the union of Eleusis with Athens some time before 600 B.C., the festival of the Greater Mysteries included a proces-sion from Athens to the sanctuary in Eleusis. The Athenian tyrant Pisistratus not only encouraged the mysteries but subsidized them so that they could be celebrated with great formal and official pomp. Occasionally the state even paid the initiation fees for poor candidates. The rites began in the evening in the Telesterion or Great Hall of the Mysteries, but because the cult practices themselves were carefully guarded secrets throughout antiquity, almost nothing is known about them. The chief priest displayed certain holy objects, as indicated by his Greek name *hierophant,* meaning one who shows something sacred; a chorus recited and chanted various hymns; and ritual acts were performed. For the participants in the liturgy there appear to have been three stages: initiation, preliminary confirmation, and final revelation. While some early Church Fathers, notably Clement of Alexandria, report that sexual objects were uncovered in the final stage, it is more likely that the ultimate manifestation of the mysteries was an ear of wheat, which could well embody the wonder of the changing seasons as well as food and famine, or life and death. However, the actual content of the final revelation remains unknown.

The main building of the sanctuary of Demeter at Eleusis was the Telesterion, a large structure some one hundred and seventy feet square at its base. Its roof was supported by forty-two columns, with banks of steps on all sides of the interior which perhaps served as seats. Here the *mystai* or initiates observed the sacred rites on the floor in front of them. The building was a final evolution of a first structure which had been small and rectangular and a second which had been square but only one fourth the size of the last building, which was designed and built by the architect Ictinus in the Periclean age. Other structures in the area were the Temple of Artemis Propylaea, the Greater and Lesser Propylaea, all of Roman times, and numerous altars and steles with inscriptions and dedications within the sanctuary proper.

Excavations at Eleusis were begun in 1882 by the Greek Archaeological Society, and have continued at varying times until the present.

Pertinent Literature

Mylonas, George E. *Eleusis and the Eleusinian Mysteries.* Princeton: Princeton University Press, 1961.

This book sums up the archaeological research of recent decades on the site of Eleusis, and also examines what is known about the mysteries celebrated there in antiquity. After an introductory chapter on the myth of Demeter and Persephone, a chronological study of the sanctuary follows: early history from the Middle Helladic Period to the seventh century B.C.; the Pisistratean work of the sixth century; construction in the time of Cimon and Pericles in the fifth century; and later building in the fourth century, the Hellenistic Period, and the Roman Period. These chapters, and the one following on the art and artifacts found at Eleusis, will be of special interest to those seeking to study the evidence of the excavations of the great sanctuary and its environs. But the last two chapters will have a wider appeal, for they consider the Eleusinian Mysteries themselves together with speculations by the Church Fathers and modern scholars concerning the nature of the rituals. The book concludes with a glossary of ancient Greek terms a selected bibliography, an index, and eighty-eight illustrations, including a map, plans, and photographs of the site.

The Greater Mysteries were held every year for eight days in the month of Boedromion, which corresponds to September and early October in our calendar. The sacred activities began in Athens on the first day of the festival when the cult herald proclaimed to the people an invitation to take part in the ceremonies and be initiated. The only ones banned were homicides, those otherwise unclean, and foreigners who could not speak Greek. On the next day all the acceptable initiants went down to the sea, each with a sacrificial pig, in order to purify himself and the animal in the sea waters. Upon the return to the city the pigs presumably were sacrificed. Nothing specific is known about the third day, but it probably centered on a formal ceremony for the two goddesses in their temple, the Eleusinion, situated below the Acropolis on the north side. The fourth day honored Asclepius, the god of healing, and finally on the fifth day a great procession of priests and priestesses, officials, initiants, and their escorts set out for Eleusis, fourteen miles away. Because of the distance the latter part of the journey had to be completed by torchlight. On the sixth day, after resting and feasting, the initiation rites began in the evening with the drinking of the *kykeon*, a mixture of meal, water, and mint. Though nothing can be stated with certainty about the ritual within the sanctuary, it seems likely that it consisted of three parts: a sacred pageant representing the story of Demeter and Persephone; a liturgical commentary on the significance of each part of that story; and the revealing of sacred objects to the newly initiated. The author maintains that the nature of these objects remains unknown, but that they could not be sheaves of wheat or a phallic image. Completion of all ritual activity came on the evening of the seventh day, and on the eighth there were libations and rites for the dead.

The return of the pilgrims to Athens occupied the ninth day, and on the tenth the Athenian Council of the Five Hundred convened in the Eleusinion to receive a formal report on the celebration. The Eleusinian Mysteries were celebrated in this manner in Attica for more than nine hundred years until they were suppressed by the Christians and the sanctuary was destroyed by the Visigoths in the late fourth century A.D.

Guthrie, W. K. C. *The Greeks and Their Gods.* Boston, Massachusetts: Beacon Press, 1950, and in paperback.

This excellent and perceptive study covers many aspects of Greek religion from its formative situation in Minoan-Mycenaean times to the influence of philosophy on it in the fourth century B.C. But, as the author states, the book does not seek to be a general manual of Greek mythology or religion, but aims rather to serve as a kind of religious companion to the Greek classics. After an introductory history of scholarship on the subject, the early chapters are devoted to the chief Olympian deities, to the gods and men as they are treated in Homer, and to the contributions of Ionian culture in the pre-Classical age. Next follow lengthy treatments on the god Dionysos, the advocate of emotional release, and on Apollo, the champion of law and order. The last third of the work discusses the chthonian or underworld spirits and the mystery religions, including the Eleusinian, which so greatly influenced the hopes and fears of the ordinary Greek. The study concludes with a short examination of the influence of the philosophies of Plato and Aristotle on Greek religion.

At the heart of this study is the delineation of two conflicting themes in Hellenic belief: the one which notes a great and unbridgeable gap between man and deity, between mortal and immortal; and the other which observes the closeness of man to the gods, and man's need to seek and join with the divine. The Olympian and Homeric ethical systems support the former viewpoint and consider it arrogant or hubristic for man to seek union with the divine, whereas the rites of the chthonian spirits recognize the validity of that quest. To be sure, these opposing views coexisted throughout the Classical Age and in some instances they were even interwoven. Yet there were also some noteworthy distinctions between the worship of Olympians and of chthonians which were generally observed: for the former the altar was high-built, the animal victim commonly a white ox, the temple the familiar Classical type, and the time of sacrifice morning; but for the latter the altar was low or even a pit or trench, the victim black and either a ram or pig or offerings of the fruits of the earth, the shrine a cave or sanctuary, and the time late evening or the dead of night. To some degree the Olympian religion represented the beliefs of the dominant group of kings and nobles in the Mycenaean social structure of the later Bronze Age as described by Homer. The gods of this dispensation were inaccessible to the ordinary man and his needs, and the afterlife was generally considered with abhorrence as a kind of shadow existence that could never replace the joys of life on earth. On the other hand the emotional and mystical forms of religion, with their multitude of cults to fertility daemons and their promises of ultimate bliss, were especially fostered by subjugated farming classes whose daily lives, beliefs, and folk practices constantly touched upon the province of these spirits. Chief among these were the Eleusinian deities, and Guthrie stresses the point that the worship of Demeter and Persephone tended to see the goddesses not only as involved in the fertility of the land but also in the immortality of the human soul. To guarantee this latter state, men underwent purification and initiation rites which in some way suggested that the mortal believer was raised thereby to divine estate. — *K.H.*

Additional Recommended Reading

Nilsson, M. P., and J. H. Croon. "Mysteries," in *Oxford Classical Dictionary*. Oxford: The Clarendon Press, 2nd ed., 1970. An excellent summary on this aspect of ancient Greek religion.

Rose, H. J. *A Handbook of Greek Mythology*. London: Methuen and Co. Ltd., 1958. A standard work containing basic information on Demeter, Persephone, and other deities.

APPEARANCE OF ZOROASTRIAN DITHEISM

Type of event: Religious: development of a new faith
Time: c.600 B.C.
Locale: Persia

Principal personages:
ZOROASTER (660-590), founder and prophet of the new faith
VISHTASPA, a prince in Media c.610

Summary of Event

Ditheism, or belief in two gods as in Zoroastrianism, attempts to provide a satisfactory answer to one of the serious problems of religion: the explanation of evil. To some extent the concept of a dual godhead has penetrated both Judaism and Christianity. The god of darkness or evil found its way into the former in attenuated fashion in the form of Satan. The Dead Sea Scrolls, for instance, speak of the war between the sons of light and the sons of darkness. In Christianity the force of evil becomes the Devil.

Zoroastrian ditheism was a theological position reached only with difficulty. The religion was developed by Indo-Europeans who wandered into the Iranian Plateau about 2000 B.C., and reflects to a great extent the environment of the old religion prior to the invasion.

Zoroaster himself may have been born in the mid-seventh century, the son of a landed proprietor. His name seems derived from a Greek corruption of the old Iranian word Zarathustra possibly meaning "one who plows with camels" or "one whose camels are old." At the age of twenty he left home to ponder religious questions, and after ten years was rewarded with a series of revelationary visions in which an angel called him to ascend a mountain as a disembodied soul to meet with the old Iranian god Ahura Mazda and his heavenly host. In eight days he was fully instructed as the god's new prophet in the doctrines and duties of true religion. For ten more years his preaching bore no tangible results beyond the conversion of his cousin, even though, like Amos, he inveighed against religious inadequacies and the social injustices visited upon peasant and herdsman.

His first important conversion, of a prince named Vishtaspa, came at a crucial time when he needed support in his struggle with the Magi, the entrenched priests of the traditional cults. When Vishtaspa contributed his influence to the new religion, the whole court was converted. For the next twenty years Zoroaster propagated the new faith, but its greatest success came only after his death at seventy-seven, victim of an assassin in a religious uprising. Darius might have been the first Achaemenid converted. In general, however, the Persian kings were never militant supporters of the religion.

Zoroaster's message was reasonably simple: he was Ahura Mazda's prophet sent to teach religion and the end of the world. Worship was to be directed toward this one god who brought everything into existence and who in a final apocalyptic event would crush evil forever and establish right and truth. Ahura Mazda was said to express his will through the Holy Spirit, *Spenta Mainyu,* and various "modes" of divine action, such as Good Thought, Power, Prosperity, Piety, and Immortality. Just how Zoroaster envisaged these modes is difficult to say. As forces in their own right, as good *genii* or angels, or as personalized abstractions, they represented a compromise with the local polytheism, a concession which makes it debatable whether Zoroaster was altogether a monotheist. While Ahura Mazda was supreme, he was not unopposed. A polarity implicit in creation characterized all existence. Over against Right, *Asha,* stood the Lie, *Druj*; Truth was confronted with Falsehood, Life with Death, the Good Spirit by the Bad.

Zoroaster's cardinal principle of ethics taught that each man's soul was the seat of war between good and evil. At creation Ahura Mazda gave each man freedom to determine his own actions and power to choose between right and wrong. Good men would naturally accept the true religion, while the evil, especially those who continued to practice old rites, would reject it. The old local sacrifices were eliminated and rituals were purged of what Zoroaster termed magic and idolatry. The sacred fire was kept, but only as a symbol of Ahura Mazda and not as an object of worship in itself. Zoroaster believed in individual judgment after death, with the state of the soul remaining

fixed until a general resurrection at the end of the world when evil would be destroyed forever. Those whose record of evil was greater than their good report would dwell in the House of the Lie, Zoroaster's Hell, while the righteous would go to the House of Song, or Paradise.

With the popularization of Zoroastrianism, more compromises entered into its original "monotheistic" theology. Moreover, the old Magi succeeded in molding a syncretistic system out of Zoroaster's teaching and the old Iranian polytheism. Old Arian gods were raised to a prominence far greater than the old modes. Thus Mithra was elevated along with a female figure, Anhita, the Spotless One, a counterpart of Ishtar, the goddess of fertility, to form a trinity: Ahura Mazda, Mithra and Anhita. Zoroaster himself was raised from human status to that of a godlike personage. His coming was said to have been foretold for three thousand years. His birth became miraculous through Ahura Mazda's intervention, and he became celebrated as an outstanding thaumaturg.

Spells and formulas again became popular to ward off evil, and ceremonial purity took more and more precedence over inward regeneration. Eventually Zoroastrianism became a religion of a book, the *Avesta,* a miscellany without inner cohesion and a remnant of a far larger literature that has since disappeared. After the *Gathas,* or Hymns, of Zoroaster, writing became more and more legalized and complex.

Eventually in the Sassanian period, the ditheism developed fully. The many contending gods were again demoted, while a god of evil rose in importance to contend Ahura Mazda's monopoly. While Zoroaster himself had spoken bitterly, but not very tangibly, of the evil spirit Shanitin or Satin, his successors rendered it more concrete in the form of an almost equal opponent of Ahura Mazda, the archfiend Ahariman, the cause of darkness and evil straining to nullify every good Ahura Mazda arranged whether by killing frost in winter, excessive heat in summer, snakes, locusts, or by disbelief and death.

The impact of Zoroastrianism on the West is difficult to assess. The old Iranian god Mithra, greatly "Zoroastrianized," became popular in the early Roman Empire; Gnosticism, and Manichaeism appear to owe some debt to the Zoroastrianism of the Sassanian period.

Pertinent Literature

Zaehner, R. C. *The Teachings of the Magi.* New York: The Macmillan Company, 1956.

While Zaehner is not particularly interested in early Zoroastrian history, he does try to establish the date of Zoroaster's birth. The one traditional date assigned to him is 248 years before Alexander, or 588 B.C., a date which supposedly marks Zoroaster's conversion of Vishtaspa, a bona fide prince of ancient Chorasmia earlier than the Achaemenids. Since the prophet was forty-two at the time, this would place his birth at 630 B.C. This reckoning of Zaehner differs, of course, from the chronology supported by other scholars.

Zaehner tries to reconstruct what might be called classical Zoroastrianism, and hence deals with the main tenets of the religion as developed and practiced during the Sassanian period (from A.D. 226 to 650). The author considers Zoroastrianism most ideally studied as a dualist orthodoxy under Shapur II in the fourth century A.D., when Zoroaster's evolving system was reduced to a compact theology. The surviving Pahlevi books, that is, books written in the language of Sassanian Persia, dealing with hymns, liturgies, rules of purification, and priestly law, amply testify to the character of the Zoroastrianism of this later period.

Zoroaster's concerns were those of many higher religions: the nature of God and the Devil, the genesis of the universe, the reasons for imperfections in creation, man's place in the universe, ethics, sacraments and sacrifices, the fate of the soul after death, and the vision of last things. The problem of evil was central. While the fundamental dualist doctrine that a good god could not be responsible for evil was never threatened, there did exist in Sassanian times a heretical sect which sought to derive the two principles of good and evil from a common nonmoral and androgynous father, Infinite Time. Arabic heresiographers speak of this heterodox sect as Zurvaniyya or Zurvanite, from Zurvan, the Pahlevi name for the Genius of Time. Teachings of the sect survive, often camouflaged, in the Pahlevi books.

The surviving sacred books of the Zoroastrians, the *Avesta,* represent a mere fragment of their holy literature. Its threefold division is indispensable for an understanding of the liturgy. The first section, the *Gathas,* songs or odes, have been only partially translated and proclaim the doctrines enunciated by Zoroaster himself. In the *Yashts,* very similar to that of the great hymn cycle of the earliest Hindu Aryans, the *Rig Veda,* sacrificial hymns are addressed to various gods and demigods often under the same name. This corpus reflects a polytheism against which Zoroaster himself had originally rebelled. Zaehner believes that the state of religion represented in the *Yashts* denotes a repaganization of the Zoroastrian reform when the old traditional Iranian religion fought its way back. Finally, there is the *Vendidad* containing regulations against demons and ritual impurity.

In the later Pahlevi books there is a return to the spirit of the *Gathas.* The old Ahura Mazda, whose name developed into Ohrmazd, becomes the principle of good while Ahariman is the principle of evil. The modes with which Zoroaster surrounded his supreme deity and the old gods are now simply created spirits subservient absolutely to the one Creator-God. Ahariman is supreme in his own realm of evil, master of all demons which he has created. During the period discussed by Zaehner's work, Zoroaster's dualism was systematized into a compact theology.

Duchesne-Guillemin, Jacques. *Symbols and Values in Zoroastrianism.* New York: Harper and Row Publishers Incorporated, 1966.

While Zaehner deals primarily with Zoroastrianism in Sassanian times, Duchesne-Guillemin traces the religion through its entire history and analyzes its confrontation with other faiths and cultural systems. He would remind his readers that Zoroastrianism remains an active faith to this day with some 115,000 devotees living primarily in Bombay and neighboring towns. Called Parsees because of their Persian origin, these Zoroastrians constitute a well-defined community outside Hinduism. These and some ten thousand Zoroastrians remaining in Iran keep the once great religion alive, distinguished still by its distinctive practices such as the cult of fire through the rituals of which man still expresses his close relationship to the deity and the cosmos. Since Zoroastrian ethics place a premium on the maintenance of life and the fight against evil, the former through earning a living and procreation, the latter by fighting against demons and whatever beings, man or animal, that belong to them, it is readily distinguished from Buddhism in rejecting a universal and unqualified respect for al life. These Zoroastrian enclaves, however, are in danger of extinction. Just as Zoroastrianism in the tenth century was threatened by forced conversion tactics in Islamic lands to such an extent that it had strength only to survive and not to renew itself, Zoroastrianism is now threatened by the new socialism, or state capitalism, in India which, in attacking private fortunes, penalizes Zoroastrians who as a rule have been successful in commerce. In addition, Zoroastrian communal schools are threatened with extinction or incorporation into the state system, a step toward the absorption of Zoroastrians into the melting pot of the new India.

Duchesne-Guillemin recalls that Zoroastrianism has gone through a complex development. Its founder had first to strike down all but one of the many gods he found in Persia. The diversified powers in local vogue such as Discipline, Retribution, War, Good, and Spirit, had to be subordinated to the sovereign Ahura Mazda as semidivine intermediary beings. After his death, Zoroaster's delicate system broke down as the old polytheism reasserted itself, establishing these subordinate forces as distinct deities so well defined that they were thought of even as being of different sexes. In the end Ahura Mazda again made good his claims to sovereignty as the god of all good, leaving to Ahariman the task of accounting for evil. — *J.R.R.*

Additional Recommended Reading

Dhalla, M. N. *History of Zoroastrianism*. New York: Oxford University Press, 1938. Probably the best book of a Parsee on his own religion.

Ghirshman, R. *Iran from the Earliest Times to the Islamic Conquest*. Harmondsworth, Middlesex: Penguin Books, 1954. An attempt to set the development of Zoroastrianism in its historical perspective.

Duchesne-Guillemin, J. *The Western Response to Zoroaster*. Oxford: The University Press, 1958. An excellent review of scholarly opinions.

Moulton, J. H. *Early Zoroastrianism*. London: Williams and Norgate, 1913. A dependable general discussion.

Zaehner, R. C. *The Dawn and Twilight of Zoroastrianism*. London: Weidenfeld and Nicholson, 1961. A study dealing with the entire history of Zoroastrianism.

Jackson, A. V. W. *Zoroastrian Studies*. New York: The Macmillan Company, 1928, and New York: AMS Press, 1965. A cautious study emphasizing the continuity in the development of Zoroastrianism.

LEGISLATION OF SOLON

Type of event: Constitutional: political and social reform
Time: c.594-580 B.C.
Locale: Athens

Principal personage:
SOLON (c.638-c.559), Athenian aristocrat

Summary of Event

At the beginning of the sixth century B.C., Athens was threatened with disaster. The aristocratic families fought among themselves for supremacy, and their struggles sometimes verged on civil war. The nobles also used their power against farmers of middle and low income in order to expand their own estates. Some poor farmers became serfs or were enslaved through debt. The resultant tendency was to diminish the class of men upon which the military strength and safety of Athens depended.

Other states had solved similar problems by resorting to tyranny, a kind of one-man benevolent despotism which tended to favor the nonaristocrats, including the poor. The great magnates of Athens, fearful lest such a tyrant arise and dispossess them, agreed to have limits set upon their power. Solon, himself a member of the aristocracy, was chosen archon about 594. In that year, and probably later as well, as special "conciliator" he brought about social and political relief by revising the laws of Athens.

His social reforms were important; he himself referred to them as the "lifting of burdens." He abolished serfdom and slavery for debt, ridding Athens of those curses once and for all. New laws on debt were enacted, though details have been lost, and in

this way the number of men eligible for military service was maintained.

Solon also appears to have considered building up Athens' commerce, possibly to provide employment for skilled foreigners such as potters and shipbuilders who were allowed to settle in Athens with the protected status of *metic* or "resident alien." How far Solon went along these lines is disputed. The tyrant Pisistratus undoubtedly did more later, so that by the end of the sixth century Athens was successfully competing with important trading states such as Aegina and Corinth.

To protect his social gains, Solon sought to strengthen political institutions through which the middle income group could at least voice its desires. The citizens were divided into four census classes based on wealth: The richest men were the *pentacosiomedimni* with an income of five hundred measures of olive oil, wine, or grain, a measure being 11.5 gallons wet or 1.85 bushels dry; next came the *hippeis* or cavalry whose farms produced three hundred measures and enabled them to keep a warhorse; then there were the *zeugitae* who plowed their land with a yoke of oxen, had an income of two hundred measures, could afford armor, and served as infantrymen; and last were the remaining

168

citizens who belonged to the lowest class of the *thetes,* the laborers or hired men.

The top three classes had certain duties and privileges in the public affairs of the city and served in the first-line field army. Only members of the two richest classes, however, could hold the office of archon, or ruler. Three archons were selected annually, each having jurisdiction over a specific sphere of public business. The *archon eponymus* had charge of internal affairs and presided over the Assembly. The *archon basileus* was responsible for the conduct of the state religion. The *archon polemarchos* commanded the army. These three officials and the other six archons called *thesmothetes* were also magistrates of the courts. Solon probably believed that only the nobility, by reason of birth and training, had sufficient knowledge and experience to carry out these important duties. The archons were, however, selected by lot by the people sitting as the *Ecclesia* or Assembly. It is disputed whether the *thetes* were members of this body. The same people differently organized were the *heliaea,* or court. All citizens now had the right of appeal to this court from a judgment handed down by one of the archons, an advantage for the poor. This right, and the right of the Assembly to examine the acceptability of candidates for archonship and to scrutinize the conduct of the magistrates in office, were safeguards of the few rights enjoyed by nonnoble Athenians. There is no reason to believe that the Assembly did more than elect the archons once a year and assent to declarations of war. There is no sure evidence that it passed laws, although it may have done so from time to time. How the laws of Solon were enacted is not known.

Solon is also said to have created an annual Council of Four Hundred whose function was to act as a steering committee for the whole Assembly. Considerable doubt has recently been cast on the existence of this body. There was certainly another council at this time, the *aereopagus,* made up of ex-archons serving for life, and it was also important. While we are unsure of its exact duties, it had some sort of power to safeguard the laws. It was also claimed in antiquity that Solon handed down a mass of detailed legislation amounting to a whole written code. It is extremely unlikely that he did, in fact, do so.

Solon's work was of great significance for Athens. He found the state dominated by a hereditary aristocracy, and he left it an aristocratic republic. The nobles had accepted limitation of their power, which gave the downtrodden peasantry a chance to develop.

Pertinent Literature

Linforth, Ivan M. *Solon the Athenian.* University of California Publications in Classical Philology, Vol. VI. Berkeley: University of California Press, 1919.

This book was written some years ago but its conclusions have stood the test of time well, and it requires amendment only on points of detail as the result of recent scholarship. Part I is a biographical essay on the Athenian statesman. Linforth cuts away the luxuriant growth of ancient tradition surrounding Solon and tries to arrive at as precise an understanding of his actual contributions to the social and political development of his country as is possible. The author stresses the importance of making a careful preliminary critique of the ancient sources before attempting to write a life of his subject, and he treats this matter in the first chapter of his work. Our most important single source is the fragmentary poetry of Solon himself. Part II of Linforth's book is a critical edition of Solon's surviving lines, with Greek text, English translation, and commentary. These fragments mention both the social reforms and the legal innovations of the statesman, but only the former are referred to in detail. The political changes are said to be only changes in the laws, an exceedingly vague statement which omits mention of the Council of Four Hundred. The first writers who came after Solon are also vague in their references to him. All that Herodotus (c.440 B.C.) says is that he made laws for the Athenians and bound them by oath to obey them for ten years. This general comment suggests that much of what we are told of Solon is later fabrication.

The same idea is confirmed by the remarks in *The Constitution of Athens* ascribed to Aristotle and written about 325 B.C. The tract gives many details concerning political reforms, including the organization of the Council of Four Hundred. This pamphlet, however, was written after the oligarchic revolution of 411 B.C. in which the nobles of Athens overthrew the democratic regime. It has been suggested subsequent to Linforth's investigation that the Solonian Council

of Four Hundred existed only in the political propaganda of the conservative revolutionaries, who sought justification for their own narrowly based Council of Four Hundred in the pretence that it had had a prototype in the days of Solon, the "Father of Athenian democracy."

Plutarch about A.D. 100 wrote a full-scale biography of Solon, replete with much detail. It is certain that this *Life* has absorbed a great deal of fiction. Solon had come to be thought of as one of the Seven Wise Men of Greece, and as such had many clever, sagacious, and witty sayings passed off under his name by later men. Such remarks Plutarch used in his obviously fictitious *Dinner of the Seven Wise Men,* and it is extremely likely that most of the details he gives in the *Life* rest on no firmer foundation than the elegant remarks made at that imaginary dinner conversation. In fact, ancient sources for Solon's life become fuller the further they are removed from the hero's time. Short of our finding fresh, contemporary evidence of his work, Solon must remain something of a shadowy figure. It is possible that some of the reforms attributed to him were really the work of the tyrant Pisistratus, who died in 528 B.C., or even of other Athenians who are known to us only as names. In ancient times reputations of famous men sometimes grew by absorbing deeds actually performed by others. For example, the famous conqueror King David was credited well before the time of Christ with the composition of the whole canonical book of Psalms, a case of authorship no scholar would care to defend today.

Legislation of Solon

French, A. *The Growth of the Athenian Economy*. London: Routledge and Kegan Paul, 1964.

This recent book examines the development of the farming and commercial sectors of the Athenian economy in the fifth and fourth centuries B.C. French opens with a picture of the economic life of Athens in the seventh century, when it was almost entirely agricultural, and then traces the changes which broke down the traditional, aristocratic order in the time of Solon and Pisistratus. These changes came about through the rise of trade and manufacturing in Attica, for by the middle of the sixth century, Athens was well on her way to becoming a center of commerce.

Ancient trade differed sharply from modern. Nowadays, an American merchant finds a market for his goods by resorting to the telephone or by media advertising. No such convenient technical means were, of course, available to the Greeks, so that an ancient merchant usually had to go away from his source of supply to find customers. It was, therefore, a great advantage for sellers and buyers to have commonly recognized places where both could congregate, and for such purposes cities like Aegina and Corinth were popular in early Greek times until Athens was able to compete successfully with them for two good reasons.

First, she had rich deposits of silver, which assured the incoming merchant of a valuable return cargo, if only of coined silver. So far as Solon's economic policies are concerned, French hesitates to follow recent scholarship on the origins of Attic coined silver. Insofar as Solon's

economic policies are concerned, agrees with the older view, which credits Solon with a reform of the currency. Before his time, according to *The Constitution of Athens,* the Athenian monetary system had been based on the heavy Aeginetan weight standard, and Solon changed it to the lighter Euboïc standard. This shift made it easier for Athenian and foreign merchants to trade with one another, since large states like Corinth and Samos were also on the Euboïc standard.

Second, there was the rise of manufacturing at Athens, carried out in part by attracting skilled *metics* to settle there. Evidence of Solon's influence in this field is, French thinks, to be found in the sudden increase of exports of Attic black-figured pottery to the northern Aegean and western Greece in the early sixth century. *Metics* certainly brought with them both industrial and commercial skills, including contacts with important merchants, and such contacts must have been at least as important in ancient times as they are today. As a result, there was the growth of an urban proletariat in the workshops and docks of the rising harbor towns of Attica, and of a commercial middle class. The effect was the gradual decline in the relative importance of the farmers, and by the late fifth century the urban population, "the nautical mob" as Plato called them, dominated both the economic and the political scene at Athens. Rural aristocrats such as Cimon and Pericles were shouldered aside by merchants and manufacturers from the city, such as Cleon and Cleophon.

French's book is packed with information, and his knowledge of recent scholarly work is extensive. His picture of the crowded, noisy, unsanitary, poverty-ridden, quarrelsome conditions of the average citizen living in the city of Athens is a valuable corrective to the romanticised version of life which some books present: the gentle citizens at leisure discussing, on a sunny afternoon, the latest contributions of poet and philosopher. — *S.K.E.*

Additional Recommended Reading

Woodhouse, William J. *Solon the Liberator*. London: Oxford University Press, 1938. Reprinted in paperback by Octagon Books, New York. Goes deeply into the social and economic problems with which Solon had to contend.

Kraay, C. M. "The Archaic Owls of Athens: Classification and Chronology," in *Numismatic Chronicle*. Volume 16 (1956), pp. 43 ff. Argues that the introduction of coinage at Athens took place after the time of Solon.

Freeman, Kathleen. *The Work and Life of Solon*. London: H. Milford, 1926. A survey of the statesman's reforms.

RISE OF PHILOSOPHY

Type of event: Philosophical: emergence of rational cosmological speculation
Time: c.580 B.C.
Locale: Miletus, an Ionian seaport in Asia Minor

Principal personages:
THALES OF MILETUS (c.640-c.548), philosopher
ANAXIMANDER OF MILETUS (c.610-?), Ionian philosopher
ANAXIMENES OF MILETUS (fl.585-524), Ionian philosopher
XENOPHANES OF COLOPHON (c.570-c.475), Ionian poet and sage

Summary of Event

Philosophical speculation, the posing of questions and answers concerning the nature of man and the universe in a spirit consciously liberated from a mythological framework, had its beginnings in the first half of the sixth century B.C. in the Ionian Greek seaport of Miletus. The intellectual atmosphere was clearly conductive to such speculation: far-traveling Ionian merchants were in contact with distinctly different cultural traditions of both Greece and the Near East; a skeptical, curious, inventive, and pragmatic mind already characterized the Homeric epic hero Odysseus, whose adventures, although situated in the Mycenaean era, reflected the attitudes of Ionian bards and the circles entertained by them. Individualism in thought and in action found expression in early Ionian poetry, and it was in Ionia that the posing and investigation of concrete questions concerning history and geography found its natural vehicle in a prose aptly termed *historie,* literally "questioning" or research. The attitudes underlying Ionian philosophical speculation found explicit expression in poems by Xenophanes of Colophon in the sec-

ond half of the century which said: Men learn the truth about man, nature, and the gods not through divine revelation but through progressive human discovery; dogmatic claims of knowledge by any man have no validity; Homeric and Hesiodic theology is unworthy of acceptance because it is patently anthropomorphic and also because it is morally unacceptable.

Despite the clear break from the mythical view of the universe and the gods represented by Hesiod's *Theogony,* Ionian cosmological speculation remains in the same intellectual tradition. From Hesiod the Ionians inherited the assumption of a rational order of nature, and used the metaphors employed by Hesiod to express an understanding of this order: organism, state, and moral maturation. The Ionians spoke of the world as *physis,* an animate, growing organism; they spoke of a *cosmos* and its laws; and Anaximander even spoke of a judicial process strictly governing the emergence and dissolution of finite natural phenomena in terms of punishment for exceeding fixed boundaries of existence. Finally, although mythological expression and person-

173

al gods had no place in their speculative systems, the Ionians each presented a cosmogony which may be
said to be conceptually derivative from
the theogonical form of Hesiod's poem.

The problem confronted by the
Milesian school was that of permanence and change. Regarding the ever-
changing phenomena of nature, they
sought to answer first of all the question: what substance within nature
is primary, the *arche*, chronologically
original in the cosmogonic process,
and fundamental as a real substance
of which all substances are but temporary formal manifestations? Then
they attempted to explain the process
of transformation by which the primary substance has differentiated itself into secondary substances and by
which these have coöperated to form
the phenomenal order of nature.

The question of the primary substance was normally answered by
identifying it with earth, air (or at
that date, mist), fire, or water, each
of which was thought to constitute
substantially the concentric spheres
of the visible world: a solid central
mass enveloped by overlaying shells
of liquid, gas, and ethereal fire (sun,
moon, stars, and other heavenly bodies). Thales, the first of the school,
identified the primary substance with
water; Anaximenes with air; Heraclitus of Ephesus, whose system is
loosely derivative from the Milesian
systems at the end of the century, with
fire. Anaximander of Miletus, chronologically intermediate between Thales
and Anaximenes, postulated as the
primary substance an undifferentiated

stuff, qualitatively and quantitatively,
which he called "the Boundless"
(apeiron) and out of which all natural
phenomena emerge as distinct entities
and into which they dissolve again.

The process of differentiation of
the primary substance is analogous to,
perhaps even suggested by, the emergence in Hesiod's *Theogony* of paired
sexual opposites which mate and give
birth to further aspects of the divine,
natural, and human order. In the cosmology of Anaximander, the primary
opposites, the hot and the cold or the
moist and the dry, emerged originally
from "the Boundless" and these opposites, by a process of rarefaction or
condensation in combination with each
other, yield the primary elements:
fire is hot and dry, air is hot and wet,
water is cold and wet, and earth is
cold and dry.

The achievement of the first philosophers must be measured by their
methods and assumptions rather than
by the empirical validity of their cosmological schemes. They sought to
answer questions about nature without resorting to divine revelation by
speculating rationally about the world
as they experienced it. Dispensing with
the older concept of personal gods
governing the world in a divine political regime, they nevertheless retained
a political concept of nature as obedient to fixed laws. They thereby
established the rationalist, humanist
principle of faith that the structure and
moving principles of nature are intelligible because they are akin to the
mode of operation of the human mind.

Pertinent Literature

Cornford, F. M. *Principium Sapientiae: The Origins of Greek Philosophical Thought.* Cambridge: The University Press, 1952. Reprinted New York: Harper & Row Publishers Incorporated, 1965.

This last work of F.M. Cornford, unfinished at the time of his death and published posthumously, comprises a wealth of perceptive insights, judicious generalizations, and provocative speculations distilled from a lifetime of intense study of the Greek philosophical tradition and its setting in ancient history. While much that is in this book is speculative and perhaps in need of considerable documentation, its fundamental thesis has been clearly demonstrated: that the speculative systems of the first philosophers of Miletus, far from being empirically founded and radically new departures in the history of thought, were essentially sophisticated rationalizations of an ancient cosmogonical myth rooted in an annually celebrated ritual of the death and resurrection of the natural order of the seasons and the political order of society.

In the first half of the book, entitled "Empiricism versus Inspiration," Cornford demonstrates the dominance throughout the tradition of Greek cosmology of an intuitive, nonempirical concept of how knowledge is acquired. It is only in the medical writers that we find a fundamental opposition to dogmatic, a priori assumptions laid down as a foundation for understanding a subject and an insistence that generalizations be made only after careful observations have been carried out. Cornford believes, however, that the cosmological thinkers inherited, ultimately from primitive shamanism, a concept of a separable intelligence having direct access to a spiritual realm of truth.

The physical thinkers of Miletus were conditioned by the cosmogonical tradition even in the questions they posed: how did the present ordered pattern of natural phenomena emerge out of a primal simple state? Anaximander's cosmogony describes a primordial *apeiron,* much like the *chaos* of Hesiod's *Theogony,* out of which have emerged the primary opposites: the hot and the cold, or the moist and the dry. The former emergent pair moved to their "natural" places, the cold to a central core and the hot to a circumferential ring or shell. The cold then further differentiated into the moist and the dry and thus dry land became distinct from water. This process in Anaximander follows essentially the same cosmogonic pattern as that described in more patently mythological terms in Hesiod's *Theogony:* in the beginning a masculine sky was sundered from a feminine earth, leaving a yawning gap between them. The interaction of sky and earth was regulated by the sexual principle, *Eros,* and differentiation then proceeded by sexual pairing and generation as sea and dry land became distinct and the features of the natural order of the world became distinct. Anaximander's fire is Hesiod's sky, and the place of Hesiod's *Eros* is taken by the process of rarefaction and condensation in Anaximander's system, as water and air alternately ascend to

175

the sky in vapor and descend again to earth in rain.

Anaximander's four primary opposites, the hot, the cold, the wet, and the dry, are surely the powers dominating the recurrent cycle of the seasons, and Cornford explains the enigmatic fragment of Anaximander concerning the "penalty" paid by existing things to each other for their aggression "according to the order of time" as a description of the everlasting war of the dominant seasonal powers against each other, the successive advance of each power in turn in "unjust aggression" and its certain retreat before a new power. It is Cornford's contention that this scheme is not simply the consequence of Anaximander's observations but is derivative from Hesiod's *Theogony* and ultimately from a common pattern of myth and ritual employed at the vernal equinox of each year in early agricultural societies in order to celebrate the re-creation of the order of nature and society in a drama wherein the king enacts the roles both of the humbled and defeated old year and of the revivified and triumphant creator of the new year.

Snell, Bruno. *The Discovery of the Mind: The Greek Origins of European Thought*. Oxford: Basil Blackwell, 1953.

Apart from the nature and impact of early Greek philosophy, there arises the interesting historical question, particularly among the Greeks, why philosophy, as we know it, happened to emerge. Several of the essays in this book are pertinent to that question. Chapters 7 through 10 discuss the liberation of speculative thought from authoritarian inhibitions, the rationalization of morals, the role of simile and metaphor in the development of significant generalizations, and the part played by the structure of the Greek language in fostering abstract thought as well as inhibiting certain kinds of thought. The essay on Greek language and philosophy is especially illuminating.

Snell stresses the primary importance of the definite article, developed from an original demonstrative pronoun, in permitting the formation of high-level abstractions. Abstract nouns are a relatively late development in Greek. Snell sees their seeds in the mythical nouns (*Phobos,* "Fear" personified) in early poetry and in the figurative use of concrete nouns. These nouns refer to the area of the nonphysical, to what is animate, dynamic, or intellectual. The development of natural science depends on the recognition of a clear distinction between the physical and the nonphysical, which means that the subjective elements of experience of nature must be reduced to what can be objectively expressed: verbs and adjectives must be reduced to nouns or substantival groups. The definite article aided in this process by permitting the substantivation of adjectives and verbs. Infinitives and participles became, with the addition of the article, objects of thought which could be easily manipulated. Likewise the adjective of quality can be made a substantive and thus become subject to meaningful discourse, as "the moist" of Anaximander or "the good" of Plato.

According to Snell, the tendency,

inherent in Greek philosophical thought, to transform, for purposes of understanding, the qualitative content of an adjective and the dynamic content of a verb into simple abstract substantives ultimately became fully explicit in the thought of Democritus. Thales of Miletus developed the content of Homer's mythological concept of Ocean as the first parent into his own concept of water as an elemental substance: he transformed a mythical noun into a universalized concrete noun. Anaximander carried the process further in distinguishing as basic cosmological formative principles the primary opposites, expressed as substantival adjectives, "the moist," and the like. In Democritus the process of abstraction has reached its logical goal: the only real properties recognized as fully objective are those which can be described in quantitative, mathematical terms such as large, round, small, many, few, for example. Even the ethics of Democritus are grounded on a concept of human psychology which is itself molded on the pattern of physical nature so that the processes of the soul are motions, or fluctuations. Pleasure, the goal of moral self-regulation, is thus amenable to calculation and so, like physical nature, is to be understood in quantitative terms.

An interesting aspect of Snell's discussion is his demonstration of the inadequacy of Greek concepts of motion as a consequence of the nature of the Greek verb tenses. As these tenses express not so much time as static condition (present), simple event (aorist), or result (perfect), the Greek verb cannot adequately express the dynamic, or as Snell says, the irrational character of motion in meaningful terms. Even Heraclitus, who comes closest to the modern physical understanding of motion in terms of tension and waves, can only employ symbols of this character of nature, and so reduces motion as a concept to a static condition.

Many other factors are involved in the emergence and development of Greek philosophy, but Snell's account of the linguistic frame of this development, what he calls the "liberation of the *logos* from the language," is one of the more significant factors. — *C.W.C.*

Additional Recommended Reading

Burnet, John. *Early Greek Philosophy*. 4th ed. London: Adam & Charles Black, 1930. A study of each of the major pre-Socratic schools of philosophy, with a chapter on the relationship between science and religion.

Guthrie, W. K. C. *A History of Greek Philosophy*. Vol. I. Cambridge: The University Press, 1962. A full discussion of Greek philosophical thought prior to Parmenides.

Jaeger, Werner. *The Theology of the Early Greek Philosophers*. Oxford: The Clarendon Press, 1947. A treatment of the significant religious aspects of early Greek philosophy.

Kahn, Charles H. *Anaximander and the Origins of Greek Cosmology*. New York: Columbia University Press, 1960. A careful evaluation of sources for reconstruction of early Greek philosophy and of the character and historical significance of Anaximander's system.

Kirk, G. S., and J. E. Raven. *The Presocratic Philosophers: A Critical History with a Selection of Texts.* Cambridge: The University Press, 1960. Greek text, English translation, and critical discussion of major pre-Socratic texts.

FALL OF BABYLON

Type of event: Military: capture of the Chaldean capital by the Persians
Time: October, 539 B.C.
Locale: Babylon, south of modern Baghdad

Principal personages:
NOBONIDUS, last independent King of Babylon 556-539
NEBUCHADREZZAR, King of Babylon 605-561
CYRUS II (CYRUS THE GREAT), Achemenian King of Persia 559-c.529
BELSHAZZAR, son of Nabonidus

Summary of Event

Babylon, centrally located in the Tigris-Euphrates valley, had been the capital city of Semitic kings who ruled most of the Fertile Crescent from 1900 to 1600 B.C. Best known of these rulers was Hammurabi. During the following millenium Babylon remained a vital economic and cultural center, acknowledged as a sacred city by the Assyrians and others. After the fall of Nineveh in 612, Babylon became the capital of a new dynasty of "Chaldean" rulers, beginning with Nabopolassar who had shared with the Medes in the overthrow of Assyria. The next Chaldean king, Nebuchadrezzar, known through the Hebrew Bible as the conqueror of Jerusalem, controlled the entire Fertile Crescent and Phoenicia, even going so far as to invade Egypt. He enlarged and beautified many cities as his part in a religious revival. Even by modern standards Babylon became a huge city covering five hundred acres with paved streets, more than a thousand temples, elaborate gateways, and sumptuous palaces. For a Median princess whom he married, the King created the famous Hanging Gardens. He designed formidable defenses including a triple circle of walls around Babylon itself and earthworks connecting the two rivers in a wider fortification which enclosed many other cities.

After Nebuchadrezzar, a short period of disorder ended in 556 when an official not directly of royal descent was crowned king. Nabu-na'id, or Nabonidus to Greek historians, was over sixty years old at the time, a pious man from a priestly family who devoted much energy to religious affairs. In an attempt to make the moon-god, Sin, the supreme diety over his kingdom, he had huge temples erected for him as well as for other gods. Fascination with the past led him to dig for ancient foundation stones and to collect historical records. During much of his reign he was absent from Babylon on expeditions to Arabia and Syria, leaving affairs at home in charge of his son Bel-shar-usur, the Belshazzar of the Bible.

When Nabonidus sought to rebuild a temple of Sin in Harran, the strategic center of northern Mesopotamia then held by the Medes, he sought military aid from Cyrus, the ruler of Persia. Cyrus used Babylonian support to overcome the Medes, and then he marched westward to capture large areas of territory formerly subject to Nebuchadrezzar. By 546 his Persian troops dominated western Asia Minor and Greek cities along the eastern Mediterranean coast. Cyrus then marched eastward into India. Only Babylon remained unconquered.

In 540 the elderly Nabonidus returned to Babylon to defend his kingdom. Lacking soldiers to maintain all the fortifications developed by Nebuchadrezzar, he concentrated on a smaller area. Belshazzar was put in charge of troops guarding a defense rectangle including the cities of Opis, Sippar, Cutha, and Borsippa, which were considered essential to the defense of Babylon. Inscriptions record efforts during a four-month period to bring into Babylon the gods of other more distant cities, making these unprotected cities cultically dependent.

By propaganda Cyrus had gained the admiration or respect of certain residents in Babylonia. His later reputation for religious tolerance and mercy is known of through the Greek historian Herodotus and through Hebrew prophets who saw Cyrus as a savior of the oppressed. Some historians believe there was resentment in Babylonian cities against Nabonidus' religious programs or as a result of economic difficulties. Perhaps it was a desire to reconcile native Babylonians that led Nabonidus, at the beginning of 539, to participate at Babylon, for the first time in eleven years, in the New Year festival, an old rite involving the triumph of Marduk over forces of evil; it also purified and reinstated the king.

Also in 539 Cyrus came. With overwhelming numerical superiority and with the support of a "fifth column" within some Babylonian cities, the Persian army quickly breached the Chaldean defenses. Early in October, Cyrus attacked the city of Opis, aided by a turncoat Babylonian governor. There was rioting within the defensive perimeter, and a battle was fought in which Belshazzar was killed. Within a few more days, remaining key cities were seized or they surrendered without siege, and Nabonidus fled from Babylon.

Herodotus enlivens his account of Babylon's capture with a story that Cyrus diverted the Euphrates river into an old floodway, allowing his army to enter the city through a nearly dry river bed. The older cuneiform record simply states that "the army of Cyrus entered Babylon without a battle" to receive the acclaim of many citizens.

While the fall of the Chaldean dynasty ended the political leadership of Babylon, it did not cause the decline of the city as an economic and cultural center. Cyrus granted the area considerable autonomy and made Babylon his winter headquarters. A century later Herodotus described it as still "surpassing in splendor any city in the known world." Indeed, one result of Cyrus' victory was the economic unification of Mesopotamia with the Iranian plateau, a move which was important for later Parthian and Moslem cultures.

Fall of Babylon

Pertinent Literature

Saggs, H. W. F. *The Greatness That Was Babylon*. New York: Hawthorn Books, Inc., 1962.

This work by a professor of the University of London is one of the best recent accounts in English summarizing the Mesopotamian civilizations as a whole from their prehistoric origins down to the fall of Babylon. Written for the general reader, it lacks documentation but it is a careful work of scholarship, introducing in simple terms much of the textual and archaeological evidence, and correlating into the story various aspects of life such as economics which were neglected in most older publications.

Saggs presents not only a broad understanding of the diverse cultures in this cradle of civilization but also an unusual thesis concerning the fall of the city of Babylon at the hands of Cyrus. Many earlier scholars tended to blame the conquest of Babylonia on the weakness of Nabonidus, his preoccupation with building temples, and his antiquarian interest in archaeological research. In sharp contrast, Saggs considers that Nabonidus was "a statesman of high ability" who recognized the serious problems facing his kingdom and who took vigorous action to remedy economic and cultural difficulties. It was precisely in order to set up some unifying symbol for his many diverse subject peoples that the King honored the moon-god Sin, since the old Babylonian deity Marduk had little appeal to Arabians and Arameans. It was to deal with famine and inflation that Nabonidus was absent from Babylon for so long. He spent the time not in mystical religious retreat, as many earlier his-

torians believed, but in concluding a military expedition to Syria and Arabia, to secure trade routes replacing those now dominated by the Medes and Persians in the East and Northeast.

The final reason for the collapse of Babylon, according to Saggs, was neither ineptitude nor inaction by Nabonidus but "the presence within the city of a 'fifth column' " of discontented citizens who still regarded a Chaldean ruler as a foreigner alien to Babylon. Resenting the religious campaign which had subordinated Marduk to Sin and blaming Nabonidus for their economic difficulties, these Babylonians led by priests of Marduk enthusiastically welcomed Cyrus. The generosity with which Cyrus treated Babylon is considered by Saggs as evidence for this view. Cyrus restored the gods of the Akkadian cities to their traditional places, and in no way was the city of Babylon itself damaged.

Saggs recognizes in the conquest of Babylon not merely the fall of an unpopular dynasty but also evidence for new forces which had sprung up from cultural influences that weakened the old system of city-states. For example, alphabetic Aramaic had begun to replace the more complex Akkadian cuneiform even before 539, reducing writing from over six hundred signs to a script which utilized twenty-two letters. Furthermore, the earlier overthrow of Assyrian rule had left the Near East fragmented; Chaldean rulers had been forced to maintain a costly standing army even when Babylonian commerce had been disrupted. Saggs relates his studies of Mesopotamian social and economic developments to these political changes.

Wohil, Howard. "A Note on the Fall of Babylon," in *Journal of the Ancient Near Eastern Society of Columbia University*. Vol. 1, no. 2 (Spring, 1969), 28-38.

This article reviews in a clear and scholarly fashion historical evidence about the fall of Babylon in 539, and proposes a fresh theory about the defense strategy of Nabonidus. Since he uses the same sources which have been used by scholars since the publication in 1891 of a "Nabonidus-Cyrus Chronicle," Wohil considers it necessary to begin by surveying such sources. The Nabonidus-Cyrus Chronicle is a narrative probably drawn from records of the temple of Marduk in Babylon. Two Akkadian inscriptions, the "Cyrus Cylinder" and the "Verse Account," are of less value, in Wohil's opinion, partly because he regards them as pieces of Persian propaganda which malign Nabonidus as a weak religious fanatic and justify rule by Cyrus. He regards Greek and Hebrew sources composed much later as even less trustworthy.

Wohil is sympathetic to Nabonidus and does not indict him for weakness or disinterest. His defeat, according to the author, was caused not so much by treachery, although that was not absent, but by the difficulties involved in defending Babylon in 540-539, apart from the fact that he was compelled to use seminomadic mercenaries commanded by Babylonian nobles some of whom were of doubtful loyalty. Analyzing the defenses developed by Nebuchdrezzar, Wohil provides an excellent map which demonstrates how Nabonidus was forced to limit the area he could defend around Babylon. Opposing the view of Olmstead and others that the movement of foreign gods into Babylon was a foolish fetish on the part of Nabonidus which supposedly turned the citizenry against him, Wohil notes that the four cities within the narrowed defense perimeter which Nabonidus set up did not send their deities to Babylon. Rather, it was only from the cities outside the area which Nabonidus despaired of defending and which was to be abandoned to Cyrus, that he gathered in the gods along with their chief priests into Babylon. The simple fact is that when Cyrus captured Opis, Wohil reasons, the integrity of Nabonidus' defenses broke down, leaving the other cities, including Babylon, vulnerable.

Wohil accepts the tale of Herodotus that Cyrus drained the Tigris River as a scheme to capture Opis, but he offers no evaluation of the other story by Herodotus about the Persians diverting the Euphrates River in order to enter Babylon. Even Wohil's logical study leaves some mystery about the quick surrender of that city.

In his footnotes, the author provides a fine bibliography of scholarship during the past eighty years relating to the fall of Babylon. — *R.B.M.*

Fall of Babylon

Additional Recommended Reading

Rogers, Robert W. *A History of Babylonia and Assyria.* 6th ed. Vol. II. New York and Cincinnati: Abingdon Press, 1915. A study of the neo-Babylonian Kingdom, blaming its fall on the weakness of Nabonidus.

Roux, Georges. *Ancient Iraq.* Cleveland: World Publishing Company, 1964 and 1965. A popular survey of Mesopotamian empires, with a brief account of Cyrus's conquests.

Herodotus. *The Persian Wars.* Book I, 178-191. Translated by G. Rawlinson. New York: Random House, 1942. An ancient source on Babylon and its capture. Many other translations are available.

Olmstead, Albert T. E. *History of the Persian Empire.* Pp. 34-58. Chicago: University of Chicago Press, 1948. An account of the capture of Babylon which emphasizes the resentment of the priests against Nabonidus.

Pritchard, James B. *Ancient Near Eastern Texts Relating to the Old Testament.* Princeton: Princeton University Press, 1950, 1955. A scholarly work including Babylonian texts.

Dougherty, Raymond P. *Nabonidus and Belshazzar.* (Yale Oriental series, Researches 15.) New Haven: Yale University Press, 1929. Translations of the cuneiform sources with commentaries may be found in the works cited above.

THE TEACHING OF SECOND ISAIAH

Type of event: Religious: culmination of Old Testament prophecy
Time: c.539 B.C.
Locale: Babylonia

Principal personages:
SECOND ISAIAH (fl.c.540), "Isaiah of the Exile"
FIRST ISAIAH (fl.738-701), "Isaiah of Jerusalem"
CYRUS THE GREAT, King of the Persians 559-529

Summary of Event

A dramatic dynastic and imperial change was wrought in the Middle East when the Babylonian Empire was destroyed by Cyrus the Great in 539 B.C. Even greater from the point of view of history than the establishment of the great Persian Empire, however, was the way in which an anonymous Jewish poet posited this momentous event into the religion of the Jews, along with the destruction of the Temple and the Babylonian Exile.

Because the style and theme of this unidentified writer were similar to the Isaiah who lived two centuries earlier in Jerusalem, his writings were included in the same book of the Hebrew canon. Changes in the character of the oracles in the composite book, together with inconsistencies of the historical background and different emphases, have enabled scholars to isolate the work of the poet generally referred to as "Second Isaiah."

The message of this Second Isaiah is broader than that of Isaiah of Jerusalem. He sees the plight of the Jews as more than simple divine punishment, and he postulates a more articulated philosophy of the unity of nature and history under one God. He seems to have written his great chapters 40-55, among the most sublime in the old Testament, against a Babylonian background at the time when Cyrus the Great led the combined Persian and Median forces in a surge of new strength against the old empire of Babylon.

Yet the victorious Persians were tolerant toward the religious beliefs of the Jews. The majority of exiles preferred to remain in Mesopotamia where they had prospered, but those who desired to return to Judah were allowed to do so. There they might restore their small nation to its former narrow nationalism. Second Isaiah suggested a more sublimated intent: the Jews could elect to be agents of a new feeling of worldly-mindedness which could be the spirit of universal justice and peace for all. Second Isaiah developed a theology of survival and purpose which he based on Jewish theology but to which he added new depth.

He explained that the sufferings of the Jews arose not only from the sins of the people but also in a sublime way from the special role which God had assigned to them. The Jews had been chosen by God from among all the nations to teach all men about the one, true, universal God. The dross had been refined away during the Ex-

184

ile, and they were now to be God's ambassadors to wayward mankind, bringing his salvation to the ends of the earth.

Second Isaiah thus differed from Ezekiel, the other prophet of the Exile, who in a vision was told by God to preach that Judah and the Temple were overcome through the wickedness of the people; but the might of Babylon would pass and the innocent would return to the Holy Land, a fallen Israel arisen again as portrayed in Ezekiel's vision of the Valley of Dry Bones. Both prophets spoke primarily to their own people, but Second Isaiah also had a profound message for the whole of mankind. Yahweh was portrayed as the Lord of all history, the omnipotent ruler of the entire universe, the Judge of all nations with none other beside him.

With this message Isaiah reached the climax of Old Testament prophecy.

He comprehended and epitomized the whole prophetic tradition. Israel as a small and weak nation might never achieve the power of Persia or the splendor of Egypt, but the dramatic focus of her faith was the redemption of all mankind through suffering. Failing politically, she would succeed spiritually as the teacher of all men. Yahweh's love and power were to be made manifest to the nations through Israel.

As crucial as Second Isaiah was for Judaism, his teachings were to have a greater effect on history through Christianity, which saw in Jesus the ideal of suffering and salvation through vicarious atonement. References to the "Suffering Servant," interpreted as prophecies applying to Jesus, became one of the most important sets of Biblical verses exploited by Christians as foretelling the divine redemptive work of Christ.

Pertinent Literature

Blank, Sheldon H. *Prophetic Faith in Israel*. New York: Harper & Row Publishers Incorporated, 1958.

This study divides the prophets into pre-Exilic challengers and chastisers, and post-Exilic harbingers of comfort and hope. The position of most scholars is accepted, that there were at least three Isaiahs. Chapters 55-66 may have been composed by several poets sharing common orientation of a hopeful faith for the future when God would again intervene in history on behalf of his chosen people.

When studying Second Isaiah, it is useful to understand First Isaiah's contrasting view of history, and Sheldon Blank is chiefly concerned with describing this view. First Isaiah

sees Israel's history as showing how Yahweh educated his children, rearing them as a heavenly Father. It was essentially a dynamic, not a static, relationship; God intervened in history but demanded loyalty from his people and this loyalty had to be exhibited in deeds, not vain words.

Following this prologue of moral imperatives, the later Isaiahs offered confidence and faith after First Isaiah had spoken of rejection and reconciliation. First Isaiah denied that Israel had a covenant-hold on God, while the others saw the covenant renewed and transformed into a divine commitment. First Isaiah looked forward to the day when God would be exalted though his people perish, while the others believed that God and Israel would triumph together. First Isaiah spoke of man's defeat and doom, while the others heralded victory and salvation. Sheldon Blank sees the composite Book of Isaiah as the only one in the Bible to present these diverse explanations of the source of human confidence and success.

Second Isaiah sees corporate Israel as God's chosen Suffering Servant, fulfilling no narrow national goal but rather God's universal purpose in history. This is a view based on Second Isaiah as the author of chapters 40-56 only, other Isaiahs having contributed the final chapters of the book.

North, Christopher R. *The Suffering Servant in Deutero-Isaiah*. London: Oxford University Press, 1948.

The Hebrew philosophy of history echoes throughout the Old Testament as an insistent, admonitory formula: the pious will be rewarded and the wicked punished. Emerging from this concept of divine retributive justice is the belief, compellingly expressed by Job's three friends, that suffering is the consequence of human sin. An alternative interpretation of suffering and death is embodied in the Servant Songs of Second Isaiah (Isaiah 42:1-4; 49:1-6; 50:4-9; 52:13-53:12).

The four songs present a servant, variously identified by Biblical exegetes as the ideal Israel, as the faithful remnant in exile, or as Isaiah himself, who bears the penalties which the iniquities of others have incurred and whose vicarious suffering thus serves to restore man to God: "He was despised, and rejected by men, . . . smitten by God, and afflicted. But he was wounded for our transgressions, he was bruised for our iniquities . . . and with his stripes we are healed." (Isaiah 53:3-5). The Suffering Servant, his divine mission not restricted to the salvation of Israel, gleams forth with a celestial glow that will illumine the entire world: "I will give you as a light to the nations, that my salvation may reach to the end of the earth." (Isaiah 49:6b).

Five centuries after the Exile, the Servant Songs attained a new significance in relation to the life and death of Jesus. From Christians in the apostolic era to modern scholars such as Christopher R. North, the servant of Second Isaiah who "bore the sin of many, and made intercessions for the transgressors," (Isaiah 53:12), seemed to impart to the events at Calvary an association between the passion of Jesus and the redemptive effect of suffering and death.

Christological commentary on the Isaianic Servant was early employed as an apologetic to accommodate the anomaly of a messianic figure who must also suffer. In Acts, for example, the evangelist Philip on one of his missionary journeys is challenged by an Ethiopian eunuch to clarify a passage from the fourth Servant Song. The evangelist's response clearly reveals his personal interpretation of the Servant: "Then Philip opened his mouth, and beginning with this scripture he told him the good news of Jesus." (Acts 8:26-39; see Isaiah 53:7-8). Similar sentiments prevail elsewhere in the New Testament, as

1 Peter explains that Jesus "himself bore our sins in his body on the tree, that we might die to sin and live to righteousness. By his wounds you have been healed." (1 Peter 2:24; compare Isaiah 53:4-5).

After summarizing the various interpretations of the Servant Songs, North concludes with a Christological rendering which incorporates this basic theme of an identity between the Servant and Jesus, but which also presents the position that the Servant Songs were "primarily intended" to inspire Jesus "upon his predestined path."

There is no question that the authors of the Gospels consciously perceived Jesus as the Suffering Servant (see, for example, Matthew 8:17 or Mark 10:34), but it is difficult to determine the extent to which Jesus himself interpreted his mission in these terms. Since North believes that Isaiah's writings were divinely inspired to afford guidance for Jesus, he contends: "If Mark 1:11 is genuine, it would seem that Jesus, from the moment of his baptism, conceived of his person and mission in terms of the Old Testament Messiah, . . . and the Servant." (Compare Isaiah 42:1). One can at least conclude that the Marcan account of the Last Supper unequivocally portrays Jesus near the end of his life as uttering Isaianic-inspired rhetoric. The statements given to Jesus that "this is my blood of the covenant, which is poured out for many" and "I shall not drink again of the fruit of the vine until that day when I drink it new in the kingdom of God," (Mark 14:24-25), reflect various themes from the Servant Songs such as atonement through suffering and death (Isaiah 53: 3-8), the Servant as a covenant of the people (Isaiah 42:6), and the ultimate vindication of the Servant through his exaltation (Isaiah 52:13).

Perhaps Jesus did, as North asserts, see "his way by the light that Isaiah 53 shed upon his predestined path." Certainly later Christians invoked the Servant Songs to transform the enigma of the Cross into a soteriological triumph, an Isaianic light for all nations. — *J.R.R.*

Additional Recommended Reading

North, C. R. *The Second Isaiah: Introduction, Translation and Commentary to Chapters XL-LV*. New York: Oxford University Press, 1964. A perceptive commentary verse by verse.

Torrey, C. C. *The Second Isaiah*. Edinburgh: T. & T. Clark, 1928. Forcefully advocates a single, great spiritual author for chapters 40-66.

Rowley, H. H. *The Servant of the Lord*. Oxford: Basil Blackwell, 1965. A scholarly survey of Second Isaiah.

Smith, Sidney. *Isaiah Chapters XL-LV: Literary Criticism and History*. London: Oxford University Press, 1944. Excellent historical background to Second Isaiah's time.

Wordsworth, W. A. *En-Roeh: The Prophecy of Isaiah the Seer with Habakkuk and Nahum*. New York: Charles Scribner's Sons, 1940. The author's thesis is that Isaiah's dominant theme was the prediction of Jesus as Messiah.

The Teaching of Second Isaiah

Smart, J. D. *History and Theology in Second Isaiah*. Philadelphia: Westminster Press, 1965. A work that differs from the views of many scholars of Second Isaiah on several issues.

RETURN FROM THE CAPTIVITY

Type of event: Politico-religious: repatriation of the Jews
Time: c.538-c.450 B.C.
Locale: Palestine

Principal personages:
CYRUS THE GREAT, King of Persia 559-c.529
ZERUBBABEL (fl.c.538), descendant of King David; governor of Judah, rebuilder of the temple between 520 and 516
HAGGAI, a prophet
ZECHARIAH, a prophet
NEHEMIAH, Governor of Palestine c.445
SANBALLAT, Samaritan leader c.445
EZRA, Jewish scribe c.425

Summary of Event

The four centuries of Jewish history from 586 until 166 comprised a period of physical weakness but of religious growth and strength. The very destruction of the Temple and the nation encouraged Second Isaiah to reach such a lofty concept as the universality of God.

The return from the Babylonian exile was made possible by an edict of Cyrus the Great in 538 which gave evidence of his appreciation for local autonomy and for the cultural and religious integrity of his peoples. The books of Chronicles record that 42,360 Jews with their servants returned under the combined leadership of the prince Zerubbabel and the high priest Joshua. The numbers appear to be exaggerated when compared to those suggested by the prophets Haggai and Zechariah, who imply that the community was weak and struggling. In order to develop a new central shrine, a second Temple was built and completed, probably by 516. Though not as large or grandiose as that of Solomon, it stood as a symbol of triumph and hope to a revived Judaism until Jerusalem was destroyed by the Romans in A.D. 70.

The returned exiles, however, had their problems. First of all, Zerubbabel, a legitimate descendant of David, plotted to reëstablish the old dynasty. Taking advantage of the death of Cyrus' son Cambyses with consequent turmoil and open rebellion in the Persian Empire, he established himself as King in Jerusalem, but was either executed or deported.

Once the exuberance of the return had passed, the Jews were faced with the harsh realities of the situation. Palestine was agriculturally poor and also isolated from trade routes. On to this mixed scene of joy and despair appeared first Nehemiah and then Ezra, presumably in that order since Nehemiah seems to set the stage for Ezra. Nehemiah, a cupbearer to the Persian King Artaxerxes, requested permission to go to Jerusalem as governor to help his coreligionists struggling to adjust to Palestine. The Temple had been rebuilt but it had been as quickly defiled, the Sabbath was regularly desecrated with commercial activities, and the city's defenses were in disrepair. Intensive work enabled Nehemiah to rebuild the city's walls and consequently to guarantee the integrity of the Jewish cult by isolating his people from their neighbors including even the Samaritans, despite the fact that under the leadership of Sanballat they had sought some political and religious rapprochement with the Jews. Disregarding considerable intermarriage between the two groups, Nehemiah preferred to exclude them as a mixed people, even going to the length of trying to separate couples who had intermarried. To thwart religious syncretism and to maintain a pure Yahwism, Nehemiah would unify only those Jews who, because of their experiences in the Exile, were highly motivated religiously.

Hoping to solidify Nehemiah's program, Ezra, a scribe, established the Law of the Pentateuch as the politico-religious constitution of the Jews. This official promulgation of the Law, tantamount to its canonization as the first part of the Hebrew Scriptures, was the first important effort since Josiah's Deuteronomic reform to establish the Jewish community on the basis of the written word of God. Ezra's dispensation fixed the basis for Judaism so effectively that normative Judaism continued to develop as a legalistic and exclusive community for the next thousand years.

The only vindication for the parochialism of both Nehemiah and Ezra, so far removed from the universalism of Amos or Second Isaiah, is its desire to enable Biblical faith to prosper in a protected environment. A new type of optimistic prophecy encouraged men such as Haggai, Zechariah, Malachi, Third Isaiah and Joel, who labored in turn by emphasizing the Temple, institutional reform, and the cult to provide a religious structure which could replace the crumbled political order. Concern for social justice and for a universal worship of God took second place.

The Jews maintained their peaceful isolation during virtually the whole Persian period, not even participating in the sole rebellion of the Syro-Palestinian provinces, that of the Phoenician cities in 351. Except for the abortive aspirations of Zerubbabel, the Jews devoted themselves to internal affairs, mainly the purification of Judaism and the maintenance of the Law as the undisputed cornerstone of the community. The solidity and depth of this reformed Judaism was soon to be tested by the impact of Hellenism which came with the Greek conquests of Alexander the Great in the fourth century.

Pertinent Literature

Welch, Adam C. *Poste-Exilic Judaism.* Edinburgh: William Blackwood and Sons Ltd., 1935.

Welch interprets the entire post-exilic development of Judaism as a defensive and conservative effort, in the face of threatening conditions of the period, to maintain Jewish identity and purity of worship. He outlines the characteristics of the new policy of retrenchment as they were determined by the ideals and convictions of the men who guided this movement. Among these Nehemiah was only nominally important. Admittedly a picturesque personality and a figure of some importance as a Persian official, he merely supported the programs already in progress and conceived of and directed by lesser known figures.

The program itself emphasized a studied hostility on the part of Jews toward alien life in general and justified their reaction against the outside world as a means to restore their own peculiar life and renew the conditions of the past. This conservative course based on institutionalized religion was decisive in determining the future. Jewish leaders rejected the extreme proposals of Ezekiel including the restoration of the kingdom with a descendant of Jehoiachim on the throne, allotting equal portions of land to the twelve tribes to unify them, and placing the Temple and the priests outside the capital. He would have new laws for priestly temple service as well as new royal obligations to the cult. The new leaders chose instead to make a descendant of Zadok high priest, and reinstated an ancient Levitical law.

Yet because conditions were different, some changes in the cult had to be made. The injunction of appearing in Jerusalem three times each year was quietly dropped because of the widespread Jewish dispersion. An offering sent to the Temple would suffice. The Temple with an elaborate priesthood and liturgy became a symbol of unity for a people bent solely on enriching their relationship with God.

While all those developments gave a *raison d'être* to the life of the scattered nation, they still offered little opportunity for personal involvement. Welch sees this gap between corporate and individual life bridged by the development of an elaborate scheme of penitential atonement, an arrangement which tied the individual Jew both to God and the Temple through sacrifices as means of justification. In this intensified ritual system sin itself became chiefly ceremonial defilement rather than moral transgression as in the Mosaic and prophetic systems. But this religion of outward forms and signs succeeded in enabling the Jews to sense quickly in a visible way any invading influences from their heathen surroundings. Sabbath observance and circumcision naturally assumed new importance in distinquishing Jews from the polyglot population of the Palestine to which the exiles returned. While such stressing of the outward signs of nationality caused the faith to lose some of its prophetic universalism, the times called for a Judaism more interested in preserving itself than in enlightening the world.

Noth, Martin. *The History of Israel.* Translated by Stanley Godman. Pp. 229-354. New York: Harper and Row Publishers Incorporated, 1958.

Noth's general view of the Jewish nation colors his entire historical interpretation and particularly the period covered in this section. He sees Israel as a unique phenomenon in the midst of other historical nations. The secret of Israel's distinction is the mystery of God's involvement, a result of which is Israel's estrangement in the world of its own time, its existence as an entity separated from the world in which it lives. For Noth, therefore, certain happenings in the history of Israel are without parallel. The idea of Israel transcends the idea of nationhood which ended in 586 B.C. The terms "Judaism" and "Israel" came to be synonymous after the national period ceased.

The beginning of this development came in the Persian period when some of the Jews returned from captivity. Unlike most conquerors who introduced their own official religions, at least in their provincial capitals, the Persians accepted the traditions and characteristics of their subject peoples even to the extent of actively supporting them. The Persian policy of toleration thus allowed the new Israel to come into being and flourish. Cyrus not only allowed the Jews to return to Palestine, but he and his successors also financed some of their projects, released valuable articles which had been taken by Nebuchadnezzar, and made outstanding Jewish government officials available to the struggling community.

Noth indicates that even with these encouragements, the Jews found the process of rebuilding their community a difficult one. Funds were in short supply, agricultural conditions were poor, and the process of changing the primarily political nature of Judaism into a religious one was difficult. Israel was now to be a religious community centered about a shrine in Jerusalem, a temple state.

Two personalities, more than any others known to us, accomplished most of this. Nehemiah built the wall, cleansed religious practice of many abuses, and improved the general welfare of the people. He excluded non-Jewish and mixed peoples from the Temple, thereby furthering the policy of strict social and religious isolation which Noth sees as characteristic of the history of Israel after the loss of its political independence. The necessary welding together of the new Israel comprising the Jews of Palestine as well as those of the Diaspora was the task of Ezra. This was done through a renewal of the ancient covenant as practiced among the Jews in Babylonia where ritual observance was stricter than in Palestine. The Pentateuch would bring stability to the Jews of Palestine as it had to those in Babylon.

The Temple was no longer simply a royal shrine but a center for public worship for Jews in Jerusalem and the religious center regardless of where they lived. This period is also seen as crucial by Noth since the Pentateuch not only acquired definitive form during it but also became a holy book binding together the whole community wherever it was located. *—J.R.R.*

Additional Recommended Reading

Meyers, Jacob M. *Ezra and Nehemiah.* New York: Doubleday & Company, Inc., 1965. A detailed analysis of the major Biblical historical sources of this period.
Meyers, Jacob M. *Chronicles.* New York: Doubleday & Company, Inc., 1966. 2 vols. A study of the Biblical history of Israel written during the postexilic

period.

Bevan, Edwyn Robert. *Jerusalem Under the High Priests*. London: E. Arnold, 1920. A history of the role of the priesthood in ancient Israel.

Browne, L. E. *From Babylon to Bethlehem*. Cambridge: Heffer, 1951. A general account of postexilic Jewish history leading to Christianity.

Robinson, T. H., and W. O. E. Oesterley. *A History of Israel*. Vol. II. Oxford: The University Press, 1932. An excellent history of the period.

Graetz, H. *History of the Jews*. Vol. I, pp. 354-411. Philadelphia: Jewish Publication Society, 1891. A standard comprehensive account of Jewish history.

193

FOUNDING OF
THE PYTHAGOREAN BROTHERHOOD

Type of event: Cultural: emergence of a philosophic way of life
Time: c.530 B.C.
Locale: Croton, in southern Italy

Principal personages:
PYTHAGORAS OF SAMOS (572-c.500), Ionian polymath
and philosopher
ALCMAEON OF CROTON (fl. early fifth century), Pythagorean
philosopher of medical interests
PHILOLAUS OF CROTON (fl. second half of fifth century),
Pythagorean philosopher
ARCHYTAS OF TARENTUM (fl. first half of fourth century),
Pythagorean philosopher and mathematician

Summary of Event

The final conversations of Socrates with his friends as described in the *Phaedo* reveal Plato's immense debt to Pythagoras and his school. The Pythagoreans stand out in the history of science as precursors of understanding the structure of the universe in terms of mathematics. It is unfortunate that the facts about Pythagoras and his brotherhood are shrouded in legends which began in his own lifetime and grew more colorful during the millennium after his death. Reliable information is scant, but it can be stated that Pythagoras was born about 572 B.C. and lived until maturity on the Ionian island of Samos when it was economically and culturally prominent. He had already acquired fame as a sage well-versed in the learning of his age and also as an exponent of doctrine about the immortality of the soul, when he left Samos about 530 B.C. He then settled in Croton, one of the Greek cities in southern Italy and Sicily which made up the region known as

Magna Graecia. According to tradition, he left Samos because he was opposed to the tyranny of Polycrates. In Croton he organized a society of mixed religious, philosophic, and political interests which by 510 had become dominant, and he played a leading role in the war between Croton and Sybaris which established the hegemony of Croton over the other cities of Magna Graecia. In 509, a democratic rebellion expelled the Pythagorean party from power in Croton, and Pythagoras moved to Metapontum, where he died about 500. Pythagorean societies of an oligarchic nature played a leading role in several cities of Magna Graecia until about the middle of the fifth century B.C., when they were expelled in a violent upheaval, following which several survivors migrated to the Greek mainland and established communities in Thebes and in Phlius. After the beginning of the fourth century, Pythagorean influence in southern Italy was reëstablished with its center

194

at Tarentum under the leadership of Archytas.

It is a matter of debate which doctrines may reasonably be attributed to Pythagoras and the society that he founded. The most prevalent view is that the society's activities were based upon a curious fusion of religious belief and speculative cosmology dominated by mathematics. The religious doctrine shared an affinity with so-called "Orphic" conceptions of the transmigration of souls. The soul, according to this doctrine, is distinct in origin from the body in which it is imprisoned during a man's life span. Originally akin to the fires of heaven, it has entered at birth into a body from which it is released at death, only to enter anew into another body in a continuing cycle of successive reincarnations. The soul cannot free itself permanently from the cycle of reincarnation until it has successfully purified itself of the corruption to which its bodily imprisonment has subjected it. The distinctive element of the Pythagorean concept of purification is that, although one must engage in ascetic practices of bodily denial, the primary purifying activity is the intellectual endeavor to understand the nature of the heavenly bodies and their harmony, on the assumption that understanding the essence of the astral harmony enables the soul to "recollect" its primal astral purity and actualize at last its divine nature. The Pythagoreans believed that the essence of the heavenly bodies and

their interrelationships was number: one came to understand the heavens by understanding the geometrical and arithmetical ratios involved in the constitution of the cosmos.

The significant features of the Pythagorean doctrine for the history of philosophy are its epistemological assumptions, which bore fruit later in Platonic dualism and the doctrine of Ideas. The sharp distinction between the sense-experience mediated by organs of the body and the intellectual awareness of pure concepts is essentially Pythagorean, as is also the notion that mathematical relationships are eternal objects of knowledge. Once Plato had taken the step of identifying the eternally valid moral concepts which Socrates sought to define as of the same nature with the Pythagorean eternal mathematical objects of knowledge, the ground was laid for the doctrine of Ideas. It was probably also through the mediation of the Pythagorean tradition that Plato came to appropriate the notions of the soul's eternal nature, its transmigration, and of learning as a process of "recollection" of truths once known by the soul when free from the corrupting influences of the bodily prison. All these notions find expression in the *Phaedo* of Plato, a dialogue deliberately fashioned so as to present Socrates as a Pythagorean sage and a paradigm of the disciplined philosophic life of progressive actualization of one's innate potential divinity through the acquisition of wisdom.

Pertinent Literature

Minar, Edwin L. *Early Pythagorean Politics in Practice and Theory.* Baltimore, Maryland: Waverly Press, Inc., 1942.

The interpretation of early Pythagoreanism presented in this book is consistent in its primary stress upon the reactionary political goals of Pythagoras and his organization in southern Italy, and in its conception of doctrinal elements as rationalizations and moral sanctions for a strictly regulated social order. To support this thesis, Minar relies heavily upon the testimony of the later sources of the Pythagorean tradition. He exercises considerable caution in doing so, and he rightly emphasizes the strength of the evidence for political activity of the earliest Pythagorean society, but at times his reconstruction seems to be unduly weighted toward testimony supporting the thesis while neglecting other important witnesses.

Pythagoras left Samos, says Minar, about 529, clearly in opposition to the tyranny of Polycrates. In Croton he gathered around himself many disciples drawn primarily from the aristocracy. This group came to exercise a dominant authority in Croton's Council of Elders and directed its policies until Pythagoras' expulsion from Croton in 509. The culmination of Pythagorean influence was the successful war of Croton against Sybaris which ended in the destruction of that city in 509.

Minar calls attention to the extensive parallelism of terminology and organization between the Pythagorean society and political clubs in later fifth century Athens. Similar titles were used for both: *hetaireia,*

synomosia. and *synodos.* Personal loyalties of "friends" to each other and oaths of secrecy, as well as common meals, were features present in both the Pythagorean society and the Athenian political clubs. Internally, according to the evidence of Timaeus of Tauromenium (c.356-260 B.C.), the membership of the organization was carefully screened and divided into degrees of the noviates and the initiates until the doctrines of the inner circle were divulged. This division distinguishes the inner circle of *mathematikoi,* whom Minar considers not so much "mathematicians" as "the indoctrinated" in the teachings or *mathemata* of a more strict nature, and *akousmatiki,* who lived a mildly ascetic life and learned and heeded the simpler precepts or *akousmata* of Pythagoras. After the breakup of the organization in 354, says Minar, the *mathematikoi* preserved the more purely philosophical side of Pythagoreanism, while the survivors of the *akousmatikoi* preserved the religious lore.

The political theory of the Pythagoreans was founded on the necessity of imposing order and limit on the unruly aspects of human nature and social life. The rule of the gods is of primary importance, and harmony in the body social is preserved through the willing submission of the ruled to a naturally superior ruling group including Pythagoras himself (more priest than king) and the aristocratic elders. Men are distinguished in age groups, each of which has its appointed

196

function to perform. Since the state is analogous as a microcosm to the macrocosm of the universe, each person or age group must fulfill his or its own function to preserve the harmonious order of the universe.

The Pythagorean concern with mathematics, Minar insists, was not essentially scientific, but had as its focus the dominant notion of harmony and proportion. The doctrine of numbers is adapted to the expression of a preëxisting attitude toward life and the world, which Minar views as fundamentally that of a social hierarchy.

In religion the Pythagoreans did indeed teach the immortality and transmigration of souls, and the certainty of retribution after death for righteousness or sinfulness in life. Minar emphasizes the usefulness of the doctrine of imminent punishment as a powerful moral sanction in preserving social order. Contrary to the more common view of the Pythagoreans, Minar sees the goal of the Pythagorean discipline not as the salvation of the individual soul by assimilation with the divine, but as the achievement of harmony in the cosmos and in human society.

Philip, J. A. *Pythagoras and Early Pythagoreans.* (Supplementary Volume VII of *Phoenix,* Journal of the Classical Association of Canada) Toronto: University of Toronto Press, 1966.

Despite the importance of Pythagoras in Greek philosophy, there is no scholarly concensus about the doctrines which he taught or about the "brotherhood" which he founded. In his introduction to this sober reëvaluation of the ancient evidence, J. A. Philip notes that Pythagoras has been used by historians of philosophy as a kind of "missing link" to solve certain problems of reconstruction of the development of pre-Socratic thought, problems such as how the shift from physical speculation to concern with quantitative abstraction emerged, and how philosophy became a disciplined way of life.

Sources for reconstructing early Pythagoreanism are divided by Philip into three groups: (1) meager statements of pre-Socratic thinkers which have been transmitted orally; (2) early written accounts of the fourth century B.C. formulated in the Academy or

in the Lyceum; and (3) a massive body of legendary biographical and doxographical accounts formulated throughout the last seven centuries of antiquity. Fancy had already become dominant in accounts of the fourth century B.C., Philip asserts, and most reconstructions of early Pythagoreanism rely too heavily and uncritically on statements made as late as the third century A.D. by the Neoplatonists Porphyry and Iamblichus. Philip believes that a careful reconstruction must be based almost exclusively upon Aristotle's scattered references throughout his treatises and surviving fragments of his monograph *On the Pythagoreans.*

For his own reconstruction, Philip finds no evidence for the foundation by Pythagoras of a monastic type of institution with community property and degrees of initiation. It is likely, however, that as a stern moralist

Pythagoras was influential in the formation of a group of adherents who became politically dominant in Croton and other cities of Magna Graecia.

There is no reason to doubt that Pythagoras shared and taught a belief in the transmigration and essential divinity of souls. Although the exact nature of his doctrine cannot be ascertained, a story in Herodotus indicates the probability that Pythagoras held such a doctrine before leaving Samos, and it is likely that some form of the doctrine was already current in Magna Graecia when he arrived there, for Empedocles of Acragas clearly professes belief in it one generation later.

Philip finds Aristotle's account of Pythagorean cosmology sufficiently consistent and primitive, phrased as it is in terms scarcely conceivable in the fifth century B.C., to indicate its sixth century origin and to warrant its attribution to Pythagoras himself. The probability is great that Pythagoras was heavily influenced by the cosmology of Anaximander of Mile-

tus, which was founded on the principle of interaction of opposites and on the primary substance of indefinite nature or *apeiron*. For Pythagoras, the cosmos originated through the primal fusion of limit or *peras,* and the limitless *apeiron,* establishing the One as a primary limit surrounded by the *apeiron.* The One then generated other numbers by "inhaling" portions of the *apeiron* to function as spacial interstices or voids between numbers, which were held by Pythagoras to be physical substances.

The Pythagorean *Symbola,* a corpus of taboos and ascetic regulations listed in Aristotle's monograph, were not by any means unique, but that Pythagoras should have adopted them is consistent with his view of the soul's divinity and transmigration. What distinguishes Pythagorean asceticism from that of the "Orphics" and the merely superstitious is its purpose in regulating the life of one who through acquisition of wisdom seeks to purify his soul and progressively recover its primal divine nature. — *C.W.C.*

Additional Recommended Reading

DeVogel, C. J. *Pythagoras and Early Pythagoreanism.* Assen: Van Gorcum & Company, N. V., 1966. An examination of late and often discounted evidence to support a more vivid reconstruction of the historical Pythagoras and his activities than is commonly believed to be possible.

Guthrie, W. K. C. *A History of Greek Philosophy.* Vol. I. Cambridge: The University Press, 1962. The Pythagorean school receives a full and careful discussion in relation to its historical context.

Heidel, W. A. "The Pythagoreans and Greek Mathematics," in *American Journal of Philology,* 51 (1940), 1-33. A disclosure of the mathematical theory of the Pythagoreans.

Kirk, G. S., and J. E. Raven. *The Presocratic Philosophers: A Critical History with a Selection of Texts.* Cambridge: The University Press, 1960. The Greek text of fragments of the pre-Socratic philosophers, including the Pythagoreans, with English translation and critical and historical commentary.

Raven, J. E. *Pythagoreans and Eleatics.* Cambridge: The University Press, 1948. A study to determine the relative earliness or lateness of doctrines ascribed to the Pythagorean school by considering its relation and reaction to doctrines of Parmenides and his successors.

APPEARANCE OF THE SIBYLLINE BOOKS

Type of event: Religious: innovation in divination
Time: c.525 B.C.
Locale: Rome

Principal personage:
TARQUINIUS SUPERBUS, King of Rome traditionally 534-510

Summary of Event

The Sibylline Books were a collection of oracles in Greek hexameters that were carefully guarded in ancient Rome and consulted in times of great distress as a result of war, famine, pestilence, or other public calamity. The Sibyls, from whom the adjective "Sibylline" is derived, were prophetesses who gave responses to questions posed to them. The etymology of the word is unknown, though numerous attempts have been made in ancient and modern times to explain it. The Sibyls originated in Asia Minor during the seventh century B.C. and spread from there to various sites throughout the Mediterranean world. The philosopher Heraclitus of Ephesus (c.560-500), the first to refer to women of this type, knew but one; Heraclides Ponticus, a philosopher and writer (c.390-310), was aware of two Sibyls, and later authors mention three, four, eight, ten, and twelve of them, or leave the number indefinite. The most famous listing of these seers is that given by Varro in his *Res Divinae* where he names all sorts of Sibyls: Persian, Libyan, Delphic, Cimmerian, Erythraean, Samian, Cumaean, Hellespontic, Phrygian, and Tiburtine.

The Sibyls could be consulted on a private or public basis, and collections of their responses were made and circulated. One of these collections reached Rome toward the end of the sixth century B.C. There it received official approval and came to be known as the *Libri Sibillini* or "Sibylline Books."

The famous story connected with the advent of these books is an obvious legend devised to increase their prestige. It is related by both Greek and Latin authors with some minor divergencies in detail. The fullest account is that found in Dionysius of Halicarnassus, who taught history and rhetoric in Rome (30-8 B.C.). According to him, Rome, through the favor of some divinity, was the recipient of wonderfully good fortune during the reign of Tarquin the Proud. A foreign woman tried to sell the king nine books of Sibylline oracles. When he refused to buy them, she burned three of the nine books and then offered him the remaining six at the original price. Rebuffed again, she burned three more of the books. When she finally offered the remaining three for the same price as the original nine, the baffled king asked the advice of his augurs. These augurs decided by certain signs that he had rejected a divine blessing in not buying all the books and urged him to purchase at

200

least those that were left. Tarquin appointed two prominent men to guard the books and gave them two public slaves to assist them in their task. Dionysius states that these books were kept in a stone chest beneath the temple of Jupiter on the Capitoline hill until the time of the Social War in 91-88 B.C., and that they perished in the fire that destroyed the temple in 83 B.C. They were replaced with oracles gathered from other Italian cities, from Eythrae in Asia Minor, and other places. These oracles, according to Dionysius, were the most guarded possession of the Romans whether sacred or profane so that the senate decreed that they could be consulted only during times of strife and misfortune in war, or when some baffling prodigy or apparition appeared.

Some attempts have been made to derive the Sibylline Books from Etruria because of their resemblance to the *Libri fatales,* or "Books of Fate," which are assumed to be of Etruscan origin. This title, however, is a generic term used for both Etruscan and Greek rituals. It seems more probable that the oracles were brought to Rome from Cumae, whence they had originally come from Erythrae. Unlike the Greeks who freely allowed private persons as well as public officials to consult their oracles and even permitted private copies of the responses to be made, the Romans surrounded the books with great secrecy and restricted their use to state officials. Not even the priests in charge could consult them without a special order of the senate.

One important result stemming from the consultation of these oracles was the progressive introduction of Greek and Eastern deities and modes of worship into Rome, a course which the books frequently advised. Among the gods introduced in this manner were Demeter, Dionysus, and Kore under their Italic names of Ceres, Liber, and Libera, and most famous of all, Cybele. Among the rites introduced were the *lectisternium,* or public offering of food to the gods as they were displayed on pillows or couches, the *supplicatio,* a general adoration of the gods on the part of the people with kneelings and prostrations, and the *taurobolium,* or baptism in blood. The original priesthood in charge of the books, the *Duoviri sacris faciundis,* was increased from two to ten, the *Decemviri,* and then to fifteen, the *Quindecimviri.* It formed one of the four major priestly colleges. As part of his religious reform, Augustus ordered a revision to be made of the oracles and had them transferred to the temple of Apollo on the Palatine hill, but by that time their days of influence were largely over. Although a new interest was taken in them under the emperors Aurelian and Julian the Apostate, they were reportedly burnt during the reign of Honorius by order of his general Stilicho.

201

Pertinent Literature

Carter, Jesse Benedict. *The Religion of Numa and Other Essays on the Religion of Ancient Rome.* New York: The Macmillan Company, 1906.

Jesse Benedict Carter was a pupil of the famed Georg Wissowa, whose *Religion und Cultus der Römer* is still one of the classic works on Roman religion. The first two essays in Carter's work deal with the period of the kings, while the third treats the first three centuries of the Republic. The latter he titles "The Coming of the Sibyl."

In general, Carter has two theses regarding the Sibylline books: first, that they were destructive of true Roman religion, and second, that the books stem more out of the early Republic milieu than the late kingdom.

As Carter points out at the outset, the Rome of the first consuls was considerably different politically, socially, and religiously from what it had been under the kings. While there was an increase in the number of gods, the new dieties did not present a serious challenge to the old pantheon. The era of the Early Republic was, according to Carter, clearly "the best and strongest period in the whole history of Roman religion." There were as yet no improper violent manifestations of religious enthusiasm but only the "conscientious formalism which was best adapted to the Roman character." This balance between the new and the old religious dispensation, however, did not last long. During the first centuries of the Republic there was a gradual increase in superstition that eventually led to a collapse of faith after 200 B.C.

Though it has been customary to attribute this decline in religion to the influence of Greek literature and philosophy, Carter believes that the real cause is to be found in an earlier phenomenon: the unnatural stimulation of religion produced by the Sibylline oracles. He is therefore interested in studying the workings of these oracles to try to apprehend why their effect was so powerful that they could in the course of three centuries "entirely change both the form and the content of Roman religion." Under the guise of increasing its zeal, they actually sapped the vitality of traditional religion to such an extent that almost two centuries of human experience and travail were necessary "before true religion was in some sense at least restored to its own place."

The control which the senate exercised over consultation of these oracles is, according to Carter, proof of how dangerous they were in the minds of the older and wiser men of the community, who appreciated the peculiarities of the Roman temperament.

Carter rejects the traditional account of the origin of the Sibylline Books because he conjectures that they may not be earlier than the Republic. The title given to the two men placed in charge of the books, *Duoviri sacris faciundis,* is not a proper name as it is in other earlier priesthoods, but resembles the titles of special committees appointed by the senate for administrative purposes. The books seem therefore to have come into use at a time when the senate was in control of the state, that is, during the early Republic rather than during the late kingdom. It is probable that the oracles came from Cumae in the wake of the Greek god Apollo, who as a newcomer was given a place in the Campus Martius outside the *pomerium*, and only in 431 B.C. was voted a temple along with his sister and mother. The more recent date may well explain the interest in enlarging the priesthood in charge of the Sibylline Books in 367 B.C., which was a victory for the plebeians since half of the new members, that is, five out of ten, were to be chosen from their ranks.

Partly by nature and partly because of Etruscan influences, the Romans were strongly inclined to superstition, and "the more they thought of the gods the more terrified they became." Since they never acquired the easy familiarity with their deities enjoyed by the Greeks, the introduction of a series of Greek gods and rituals could only be harmful. Outwardly the Sibylline Books introduced new deities to Rome that were respectable enough, but by so doing they inwardly corrupted primitive beliefs and increased a craving for magic. In times of peril the Sibylline Books seemingly gave good advice, and this occasional use apparently deserved the gratitude of Rome; actually, however, the oracles took their toll with the passage of time when "the abuse of faith, the substitution of incantation for devotion, was destructive of true religion."

Lanchester, H. C. O. "Sibylline Oracles," in *Encyclopaedia of Religion and Ethics*. Edited by James Hastings. Vol. XI, pp. 496-500. New York: Charles Scribner's Sons, 1934.

Though a shorter article can be read in the *Oxford Dictionary of the Christian Church,* Hastings' somewhat dated *Encyclopaedia of Religion and Ethics* is still the only scholarly source of information in English on many aspects of ancient religions. Such seems to be the case regarding the Sibylline oracles, those "curiosities of ancient literature," especially in respect to their usage as instruments of proselytization of Jews and Christians.

Neither witches nor divinities, the Sibyls built up such a reputation as persons enjoying occult ability to predict the future and to communicate with deity that they were universally revered. Three were associated with Apollo: the sibyl of Erythrae in Asia Minor; that of Cumae in Campania mentioned by Vergil in both his *Eclogues* and the *Aeneid*; and that of Delphi. Imitations were made of the verses of Erythrae, the most famous of sibyls, by Musaeus of Athens whose writings reputedly were collected by Onamacritus by order of Pisistratus. Tarquin, of course, saw fit to buy the oracles for Rome. Even if these books had confined themselves to Greece and Rome they would deserve serious study as "a very curious and interesting phenomenon in the ancient world." However, the modern student is likely to be intrigued equally by the fact that employment of the oracles did not confine itself to pagan circles but extended even into the Jewish and Christian worlds.

Fifteen such books, three of which are missing, purport to be prophecies by Greek sibyls concerning Jewish monotheism and the nature of Christ. As such they were taken seriously by several Christian Fathers including Clement of Alexandria. Although some bona-fide Greek oracles are included in the collection, the bulk is too monotheistic and messianic to be anything in the eyes of modern scholars but compositions, to a lesser or greater degree, of Jewish and Christian writers extending from the first half of the second century B.C. to the fourth century A.D. The purpose apparently was to use the weight of an ancient sibyl to foster conversions from the pagan world, a tribute to the great influence these prophetesses enjoyed in ancient times.

The first to hit upon this device seems to have been an Egyptian Jew living probably in Alexandria about 150 B.C. in effervescent Maccabean times. His work, cast in the future tense in the style of the oracles, mingles the history of the Old Testament with pagan legends. Thus the destruction of the Tower of Babel is to be followed by the reign of Kronos, Titan, Iapetus, and the birth of Zeus. These Jewish Sibylline oracles continued to be produced until the time of Hadrian, and interested Christian writers interlaced them with pagan oracles and snatches of existing Christian literature in order to impress them into the service of the new faith. The Christian portions seem to appear not earlier than the third century. Book six is a hymn to Christ sufficiently important to attract the admiration of Lactantius and the notice of Augustine in his *City of God*. Book eight deals with the nature of Christ and his Second Coming.

Though Lanchester does not pursue the Sibylline influence upon Christian writers of the Middle Ages, there is an obvious reference to them in the great medieval sequence the *Dies irae* where the sibyl is cited as a seer alongside King David: *"Teste David cum Sibylla."* The Cumaean sibyl is portrayed with verses from Vergil as a prophetess of Christ in the marble floor of the cathedral of Siena. Their greatest inspiration for art is, however, to be found in the Renaissance painting of Michelangelo on the ceiling of the Sistine Chapel. — *M.J.C.*

Additional Recommended Reading

Bailey, Cyril. *Phases in the Religion of Ancient Rome.* Berkeley: University of California Press, 1932. A judgment of the Sibylline oracles as destructive of old Roman animism in favor of new Greco-Roman anthropomorphisms.

Halliday, W. A. *Lectures on the History of Roman Religion.* Liverpool: The University Press of Liverpool, Ltd., 1923. A brief evaluation of the Sibylline Books as a Hellenizing agent.

Fowler, W. Warde. *The Religious Experience of the Roman People.* New York: The Macmillan Company, 1911, reprinted 1922. An excellent and sympathetic survey of Roman religion.

Bailey, Cyril. "Roman Religion and the Advent of Philosophy," in *The Cambridge Ancient History.* Vol. 8, pp. 451-454. New York: The Macmillan Company, 1930. A study maintaining that the failure of the artificial state-cult naturally led to the kind of innovations suggested by the Sibylline books.

THE REFORMS OF CLEISTHENES

Type of event: Constitutional: inauguration of political reform
Time: 508-507 B.C.
Locale: Athens

> *Principal personages:*
> CLEISTHENES, Athenian aristocrat of the Alcmaeonid family fl.c.510
> CLEOMENES, King of Sparta c.519-487
> ISAGORAS, Athenian aristocrat who opposed Cleisthenes

Summary of Event

After the passage of Solon's legislation early in the sixth century, Athens continued to experience stormy times. Pisistratus established a tyranny which after his death in 527 passed to his two sons, one of whom was assassinated in 514 and the other was expelled with the assistance of King Cleomenes of Sparta in 510. The tyranny was followed by government by the nobility, apparently a narrow oligarchy whose leader was the aristocrat Isagoras. Cleisthenes, of the noble family of the Alcmaeonidae, incited the common people against the oligarchs. In 508-507, he besieged the conservatives and their Spartan supporters on the Acropolis. The Spartans acknowledged defeat and were permitted to withdraw, whereupon the aristocratic faction surrendered.

Cleisthenes, with the support of most Athenians, then drew up a fresh series of laws which superseded the constitution set up by Solon. The reform was essentially political in nature, although it inevitably had repercussions on Attic society as a whole.

Social change was made mainly through abolishing the four traditional tribes of citizens and creating ten new ones which were not territorial, though they were made up of members of the old *demes*, the villages of Attica. There were then about 170 *demes* of varying sizes. Groups of ten *demes* called *trittyes* were formed by assigning *demes* by lot from the three geographical regions of Attica: the city itself and the countryside immediately around it; the coastal district; and the interior. The *demes* were not necessarily contiguous, especially as Cleisthenes intended to break up regional interest groups of the nobility which had hitherto caused civil unrest, but they were approximately equal in population. New cults were created for the tribes with the approval of the Delphic Apollo in order to bind new loyalties.

The organization of Solon's Assembly was also changed, and there is reason to suppose that Cleisthenes assigned to it a more active and important role. It continued to see to the annual election of magistrates and to be consulted on the issue of war or peace, but it now passed new laws from time to time. With thirty thou-

205

sand male citizens including the *thetes* eligible to attend, though not to vote, the Assembly was unwieldy. An important constitutional innovation of Cleisthenes was creation of the *Boule* or Council, an executive committee of the Assembly made up of five hundred councilors, fifty from each tribe. Each *deme* elected councilors in proportion to its population. It is a matter of controversy whether the *Boule* was a new institution or merely replaced the Council of Four Hundred said to have been constituted by Solon.

Though the precise functions of the *Boule* in the time of Cleisthenes are not clear, it began somewhat later to draw up formal bills for consideration by the Assembly, receive foreign embassies, discharge certain judicial functions, and look after the construction of warships, fortifications, and other public works.

Each tribal group of fifty men, a *Prytany*, lived continuously at public expense in the city of Athens for a tenth of the year, an arrangement which was the closest Cleisthenes came to giving payment for holding public office. These groups were ready in emergency to call either the full *Boule* or the Assembly into session. One man of the *Prytany* was chosen each day to be the *Prytanis* or "President" of Athens for twenty-four hours. He was responsible for the safekeeping of keys to the temples and treasuries, and he presided over any sessions of the Council or Assembly which might take place on his day in office. The *Boule* familiarized the people of Athens with the organization, finances, and resources of the state. It also prepared the generation which followed Cleisthenes for the more democratic 460's and 450's under Pericles.

The nine archons continued to function as heretofore, but Cleisthenes has also been credited by some authorities with creating the new office of "General" or *Strategos*, which was a more democratic office than archon because generals were elected without regard to census rating. As the office actually dates from 501/500, it was probably the creation of some other man because Cleisthenes drops out of Athenian history abruptly after 507. Some ancient writers also ascribed to him the honorable form of legalized exile known as "ostracism," but since it was not used until 487, it too was in all probability the creation of someone else.

Pertinent Literature

Hignett, C. *A History of the Athenian Constitution to the End of the Fifth Century B.C.* Oxford: The Clarendon Press, 1952.

In this thorough, candid, and well-presented book, C. Hignett begins with a valuable criticism of the scant evidence for Athenian constitutional history. We are severely handicapped by having almost no reliable contemporary witnesses to the various changes which occurred early in Attic history, such as replacement of the monarchy by the archonship (c.750 B.C.), the promulgation of the laws of Draco (c.620), the legislation of Solon (c.590), or even of the reforms of Cleisthenes. The earliest trustworthy ancient historian whose work has been preserved is Herodotus, and since he wrote as late as the 430's, he was sometimes led astray by stories which descendants of famous men told him about their forebears.

As Hignett shows, one ancient authority that has been trusted too much by modern scholars is *The Constitution of Athens,* ascribed to Aristotle though wrongly in the opinion of Hignett. Whether this book was actually written by Aristotle or not, it certainly was written about 325 B.C. by someone in Aristotelian circles. It makes statements about the early legal changes mentioned above, but its value is small since there were virtually no written records from the sixth century for its author to consult. He was driven to depend upon oral traditions still circulating, not all of which were wrong; upon political pamphlets, which were generally tendentious and partisan; and upon the books of the Atthidographers. These last were men who, beginning with Hellanicus in the 430's, wrote down the local traditions of Attic history. Hellanicus' book was, according to Thucydides, short, jejune, and somewhat inaccurate. The Atthidographers were able, we know, to read public inscriptions no longer extant today, and such inscriptions may have recorded constitutional innovations and honest memories of famous men of the past such as Cleisthenes. Unfortunately, none of the *Atthides* has come down to us complete, so that we can never be sure how much they were used by Pseudo-Aristotle, and his ability to extract genuine and accurate information from them cannot be tested. What is beyond dispute, however, is that the Atthidographers too often believed political propaganda to be sober fact. Hignett can show, with earlier scholars, that the constitution of Draco, as outlined in *The Constitution of Athens,* is a forgery of the late fourth century B.C. In the past there has been considerable disagreement among scholars as to the exact provisions of this or that reform because we are uncertain how far the early chapters of *The Constitution of Athens* can be trusted, if at all.

Hignett's version of the reforms of Cleisthenes, therefore, is based upon a skeptical view of the ancient sources. In the case of the attribution of the law of ostracism to Cleisthenes, he shows that there are no cases of ostracism earlier than 488/487 mentioned in the ancient literary authorities. They are probably correct, for we can now associate with the tradition a few actual *ostraca,* the fragments of pottery upon which was written the name of the candidate for exile; none of these is earlier than about 485 B.C. Since it is a reasonable assumption that where no use was made of a law the law did not exist, the law of ostracism is far more likely to have been passed close to 488 B.C. than back in 507 B.C.

If Hignett's book has any weakness, it is that there is so little said about the economic history of Athens, for social and economic conditions both before and after Cleisthenes had their effects on constitutional history.

The Reforms of Cleisthenes

Jones, A. H. M. *Athenian Democracy*. Oxford: Basil Blackwell, 1957.

Three of the five chapters in this short but admirable book bear directly on questions related to the Athens of the days of Cleisthenes and Pericles, including the one entitled, "The Economic Basis of Athenian Democracy." There is an old cliché in some handbooks of Greek history that the classical city-state was a society based on slave labor, and that the voting classes were leisured and parasitic living off the labor of others. The Greeks, so the argument runs, shunned manual labor, as we learn from some statements in writers such as Plato and Aristotle. Jones is able to refute this view. The two philosophers were men with highly individualized points of view. Aristotle was not an Athenian, although he did live at Athens for some years, and Plato was a leisured aristocrat who presumably was quite wealthy. But the average Athenian, no doubt, had to work hard in his shop or on his farm, and we are certain that the free men who manned the Athenian navy led no restful life while toiling at the oars. Slavery certainly existed at Athens, and the life of the slave in the silver mines must have been brutal, and was probably short; nevertheless, slavery seems to have been less widespread than previously thought, and certainly its general character should not be equated with our own concept of the institution as chattel bondage. Unfortunately, we have no certain statistics, and estimates of the size of the slave population have to be based on chance remarks of various authors. Taken together, Jones believes, these indicate that most Athenians did not own domestic slaves, and that possibly two-thirds to three-fourths of the citizens owned no slaves at all. If slavery could have been abolished, its passing would not have seriously injured Athens' economic life.

Jones also discusses "Athenian Democracy and Its Critics," and draws attention to the interesting fact that no reasoned, theoretical defense of democracy as a political way of life has come down to us. Instead, we have the hostile statements and tracts of Athens' intellectuals: Socrates, Plato, Aristotle, and Thucydides. Socrates was highly critical of democracy, and Plato was outspoken against the personal liberties guaranteed by the democratic regime. He was deeply committed to certain moral and intellectual standards, and he was horrified at the right of the average Athenian publicly to make his opinions of great issues known in the Assembly. Free speech might lead to lying, to proposals for unjust wars, and even to slighting of the divine. Plato also abhorred the notion of equality for all, since to him men differed widely in education, goodness, and love of morality. Aristotle favored widely based oligarchies, and, like Plato, attacked the idea that men should be so free of constraint as to be enabled to live as they pleased. He believed that such a society would in time overthrow traditional law, and thereby pave the way for mob-rule or anarchy. Thucydides disliked democracy because of its fickleness and incompetence, especially in wartime.

Jones also explains the working of Athenian democracy in the technical sense. He gives an interesting outline of the day-by-day functioning of the almost entirely amateur government of the state. The duties of the various boards of citizens which administered the funds of the city, the role of the Council *vis-à-vis* the Assembly, and the methods by which bills might be amended during debate are all discussed fully and carefully.

The book ends with an appendix on the size of the population of Athens at the end of the fifth century B.C. This is an important matter, even if the work of the scholar is made difficult by the very few good figures we have. How many rich men were there? How many *zeugitae*? How many *thetes*? Jones attempts to find answers to all these questions. — *S.K.E.*

Additional Recommended Reading

Gomme, A. W. *The Population of Athens in the Fifth and Fourth Centuries B.C.* Oxford: Basil Blackwell, 1933. In spite of Jones' work mentioned above, Gomme's estimates are more soundly based.

Von Fritz, Kurt, and Ernst Kapp. *Aristotle's Constitution of Athens.* New York: Hafner, 1950. This book has the Greek text, English translation, and a detailed commentary; it is an important work on the history and functioning of the Athenian democracy.

Stecchini, Livio C. *Athenaion Politeia: The Constitution of Athens.* Glencoe: Free Press, 1950. This slim volume contains annotated translations of the tracts on constitutional history of both Pseudo-Aristotle and Pseudo-Xenophon (the "Old Oligarch"), a bitter opponent of Athenian democracy c.430 B.C.

Kourouniotes, K., and H. A. Thompson. "The Pnyx of Athens," in *Hesperia,* Volume 1 (1932), pp. 90-217. A discussion of the results of excavation of the hill where the Athenian Assembly held its sessions.

POSTULATION OF THE LOGOS

Type of event: Philosophical: formulation of a new concept
Time: c.500 B.C.
Locale: Ephesus

Principal personages:
HERACLITUS OF EPHESUS (c.530-470), Ionian philosopher
ZENO OF CITIUM (335-263), founder of the Stoic school
    of philosophy
PHILO OF ALEXANDRIA (c.30 B.C.-A.D.45), eclectic Hellen-
    istic Jewish philosopher
JOHN THE EVANGELIST (fl. second half of first century A.D.),
    reputed author of the Fourth Gospel and possibly one or
    more of the Johannine epistles

Summary of Event

The concept of the logos, which was formally postulated by Heraclitus in his book *On Nature,* published about 500 B.C., has its roots in the earlier Greek cosmological tradition; implicit in the *Theogony* of Hesiod (currently dated c.730 B.C.) is an anthropomorphic concept of the world as an organism endowed with an innate impulse toward rational order which ultimately becomes consciously directed in the cosmic political regime of Zeus. More immediately influential for Heraclitus was the cultural climate of his period in Ionia: a sense of the fundamental instability of human life as well as of nature was balanced in popular thought by the belief in an underlying pattern of change recognizable by the wise man and forming the basis of his moral response to life. Thus the poet Archilochus, whose date of c.700 B.C. is, like Hesiod's, widely disputed, speaks of an unending ebb and flow of fortune comparable to the movement of the waves of the sea, and he advises a morality of moderation based on recognition of the *rhythmos,* the law of constantly repetitive reversal of fortune. The philosophical school of Miletus, a city neighboring Ephesus, had postulated a materialistic philosophy explaining the cosmological phenomena of nature as transformations of some single substance in obedience to some strict law. Influenced by the concepts of the Milesian school, yet himself a tough-minded aristocrat of independent thought, Heraclitus viewed constant change as the fundamental reality of nature. For him fire was both the ultimate real material element of nature, constantly transformed into earth and water and back into fire, and also a symbol of the very process of cosmic flux. The human soul itself he saw as an active fiery efflux intermediate between the terrestrial water and the cosmic fire. Yet the cosmic transformations of fire were governed by an inner law of balance: the upward transformation of earth and water into fire was compensated by a downward transformation of fire into earth and water

210

occurring at the same time. "Harmony consists in opposing tension, like that of the bow and the lyre."

Although he conceived this cosmic process of transformation as necessary and mechanically rigid, Heraclitus nevertheless paradoxically understood it as the expression of a universal intelligence which is present in some measure in the human soul, and it is here that his doctrine of the logos has its place. Logos, literally "word" in Greek, is a term of almost infinite flexibility in its application to every kind of communication and communicability. Logos is active intelligence coextensive with the cosmic fire; logos is the pattern of transformation through which the cosmic intelligence "expresses" itself. Logos is the active intelligence of the human soul which is potentially cognizant of and communes with the cosmic intelligence and its pattern of transformation. Finally, logos is the pattern of moral behavior achieved by the human soul when it consciously recognizes and obeys the cosmic logos.

There is a disquieting paradox and perhaps an inner contradiction in the Heraclitean conception of the logos. Although the doctrine expressed a kind of faith in the rationality of the universe and provided an epistemological ground for man's knowledge of the order of the universe, the process of cosmic transformation was essentially deterministic, void of the purposeful direction of activity which is an essential quality of active intelligence. The logical problem presented by this contradiction was never really resolved even after Zeno of Citium, who founded the Stoic school of philosophy in the middle of the third century B.C.,

appropriated the cosmology and logos doctrine of Heraclitus for the Stoa, incorporating into it the Socratic concept of a purposive divine intelligence providentially guiding the course of universal nature. Nevertheless, the logos concept provided the foundation for the Stoic notion of a *cosmopolis,* a universal natural community of all rational beings, that is of God and all men, as participants in the common logos and as moral agents bound to each other by shared recognition of its common bonds. When Stoic thought was naturalized in Rome in the circle of Scipio Aemilianus and in the philosophical works of Cicero, logos became *ratio* or "right reason," and the doctrine of the universal rational community served as a moral foundation for the *jus gentium* of Roman law.

In the cosmopolitan Hellenistic period the logos doctrine provided the necessary link between Greek philosophy and the Hebraic tradition, and ultimately formed the foundation of rational theology in early Christendom. Philo of Alexandria (c.30 B.C.-A.D. 45) postulated a logos which was evidently a fusion of the Heraclitean-Stoic concept with the Hebraic conception of the Word of God. Philo's logos, however, was not identical with the essential "Being" of God but rather an intermediary being between God and man, pure thought through which man comes to know the nature and will of God. In the prologue of the Fourth Gospel, now thought to date from the second half of the first century A.D., the logos is fully identical with God the Creator and is declared to have entered human history in the incarnate Logos, Jesus Christ.

211

Pertinent Literature

Kirk, G. S. *Heraclitus, the Cosmic Fragments.* Cambridge: The University Press, 1954.

In this book, surely the single most important work on Heraclitus in English, G. S. Kirk has grouped together in several sections the cosmological fragments treating common themes. For each fragment he offers a full text in the original Greek, including the context of the fragment in the source from which it is cited, a careful translation into English, and an exhaustive commentary explaining variant interpretations that have been offered. He also gives his own reasons for his choice of terms of translation, and the implications of the fragment and its relation to the Greek philosophical and cultural tradition. The book does not provide a comprehensive interpretation of Heraclitean cosmology, but it reviews the available information on the dates and life of Heraclitus and discusses the reliability of ancient sources in an introduction. In a brief epilogue, Kirk presents "a few synthetic impressions" on the nature of Heraclitus' thought and its relation to his philosophic environment.

Kirk's first group of fragments includes those which bear the most significance for Heraclitus' concept of the logos, nos. 1, 114, 2, and 50 from the authoritative collection of pre-Socratic fragments compiled by Diels and Kranz. Of the great variety of meanings which the word logos certainly could express in Heraclitus' day, Kirk prefers the phrase, "formula of things," or "the organized way in which all things work." "Plan" is a reasonable one-word translation, provided one is well aware that a teleological sense is altogether absent from Heraclitus' notion. Kirk argues vehemently against those who have sought to attribute a subjective sense of "reason" or "rational apprehension" to the logos: it is the "object" of recognition, not a mode of apprehending the object.

Most interesting of this group of fragments and richest from the standpoint of later developments of the concept of the logos is no. 114. In Kirk's translation: "Those who speak with sense must rely upon what is common to all, as a city must rely on its law, and with a much greater reliance; for all the laws of men are nourished by one law, the divine law; for it has as much power as it wishes and is sufficient for all and is still left over."

Here the logos is not quite identified with the divine law, *theios nomos,* but the sentence links Heraclitus' concept of cosmic process with religious and social ideas of his Greek tradition, and hence the two concepts are complementary. The significant link between the two notions is the declaration that each constitutes a community, and each binds its members in obedience to a common principle. Therefore, accommodation of one's actions to the recognized laws of nature is similar to accommodation of one's relations to other persons in the constitution of his community. To sail in the stormy season is as much an act of *hubris* as to disregard violently the rights of a neighbor.

The notion of accommodation of

one's self to the law of the cosmos finds expression in fragment 50 in explicit verbal form: "Listening not to me but to the *logos,* it is wise to agree [*homo-log-ein*] that all things are one." Here the verb form *homologein* neatly expresses the rational consent of an individual who "attunes" himself to the logos. This is precisely the aspect of Heraclitus' doctrine developed by the Stoics in their concept of the life lived in accordance with nature.

Heraclitus, says J. E. Raven in *The Presocratic Philosophers* (coauthored with G. S. Kirk), was the first thinker to provide an explicit definition of the underlying unity of the plurality of existing things which all thinkers had hitherto taken for granted. Heraclitus emphasized, more than any previous thinker, the degree to which a man is part of his contextual world, and he stressed that man's effective functioning depends upon his recognizing, and accommodating himself to, the structural principle of that contextual world, the *logos.*

Wheelwright, Philip. *Heraclitus.* Princeton: Princeton University Press, 1959.

Wheelwright's book is a systematic presentation and interpretation of the doctrines of Heraclitus. In his sequence of chapters, each headed by a translation of the surviving fragments relevant to the chapter's theme, the author moves from the method and the basic assumptions of Heraclitus through his cosmology and psychology to a consideration of the philosopher's religious perspective and views on morality, ending with a discussion of the paradoxical hidden harmony underlying the whole philosophical system.

There are special virtues in Wheelwright's presentation which make his exposition pleasantly lucid to a modern reader unfamiliar with Greek or with the cultural context of Heraclitus. In his introduction, the author points out the overlapping spheres of the Greek noun, verb, and adjective, and he clarifies Heraclitus' failure to distinguish clearly between things, actions, and qualities. Other distinctions taken for granted by moderns but absent or unclear in Heraclitus

are those between concrete and abstract, and subject and object. In a later chapter Wheelwright makes a distinction between surface and indepth metaphors and paradoxes, thereby elucidating a fundamental aspect of the Heraclitean world view and its intuition that paradox is an ultimate constitutive principle in the universe.

Fire for Heraclitus is both a primary element of the phenomenal world and a symbol of the constant natural process of change and self-transformation. Fire is forever in process of "kindling" and "being extinguished"; the world is formed by the transformation of cosmic fire into elemental terrestrial earth and water, which in turn liquefy and evaporate back into the cosmic fire.

"Soul" in living things consists of the elemental fiery substance hovering between the condition of water and fire. Self-kindling and self-extinguishing, "soul" is "a microcosm reflecting, in minuscule, the essential nature of reality at large." The nature

213

Postulation of the Logos

of soul is paradoxical in that it is both an emergent and a finite phenomenon within the larger world-order and a substance endowed with a limited degree of autonomy of its own. Although soul is essentially a transient phenomenon, Heraclitus seems to have held that the more actively "self-kindling" souls might outlive the body and endure for a time as mortal deities, vigilant "guardians of the living and the dead." Ultimately, however, they too must dissolve and perish.

Genuine divinity endowed with immortality is ascribed by Heraclitus only to the logos itself, the fundamental principle of change which regulates the perpetual upward and downward transformations of elemental fire and assures the unity of opposites. Wheelwright stresses that although Heraclitus in many fragments employs the traditional language of religion for the principle, it is nonteleological and hardly to be described adequately in anthropomorphic terms unless one accepts the analogy of an

irresponsible child "moving counters in a game; the royal power is a child's."

In his chapter entitled "Man among men," Wheelwright argues that in the human community also the characteristically Heraclitean complementarity of opposing perspectives holds true. A genuine community can exist only insofar as there is something "common," some shared awareness among citizens which is nourished by a divine source analogous and perhaps identical with the logos. Yet communities are also representative of the warring nature of opposites in the universe at large, and although the aristocrat Heraclitus expressed his disapproval of flagrant self-assertive *hybris* on the part of individuals, he is confirmed in his misanthropy by his observation of the prevalent insentient nature of most men and by his assumption that in nature, as well as in society, strife is the dominant principle and harmony is to be perceived with difficulty only by one who looks intently beyond appearances. — C.W.C.

Additional Recommended Reading

Fränkel, Hermann. "Heraclitus on God and the Phenomenal World," in *Transactions and Proceedings of the American Philological Association.* 69 (1938), 230-244. A discussion of the concept of God in Heraclitus with special attention devoted to fragment 67DK.

Jaeger, Werner. *The Theology of the Early Greek Philosophers.* Ch. VII. Oxford: The Clarendon Press, 1947. An analysis of the religious content and implications of the doctrines of Heraclitus.

Kirk, G. S., and J. E. Raven. *The Presocratic Philosophers: A Critical History with a Selection of Texts.* Cambridge: The University Press, 1960. The Greek text of fragments of the pre-Socratic philosophers, including Heraclitus, with English translation supplemented by a critical and historical commentary.

Minar, F. L. "The Logos of Heraclitus," in *Classical Philology.* 34 (1939), 323 ff. An investigation of the several possible meanings of *logos* in Heraclitus.

PERFECTION OF
THE GREEK CHORAL LYRIC

Type of event: Cultural: development in poetry
Time: c.500 B.C.
Locale: Greece and Greek colonies in the Mediterranean area

Principal personages:
SIMONIDES OF CEOS (c.556-468), first of the great writers of
choral lyrics
BACCHYLIDES (c.505-c.450), Simonides' nephew and another outstanding poet
PINDAR (c.518-c.453), the renowned Boeotian poet, master of the lyric honoring winners in athletic contests

Summary of Event

From the time of Homer, and probably even earlier, the Greeks celebrated important religious, political, and athletic events with performances of choral lyrics and accompanying dances composed in honor of the occasion. Appropriate forms, each with its own conventions, were developed to suit different situations. Extant poems and fragments include paeans in honor of Apollo, dithyrambs in praise of Dionysus, parthenia to be sung only by women, heroic hymns for epic heroes, encomia for famous men, and epinicia commemorating victors in the Olympic, Pythian, Isthmian, and Nemean Games.

Unlike the highly personal poems of Sappho and Anacreon, the choral lyrics were public statements, generally commissioned by rulers and noblemen. The poets and the singers and dancers who interpreted the lyrics were professionals, expected to give polished performances. Since only the words have survived, it is impossible to recreate the total effect of the lyrics; understanding them is made somewhat easier if we think of them in connec-

tion with the masques and entertainments of the Renaissance courts of Italy, France, and England, where music, dance, and poetry were also combined to compliment monarchs.

The first important choral lyrist whose works have survived was Stesichorus, who lived in Sicily around 600 B.C. Literary historian Albin Lesky calls him a bridge between epic and tragedy, for his poems gave special emphasis to tales of gods and heroes. Surviving fragments of his work refer to events and legends related in the *Odyssey,* the *Oresteia,* and the life of Heracles.

Ibycus, a native of the Greek colony of Rhegium in southern Italy, followed Stesichorus in using myths extensively in his early work. Later, writing at the court of the tyrant Polycrates of Samos, he turned to erotic love as his main theme.

The choral lyric reached its full flowering between 525 and 475 B.C. in the hands of three fine poets: Simonides of Ceos, his nephew Bacchylides, and the greatest master of all, Pindar.

Simonides, who was born about 556 B.C., is said to have been first a chorus master at a temple of Apollo, and later a traveling performer of lyrics at the courts of wealthy rulers, a position which gained him the reputation of being mercenary. He wrote for Pisistratus and his son Hipparchus in Athens and, at the end of his life, for Hiero of Syracuse, a noted patron of the arts.

It was Simonides who popularized the epinicia or victory songs for winners in the great games, preparing the way for Pindar's achievements in that genre. He also developed the threnos, the lament for the dead; his most famous poem is the epitaph on those who fell at Thermopylae, defending Greece against Persian invaders.

Bacchylides and Pindar, a generation younger than Simonides, seem to have been rivals for important commissions in their own lifetimes, and they have traditionally been compared. The author of the ancient treatise "On the Sublime" uses the two as representative types: Bacchylides of the polished, elegant, flawless style that never rises to great heights; and Pindar of the inspired, impassioned tone that redeems occasional lapses.

Bacchylides' extant epinicia reveal his strong interest in narrative. He generally emphasized plot in his mythological episodes, while Pindar focussed on their symbolic value. Critics have given high praise to Bacchylides' talents as a dramatic writer, especially in the scenes from the life of Theseus in two of his poems.

It is Pindar, however, who has, throughout the centuries, been acknowledged as the supreme master of the choral lyric, in spite of the fact that he is perhaps the most difficult of all the Greek poets to read and translate. Only a fraction of the many groups of his poems catalogued by Alexandrian scholars has survived, and his modern reputation rests largely on the epinicia, the only group that remains nearly intact.

These poems were written either in stanzaic verse or in the form traditionally known as the "Pindaric Ode." In the latter form, the poem consists of symmetrical sections, each divided into three parts: the strophe, the antistrophe, and the epode. Line length and meter could be varied to produce the desired effect rhythmically and emotionally. Without the music that accompanied every ode and without a full understanding of quantitative metrics based on length of syllable rather than stress, the modern reader can never fully appreciate Pindar's accomplishment, but those who can read him in the original marvel at the power of his verse.

All of Pindar's epinicia share certain elements. Each one contains some reference to the victory being commemorated, although, perhaps surprisingly, there is nowhere a lengthy description of the event itself. Sometimes the family of the victor is praised; the commission might specify the inclusion of certain items. One family even demanded that every one of their more than sixty victories in various contests be mentioned in their ode. Pindar wryly comments in the poem that moderation has value in all things. Each ode also alludes to famous myths, sometimes to stories about legendary ancestors of the victor or founders of his city, sometimes to tales illustrating

216

a particular moral point. Like earlier choral lyrists, Pindar nearly always included "gnomes" or moral proverbs.

Implicit in all of Pindar's odes, whatever their individual themes, is his conservative, aristocratic bias, his faith in the values of his class, which prevented him from understanding or sympathizing with the new spirit of democracy growing up in Athens; he stood with the neutral Thebans rather than with the city-states that defended their land against the Persians. It seems strange to a modern reader that a poet should find an

ideal in the winner of a chariot race, but victory in the games was for Pindar a symbol of the *arete*, the innate excellence that was the birthright of the aristocracy. Success at Olympus or Delphi brought a momentary radiance, a kind of glory, to a man or a city, bestowing a transient beauty upon the "dream of a shadow" that is man. It is this radiance, this beauty, that Pindar communicates in his lyrics, not the dust and excitement of the finish line; it is his poetic vision of the nature of man that has made him immortal.

Pertinent Literature

Norwood, Gilbert. *Pindar*. Berkeley: University of California Press, 1945.

Gilbert Norwood's lectures are highly illuminating for their insights into both the historical background of Pindar's work and the structure and imagery of the poems themselves. Although Norwood is writing primarily for those who read Pindar in the original Greek, his lucid discussions offer much to the layman as well.

The first chapter describes the stages by which Pindar became the most illustrious professional poet in the Greek world. His career began formally when he was commissioned at twenty by a Thessalian nobleman to commemorate the victory of a Thessalian boy in the Pythian games at Delphi. As his fame spread, he celebrated athletes and monarchs (who often owned winning chariot teams and race horses) in every corner of the Greek world. Diagoras of Rhodes, Hiero and Hagesias of Syracuse, Arcesilas IV of Cyrene, victors from Thebes, Aegina, even Locri in Italy all were honored in the epinicia. As poet and aristocrat,

Pindar felt able on most occasions to speak his mind freely, and at the height of his success he even gave advice on governing to Hiero and asked Arcesilas to restore to citizenship the banished nobleman who had commissioned the poem.

One of Norwood's central theses is that Pindar must be considered as a poet, not as a thinker; he devotes his lecture on Pindar's "Views on the Life of Man" to the premise that the poet had, in fact, very few coherent or consistent theories of philosophy, religion, or politics. He argues that Pindar lived in an age that was essentially prelogical. Attempts to create consistent systems began a generation later.

Therefore, in reading Pindar one must look not for theologies but for almost intuitive flashes of insight and feeling, such as his affirmation in the Sixth Nemean Ode of the divine origin and immortality of the soul, or the picture of the Last Judgment in the

217

Second Olympian. Norwood does not, of course, deny that Pindar had ideas, but he points out clearly that the poet's reputation rests on the greatness of his language and his ability to create beauty, rather than on his somewhat commonplace moral and religious maxims.

More than half of Norwood's study is devoted to close internal analysis of Pindar's odes. He suggests that earlier scholars have misdirected their efforts in trying to find unity for each of the odes in a particular idea that links the victory, the myths, and the morals. His view is that Pindar's odes achieve unity through a pervasive image or symbol that controls both the vivid pictorial effects and the choice of words throughout the poem. He demonstrates in detail the working out of these central symbols in several lyrics, discussing the use of the War-horse in the Seventh Isthmian, the Triple Diadem in the Seventh Nemean, and the Hunter in the Second Olympian, written to Thero of Agrigentum, whose name is the Greek word for hunter.

In his final chapter Norwood discusses Pindar's concept of the role of the poet, citing from the odes passages that relate to artistic creation. Pindar often spoke of poetry as something inspired, either by the gods, by the glory of his subject, or by his own spirit, meaning, perhaps, that part of himself which was divine. He emphasized, too, the obligation of the poet to speak the truth, although he did not allow this duty to prevent his altering myths to suit his purposes.

Pindar's best description of the kind of poetry he wrote comes, in Norwood's opinion, in the Ninth Pythian where the poet expresses his belief that the best way to treat legends is to "embroider" the essential moment in a story rather than go through the whole tale. It is significant that in the same passage Pindar speaks of his hearers as "cultured"; his work was clearly directed to a sophisticated audience.

Not all students of Pindar will agree with some of Norwood's theories and interpretations of the poet's techniques and symbols. He does, however, offer many stimulating new perspectives for the study of the great odes.

Hamilton, Edith. "Pindar: The Last Greek Aristocrat," in *The Greek Way to Western Civilization.* New York: W. W. Norton & Company, Inc., 1930. Also in Modern Library paperback.

Miss Hamilton's essay is a brilliant analysis of the essential elements of Pindar's philosophy and poetic genius. She sees him as, in some respects, a tragic figure, looking back at an ideal that never reached fulfillment, and incapable of sympathizing with the forces of nationalism, humanism, and democracy that inspired the great Athenian civilization of the fifth century B.C. and, through it, much of Western thought. Nonetheless, she says, an understanding of the aristocratic ideal of Pindar is necessary for full comprehension of the genius of his people.

In Pindar's view, society should be ruled by aristocrats, men born into a certain class, whose excellence rested in their blood, rather than on their wealth. Since they were, so to speak, "born at the top," they should theoretically be free of all pressure to compete for power and therefore able to act for virtue's sake alone. The responsibilities of the aristocrat should be as great as his privileges; Hamilton outlines the demanding code of conduct which he was expected to uphold. The result of the privileges and self-discipline of the ruling class was expected to be just, disinterested government of the less privileged. As Hamilton says, this ideal is "impeccable" in theory but impossible in practice, for noble birth has never been a guarantee of integrity. Men born with power tend to seek more, and privilege easily degenerates into prejudice.

Pindar apparently never perceived the inevitability of the downfall of the aristocratic ideal, and he went on year after year glorifying the victors in the games, which were solely the province of the nobility in his day, as "the noble representatives of the noble, showing in themselves the true ideal for humanity."

Hamilton points out many aristocratic characteristics and attitudes in Pindar himself. Though paid for his work, he spoke in his odes to noble-men and princes as their equal or superior, urging them to fulfill their aristocratic destiny. The very tone of the poetry, cold, austere, magnificent, but always remote from common humanity, suggests his aristocratic stance.

Hamilton's great lament for Pindar, however, is that he was bound by an innate conservative, cautious, defensive frame of mind which led him to urge the nobility to preserve what they had, to accept their destiny, to strive for what was in their power rather than to risk all in reaching for something greater. There is, therefore, in Pindar's poetry, the sadness that accompanies the accomplishment of all goals; there is nothing to look forward to, for the best has already been, and the worst might be yet to come.

In conclusion, Hamilton speaks of our double loss in relation to Pindar. The language barrier prevents the English-speaking reader from ever comprehending his "peculiar beauties of language and rhythm." The far greater deprivation, however, is that "this man of genius used his great gifts to shed light only upon the past and turned away from the present which was so full of promise for the future of all the world to come." — *E.J.L.*

Additional Recommended Reading

Hadas, Moses. *A History of Greek Literature.* Ch. 6. New York: Columbia University Press, 1950. A work including the development of the choral lyric and a discussion of its major practitioners, giving a helpful analysis of the structure of Pindar's odes.

Higham, T. F., and C. M. Bowra, eds. *The Oxford Book of Greek Verse in Translation.* Oxford: The Clarendon Press, 1938. A useful anthology that includes selections from the poets discussed.

Perfection of the Greek Choral Lyric

Lesky, Albin. *A History of Greek Literature.* Translated by James Willis and Cornelius de Heer. Pt. IV. New York: Thomas Y. Crowell Company, 1966. A survey of the origins of the lyric, the major poets, and extant texts and translations.

Murray, Gilbert. *The Literature of Ancient Greece.* 3rd ed. Chicago: University of Chicago Press, 1956. A good general discussion of the development of the "choir song," its performance by professional singers and dancers, and of the important writers in the genre.

Oxford Classical Dictionary. Edited by M. Cary *et al.* Oxford: The Clarendon Press, 1949. Brief, cogent entries on both poets and poetic forms.

Pindar. *The Odes of Pindar.* Translated by Richmond Lattimore. Chicago: University of Chicago Press, 1947. A fine poetic translation with a comprehensive but concise introduction.

INSTITUTION OF THE PLEBEIAN TRIBUNATE

Type of event: Constitutional: recognition of the rights of the lower orders of
society
Time: 494/493 B.C.
Locale: Rome

Principal personages:

MANIUS VALERIUS, dictator in 494
MENENIUS AGRIPPA, ambassador of the senate to the dissi-
dent plebeians
SICINIUS, leader of the plebeian revolt
GAIUS LICINIUS and
LUCIUS ALBINUS, first tribunes to be chosen by the plebeians

Summary of Event

Because of the lack of contemporary sources, and because evidence
was at times deliberately suppressed
and falsified for purposes of family
aggrandizement or for purposes of
moral or artistic edification, much
early Roman history lies shrouded in
obscurity and myth. Despite conflicting details, however, there seems to
be a hard core of fact relating to the
institution of the plebeian tribunate
as described by Dionysius of Halicarnassus and Livy. A secession of the
plebs, prompted by their abuse at the
hands of patricians, was followed by
the election of officers to represent
plebeians and defend their rights; ultimately an oath was sworn by the
plebeians to regard as inviolable the
persons of their new tribunes. Conflicting accounts exist about the place
of secession, whether on the Aventine
hill or the Sacred Mount; about the
number of tribunes elected, whether
two, four, or five; about the manner
of their election; and about the oath
taken making them sacrosanct.

According to Livy, trouble broke
Appius Claudius and Publius Servil-

ius; the plebeians complained that
while they were fighting in the army to
preserve Roman independence, they
were being enslaved at home by patrician creditors. Their feelings were
particularly exasperated by the pitiful
sight of a former soldier who, having
lost his home and his crops to the
enemy, had to borrow money in order
to pay his taxes. To induce plebeians
to take up arms against a Volscian
army, Servilius was forced to order
that no Roman citizen should be held
in chains or in prison to prevent him
from enlisting, that no one should
seize or sell a soldier's property while
he was in service, and that no one
should harass his children or grand-
children. But continued pressure on
debtors caused the plebs to become
violent; they began to assemble at
night on the Aventine and Esquiline,
and they refused to fight against the
invading Sabines. An edict by the
dictator Manius Valerius giving greater protection to plebeians from their
creditors made it possible to muster
an army; but in the absence of permanent adjustments, the plebs took

221

the advice of a certain Sicinius and withdrew to the Sacred Mount three miles from the city across the Anio River. This secession caused panic in the city among the patricians who were at one and the same time afraid of hostile foreign invaders and also of those plebeians who remained behind. According to Livy, the senate compromised with a constitutional innovation.

This new agreement, a milestone in the struggle between the orders, created an exclusive plebeian office to protect "the people" from the aristocratic consuls. The "tribunes of the people" at first had only a negative function because they could do no more than "forbid" overt acts inimical to a plebeian at the instant of its perpetration. Moreover, aid had to be initiated by a complaining plebeian, so a tribune could not absent himself from the city for a whole night nor shut his doors at any time. The person of the tribune was declared sacrosanct by a *lex sacrata*; anyone who interfered with a tribune doing his duty became an outlaw, liable to be killed by plebeians.

At first there were two tribunes, or four or five according to some sources, but the number grew to ten. This strange negative office, creating a set of parallel officials working at cross-purposes with the old magistrates of the state, was intended partly to satisfy plebeian unrest and partly to keep plebeians from becoming regular magistrates which would have usurped the prerogative of the nobility. In 471 a law transferred the election of tribunes from the assembly of the *curiae* to that of the *comitia tributa,* an event and date which Eduard Meyer and some other authorities associate with the actual creation of the plebeian tribunate itself. Eventually the veto of a plebeian tribune permitted him to negate the passage of any legislation prejudicial to plebeian concerns. So it was only natural that tribunes began to sit in the senate to make known their objection to laws before they were actually passed, or to suggest legislation and even to call together the senate. The tribunes were also able to veto acts of the consuls and other magistrates except dictators. In 287, plebiscites of their *comitia tributa* were given the same force as laws passed by the senate or the *comitia centuriata.*

Because of its invaluable power of veto, the office of plebeian tribune came to be sought after avidly. Even patricians had themselves adopted by plebeians in order to become eligible. It is ironic that this weak, plebeian, negative, makeshift office became so powerful that the Emperor Augustus used the authority of the plebeian tribunate to rule Rome in preference to consular *imperium* because of the unique right of the former to initiate or veto legislation.

Pertinent Literature

Greenidge, A. H. J. *Roman Public Life.* London: Macmillan & Company, 1922.

A.H.J. Greenidge was the author of a number of excellent works on problems of Roman law and consti- tution. Among these is his *Roman Public Life*; though first published in 1901, it remains a standard item in any bibliography on the subject.

Greenidge's exposition of the power of the tribunate is largely concerned with the constitutional aspects of this strange office which in some ways set up a state within a state. He notes that from the beginning the tribunate involved a dual authority: a negative control over the whole people represented in the person of their magistrates, all of whom at this stage in Roman history were aristocrats, and a positive authority within the plebeian or nonnoble community of Rome. Evidence of their power is seen in the right of veto and the right to elicit "plebiscites," *scita plebei* or *plebiscita,* from the plebeian *concilium* or "assembly." The tribunate was established in order to counteract the consular *imperium,* and any plebeian who felt that he had been injured by the order of a magistrate could ask for a tribune's help or *auxilium.* If granted, the tribune's response took the form of a veto of the offensive decree. Since this power of intercession had to be exercised by the tribune in person, he was expected to be available at all times for on-the-spot action.

This negative control which the tribunes exercised over Roman magistrates would have been meaningless without means of enforcement. Such enforcement could have been arranged for through judicial prosecution before the regular courts of the community, but such dependence upon agencies outside an officer himself was not consonant with the Roman idea of magistracy. Every magistrate, by virtue of being a magistrate, had to have to a greater or less degree the power to enforce his own decrees.

This power, known as *coercitio,* belonged to the tribunes as a logical consequence of their right of veto. The sanctity of their persons, guaranteed by the plebs, made resistance impossible; and where necessary they could use almost any means—arrest, imprisonment, fines, scourgings, and even executions—in their defense of the plebs. In time, the exercise of summary jurisdiction over citizens in matters involving severe penalties became subject to the right of appeal on the part of the accused. When an appeal was made, the tribune brought the case before the plebeian assembly.

This right of dealing with the plebs, a necessary consequence of the tribune's *auxilium,* was extended so that the tribunes could propose measures of concern to the plebeians for debate in the assembly. Eventually in 287, such *plebiscita* were raised to the level of laws and made binding not only upon plebeians but upon patricians as well.

The community of the plebs was modeled upon that of the larger community of the *populus.* Two aediles were assigned to the tribunes in imitation of the two quaestors who assisted the consuls. But since the plebs was not strictly the community of the *populus,* nor even in the beginning a legalized corporation within the city, the tribunes were therefore not magistrates in the constitutional sense of the term. They enjoyed no use of *imperium,* no right to perform *auspicia,* and did not even earn the distinction of wearing *insignia* of office. Their power rested upon a religious sanction, upon the oath which the plebeians took to eliminate anyone who attacked their tribunes. This oath prompts Greenidge

223

to say: "Perhaps Rome is the only state that has definitely invested the demagogue or 'champion of the people' with a halo of sanctity."

Taylor, L. R. "Forerunners of the Gracchi," in *Journal of Roman Studies.* Vol. LII, 1962, pp. 19-27.

While Cicero called the tribunate an office born in sedition to create sedition, L.R. Taylor sees it only gradually transformed into an instrument of revolution, and then more as a symptom than a cause of decline. There were two periods when this office was especially active: from the beginning until the passing of the *lex Hortensia* in 287; and from the tribunate of Tiberius Gracchus in 133 until Caesar's dictatorship, a period when the tribunate was especially revolutionary and violent.

The author is interested primarily in the interim period when it is generally held that the tribunate was placidly coöperative with the senate. Indeed, after the acceptance of plebeians into the consulship there was a period of coöperation even though the tribune Gaius Flaminius and his followers between 232 and 216 generally bypassed the senate in order to appeal directly to the people. The war with Hannibal naturally encouraged unity. But in 171, centurions who were disgruntled with the conditions of recall into service during the Macedonian Wars appealed to the tribunes to help them defy the levy. To the author it was the year 151 which inaugurated the "period of defiance of the will of the senate" leading directly to the rise of the Gracchi. Trouble broke out when forces were needed for new wars in Spain. The common soldiers, anticipating little booty and a long engagement, appealed to the tribunes. In obstructing the levy of troops the tribunes were, indeed, following a tradition established when the first tribunes seceded to the Sacred Mount to avoid a levy. In the fracas, the tribunes illegally seized the consuls and put them in prison, a new departure establishing "a precedent which was to be followed several times in the next century." In the eighteen years following this event and preceding the tribunate of Tiberius Gracchus, twenty-three episodes are recorded involving relatively unknown tribunes, which show serious strife between them and the magistrates and the senatorial majority. Tribunitian legislation proposed in defiance of senatorial authority must have been frequent judging from the *lex Aelia* and the *lex Fufia,* passed about the year 150, which tried to curb troublesome legislation and the "fury of the tribunes" by regulating the manner and time of proposing bills. The main items of contention were terms concerning soldiers' enlistments and agrarian laws. When in 149 a tribunitian bill vainly called for an investigation of a treacherous attack on the Lusitanians, the tribune L. Calpurnius Piso sponsored the law which established a permanent court to try magistrates accused of extortion from allies and provincials. Further tribunitian laws interfered in the distribution of provinces and appointments to major commands. Tribunes presented the *lex Gabinia* in 139 and the *lex Cassia* in 137, which, though

224

never passed, threatened patrician political monopolies by demanding a secret ballot in judicial assemblies. Continued strife came out of the long Spanish wars when tribunes supported battle-tired veterans demanding release from service. In 140 a tribune even tried to prevent the departure of a consul for Spain. In 138 two tribunes, one of whom was regarded by Cicero as the foulest of men, demanded that the consuls release veterans from service. When the consuls refused to act, they were, in the manner of 138, led off to prison. Continuing troubles in Spain, over which Scipio was put in charge supported by the tribunes, and the slave war in Sicily with possible repercussions in Italy, form the background for the election of Tiberius Gracchus to the tribunate in 133.

Taylor considers tribunitian defiance of the authority of the senate, especially in military matters, a sign of decay in the mixed Roman constitution which Polybius saw distributed evenly among the magistrates, the senate, and the people. Between 155 and 134 the tribunes were men of small stature who helped to deepen the growing factionalism in the ruling classes by carrying out the designs of ambitious individuals. While, indeed, the imprisonment of the two consuls in 138 was the only revolutionary act during this period, the continual interference of tribunes in levies, army discipline, and the relations of subject peoples make them true forerunners of the Gracchi and the later demagogues of the great age of revolution which was to follow. — *M.J.C.*

Additional Recommended Reading

Heitland, W. E. *The Roman Republic.* Cambridge: The University Press, 1923. 3 vols. A classic general study first published in 1909 but still valuable.

Jolowicz, H. F. *Historical Introduction to the Study of Roman Law.* 2nd ed. Cambridge: The University Press, 1952. The author sees the tribunate, although an integral part of the Roman constitution, as an instrument of party strife.

Jones, H. Stuart. "Plebeian Institutions," in *Cambridge Ancient History.* Vol. VII, pp. 450-456. New York: The Macmillan Company, 1928. A view holding traditional accounts of the plebeian tribunate to be later efforts to read some legality into the office.

Lewis, Naphtali, and Meyer Reinhold. *Roman Civilization.* Volume I: *The Republic.* New York: Columbia University Press, 1951. Translations of passages from Dionysius of Halicarnassus, Valerius Maximus, and Plutarch describe the creation of the tribunate together with its powers and duties.

Wolff, Hans Julius. *Roman Law: An Historical Introduction.* Norman: University of Oklahoma Press, 1951. A thesis that the democratic character of the tribunate disappeared in the later Republic so that it became the willing tool of the senatorial aristocracy.

Lintott, A. W. *Violence in Republican Rome.* London: Oxford University Press, 1968. A view of the tribunate as a formalization of the conflict between the oligarchic and democratic elements in Roman society.

THE NAVAL LAW OF THEMISTOCLES

Type of event: Military and political: enactment of defense measures
Time: c.483 B.C.
Locale: Athens

Principal personages:
THEMISTOCLES (c.528-462), son of Neocles, archon and general
ARISTIDES (c.520-468), son of Lysimachus, Athenian statesman
PERICLES (c.495-429), son of Xanthippus, Athenian statesman and general

Summary of Event

About 488 B.C., war broke out between Athens and the island state of Aegina over commercial rivalry. For some time each side was content to raid the other's shipping, but in about 485, Athens determined to bring the conflict to a decisive finish. Building her navy up to a strength of seventy ships, approximating her rival's well-manned fleet, Athens boldly invaded the island state. The attempt, however, proved abortive.

About 484 B.C., fresh and rich veins of silver-bearing ore were discovered near Laurium in southern Attica. What to do with the sudden new wealth that poured into the state's treasury from these mines became a major political issue. Under Aristides' leadership, conservatives called for distributing the surplus money among the citizens; Themistocles had other ideas, based on his conviction that security of Athens' trade and safety of her vital imports of food, timber, and industrial metals depended upon her control of the sea. As archon in 493 he had already begun giving this conviction tangible form by successfully pressing for construction of a new and better harbor at Piraeus. He now proposed to use the state's new income to build an invincible navy, and moved the passage of a naval law providing for a fleet of two hundred warships. Aegina, with no silver mines under her direct control, could scarcely hope to compete with such an armada. The assembly voted the proposal into law and incidentally, though not without encouragement from the faction supporting Themistocles, ostracized Aristides.

Between 483 and 480 the ships were built, and when, in the latter year, the Persians invaded Greece, relations were hastily patched up with Aegina and Aristides was recalled. In the naval campaigns against Xerxes, the Athenian ships were the mainstay of the united Greek fleet. Operations steadily reduced Persian naval power, and the Athenian navy emerged from the war as the most powerful fleet in Greek waters. By 460 Athens was able to turn her attention to Aegina again, and after the Aeginetan fleet had been destroyed in a great battle, she successfully invaded the island. In 457, after a siege, Aegina surren-

226

dered to Athens and agreed to pay tribute.

Historically, the creation of a new military institution has frequently carried with it unforeseen social and political consequences. This condition now occurred at Athens because of her huge new navy. The crew of a single trireme consisted of almost two hundred men, including a captain, six subordinate officers, some half-dozen sailors, and 170 oarsmen. The rowers were freemen recruited from the class of *thetes,* the poorest and up until this time the least important politically of the four census groups. But now, as maritime power became a major factor in the total strength of the state, the Athenians realized that their continued supremacy depended as much on the lowly oar-pulling *thetes* as it did on the middle-class infantry. Statesmen such as Ephialtes and Pericles began marshaling the voting strength of the *thetes* in the Assembly and made them conscious of their political power as a class. Since the sailors resided for the most part in the port of Piraeus or in the city of Athens, they found it easier to attend meetings of the assembly than did the rural population, and they gradually came to dominate action in that body. Thus, for example, Pericles was able to secure the ostracism of the aristocratic statesmen Cimon and Thucydides (son of Melesias), whose followings came mostly from rural areas.

Over the next several decades, the power of the urban democrats led to enactment of reforms suggested by Ephialtes and Pericles. The upper-class *aeroeopagus* was stripped of all its powers except that of trying cases of murder. *Zeugitae,* or middle-class farmers, were admitted to the archonships. Athenian citizenship was restricted to persons both of whose parents were native born. Instituting state pay for service on the Council or juries made it possible for *thetes* of the lowest class to take a direct part in government, thereby rendering a more democratic, popular tone to the Assembly and courts. The result was what many ancient commentators called "radical democracy."

The furthering of democracy was accompanied by development of a theory of seapower. Athens' fleet made her mistress of the maritime trade routes in the Aegean Sea, and she could therefore manipulate to a considerable degree the flow of important commodities such as grain, timber, and metal. By supervising movement and importation of these materials, Athens could control the power of the Aegean states. Such use of seapower, propounded in modern times in the doctrine of the American Admiral Mahan that "he who rules the sea rules the land," was to be exploited to its fullest by Pericles in the years immediately preceding the Peloponnesian War. As part of his program to make Athens invulnerable, Themistocles supervised the erection of massive walls which transformed Piraeus and Athens into a single impregnable fortress. Recognizing the relative weakness of Athens' land army, and that in time of war an efficient hostile army would have little trouble devastating the Attic countryside, Themistocles reasoned that Athens' citizenry could find shelter inside the walls and could survive on

227

food brought in on merchant ships convoyed and protected by the fore- most navy of Greece, the fleet begun by Themistocles.

Pertinent Literature

Frisch, Hartvig. *The Constitution of the Athenians.* Copenhagen: Nordisk Vorlag, 1942.

Athens is generally associated with ancient democracy and enlightened idealism. It comes, therefore, as something of a surprise to realize that most Athenian writers whose work has survived show a strong antidemocratic point of view. One such was the pamphleteer who wrote *The Constitution of the Athenians.* Frisch has produced an English translation together with an admirable commentary, full notes, and discussion. The name of the author of the pamphlet is unknown. Since the manuscript has come down to us in the corpus of Xenophon's work, he is sometimes called Pseudo-Xenophon, but more often the Old Oligarch. The exact date at which he wrote is also unknown. Frisch ably argues a case for 432 B.C. some months in advance of the outbreak of the Peloponnesian War, and a date about 430 B.C. is probably correct. An oligarch he certainly was, a man possibly of noble birth and certainly of the upper class. He was horrified to see the lowest born citizens rising to prominence, holding office, making a stir in the courts, and voicing their uneducated opinions in the Assembly. While he disliked democracy, he nonetheless realized that the sailors had greatly increased the power of Athens, and he gave the *thetes* full credit for having done so. If it was power for themselves they had wanted, power they had received, and they now managed it well in their interest.

In the chapter titled "Sea-Power and Defensive Theory," Frisch shows that the Athenians well understood the naval and military strategy developed by Themistocles and Pericles. The former, Frisch thinks, was the originator of the idea. It was given final, concrete expression in the fortification of Athens by Pericles. The defense works included ringwalls around Athens and Piraeus, and three Long Walls, each stretching about five miles to connect the two cities. The whole complex was an impregnable stronghold; given the military technique of the fifth century, Athens could not be successfully carried by storm. It held powerful weapons in its own hands. No Greek state was entirely self-sufficient. If one was rich in a commodity such as iron, it was poor in another such as grain. Athens, by controlling the exchange of goods by sea, controlled the power of many of the Greek states, since no state could import what it required without permission from Athens, whose citizens could secure all their needs from overseas. In the naval sphere Athenian strategy was offensive: to raid the enemy by landing troops from the fleet in his territory. On the mainland front its strategy was defensive, based on holding the fortifications. Pitched battles would not be fought against powerful armies. Only small states might be attacked. The Old Oligarch complained that

228

such strategy made the role of the middle and upper classes in the army secondary to that of the lowest classes operating the fleet.

The Old Oligarch ends his tract with an interesting section on the possibility of overthrowing the democratic regime in favor of a more narrowly based government. He says that such an action, to be successful, would have to have many men supporting it, and that the antidemocratic forces were too few to accomplish it in the face of the numerous *thetes*. His extreme, if cynical, dislike of democracy shows the unfortunate factionalism which had arisen in Athens, the unhappy result of the creation of that "radical democracy" which had grown out of the dockyards and fleet.

Singer, Charles, ed. *A History of Technology*. Vol. 2: *The Mediterranean Civilization and the Middle Ages*. Oxford: The Clarendon Press, 1956.

The Naval Law of Themistocles was a political act of the Athenian Assembly. It was, however, one thing to vote for a fleet of two hundred warships, and another matter of technique and hard work to have them built. Most books on Greek history have little or nothing to say about ancient technology, but Singer and his colleagues have produced a book on the technical knowledge of the ancient world which covers such subjects as shipbuilding, metallurgy, mining, and so on, explaining the methods necessary for going about the actual procurement of Themistocles' ships.

The construction of the ships would not have been possible without silver money to pay the shipwrights and to purchase timber. Athens had one of the few sources of silver in the Aegean region, and C. N. Bromehead explains in the chapter on "Mining and Quarrying" in *A History of Technology*, how it was exploited. Silver-bearing lead sulphide ore (galena) had been discovered at Laurium in Mycenean times, but Athenian mining did not begin until the sixth century, as we know from the archaeological investigation of the ancient pits. The finding of the most valuable deposits of ore was made about 484 B.C. by a man named Callias, who must have been a persistent and imaginative man, for the rich veins of galena lie under two layers of limestone which are themselves some distance underground. Eventually, over two thousand vertical shafts were dug to reach the ore, the deepest descending nearly four hundred feet. Forced ventilation was provided by means of baffles which caught surface winds and deflected air down the shafts. Fires could also be built at the bottoms of some shafts to force the air in the mines up and out, thus creating down drafts in adjacent shafts and along the connecting galleries which were being worked. The miners used small oil lamps set in niches for light, and iron chisels, hammers, and picks for digging. By the end of the first century A.D. when the mines were exhausted the Athenian miners had excavated more than two million tons of material a shovelful at a time, and from their smelting operations they left behind enormous slag heaps which extracted less than sixty ounces of pure silver per ton of ore.

T. C. Lethbridge's chapter on

"Shipbuilding" is a brief survey of the evolution of Greek and Roman designs and methods. The standard warship before Themistocles' generation had been the penteconter, a ship driven by fifty oars. Towards the end of the sixth century the need for more speed suggested an increase in oarpower. But wooden ships could not be lengthened indefinitely because they tended to warp. The solution was to lengthen the ship only slightly and to superimpose two additional banks of oarsmen above the original one so that 170 men could be employed. The invention of this kind of warship, the trireme, is attributed to Aminocles of Corinth. A trireme was about 120 feet long, with a beam of fourteen feet and a draft of three. It displaced about eighty tons. Two hundred ships would require, allowing for the inevitable wastage of woodworking, well over sixteen thousand tons of timber. Tall trees were required for keels and masts, and the best came to Athens from Macedonia and the north shore of the Aegean. The Athenians' organization for the transport of this mass of lumber must itself have been impressive. Triremes were built from a keel and latitudinal framing, with the hull planking sawed with considerable skill to fit the curving lines of the ship's body. The few fragments of Greek ships which have been found show that the standard of their carpentry and joinery was high. — *S.K.E.*

Additional Recommended Reading

Perrin, Bernadotte. *Plutarch's Themistocles and Aristides.* New York: Charles Scribner's Sons, 1901. There are no adequate biographies of Themistocles or of Aristides; Plutarch's ancient versions are here translated, and the reader is helped with introductions and copious notes.

Havelock, Eric A. *The Liberal Temper in Greek Politics.* New Haven: Yale University Press, 1957. A treatise discussing the democratic views of Greek liberals.

Morrison, J. S. "Notes on Certain Greek Nautical Terms," in *Classical Quarterly.* Vol. 41 (1947), pp. 122-135. A short study describing the trireme and its equipment.

Cary, Max. "*Callias o Laccoplutos,*" in *Classical Review.* Vol. 50 (1936), p. 55. The title of this article, which is written in English, means "Callias the Pit-Wealthy"; it contains what little information is available about a remarkable man.

BEGINNINGS OF METAPHYSICS

Type of event: Philosophical: formulation of basic principles
Time: c.480 B.C.
Locale: Elea in southern Italy

Principal personages:
PARMENIDES OF ELEA (born c.515), Eleatic philosopher
ZENO OF ELEA (born c.490), Eleatic philosopher, successor to Parmenides

Summary of Event

Parmenides of Elea, according to Plato, visited Athens as an old man in the company of his disciple Zeno and there met and conversed with the young Socrates. As this encounter must have taken place soon after the middle of the fifth century B.C., the publication of Parmenides' poem *On Nature,* clearly designated within its proem as a work of the philosopher's youth, must be dated about the second decade of the century. Tradition presents Parmenides as a disciple at one time of the Pythagorean philosopher Ameinias, and although nothing further is known about this Ameinias, it is clear that despite its radical break with Pythagoreanism, the doctrine of Parmenides is a development out of Pythagoreanism. The surviving fragments of the poem also indicate that Parmenides was familiar with the traditions of Ionian speculative cosmology and that he deliberately affiliated himself with a tradition of religious cosmological poetry as old as Hesiod.

The treatise *On Nature,* which survives only in fragments, was composed in dactylic hexameters. It is thus formally set off from the scientific prose style accepted by Ionian cosmological thinkers, following instead a tradition of cosmological poetry to which Hesiod, Xenophanes, the Orphics, Empedocles, and even Lucretius belong. The poem begins with a proem describing a mystical journey taken by the author to the abode of the great goddess of Truth who presides over the portals of Night and Day and who, persuaded by the young man's zeal for wisdom, undertakes to reveal to him the two opposed perspectives open to men, "The Way of Truth" and "The Way of Opinion." The proem thus depicts the doctrine of Parmenides as a mystical revelation much in the manner of Hesiod's *Theogony.* Nevertheless, despite the strong religious color of the language, it is clear that the truth communicated to Parmenides commands rational assent through its own persuasive cogency and hence is not by any means an intuitive vision describable only in mythical terms; the formulation of the doctrine as a revelation perhaps enhances its authority, but the doctrine does not depend on the revelation for its cogency.

There are, says the goddess, only two premises of thought open to the mind: either "it is" or "it is not." Although the subject of the verb is not specified (in the English translation,

231

"it" is an expletive, not a pronominal subject), it is generally agreed by interpreters that Parmenides is asserting the logical impossibility of formulating a negative predication about anything without at the same time implying its nonexistence: if a thing "is" at all, one cannot logically assert that it "is not" red or black, or anything else. Thus a negative predication about what really exists is logically impossible, as is also any mixed affirmation of a thing's existence and negative predication. Consequently, the only logically admissible propositions are that "it is" or "Being exists," and logical predications about Being that are free from contradition within that proposition. Consequently, Being is eternal, one, uniformly continuous, homogeneous, indivisible, and motionless. This doctrine seems to be related, on the one hand, to a Pythagorean list of opposites, one column of which Parmenides affirms while rejecting the other. On the other hand, the doctrine is related to the dominant conception of the Ionian cosmological tradition: that nature is essentially a single substance. Parmenides, however, will not allow any logical validity to the Ionian view that the cosmos known to experience represents modifications or qualitative differentiations of this primary substance. Qualitative differentiations, he holds, are themselves logically inconceivable, and therefore he simply rejects sense experience as a valid source of knowledge in favor of an intellectual criterion of logical consistency.

In the second major portion of his poem, of which much less has survived than of "The Way of Truth," Parmenides presents a cosmogony of a more traditional kind in terms of sensible opposites. This cosmogony has no absolutely valid logical ground but only a relative validity: it is an account of the physical world known to human sense experience, a world whose features cannot be explained without resort to logical paradox.

Parmenides' disciple and successor, Zeno of Elea, elaborated further the logical problems in the common-sense view of the world in a famous set of paradoxes demonstrating the impossibility of formulating a logical concept of motion. As a consequence of Parmenides' distinction between a realm of absolute logical truth and a realm of paradoxical sense experience concerning which only paradoxical opinions can be asserted, Greek philosophy after Parmenides was dominated by a concern to clarify the relation between logically impeccable assertions guaranteed by the principle of noncontradiction, and affirmations about the physical world having only relative validity. On the one hand, there emerged the epistemological skepticism of the Sophists, who argued that all opinions regarding the world of sense experience are relative and void of truth-value, though not necessarily of persuasive cogency. On the other hand, the implicit dualism of Parmenides' realms of logical truth about Being, and contradictory opinion about Appearances, served as a foundation for Platonic idealism's explicit dualism of (1) a realm of thought wherein Form or Ideas, each characterized by the predications of Parmenides' Being (unity, eternity, changelessness), exist absolutely, and (2) a realm of sense experience of physical nature, concerning whose flux of contradictory impressions no genuinely valid account can be given. Finally, the Greek cosmological speculation proceeded after Parmenides on a new level: henceforth no important thinker sought to explain the world of sense experience in terms of differentiation of a primary sub-stance. Empedocles of Acragas, Anaxagoras of Clazomenae, and the atomists Leucippus and Democritus all formulated pluralistic systems recognizing in one way or another the logical requisites of Being laid down by Parmenides.

Pertinent Literature

De Santillana, Giorgio. *Prologue to Parmenides*. (Lectures in memory of Louise Taft Semple delivered March 28 and April 1, 1964). Cincinnati: University of Cincinnati, 1964.

The interpretation of Parmenides' poem sketched out in these two brief lectures of Santillana is fresh and provocative in that it is presented from a perspective of the history of science rather than from the perspective from which pre-Socratic philosophy has usually been viewed, that of the history of cosmological systems. Santillana argues that Parmenides must be restored to the world of science without removing him from the realm of metaphysics, where he is rightly considered a founder. The criticism of Parmenides has been vitiated, says Santillana, in antiquity by Plato's use of his doctrine and in the modern era by idealist philosphers' efforts to make him the "banner-bearer of the anti-scientific attitude" as well as by the concern of linguistic analysts to demonstrate a confusion in Parmenides' mind between the existential and copulative functions of the verb "to be." Attention is here called to Parmenides' reputation as a mathematician who classified geometrical figures, first taught that the earth is round, and divided the earth into zones. The achievement of Parmenides lies in having distinguished the metamathe-matical foundation of physical science, a foundation with rigidly precise logical interrelations, from physical science itself, wherein any and all assertions or hypotheses have only a limited and relative validity which is nonetheless significant for its character of limitation and relativity. In defense of his assertion that this is a genuinely scientific distinction, Santillana cites Einstein: "If it is certain, it is not physics. If it is physics, it is not certain."

Too much effort has been expended, according to Santillana, on the linguistic analysis of Parmenides' use of the verb "to be" and too little on the content ascribed by Parmenides to Being. He suggests that the word "Being" be replaced by an X and an effort made to determine its meaning from the context of qualities predicated of it. If this is done honestly, then the only concept that fits the context is that of geometrical space. The insistent denial of spatial qualities in Parmenides "Being" by interpreters is based on Aristotelian conceptions of space as an aggregate of qualitatively distinct local units rather than on Euclidean concepts. There are, says Santillana, three essential requisites of Euclidean space: continuity, homogeneity, and isotropy. The first two of these are unquestionably predicated of Being by Parmenides as is demonstrable by citation of relevant statements from the text of the poem; the third, isotropy, is implicit in Parmenides' description of Being as a sphere of infinite radius. This concept of geometrical space is equally suited to serve as a substratum for physical form and for matter. Thus, standing at the point of convergence of the eastern Ionian cosmological tradition and the western Pythagorean tradition, Parmenides postulated a spatial continuum capable of filling the same role as the Ionian Anaximander's undifferentiated *apeiron* and the Pythagorean numbers.

Although his treatment of the religious aspect of Parmenides' poem is in need of considerable expansion and elucidation, Santillana is original and provocative in this area also. The

goddess of truth and justice named in the proem of Parmenides' poem as the revealer of the Way of Truth, and the Way of Opinion is the same *daimon* who in "The Way of Opinion" is called "the goddess who guides everything." She is the cosmic feminine power named with many names throughout the ancient world and associated especially with the planet Venus, whose heliacal risings in the course of an eight-year period are a model of recurrent precise regularity. As the precise and predictable movement of the heavenly bodies was a guarantee of correct measures of every sort in the ancient world, and as Venus is the brightest heavenly body with the shortest measurable cycle, she is, as a divine power, the guarantor of absolute and necessary truth (her role in Parmenides' proem) and also the ruler of time and events (her role in the second half of the poem, "The Way of Opinion").

Taran, Leonardo. *Parmenides: A Text with Translation, Commentary and Critical Essays*. Princeton: Princeton University Press, 1965.

The title of Taran's book describes its content. A close analysis of the text of Parmenides, line by line, permits the author to comment at once on precisely what Parmenides says and on the validity of the many scholarly interpretations of the text. Perhaps the primary achievement of Taran is his negative critique of more fanciful speculative interpretations of the poem which are not justified by a close scrutiny of the text.

In his essay on Parmenides' concept of Being, Taran concentrates on what cannot be affirmed of Parmenides' doctrine. Parmenides' Being is not atemporally eternal, for

Parmenides, apparently unaware of the logical relationship of time and process, denies process but affirms the perpetual duration of Being. There is no *tertium quid* between Being and Non-Being. Since Non-Being is inconceivable, what exists can have no positive characteristic other than being itself; the predications attributed by Parmenides to Being are either negative (denials of difference) or positive affirmations of the identity of Being. It is illegitimate to consider Parmenides as a materialist or an idealist; any statement that Being is matter or thought would presuppose the reality of difference. Being is not identical with thought: Parmenides held that only what is logically conceivable is existent; it was Plato who first recognized the problem of the existence of thought and language.

In his essay on the relationship between the two parts of Parmenides' poem, Taran gives an account of the variety of explanations given by scholars for Parmenides' offering a traditional cosmogony. Taran utterly rejects every view which would attribute some degree of reality to the physical world. Taran's own view is that Parmenides, in the second half of his poem, is showing that men's acceptance of a phenomenal world as real depends upon their illegitimate allowance of difference as real, even a minimal difference of two distinct classes of reality. That initial error necessarily commits men to a string of additional errors. For Parmenides himself there is no real phenomenal world, and his purpose in describing "The Way of Opinion" is to show exactly how men have fallen into error. A further implication of this view of "The Way of Opinion" is that Taran believes the goddess of the poem cannot be real to Parmenides, but her revelation is employed as a literary device to emphasize the objectivity of his method and doctrine.

Taran's final essay is concerned not with the impact of Parmenides' doctrines on subsequent Greek philosophy so much as with the adequacy of later representations of Parmenides' doctrine. Plato, says Taran, consciously and deliberately misrepresented Parmenides' doctrine to be that "all things are one and there is no change or movement in this one reality." Parmenides himself, however, proceeded from the premise of Being, not of the One. Plato did formulate an adequate criticism of Parmenides, however, by establishing that Non-Being is an Idea, the idea of difference, which is a necessary logical complement to the idea of identity. Plato further demonstrated what Parmenides himself failed to recognize, that the sole existence of Being cannot account for thought. Aristotle's criticisms of Parmenides utterly misrepresent the doctrine of Parmenides because Aristotle assumes the earlier thinker was attacking the same problem of causality that he himself was and in the same way. Aristotle's view of Parmenides' Being as a unified concept of the physical world, essentially material, is unhistorical, but Aristotle's view influenced all subsequent ancient histories of philosophy and many modern reconstructions of pre-Socratic thought as well.

The achievement of Parmenides, in Taran's eyes, was the establishment of the ontological priority of the problem of identity and difference. Earlier Greek thinkers had failed to recognize this problem; all later thinkers were compelled to grapple with it. — *C.W.C.*

Additional Recommended Reading

Cornford, F. M. *Plato and Parmenides*. London: Routledge & Kegan Paul, 1939. Though this book is primarily concerned with Plato's *Parmenides*, the first chapter offers a translation and commentary on the poem of Parmenides.

Jaegar, Werner. "Parmenides' Mystery of Being," in *The Theology of the Early*

Greek Philosophers. Oxford: The Clarendon Press, 1947. A study of the theological aspects of Parmenides' poem.

Kirk, G. S., and J. E. Raven. *The Presocratic Philosophers: A Critical History with a Selection of Texts.* Cambridge: The University Press, 1960. The Greek text with an English translation, and critical and historical commentary, of the pre-Socratic philosophers, including Parmenides.

Raven, J. E. *Pythagoreans and Eleatics.* Cambridge: The University Press, 1948. An examination of the traditions of Parmenides and Pythagoreanism which seeks to clarify the relationship and interaction between the two schools of thought.

PERSIAN INVASION OF GREECE

Type of event: Military: occupation of northern Greece
Time: 480-479 B.C.
Locale: Greece, the Aegean Sea, and western Asia Minor

Principal personages:
XERXES, King of the Kings of the Persian Empire 486-465
LEONIDAS, King of Sparta 487-480
THEMISTOCLES, (c.528-c.462), Athenian general
EURYBIADES, Spartan admiral, commander in chief of the Greek fleet 481-480
ADIMANTUS, Corinthian general 480
PAUSANIAS, nephew of Leonidas and Regent of Sparta 480-c.470

Summary of Event

Cyrus the Great, founder of the Persian empire, subjected the Greek states of western Asia Minor, or Ionia, to Persia. The Ionians resented the loss of their sovereignty, and in 499, they rebelled against Cyrus' successor, Darius I. Their action was supported by two states in Old Hellas, Eretria and Athens. At first the Ionian revolt went well, but Darius soon gathered overwhelming forces and reimposed Persian authority by 493 B.C. He then determined to invade Old Greece, to punish the states which had assisted the Ionian cities, and to end a vexatious frontier problem. His first attack in 492 miscarried when much of the Persian fleet was wrecked in a storm, and his second attempt in 490 failed when his army was driven into the sea at Marathon in Attica. He therefore planned a third invasion on a lavish scale. Darius, however, died in 486, and it fell to his son Xerxes to complete the preparation of his empire's forces.

The great invasion finally began in the spring of 480. An enormous host of more than one hundred thousand soldiers was supported by a fleet of six hundred warships. The Greeks could not fail to learn about the assembling of such masses, and in the winter of 481-480 representatives of the larger states met at Corinth to discuss resistance. The Delphic Oracle had to be persuaded to modify its initial prophecy of doom to one of doubtful outcome, and it was with some trepidation that a decision was taken to fight under Spartan leadership. Appeals to other Greek states to join the patriotic cities were rejected by some of the more important ones, notably anti-Spartan Argos. Ultimately, only thirty-one states fought on the Greek side. There were actually more Greek states on the side of Xerxes, although these served under compulsion.

The Greeks decided to delay the Persians' advance by holding the narrow pass at Thermopylae with eight thousand men and the adjacent strait

237

between Thermopylae and the island of Euboea with their fleet. It was not until August that the Persians came up against these fortified positions. Three days passed as Xerxes vainly sent his best troops against the well-armored Peloponnesian infantry fighting under King Leonidas of Sparta. Simultaneously, a series of inconclusive but costly naval engagements were fought off Cape Artemisium on Euboea; the Persians had earlier lost about two hundred warships in a storm. Xerxes, however, turned the position at Thermopylae by marching around it through the mountains. Most of the Greeks escaped encirclement in time, but Leonidas with his bodyguard of three hundred Spartans and the seven-hundred-man army of Tespiae were cut off and could only die resisting bravely to the end.

With the position on land lost, the Greek fleet retreated and took station on the island of Salamis off the western coast of Attica. The population of Athens had already been evacuated to the Peloponnesus. There was more wavering among the Greeks at Salamis, some even considering defection, but at last honor prevailed, and, led by Eurybiades of Sparta, Themistocles of Athens, and Adimantus of Corinth, the Greek sailors prepared to fight. The Persians, fearing that the Greek fleet might escape westward, decided upon an immediate attack, and late in September the Battle of Salamis was fought in the narrow strait between the island and the mainland. The Persians had about 350 ships, the Greeks probably 310, of which the majority were Athenian. The conflict lasted most of the day, and by sunset

the Greeks were victorious. With the campaigning season nearly over, Xerxes withdrew from devastated Attica and left half his army to winter in Boeotia. The rest of the army and the shattered fleet retired with the King to Asia.

The war was resumed the following spring. After a second Persian devastation of Attica, a hard-fought land battle took place at Plataea, a small state between Athens and Boeotia. Under the command of the Spartan Regent Pausanias, the Greeks gained the victory, and the Spartan infantry showed once more their undoubted excellence. The Persian army was forced into rapid retreat.

While this campaign was being fought in Greece, the Hellenic fleet had crossed the Aegean to seek out the remnants of Xerxes' navy. Off the island of Mycale the Greeks completed its destruction. Thus, the great force which Xerxes had led against the Hellenes was either destroyed or forced back into Asia, and, as the poet Simonides wrote, "Hellas put on the crown of freedom."

These victories did not end the war with Persia, but they did end Persian efforts to invade Greece. The liberation of Ionia now became the goal of the Greek states and by 477 most of it had been freed. As a result of these campaigns Athens became one of the most important military powers of Greece.

The successful repulsion of the horde of Xerxes had an effect that is hard to document. It seems that the spiritual euphoria resulting from their naval and military successes added to the Greeks' awareness of their specifically Hellenic virtues and imparted a special keenness to succeeding generations. We see this in the drama of Aeschylus of Athens and in the poetry of Pindar of Thebes.

Pertinent Literature

Herodotus. *The Histories.* Translated from the Greek by A. de Sélincourt. Baltimore: Penguin Books, 1954.

Herodotus, the historian of the Persian Wars, was born about 485 B.C. at Halicarnassus, a city on the coast of Asia Minor where Greek and Carian freely mingled. He apparently came from a prominent family, for he was forced to flee the city at a time of political turmoil. He was, therefore, a man accustomed to looking at the world as a member of its ruling class. After his exile he traveled extensively, visiting Egypt, the Levant, Mesopotamia, the Black Sea regions, Greece itself, and, finally, southern Italy. All this gave him an awareness of the diversity of humanity and an opportunity to gain knowledge from veterans of the Persian Wars, probably from both sides.

Herodotus wrote his account of what was then the greatest event in Greek experience in order that "the memory of the past may not be blotted out from among men by time, and that great and marvelous deeds done by Greeks and foreigners against each other may not lack renown." By this he shows himself to have two strong qualities. First, he was keenly excited by the manly and virtuous deeds of famous men; his book abounds in biographical detail: Polycritus of Aegina, he tells us, fought best in the Battle of Salamis. Second, he was as deeply interested in the history of Asia as in that of Greece. In fact, his impartiality towards the Persians earned him the epithet: "barbaro-

phile."

In his first five books Herodotus describes, often with amusing and charming digressions on their culture and ethnography, the countries that took part in the war. At the end of Book 5 he begins the main narrative of the campaigns and proceeds with it to the end of Book 9, where the Persians are in full retreat. Herodotus then makes a Persian nobleman give his own moral on Xerxes' defeat: the Persians, by conquering the rich plains of the Near East, had grown luxurious and soft, so that they could be beaten by the poor but tough hill peoples of Greece.

To Herodotus this denouement took place in a world in which gods and men mingled and interacted. Men were responsible for what they did, and by their actions they might win fair fame and glory. But they might also earn blame, guilt, and defeat, for the gods were guardians of the cosmic order. Xerxes, arrogantly aspiring to conquer Greece, committed the fault of *hybris,* that is, of overstepping the bounds of his rightful position as King of Asia. The gods therefore afflicted him with *ate,* blind infatuation, and in this state he crazily and recklessly invaded Greece. He even ordered the waters of the Hellespont lashed for disobedience to himself. In this condition he inevitably and deservedly suffered his *nemesis:* defeat on the battlegrounds of Greece.

239

As a historian Herodotus had certain limitations. He had for the most part only oral traditions of varying reliability to draw on, but he was not uncritical of them. His remarks on the book written by Hecataeus of Miletus show this, as does his often-used phrase, "They say this, but I do not believe it." Yet, he naïvely calculated the strengh of the Persian forces at over five million men, a clearly impossible figure, and he became a biased partisan of Athens. In his account of the Battle of Salamis he tells outrageously untrue stories of the Corinthian General Adimantus. The best that can be said of Herodotus here is that he also admits he had heard the stories were false.

In spite of his limitations Herodotus deserves our respect, for his work showed a great advance in Greek historical thought. His predecessors had been content with short and simple chronicles. Herodotus was the first Greek to write narrative history in which a mass of individual facts was collected and set forth within a unifying, interpretive context.

Hignett, C. H. *Xerxes' Invasion of Greece.* Oxford: The Clarendon Press, 1963.

C. H. Hignett's book is the product of some forty years of research and reflection on the problems connected with the reconstruction of the history of the Persian invasion. Its principal thesis is that the only reliable source of knowledge of the war is Herodotus. Hignett, in a valuable introduction, reviews what is known of the books of ancient writers other than Herodotus, and is able to demonstrate that their work was, on the whole, shorter, more jejune, and less accurate than the history of the great Halicarnassian. For example, an important secondary account is the *Hellenica* of Ephorus of Cymae, a universal history from remote times down to the fourth century B.C. Ephorus tells us that Leonidas' Spartans one night actually raided the camp of the Great King and very nearly laid hands on Xerxes himself. This story is highly improbable on the face of it, since the Greeks had chosen to fight at Thermopylae because they could fight defensively behind fortifications in a narrow place and thus nullify the effect of the Persians' vast numbers. Why, then, should they risk disaster by striking straight into the middle of the Persian camp? Herodotus says nothing of this adventurous incident, and Hignett regards it as romantic invention. In consequence, the modern scholar must use the work of the other ancient historians only with the greatest care and skepticism.

Hignett is also penetrating in his criticism of Herodotus' own account. Herodotus says that at some time before the Battle of Thermopylae the Spartans received an oracle from Delphi that one of their kings must die in the war or the state itself would fall. Herodotus, a pious man, was likely to believe Delphic prophecies. Leonidas, we are to believe, during the retreat from Thermopylae, remained behind when the Persians had turned his position and bravely died to save the state. This, Hignett thinks, is Spartan propaganda, probably invented to explain away the disaster of the death of one of its kings. Since the whole Thespian army

240

died along with Leonidas' three hundred Spartans, and since it is inconceivable that the Thespians would have allowed the whole flower of their manhood to perish merely to help fulfill a prophecy of doubtful authenticity which was to them irrelevant, the story must be an invention. Hignett then goes on to speculate on why Leonidas did not withdraw from the pass in time, and concludes that unless fresh evidence comes to hand we can never know.

This book is not easy reading, since much of it is taken up with technical, critical analyses concerning the credibility of parts of Herodotus' narrative. Moreover, narratives of battles are interrupted by discussions about the topography of the battlefields, and Hignett admits that he has little direct familiarity with them. Despite such defects, together with a few details of chronology in which he differs from general scholarly opinion, Hignett's book is the most careful treatment of the campaigns of 480 and 479 B.C. — *S.K.E.*

Additional Recommended Reading

Burn, A. R. *Persia and the Greeks.* New York: St. Martin's Press, 1962. A narrative covering events from the sixth century to Xerxes' defeats in 479.

Olmstead, A. T. *A History of the Persian Empire.* Chicago: University of Chicago Press, 1948. A somewhat uncritical account of the wars from the Persian viewpoint by a distinguished Orientalist.

How, W. W., and J. A. Wells. *A Commentary on Herodotus.* Oxford: The Clarendon Press, 1912. 2 vols. An obsolescent work but one still useful for bringing together passages in ancient literature which supplement and explain Herodotus.

CREATION OF THE ATHENIAN EMPIRE

Type of event: Political: establishment of a large political unit
Time: 470-448 B.C.
Locale: The Aegean Sea

Principal personages:
ARISTIDES (c.525-c.468), son of Lysimachus, Athenian statesman
CIMON (c.512-449), son of Miltiades, Athenian general and statesman
PERICLES (c.495-429), son of Xanthippus, Athenian general and statesman
THUCYDIDES (c.485-c.425), son of Melesias, Athenian statesman

Summary of Event

After the Persian invasion of Greece had been repulsed in the spring of 477 B.C., delegates from the liberated Greek cities of Ionia and Athens assembled and agreed to combine forces in a league whose stated aims were to protect the Aegean area from fresh Persian offensives and to ravage Xerxes' territory. The headquarters of this confederacy was located on the sacred island of Delos, and it came to be called the Delian League. In the beginning an assembly of representatives determined policy, with each state, large or small, exercising one vote. Each member contributed either ships or money; the respective assessments of ships and money were the work of Aristides of Athens, whose determinations were so fair that he was afterwards called "The Just." The money was kept on Delos under the supervision of a board of Athenians called Hellenic Treasurers. Fleet and army were both commanded by Athenians since Athens was the largest and most powerful of the allied states and Athenians had

won great prestige in defeating the Persians.

At first all went well. The league fleet maintained the security of the Aegean and even successfully attacked the Persian-held island of Cyprus. Such victories led some members of the confederacy to regard the Persian menace as broken, and about 470 B.C. Naxos, tired of onerous naval service, unilaterally seceded. The Athenians, supported by a majority of the allies, felt that the withdrawal of Naxos might portend the dissolution of the league to Persia's advantage. Naxos was therefore besieged and reduced to obedience. This act set an important precedent. Moreover, the league's assessment of the situation was shown to be correct the next year when the reconstituted Persian Navy sailed towards the Aegean but was defeated in the Battle of Eurymedon by the league fleet led by Athens' excellent general Cimon.

Because providing ships year after year was a hardship for some members, Athens, upon the suggestion of Cimon,

242

introduced the policy of allowing any state to convert its obligation of furnishing ships to one of paying money. Gradually most did so, until by 445 only seven states of a regular membership of some 150 still contributed triremes. At the time the change must have seemed statesmanlike, but it actually cloaked a great danger to the league. As time went on only the Athenians and the few other states with fleets were capable of serious naval action; the ships of the money-paying cities decayed and their crews lacked practice. The Athenians, meanwhile, not only increased the size of their navy but also introduced improved models of triremes and new naval tactics, so that by the 440's their navy was a virtually invincible force.

In 460 B.C., the Delian confederates attacked the Persians in Egypt, but the offensive ended with the annihilation of a league fleet in 454. For a time it seemed that the Persian naval forces might again invade the Aegean. To meet the immediate danger this threat posed to the league's accumulated treasure on the unfortified island of Delos it was agreed to move the fund to the heavily guarded Acropolis at Athens. When peace was made with Persia in 448, however, the money was not moved back. Athens assumed sole control of this enormous sum of five thousand talents and insisted that the annual sums thereafter be paid to her. Over the next decades this money was used to maintain Athens' navy, to build the remarkable series of buildings erected on the Acropolis, and to finance future wars. Meetings of the league's assembly stopped; the league had become an Athenian empire.

Some members of the league strongly objected to this new regime and rebelled against it, but their naval weakness made them easy to suppress. Rebellious states were compelled to accept democratic, pro-Athenian governments; other states had their legal and commercial relations with Athens subjected to regulation. A few were forced to accept Athenian garrisons or to cede territory for Athenian settlers. The man mainly responsible for this program was Pericles. He was filled with the vision of an idealized Athens, not only as a supreme military power but also as a model of political organization and advanced culture. "Our state," he once said, "is the education of Hellas." His more extreme acts of imperialism were condemned by conservatives such as the statesman Thucydides, son of Melesias, but by the 440's some thousands of Athenians received wages for various services from the annual payments of the allies. As a result the masses backed Pericles, and Thucydides was ostracized. "It may have been wrong to acquire the empire," said Pericles, "but it would certainly be dangerous to let it go." Thus, while necessity had dictated the punishment of Naxos, greed and fear compelled the Athenians to keep their grip on their former allies. Athens, in her own eyes "the Hellas of Hellas," was the tyrant-city in the eyes of other Greeks. Certain members of the former league appealed to Sparta for help, and, when the Peloponnesian War broke out in 431, most Greeks supported Sparta in the hope of seeing Athenian power destroyed.

All this was unfortunate because Athens was, in other ways, the most humane and liberal state in Greece. She was democratic. She tolerated free speech to a remarkable degree. She provided work for her poor and treated her slaves with relative humanity. From all parts of the Hellenic world artists, poets, and philosophers streamed in to visit her, so that she became the intellectual and moral beacon of the Aegean world, a true city of light. But her crass subjection of allies turned much of the world against her and may have prevented the Delian League from becoming an instrument for the gradual and voluntary unification of the innumerable small, quarrelsome, and warlike Greek states.

Pertinent Literature

Tod, Marcus N., E. M. Walker, and F. E. Adcock. *The Cambridge Ancient History*. Vol. V, pp. 1-112; 165-192. Cambridge: The University Press, 1927.

It must be made clear, before discussing this book, that there is no one work that gives an adequate account of Athens' conversion from leader of a voluntary confederation to the ruler of an empire. The reason is that the evidence is hard to interpret. The literary evidence for the period 477-439 B.C. is of uneven quantity and uncertain quality. We have an excellent, nearly contemporary authority in the Athenian historian Thucydides. His subject, however, was the war of 431-404 B.C., and he felt that he did not have to detail events of the preceding fifty years when the empire was being formed. There is also the history of Diodorus Siculus, who lived in the time of Julius Caesar. His account, based on the *Hellenica* of Ephorus, who wrote in the fourth century, covers the whole of the fifth century. Ephorus, however, was uncritical, and unfortunately his narrative is often inaccurate; moreover, Diodorus, an unskillful man, debased the work still more. Plutarch, the famous biographer and ultra-moralist of the early second century, was somewhat more careful than either Ephorus or Diodorus, and he records valuable details concerning Aristides, Cimon, and Pericles in his *Parallel Lives*. His most trustworthy passages are those based on the work of Thucydides, but sections derived from other fifth century writers, such as Ion of Chios, are regarded with some suspicion by modern scholars and, as a result, valuable time and effort has had to be expended on source criticism to the detriment of historical narrative.

Apart from the ancient writers, there is a considerable amount of epigraphic evidence in the form of inscriptions recording decrees of the Athenian Assembly, some of which have only recently been found. Here too, however, there are problems. The series of inscriptions which indirectly record the amounts of tribute paid by each allied state after 454, for example, received definitive publication only in 1948, and since then the accuracy of the publication has been questioned. Other inscriptions, usually mutilated but more or less restorable, contain the texts of various treaties between the subject allies and Athens. The dates assigned to many of these inscriptions have lately been chal-

244

lenged by Harold Mattingly among others. Many of the objections have been answered by Benjamin D. Meritt, but the controversy has tended to create doubt and hesitation rather than stimulate constructive reëvaluation.

Given the necessity for meticulous criticism of ancient literary sources and for careful restoration of inscriptions, then, historians have often overspecialized, in the process losing sight of the whole problem. Admittedly, for example, Athenian imperialism was decisively affected by purely internal events at Athens, such as the quarrel between Pericles and the statesman Thucydides over democratic reform, but while we have an excellent book on the constitutional history of Athens, with some remarks on foreign affairs, and an excellent book on the financial and imperial policies of Athens, with some remarks on internal affairs, the overall result is that we do not have a single book combining both subjects which is up-to-date and takes economic history into account. Writers are reluctant to deal with the biographies of the men of this period because they are uncertain about Plutarch's trustworthiness. Thus, no one book adequately covers all facets of the creation of the Athenian empire.

Now to return to the literature cited above.

Tod, Walker, and Adcock contributed five chapters to the fifth volume of *The Cambridge Ancient History* which appeared in 1927. Tod, a famous epigrapher, wrote on the economic history of the fifth century, which explains with little detail one reason for Athens' early successes, namely her wealth. The Rev. E. M. Walker contributed three chapters on the creation of the Delian League, interstate relations, and the democratic reforms of Pericles. Professor Adcock wrote on the years from 445 to 431 and of Athens' relations with her subject allies.

Though written before the important studies of B. D. Meritt and other scholars on the texts of the Athenian inscriptions were completed, these chapters are not entirely obsolete. Each man was an expert. Walker was, perhaps, the least skilled of the three men because he wrote under the influence of perverse conceptions such as the claim that Athens insisted upon the establishment of democratic constitutions everywhere in her empire. We are certain today that such was not the case. Athens was imperialistic but not ideologically fanatic. Volume V of *The Cambridge Ancient History* does combine some economic history of the fifth century with the internal and external history of Athens and her allies.

Meritt, B. D., H. T. Wade-Gery, and M. F. McGregor. *The Athenian Tribute Lists.* Vol. III. The American School of Classical Studies at Athens. Princeton: Princeton University Press, 1950.

No student of Greek history should ignore this important book. B. D. Meritt is a veteran epigrapher of great reputation who has worked to reconstitute and interpret the chipped and mutilated surfaces of the Athenian inscriptions. With his no less distinguished colleagues, he undertook the publication of the surviving fragments of the Athenian tribute-quota lists, and the first volume of this work appeared in 1939. Volume II, a republication of the old fragments along with a few new ones, appeared in 1948. Finally, Volume III was published in 1950. It is divided into three sections. Part I is a critical and highly technical discussion of the contents of the lists themselves. Part II is a learned analysis of various problems connected with the literary sources, including a consideration of textual problems in Thucydides and a carefully reasoned outline of the chronology of the period from 477 to 431 B.C. Part III is a history of the Delian League from its inception until the fall of Athens in 404.

It is a detailed account which necessarily concentrates on Athens. Little is said about the Athenian allies, and even less about Sparta and her allies. It is based on more and better evidence than was available to Walker and Adcock. Considerable attention

is given to the financial history of Athens. On this point we are in a tantalizing position. With part of the evidence for the administration of Athens' money in our hands, we can partially reconstruct a detailed picture of the economic resources available to the Athenian government at various stages between 454 and 420 B.C. But in going into this matter, Meritt and his colleagues overreach themselves. They appear to think that the epigraphical record combined with literary evidence gives us virtually a complete picture of Athenian finance, that, as A. W. Gomme said, these fragmentary stones are like the pieces of a puzzle which fit side by side. But in fact they do not; there are important gaps in the surviving inscriptions, and the three authors have gone too far in filling them in by what amounts to guesswork. Still, *The Athenian Tribute Lists* is a useful book, indispensable for the study of Athens' change from *hegemon* to master of the Aegean. — *S.K.E.*

Additional Recommended Reading

Laistner, M. L. W. *A History of the Greek World from 479 to 323 B.C.* London: Methuen, 1936. An older but competent survey of Greek history which includes the history of the transformation of the Delian League.

Laidlaw, W. A. *A History of Delos.* Oxford: Basil Blackwell, 1933. A narrative of the island's history including a survey of its impressive archaeological remains.

Ste. Croix, G. E. M. de "The Character of the Athenian Empire," in *Historia.* Vol. III (1954), pp. 1-41. This work argues that most Greeks in the Empire did not hate Athens by 431 B.C.

Bradeen, Donald W. "The Popularity of the Athenian Empire," in *Historia.* Vol. IX (1960), pp. 257-269. An answer to Ste. Croix' article.

Mattingly, Harold B. "The Growth of Athenian Imperialism," in *Historia.* Vol. XII (1963), pp. 257-273. One of the author's more recent articles revising the accepted dating of Athenian inscriptions.

Meritt, B. D., and H. T. Wade-Gery. "The Dating of Documents to the Mid-Fifth Century," in *Journal of Hellenic Studies.* Vol. 83 (1963), pp. 100-117. An answer to Mattingly's approach and methods.

Andreades, A. M. *A History of Greek Public Finance*. Translated from the Greek by C. N. Brown. Rev. ed. Cambridge: Harvard University Press, 1933. An older survey of what is known of the financial institutions and practices of the Greek states.

Barron, John P. "Religious Propaganda of the Delian League," in *Journal of Hellenic Studies*. Vol. 84 (1964), pp. 35-48. A study of Athens' attempt to distill an opiate for the masses in the subject states.

AESCHYLUS WRITES THE *ORESTEIA*

Type of event: Literary: creation of a dramatic production
Time: 458 B.C.
Locale: Athens

Principal personage:
AESCHYLUS (c.525-456 B.C.), Athenian tragic dramatist

Summary of Event

As a historical phenomenon, tragic drama stands witness to the characteristically Greek synoptic view of man's greatness and weakness while at the same time testifying to the success of the Athenians in developing a workable social order which allowed maximum individual freedom and self-expression. Tragedies were produced at the *Dionysia,* a religious festival lasting several days in honor of the god Dionysus. Competing poets submitted groups of four plays to the *archon eponymos* who selected three poets, giving them actors and a chorus to present their productions on three successive days.

The origins of tragedy are greatly disputed. It is an artificial and highly stylized form of dramatic action consisting of alternating sections of dialogue spoken in conversational Attic dialect composed in iambic trimeters, and of choral lyrics sung by dancers in a variety of meters written in a more dignified language colored by Doric dialect forms. From its beginnings, tragedy seems to have employed myths from the early heroic age and to have reinterpreted them as symbolic expressions of the human condition. Almost invariably the tragic plot relates the suffering of a hero and portrays the response of an onlooking public through the meditations of the chorus.

The surviving plays of the first great tragic dramatist, Aeschylus, are political and theological in nature. They are exuberant and optimistic expressions of faith in man's ability, through the democratic *polis,* to solve the problems of personal and social life. At the same time they are probing efforts to formulate a new theology expressing divine sanctions for the *polis.* The earlier literary theologies, implicit in the Homeric poems and explicit in those of Hesiod, had portrayed the Olympian gods as hostile or indifferent to human efforts aimed at improving man's lot in life.

The theme of the *Oresteia* trilogy illustrates the transition from conditions where wrongs were vindicated by members of the family of the injured party, to a state where such wrongs are satisfied through the justice of the *polis* and its institutionalized court system. The mythical vehicle chosen by Aeschylus to express this theme is the ancient tale of the family of Atreus, stained by guilt from acts of bloodshed in each generation until responsibility for vindication is removed from the family and placed in the hands of the Athenian court of the Areopagus.

Atreus, King of Argos, had entertained his brother, Thyestes, in a banquet at which he had served the flesh of Thyestes's children. In the following generation, Agamemnon, a son of Atreus, assembled an army and a fleet of Greek ships to avenge the rape of Helen, wife of his brother Menelaus, by Paris, a Trojan prince. When winds sent by Artemis prevented the sailing of the fleet from Aulis, Agamemnon felt compelled to sacrifice his daughter Iphigeneia to the angry goddess before sailing to Troy and eventually sacking it after a ten-year siege. During his absence, his wife Clytemnestra, offended by the sacrifice of Iphigeneia, plotted with Aegisthus, another son of Thyestes, to murder Agamemnon upon his victorious return from Troy. The first play of the trilogy, *Agamemnon,* ends with the success of this plot. In the second play, *Choephoroe,* Agamemnon's son Orestes, now grown to manhood, returns to Argos and avenges his father's murder in accordance with a command of Apollo, by killing his mother Clytemnestra and her paramour Aegisthus, only to find himself confronted by the Furies, the avenging spirits of kindred blood, demanding his own death in requital for his mother's blood. The third play, *Eumenides,* presents the absolution of Orestes by an Athenian court established by Athena to hold jurisdiction over homicide cases. The chief action of the *Eumenides* is a confrontation at the divine level between Athena and the Furies. At stake is the place of fear of punishment in restraining acts of violence. The Furies fear that, should Orestes be acquitted, there may be no more personal security from threats of violence. Athena, however, determines that homicide cases should be judged on their individual merits by a citizen jury, and she secures the support of the Furies, now transformed into the "Kindly Spirits," as sanctions of the institutionalized court's power to punish acts of violence on behalf of the *polis.*

The choral odes of the first play of the trilogy are brooding speculations on the problem of theodicy, on the dilemma of the individual faced with conflicting responsibilities to his family and to his community, and on the agony of the moral agent directed by conflicting divine sanctions of equally persuasive cogency to carry out ruinous acts of self-humiliation and social destructiveness. The choral odes further speculate on the awesome ambiguity of human motivation as men are spurred on to acts of violence partly through private greed and partly through a will to execute what they believe are divine commands. The law of Zeus, says the chorus, is that men must learn wisdom through brooding over their sufferings. Although in the *Oresteia* this law ultimately finds expression in the transferal of the right to avenge wrongs from the family to the state, yet Aeschylus portrays the tragic suffering of the individual moral agent and of whole societies as the price of the long slow process of purification of human moral vision.

249

Aeschylus Writes the Oresteia

Pertinent Literature

Snell, Bruno. "Myth and Reality in Greek Tragedy" (1941), in *The Discovery of the Mind: The Greek Origins of European Thought*. Oxford: Basil Blackwell, 1953.

Since the emergence of tragic drama as a historical phenomenon is of greater import than the production of the *Oresteia,* the literature here discussed is concerned more generally with the significance of the genre and of the political context of its emergence than with particular aspects of Aeschylean tragedy. Bruno Snell's article, "Myth and Reality in Greek Tragedy," brings into focus the significance of tragic drama in human intellectual history.

Beginning with Aristotle's distinction of poetry from history and his assertion that poetry is more serious and more universal than history, Snell seeks to categorize the kind of reality with which tragic drama is concerned, the reality of man's inner life as distinct from the objective reality of concrete events. Snell follows the traditional view that tragedy emerged from the ritual context of the choral ode, which recreated an event of the mythical past as present reality. In tragic drama, however, the mythical event is acted out, not simply narrated, and therefore becomes a self-subsistent reality in its own right. Snell notes further that the choral odes of tragedy are akin in mood to the older personal lyric wherein a sense of helplessness is expressed and the individual seeks to relate his suffering to the framework of fate and the rule of the gods.

The distinctive feature of Aeschylean tragedy, according to Snell, is a vital decision thrust upon the individ-

ual hero, a decision requiring reflection within the soul on the vying claims of mutually exclusive alternatives, each of weighty consequence for his own and his community's future. Thus Pelasgus in the *Suppliants* of Aeschylus must determine whether he will risk a clash between the Argive people over whom he rules and the sons of Aegyptus, a clash which will inevitably follow if he undertakes to protect the daughters of Danaus who have fled to him claiming the right of sanctuary.

Using Homer and tragedy as comparisons, Snell discusses the decision-making process and the role of the gods. Homeric man's decisions are quickly reached on the basis of objective criteria of personal advantage and an unambiguous awareness of the will of the gods; the Aeschylean hero's decisions are agonizingly personal, complicated by a more distant and self-contradictory divine will involving danger or even death as a consequence of choice of the just alternative.

The tragic dramatist, says Snell, deliberately chooses the myth that is removed from everyday concrete historical life and further strips it down to its essentials: "A chemist combines in the test tube several substances which are rarely or never found together in nature to form a clear and precise idea of their reactions. Likewise the dramatist constructs his actions with a view to isolating the quintessence of the action."

As tragedy developed in the course

250

of the fifth century B.C., it tended to concentrate in growing measure on the inner life of the protagonist and therefore it also tended to transform the use of myth. Externals, such as stage props, the political context, or the gods, became increasingly less vital as the focus shifted ever more to the subjective. Sophocles' heroes are already more isolated than those of Aeschylus: it is their character that is the primary focus of the plays' action. In Euripides the focus shifts all the more decisively to inner psychology. In the course of the whole development, myth lost all historical or concrete reality; it became an expression of universal human experience.

Else, G. F., *The Origin and Form of Early Greek Tragedy.* Cambridge: Harvard University Press, 1965.

As a historical phenomenon, Greek tragedy is uniquely Attic and intimately related to the emergence of Athenian democracy. Although this fact is beyond dispute, the view still prevalent among literary historians outside the the field of classical philology is that the genre of tragedy developed out of cultic ritual and the Dorian choral lyric. Else not only demonstrates the absence of any convincing foundation for this view but also expounds a theory of the origins of tragedy which does justice to the context of Athenian politics.

In Else's view, the two major foundations for the development of tragedy were laid by the poetry of Solon and the establishment of regular readings of the Homeric epics at the Attic festival of the *Panathenaea.* In his elegiac *Hymn to the Muses,* Solon set forth a personal view of human destiny in a political and theological frame of reference. In his other long elegy he presented to the Athenian people his views on political order and justice which were instrumental in his being selected to carry through a program of political and economic reform in Athens. Later he presented a justification for his actions in iambic and trochaic verses. His poems thus have the character of exhortation and self-presentation to a listening community. On the other hand, the Homeric recitations instituted by Pisistratus as a regular feature of the *Panathenaea* provided a literary education for the Athenian populace and established the epic tradition as a part of the cultural heritage of Athenians.

Tragedy as an art form did not develop out of ritual origins. Instead, says Else, it was created by Thespis in the last quarter of the sixth century B.C. Thespis, the first *tragoidos,* or actor-poet, invented the spoken portion of the play as the self-presentation of a hero's *pathos,* or experience, to which a chorus responded with an ode expressing communal sorrow.

The spoken parts of tragedy instituted by Thespis were the prologue, and the *rhesis,* or direct address. Else doubts whether the prologue was originally spoken by a god; he thinks rather that the tragic prologue was modeled on the *prooimia* spoken by *rhapsodes* to introduce their recitations of Homer. The *rhesis* of Thespis took the form of either an exhortation addressed by the hero to the chorus or a narrative description meant to elicit the response of the chorus. Else sees the elegiac *paraenesis* of Solon as the inspiration for the content, and Solon's use of iambic triameter and trochaic tetrameter as the model for Thespis' adoption of these meters for the *rhesis*.

Two types of choral ode are found in early tragedy. Hymns appear frequently in the *parodos,* the verses sung by the chorus as it makes its entry into the orchestra. *Threnoi, songs* of lamentation, appear toward the end of the play. The *threnos* is indeed a ritual element taken from cultic funeral celebrations, but here it is deliberately put to use in a nonritual setting to bewail the death or suffering of a hero of poetry rather than a real historical personage. The Doric coloring of the ode, says Else, is probably explained by the stylistic influence of the dithyramb, a choral ode imported into Athens from Corinth at about the same time and made a part of the festival of the *Dionysia* along with tragic drama.

Thespis invented the form of tragedy in the sixth century B.C., but Aeschylus, in the first half of the fifth century, became a second creator by adding second and third actors—thereby making dramatic development possible within a play—and by expounding the Solonian themes of theodicy and individual fate in a communal context. — *C.W.C.*

Additional Recommended Reading

Kitto, H. D. F. *Greek Tragedy: A Literary Study.* 2nd ed. New York: Barnes and Noble, 1950. An emphasis on the development of dramatic form by the great writers of Greek tragedy.

Murray, Gilbert. *Aeschylus, the Creator of Tragedy.* Oxford: The Clarendon Press, 1940. A study of the origins of tragedy, the stage technique and theology of Aeschylus, and interpretations of the extant plays.

Podlecki, Anthony J. *The Political Background of Aeschylean Tragedy.* Ann Arbor: University of Michigan Press, 1966. An analysis of the political context of the plays of Aeschylus.

Solmsen, Friedrich. *Hesiod and Aeschylus.* Ithaca: Cornell University Press, 1949. An investigation of Aeschylus as a theological reformer.

Thomson, George. *Aeschylus and Athens.* London: Lawrence & Wishart, 1941. A Marxist interpretation of the social and political background of Aeschylean tragedy.

FORMULATION OF THE "TWELVE TABLES" OF ROMAN LAW

Type of event: Legal: enactment of a code of laws
Time: 451-449 B.C.
Locale: Rome

Principal personages:
APPIUS CLAUDIUS,
TITUS GENUCIUS,
PUBLIUS SESTIUS,
LUCIUS VETURIUS,
GAIUS JULIUS,
AULUS MANLIUS,
PUBLIUS SULPICIUS,
PUBLIUS CURIATIUS,
TITUS ROMILIUS, and
SPURIUS POSTUMIUS, decemvirs in 451 B.C.

APPIUS CLAUDIUS,
MARCUS CORNELIUS MALUGINENSIS,
MARCUS SERGIUS,
LUCIUS MINUCIUS,
QUINTUS FABIUS VIBULANUS,
QUINTUS POETELIUS,
TITUS ANTONIUS MERENDA,
CAESO DUILLIUS,
SPURIUS OPPIUS CORNICEN, and
MANIUS RABULEUS, decemvirs in 450 B.C.

Summary of Event

The formulation of the Twelve Tables of Roman Law, as recorded by Livy and Dionysius of Halicarnassus, was one of the most significant events in the "struggle of the orders" between patricians and plebeians in Rome during the fifth century B.C. In 462, according to the traditional date of the *fasti,* Gaius Terentilius Harsa, a tribune of the plebs, made a spirited attack on the authority of the consuls, saying that their unregulated and unlimited power brought down all the terrors and penalties of the law upon the plebs. Harsa suggested that five men should be appointed to compose a code of laws which would put a check upon the patricians who as judges were interpreters of the unwritten customary law and who as priests determined the validity of the complex legal procedures. His proposal was rejected, as was another in 454 when the tribunes suggested that a commission composed of both patricians and plebeians should draw up the code.

In 452 the tribunes insisted that the work of codification should begin. To

253

expedite the task it was decided that the ordinary magistracies should be suspended and that, instead, *decemviri legibus scribundis,* "ten men for writing the laws," should be chosen to rule the state the following year without being subject to appeal. After some debate, the plebeians agreed to surrender their demand to be represented on the board along with the patricians, but they did so with the understanding that their sacral laws would not be abrogated.

The ten elected decemvirs set about framing the laws and set them up on ten tables in the Forum. After amending them according to suggestions received, they presented their work to the *comitia centuriata* for formal ratification. It soon became apparent that two more tables would have to be added to make the corpus complete, and so decemvirs were again elected by the *comitia centuriata* after considerable canvassing. Appius Claudius, who had been chairman of the first decemvirate was reëlected with nine new colleagues.

The second decemvirate is traditionally pictured as drafting the two additional tables amidst a reign of terror. For some unknown reason they began to act like tyrants by oppressing the plebeians, and only a secession of the plebs forced them out of office at the expiration of their commission.

Legendary though much of this account of the formulation of the Twelve Tables may be, there is little doubt about the antiquity of the ancient code which Livy, with some exaggeration, describes as "the source of all public and private law" for Rome.

While the original text of the Twelve Tables is said to have been lost in the sack of Rome by the Gauls about 390 B.C., copies remained so that Cicero reported in his *De legibus* that boys still had to memorize them in his day. Provisions of the code were never repealed although many lapsed through neglect and irrelevancy. Some one hundred and forty fragments or paraphrases show that the code was genuinely Roman in content and largely a codification of already existing custom. The code had only two constitutional provisions: one forbidding *privilegia,* and the other forbidding trial of a citizen on a capital charge by any assembly except the *comitia centuriata.* Assembly at night was forbidden. Dealing with private, public, and sacral law, the code concerned itself, among other matters, with the guardianship and status of women and property, the guardianship of lunatics and prodigals, division of inheritances, and rights concerning land. The laws were absolute imperatives and protected property above life; an insolvent debtor, for instance, could be fettered for sixty days and then executed or put up for sale, and many believed that the code allowed dismemberment of a debtor's body to satisfy several creditors. One was permitted to kill a thief only if he came at night or actually used a weapon. Dreadfully deformed children were to be killed. Blood revenge was recognized if satisfaction was denied in other ways. The father, as absolute head of the family could sell, with certain safeguards, his sons into slavery. Although marriage rites were simple, intermarriage between plebeian and patrician was forbidden. Penalties were harsh, death being meted out in five different ways including burning at the stake and casting from the Tarpeian rock. Bribery, libel, sorcery, cutting other people's crops, and even theft were capital offenses. Besides the death penalty other forms of punishment recognized were being fined, fettered, or flogged; retaliation in kind; civil disgrace; banishment; and slavery. Fines for injuring persons were graduated according to the value traditionally ascribed to individuals. Plebeians gained through a law allowing a thirty-day interval to discharge a debt before the infliction of penalty. Interest was fixed, probably at eight and one third percent, and "not according to the free choice of the wealthy."

Apart from obvious legal significance, the Twelve Tables are of great interest to philologists because of the archaic language used and to historians because the ordinances provide the best information available on the economic and social conditions of Rome during the fifth century.

Pertinent Literature

Pais, Ettore, *Ancient Italy*. Translated by C. Densmore Curtis. Chicago: University of Chicago Press, 1908.

Pais has been in the forefront of discussion concerning the relationship of the Twelve Tables of Roman law to Athenian and other Greek law. The subject was brought up by the ancients themselves who unanimously believed that the Roman Law was modeled upon Athenian legislation. Tradition had it that three commissioners were sent from Rome to study the laws of Athens before beginning work on the Roman code. Since only short, matter-of-fact fragments of the Twelve Tables exist, the question is made so difficult that Pais feels he can give no conclusive answers. Mommsen, the great authority on Roman law, accepted the Greek origin of the laws of the Twelve Tables, but Pais believes that he should have drawn his conclusions from a wider study than mere consideration of linguistics.

Pais points out that three contradictory stories exist explaining how Rome received knowledge of Greek jurisprudence: one records that such information came in the form of an embassy from Greece; another gives credit to a Greek philosopher who came to Rome; and a third postulates a Roman embassy sent to Greece on a mission of inquiry. He also points out that the general character of Greek law is different from the specific character of the Twelve Tables, and that the latter differs sharply in the matter of strict agnation. There is no evidence of direct borrowings from very early Greek law and yet the Roman fragments indicate a tradition of legal procedure, especially in the case of retaliation, more ancient than any used in contemporary Greek cities, especially Athens. Clearly the laws of Solon are not transported bodily to Rome, although portions of the funerary laws may be related to Solon's enactments. Furthermore, Pais suggests that there was no need for Rome to go to Athens to survey her code, since the Twelve Tables emanated, he believes, from the time of the censor Appius Claudius (not the decemvir) between 312 and 304. Thus Rome had plenty of time to learn about Greek law from the new Athenian colony of

255

Thurii founded in 446. It seems relevant, too, that even Magna Graecia itself did not await the spread of Athenian influence before building its own codes such as that made by the famous Zeleucus for Locri, or that by the still-more-famous Charondas for the Chalcidian cities of Italy.

Pais favors Tacitus' thesis that the code came from all cities who could offer model laws. Dionysius of Halicarnassus seems to reflect the same view in remarking that an embassy was sent not only to Athens but to many Greek cities of Italy. Pais is partial to the influence of Thurii where an Attic code was put into effect in 446 after being compiled under a commission by the sage Protagoras of Abdera. This code, in turn, was a composite of items from Locri, the Chalcidian cities, cities of the Peloponnesus, and Crete, as well as Athens. Given out under the venerable name of Charondas it spread from Thurii to Athens, thence to Sicily and apparently to Cappadocia in Asia Minor. Zeleucus of Locri, too, was said to have incorporated the laws of many codes, especially those of Ly-

curgus, Solon, and Minor. If in compiling a code for cosmopolitan Thurii, where Dorian, Ionian, and Athenian cultures met, Protagoras leaned heavily on the code of Locri, it is easy to see why Zeleucus in some traditions is regarded as the lawgiver of Thurii. Pais asks whether this code which spread to Athens could possibly have moved to Naples and from there to Latium. He believes that a study of the code of Charondas, as does the one from Thurii, reveals that the Romans adopted certain legislation, such as laws relating to the obligation to and care of orphans, which was not in harmony with their national character.

Whatever the case, it is clear that Magna Graecia is foremost in legal codification and that these compilations represent, in virtually all cases, the experiences of more than one city.

Finally Pais tries to argue for a composite influence of Magna Graecia, especially Thurii, on Roman law by showing that much of Roman religion and attitudes toward education stem from Italian Greece rather than Athens proper.

Jolowicz, H. F. *Historical Introduction to the Study of Roman Law.* Cambridge: The University Press, 1952.

Until the end of the nineteenth century the Twelve Tables were generally accepted as authentic. In his *Storia di Roma,* published in 1898, Pais sowed considerable doubt not only about the details surrounding the story of the Tables, such as the palpably legendary account of Virginia, but also concerning the entire historical tradition of the code itself. He believes that the fifth century decemvirate is historically indefensible and holds that this fictious board was a variant of the *de-*

cemviri stlitibus judicandis known to have been established about the same time to decide cases involving the status of a freeman. This interpretation would make Appius Claudius the decemvir a "legendary double" for Appius Claudius the blind, who was censor in 312. The Tables, most likely the result of several legislative acts according to this view, grew up gradually over many years and received their final form in the fourth century. Only in that century, Pais thinks, was pontifical authority sufficiently blunted to allow law to be so secularized.

The whole episode, he holds, is clarified if one sees some relationships between the Twelve Tables and the so-called *Jus Flavianum* exacted when Gnaeus Flavius was aedile in 304. Flavius, a secretary to Appius Claudius the censor, is reputed to have stolen and published a collection of laws made by his master which revealed on what days a legal action could be taken. This popularization of law and the opening of the pontificate to plebeians by the Ogulnian Law of 300 convince Pais that the fourth century fits the whole situation better than the mid-fifth. Consequently the decemvirate should be discarded and the event placed in the late fourth century.

Many other matters contribute to his doubts. In general, he makes it clear that reliable information for Roman history is simply not available before the burning of Rome about 390. More specifically, the provisions of the Twelve Tables are too divergent; some are barbaric and others reveal a sophistication in which Greek influence seems at work. Traditions concerning the decemviri are unbelievable. The last two tables are said to be unfair because they forbade intermarriage between the orders yet they were not repealed in 449 by Valerius and Horatius, who were clearly sympathetic to the plebs.

Lambert, a French writer of the early 1920's, is even more iconoclastic than Pais. He considers that the so-called Twelve Tables code is actually a collection of antiquarian materials made in the first half of the second century probably by a Sextus Aelius. As such it was never an actual legisla-tive instrument.

H. F. Jolowicz points out that scholars were generally unconvinced by the work of Pais and Lambert. While admitting that interpolations were made easy by the absence of a standard text of the code, they considered it inconceivable that Romans of the first century should be misled about an episode as recent as these authors would make it. As Jolowicz puts it, both Sextus Aelius' and Gnaeus Flavius' times lay in the full view of history. Moreover, tradition so firmly held the Twelve Tables to be an organic whole that it affected the entire subsequent history of Roman jurisprudence. Furthermore, considering how archaic the laws are, far too much so for 200 or 300 B.C., it would have been virtually impossible for the Roman Law to grow into the sophisticated system it became by the time of Cicero if the Twelve Tables were as late as these scholars assert.

It is now generally accepted that the Twelve Tables were an enacted code of laws and that, as a law of peasant proprietors suited to a day of little commerce, they fit the period around 450. Modern scholars assume that details surrounding adoption of the code are fictitious or glamorized. As a product of the fifth century the code remains a tribute to the precocious Roman mind in that it so early separated law from religion and that it devotes itself almost exclusively to private law. Apparently it never introduced any constitutional change; otherwise, it would be difficult to explain how the old constitution could have been so easily restored when the decemvirate was abolished. — *M.J.C.*

Formulation of the "Twelve Tables" of Roman Law

Additional Recommended Reading

Coleman-Norton, P. R. *The Twelve Tables Prefaced, Arranged, Translated, Annotated.* Princeton: Princeton University Press, 1952. A work extremely helpful in explaining the significance of individual laws.

Frank, Tenney. *An Economic Survey of Ancient Rome.* Vol. I. Baltimore: The Johns Hopkins Press, 1933. This survey deals with the laws of the Twelve Tables in relation to the economic history of Rome.

Wolff, Hans Julius. *Roman Law. An Historical Introduction.* Norman: University of Oklahoma Press, 1951. Wolff notes that codifications of Roman law in the fifth century B.C. and the sixth century A.D. stand at the beginning and end of the Law of the Roman state.

Warmington, E. H., ed. *Remains of Old Latin.* Newly edited and translated by E. H. Warmington. Vol. III: *Lucilius; The Twelve Tables.* Cambridge: Harvard University Press, 1938. This volume in the Loeb Classical Library contains the Latin text, an English translation, and the contexts in which individual laws are cited.

PROFESSIONALIZATION OF HISTORY

Type of event: Cultural: establishment of history as a literary genre
Time: c.450-425 B.C.
Locale: Samos, Athens, and the Greek colony of Thurii in Italy

Principal personages:
HECATAEUS OF MILETUS (fl.c.575), early geographer and genealogist
HERODOTUS (484-c.425), Greek historian

Summary of Event

Herodotus' monumental history of the Persian wars, written during the second half of the fifth century B.C., established its author as in Cicero's words, "the father of history." It is an extraordinary work, combining history in the modern sense with geography, anthropology, and comparative religion.

Like most genres, history did not achieve maturity in its first form. Herodotus, while groping for the historical perspective mastered by Thucydides a generation later, retained many characteristics of his diverse predecessors. Homer influenced him significantly; critics have pointed out that epic poetry, for centuries the repository of records of the Greek past, probably hindered the development of history as a discipline through its emphasis on the biographical, rather than the institutional, its theistic-humanistic philosophy, and its appeal to romance and excitement.

Herodotus clearly derived much from the poets: the art of holding interest by intermingling digressions with narrative, the significance put on characterization of leaders, and, most important, a view of history as controlled to a great degree by the gods. Like his contemporaries, the great dramatists Sophocles and Aeschylus, Herodotus followed Homer in viewing human affairs as divinely ordained; man is a creature of fate, often a suffering victim. Like the heroes of classical tragedy, Herodotus' kings and princes become arrogant in their wealth and power and bring catastrophe upon themselves. Once Xerxes chastizes the sea, the reader knows his great host crossing the Hellespont is headed toward its destruction.

While epic was the most popular record of the past in the Greek world of the seventh and sixth centuries B.C., Ionian writers were gradually developing prose accounts of the geography and customs of the areas they visited as they sailed on trading expeditions around the Mediterranean. The exposure to a variety of cultures seems to have developed in them a rational, often skeptical spirit, and they began to cast the eye of reason upon the myths that passed for history among their people. Only fragments have survived to indicate the nature of these semihistorical works. The remains of two treatises by Hecataeus of Miletus, who wrote during the latter part of the sixth century B.C., are probably representative of the new school of

259

thought. In his *Genealogies* he attemped to give rational explanations for familiar tales of the gods and heroes who were purportedly the ancestors of the Greeks of his own day. More significant for Herodotus was Hecataeus' *Periezesis,* his account of his observations on his journeys into Egypt, Persia, mainland Greece, and the countries near the Black Sea.

Thus, Herodotus began his work with a foundation in the epic concept of the relationship of god and man, and an Ionian-inspired curiosity about man and society, along with a rationalistic and skeptical approach to mythical history. To these perspectives must be added his strong pro-Athenian bias. Born in the Dorian city of Halicarnassus on the coast of Asia Minor, Herodotus lived in Athens for much of the period between 454 and 443, when he helped to colonize Thurii in Italy. He was thus a part of the flowering of Periclean Athens during the years between the end of the Persian wars in 479 and the beginning of the Peloponnesian conflict in 431. It was during these years that he probably derived his strong faith in the free state and its ability to triumph over tyranny, a belief that becomes a significant theme in the histories.

To assess the *Persian Wars* as history, it is perhaps useful to note that the Greek word *histor* means "observer," or "recorder," rather than "analyst of facts," and Herodotus is a historian in this sense more than in the modern one. Especially in the first six books he refers over and over again to what he has seen or what he has been told. He does not uncritically accept everything he hears, but neither does he attempt to sort out every conflicting account.

Herodotus' work begins with a discussion of the earliest conflicts between the near-eastern and western Mediterranean cultures and an account of the growth of the Persian empire. As he recounts each new conquest, he digresses to describe the customs of the soon-to-be-invaded nation: Lydia, ruled by the legendary Croesus, Assyria, Egypt, Ethiopia, Scythia, India, and Arabia. He traces the careers of successive Persian monarchs, Cyrus, Cambyses, and Darius, setting the stage for the massive expedition of Xerxes against the Greeks. Initially more digression than narrative, Herodotus' work sharpens its focus as it moves toward the climax, the account of the battles that culminated in the Persian defeat at Salamis. Though the organization seems haphazard at times, as when Herodotus is describing three common methods of embalming in Egypt and similar abstruse pieces of information, he never loses sight of his purpose, stated in his first paragraph, "of preserving from decay the remembrance of what men have done and of preventing the great and wonderful actions of the Greeks and the Barbarians from losing their due need of glory." Whatever his deficiencies in modern research techniques, Herodotus accomplished his primary goal. It is his vast perspective and his superb talent as a storyteller that have preserved the memory of the world-shaping victory of the Greeks for 2500 years.

Pertinent Literature

Myers, John L. *Herodotus, Father of History*. Oxford: The University Press, 1953.

Even in ancient times Herodotus' purpose, methodology, and stature were disputed. On the whole, early evaluations treated him harshly as a liar, or as an incompetent, biased narrator of gossip. Diodorus, it is true, thought that Herodotus should be listed among "principal historians" but chiefly on literary grounds. Cicero treats him kindly as the "father of history." Plutarch, on the other hand, dubbed him little more than a biased flatterer of Athens.

Later, Niebuhr, while skeptical of much of Greek historical tradition, came to appreciate the difficulties encountered by Herodotus in the use of formless and heterogeneous sources. K. W. Nitzsch, after postulating the radical thesis that Herodotus depended on a formal written source, declared him an "industrious but unintelligent compiler." Others saw Herodotus as a moralizer, or a mere inventor of historical causes. As late as 1887 the famous work of Delbruck exposed Herodotus' incompetence in regard to military numbers by comparing possible maneuvers of Greek armed forces with those of the Swiss cantons in the fifteenth century.

Nineteenth century studies, stressing investigation into the sequence in which the various books of Herodotus were written, began to be more considerate. Constructive criticism began with A. Bauer, who postulated the explanation that Herodotus' defects were due more to inadequate editing in combining separate drafts written over a long period and in various places, than to shortcomings in planning an overall composition. About the same time, however, the noted A. H. Sayce was accusing Herodotus of plagiarism in not acknowledging his indebtedness to Ionian chroniclers and of dishonesty in claiming reliance on eyewitnesses. Sayce, in turn, was attacked by R. C. Jebb and A. Croiset.

At this juncture, when a general review of the earlier criticism was timely, Amédée Hauvette did much to restore Herodotus' reputation by stressing his "industry, good faith, and discernment." The weighty reputation of Eduard Meyer, about 1890, reinforced this positive view. Yet when modern conditions made access to Egypt and Greece easier and provided new resources for study, Herodotus came in for more criticism. G. B. Grundy, for example, after surveying sites of ancient battlefields, subjected the historian to severe reproach as being inept in military experience.

When F. Jacoby reëxamined all the evidence in his Pauly-Wissowa article of 1913, Herodotus emerged as an original artist who skillfully combined various phases of composition and sundry ingredients such as travel accounts, studies in ethnography, and lectures on regional areas into a composite whole after developing a belated historical consciousness from his experience in Athens. Jacoby saw the epic as Herodotus' model. A rash of studies continued to appear commending various virtues in Herodotus: some stressed his political insights, others his capacity for human interest, his emphasis on the divine, or his message of free will and responsibility. F. Hellman in 1934, for instance, pictured Herodotus essentially as a philosopher of history who in making a "tragic reference of all human actions to the will of God" posited an unpredictable "divine predestination and cycle of human affairs." In failing to fathom this divine fate correctly, man invited retribution as an aggressor. Pohlenz, in turn pointed out that Herodotus, in deliberately relating the cause of events after the events themselves, was using a legitimate epic device which permitted logical retrogressions in background material. Myers preferred to stress the tragic element in Herodotus.

Modern study, emphasizing an investigation into the sequence of Herodotus' different books and the circumstances or production, have conjured up more and more respect for the ancient historian as an "intelligent and observant man of his age" who accepted only what to him at the time seemed plausible whether gathered from eyewitnesses or from hearsay.

Hadas, Moses. *A History of Greek Literature*. New York: Columbia University Press, 1950.

Professor Hadas' short introduction to Herodotus is a brilliant distillation of the qualities that have given the *Persian Wars* their lasting appeal. Hadas suggests that it is Herodotus alone who has preserved for modern readers what he calls the "Logos," the "Thing Said," the vast, valuable body of folk history that makes up much of the Greek writer's work. He was the culmination of a long tradition of oral tales in much the same way that Homer was the last and greatest of the Ionian court bards, building his epics on theirs.

Hadas emphasizes the essential unity of Herodotus' work, "a mighty stream, to which lesser tributaries, traced from their sources, are from time to time joined to swell the flood." A part of this unity results from the historian's world-view, the tolerance that enabled him to observe and describe other cultures without making constant judgments upon them. His epic concept of history as mankind's tragedy is another unifying factor. Hadas sees Croesus and Xerxes as Aristotelian heroes akin to Oedipus and Agamemnon, men essentially noble whose *hubris,* or passion, literally brings the wrath of the gods upon them.

Hadas gives an astute analysis of Herodotus as a historian. He points out his obvious failings: the lack of a consistent chronology made almost inevitable by the absence of a unified calendar in the Greek states; the clearly impossible statistics, especially those involving the size of the Persian army, which he estimates at five million; his inevitably faulty calculations; his confusion about military tactics; and his over-emphasis on divine intervention and the effects of the oracles. However, Hadas vociferously denies the contention that Herodotus uncritically accepted everything he was told. His primary difficulty was that he had little evidence for verifying what he heard. He was careful to evaluate what he was told against his own sense of probability, and he stated his concept of his function clearly in

Book VII: "My duty is to report all that is said, but I am not obliged to believe it all alike." He generally distinguished between the things he himself had seen and things he reported on the authority of others, and modern geographers and anthropologists have confirmed some of his observations that were ridiculed a century or two ago. Whenever possible, he made use of inscriptions on monuments and official documents relating to such matters as Persian satrapies and aspects of Athenian and Spartan history. He also quotes extensively from the temple records at Delphi.

Hadas agrees that Herodotus may be considered too "theological" for modern tastes. He was a deeply religious man and a believer in the validity of the oracles he quotes so often. For analytical, dispassionate history, Thucydides is clearly superior, but for the picture of a "whole wide world teeming with life," the work of Herodotus is unsurpassed. Had his book not survived, Hadas concludes, we "would have been impoverished of an incalculable treasure of enchantment."

— *E.J.L.*

Additional Recommended Reading

Bury, J. B. *The Ancient Greek Historians.* New York: Dover Publications, 1958. The classical account of Greek historiography.

Herodotus. With an English translation by A. D. Godley. (Loeb Classical Library.) Cambridge: Harvard University Press, 1966. 4 vols. A good literal translation with brief introductory materials on Herodotus' life and the general characteristics of his work.

Pearson, Lionel I. C. *The Early Ionian Historians.* Oxford: The Clarendon Press, 1939. An indispensable study of primitive "history" writing.

Lesky, Albin. *A History of Greek Literature.* Translated by James Willis and Cornelis de Heer. New York: Thomas Y. Crowell Company, 1966. A scholarly introduction to early prose treatises as well as to the work of Herodotus.

Hamilton, Edith. "Herodotus, the First Sight-Seer," in *The Greek Way.* New York: W. W. Norton and Company, Inc., 1942. A treatise focusing on the great breadth of Herodotus' interests and the bases on which he evaluated what he saw and heard.

Shotwell, James T. *The History of History.* New York: Columbia University Press, 1939. A survey of Herodotus' predecessors pointing out his special contributions to historical writing.

Godolphin, Francis R. B., ed. *The Greek Historians.* New York: Random House, 1942. 2 vols. An edition of the works of Herodotus. Thucydides, Xenophon, and Arrian, with an introductory survey of the development of Greek history.

CONCEPTION OF MECHANISTIC ATOMISM

Type of event: Intellectual: emergence of a school of philosophy
Time: c.450 B.C.
Locale: Miletus in Ionia; and Abdera in Thrace

Principal personages:
LEUCIPPUS OF MILETUS (fl. mid-fifth century), Greek philosopher who propounded an atomic theory
DEMOCRITUS OF ABDERA (c.460-370), Greek thinker who systematically elaborated the atomic theory of Leucippus
EPICURUS OF SAMOS (342-270), Greek philosopher who constructed a system of moral philosophy based on the same atomic theory
TITUS LUCRETIUS CARUS (94-55), Latin poet and author of *De Rerum Natura*, a systematic exposition of Epicurean natural and moral doctrine

Summary of Event

The theory that physical nature and its phenomena can best be explained in terms of ultimate material particles and their interaction has played a major role in the development of modern science. This theory first emerged in the ancient world in the middle of the fifth century B.C., not as a scientific hypothesis formulated to account for observed phenomena of nature but as a philosophical solution to a philosophical problem. Since its beginnings in the sixth century B.C., Greek natural philosophy had been concerned with explaining the underlying causes of the phenomena of change. Early in the fifth century, however, Parmenides of Elea had demonstrated the apparent impossibility of giving a rational account of change; anything really existing (Being) must be homogeneous, permanent, indivisible, and immutable, and Parmenides concluded that because Being must

be one, it followed that a plurality of existent things and change were rationally incompatible. There were three significant attempts to solve the problem posed by Parmenides in the fifth century: those of Empedocles of Acragas, Anaxagoras of Clazomenae, and Leucippus of Miletus and his pupil Democritus of Abdera. The most rational of the three solutions, however, was the atomic theory first proposed by Leucippus and elaborated by Democritus.

Leucippus exists as little more than a name in history; although a book entitled *The Great World System* is attributed to him, nothing significant remains of it. Democritus wrote voluminously, but relatively little of his book *The Small World System* survives. Nevertheless, the atomic theory of Democritus is presented in considerable detail in the writings of Aristotle, who found it necessary to criticize it extensively in favor of his

264

own solution to the Parmenidean problem.

Leucippus and Democritus postulated, as fundamental principles of physical nature, two concepts representing respectively the Parmenidean concepts of Being and Non-Being: atoms and void. Atoms are ultimate units of matter, infinite in number and all sharing the properties of Parmenidean Being: indivisibility, immutability, permanent existence, and homogeneity. Void is infinite in extension and is not to be understood as space occupied by atoms but rather as a negative principle, emptiness, a separator of the distinct atomic units. The atoms themselves, although homogeneous in substance, differ from each other in size, shape, position, and arrangement. All phenomena in nature are explained as functions of aggregation and dissociation of the atoms. The qualitative differences between these aggregate things are dependent only on quantitative and local differences.

Democritus held that there are infinite worlds in process of formation and dissolution through the association and separation of atoms. Worlds come into existence through the mingling of a large collection of atoms isolated in a large patch of void. These atoms form a vortex, causing larger atoms to congregate at the center of the vortex while smaller atoms are squeezed out to the perimeter, where a filmy membrane forms to enclose the whole. Within the world, distinct aggregates of atoms form bodies through the temporary association of atoms of congruent or similar shapes.

The interaction of the atoms in the system of Democritus takes place according to strict mechanistic necessity. He seems to have attributed an original motion, perhaps simply vibration, to the atoms, causing collisions and temporary association of them, but the significant motion of the atoms is that derived from their collisions. At any rate, it is an essential feature of Democritus' concept of the atoms that they have always been in motion and have always been colliding with one another.

The fate of the atomic theory in antiquity rests upon its nature as one feature in a whole system of philosophy rather than as a scientific theory of the structure of matter. The contemporaries and immediate successors of Democritus rejected the whole system because of its fundamental materialism and its failure to account adequately for human intellectual and spiritual experience, and perhaps most of all because of its strict mechanistic character and exclusion of the possibility of teleological causation. The atomic theory could not become scientifically fruitful until the examination of natural phenomena became distinct from philosophy and had begun to be supported by the gathering of experimental data. As was noted earlier, the theory of Democritus emerged as a speculative solution of a philosophical problem, not as a hypothesis to account for observed facts.

The very mechanistic, nonteleological qualities of the atomic theory which led to its rejection by most subsequent thinkers of antiquity account for its acceptance by Epicurus of Samos early in the third century B.C. as the foundation for a

Conception of Mechanistic Atomism

system of moral philosophy, the positive goal of which was personal freedom from spiritual anxiety. A strictly deterministic, nonteleological world order wherein death is explained simply as the final dissolution of the component atoms of personal existence left no room for a concept of an afterlife and hence no ground for anxious fears about post-mortal punishments. Such a world-order also provided a rational ground for a

morality of self-preservation and simple pleasures. For many men spiritually troubled in the later centuries of antiquity, this was a comforting philosophy of life, and its appeal was broad. Atomism and the Epicurean ethic founded upon it received its fullest exposition in the six books of the poetic treatise, *De Rerum Natura,* composed by the Roman poet Lucretius in the middle of the first century B.C.

Pertinent Literature

Van Melsen, Andrew G. *From Atomos to Atom.* Pittsburgh: Duquesne University Press, 1952. Reprinted New York: Harper & Row Publishers Incorporated, 1960.

This book is primarily a historical account of the development of the concept of ultimate particles from its origin in Greek philosophy to its systematic elaboration in modern nuclear physics. A major theme running through the whole account, however, is the relationship between natural philosophy and science proper at each stage of development and the essential interdependence of the two.

Van Melsen stresses the importance of philosophy in general to the development of science and Greek philosophy in particular as a necessary foundation for the very initiation of genuine scientific investigation. That the vocabulary of science was developed in the Greek philsophical tradition is, according to Van Melsen, no accident. The development of natural science was made possible only by the philosophic investigation of problems centering around the apparent contradiction between the data of experience and the postulates of reason. Specifically, the problem

of change must be understood in adequate philosophical terms, inasmuch as a universal aspect of matter is its mutability. Since the philosophical problem of change does not depend for its solution upon a mass of empirical data, the Greek thinkers were as adequately equipped to deal with it as are moderns.

It was Parmenides who pushed to the ultimate limit insistence that the explanation of phenomena must be thoroughly rational. All that is real must be explained in terms conforming to certain metaphysical canons. Thus no account of change can be given that does not preserve the principle of identity. Van Melsen is particularly illuminating with regard to the significance of Parmenides' canons: he notes that when a change has been adequately explained, the alteration of conditions ceases to contradict the principle of identity because the underlying identity of the changing substance is affirmed. Hence, the chemical equation $Hgo{\rightarrow}Hg+O$ af-

266

firms the identity of the elements in the process of chemical change.

Van Melsen discusses the atomic theory of Democritus rather briefly and shows how the postulation of homogeneous atoms meets the Parmenidean canons. He also discusses the alternative solutions of Anaxagoras and Empedocles and notes that, while the atomic theory of Democritus is the most rational of the three proposed solutions, that of Empedocles is more empirical because it accounts for our experience with fundamentally different types of matter.

Later Greek philosophers are discussed at greater length than Democritus himself because they contributed in one way or another to the development of the atomic theory. Hence Socrates receives credit for the creation of the inductive method and Plato for recognizing the significance of mathematics in determining the structure of the building-blocks of matter. While Aristotle's alternative solution to the Parmenidean dilemma retarded the development of the Democritean atomic theory, Aristotle's insistence that the compounding of elements involves an internal change in the elements themselves was to prove fruitful later. Finally, Aristotle proposed a theoretical concept of minimal particles which was developed by his commentators in later antiquity into an assertion of the real existence of such particles, technically terms *elachista* in Greek, *minima* in Latin.

Only gradually came the discovery that one sector of experience could be investigated apart from a systematic account of all general problems of philosophy. When, in the seventeenth century, the deductive method of mathematics and philosophy began to be combined with the inductive method developed in the practice of the technical arts, it at last became possible to gather a body of chemical and physical data sufficiently large to permit an adequate judgment of the usefulness of the theory of Democritus. The further development of the atomic theory has continued to issue, in Van Melsen's view, from the fruitful meeting of experimental results with philosophical vision.

Kirk, G. S., and J. E. Raven. *The Presocratic Philosophers: A Critical History with a Selection of Texts.* Cambridge: The University Press, 1960.

This work is now a standard reference in English for the history of pre-Socratic philosophy. After a discussion, with a selection of texts, of the mythical antecedents of Greek cosmology, the authors proceed to a presentation of the major groups of early Greek thinkers: Ionian and Italian schools and the post-Parmenidean systems. Each philosopher of importance is given a chapter subdivided into major topics, and a discussion of each topic devoted to what positive conclusions may be drawn from the trustworthy evidence follows on a Greek text and English translation of the most important witnesses.

The atomists are here set within the context generally accepted for them: along with Empedocles and Anaxagoras and the lesser figures

Archelaus of Athens and Diogenes of Apollonia, they attempted to formulate a cosmology consistent with the metaphysical requisites laid down by Parmenides. Kirk, the author of the chapter on the atomists, does not attempt to distinguish clearly between the personal contributions of Leucippus and Democritus to the fully developed atomic theory.

Kirk believes it probable that Leucippus, in originally formulating the concept of atoms, was following out the consequence of a suggestion originally presented as an absurdity by Melissus of Elea, the pupil of Parmenides: "If there were a plurality, things would have to be of just the same nature as the one." Such is precisely the character of the atoms of Leucippus and Democritus: they are homogeneous, indivisible, permanent, and immutable.

The fundamental features of the atomic theory have already been presented, but it is worth noting how Democritus explained sensation, thought, and knowledge in terms of his atomic theory. All sensation must clearly be explained as a form of contact or touch. Soul is explained as consisting of tiny spherical atoms spread throughout the body and present wherever sensation occurs. Mind must be a concentration of soul-atoms, and thought is analogous

to sensation: it is occasioned by the disturbance of soul-atoms by contact with incoming congruent atoms from outside the body. Vision is explained in terms that will not stand close examination: objects of vision give off "effluences" which meet other "effluences" from the observer and form a solid impression in mid-air. This impression then enters the pupil of the eye.

Implicit in Democritus' theory of sensation and knowledge is a doctrine of primary and secondary such as that developed by the English empiricist John Locke (1632-1704). "Genuine" opinions for Democritus are essentially intellectual, those concerning atoms and the void, while "obscure" opinions are those based only on direct sense-experience.

There are a greater number of Democritus' fragments relating to ethics than physics, but Kirk presents only a small selection of them. While granting that Democritus' concept of contentment based on moral well-being is developed in naturalistic terms, he notes that it is not based directly on atomist physical assumptions and that atoms are never mentioned in any extant fragment dealing with ethics. On the whole, Democritus' moral concepts seem to reflect the traditional Greek aristocratic ethic of restraint. — *C.W.C.*

Additional Recommended Reading

Bailey, Cyril. *The Greek Atomists and Epicurus*. Oxford: The Clarendon Press, 1928. In addition to describing the origins of Greek atomism and the theories of Leucippus and Democritus, this work describes modifications of atomic theory made by Epicurus in formulating his philosophical system.

Burnet, John. *Early Greek Philosophy*. 4th ed. Ch. IX. London: Adams & Charles Black, 1930. A study presenting an account of the atomic theory of Leucippus.

Freeman, Kathleen. *Ancilla to the Pre-Socratic Philosophers*. Oxford: Basil Blackwell, 1952. English translations of fragments of pre-Socratic philosophers (without commentary), including Leucippus and Democritus.

Guthrie, W. K. C. *A History of Greek Philosophy.* Vol. II, ch. VIII. Cambridge: The University Press, 1965. A well-known work offering an extensive account of atomic theory in the fifth century B.C.

Vlastes, Gregory. "Ethics and Physics in Democritus," in *Philosophical Review.* 54 (1945), 578ff.; and 55 (1946), 53ff. A discussion of the ethical theory of Democritus as being consistent with his physical theory.

FORMULATION OF THE
MULTIPLE-ELEMENT HYPOTHESIS

Type of event: Intellectual: attempt to define basic reality
Time: c.450 B.C.
Locale: Acragas, Sicily

Principal personages:
EMPEDOCLES OF ACRAGAS (c.493-443 B.C.) Sicilian philosopher and religious thinker
ANAXAGORAS OF CLAZOMENAE (c.500-428), Ionian natural philosopher

Summary of Event

Historians of science recognize the beginnings of a serious effort to understand the nature and operating principles of the physical world in the speculations of ancient Greek philosophers whose assumptions were dogmatic and not based on experiment but who posed questions which are still recognized as meaningful by modern scientists. These ancient philosophers laid down several basic notions and hypotheses which proved fruitful in post-Renaissance physical science. One such hypothesis was formulated by Empedocles of Acragas in the middle of the fifth century B.C. All substances in the physical world, Empedocles declared, are either pure forms or proportionate mixtures of four elemental substances: earth, water, air, and fire.

The systematic explanation of natural phenomena constructed by Empedocles on the foundation of this hypothesis was itself a synthesis of speculative doctrines and rational criticisms of them developed over a century of earlier Greek philosophical thought. The same four elements already played dominant roles in the cosmogonic speculations of the Milesian philoso-

phers in the sixth century B.C. These thinkers, under the influence of the cosmogonic myth of Hesiod, supposed that one of the four elements (water, according to Thales; air, according to Anaximenes) was the primary "stuff" of the world, and that the other three were qualitative modifications of this material which emerged in the course of the development of a complex world order out of an original unity. By the early years of the fifth century B.C. the Milesian view of the differentiation of one primary substance into several qualitatively distinct substances was subjected to logical criticism by Parmenides of Elea. Parmenides insisted that anything real must itself be ungenerated and indestructible; a plurality of substances could not be derived from a single qualitatively distinct substance. After Parmenides, therefore, every thinker constructing an explanation of the order of physical nature began with an assumption that there must be a plurality of substances in nature. Empedocles' system based on a doctrine of four primary substances was approximately contemporaneous with two other

270

pluralist systems: Anaxagoras of Clazomenae (c.500-428) postulated the existence of infinite qualitatively distinct primary substances, while Democritus of Abdera (c.460-370) constructed a theory that an infinite number of indivisible substances, which he called "atoms" moved at random in a void to form groups appearing qualitatively distinct due to the sizes, shapes, and positions of their components.

Empedocles' own system explained natural phenomena through the mingling and dissociation in alternate cycles of the four primary substances under the motive influence of Love and Strife (themselves also conceived as being somehow corporeal). In an everlasting cyclical process consisting of four phases, the elements pass from a state of full intermingling under Love's dominance, through a transition to an opposite stage of complete differentiation under the domination of Strife, and back again through a second transition to the original state of perfect union. In the initial stage, the fully mingled elements are held together in a sphere by Love, and Strife is excluded; at the other end of the cycle, Strife has brought about separation of the elements so that they are arranged in concentric spheres with all earth at the core and successive spherical layers of water, air, and fire enveloping the terrestrial core. In the transitional stages, the elements mingle in various proportions to form the phenomena of nature and living organisms.

It is clear that the dualistic motive forces of Love and Strife are derived from an "Orphic" religious scheme represented more directly in another poem of Empedocles, the *Purifications*. Essential to this religious scheme are a conception of the soul's immortality, its fall from a state of primal purity into corruption, its successive reincarnation in a number of physical forms of life, and its ultimate purification with restoration to original purity. The relationship of the *Purifications* to Empedocles' cosmological poem *On Nature* is disputed, but one suggestion is that the soul as understood by Empedocles is a mixture of the four elements in nearly equal proportions; hence the principle of the soul might be regarded as a harmony, an attunement, or a proportional formula of the nature of Love.

The significance of Empedocles' system must be seen as a kind of classical synthesis of many physical and religious conceptions held at different times in Greek antiquity, especially in the pre-Socratic era. One of these conceptions is that of a world order formed from four primary substances emerging from a primal unity through processes of separation, rarefaction, condensation, and mingling. A second conception widespread in antiquity is that of the cyclical nature of time. A third conception is the identification of life and consciousness, or soul, with blood.

From the standpoint of the history of science, the system of Empedocles must be seen as a vague anticipation of the modern physical hypothesis of a plurality of elemental substances (far more, of course, than the four of Empedocles). Perhaps it is also fair to say that the distinction of earth, water, air, and fire as primary substances is a vague anticipation of the modern view of primary qualitative

forms of physical nature: solid, liquid, gas, and energy.

Pertinent Literature

Burnet, John. *Early Greek Philosophy.* 4th ed. London: Adam & Charles Black, 1930.

In this concise but detailed presentation of the doctrines of the major pre-Socratic natural philosophers and schools, Empedocles is fully treated in a lengthy chapter. Burnet includes an English translation of all the extant fragments in the order in which they appear in the Diels-Kranz authoritative edition of the collected fragments of the Pre-Socratics.

While Empedocles, like Pythagoras before him, was the focus of a growing body of legends in antiquity, Burnet notes an extraordinary range of interests and activities attributed to him by traditions that need not be doubted. He was politically active as an extreme democrat in his native city of Acragas. He was a religious teacher and, as is directly stated in his poem *Purifications,* claimed divinity for himself. He evolved the technique of rhetoric which was elaborated and taught by his disciple, the Sophist Gorgias. He was also the founder of a school of medicine which was still extant in Plato's day and competed with the Cosan school of Hippocrates.

Burnet sees Empedocles' world view as developing directly out of Parmenides'. Some of the earlier fragments of the poem *On Nature* reproduce very closely Parmenides' argument that Being alone is real and indestructible. Although Empedocles postulated a multiplicity of real and

indestructible substances rather than the one of Parmenides, his cosmogony has as its initial stage the very sphere of Being conceived by Parmenides. Where Parmenides, however, had denied the validity of sense-experience, it was a primary concern of Empedocles, in Burnet's view, to preserve the logical requisites of reality as enunciated by Parmenides and still do justice to the evidence of the senses. Empedocles was of all Greek thinkers before Aristotle the one who observed natural phenomena most keenly; and while certainly no empirical scientist, he incorporated into his system a number of reasoned conclusions based on observations. He understood the true cause of eclipses, recognized that the moon shines with reflected light, observed that plants reproduce bisexually, and even postulated a scheme of biological evolution dominated by the principle of survival of the fittest.

The cosmogonic process envisioned by Empedocles begins when Strife penetrates the body of the spherical mixture and effects the separation of air from the rest. The air moves to the surface of the sphere as a mist enveloping it and the outer circle of this air becomes solidified to form a glassy shell bounding the cosmos. In the next stage of the process, two hemispheres, diurnal and nocturnal, are formed when fire displaces a portion of the air in the upper half of the sphere; this air sinks downward and carries with it a small portion of fire. The equilibrium of the heavens is upset by the accumulation of fire in the upper hemisphere; hence the heavens begin to revolve and the alternation of day and night commences. The sun is conceived by Empedocles to be a concentrated flash of reflected light of the fiery hemisphere from the earth. The moon is a disk of frozen air reflecting the light of the sun. Within the central portion of the sphere there still remain earth and water, in addition to remnants of the original fire and water diffused throughout the mixture. Water is squeezed out as a consequence of compression caused by the revolution of the heavens, and Empedocles calls the sea the "sweat" of the earth. Next, through the interaction of the

elements subject to the opposite influences of Love and Strife, compounds of organic nature form through the strictly proportionate mingling of the elements. Plants are the first living creatures to develop, and animals come into being through four stages of evolution. Our own stage, as Burnet interprets the scanty evidence, is that of the growing domination of Strife.

Burnet treats the Empedoclean poem *Purifications* very briefly and sees only minor relationships between it and the poem *On Nature*. Since the cosmological poem, as Burnet interprets it, leaves no room for an immortal soul, he sees Empedocles as a man who kept his science and religion rigidly compartmentalized, apparently unaware of any conflict between the two.

Long, Herbert S. "The Unity of Empedocles Thought," in *American Journal of Philology*. 70 (1949), 142-158.

A fundamental problem in interpreting the extant fragments of Empedocles' two poems is that of the inconsistent manner in which souls, especially human souls, are discussed in the two works. In *On Nature,* all things compounded of the primary elements dissolve and perish including, it would seem, the soul. In *Purifications,* however, the immortality of souls successively reincarnated in new bodies is a fundamental assumption. How is the inconsistency to be explained? In this article, Long notes the attitudes most commonly expressed toward the problem: some admit the inconsistency and assert that Empedocles was probably never aware of it; others argue that Emped-

ocles radically changed his world view in the course of his life, either because he was converted to a religion of transmigration after he had composed *On Nature,* or because he lost his faith in such a religious view before he wrote the cosmological poem.

Long's discussion of this problem is illuminating and relevant to understanding Empedocles' doctrine of elements, not so much because of his solution to the problem but because it brings into sharp focus the difficulty experienced by early Greek thinkers in considering immaterial realities. Long notes that our sources for Empedocles are sharply divided into two groups: Peripatetic writers who described the physical theory of Empedocles and sought to understand it in terms of an Aristotelian distinction of material and efficient causes; and Academic or Neo-Platonic writers interested primarily in the religious doctrine of the soul. Each group seems to have concentrated on that part of Empedocles' thought relevant to their own concerns alone. Neither group seems to have fully appreciated the certainty for Empedocles that Love and Strife, even the immortal soul of the *Purifications,* were corporeal in nature.

Aristotle, noting that Love and Strife are moral terms and that they function causally in a different way from earth, water, air, and fire, sought to classify them as efficient rather than material causes, and he accused Empedocles of confusion caused by the latter's view of them as material substances. There is, Long insists, no single extant fragment of Empedocles wherein Love and Strife cannot be understood as material, and there are undeniable indications in other fragments that they were understood to be material.

Long sees the poems *On Nature* and *Purifications* as complementary accounts of the macrocosmic world order and the microcosmic soul order. Both the world and the soul are composed of the six elemental substances. Intellect, the capacity for perception, is associated by Empedocles with blood, a perfectly harmonious mixture of all six elements. Mind is especially associated with the proportions of earth, water, air, and fire and is, says Long, "in a sense, a subdivision of perception." Long's interesting positive solution of the problem of the relationship between the two poems is that a combination of Love and Strife is "the organizing principle of the body and the moral character of the individual man, his personality considered in its ethical aspect." The mixture of these two elements is the *daimon* of a man which survives the dissolution of the other four elements and later enters into a new body. This *diamon* does not have a constant composition, but changes slowly according to its upward movement toward the purity of Love or downward movement toward the absolute domination of Strife.

This explanation has the advantage of clarifying the presence of the Orphic cyclical process and dualism of opposed ethical absolutes in Empedocles' cosmology. If valid, it also places Empedocles in the category, not of scientists who keep science and religion in separate compartments, but rather of Greek systematic thinkers who saw man and the universe as analogous microcosmic and macrocosmic structures. — *C.W.C.*

Additional Recommended Reading

Gershenson, Daniel E., and Daniel A. Greenberg. *Anaxagoras and the Birth of Physics.* New York: Blaisdell Publishing Company, 1964. An account of Anaxagoras' theories of physics, with a full collection of ancient sources in translation and a review of ancient and modern interpretations.

Guthrie, W. K. C. *A History of Greek Philosophy.* Vol. II, chs. III and IV. Cambridge: The University Press, 1965. A systematic account of the doctrines of

Empedocles and Anaxagoras is presented in this work.

Jaeger, Werner. *The Theology of the Early Greek Philosophers*. Chs. VIII and IX. Oxford: The Clarendon Press, 1947. Here a famous scholar discusses the religious aspects of the philosophies of Empedocles and Anaxagoras.

Kirk, G. S., and J. E. Raven. *The Presocratic Philosophers: A Critical History with a Selection of Texts*. Chs. XIV and XV. Cambridge: The University Press, 1960. Systematic accounts of the systems of Empedocles and Anaxagoras with Greek texts, English translations, and commentaries.

BUILDING OF THE PARTHENON

Type of event: Artistic: construction of a Greek temple
Time: 447-432 B.C.
Locale: The Acropolis at Athens

Principal personages:
PERICLES, political leader of Athens 461-429
PHIDIAS (475-430), master sculptor and overseer of art work
for the Parthenon
ICTINUS and
CALLICRATES (fl.440), architects in charge of design and
construction

Summary of Event

The Parthenon, dedicated to Athena the Maiden, is the most famous of Greek temples, the crowning monument of the Athenian Acropolis. Of the Doric order but with Ionic architectural features such as the continuous frieze, it was built under Pericles in 447-432 B.C. by the architects Ictinus and Callicrates. The sculptor Phidias was responsible for the design and composition of its decorative reliefs and statuary. Constructed entirely of Pentelic marble upon a limestone foundation, it is peripteral octastyle in plan, being encompassed by a single row of columns, with eight at each end and in this instance seventeen on each side. At the top step of the stylobate or substructure, the building measures 228 feet by 101 feet, so that it is exceptionally wide in proportion to its length. Within the peristyle of columns stood the enclosed cella or main room, and a back chamber, each fronted by a porch with six columns. At both ends metal grilles between these columns completely enclosed the two chambers. The cella, with its door facing east, had interior columns in two

levels at the sides and rear. Within this main gallery visitors could view the colossal cult statue, the gold and ivory Athena of Phidias set at the far end of the room. The foundation of the pedestal, all that remains of this great work, measures twenty-six by thirteen feet. The back chamber or *opisthodomos,* with its door opening to the west and with four interior columns, may have served as a treasury for gifts dedicated to the goddess.

Chief among the sculptural decorations of the Parthenon were the metopes in high relief on the entablature, the continuous frieze in low relief above the wall of the two chambers, and the fully sculptured groups in the pediments at each end of the temple. The themes of this art glorified the goddess and the city of which she was patron; the metopes depicted notable combats—Lapiths against Centaurs, Olympians against giants, and Greeks against Amazons or Trojans—to symbolize the victory of civilization over barbarism; the frieze showed the citizenry in the great Panathenaic procession in honor of the goddess; the western pediment

276

portrayed the contest between Athena and Poseidon for dominion over the city, while the eastern one depicted the birth of Athena. Of the purely architectural features the columns stand thirty-four and a half feet high, the equal of about five and a half lower diameters of the columns. From the stylobate to the peak of the gabled roof the structure stood over sixty-one feet in height. Rectangular coffered blocks of marble supported by the sequence of pillars, beams, and walls made up the ceiling, above which was the network of timbers to sustain the low-pitched roof. But even the roof tiles were cut from marble.

Though the earliest Greek temples were constructed of sun-dried brick and wood, after the seventh century hard limestone, conglomerate, and marble became the chief materials. Athens was well endowed with marble from Mount Pentelicus to the northeast of the city. After being roughly cut in the quarries there, the blocks were brought to the Acropolis in wagons. Hoisting was accomplished by means of pulleys and tongs, the lewis or iron tenon fitting into a dovetailed mortise in the stone. To bond the stones set vertically, such as the individual drums of the columns, iron or bronze dowels set in molten lead connected the top of one drum to the bottom of the one above it. Horizontal bonding of stone beams was achieved by the double-T or H type of cramp. The Greeks never used mortar or nails in this kind of construction, and great care was taken to assure perfect contacts along the surface joins of the marble. Even today many of these joins are so tight that a razor blade cannot be inserted between the blocks.

Many elements in the Hellenic temple came from other Mediterranean cultures—the floor plan from Crete, the columnar structure from Egypt, and the capitals from Assyria —but the genius of the evolving Doric form was typically Greek in its simplicity, its balance of proportions, and its complementary use of sculpture and decoration. As the perfection of this type the Parthenon also includes a number of unique refinements which make it a dynamic creation and a moving visual experience. Among these are the drooping or horizontal curvature of the stylobate toward all four corners, so that, for example, on the long sides the rise from the ends to the center of the structure is about four inches. The columns have both diminution or tapering of the shaft from the bottom up and also entasis or a slight convex swelling in the shaft. Furthermore, all the outside columns incline slightly toward the cella walls; the four angle columns are thicker than the others and by virtue of their position have a double inclination. Last, the chief vertical surfaces such as the cella wall have a backward slope, but the entablature above the columns has a slightly forward tilt. These and other refinements were probably incorporated to correct optical illusions which would otherwise make the stylobate appear to sag, the entablature to recede, and the angle columns to appear thin against the sky. Whatever the reasons, the refinements combine with other features of the Parthenon to make it nearly perfect. It survived in fairly whole condition until 1687, when it was badly damaged by an explosion during a war between the Turks and the Venetians. More than a century later Lord Elgin brought most of the surviving sculptures to London in order to save them from piecemeal destruction. Consequently a full appreciation of the Parthenon now requires a visit to the British Museum in London, where the so-called Elgin Marbles are on display, and to Athens, to view the partially restored temple.

Pertinent Literature

Lullies, R., and M. Hirmer. *Greek Sculpture*. London: Thames and Hudson, 1957.

This excellent study of the whole of Greek sculpture from the Archaic period through the Hellenistic age is especially useful for an appreciation of the decorative art that survives from the Parthenon. The straightforward, factual text is by Lullies, and the superb photography is by Hirmer who has made a distinguished career of illustrating works of antiquity. Plates in the book give a selection of the metope and frieze reliefs and of the sculptures in the round from the pediments of the great temple. All this work was created under the leadership of the Athenian Phidias, whom Pericles commissioned for the task and who was responsible for the design and composition of the sculptures. He created the models in clay and plaster which his corps of artists then rendered in the actual stone. In his own right Phidias also created the thirty-foot-high bronze Athena Promachos, which stood on the Acropolis to the northwest of the Parthenon, and the colossal gold and ivory Athena Parthenos, the cult statue inside the temple itself.

The sculptural work adorning the exterior of Athena's temple was entirely original and brilliant in mastering problems of form and composition while employing suitable mythological and processional events to enhance the great structure. Stylistically the oldest sculptures are the metopes, seventy-four of which were set in the entablature, each one being four feet eight inches wide by four feet two inches high. The best preserved of these come from the south side of the temple and depict in part the struggle between the Lapiths and Centaurs. In the myth, Peirithous, King of the Lapiths, invited the Centaurs to his wedding feast, but these creatures, half man and half horse, became drunk and attacked the bride and other women present. The resulting melee is the subject of the separate panels of the metopes, of which perhaps that in Plate 143, with close-up in Plate 145, is the best preserved. In it the Centaur on the left and the Lapith on the right come to grips with each other in a perfect balance of blows and struggling bodies.

The frieze, standing three feet seven inches high but running in a continuous panel some 530 feet long at the top of the walls of the chambers and their colonnaded porches, depicts the Panathenaic procession in honor of Athena. On the west side of the temple the story begins as cavalrymen are depicted in preparation for the parade. The tempo picks up on the north side as horsemen pass along in full stride. In front of them are a number of chariots, elders, musicians, acolytes with water jars for the ritual, and a group of sacrificial animals. The south side shows a somewhat similar array, but with the marchers in this case also proceeding toward the east end where the two streams of celebrants converge upon the main scene. On the east or front side appears the van of the procession, a group of maidens being received by the magistrates and handing over the sacred peplos for the statue of Athena as the seated assembly of the twelve Olympians looks on. Plates 146-151 illustrate selected parts of the frieze, of which that on the west side of the temple remains *in situ* (Plate 146). Various equestrian groups are shown in Plates 147-152 and Poseidon, Apollo, and Artemis appear among the seated gods on the east side in Plates 154-155.

The best preserved of the free-standing pedimental sculptures comes from the east side of the Parthenon. They include the famous reclining figure of the nude god Dionysos (Plates 162-163) and the two female groups: one of Demeter, Persephone, and Artemis; and the other of Hestia with Aphrodite in the lap of her mother Dione (Plates 164-165). The sculptural decoration of the Parthenon portrays the whole range of the cosmic order of fifth century Greece: the mythological past, the worship of the patron deities, and the beneficent rule of the gods themselves.

Robertson, D. S. *A Handbook of Greek and Roman Architecture*. 2nd ed. Cambridge: The University Press, 1959.

The Parthenon cannot be fully understood as the most beautiful of Greek temples unless it be considered within the history and development of Greek architecture; nor can it be fully appreciated in its setting unless the other surviving monuments of the Acropolis receive their due. This book offers the reader detailed information on both these subjects as well as a concise but adequate treatment of the great temple itself. In fifteen chapters the author treats in historical sequence every topic from the palaces of Minoan Crete to Roman private houses, with numerous useful illustrations in the text and plates. A useful appendix is the table entitled "Select Chronological Tables of Greek, Etruscan, and Roman Buildings from 1000 B.C. to A.D. 330." For each structure listed there is given its date, place, dedication or name, dimensions of plan, and many other technical details. From these pages the reader may quickly learn that of the four remaining ancient structures on the Acropolis, the Doric Temple of Athena Parthenos was constructed in the years 447-432 B.C., the Ionic Temples of Athena Nike about 425 B.C. and of the Erechtheum mainly in the years 421-407 B.C., and the monumental entrance known as the Propylaea in 437-432 B.C. These dates indicate that in great part the planning of this immortal complex and the erection of the Parthenon and Propylaea occurred under the guidance of the great Pericles, who died in 429 B.C.

From the late seventh to the early fifth centuries the form of the Doric temple evolved in Greece in a style

279

that emphasized simplicity, integrity, and suitable decorative elements. In the early period the proportions of the columns and other aspects of the form convey an impression of heaviness and massiveness. The illustrations of the "Basilica" at Paestum, of the "Temple of Ceres" also at Paestum, and of "Temple G (T)" at Selinus are good examples of these qualities. With the Parthenon the Doric order reached the summit of perfection by a more delicate balance of proportions and the use of subtle refinements of curvature, inclination, and entasis or the slight convex curve of the columns. Lines which at first sight appear to be straight are found upon close inspection to be tilted or curved in an almost imperceptible manner, and the thickness of the seemingly identical columns is in fact varied according to fixed rules. The result of these developments and techniques is a structure that even today remains dynamic, vital, and unsurpassed. — *K.H.*

Additional Recommended Reading

Dinsmoor, W. B. *The Architecture of Ancient Greece.* 3rd ed. London: Batsford, 1950. A comprehensive and reliable handbook with copious illustrations.

Rodenwaldt, G. *The Acropolis.* Norman: University of Oklahoma Press, 1958. A recent reprint of an older work describing in detail the monuments on the Acropolis.

Corbett, P. E. *The Sculpture of the Parthenon.* Baltimore: Penguin Books, 1959. A concise and authoritative analysis of the decorative sculpture, fully illustrated.

Stevens, G. P. *Restorations of Classical Buildings.* Princeton, New Jersey: American School of Classical Studies at Athens, 1958. A superb set of architectural reconstructions, devoted chiefly to the Parthenon and other monuments of the Acropolis.

ENACTMENT OF THE CANULEIAN LAW

Type of event: Legal: issuance of social legislation
Time: 445 B.C.
Locale: Rome

Principal personage:
GAIUS CANULEIUS, plebeian tribune in 445 B.C.

Summary of Event

During the last decade of the sixth century B.C., the political community already established at Rome started on the long road of political development that led to the Republican constitution of the first century B.C. The traditional system of kingship was overthrown and replaced by two annually-elected magistrates equipped with broad executive powers. Legislative initiative and a general intangible but effective substance of political power was vested in the senate, a self-sustaining body of elder counselors. Although both these organs of government appeared to be republican in character, they were unable to forestall civil strife at Rome and, in fact, they reflected the basic discrepancy in Roman society that engendered that strife. This dichotomy was the so-called "struggle of the orders," a patterned class conflict which was contested on almost all levels of communal life.

The two classes engaged in the struggle were known as patricians and plebeians. After 509, the traditional date for the beginning of the Roman Republic, the plebeians held an inferior position within the Roman state. They were excluded from political office and from the senate, since such honors were reserved for the patricians. Furthermore the plebeians were barred from the official religious bodies of the state and, by one of the laws in the Twelve Tables, from intermarriage with the patricians. The cause and significance of these prohibitions can be found in the underlying social structure of Rome.

The predominant social unit was the *gens* or clan, which was composed of a group of families linked by a common name and the veneration of a common male ancestor. The origin of the *gens* structure has been keenly disputed, but there is general agreement today that it was an outgrowth of the economic progress within the early agrarian society of Rome. Increased wealth caused a split into upper and lower classes that hardened into richer and poorer families. Members of the richer and more powerful clans called themselves patricians, perhaps because of their exclusive hold on the senate, whose original members were termed *patres,* or fathers. This nobility of wealth eventually became a nobility of blood which claimed for itself the fullness of citizenship and total dominance in all aspects of political life. For the fifth century B.C. there is evidence for the existence of fifty such patrician clans, entrenched in power and maintained by privilege.

Opposed to the patricians were the

281

plebeians. There is also some debate as to their origin but they were probably not racially distinct from the patricians. In general they were the poorer elements of Roman society who had not shared in the economic advances of the early years of Roman history. This original core was augmented by the workers and peasants who had been either attracted to Rome by its commercial growth or engulfed by the spread of Roman conquest. Together these various strands formed the *plebs,* or multitude. It must be understood that the plebeians were not a servile class; they always possessed a number of political and civil rights. Furthermore the plebeians also had a *gens* structure within which individual plebeian clans gradually increased in size and wealth. Gradually they became discontented with their second-class status: throughout the first half of the fifth century they repeatedly demanded, and obtained, greater equity within the state. They acquired their own officials, the tribunes of the *plebs,* to act as their protectors and leaders. In 449, a special commission completed the first written codification of law at Rome, the famous Twelve Tables, which made knowledge of the law accessible to everyone so that it was no longer the private province of the patricians. These gains were not obtained without patrician resistance, as evidenced by the inclusion in the Twelve Tables of the ban on intermarriage, a blatant reminder that the plebeians did not enjoy total equality.

In this regard it is misleading to say that marriage between the two groups was interdicted. The Roman Law recognized various forms of marriage, the simplest being the mere living together of a man and woman. If such an arrangement persisted uninterruptedly for one year, the two parties were considered legally married, except in the case of patricians and plebeians. A plebeian woman could share the house of a partician man for the required period without her, or the children of such a union, becoming patrician, results which normally followed in a legal marriage. The decisive factor in this bizarre arrangement was a religious one. The only valid marriage ceremony for patricians was the solemn, religious one called *confarreatio.* For a valid marriage between the two groups, therefore, the plebeians would have to be permitted entrance into the tenaciously guarded domain of patrician religion.

This impasse was circumvented in 445 by Gaius Canuleius, a tribune of the people, who proposed a law rescinding the ban on intermarriage. The law did not eliminate the exclusion of plebeians from the ceremony of *confarreatio;* instead it recognized cohabitation and another secular form of marriage as legally binding so that the wife and her children gained patrician status. It seems probable that the patricians at first rejected even this compromise which left their religion intact. The plebeians countered with their most effective weapon, a mass withdrawal from the communal life of the city. This drastic measure compelled the patricians to accept the law. With its enactment, the plebeians shed another vestige of their inferior status. Civil strife between the two classes persisted, but for the plebeians the Canuleian law came to stand as one of their more gratifying victories.

Pertinent Literature

Mommsen, Theodore. *The History of Rome.* New York: Charles Scribner and Sons, 1900.

Although Mommsen's original work in German is more than one hundred years old, it wears its age extremely well. Clearly wrong in many of his conclusions and occasionally haphazard in his use of evidence, Mommsen's nonetheless remains one of the most comprehensive and in many respects the most stimulating account of the Republic of Rome. For the very early period of the Republic, Mommsen did not hesitate to reconstruct a cohesive and detailed account of the struggles between the patricians and plebeians.

This reconstruction requires as its basic hypothesis that the plebeians were originally a client class. In the Rome of the kings, to be a citizen meant to be a member of a *gens.* Membership in a *gens* was determined solely by patrilinear descent, and as a result citizens were termed *patricii,* or those who could lay claim to a legitimate father. Anyone not in this position was either a slave or a client. Whereas a slave was a mere chattel, a client, although deprived of all legally established rights, enjoyed a sort of protected freedom as a result of his special relation to a patrician patron. While the patron possessed complete control over his client, *dominium,* the Roman Law provided that once this control was allowed to lapse through disuse, it could never revert to the original patron or his heirs.

This class of independent clients was augmented through the territorial expansion of the Roman kings. While the aristocratic families of conquered areas were admitted into the circle of patricians, the majority of the conquered peoples were incorporated as clients, often under the patronage of the king himself. Protected from abuse, they combined with the independent clients by marriage and other legal relationships that soon formed a new *gens* framework. The normal birth increase of this group was accelerated by the citizens' traditional tolerance of foreigners. Its size became even more pronounced since the patricians, as the exclusive holders of citizenship, were alone capable of fighting and dying in Rome's wars of expansion.

Out of this background emerged the plebeians, numerous and deprived of civil rights. Mommsen found the first adjustment of this situation in the constitutional reforms of the sixth king of Rome, Servius Tullius, traditionally 578-535 B.C. He established the *comitiae curiatae,* which organized the populace of Rome along military capabilities and admitted into its ranks the wealthier plebeians. The Servian reforms also imposed on this group of plebeians the duty of tax payments, but in return did not provide them with any secure political rights. This anomalous situation only increased plebeian clamor for political equity, which was not satisfied by the grudging concessions made by the patricians during the early decades of the Republic. The wealthier plebeians were admitted into the senate, but only as silent members, allowed neither to vote nor to advise. For Mommsen, the eventual loss of all patrician privileges resulted from their failure to admit the wealthier plebeians to full equality of rights. Through their narrow-minded self-esteem, they clung to the obsolete arrangement of a previous generation and contributed significantly to the growing factionalism which was only eradicated by passage of a whole array of new laws. Much of this reconstruction is tenuous at best and at worst totally wrong, as the next suggested reading makes clear. Yet Mommsen's work contains, along with a wealth of information, a consistent analysis of many of the political attitudes that dominated Rome's later development.

Jones, H. Stuart. "The Primitive Institutions of Rome," in *Cambridge Ancient History*, Vol. VII, ch. 13. Cambridge: The University Press, 1954.

The Canuleian Law presents a number of distinct historical problems. Information about it is meager and many of its aspects as highly problematical. In this situation by far the best guide is H. Stuart Jones. In any evaluation of the early political developments of Rome, a sober eye must be focused on the nature of the evidence since much of it is either legendary or the product of later Roman historians who attempted to explain customs and ceremonies whose original significance had long since faded from historical memory. With these strictures in mind, at least some negative judgments can be made about the primitive status of patricians and plebeians.

It has been argued by Mommsen and other ancient historians that the leading men of the patrician *gentes,* the so-called *patres familiarum,* were the chief organizers of the overthrow of the Etruscan-dominated monarchy, and that they afterwards monopolized the running of the newly-fashioned republican government. Proponents of this view point to the plebeian name of the third king of Rome, Marcius, and to the plebeian names of three of the seven hills of Rome as evidence that the plebeians were in the ascendancy in the city and were supported by the Etruscan kings to offset and isolate the power of the patricians. This situation was reversed in the patrician dominance of the early Republic when new tribes incorporated into the state were designated by the names of existing patrician *gentes.*

This theory, however attractive, runs counter to other, reliable ancient traditions. It is reported of the early kings that when they spread Roman dominion over nearby cities, they incorporated the members of those cities into the citizen population of Rome and bestowed patrician standing on the more powerful families. A clear indication of the early power of the patricians is that the kingship at Rome was not a hereditary title that automatically passed from the father to his eldest son. Instead, the *patres* had the duty of ratifying the selection of the new king. Furthermore the patrician claim of being the sole repository of the knowledge of divine and human law, and especially of maintaining correct relations with the gods, would have been scarcely tenable if they owed this position to a violent usurpation of primacy. In his refutation of this theory, Jones advances positive conclusions. The plebeians were an essential ingredient of pre-Republican Rome, equipped with their own *gens* structure and with a limited amount of political rights.

These conclusions rule out the explanation of the plebeians as originally a client class, totally dependent on the patricians, especially in the light of ancient accounts that the patricians and their clients often united in elections to stifle the opposition of the plebeians. The client system does represent, however, one of the main causes of the rapid growth of the plebeians. As the limited number of patrician families suffered the inevit-able decline to which every exclusive caste is liable, clients who had thereby lost their patrician patronage joined the ranks of the plebeians and added their own grievances to the list of plebeian complaints. The rapidly increasing number of plebeians and the persistent demand made on Rome for a more efficient military organization made the removal of plebeian discontent imperative. The Canuleian law eliminated one of the more obvious causes of unrest by permitting free interchange between plebeians and patricians and eventually producing the patricio-plebeian nobility of the later Republic that led Rome to internal stability and foreign supremacy.
— *G.M.P.*

Additional Recommended Reading

De Coulanges, Fustel. *The Ancient City*. Boston: Lothrop, Lee and Shepard Co., 1901. Also in paperback by Doubleday. A provocative and speculative account of the origins of Roman society.

Rose, H. J. "Patricians and Plebeians at Rome," in *Journal of Roman Studies* XII (1922) pp. 106-133. An argument that the distinction between the two groups developed out of the value attached to private ownership of landed property.

Nilsson, M. P. "The Introduction of Hoplite Tactics at Rome: Its Date and Its Consequences," in *Journal of Roman Studies*. XIX (1929), 1-11. A suggestion that the new military formation, in which plebeians fought side-by-side with patricians, required that plebeians be accorded equality in political and social life as well as on the battlefield.

Last, Hugh. "The Servian Reforms," in *Journal of Roman Studies*. XXXV (1945), 30-48. An attempt to demonstrate that plebeians and patricians used to intermarry, and that the ban was an innovation which indicates an increasing split, not present earlier, between the two groups.

THE TEACHINGS OF THE SOPHISTS

Type of event: Cultural: emergence of an educational movement
Time: c.440 B.C.
Locale: Greek-speaking communities throughout the Mediterranean world

Principal personages:
PROTAGORAS OF ABDERA (c.481-411), Greek Sophist prominent for doctrines of epistemological relativism and agnosticism
GORGIAS OF LEONTINI (c.483-376), Greek Sophist important in the development of rhetorical theory
PRODICUS OF CEOS (c.470-400), Greek Sophist noted for his concern with precise language
HIPPIAS OF ELIS (c.475-400), prominent Greek Sophist
ANTIPHON THE SOPHIST (c.480-410), Athenian Sophist and rhetorician associated with distinguishing between *nomos* and *physis*

Summary of Event

The Sophists, literally "educators," arose in the second half of the fifth century B.C. in response to a recognized need in the more advanced Greek states for training in the skills needed for active participation in political life. Traditional education consisted of appropriation of aristocratic ideals embodied in the poetic tradition and in military education, but this training was felt to be inadequate to impart the skills of political leadership in states where success depended upon the ability to sway votes in the courts and the popular assembly, and upon awareness of the principles of community organization. To meet this need, the Sophists emerged as itinerant educators making the rounds of Greek cities and offering courses of instruction to groups of disciples for a fee. They claimed to teach *politite arete,* competence in citizenship. One of the more well-known Sophists, Protagoras, claimed that any man who went

through his course of instruction would learn "to order his own house in the best manner and be able to speak and act for the best in the affairs of the state."

Since the ability to sway votes in courtroom or assembly was a fundamental political skill, the Sophists taught rhetoric and were the first to organize it into an art. Protagoras defined the nature and function of the orator as the ability to speak persuasively on either side of any controversial question and to fortify a weaker argument so as to make it the most convincing. Gorgias simply defined rhetoric as "the art of persuasion."

The methods of rhetorical training employed by the Sophists were the debate and the set speech. The debate was an imitation of the courtroom situation wherein speakers had to present as convincingly as possible the arguments for both the prosecution and the defense. The set speech might exemplify the presentation of a policy before the popular assembly or present a persuasive reinterpretation of some conventional myth, offering a convincing reversal of value-judgments on characters in the myth. Thus the *Encomium of Helen,* a set speech by Gorgias, argued the view that Helen, far from being guilty of criminal adultery, was the innocent victim of forces beyond her control. Gorgias' *Encomium of Helen* neatly exemplifies some of the assumptions of Sophistic rhetorical theory: that human psychology may be understood in terms of physico-chemical causation, that speech bears no necessary relationship to objective reality but plays upon men's hopes and fears to dislodge firmly held convictions and moral principles, and implant new perspectives with the same inevitable efficacy that drugs have when administered to the body.

The impact of Sophistic rhetorical training on Athenian life is clearly evident in the literature of the later years of the fifth century B.C., especially in the history of Thucydides and the plays of Euripides and Aristophanes. A critical disposition of mind toward traditional values was fostered; eloquence of speech came to be admired and often to be practiced with a cynical awareness that an argument need not be valid to be persuasive; and there were growing doubts of the efficacy of traditional values to govern human conduct, which was increasingly viewed as governed by nonpredictable compulsions.

Sophistic anthropology and political science were consciously founded on humanistic assumptions rather than upon traditionally recognized divinely sanctioned principles. Protagoras made the first widely publicized open declaration of agnosticism concerning the nature and activities of the gods and it was he also who propounded the doctrine of the relativity of human knowledge: "Of all things the measure is [each single] man, of things that are, that they are, and of things that are not, that they are not." With the logical priority of the individual over the group thus assumed, it is only reasonable to argue that the Sophists saw the values of any particular human community as artificial conventions, distinct from the conventions of other communities and imposing arbitrary limitations upon an individual human being, whose natural inclination could be empirically recognized as essentially self-interested and aggressive. That *nomos,* the conventional values and laws of a particular community, were artificial limitations imposed upon the universally self-assertive nature, or *physics,* of the individual man thus became a widely accepted view in the later years of the fifth century, a view finding varied expression in literature as well as in formulations of public policy. As a consequence of this view of the nature of individual man and of human communities, the principle of justice came to be defined by some Sophists as the "advantage of the stronger party" in any community. Traditionally, justice had been held to be a divinely sanctioned principle of distribution of rights and privileges in the human community, but it was now held by the Sophists to be a reflection of the power structure in any state. For example, in an oligarchy, a minority, by virtue of its control of army and police, enforces a distribution of wealth and privileges which benefits itself; in a democracy, the majority has seized and maintains power to assure an equality of distribution of rights and privileges. The impact of this analysis of human society in terms divorced from traditional moral sanctions was to undermine public confidence in, and voluntary submission to, constituted authority. Encouraged by the new perspective on man and society, groups of young noblemen, who were naturally most directly influenced because they were best able to afford Sophistic instruction, carefully studied the means of gaining power without scruples, and the later years of the Peloponnesian War were marked by violent social upheavals in many Greek states, upheavals made the more violent by the undermining of traditional moral scruples.

Pertinent Literature

Gomperz, Theodor, *Greek Thinkers: A History of Ancient Philosophy*. Vol. I. Translated by Laurie Magnus. London: John Murray Publisher, 1901.

Theodor Gomperz's three-volume comprehensive presentation of ancient Greek philosophy is patently a work of nineteenth century scholarship. Its vast scope and the singularly erudite approach to the subject, however, are sufficient to account for its repeated reprinting for over sixty years. The chapters in Volume I which treat the Sophists are valuable partly because there are few treatments of the subject in English, and partly because Gomperz is one of the few scholars who have shaken off the spell of Plato's anti-Sophistic bias sufficiently to give a sympathetic account of the Sophists and their views.

In a general discussion of the nature and teaching activity of the Sophists, Gomperz treats thoroughly the linguistic history of their title. Only briefly was it free of pejorative connotations and applied to any man achieving a high degree of competence in any field. When the itinerant purveyors of higher education took the title for themselves, they fell into disfavor from the general public for several reasons: distrust by the pious of efforts to probe nature's secrets, an aristocratic contempt for wage-earners of any sort, the jealousy of those who could not afford Sophistic training, and most important of all, the impact of Plato's powerful literary attacks on them. Gomperz emphasizes the moderate, nonradical nature of their teaching in general and quotes with approval the assertion of Grote that the Sophists "were the regular teachers of Greek morality, neither above nor below the standard of the age." They were, in fact, distinct individuals with distinct programs of study to offer, rhetoric as an indispensable tool of practical politics being the single common subject of importance. They certainly cannot be considered members of any particular school of philosophy, and they are linked together arbitrarily in the history of thought, Gomperz feels, because they taught in the same era under the same conditions.

Gomperz presents a brief review of the activities of three lesser Sophists, Prodicus, Hippias, and Antiphon (who was a younger contemporary of Antiphon the Orator), in his general chapter on the whole group. Two separate chapters are devoted to Protagoras and Gorgias. The chapter on Protagoras is significant for interpretations of two of the most significant preserved statements that differ radically from the widely held ways of looking at them. The agnostic declaration which prefaced Protagoras' book *On the Gods,* "concerning the gods, I am unable to know whether they exist or do not exist, nor what they are like in form," is not, Gomperz insists, an attack on *belief* in the gods, but on the claim to have any authoritative cognition of them. They are not subject to scientific understanding because they are outside the realm of sense-perception, and an adequate investigation of them could not be conducted within the brief span of a man's life. Gomperz does not dispute, however, the fact that Protagoras was publicly prosecuted for impiety in Periclean Athens as a result of this statement and copies of his book *On the Gods* were

publicly burned.

The declaration that man is the measure of the existence of all things is not an assertion of moral relativism either. Gomperz insists that Protagoras, in the book from which this statement was taken, is attacking the Parmenidean rejection of the validity of sense-experience. The statement refers, moreover, not to the individual man as a measure, as generally held by scholars, but to universal man, and asserts that universal human experience of the multiplicity and movement and change of natural phenomena cannot be fallacious. When Plato in the *Theaetetus* interprets Protagoras to mean that each man's experience of reality has a truth-value absolute for himself only, he is using Protagoras' name to attack his own contemporary Aristippus, but setting this polemic in the chronological framework of the previous century in which the dialogue is set.

Jaeger, Werner. *Paideia: The Ideals of Greek Culture.* Translated from the second German edition by Gilbert Highet. Vol. I. Oxford: Basil Blackwell, 1954.

Although it is admitted by historians of Greek civilization that the Sophists were essentially educators, the role in which they have most commonly been surveyed is that of the major target of Socratic and Platonic efforts to construct an objective science of morality. The great virtue of Werner Jaeger's chapter on the Sophists in his survey of the Greek cultural tradition, a work dominated by the theme of development of education, is its focus on the Sophists' role in the creation of the humanist cultural ideal and of the theory underlying the tradition of liberal education in the West.

Jaeger defines the position of the Sophists in the history of culture as representing the leading edge of several main trends of the spirit of their century: The rationalization of community life, the effort to integrate the philosophical understanding of the universe as an ordered structure with the poetic tradition's dominant concern with man and his community, and the growing individualism of the age. Perhaps especially significant is the shift the Sophists represent, a movement away from the dominant concern of earlier systematic scrutiny of man as a social animal. The Sophists, Jaeger emphasizes, were successors not so much of the philosophical as of the poetic traditions of Greece. Yet they regarded the poetic tradition in a new way, as an enclyclopedic repository of useful information to be cultivated for utilitarian ends. Their new systematic, rational approach to this tradition is marked by their cultivation of prose rather than poetry as a vehicle of communication.

The second portion of Jaeger's discussion treats the development of Humanism as a distinct ideal and the beginnings of educational theory. Here he draws heavily upon the presentation of the Sophistic educational ideal by Protagoras in Plato's dialogue of that name. Protagoras there distinguishes two complementary aspects of human civilization: technical skills, and justice and law; he then announces his aim of making the latter aspect, statesmanship, a technical skill. The standards for such a science, Jaeger says, had to be drawn from man's own nature, and this could only have happened in an age when traditional standards were being questioned. Hence the initial formulation of the humanistic ideal is associated with skepticism and relativism.

The Sophists made a conception of human nature the foundation of their educational theory. The concept of human nature was a fifth century development issuing from both Greek medicine and Ionian cosmology: the notion of nature, *physis,* was transferred from the universe as a whole to the part, man. The assumption of the Sophists was that human nature is educable because it is plastic, capable of being molded and formed by good teachers and adequate methods. Jaeger believes that the application of the agricultural metaphor to education was probably originated by Protagoras: the mind of the pupil is fertile soil, the teacher is an industrious cultivator, and the curriculum is good seed. The process of education rightly conducted ought therefore to produce healthy individuals with well-formed character. The mind was to be formed by disciplines training it in the form of language, or grammar; the form of oratory, or rhetoric; and the form of thought, or dialectic. To this classical trivium the Sophists added the Pythagorean *mathemata:* arithmetic, geometry, astronomy, and harmonics. They thus established the pattern of the "seven liberal arts" that have long formed the basic curriculum in ancient, medieval, and early modern programs of humanistic education. Granted that the intellectual and moral foundations of Sophistic education were weak, Jaeger nevertheless insists that the formalization of education by the Sophists was a major contribution to Western culture. — C.W.C.

Additional Recommended Reading

Freeman, Kathleen. *Ancilla to the Pre-Socratic Philosophers.* Oxford: Basil Blackwell, 1952. A translation of the extant fragments of the Sophists is included in this comprehensive translation of pre-Socratic fragments.

Havelock, Eric A. *The Liberal Temper in Greek Politics.* New Haven: Yale University Press, 1957. A work devoting a large section to the Sophistic contributions to the theory and practice of democratic politics.

Plato. *Protagoras, Gorgias.* These two dialogues, although considerably biased against the Sophists, present a vivid picture of the two greatest of them, their methods and basic concerns.

Segal, Charles P. "Gorgias and the Psychology of the Logos," in *Harvard Studies in Classical Philology.* 66 (1962), 99-155. A close study of the psychological and epistemological foundations of the rhetorical theory of Gorgias, revealing especially the nature and uses of skepticism and psychological determinism.

Untersteiner, Mario. *The Sophists.* Translated by Kathleen Freeman. Oxford: Basil Blackwell, 1954. A thorough but difficult and somewhat controversial examination of the doctrines of all the Sophists.

THUCYDIDES WRITES THE *HISTORY* OF THE *PELOPONNESIAN WAR*

Type of event: Literary: an account of contemporary history
Time: 433-c.403 B.C.
Locale: Athens and other parts of Greece

Principal personage:
THUCYDIDES (c.460-c.403), son of Olorus, Athenian general and historian

Summary of Event

The Peloponnesian War broke out in March, 431 B.C., with a sudden night attack by Thebes upon Plataea, a small Greek state allied to Athens. More serious fighting began in May, when Sparta and her Peloponnesian allies invaded and laid waste the northwestern districts of Attica. At the same time an Athenian fleet landed troops in the Peloponnesus to ravage parts of it. The hostilities thus begun lasted for twenty-seven years, with some intervals of peace, and only ended with the complete overthrow of Athens and her empire. The war was the greatest event in Greek history in the fifth century, surpassing in importance even the Persian wars because it left Greece transformed. The war was responsible for political revolutions, the forcible transfer of some entire populations, and the wholesale slaughter of others. The invasion of Sicily by Athens brought in the western Greeks so that almost the whole Hellenic world and part of the non-Hellenic were involved. The material destruction caused was reparable; the moral havoc was not.

When the fighting commenced, Thucydides began to write a history of the war which was to be, as he put it, a "possession for all time." His account was primarily a description of the results of Athens' imperialist policy, which he regarded as the fundamental cause of the war and its prime driving force. The restless activity of Athens and her desire to dominate more and more states caused Sparta to attack her in self-defense to avoid her becoming so rich and powerful that she controlled the whole Greek world. Imperialist motives kept the war going especially when Athens became involved in the invasion of Sicily. To Thucydides this greed for power was a fundamental characteristic of some men. Granted the consistency of human nature from one generation to the next, imperialist states would rise again, and the "possession for all time" was intended to be a case study of the virulence of such a disease.

Thucydides tells us that he began to collect information on the events of the war as soon as it began, which probably means 433 B.C. when Athens sent out warships to engage the Corinthians if the latter continued their war with the Athenian ally Corcyra. Until 424 the historian lived in his native Athens, and he must have culled most of his information from Athenian sources; he was then a general, but the Assembly judged that he

292

failed to carry out Athens' policy efficiently, and he was exiled. He lost his commission but gained the opportunity to study the war from a non-Athenian point of view, and the details he gives of the activity of some of Athens' enemies, soldiers such as Aristeus of Corinth and Brasidas of Sparta, show that he was able to supplement extensively his knowledge of the war outside Athens.

Thucydides was not completely impartial, but he did attempt, with some success, to be objective. He soon realized that inconsistencies among the reports of the eyewitnesses of an event could be resolved only by the most careful collection and sifting of evidence. Such continuous questioning led him occasionally to make revisions in earlier parts of his narrative, so that there are a few passages in conflict with others. The reason that they survive is that Thucydides died while his work was incomplete; he never had the opportunity to give it the final revision and polish which no doubt he intended.

He was an accurate writer. He gives the text of a treaty made by Athens and Argos in 420 B.C. Fortunately, the stone recording the alliance has been found, and in a document which amounts to about a page and a half of English, the official Athenian version and its reproduction by the historian differ in only a few unimportant words, and some of the differences

may be due to faulty transmission of the text, for Thucydides was not in Athens to read it and may never have visited Argos. The objectivity of the writer is consequently beyond dispute and is seen best, perhaps, in his treatment of Cleon, the man who did the most to secure his exile. While Thucydides might have wished to misrepresent Cleon's role at Athens, he contented himself with one introductory remark on Cleon, calling him "the most violent of the citizens," and then proceeded with his narrative.

The *History of the Peloponnesian War* contains many speeches of the principal protagonists such as Archidamus of Sparta and Pericles of Athens. The insertion of these extended remarks was a clever artistic device in an age which prized highly the art of public speaking, and the speeches add a sense of immediacy to the narrative. There is, however, considerable modern controversy concerning their accuracy.

Thucydides' precision, detachment, and passionate desire to tell the truth captured the imagination of the next generation of Greek historians, and no less than three writers of the fourth century, Cratippus, Theopompus, and Xenophon, paid him the enormous compliment of beginning their histories of Greece from the point in 411 B.C. where the unfinished text of Thucydides abruptly ends.

Pertinent Literature

Gomme, A. W. *A Historical Commentary on Thucydides.* Oxford: The Clarendon Press, 1945-56. 3 vols.

A. W. Gomme, formerly Lecturer in Classics at the University of Glasgow, has written a commentary on

Thucydides which is an ornament of British scholarship, indispensable for a well-rounded study of Thucydides, the Peloponnesian War, and the history of Greece in the fifth century. Unfortunately Gomme, like Thucydides, did not live to complete his work; the third volume ends at Book V, chapter 24 of Thucydides in the year 421 B.C.

Gomme opens with an essay of eighty-eight pages on some necessary preliminary considerations, and in it he lays down principles for the use of Thucydides' work by modern historians. There is an important section on those aspects of Greek life about which Thucydides assumes his readers will know and of which he says little. These aspects include economic conditions, the political constitutions of the Greek states, and the military and naval techniques. Thucydides, of course, knew much about these matters; for example, his book shows that he understood the extraordinary value that economic strength and accumulated capital had for the military power of a state. But he does not go into the details of economic life because he could assume that his readers knew of them, much as a modern historian of, say, the foreign policy of President Kennedy might assume that his readers had a basic understanding of the Constitution of the United States. It is unfortunate that Thucydides did not say more on these subjects. He certainly had the knowledge, and critics who say that he was blind in these areas are incorrect.

Having made this point, Gomme continues with an extremely valuable assessment of surviving histories of Greek writers other than Thucydides. He disposes of the incompetent Diodorus Siculus (who based his books on the scarcely more competent Ephorus of Cymae) in short order, and passes on to the more important Plutarch, biographer and essayist of A.D. 100. Gomme knew Plutarch's work intimately, and obviously admired him as a charming, honest, and sensible man, but he shows that Plutarch did not have the same deep understanding of the realities of Greek political life of the fifth century which even Ephorus had. Plutarch could not be expected to have such insight for he lived six centuries later in an age of monarchs.

Gomme expended considerable effort on the problems raised by Thucydides' use of speeches, and he has satisfactorily answered them. Thucydides claimed that his versions of the speeches were either as close to the actual words used as he could make them, or that they recounted the things that had to be said on specific occasions. This curious language led several modern scholars to attack the accuracy of the speeches on the ground that they were Thucydidean inventions, pure literary creations. Gomme counterattacked this view and showed that the speeches, if we are to think Thycydides an honest historian, must be approximations to what was actually said. The speeches are certainly not exact transcriptions of the orators' words, for Spartans did not speak Doric nor eastern Greeks Aeolic or Ionic. All the speakers are recorded in Thucydidean style; but there is no reason to think that because of this fact the accounts are anything but paraphrases of the original speeches.

The rest of Gomme's work is given over to a close, detailed, and precise commentary on the text of Thucydides, often taken sentence by sentence,

294

occasionally word by word. To be fully appreciated, Gomme's well-reasoned remarks must be read. A knowledge of Greek is essential here and there. He has made important contributions not only to the restoration of corrupt manuscript readings, but, above all, to our understanding of the history of the late fifth century. His comments reveal a scholar of enormous erudition, well read in European languages, careful, judicious, and incisive. In him the greatest historian of ancient times found a worthy commentator.

Adcock, F. E. *Thucydides and His History.* Cambridge: The University Press, 1963.

Sir Frank Adcock's slim volume on Thucydides is the best short introduction to the man and his work which we have in English, and ably presents a summary of previous scholarship on these subjects, to which he himself has been a notable contributor.

The author begins with a brief account of Thucydides' life and environment. Thucydides was born before 455 B.C. at Athens, and thus grew up in a milieu touched by the first rationalists of European history, the Sophists. It was also the time when the medical school of Hippocrates of Cos was making studies of disease based on empirical methods. Much of this rational, empirical attitude is apparent in Thucydides' idea of history. The gods do not intervene in human affairs, as Herodotus had thought, but instead man is the sole agency of cause. The history is written not so much to show why the war occurred as to show how the course of the war unfolded. In this, Thucydides resembles Hippocrates, who was less concerned with the origins of disease than with the effects of illness on the patient. Thucydides, however, was more than a cold observer; he was a political man with a concern for the interests of the city-state. The affairs and well-being of the individual citizen had to be subordinated to the good of all, that is, to the good of the state. The ability of a statesman to realize practical results seems to have impressed him as much as considerations of good and evil, although that is not to say that Thucydides had a light approach to morals. He was, on the whole, antidemocratic, distrusting the decisions of popular assemblies as subject to ignorance and mob psychology.

Sir Frank raises a number of interesting side issues. He goes into the matter of the speeches and backs up Gomme's interpretation. He thinks that the obvious lies told in some speeches are sure evidence that the general accuracy of what was really said is maintained. As a veteran of Athenian public life Thucydides was, of course, aware that some Greek statesmen took as their model the Homeric "Odysseus of many wiles." There is a fascinating page on the official secrecy of the Greek governments, of which there was certainly less then than exists today, although Sparta was an exception to this general rule. Adcock is also good on Thucydides' methods of composition, and his argument that the historian wrote as the war proceeded is entirely convincing. He shows conclusively

295

that Thucydides did not merely accumulate material during the war and then compose the history after the end of hostilities. His conjecture that Thucydides was drowned at sea about 403 B.C. while returning to Athens from exile cannot be proved, as Sir Frank knows, but it is certainly plausible and accounts for the broken ending of the history in 411 B.C. On the other hand, some scholars believe that Thucydides was murdered, perhaps in Thrace.

There is one quality in this book, however, which is unfortunate, and that is Adcock's prejudice. In discussing the responsibility for the outbreak of the war he asserts that Athens was in the right and the Peloponnesians were the aggressors. This contradicts what Thucydides himself says. It is true that the Spartans crossed the Attic frontier before a single Athe-

nian marine landed in the Peloponnesus, but Thucydides says that Sparta was compelled to attack by reason of Athens' forward policy and tireless efforts to gain new allies. Athens was guilty of indirect aggression at Corcyra in 433 and at Potidaea in 432 before the Peloponnesians struck in 431. Adcock even seems to adopt Athens' own evaluation of her imperial position and lack of war-guilt. On the origin of the Peloponnesian War, he says, in tortuous language, "The defence of the Athenian empire, because it was deserved not so much morally as by its very existence, raised it (the empire) above challenge, like the Statue of Athena Promachos on the Acropolis, inspired by wisdom like the Athena of legend embodied in the Athena of the Parthenon." This is a curious doctrine of phil-Atticism. — *S.K.E.*

Additional Recommended Reading

Thucydides. *The Peloponnesian War.* Translated from the Greek by Rex Warner. Baltimore, Maryland: Penguin Books, Inc., 1954. An accurate and readable translation of the ancient historian's masterpiece.

Finley, M. I. *Thucydides.* Ann Arbor: University of Michigan Press, 1963, and in paperback. An analysis of Thucydidean thought and methods.

De Romilly, Jacqueline. *Thucydides and Athenian Imperialism.* Translated from the French by Philip Trody. New York: Barnes and Noble, Inc., 1947, reissued 1964. A thesis that imperialism is the unifying theme of Thucydides' work.

Brunt, P. A. "Thucydides and Alcibiades," in *Revue de études grecques.* Vol. 65 (1952), 59-96. Written in English, this article demonstrates Thucydides' methods of obtaining information from participants in the war, in this case from the Athenian Alcibiades.

PHIDIAS CREATES THE STATUE
OF ZEUS AT OLYMPIA

Type of event: Religious and artistic: creation of one of the greatest cult statues of
Classical Greece
Time: c.432-430 B.C.
Locale: Olympia, Greece

> *Principal personages:*
> PHIDIAS (fl.475-430), one of the greatest sculptors of
> Greece
> PANAINOS (fl.448), his nephew or brother and chief assistant

Summary of Event

Phidias, the son of Charmides, was born at Athens about 490 B.C. As a youth he studied sculpture under the early classical artists Hegias and Ageladas of Argos, and he achieved his first great success with the colossal bronze Athena Promachos, created about 460, to commemorate the Battle of Marathon in 490. Standing some thirty feet high including its base, it was the chief feature of the entrance court of the Acropolis behind the Propylaea, and because of its height, reflections from the shining upper parts could be seen by sailors in the Bay of Phalerum, some six miles away. Part of its base survives, but no copy of the work is extant. The next major commission of the artist was the Athena Lemnia, also created in bronze and set upon the Acropolis on behalf of colonists of the island of Lemnos in the northeast Aegean. In this case, however, Roman copies apparently survive in the elegant head in the Museo Civico, Bologna, and in the statue in the Albertinum, Dresden. The Bologna head is one of the most noble and artistic portraits to survive from antiquity.

A major phase in the career of Phidias then followed when he was chosen by Pericles to design the sculptures of the Parthenon and to supervise a corps of sculptors in the actual work of cutting them. Since he was mainly a worker in bronze, he probably made models in clay or plaster, which were then reproduced exactly in stone by his craftsmen. This method of production was necessary for the large amount of sculpture intended for the metopes, frieze, and pediments of the Parthenon, but it also had a significant influence on the development of Greek sculpture. In effect it subordinated carving to modeling, and led artists to new concepts in the treatment of marble drapery through the plastic qualities of the models. As a result, the Phidian conception of noble heads, self-possessed attitudes, and fluid treatment of drapery came to dominate Greek sculpture in the second half of the fifth century, with the sole exception of the Peloponnesian school which specialized in portraying naturalistic, muscular athletes. To crown his work on the Parthenon, Phidias created the

297

then unique ivory and gold cult statue of Athena Parthenos. The colossal standing figure had a face, arms, hands, and feet of ivory, and her clothing consisted of gold sheets, probably attached to bronze plates over a wooden frame. In spite of this brilliant achievement, the political enemies of Pericles attacked Phidias for withholding a certain amount of the gold designated for the statue, and consequently the great sculptor went into exile to Olympia in Elis, in the Peloponnese.

Though he was nearing sixty years of age, his greatest work was still to be accomplished. Olympia was the main sanctuary of Zeus in all Greece and had been the site of the great Olympic Games since 776 B.C. The chief temple of Olympia, dedicated to Zeus, was built in the years 470-457 B.C., but the main cult statue of the great god was not commissioned, perhaps because the treasury had been exhausted by the expenses of constructing the temple. Later, when the fame of Phidias' Athena Parthenos had spread throughout Greece, there seems to be no doubt that after the charges of peculation against him sent him into exile from Athens, he was invited to come to Olympia to create a statue of Zeus in the same style as that of the Athena.

Many ancient commentators speak of the admirable qualities of the finished statue, but Pausanias in his *Description of Greece* Vol. 11, pp. 1 ff. gives the most detailed analysis of it. He says that the gold and ivory figure was seated on his throne, crowned with an olive garland, and holding in his right hand a Victory, also of ivory and gold, and in his left an eagle-topped scepter inlaid with many metals. On his golden robe were wrought figures and lilies, and on the throne a great variety of decorations were displayed in gold, precious stones, ebony, and ivory. In effect this colossal, seven times life-size representation of the father of gods and men was an advance beyond the more anthropomorphic treatment of divinity and the creation of a figure that in the words of Quintilian "added something to traditional religion, so adequate to divine nature is the majesty of [the] work." Whereas the Athena Parthenos was a standing figure, the Olympian Zeus gained in dignity by being seated on a raised throne. When the ancients saw this impressive figure with its golden robe completely covering the lower body and draped over the left shoulder, the majestic face of ivory framed by a full beard and the olive crown, and the figure seated upon the great throne, there can be no doubt why they considered the Olympian Zeus to be the supreme achievement of Phidias, the greatest sculptor of the fifth century. The statue remained in its temple for over 800 years until it was destroyed sometime after the Olympic Games were abolished by the Emperor Theodosius I in A.D. 394.

Phidias Creates the Statue of Zeus at Olympia

Pertinent Literature

Richter, Gisela M. A. *The Sculpture and Sculptors of the Greeks.* 2nd ed. New Haven: Yale University Press, 1950.

This comprehensive study considers the major art form of the Greeks from two points of view: that of anatomy, technique, and composition; and that of periods and individual artists. There are also a bibliography, 775 illustrations comprising fully a third of the entire volume, and indexes to both the text and the figures. By way of introduction the author also wisely offers a short but useful treatment of the historical background to Greek sculpture, its general characteristics, and a tentative chronology of its outstanding works of art.

In the full treatment of Phidias, our understanding of his lost work is greatly assisted by the use of illustrations of Roman copies, miniature imitations, or representations of the statues on later coins. The sculptures and reliefs from the Parthenon at Athens are the chief examples of the Phidian style remaining to us, but none of this work can be identified as coming directly from the hand of the master, whose efforts at this time were probably wholly given over to design and supervision. None of the artist's famous colossal statues, including the bronze Athena Promachos and the two gold and ivory works, the Athena Parthenos and the Olympian Zeus, have survived. Yet in each case evidence of various kinds enables us to surmise their general features. For example, two Athenian coins of the Roman Imperial Age illustrate the Promachos figure and show that Athena held her shield at chest level, whereas on another coin

of the same period the Parthenos appears with the shield resting on the ground but held by the left hand. But the appearance of the Parthenos presents few problems because a number of statuettes have survived, doubtless made as mementoes for pious tourists. The most famous of these is the well-preserved Varvakeion Athena, which is in the National Museum at Athens. Unfortunately, however, evidence of this kind for the Olympian Zeus is less adequate. On the reverse of two coins of Elis from the reign of the Emperor Hadrian, the head in right profile and the complete seated figure in left profile are shown. The latter is especially useful, for it depicts the god on his elaborate throne with footrest, as he holds the Victory in his right hand and his upright scepter in the left. Various later works of art which survive also reflect the influence of the great statue, especially the superb marble head of Zeus in the Museum of Fine Arts, Boston, and the fresco painting from Eleusis. A comparison of all this evidence with that for the Athena Parthenos leads to the conclusion that the Olympian Zeus was the greater work, for its elements are more harmonious and its total effect one of dignity combined with power.

After one has considered the style of the Parthenon sculptures and the scattered evidence for the lost colossal works of Phidias, the Roman copy in Bologna of the head of his Athena Lemnia offers the best means for appreciating his work. Richter considers

Phidias Creates the Statue of Zeus at Olympia

that the evidence for identification of the Bologna head with the Lemnia is uncertain, but surely this magnificent face is in the Phidian style. The sharply delineated features of the per-

fect eyes, nose, and mouth, the delicate facial structure, the serene gaze, and the simple treatment of the hair all combine to produce a vision of nobility and beauty rare in any age.

MacKendrick, Paul. *The Greek Stones Speak: The Story of Archaeology in Greek Lands*. London: Methuen and Co., Ltd., 1962.

A popular study of Greek archaeology and its achievements in the past century, this book considers sites, art, and architecture in eight chapters which cover the Aegean in prehistory, Mycenae and the Late Bronze Age, Mycenaean Athens and later, the Archaic and the Classical Periods, the fourth century, the Hellenistic Age, and the Greco-Roman Period. There are 175 figures, plans, reconstructions, a bibliography, and an index of proper names. Since the Phidian Zeus stood in the god's temple within the sanctuary at Olympia, it seems desirable to consider this great religious and athletic center in its entirety. The book devotes nine pages to Olympia, including photographs of a model of the area and of the famous sculpture of Apollo from the west pediment of the Temple of Zeus.

As the photograph of the model reconstructions shows, the great temple dominated the entire area. It was in the Doric style, with six columns at each end and thirteen on the sides, measured 210 feet by 90½ feet on the stylobate, and was completed about 457 B.C., some thirty years before the great cult statue of Phidias was raised within it. Although it was built of local shell conglomerate covered with stucco, the roof tiles and the sculptural decoration consisted of marble. Directly west of the

temple is a windowed building which has been identified as the studio of Phidias. Its ruins are mainly covered today by a Byzantine church, but in 1876 German excavators of the site noted that the foundations of the ancient building exactly matched the dimensions of the temple cella. They deduced that the size of this building was planned as a perfect replica of the cella so that the artist might create his great work in proper scale to the room it would occupy. This brilliant theory was not to be confirmed until excavations in this area in 1955-1956 revealed a pit for the casting of bronze, its slag refuse, pieces of modeling plaster, worked objects, and sculptors' tools, and, most interesting of all, terracotta molds over which were hammered the sheets of gold that formed the drapery of the great statue. These molds are even marked with serial letters on the backs to indicate their location in the total pattern. In another section of the studio complex the archaeologists also found the core of an ivory tusk, from which sections for the flesh portions of the statue had been cut.

North of the studio buildings are the remains of the palaestra and gymnasium, south of it the Leonidaion, a hotel for distinguished visitors. North of the temple within the sanctuary proper stood a temple to Hera, the Prytaneion or town hall, the round

300

Philippeion built by Philip II of Macedon, the exedra of Herodes Atticus, and a series of treasure houses built by various cities for the valuables they had dedicated to the god. Beyond this row of buildings to the east lie the remains of the stadium where the foot races of the Olympic Games were held. Since 1937, over seventy thousand cubic meters of earth have been removed to reveal that this structure evolved through five separate phases from the sixth century B.C. onward. The track is 640 feet in length, and even the marble starting blocks for the runners have been found. But the hippodrome for the chariot races, located further to the east, was long ago destroyed by the floodwaters of the nearby Alpheus River. Such were the main structures which with other lesser buildings and monuments formed the center for the quadrennial athletic contests at Olympia, but to which every day of every year came visitors to see and marvel at the great cult figure of Zeus by Phidias. — *K.H.*

Additional Recommended Reading

Boardman, J., *et al. Greek Art and Architecture*. Pp. 355-360. Figs. 199-215. New York: Harry N. Abrams, Inc., 1967. This superbly illustrated work has a section devoted to Phidias.

Gardiner, E. N. *Olympia, Its History and Remains*. Oxford: The Clarendon Press, 1925. Though dated, this work is still an excellent introduction to the subject.

EMERGENCE OF GREEK MEDICINE

Type of event: Scientific: isolation of medicine as a distinct discipline
Time: c.420 B.C.
Locale: Greece

Principal personages:
ASCLEPIUS, Greek god of medicine
ALCMAEON OF CROTON, Pythagorean philosopher and physician active in the first half of the fifth century
HIPPOCRATES, physician active toward the end of the fifth century on the island of Cos

Summary of Event

At the time of the Homeric poems, Greek medicine had reached a decisive phase in its development; magical superstition and empirical technique, its chief components, were uneasy allies. In the Homeric poems disease is a product of divine interference, and health is restored through propitiation of the deity involved. Wounds suffered in battle, however, belong to a different category. Although on occasion the gods are invoked to heal such wounds, human beings are themselves able to treat them unassisted. The heroes at Troy, for example, deal with arrow wounds by pulling the point out of the wound, sucking out the blood, and then applying "soothing drugs," a slightly magical phrase but perhaps describing nothing more mysterious than an astringent, such as onion juice, as an effective agent against infections. In addition, medicine was an independent and esteemed craft as the prominence in the *Iliad* of the two sons of Asclepius, the physicians Machon and Poliadorus, indicates.

Asclepius himself is the central figure for the later career of the magical branch of Greek medicine.

While Homer describes him only as a mortal who had learned the art of healing from the centaur Chiron, in the succeeding centuries he had become the presiding religious figure of Greek medicine. By the fifth century, Asclepius had become fully deified as the supreme god of healing with the center of his cult at Epidaurus in the northeast area of the Peloponnesus. The sick were brought to this spot from all parts of Greece to sleep for one night inside the sacred temple of Asclepius, where they might be visited either by the god himself or by his cult animal, the snake. They arose the next morning presumably healed. However absurdly superstitious such a practice may seem (although it does have its modern parallels), it enjoyed such extensive popularity that in 420 B.C. the cult of Asclepius was officially welcomed into Athens.

It is an over-simplification to envision the medical career of Hippocrates as the first ray of light in the long night of superstitious fantasies about the human body and its conditions. There were skillful doctors before Hippocrates, such as the physician Democeides, who healed the fractured leg of the Persian King Darius. The practice of medicine was also an activity prominent among the adherents of Pythagoreanism. Its most successful practitioner was Alcmaeon, who performed dissections on animals, including the delicate removal of an eye, and who postulated the brain as the center of nervous sensations. Nonetheless, it remains true that all later generations recognized Hippocrates as the most important Greek physician and the founder of scientific medicine.

Compared to his later renown, there is surprisingly scanty information about the life of Hippocrates. He was certainly born on the Aegean island of Cos, which housed a thriving school of medicine, but his dates are far from exact. His career reached its height around 400 B.C. and so he was probably born about 460 B.C. A descendant of the family of Asclepius, according to tradition of doubtful reliability, he is said to have traveled widely, to have visited Athens, and to have died at a very advanced age. Plato mentions him twice in a respectful but cursory fashion. Beyond these meager notices, nothing is known for certain about him.

Our knowledge of his medical accomplishments is equally disappointing. Although a considerable amount of Greek medical writing has survived under the title *Hippocratic Corpus,* its contents range in date of composition from the fifth century B.C. to the third century A.D., and represent the theories of many doctors and conflicting medical schools. Its most celebrated part, the *Hippocratic Oath,* is judged by many scholars to be a late addition to the collection and

even alien to the doctrines of the Hippocratic school.

Even against this discouraging background it is still possible to attempt some definite statements about Hippocrates. Later medical writers praised him for "having separated medicine from philosophy." Thus, whereas a physician such as Alcmaeon was probably influenced in his medical research by the tenets of Pythagoreanism, Hippocrates appears to have been free from the influence of philosophical preconceptions in his medical observations and conclusions.

This spirit is evident in the work of probable Hippocratic authorship, *The Sacred Disease,* which argues that epilepsy is no more divine than any other disease since it has a natural cause and a natural method of treatment, and since all diseases are produced by the intrusion of a foreign element, such as air, into the body. The effect of external conditions on bodily health is treated in detail in another work, probably Hippocratic, *Air, Places, and Waters,* which records perceptive observations on the correlation between climatic or geographic factors and certain diseases. In the treatment of disease, the Hippocratic doctor concentrated on the individuality of the sick person, by ascertaining relevant information about the childhood, diet, habits, and similar details of the patient. The doctor meticulously observed the daily progress of the disease, while attempting to arrest it with the limited therapeutic remedies available. Although some surgery was performed under requirements of cleanliness that are strikingly modern, it is not in the fields of technical medical skill and

303

knowledge that Hippocrates' achievement should be sought. What he did
accomplish was to establish medicine
irrevocably as an independent science

with its own methodology requiring
skill and instruction free from religious and philosophical influences.

Pertinent Literature

Edelstein, Ludwig. "Greek Medicine in Its Relation to Religion and Magic," in
Bulletin of the Institute of the History of Medicine. V, March, 1937, 201-246.

This comparatively short article by
one of the world's foremost authorities on ancient Greek medicine discusses a topic that is of central importance in any consideration of the
place of Greek medicine in the history
of scientific thought. Greek medicine
is often applauded as one of the early
triumphs of the enlightened human
mind, and Hippocrates has been celebrated as the liberator of mankind
from the shackles of religious superstition. Edelstein regards this idea as
an over-simplified assessment of a
complex relationship. Instead, he attempts a more precise delineation of
the interaction between Greek medicine and religion.

While many historians of Greek
medicine admit that in its later stages
medicine suffered a relapse into a
primitive level of superstition and
charlatanism as part of the general
cultural decline of the ancient world,
they still stoutly maintain that the
earlier period of Greek medicine was
not infected with such perversities,
and embodied a genuine triumph of
unencumbered human intelligence.
Edelstein argues that such a view
neglects some essential religious sup-
positions of ancient medicine and that
much of the progress made by ancient
medicine is directly attributable to its
reliance on a theistic conception of
the universe.

To support his contention, Edelstein refers to the Hippocratic explanation of the causes of disease. Disease was the result of penetration of
the body by external elements, such as
cold, heat, air, or climatic conditions.
Since it was a commonly held belief
of the fifth century B.C. that all
planetary bodies were divine, the
ancient doctors were in effect posit-
ing divine elements as the cause of
disease. Although there were isolated
thinkers at the time who denied divine
status to such objects as the sun, Edelstein considers it significant that physicians are not found among them.
Furthermore the fifth century doctor,
probably Hippocrates, who is quoted
as denying any "divine quality" to
epilepsy, actually defends this view by
demonstrating that all diseases are
equally divine in origin, since they are
all produced by divine elements. While
Edelstein may be placing too much
weight on what may only have been
circumspection by doctors to avoid
direct challenge to a belief cherished
by the common people, he does call
into question a widespread assumption about the irreligious attitude of
Hippocrates toward disease.

A larger question that affects this
problem is understanding the idea of
nature. Edelstein contends that while
ancient doctors considered all diseases
to possess their own distinct natures,

at the same time they considered the nature of things as a whole to have been created and permeated by God. Thus one of the supposedly Hippocratic writings maintains that the nature of all things was arranged by the gods, and that as a result all things occur through a divine necessity. Although the later methodist school of medicine explained nature as nothing more than a mechanical and dynamic process devoid of any divine immanence, their position was definitely a minority viewpoint. In fact, most ancient doctors deliberately embraced the notion that every physical process was regulated by divine guidance, since without such an intelligent agency behind it, nature would be only the product of haphazard chance and not of intelligible laws that could be discovered by human reason and employed to benefit mankind.

In conclusion, Edelstein emphasizes that this kind of religious framework has nothing to do with the superstitious magic and sorcery that as a result of oriental influences came to characterize later stages of ancient medicine. Greek doctors never considered demons to be the cause of disease nor did they resort to magical remedies. On the other hand, they ought not to be pictured as irreligious modern scientists. Greek medicine was a science, but a science that emerged only out of a positive religious foundation and background.

Sigerist, Henry E. *A History of Medicine.* New York: Oxford University Press, 1961.

This work is the second volume of a projected eight-volume history of medicine from its earliest beginnings to the present day. Unfortunately the untimely death of the author, one of the foremost authorities on the history of medicine, prevented the completion of the concluding six volumes and even the second volume lacks revision. Nonetheless, the work still offers the best treatment in English of the various phases of Greek medicine.

Sigerist's treatment of Hippocrates concentrates on the glaring discrepancy between the renown of Hippocrates and the almost total absence of reliable information about his life or work. Sigerist examines all the available ancient sources in an effort to uncover some facts hidden beneath layers of legend and fancy, but all that can be discovered in this way is the meager information already mentioned. Sigerist's examination of the references to Hippocrates in Plato produces the same dearth of facts. For Plato, Hippocrates was a physician who may also have been a professional teacher of medicine and who may have used the dialectical method of division to analyze the nature of disease. Such information is too general and too terse to give a clear idea of Hippocrates' teaching. In short, there is no detailed or accurate information about Hippocrates preserved in any ancient writer.

Sigerist is equally negative in his examination of the *Hippocratic Corpus.* In his judgment there is not one treatise in the entire collection which can be ascribed to Hippocrates with any degree of certainty. Yet he is also convinced that the *Corpus* does contain genuine works by Hippocrates, although he admits this is a claim which he cannot substantiate. However, unless Hippocrates' writings formed at least a part of the collection, there would be no adequate explanation for the *Corpus* bearing his name. In accord with this explanation, Sigerist proposes a provisional solution to this vexing problem about Hippocrates.

Why is so little known about a man who has been so long regarded as the father of Western medicine? Sigerist's answer is essentially an expansion of a theory advanced in an inaccessible work by Edelstein. According to this theory, Hippocrates was in his own lifetime merely one of a number of eminent doctors, as indicated by Plato's allusions to other physicians. At the beginning of the third century B.C., during the rise of Alexandrian scholarship, there was increased interest in the history of the past, especially in its cultural evolution. The standard methodology was to explain cultural progress as the result of the pioneering efforts of early practitioners of the various arts and sciences. Thus the rise of medicine was associated with the activities of three separate doctors: Hippocrates, Praxagoras, and Chrysippus. Inasmuch as the latter two had lived in the fourth century, Hippocrates enjoyed a distinct prominence as the oldest innovator and since there were available at the same

time anonymous medical writings from the fifth century, there was an overwhelming plausibility in assigning these works to the pen of Hippocrates.

In the course of time other anonymous works were also attributed to him, so that he became the only medical writer worth reading: Hippocrates' later fame is a direct result of this process. By the beginning of the Christian era, he had become the father of Greek medicine. Originally no more than a well-known, competent physician, he had come to occupy a position unique in the history of medicine.

While much of this theory must remain pure speculation, it does illuminate an important aspect of Hippocrates' fame; he came to be not only the author of many books, but also the model of the ideal physician. Sigerist argues that every period must have an ideal physician in order to determine not only the education but also the ethics of the individual doctor. Hippocrates gradually came to be regarded as embodying the values required of the medical profession. In this role the influence he exercised over later Greek physicians, and beyond them to all succeeding physicians, rightfully justfies his title as "Father of Western medicine." — *G.M.P.*

Additional Recommended Reading

Jones, W. S., and E. T. Withington. *Hippocratic Writings*. Cambridge: Harvard University Press, 1922-1931. The best modern English translation of the *Hippocratic Corpus*.

Edelstein, E. J. and L. *Asclepius*. Baltimore: The Johns Hopkins Press, 1946. The definitive study on the origin and history of the cult of Asclepius.

Edelstein, L. *The Hippocratic Oath*. Baltimore: The Johns Hopkins Press, 1943. A thesis arguing that the oath was devised very late by and for Pythagorean

306

physicians.

Heidel, W. A. *Hippocratic Medicine*. New York: Columbia University Press, 1941. A thorough survey of fifth century B.C. medicine that relies basically on ancient medical writings.

ATHENIAN INVASION OF SICILY

Type of event: Military: launching of naval attack
Time: June, 415-September, 413 B.C.
Locale: Syracuse

Principal personages:

NICIAS (c.470-413), conservative Athenian statesman and
general

ALCIBIADES (c.450-404), radical Athenian politician and
general

DEMOSTHENES (d.413), Athenian general

HERMOCRATES (c.455-407), Syracusan statesman and general

GYLIPPUS (c.450-400), Spartan soldier

GONGYLUS, fifth century Corinthian naval officer

Summary of Event

In 421 B.C., the first phase of the Peloponnesian War ended. As soon as Athens had regained her strength, she began under the leadership of Alcibiades, young and brilliant but sinister, to attempt a decisive victory over Sparta and her Peloponnesian allies. In early 415, this leader proposed attacking Sicily, using the pretext of assisting an ally of Athens there and of stopping the supply of Sicilian grain to the Peloponnesians. Victory over the latter could be secured, Alcibiades contended, if Athens captured the vital Sicilian source of food and recruited mercenaries. The Sicilian Greeks, he went on erroneously, were a mongrel people, unskilled at war, and they would be easy prey. This program of aggression was opposed by the cautious Nicias without success. In June, 415, the Athenians sent out a fleet hitherto unrivaled in Greek history for its magnificence. There were 134 warships, of which thirty-four came from Athens' allies, who were thus dragged into a war which was not of their making. The embarked army numbered 6,500 men, of whom only a third were Athenian.

The expedition sailed under the command of Alcibiades and Nicias. Shortly before it did so, however, certain religious statues in Athens were mutilated by unknown persons. After the fleet had sailed, a formal indictment for this sacrilege was made against Alcibiades, and he was ordered home for trial. Fearing that he would be unjustly condemned, Alcibiades defected to Sparta and in revenge urged an attack against Athens.

His desertion did not stop the Athenians' effort in Sicily under the hesitant Nicias. His offensive soon became an attack on the chief Sicilian state of Syracuse, a colony of Corinth. Nicias procrastinated and the campaigning season of 415 ended with Syracuse scarcely damaged. The Athenians were forced to withdraw into winter quarters.

The Syracusans, efficiently led by

308

Hermocrates, meanwhile managed to dispatch envoys past the Athenian fleet to beg the mother city, Corinth, for help; Corinth, in turn, appealed to Sparta. The Peloponnesian response was good, the Spartans sending one contingent under Gylippus and the Corinthians another under Gongylus.

In 414, a few more Athenian troops arrived in Sicily, and Nicias pressed the siege of Syracuse, a strong, walled city built on a peninsula which separated a large bay, the Grand Harbor, from the sea. The Athenians seized part of the Grand Harbor, fortified it, and blockaded the city by sea, hoping by building a wall across the landward end of the peninsula to invest Syracuse completely and force her surrender through lack of food. With each Athenian victory the wall advanced. Syracuse despaired. Blockaded by sea, she now looked on helplessly as her land routes too were choked off. There seemed no other course but to capitulate. Then, just in time to keep Syracuse from negotiating, Gongylus slipped inside the city to report Gylippus' approach with relief forces. Gylippus' strategy was to extend a counterwall out of Syracuse at right angles to Nicias' five-foot wall to head off its completion. During the summer fierce combats raged around the ends of the two walls. By a narrow margin Gylippus carried his fortifications past Nicias' and thus frustrated the Athenian offensive. In the autumn, operations stalled and Nicias asked for reinforcements.

In the winter of 414-413, the Spartans, finally determined to renew the conflict in Old Hellas, attacked Athens, so that the latter was now fully engaged in two theaters. Athens nonetheless responded to Nicias' appeals, and seventy-three additional triremes (fifty-one Athenian) along with five thousand hoplites (twelve hundred Athenian) were dispatched under the command of Demosthenes. Before he could join Nicias, fresh naval forces reached Syracuse from the Peloponnesus and parts of Sicily. The Syracusans made a bid for victory, and in June and July, 413, they won a series of naval actions in the Grand Harbor. At this point Demosthenes arrived, reëstablished Athenian naval supremacy, and dashed Syracusan hopes.

Demosthenes and Nicias next decided to capture Gylippus' counterwall in order to retrieve gains made in the campaign of the year before. The Athenian army went forward by night and came extremely close to success, but in the darkness it lost cohesion and was repulsed. Demosthenes promptly advised Nicias to begin immediate withdrawal by sea, but once more Nicias delayed, believing an eclipse of the moon an omen against evacuation. The Syracusans then resumed their naval offensive, and in September defeated the Athenian fleet in a great battle in the Grand Harbor, compelling Nicias to resort to the forlorn hope of escaping by land. Complete disaster followed. The Syracusan cavalry and light troops harried their enemy and wore them down under a hail of missiles until Nicias surrendered. The Syracusans executed both him and Demosthenes, and imprisoned their men in quarries for months. Those who did not die under these conditions were sold into slavery.

309

The defeat of Athens was complete. She had lost over two hundred triremes and nearly fifty thousand men, mostly soldiers and sailors of her allies. These appalling losses convinced many statesmen that Athens was finished. In the winter of 413-412, the allied states began to revolt and join Sparta. The Persians, too, entered the war against Athens, thus effecting the grand coalition which was to bring the proud city-state to her knees.

Pertinent Literature

Ferguson, W. S. "The Athenian Expedition to Sicily"; "The Oligarchic Movement in Athens"; and "The Fall of the Athenian Empire," in *The Cambridge Ancient History.* 5th impression. Vol. V, pp. 282-375. Cambridge: The University Press, 1958.

Our main sources of information on the Athenian invasion of Sicily are the sixth and seventh books of the history of the Athenian Thycydides, one of the literary monuments of antiquity. Thucydides' narrative is thoughtful, vivid, and dramatic. We sit in the assembly at Athens as Alcibiades and Nicias debate the merits of making the attack; we watch the first grand armada row out of Piraeus after libations have been poured to the gods; we storm the heights of Epipolae with Demosthenes' men.

Little can be added to this great account. Since only details can be gleaned from Plutarch's biographies of Alcibiades and Nicias and from the corpus of Greek inscriptions, the task of the modern historian, as Ferguson reminds us, is really little more than that of paraphrasing Thucydides and adding a few items from other authorities. Ferguson does so succinctly in less than forty pages. He points out the ignorance of both the Athenian and Syracusan popular assemblies concerning the size, resources, and intentions of the other. The Athenians grossly misjudged the numbers and fighting quality of the Syracusans, and the latter completely disregarded the reports, which Her-mocrates believed, of the approach of Nicias' fleet in 415. Neither state had a professional staff of any kind to collect information about foreign powers for the benefit of policy-making bodies.

Thucydides' contention that the Athenians might have won if Nicias had acted more decisively is a point still being argued by historians. Thucydides' opinion has been accepted by some modern authorities, although there are others who feel that in the realm of grand strategy Thucydides' judgment was only that of a regimental commander with above-average competence. While no certain answer can be given, we can say that even if Athens had forced Syracuse to surrender in 415, she could not have held the state indefinitely without committing part of her strength to garrison it, and that, given time, Syracuse and her allies could have raised much of the island against Athens and broken her hold. In this sense, as Thucydides knew, the expedition was a fatal blunder.

The effect of the destruction of the expedition on Athens herself, as Ferguson shows, was ruinous. Outraged oligarchs overthrew the democrats in 411. The conservatives, in turn, speedily showed their incompetence either to win the war by military victory or to end it by negotiation, and the resurgent democrats soon overthrew them. In the poisoned atmosphere at Athens men distrusted one another, and the single-minded effort which Athens should have mounted against her enemies was blunted.

Ferguson's third chapter recounts the last years of the Peloponnesian War. Athens was able to keep alive the long naval conflict, in Ionian waters, against Sparta and Persia until 405. Simultaneously, operations of the Peloponnesian and Boeotian armies in Attica slowly but systematically devastated the country. It is indeed remarkable that Athens, assailed by so many enemies, was able to hold off their superior numbers for so long. Finally, closely besieged, with her fleets sunk or captured, supported only by a single ally of the once great Delian League, she surrendered in 404, compelled to give up her imperial ambitions.

Adcock, F. E. *The Greek and Macedonian Art of War.* (Sather Classical Lectures, Vol. 30). Berkeley: The University of California Press, 1957.

The fighting in Sicily involved almost all forms of classical Greek warfare. This short volume of essays covers the development of the various modes of Greek warfare from the sixth to the second century B.C.

The main force of a city-state's army was made up of slow-moving, heavily armored infantrymen called "hoplites" who fought in close order in formal ranks. This formation, called the phalanx, was usually made up of columns eight hoplites deep and as broad as the manpower of the state permitted. There was little tactical maneuvering and little use of reserves, so that a battle was decided in a short time by the spearmanship of the front ranks of hoplites or even by the sheer weight of their charge. In a country as mountainous as Greece, it is strange that such cumbersome soldiers in such an unwieldy formation predominated, and that fast-moving light infantry was slow to develop. But warfare was mainly a matter of attacking or defending crops, of bringing about or preventing starvation. Therefore, the development of mobile troops suitable for mountain fighting seemed irrelevant for warfare that went on in the plains where the food was grown. Light-armed troops, however, were known and were of some use to the Syracusans, especially during the final retreat of the Athenians.

The Greeks did not possess effective cavalry. The Syracusan horse were of greatest use not in the pitched battles between hoplites around the heads of the walls, but in harassing tactics. The Athenians had to feed themselves in part by living off the country, and the Syracusan cavalry often fell upon foraging parties. But against an unbroken phalanx Greek cavalry was useless.

The technique of the siege was almost always simple circumvallation and starvation of the enemy. Before the Peloponnesian War we know of no certain case of successful assault on a walled city. The Greeks knew that fortified places might be stormed, but until the fourth century they had no specialized equipment, such as catapults, to assist them in doing so. They therefore shrank from direct assaults since such tactics were always very expensive in men. For Nicias to have stormed Syracuse was unthinkable, and this fact explains the rival strategies of wall and counter-wall.

Greek navies were made up of a nucleus of triremes. On long passages they could be propelled by sails, but in action they relied exclusively on oarpower. Such a ship was so packed with the two hundred men of its crew that it could not carry enough food or water to give it long range. Hence, Greek navies could scarcely operate more than one or two days' row, about thirty-five or seventy miles, from home base. Nicias therefore first had to make a base for his ships before he could begin work

with his army. Battles between fleets had been decided in early times by the smothering fire of arrows and javelins and by boarding, but by the time of the Peloponnesian War complex fleet tactics employing ramming were well understood, as were defensive formations for coping with them. In the last battle in the Grand Harbor the Corinthians showed the Syracusans a variant form of ramming by hitting head on. Normally, this tactic would have resulted in the crippling of both lightly built triremes, but the Corinthians had incorporated a special strengthening in their prows; and with this innovation their ships survived while the enemy's were disabled. Thus, often the fortunes of war turn upon the employment of a new strategy. — *S.K.E.*

Additional Recommended Reading

Benson, E. F. *The Life of Alcibiades.* London: E. Benn, 1928. The life of the most remarkable Greek of his time.

Brunt, P. A. "Thucydides and Alcibiades," in *Revue des études grecques.* Vol. 65 (1952), 59-96. This interesting and ingenious article in English deals with the relations between the two men and the historian's assessment of the General.

Meritt, Benjamin D. "The Alliance Between Athens and Egesta," in *Bulletin de correspondence hellénique.* Vol. 88 (1964), 413-415. A discussion in English of the text of the treaty with Egesta (Segesta), the city in Sicily which was allied with Athens.

Westlake, H. D. "Athenian Aims in Sicily, 427-424 B.C.," in *Historia.* Vol. IX (1960), 385-402. A disclosure of Athens' relations with Sicily before the invasion of 415.

MARCH OF THE TEN THOUSAND

Type of event: Military: invasion and retreat of an army
Time: 401-404 B.C.
Locale: Persian Empire

Principal personages:

CYRUS II (d.401), Persian satrap of western Asia Minor, brother of Artaxerxes

ARTAXERXES II, King of Persia 404-359

XENOPHON (c.434-c.355), chronicler of the march

CLEARCHUS (fl.c.400), Spartan general in Cyrus' army

TISSAPHERNES (fl.c.400), Persian commander at Cunaxa

Summary of Event

The epic March of the Ten Thousand took place against the background of Sparta's newly acquired hegemony in Greece after the disastrous Peloponnesian War (431-404 B.C.) and Persia's slowly declining strength in Asia Minor. Cyrus II, a Persian satrap in the area, was willing to foment dynastic troubles in the empire because of his ambition to seize the Persian throne from his recently crowned brother, Artaxerxes II Memnon. Cyrus was supported by the Ionian Greeks who, having been treated as pawns of military policy and treachery during the period of Sparta's domination, hoped for concessions from Cyrus. At the same time they hoped to weaken the Persian colossus by supporting dynastic division.

Cyrus apparently experienced little difficulty in recruiting a large mercenary army, of which some thirteen thousand were Greeks, mostly Spartans, more or less fresh from recent fighting at home. In the spring of 401, his army broke camp at Sardis and began what turned out to be one of the most famous marches in history.

The army mutinied when it learned that it was to invade the very depths of the Persian empire and not merely to reduce some hill tribes to obedience in southern Asia Minor. Only the entreaties of Clearchus, who was Cyrus' leading general from Sparta, promises of additional pay, and the arrival of timely reinforcements induced the mercenaries to continue the journey. The Persians, whether out of weakness or in pursuit of a policy of attrition against the Greeks, did not seriously challenge the passage of the army. Near the village of Cunaxa, not far north of the Persian city of Babylon, the dispute over the throne was decided in the summer of 401. Cyrus managed to defeat his brother's army, but his rashness in wishing to dispatch Artaxerxes personally induced him to ride into the heart of the battle where the King's picked guard was protecting him. Cyrus' impetuosity cost him his life as a javelin pierced him under the eye. His death left the expedition stranded deep in hostile country. The Greek leaders, refusing to surrender, naïvely tried to negotiate with

313

Tissaphernes, the leading Persian military commander at Cunaxa, for safe passage of their troops out of Persia. Tissaphernes, as might be expected, responded by having many of them seized and put to death.

The ten thousand Greeks who survived, instead of following the western route by which they had come into Persia, decided to move northward up the Tigris valley. Upon learning of the fate of their negotiating generals, they elected new ones from their ranks to lead their forces home. One of those chosen was the Athenian Xenophon, who after his return to Greece leisurely recorded the whole dramatic episode in his famous *Anabasis,* characterized by a simple straightforward style that has since become the traditional primer for aspiring Greek scholars. On the march up the valley, the retreating army was constantly harassed by the forces of Tissaphernes who, however, never risked a pitched battle. Further north, when the Persians had been left behind, savage hillmen rolled masses of rock down upon the straggling units of the army as they struggled through narrow passes. Snow, cold, and hunger took their toll in the vast barren winter wasteland of Armenia. With great rejoicing, the Greeks finally reached Trapezus on the coast where they could again behold the familiar waves of the sea even though these were only the waters of the Black Sea which meant they were still far from home. Here they foraged for supplies, became involved in frays with local cities, and

generally made a nuisance of themselves while resting for a month before setting out for home. The last part of the retreat from Trapezus to Chalcedon was somewhat anticlimactic, a journey undertaken by land and sea. Upon returning home some of the "ten thousand," now reduced to six thousand, entered the service of Thracian chieftains or of Sparta, who was then in the process of preparing for a war with Persia.

The whole episode took on major significance. A direct consequence was war between Sparta and Persia between 400 and 387, Sparta having responded to urgings from Ionian cities trying to defend themselves against the strenuous efforts of Tissaphernes, who had been made satrap of Asia Minor and was commissioned to recapture them. After initial successes by the Greeks, Persian money stirred up trouble in Greece. So prolonged was the struggle and so weakening to the Greek cities involved, especially Athens, Thebes, Corinth, and Sparta itself, that in 387 Persia was able to dictate the King's Peace, which brought the Ionian cities once more under Persian control. This disaster, together with the open display of Persian weakness revealed during the March of the Ten Thousand—as well as initial Spartan victories in the war of 400-387, and the general exhaustion of Greece itself—encouraged first Philip of Macedon and later his son Alexander to undertake not only the conquest of Persia but the occupation of all Greece as well.

March of the Ten Thousand

Pertinent Literature

Mahaffy, J. P. *The Progress of Hellenism in Alexander's Empire*. Chicago: University of Chicago Press. 1905.

The standard interpretation of the March of the Ten Thousand regards it as a foreshadowing of Alexander's conquest some sixty years later. Mahaffy, the well-known classics scholar of the early twentieth century, in the first of a series of lectures delivered at the University of Chicago, prefers to go further. He sees in Xenophon, the leader and chronicler of the retreat, a distinct "precursor" of the coming Hellenistic Age. Mahaffy views the coming era with mixed feelings, an age when a new civility and novel slants in art and literature "could not but dilute the purity of Hellenic civilization."

The new age, rather than beginning with Alexander, was a "thing of older growth" dating from the time when Athens lost its central position "in politics as well as in letters." The dispersion of Greeks after the Peloponnesian War brought other peoples more and more into the Greek overall view of the world. The growing use of Greek mercenaries by Persians and Egyptians, as well as the friendliness of Cyrus toward the Ionian cities, point to a new cosmopolitanism. Intellectuals, too, were loosening "the bonds of city patriotism." Men such as Isocrates saw that being an Athenian "was not a matter of birth but of culture." If Socrates thought in wider terms, Xenophon in his own way betrayed the same inclinations in his lesser known works.

Indeed, to Mahaffy, Xenophon, the hero of the March of the Ten Thousand, represents almost "the first step in the transition from 'Hellenedom' to Hellenism." He sees indications of this outlook not only in Xenophon's eclectic Greek vocabulary and simple style foreshadowing the *lingua franca* of the Hellenistic world, but also in his adoption of foreign niceties such as hunting (a sport unknown to Greeks in the Classical Age), his fondness for using Persian examples whenever he speaks of gracious living, and his wide travels in the Persian Empire, Asia Minor, and Thrace while he was in the service of Cyrus and later of Agesilaus. Mahaffy apologizes for his failure to be ultra-modern in not deciding "to go West." One of the most significant indications that Xenophon was a precursor of attitudes yet to come, Mahaffy insists, is his mistrust of democracy as unworkable and antiquated. He supposedly realized that any government which "exposes its executive government to constant criticism" and to consequent changes of military plans is "wholly unfit to make foreign conquests and to rule an extended empire." Xenophon's admiration for the strict discipline of aristocratic Sparta is clearly evinced in his tract *On the Lacedaemonian Polity*. Here is no "capricious tyrant" in the form of a popular assembly tending to misuse liberty. Even in his early career as a writer Xenophon in his *Hiero* regarded the "attaining to a tyranny as the very acme" of ambitious Greeks' desires. His most revealing endorsement of monarchy is to be found in his neglected work *On the Education of Cyrus*.

315

While his *Oeconomicus* merely urges that a man with a "ruling soul" (in Socratic terms) necessarily should be put in charge of things, his work on Cyrus openly vindicates monarchy built on the Persian model and the tract is virtually a monarch's handbook. Xenophon greatly admired the loyalty and discipline of Persian nobles, whose devotion to Cyrus causes them to perform menial tasks for him without complaint, men who are "far greater gentlemen than the Greeks." Xenophon, according to Mahaffy, is practically saying that a Ptolemy or a Seleucus must come if a great empire is to be managed. Even if one dismisses the more unpleasant aspects of this book as "semisophisti-cal argumentation," Xenophon basically subscribes to all of it as a man fully convinced of the necessity of monarchy for the coming age. That his *On the Education of Cyrus* accurately forecast the future seems obvious considering the fact that within a hundred years there was scarcely a Greek city that "was not directly or indirectly under the control of a king." Mahaffy wonders if Alexander managed to read it or whether Aristotle, as his conservative mentor, kept such a book from his pupil as being incompatible with the Hellenic mind. It is obvious that Mahaffy's lecture is strained and has serious limitations. It is, however, interesting and provocative.

Nussbaum, G. B. *The Ten Thousand. A Study in Social Organization and Action in Xenophon's* Anabasis. Leiden: E. J. Brill, 1967.

G. B. Nussbaum, a historian of ancient history at the University of Kiel, has added an important dimension to a full understanding of the March of the Ten Thousand. The central theme of Nussbaum's work is that the Ten Thousand constituted a bona-fide communal or political organization.

The real story of the *Anabasis,* the author observes, began with the death of Cyrus, the rebellious younger brother of Artaxerxes II, in the Battle of Cunaxa. Until then the ten thousand or so Greek mercenaries fighting under Cyrus had remained a self-contained military unit. After the battle, the Ten Thousand (whose number was roughly equal to the population of a Greek *polis*) reacted to their isolation by becoming a moving *polis* seeking to find its way home to the Greek world. Nussbaum holds that the political character of the army did not manifest itself until they reached the Black Sea, but thereafter their identity assumed greater importance than before because they were out of danger and able to consolidate their political feelings.

Nussbaum states that while the Army of the Ten Thousand naturally had three subdivisions—soldiers, captains, and generals—a fourth element, the "assembly," representing the army as a whole, welded the three groups together into a political community. Nussbaum's observations on the nature and functioning of the assembly are especially interesting.

The author holds that from the time the Ten Thousand entered the service of Cyrus, the assembly played an important role as the "one natural and proper vehicle for the governing activity in the community and espe-

316

cially for directive decisions." Xenophon, however, does not record in the *Anabasis* any assembly meetings between the Battle of Cunaxa and the army's arrival on the shores of the Black Sea, except the one held to consider a course of action following the kidnaping of the generals by the Persians. It was then that the soldiers chose new generals to lead them home, one of whom was Xenophon. During the final stage of the march from Trapezus on the Black Sea to western Asia Minor, however, the assembly met more frequently, according to Nussbaum, than indicated by the twenty assemblies described in Books V through VII of the *Anabasis*. The function of the assembly was, in most cases, to give backing and authority to the leaders in their plans of action.

Elsewhere in his book, Nussbaum paints an interesting contrast between the motivations of leadership shown by Clearchus and Xenophon. Clearchus is depicted as the typical military-minded Spartan to whom organization meant discipline and discipline meant fear. On the other hand, Xenophon, the cultivated Athenian, exercised a civil and political leadership based upon his men's consent and incentive. Even when it was justified, he was apparently reluctant to use compulsion, which in the army invariably meant physical punishment. Once the army was out of extreme danger, he avoided it entirely as he then considered the army as virtually a state above such treatment and the ordinary soldier as a citizen above such degradation. As a citizen, Xenophon himself tolerated criticism; once, to the shame of his soldiers, he descended from his mount to give orders when an infantryman complained about his issuing directions while comfortably seated on horseback. This incident vividly illustrates the difference between the totalitarian approach of Clearchus and the democratic concepts of Xenophon as to relations between the rulers and the ruled. Whether the extenuating circumstances of warfare demand at all times a rigid totalitarian approach, however, is a question social philosophers have long debated. — *E.P.K.*

Additional Recommended Reading

Xenophon. *Anabasis*. Translated by Carleton L. Brownson. Cambridge: Harvard University Press, 1921. Xenophon's own account of the epic march.

Anderson, J. K. *Military Theory and Practice in the Age of Xenophon*. Berkeley: University of California Press, 1970. A study of Sparta's military techniques during her brief hegemony over Greece early in the fourth century.

Parke, H. W. *Greek Mercenary Soldiers. From the Earliest Times to the Battle of Ipsus*. Oxford: The Clarendon Press, 1933. Chapter V deals with the recruitment and organization of the Ten Thousand.

Bury, J. B. *A History of Greece to the Death of Alexander the Great*. Revised by Russell Meiggs. 3rd ed. New York: St. Martin's Press, 1966. A good classic introduction to the story of the March of the Ten Thousand.

Cook, J. M. *Greeks in Ionia and the East*. London: Thames and Hudson. 1962. A study of the Greeks who lived under Persian rule.

DEATH OF SOCRATES

Type of event: Political: state execution
Time: 399 B.C.
Locale: Athens

Principal personages:
SOCRATES (469-399), Athenian citizen and informal teacher
MELETUS AND ANYTUS, contemporary Athenian citizens who brought the indictment against Socrates
ARISTOPHANES (c.448-c.385), Athenian comic dramatist
CRITO (fl.490), wealthy Athenian disciple of Socrates who sought acquittal, but later a means of escape, for the condemned Socrates
ALCIBIADES (c.450-404), talented Athenian citizen
CRITIAS (?-403), Athenian oligarchic leader of the Thirty Tyrants in 404
PLATO (c.427-347), Athenian disciple of Socrates who wrote the most vivid account of the trial, imprisonment, and death of Socrates in his *Apology, Crito* and *Phaedo.*

Summary of Event

The conclusion and aftermath of the Peloponnesian War left Athenian democrats bitter and resentful. The empire had crumbled, the fleet and walls of Athens had been dismantled, and democracy had been restored only after a period of oppressive oligarchic rule and bloody civil war. In the person of Socrates there seemed to stand the symbol, if not the principal cause, of all the factors of intellectual and moral enervation which had destroyed from within the power of Athenian democracy to prosecute the war successfully and to sustain the integrity of its own governmental institutions. An indictment was therefore brought against Socrates in 399 by a religious fanatic, Meletus, supported by the politician Anytus and by the orator Lycon, on the charge of impiety. Socrates was officially

charged with failing to worship the gods of the state, introducing new gods of his own, and corrupting the youth of Athens. Although his accusers demanded the death penalty, their intention seems to have been to drive Socrates into self-imposed exile, a sentence which they believed he himself would propose if found guilty.

Plato's *Apology* makes it clear that Socrates was identified in his accusers' minds with the natural philosophers and Sophists whose teachings had indeed contributed to the deterioration of the traditional Athenian religious and political values. The natural philosophers had promulgated doctrines of a world sustained by impersonal laws rather than by personal deities, and the Sophists had encouraged their young noble pupils to be skeptical of all forms of institu-

318

tional authority. Most damaging of all in their teaching was the doctrine of political power based on the assumptions that every individual's natural inclination was toward self-aggrandizement, and that the law of the state was an artificial restriction upon the individual's self-realization.

It was the Sophists rather than Socrates who were responsible for these demoralizing ideas. Socrates himself scrupulously lived by the laws of Athens and fully participated in the formal religion of the state. He did, however, openly criticize the tendency of the democracy to entrust tasks of professional competence to amateurs chosen by popularity or, worse still, by lot. Moreover, he freely associated with the young aristocrats who were the most conspicuous pupils of the Sophists. To the Athenian who did not know him intimately, Socrates must have appeared to be a typical Sophist, and it was as such that he was caricatured in the *Clouds* of Aristophanes in 423, a play which must have left an indelible impression on many Athenian minds. After the double humiliation of defeat and revolution in 404, people remembered Alcibiades, who had deserted to the enemy during the war and severely damaged the Athenian war effort, and Critias, who had been instrumental in the oligarchic revolutions of 411 and 404; they also recalled that these two men had been associates of Socrates in their youth, and so Socrates seemed an ideal scapegoat for the frustrated resentment of many Athenians. A majority of 280 out of 400 voted for condemnation at his trial.

The *Apology* of Plato presents a portrait of Socrates as an earnest moralist who, though no Sophist, was indeed a real threat to whatever aspects of the Athenian tradition could not be rationally grounded. Far from the atheist his accusers would have proved him, he believed in objective moral values and a transcendent diety of truth. Athenians who were personally confronted by him were faced with a relentless challenge to their pretense of certain knowledge in matters of religion and morals. Although he himself professed ignorance in these areas, he claimed a wisdom unique among men by virtue of his awareness of ignorance. Socrates stood on common ground with the Sophists in refusing to acknowledge any self-evident authority in traditional Greek theological and moral ideals. Yet he differed from them in that his skepticism was methodological rather than radical; he believed that valid moral ideals could ultimately be grounded rationally, although the effort might be long and arduous. To this end he committed himself to a life of intellectual inquiry through conversation with any who would join him, and he honestly believed that his informal intercourse with the Athenian man-in-the-street was a divine commission of vital concern to Athens. The only life worth living, he insisted, was the life based on values formulated through rigorous, honest, personal self-examination. Through such individual self-examination alone might come about eventual moral regeneration in the state.

Once condemned, Socrates refused the option of voluntary exile and obstinately insisted that only death would make him cease from his customary activities in Athens, whereupon the jury felt compelled to sentence him to execution by poison. During the interval between his trial and death, he conversed freely with his disciples, who sought to persuade him to go into exile. Plato's *Crito* gives Socrates' reason for resisting these entreaties: the command of the state, which he had heeded throughout his life, must be heeded now even though the condemnation was unjust.

The death of Socrates is dramatically portrayed in the *Phaedo* of Plato. Ostensibly the dialogue is concerned with the immortality of the soul, but its essential purpose is to exalt the pattern of philosophic life consummated in Socrates' death to a transcendent ideal for all men.

Pertinent Literature

Taylor, A. E. *Socrates.* London: Davies, 1932. Reprinted in paperback by Doubleday Anchor Books.

While the facts concerning the trial and execution of Socrates are reasonably clear and beyond dispute, the character of Socrates and the actual nature of his thought are not. Since Socrates himself left no written documents, a portrait of his career must be drawn from the conflicting accounts of Aristophanes, Xenophon, and Plato. The outstanding question is whether the celebrated "Doctrine of Ideas" formulated in the *Phaedo* was the distinct creation of Socrates himself or rather the distillation by Plato of metaphysical implications of the Socratic dialectic method of clarification and definition. One of the more significant answers to this question is that formulated by John Burnet and A. E. Taylor and expressed in the popular biography by Taylor, *Socrates.*

Taylor seeks to harmonize the evidence of the witnesses by postulating two distinct phases in the life of Socrates. Relying heavily on the autobiographical narrative in the central portion of the *Phaedo* and on the *Clouds* of Aristophanes, Taylor argues for a youthful association of Socrates with Anaxagoras and his disciple Archelaus, and suggests that Socrates must have been a scholarch, perhaps a successor to Archelaus, with a circle of disciples. During this period Socrates associated freely with Sophists visiting Athens and with the intellectual circles of Pericles and Aspasia, thus gaining a reputation as one of the wisest men in Greece.

Taylor suggests that this phase lasted until about the beginning of the Peloponnesian War in 431 B.C. and was brought to a close by the negative response of the oracle at Delphi to a question put by Chaerephon: "Is there any man wiser than Socrates?" Brooding upon the oracle, Socrates experienced a spiritual crisis and henceforth set out on the mission he describes in the *Apology,* urging every Athenian to attend to his own soul and its health. He developed the "Orphic" concept of the personal soul into a new notion of a moral center of personality. The essential function of the soul is to know the good; the health of the soul, or "virtue," is the knowledge and obligatory performance of the good as recognized by the soul. Hence arise the ethical postulates accepted by all scholars as genuinely Socratic: virtue is knowledge; vice is ignorance; wrongdoing is always involuntary. The problem of the human condition is that men are ignorant of the good which is transcendent and apprehended only in earnest dialogue with others or in searching one's own soul. Taylor argues that Socrates himself formulated the Doctrine of Ideas by fusing the Orphic notion of an eternal personal soul, the Pythagorean notion of eternal mathematical objects of knowledge, and the notion suggested, but not developed, by Anaxagoras of a teleological order of nature governed by a universal Mind. The soul, in a process of dialogue and self-examination, comes to distinguish in clear intellectual vision the eternal and absolute moral standards through knowledge of which it may rationally order personal life. Socrates himself seems to have concerned himself primarily with the knowledge of transcendent moral standards, but the Doctrine of Ideas as developed in the Platonic dialogues is of course much more inclusive in its applicability to all kinds of knowledge. Many scholars today, perhaps the majority, question the argument that the Doctrine of Ideas was thus fully formulated by Socrates himself at the time of his death. Taylor's thesis is plausible, but it depends on the absolute reliability of the *Phaedo* as a witness of Socrates' own ideas rather than to those of Plato.

Jaeger, Werner. "The Memory of Socrates," in *Paideia, the Ideals of Greek Culture*. Vol. II, Bk. 3, ch. 2. Oxford: Basil Blackwell, 1947.

Set within the context of his monumental study of the history of Greek ideals, Werner Jaeger's discussion of the character of Socrates begins with a brief review of the work of critical scholars. He insists that neither the Scottish school of Burnet and Taylor nor the Berlin philosopher Heinrich Maier has adequately explained the dual role of Socrates as moral paradigm and intellectual midwife. Jaeger himself sees Socrates primarily as a teacher interested in developing the moral potentialities of his fellow Athenians, and in his chapter on Socrates he concentrates more on the attitudes and methods of the teacher than upon his theological and metaphysical doctrines, which he feels are products of Plato's efforts to make explicit what is latent in these attitudes and methods.

Like any thoughtful Athenian of his day, Socrates knew the doctrines of the current natural philosophers, but his own approach to natural science was always anthropocentric and akin to that of the medical scientists whose influence on him was much more significant. The autobiographical passage in the *Phaedo* indicates that teleological explanations appealed to him even before he read Anaxagoras for the first time. Certainly his conception of wisdom was practical rather than theoretical; its model was the *techne* of the craftsmen and physicians: an organized body of principles underlying the achievement of distinct goals.

Jaeger denies any serious influence of Orphism, a religious movement much disputed as to date and character, upon the Socratic notion of the

soul. Without speculating on its ontological status, Socrates urged each
man he met to tend to the health of
his own soul as the center of knowing
and willing moral personality. It was
self-consciousness, an intense awareness of personal goals in the light of
rigorous rational criticism, that he
sought to arouse in his young friends.

Like the Sophists, Socrates discussed political questions frequently
and intensely, but the keynote of his
treatment of these matters was inter-
nalization, a focus on ends as well as
on means. Thus the virtues of a general or a ruler were reduced to
fundamental virtues of leadership,
of mastery over one's own person in
the light of clearly defined goals.

Jaeger accepts the judgment of
Aristotle that Socrates did not formulate the Doctrine of Ideas, but he
notes that Xenophon as much as
Plato depicts Socrates as trying to
define morality in concepts harmonious with experience yet free from

inner contradiction. Socrates challenged his partner to lay down a general hypothesis, and then proceeded
to subject it to rigorous logical analysis. By this method, he sought to draw
out of his partner a feeling for moral
truth which he optimistically felt was
innate in every human soul.

The Socratic postulates that virtue
is knowledge, that all virtues are ultimately identical, and that no man
willingly does evil were not enunciated as dogmas; they emerged during
discussions as assumptions which
alone seemed plausible and free from
inner contradictions, thereby providing the basis for fruitful analysis of
moral questions. It is from these
postulates and from Socrates' dialectic method that the metaphysics and
epistemology of Plato were developed
later. The fundamental achievement
of Socrates, in Jaeger's view, was the
advance of moral education through
introspection and the new focus on
the goals of human life. — *C.W.C.*

Additional Recommended Reading

Cornford, Francis Macdonald. *Before and After Socrates.* Cambridge: The Uni-
versity Press, 1932, reprinted 1962. Lectures on the impact on Greek cosmo-
logical tradition of the teleology implicit in Socrates' "morality of aspiration."
Levin, Richard, ed. *The Question of Socrates.* New York: Harcourt, Brace & World,
Inc., 1961. A collection of ancient source material on Socrates.
Spiegelberg, Herbert, and B. Q. Morgan, eds. *The Socratic Enigma.* Indianapolis:
Bobbs-Merrill Company, Inc., 1964. A collection of testimonies concerning the
character and influence of Socrates from antiquity to the present day.
Versenyi, Laszlo. *Socratic Humanism.* New Haven: Yale University Press, 1963.
An emphasis on the humanism and irony of Socrates, relying heavily on the
early Platonic dialogues and rejecting the mystical elements of the middle
group of Platonic dialogues.
Winspear, Alban D., and Tom Silverberg. *Who Was Socrates?* 2nd ed. New York:
Russell & Russell, 1960. A critical restudy of evidence of the opposition aroused
by Socrates, with special consideration being given to its nature.

PLATO DEVELOPS THE THEORY OF IDEAS

Type of event: Philosophical: formulation of an epistemological concept
Time: c.380 B.C.
Locale: Athens, Southern Italy, and Sicily

Principal personages:
SOCRATES (469-399), Athenian citizen and informal teacher
PLATO (429-347), Athenian philosopher, disciple of Socrates
and founder of the Academy

Summary of Event

The most lasting and influential treatment of Plato's long years of philosophical activity was the formulation of the epistemological theory of Forms or Ideas. In one sense, the emergence of this theory is the consummate logical expression of the classical Greek way of viewing human experience of the world, but in another it is possible to trace the emergence of Plato's theory in the context of pre-Socratic and Socratic thought.

Plato's master and spiritual father, Socrates, had sought in the later years of the fifth century B.C. to discover a science of life, an objective system of knowledge of life's goals, and the means by which such goals might be achieved. While questioning his young aristocratic friends, Socrates found that no man had made this discovery, and that all men held no more than mere opinions about these ends and means of life. Yet Socrates was convinced that the technique of life was a matter of the mind's knowing objective principles and, once they were known, communicating them rationally; at the divine level he was convinced that they were grasped by a deity essentially good and truthful. The individual mind, or psyche, had intuitive access to these divinely known principles; moreover, Socrates believed that the psyche was obligated to bring them to explicit rational formulation in dialogue with other men. The earlier Socratic dialogues, notably the *Euthyphro, Charmides,* and *Laches* of Plato, which are generally held to be reasonably accurate descriptions of the characteristic aims and procedure of Socrates, portray him as engaged in the effort to define inductively the precise nature of the traditional Greek moral virtues of piety, temperance, and courage. Thus, implicit in the philosophical activity of Socrates is a dualism of common opinion and transcendental moral truth to which the psyche has intuitive access.

These dualistic assumptions of Socrates gained clarity in the context of certain developments within pre-Socratic philosophy and a characteristic predisposition of the Greek mind. The Ionian philosophical tradition had already distinguished two types of experience: that of the senses on the one hand, revealing a multiplicity of distinct impressions; and that of the mind on the other, comprehending a rational pattern having the character of unity, order, and permanence. It was characteristic of the

323

Greek mind, moreover, to value more highly, and attribute greater reality to, the static pattern of order —visualized by the mind and recognized as a recurrent feature of experience—than the continually shifting flux of concrete phenomena. Greek art and literature, especially the richly exploited store of mythical paradigms, amply exemplify this Greek preoccupation with the eternal and recurrent pattern. It is consistent with this intellectual perspective that the Pythagorean community of southern Italy discovered that meaningful patterns of sense-experience are based on mathematical relations grasped not by the senses but by the psyche alone in inner vision. It was thus the Pythagoreans who distinguished the universal (the triangle, the square, the circle), seen by the mind alone, from the particular mode of the universal seen by the eye and found meaningful only by virtue of the psyche's grasp of the universal.

Plato, who spent some time following the death of Socrates in 399 B.C. in southern Italy and Sicily in company with Pythagoreans, appears to have brought together the Pythagorean idea of the universal and the Socratic idea of the objective and eternally valid moral concept. All meaningful patterns of human experience, Plato felt, must be founded on an eternal Form or Idea known by the psyche through intuitive experience and recognized by the senses as immanent in or imitated by concrete particular objects or phenomena. In the Meno, a transitional dialogue between his early and middle period, Plato gave the first clear formulation of this doctrine in terms of Orphic-Pythagorean dualistic mysticism. The doctrine is given ample expression in several dialogues of the middle period of Plato, notably in the Phaedo and the Republic. The destiny of the individual psyche is a function of its participation in successive life-periods, in two distinct realms of experience: a transcendental realm wherein the psyche, free from the bodily limitations of sense-experience, apprehends the eternal forms in their purity; and a physical realm of generation and corruption wherein the psyche, through the bodily medium of the senses, apprehends imperfect and perishable concrete exemplifications of eternal forms. The function of the philosopher is to purify his vision of the eternal forms in their ideal transcendental order so that in the physical realm he may creatively order his own life and, if permitted, the life of his human community, in accordance with this vision.

The Doctrine of Ideas has its own logical difficulties of which Plato himself was keenly aware and which he explored intensely in his own later dialogues, especially the Parmenides. The impact of this doctrine upon the history of philosophy, however, is immeasurable. With certain modifications, Aristotle made it the basis of the first great systematic understanding of all human experience. The ontological status of Forms, be they mathematical concepts or moral ideals, has been a major subject of controversy between opposing philosophical schools throughout the Western tradition, and empiricists' logical objections to the Doctrine of Ideas have never fully succeeded in dismissing its cogency and appeal as a necessary foundation for a secure epistemology.

Plato Develops the Theory of Ideas

Pertinent Literature

Friedländer, Paul. *Plato, an Introduction.* New York: Pantheon Books, 1945. Reprinted in paperback by Harper Torchbooks.

The outstanding virtue of Paul Friedländer's introduction to Plato lies in what might be called his "existentialist" approach to the philosopher as a man. Instead of relating Plato's life and thought to each other artificially, he proceeds to treat Plato's thought as an entity in itself. Friedländer presents Plato as a man seeking to communicate a vision of reality mediated through Socrates in a language never fully adequate for rendering such a vision. Friedländer's discussion of the Doctrine of Ideas, therefore, is focused more on the life experience of Plato the man than on links in the chain of the history of ideas binding Plato to Socrates and earlier Greek philosophical tradition.

At the outset, Friedländer emphasizes that Plato's initial quest in life was political rather than metaphysical. A political career was closed to him because the state, originally founded on a divine order of *dike* or "cosmic justice," had disintegrated in Athens. Plato had to build a new life based upon a new vision of *dike*. It was precisely such a vision that Socrates was seeking and urging his disciples to seek, but Plato "saw" it, with the "eye of the soul," embodied in Socrates himself. The reality of the "just" or the "beautiful" was no problem either for Socrates or for Plato; the problem was to communicate the nature of such Ideas. Plato, however, saw them in Socrates himself and called them by the words "*eidos*" and "Idea," both derived from the Greek word for "vision"

and having fundamental reference to visible Form, although used hitherto in a variety of ways by natural philosophers, medical writers, and rhetoricians to express the notion of classification.

Essential to Plato's concept of Forms are the notions that they are intuitively grasped and that they can never be fully defined in conceptual terms. Plato's problem was to discover language adequate for communicating his own vision of the Forms so that others could share his own intuitive experience. At this point Friedländer emphasizes that Plato's philosophy is not the fusion of earlier notions of an intuitive understanding of reality at which he had already arrived. The earlier notions exploited by Plato were derived from Parmenides, Heraclitus, and Pythagoras.

From Parmenides, through the mediating influence of the Sophists, Plato derived the language which he used to describe the nature of the Forms and their place in the totality of human experience: they are whole, simple, and immutable, and they have a status of being which sets them off from the realm of perishable existent things about which we have only opinion. From Heraclitus Plato derived the language whereby he related the Forms to existent things in the realm of sense experience: "the one *Eidos* gives to the many individual things a share in true being; the things, in turn, strive for the completeness of the *Eidos*." Thus the Heraclitean logos binds together the Forms in their transcendental simplicity and the existent things wherein the Forms are immanent. Finally, from the Pythagoreans Plato derived the language whereby he expressed the transcendence of the Forms in a heavenly realm of harmonious order, and the human soul's dual citizenship in both the transcendental realm of being and the phenomenal realm of perishable physical objects.

Havelock, Eric A. *Preface to Plato.* Cambridge: Harvard University Press, 1963. Reprinted New York: Grosset & Dunlap, 1967.

This book is a fresh evaluation of the historical significance of Plato's work in the context of a cultural revolution within Greek culture, a revolution brought on in large measure by the transition from oral to written communication. Havelock takes as a starting point the seriousness of Plato's attack upon the poetic tradition of Greece and sees this attack in terms of Plato's determination to replace the habitual mode of thought associated with poetry by a new mode of abstract thinking.

Poetry in Greek society functioned as the means of preserving the ethos of the community and of transmitting this ethos to new generations. It is important to realize that poetry functioned as an educational instrument through the memorization by successive generations of a manifold array of paradigmatic actions and events concerning heroic characters of old. The young of successive eras appropriated this tradition through self-identification with its content, informed as that content was by temporal succession of events, multiple sensible qualities, and contradictory judgments of persons and events. The new mode of thought of which Plato was an ardent sponsor was entirely antithetical to the old, for it is characterized by the clear distinction of the knowing subject and the content of knowledge. The autonomous psyche is here an active and self-conscious ego molding its own identity through reasoned calculation. The content of knowledge, on the other hand, is integrated in such a way that essential content stands out distinctly in its timeless unity of being and invisibility: that is, the content of knowledge is not visual images but concepts, logical relations.

Havelock argues that Platonic dualism is not so much metaphysical as it is methodological; the "realm" of opinion (*doxa*) which he wishes to transcend is the realm of poetic imagination with its passive receptiveness to a temporal succession of a multiplicity of events represented through sensible images. The "realm" of science or knowledge (*epistome*) is the realm of pure intellectual entertainment of logical relations in their abstract timelessness, consistency, and unity.

It is to this realm of knowledge that the Forms or Ideas belong. The Forms include primarily mathematical and moral concepts which are comparable "because they all alike represent the same kind of psychic effort which breaks away from the many and unifies experience into ones." For the "image-world of epic" Plato sought to substitute the "abstract world of scientific discourse." The appropriate

326

modern term would be "concept." The fact that Plato chose to use the word "form" (*eidos*), Havelock explains partly from the prior use of the word by mathematicians and medical writers, and partly from Plato's own opposition to moral relativism, the way to which might be left open by the use of the term "concept." Social background and class prejudice, as Havelock notes, inclined Plato "to the proposition that social relations between men should be not only stable but also authoritarian." There are, however, serious disadvantages to Plato's choice of the term; for Plato's language suggests that the new kind of knowledge, like the old, is closely akin to the visual, and Plato's use of visual metaphors and language describing phenomena as "imitating" the Forms obscures the purity and distinctness of the intellectual process he is sponsoring.

Havelock's account of the historical context and achievement of Plato's revolution in thought certainly throws new light on an important feature of Greek intellectual history, but it may be asked whether, in his concentration on Plato's sponsorship of a new mode of thought, he may not have obscured Plato's primary moral concern for the reconstruction of human society. — *C.W.C.*

Additional Recommended Reading

Crombie, I. M. *An Examination of Plato's Doctrines.* Volume II: *Plato on Knowledge and Reality.* New York: The Humanities Press, 1963. The central portion of this work analyzes the Doctrine of Ideas and differing accounts of it in various Platonic dialogues.

Frazer, J. G. *The Growth of Plato's Ideal Theory.* London: Macmillan & Company, 1930. An account of the development of the Doctrine of Ideas and Plato's own criticism of it.

Ross, David. *Plato's Theory of Ideas.* 2nd. ed. Oxford: The Clarendon Press, 1953. An account of the development and ramifications of Plato's theory.

Stewart, J. A. *Plato's Doctrine of Ideas.* Oxford: The Clarendon Press, 1910. An older work which presents aspects of Plato's Doctrine of Ideas in Specific Platonic dialogues, and describes the role of the doctrine in aesthetic theory.

RATIONALIZATION OF ETHICS

Type of event: Philosophical: investigation into human conduct
Time: c.345-330 B.C.
Locale: Athens

Principal personages:
SOCRATES (469-399), Plato's teacher
PLATO (427-347), founder of the Academy
ARISTOTLE (384-322), founder of the Lyceum

Summary of Event

Although Greek thought from early times had been rational even when applied to human conduct, Aristotle's *Nicomachean Ethics* stands out as the greatest effort of the Greeks to rationalize behavior. Moreover, the fact that later thinkers, especially Thomas Aquinas, considered this work (despite its peculiar Aristotelian flavor) to be the best summary of Greek ethical thought, makes its publication a signal event in the development of Western thought. Aristotle's work is the supreme effort of the Greeks to establish a norm of human conduct through rational analysis. As such, Aristotle's system stood in the West alongside the dicta of Yahweh and Jesus.

Although Aristotle had already concerned himself with ethics in the *Protrepticus,* written about 353 B.C., the treatment then was short and aimed at a popular audience; the *Eudemian Ethics,* in eight books, was probably written between 348 and 343 B.C. The fullest expression of his interest in ethics came with the publication of the *Nicomachean Ethics,* some fifteen years later. The underlying premise of Aristotle's ethical thought is to be found in the introductory first book of this work, where, as in other places, Aristotle argues that since every undertaking and activity seems to aim at some good, there must be some single goal at which everything aims. Thus, all human activities, such as medicine, shipbuilding, and politics, can be arranged in a pyramid-like hierarchy culminating in only one supreme activity. Aristotle has been criticized for the less-than-strict logical force of this argument, since he rules out the possibility that there may be two or more independent ends to our activities. To Aristotle, however, it is clear that not only do men have one goal, but that this goal is happiness, which is "the best, the noblest, and the most pleasurable" of all activities.

Aristotle several times makes it clear that the final goal of happiness for the individual is not a feeling, or even knowledge which might attend activity, but action itself; happiness is living and doing well. For the individual, it is "an activity of the mind in accord with the most perfect virtue" and not to be confounded with mere motion. Book 10 states that an activity, such as happiness, pleasure, or thought, is its own end and requires nothing more for its perfection; a motion, on the other hand, such as learning and walk-

328

ing, aims at something other than itself, and is never complete until it is over. For the city-state, happiness means prosperity. Since in Aristotle's view man is a political animal, and since justice, as he says in Book 5, is nearly equal to the whole of virtue, and alone of virtues is concerned with the good of others, the happiness discussed in the *Nichomachean Ethics* pertains to a person both as a private individual and as a citizen of a state. As such it has close relationship to the law.

The actions which concern Aristotle most are those performed voluntarily. It is these actions that are praised (sometimes with public honors) or blamed (sometimes in a court of law). The first half of Book 3, in analyzing actions, distinguishes between voluntary, nonvoluntary, and involuntary acts. An act is involuntary when it is done because of an external force or through ignorance. If an act subsequently causes the doer sorrow and psychological pain, the act was involuntary; if not, it was nonvoluntary.

A further distinction that Aristotle makes here is between acts done in ignorance and acts done through ignorance. A drunkard, for example, is said to act in, and not through, ignorance. He can thus be blamed, since he acts through drunkenness, whereas a person who acts through ignorance of the particular circumstances of his act can be pardoned.

A major problem concerns the question: how may a person voluntarily choose to do wrong? In Book 7, Aristotle discusses the concept of unrestraint, refusing to support the famous paradox of Socrates that no one does wrong willingly. His analysis of unrestraint and of the thinking vicious man is complex, and leads to the notion of the practical syllogism, which concludes not in a statement, but in action. For example, the statements: "I should eat all sweets" and "this is sweet" lead to the eating and not to the conclusion "therefore I should eat this."

Throughout the *Nicomachean Ethics* there are discussions of individual virtues: courage (Book 3), justice (Book 5), friendship (Books 8 and 9), intellectual virtue and practical wisdom (Book 6), liberality, magnificence, greatness of soul, gentleness, agreeableness, sincerity and modesty, (all in Book 4). In a preface to these discussions, Aristotle, in Book 2, considers virtue in general. The most important features of this discussion are, first, that virtue does not lie merely in the performance of a correct action, but in a correct action which is done for the right reason, a matter which requires the person to perform the action repeatedly until it becomes a fixed disposition. Another conclusion of this discussion is that most virtues represent some balance between extremes (the doctrine of the mean). Furthermore, the idea that virtue is a fixed disposition leads Aristotle to conclude that virtue is pleasurable, an idea which is elaborated in two later accounts of pleasure, in Books 7 and 10, where it is said that happiness is accompanied by pleasure.

In conclusion (Book 10), Aristotle says that the way to true happiness is through contemplation, for contemplation is what distinguishes men from animals.

Pertinent Literature

Jaeger, Werner W. *Aristotle, Fundamentals of the History of His Development.* Oxford: The University Press, 1948.

Werner Jaeger is perhaps the most influential Aristotelian scholar of this century. Before this book was first published in German in 1923, it was generally assumed one could not construct a unified system of thought from Aristotle's works. The result was a complicated scheme often requiring special pleading to explain apparent inconsistencies. Jaeger's contribution was an attempt to place Aristotle's writings in a chronological order that would explain his interests at different times of his life, and would, as the subtitle of his book makes clear, trace the history of Aristotle's development as a thinker. Although details of Jaeger's findings have been challenged, the impetus he gave to modern Aristotelian studies is still so felt by present-day scholars that his book serves as a basic text.

In the case of Aristotle's ethical writings, Jaeger had to determine the relationship between the *Protrepticus,* the *Eudemian Ethics,* the *Magna Moralia,* and the *Nicomachean Ethics,* all of which are found in the manuscript collections of Aristotle's works. Before Jaeger, almost all possible views had been held about the relative dates and the authenticity of these works, the most outlandish being that only the *Magna Moralia* was genuine. A commonly held view, opposed by Jaeger, held that the *Eudemian Ethics* was so named because it was the work of Eudemus of Rhodes, a student of Aristotle.

Jaeger's view of Aristotle started out from the fact that he was at first a devoted student of Plato, then slowly developed his own theories, some of which came to oppose his earlier Platonic views. This development holds true, Jaeger maintains, for ethical writings as well. The *Protrepticus* is Platonic in thought and medium, probably being cast in Platonic dialogue form.

Jaeger considers that the *Eudemian Ethics* is a genuine work of Aristotle, and that it was written after the *Protrepticus* and before the *Nicomachean Ethics.* Jaeger's analysis shows that on several points the *Eudemian Ethics* seems to hold an Aristotelian position midway between the two other works. For example, the Greek word *"phronesis"* in the *Protrepticus* and the *Eudemian Ethics* stands for a Platonic notion of apprehension that is both rational and intuitive; whereas in Aristotle's later works, including the *Nicomachean Ethics,* the same word stands for a sort of fixed disposition towards practical action. Although a few scholars today maintain that the *Eudemian Ethics* was written after the *Nicomachean Ethics,* Jaeger's view generally prevails.

Jaeger argues that the *Magna Moralia* is not a genuine work of Aristotle, and although not the first to hold this position, he bases his conclusion on a more comprehensive argument than any of his predecessors and his view generally prevails. Scholars still debate whether the work was written shortly after Aristotle or centuries after, but very few believe that it is an authentic work of the master himself.

The *Nicomachean Ethics* is interpreted by Jaeger as representing a third stage in the development of Aristotle's ethical thought. In almost every topic, Aristotle goes beyond the "reformed Platonism" of the *Eudemian Ethics,* taking from it what he still considered valid, but on the whole reworking his earlier speculations into something more in harmony with his later metaphysical thought.

Hardie, W. F. R. *Aristotle's Ethical Theory.* Oxford: The University Press, 1968.

Hardie's recent book, intended for the reader who knows no Greek, treats the *Nicomachean Ethics* comprehensively. After an introductory chapter in which Hardie comments briefly on current views about the nature of the texts of the *Nicomachean Ethics,* the *Eudemian Ethics,* and the *Magna Moralia,* there follow fifteen chapters dealing in detail with most of the topics which interest present-day philosophers, including the final good for man, virtue as a mean, justice, moral weakness, and theoretical activity and the nature of reason.

Chapter 2, "The Final Good for Man," may be singled out as indicative of the value of the whole work, a chapter which appears in a different form in a paperback anthology entitled *Aristotle* edited by J. M. E. Moravcsik. Hardie suggests that Aristotle in the first book of the *Nicomachean Ethics* confounds two notions of a final end, which should be kept separate. Aristotle's account reflects his own confusion about what the final good actually is and leads him to commit himself theoretically to positions which he does not apply in practice.

For example, Hardie doubts whether the pursuit of human good, understood in terms of Aristotle's conception of the dominant end, can be harmonized with the morality of altruism, especially that which inspires a man to give his life for his friends or his country. Hardie objects to Aristotle's belief that happiness may lead one to lay down his life in battle for his city, because such an action is inconsistent with statements made elsewhere in Book 1 to the effect that happiness requires a "complete life." Only survivors of the battle may go on to enjoy a full life performing actions in the way Aristotle's ethics require.

This confusion, Hardie maintains, arises on one hand from Aristotle's definition of happiness as a dominant end, the one goal that supersedes all others. On the other hand, in his extended discussion, he more generally treats happiness as an inclusive end, that is, one that consists of the harmonious achievement of all that leads up to the final goal of happiness. Sometimes these two concepts can be reconciled. The man who survives the battle may, after a complete life, achieve happiness as a dominant end in the normal way Aristotle defines. Yet the man who dies for his city cannot order his life and actions so as to develop dispositions toward virtue which eventually bring happiness in the end. — *D.S.*

Additional Recommended Reading

Chroust, Anton-Hermann, *Aristotle: Protrepticus. A Reconstruction*. Notre Dame: University of Notre Dame Press, 1964. An attempt to arrange the fragments of Aristotle's earliest work in a systematic order, with commentary.

Grene, Marjorie. *A Portrait of Aristotle*. Chicago: University of Chicago Press, 1963. An excellent introduction to Aristotle's thought with a chapter on Werner Jaeger's influence on Aristotelian studies.

Huby, Pamela. *Greek Ethics*. New York: St. Martin's Press, 1967. A history of Greek ethics from the beginning to post-Aristotelian times.

Monan, J. Donald. *Moral Knowledge and Its Methodology in Aristotle*. Oxford: The University Press, 1968. A study of Aristotle's views on the nature of moral knowledge, concluding that the *Eudemian Ethics* was written after the *Nicomachean Ethics*.

ORIGIN OF *MUNICIPIA*

Type of event: Political: development in diplomatic relations
Time: 340-338 B.C.
Locale: Rome, Latium, and Campania in Central Italy

Principal personage:
TITUS MANLIUS TORQUATUS, military tribune 362; dictator
353, 349; consul 347, 344, 340; and general in 340
against the Latin League

Summary of Event

Vital to the expansion of Roman dominance in Italy and for its later imperial development and organization was the discovery of a way to cement close relationships with other small neighboring states. Although the bonds gradually forged with Italian towns and tribal groups were diverse in character, a highly significant step in Roman diplomacy can be identified about 338 B.C. when Rome granted limited Roman citizenship to several cities of Latium and Campania.

In the middle of the fourth century B.C., Rome was becoming the strongest state in central Italy although encircled by unfriendly and ambitious rivals. Gallic tribes, which had captured Rome in 390 B.C., continued to invade the northern half of the peninsula. The most dangerous enemies of Rome, however, were the Samnite tribes in the southern Apennine mountains, which had more territory and a greater population than the Romans. The smaller states of central Italy, chiefly Etruscan and Latin, had been forced to seek Roman protection against both the plundering Gauls and the expanding Samnites, but these smaller neighbors resented and feared increasing Roman superiority.

Some thirty to forty smaller communities in the plain of Latium south of Rome had long been united in a league for mutual defense and common religious rites before Rome itself entered into agreement with them possibly as early as 493 B.C. by renouncing all claims to domination and by exchanging some citizenship privileges such as intermarriage and recognition of commercial contracts. Nevertheless aboue 358 B.C. several Latin League towns supported an attack by mountain tribes against Rome, and in 340 the entire league took up arms against Roman hegemony. Led by Titus Manlius Torquatus, hero of a famous duel in 361 against a giant Gaul, the Romans suppressed this revolt and in 338 proceeded to dissolve the league, making separate peace treaties with each of the former confederates. A few small towns near Rome were simply incorporated into the Roman state with full citizenship rights, while other Latin cities were given partial Roman citizenship but were required to supply troops for the Roman army.

Further south there were a number of populous communities that controlled the fertile lowland plain called

333

Campania, situated between the Samnites to the East and South, and the Romans to the North. Capua, the largest city in Campania, appealed in 343 for Roman aid against Samnite aggression and received help. During the Latin Revolt of 340-338, citizens of Capua and other Campanian communities assisted the Latins against Rome, but the upper-class Campanian cavalry remained loyal to Rome. Rome consequently rewarded the nobles of Capua and several smaller towns in Campania with what the historian Livy calls *civitas romana,* that is, Roman citizenship. Also described as *civitas sine suffragio,* or "citizenship without suffrage," this qualified citizenship, similar to the kind granted earlier to Latin cities, specifically excluded the right to vote in Roman elections or to hold offices in Rome, but it did include the obligation to serve with the Roman legions when called upon to do so. Communities whose leading citizens were so bound came to be called *municipia* after 338. One or more Etruscan cities near Rome were given similar status.

This partial Roman citizenship subordinated the *municipia* to the military and diplomatic dominance of Rome, but it also allowed Italian cities to retain almost complete freedom in local self-government. Inscriptions show that Capua continued to be governed by its own traditional magistrates.

Since it was in the period after 338 B.C. that Roman power expanded most rapidly, it seems evident that the *municipium* relationship proved advantageous for Rome and also for the towns drawn into such close relationship. An increasing number of Italian towns became *municipia,* many of them forced to accept the status after being conquered by Roman armies. However, most of the towns showed remarkable loyalty during the Samnite Wars between 327 and 303 and again between 298 and 290, as well as during Hannibal's invasion of Italy. Apparently Rome gave the *municipia* more security and less freedom than an alliance between equals, yet the *municipia* had the opportunity to share some of the fruits of Roman military victories and at the same time preserve their own self-government.

As Rome's domination extended in later centuries beyond Italy, terms such as *municipia* changed in meaning. By 80 B.C., all peoples living in Italy had been granted full Roman citizenship and all towns in Italy came to be called *municipia.* Moreover, by the Imperial period, independent Greek allies together with cities in Gaul and Spain came to be treated in much the same way as towns in Italy and were called *municipia.*

A major factor in the stability and longevity of the Roman Empire was the system which grew out of the *municipium* concept which originated about 338 B.C. Hundreds of cities were each given control of their own local affairs while the citizens were also Roman citizens with strong loyalties to the Empire. The concept was later to develop into the idea of a city being a corporation with a charter of its own.

334

Origin of Municipia

Pertinent Literature

Sherwin-White, Adrian N. *The Roman Citizenship.* Oxford: The Clarendon Press, 1939.

This book was the first thorough study in English on how and why the Romans gradually extended their rights of citizenship throughout Italy and the provinces. The author carefully examines many German and Italian studies in Roman political forms, and skillfully sifts ancient literary and epigraphic sources. No later English scholar has attempted any sharply different interpretation of the confusing records of the early Republic.

Sherwin-White accepts as generally accurate the tradition used by Livy which describes the reorganization of Rome's confederation after the Latin Revolt of 340-338 B.C. He concludes that Rome used ingenious and flexible diplomacy to secure the support of allies and conquered neighbors, arguing that the partial citizenship granted to several Latin city-states in 338 was the "first large breach in the older conception of a city-state." He rejects as a later confusion Livy's story that the non-Latin city of Caere, about fifteen miles north of Rome, had been given limited Roman citizenship before 350.

In a chapter on "The Settlement of 338 B.C. and the Origin of the Municeps," Sherwin-White examines the status of the Campanian towns made *municipia* in 338. At first a generous extension of the older "Latin rights" to non-Latin allies, their partial citizenship was subtly downgraded with the advance of Roman prestige. He states that originally citizens of these *municipia* could claim full rights as Romans if they migrated to Rome, and that later, as a result of support given to Hannibal, the Campanian towns lost some of their status when Roman officials were sent to share with local authorities in the governing of their towns. Although it is debatable how regularly the Romans sent "prefects" to supervise the *municipia,* Sherwin-White argues that such actions were infrequent before the invasion by Hannibal. Nevertheless, local autonomy was never entirely abolished, and as the number of *municipia* increased in Italy, they gradually came to be treated much as were the more fully incorporated Latin towns.

The author traces in detail the extension of the *municipium* until it included by the final century of the Republic military and "Latin" colonies. The military colonists were Roman citizen-soldiers sent out by Rome, and eventually they were treated much like the *municipia.* Various "allies" throughout Italy also became self-governing *municipia,* incorporated into Roman citizenship as communities rather than as individuals. Extension of the franchise in 89 B.C. along with grants of citizenship by Sulla and Julius Caesar fully municipalized Italy by 80 B.C. When the model of *municipium* was extended to communities outside Italy, it had come to mean "a self-governing community, irrespective of its origin." Eventually "free cities" in Greece, Asia, and Africa were equated with the *municipia* in Italy. By the second century of the Empire, *municipia* grew even along the banks of the Danube River out of army camps, but after the decree early in the third century which granted citizenship to all residents of the Empire, only places of secondary importance remained *municipia;* cities obtained more renown by being called *coloniae,* a status which allowed them more freedom.

Finally, Sherwin-White discusses how far and why Rome managed to win genuine loyalty in its provinces. He points to some evidences of continuing tension in eastern areas between Hellenistic and Roman traditions, but he declares that the development of the "municipal system" was Rome's most valuable accomplishment politically.

Badian, E. *Foreign Clientelae (264-70 B.C.).* Oxford: The Clarendon Press, 1958.

This review of the patron-client relationship in Roman diplomacy includes a chapter which considers Rome's relationships with other cities in Italy before the Hannibalic War. Although Badian recognizes Sherwin-White's *Roman Citizenship* as "the standard work" on this subject in English, and states that the origins of the concept of *municipium* are "wrapped in obscurity," he disagrees sharply with Sherwin-White's judgment on the earliest known instance of a non-Latin city being granted partial Roman citizenship. Badian believes it likely that Caere, an Etrurian neighbor of Rome north of the Tiber River, was the first city to receive the status *civitas sine suffragio,* or "citizenship without suffrage." Since the Caerites had aided Rome against the Gauls in 390 B.C., Rome treated Caere generously after defeating the city in war about the middle of the fourth century. Badian, accepting as authentic an old description of a Roman list of Caerite citizens drawn up by Roman censors, considers that the treatment of Caere by Rome was the original pattern which was later copied in regard to Campanian cities in 338 and thereafter.

Another point on which Badian disagrees with earlier studies involves the *foedus iniquum,* or "unequal alliance," a Roman device which Sherwin-White calls "the chief instrument in the formation of the federation of allies." Badian doubts whether this unequal alliance was ever actually articulated in any early Roman treaties, despite the fact that Rome from very early times considered many allies subject in some degree to Roman authority. However, Badian considers that it was no more than a "natural development" in any alliance between a powerful and a weaker state. The same thing happened in Greece during the fifth century when Athens predominated in the Delian League.

By correlating the patron-client concept with other diplomatic forms, Badian clarifies many changes which took place in Roman foreign policy, especially when Rome became dominant in the eastern Mediterranean. He argues that Greek cities such as Naples were first accepted as independent allies of Rome, but when Rome claimed the right to "protect" its allies, the *municipium* concept originating in Italy in the fourth century B.C. was subsequently blended with the ideas of "free cities" and "client states" through which Rome was able to dominate Greek cities. Hence Badian's perspective on many incidents in Roman foreign policy differs from that of earlier historians who gave little attention to the patron-client relationship, ingrained in Roman private life, which Badian sees as being applied analagously to inter-state liaisons, especially after Rome became the predominant military force in the Mediterranean world. Although Badian's focus is wider than most earlier studies, including Sherwin-White's, his book offers valuable insights even in the earliest of Rome's diplomatic negotiations in Italy. — *R.B.M.*

Additional Recommended Reading

Abbott, Frank F., and Allan C. Johnson. *Municipal Administration in the Roman Empire*. Princeton: Princeton University Press, 1926. A compendium of more than two hundred documents illustrating Roman municipal development, without full English translation but with careful notes.

Adcock, F. E. "The Conquest of Central Italy," in *The Cambridge Ancient History*. Vol. VII, ch. XVIII. Cambridge: The University Press, 1928. A detailed account of Roman wars and diplomacy from 360 to 290 B.C.

Heitland, W. E. *The Roman Republic*. Vol. I, chs. XVII-XIX. Cambridge: The University Press, 1923. A study of Roman conquests from 366 to 265 B.C., with the correlative development of politico-diplomatic forms.

Pinsent, John. "The Original Meaning of Municeps," in *Classical Quarterly*. n.s. 4 (1954), 158-164. A linguistic study of Republican usage of vital terms relating to *municipia*.

Reid, James S. *The Municipalities of the Roman Empire*. Cambridge: The University Press, 1913. A valuable account of the development of cities in the Republic and Empire, although it lacks precise definition of terms and references to ancient sources.

Yeo, Cedric A. "The Founding and Function of Roman Colonies," in *The Classical World*. 52 (1959), 104-107, 129-130. A study of the earliest *municipia* and their relationship to the colonies established by the Republic.

BATTLE OF CHAERONEA

Type of event: Military: Macedonian victory which heralded the dawn of Hellenistic times

Time: August 2, 338 B.C.

Locale: Chaeronea, in Boeotia northwest of Thebes

Principal personages:

PHILIP II, King of Macedon 359-336

ALEXANDER, son of Philip, King of Macedon 336-323

DEMOSTHENES (384-322 B.C., Athenian statesman and orator

ISOCRATES (436-338 B.C.), Athenian publicist and rhetorician

Summary of Event

The Peloponnesian War ended Athens' hegemony in Greece; Spartan dominance replaced it. The result was the outbreak of new destructive wars aimed at the overthrow of the latter. At the Battle of Leuctra in 371, the Thebans, allies of Athens, inflicted a decisive defeat on the Spartans, and Greece passed to the hegemony of Thebes. It proved to be exceedingly short-lived. Athens changed sides, and in concert with Sparta and other states overcame Thebes in the closely fought Battle of Mantinea in 362. Athens, meanwhile, had revived the Delian confederacy, but most of her allies successfully revolted against her in the Social War of 357-355, and Athenian power was badly shaken.

Men who participated in these unsuccessful, melancholy wars for the hegemony of Greece called out for relief from them. The Athenian Isocrates advocated, as the vital necessity for escaping continual competition and bloodshed, the unification of Greece under the leadership of some strong state and some strong men. Demosthenes of Athens dreamed of an Athens revitalized culturally and militarily and preëminent in Greece. The philosopher Plato hoped for government by philosophers.

A more likely savior than one of Plato's scholars appeared in Philip of Macedon, who began his reign in 359 B.C. He set about to Hellenize and modernize Macedonia with ingenuity and energy. He brought the factious nobility of his country to heel and taught them to serve him with heavy cavalry. He also created an infantry phalanx better drilled and more effective than that of the Greeks. His army was of professional quality, far superior to the citizen militias or hired mercenaries which made up the bulk of the armies of the Hellenic cities. The Macedonian army was, moreover, supported by efficient financial institutions. Philip intended to establish his own hegemony over Greece, although he wished it to be merciful and enlightened. Already in the 340's he began to penetrate southward through Thessaly. The principal Greek states of Athens, Sparta, and Thebes, distracted by their own per-

338

petual feuds and weakened by their precarious fiscal circumstances, resisted Philip, but only halfheartedly.

In 340 B.C., the decisive war broke out between Macedonia and the Greeks. In August, 338, the Macedonian army of two thousand cavalry and thirty thousand infantry came face to face with the united Greek armies of weak cavalry and thirty-five thousand infantry near the small town of Chaeronea in northwestern Boeotia. The Greeks deployed with their right flank covered by a small stream; it was held by twelve thousand Thebans and Boeotians. The center was composed of various allies from central Greece and the Peloponnesus, and the left was made up of ten thousand Athenians. The Greek phalanx was to make its usual straightforward attack, hoping to crush the enemy by the weight of its charge. Philip, on the other side, was a master of more subtle tactics, combining the use of cavalry and infantry. His own left, opposite the Thebans, was headed by his cavalry, which was to thrust itself into a gap to be made in the Greek line. The gap would be opened by luring the Athenians into charging his own right as it purposefully drew back in pretended retreat.

It was probably on August 2, 338, that the battle was fought, and everything went according to Philip's plan. The Athenians rushed forward shouting, "On to Pella!" (the capital of Macedonia), and when the Greek center and the left of the Thebans moved obliquely forward to keep in close ranks with them, a hole opened in the ranks of the Thebans. Into it, resolutely led by the eighteen-year-old crown prince Alexander, the Macedonian heavy cavalry crashed, charging in wedge formation. They were followed by crack formations of infantry, which attacked the flanks on either side of the gap. The Thebans, after heroic resistance, were beaten; the Greek center and left, panic-stricken, broke and ran. The result was a decisive victory for Philip.

During the next few weeks, the Greek states surrendered one after another. In 337, Philip organized them into a Hellenic League with its seat at Corinth. He was himself president of the league, and members were forced to follow his foreign policy. Wars among them were forbidden, as was internal constitutional change except by constitutional methods. Philip's intentions were to secure a tranquil and contented Greece as the necessary first step in his new plan to liberate the Greeks of Asia Minor from the Persian Empire.

The Battle of Chaeronea was the great event that destroyed the sovereignty of the Greek states. There was, it is true, a revolt against Macedonia in 323-321 called the "Lamian War," and several more in the third century which brought temporary freedom, but the era of the old, unbridled parochialism and imperialism of Athens, Sparta, and Thebes was over.

Pertinent Literature

Hammond, B. G. L. *A History of Greece to 322 B.C.* Oxford: The Clarendon Press, 1959.

Hammond's book covers Greek history from 3,000 B.C., when the ancestors of the Greeks were still living in southern Russia, to the year when Antipater and Craterus were on the verge of overcoming the Greek revolt of 323 against the control which Macedonia exercised as victor in the Battle of Chaeronea. It is a general history, including chapters on international relations, constitutional history, and the evolution of Hellenic art and thought. The first section on the Mycenean period is weak, but as Hammond approaches the fourth century B.C., the age with which he is most familiar, his interpretation of events becomes more and more interesting.

The wars fought between 431 and 338 B.C. gave rise to considerable anguish in Athens and elsewhere, as well they might. Conflict was attended by social upheaval and economic depression. Isocrates of Athens became a pan-Hellenist, believing that the unity of Greece must be achieved at any cost to win freedom from bloodshed. This unity could be brought about only by a strong leader. As the power of Macedonia increased, Isocrates hailed Philip as the natural *hegemon* of Greece, a king who could unite the warring states and cement their alliance by leading them in a national crusade against Persia. Isocrates, however, was a rhetorician and publicist who took little part in politics, so that his influence on events was small.

It was far different with Demos-thenes, a leading politician at Athens, a figure of considerable oratorical skill and persuasive power, and an imperialist after the manner of Pericles. He was a proponent of Athens' resuming her role of leader of Greece, both in a military sense as *hegemon* of a revived naval confederacy, and in a cultural sense as the intellectual and moral school of Hellas. He saw that if Athens were to lead, she would inevitably come into conflict with Philip, and he never missed an occasion to denounce the King as an aggressor bent on the conquest of Athens to end her freedom. With Philip extending his power southward, collision was inevitable; the result was Chaeronea.

Hammond concludes his book with a short discussion of what the word "freedom" meant to the Greeks and to the Greek states. Freedom was a word always on the lips of Athenian statesmen, who, like Pericles, praised to the skies the men who had preserved the freedom of Athens at Marathon and Salamis, or who, like Demosthenes, exhorted their listeners to defend the freedom of Athens once more on the eve of Chaeronea. Hammond believes that there were two kinds of freedom, the old-fashioned freedom of Demosthenes, and the new kind of freedom preached by Isocrates and practiced by Philip through the Hellenic League. The old freedom meant the right of each of the major Greek states to exercise their full sovereignty. In actuality this meant the right of each to coerce or attack weaker states, making them parts of an empire, ending their freedom, and inflicting garrisons and tribute on them. As far as the Greeks of the lesser states were concerned, freedom for Athens or Thebes meant subjection for them. Unhappily, experience showed conclusively that none of the major city-states was strong enough to conquer the other permanently. The result was continual marching, fighting, bloodshed, and agony. The new freedom of Philip and the Hellenic League was freedom from interstate war, freedom from domestic revolution, and freedom to work for the prosperity of Hellas.

Tarn, Sir William, and G. T. Griffith. *Hellenistic Civilization.* 3rd ed. London: Edward Arnold, 1952.

The Battle of Chaeronea cast down the classical city-states from their central position in Hellenic affairs, and gave Macedonia the leadership during the following generation which ushered in a new age and a new style of Greek culture. *Hellenistic Civilization* has justly been called a classic book, and it is certainly among the best one-volume introductions to this period of history. Sir William Tarn was, in fact, a respected British scholar who enriched our knowledge and enhanced our understanding of the Hellenistic Age. This edition of the book is a revision made by G. T. Griffith.

The first chapter is a brief, hard-to-digest chronological outline of the major political and military events of the period. Once past this point, one encounters the marvelously diverse, rich account of Hellenistic history. The political, social, and economic institutions of the Greek cities are reviewed. Here there is a wealth of fascinating detail, including a sketch of the unsuccessful but interesting attempts to found utopian communities in which all citizens were political and economic equals.

Tarn next surveys the Asian empire of the Seleucids, a vast monarchy stretching at its widest extent from the banks of the Indus River to the shores of the Aegean Sea and including among its subjects the Greeks of its teeming cities, the robed Persian grandees of Iran, and the scarcely civilized hill men of eastern Anatolia and northern Iraq. Then the author presents a description of the highly centralized Egypt of the Ptolemies, with its complex system of economic exploitation which, by means of planned planting controlled from a central bureau, caused a stream of grain to pour down the Nile into the royal warehouses at Alexandria for export to overseas markets at the best prices. Typically, Tarn adds the intimate detail that one of the finance ministers of this remarkable state thriftily offered for sale roses from his private garden.

Chapters follow on a wide variety of topics. "Trade and Exploration" tells how Pytheas of Massilia sailed into the North Sea, discovered the fjords of Norway and reported on them, only to be called a preposterous liar. It also reports that by the end of the second century B.C., regular contact by sea was maintained between Egypt and India. "Literature and Learning" presents the Hellenistic period as a time of tireless literary industry. The scholar Didymus wrote, it is said, thirty-five hundred books on biography and literary criticism and well earned his nickname, "Brazen-Guts." Sober and gifted historians such as Polybius had to compete with writers of cheap scandal such as Aristippus. "Science and Art" is a particularly successful essay setting forth the extraordinary achievements of Hellenistic science. We are told of the great physician Erasistratus, whose astonishing accomplishments gave credit to the story that he had raised a man from the dead. We also see dark glimpses of vivisections performed on criminals condemned to death.

Finally there is "Philosophy and Religion," those rich tapestries of Hellenistic thought and feeling exemplified by the ethical philosophies of Epicurus and Zeno, and the complete skepticism of Pyrrho. There is the rise of new and emotional religions from the Orient, tamed, or partly tamed, by Hellenism. Some men begin the grotesque practice of magic, and other men create the god Sarapis.

Sir William's book has done much to rescue Hellenistic culture from the limbo where devotees of classical Hellenism have too often wished to assign it. — *S.K.E.*

Additional Recommended Reading

Cary, Max. *History of the Greek World from 323 to 146 B.C.* 2nd ed. London: Methuen & Co., 1951. A comprehensive survey of Greek history after the Lamian War.

Gomme, A. W. "The End of the City-State," in *Essays in Greek History and Literature.* Oxford: Basil Blackwell, 1937. A thesis that the liberty of the Greek cities was not ended by the Battle of Chaeronea, nor did it curtail the vigor of their political life.

Jones, A. H. M. "The Athens of Demosthenes," in *Athenian Democracy.* Oxford: Basil Blackwell, 1953. An argument that financial stringency caused Athens to hesitate about opposing Macedon in the 340's more than the "moral decay" which Demosthenes and some modern scholars have postulated.

Jaeger, Werner. "Demosthenes: The Death Struggle and Transfiguration of the City-State," and "Isocrates Defends His Paideia," in *Paideia.* Volume 3: *The Conflict of Cultural Ideals in the Age of Plato.* 2nd ed. London: Oxford University Press, 1945. An important exposition of the life and doctrine of this Athenian statesman.

ARISTOTLE WRITES THE *POLITICS*

Type of event: Philosophical: formulation of a theory of political living
Time: c.340 B.C.
Locale: Athens

Principal personage:
ARISTOTLE OF STAGIRA (384-322 B.C.), major Greek philosopher and founder of the Lyceum

Summary of Event

Aristotle's *Politics* is but one of a number of treatises compiled in the Lyceum from school discussions of the philosopher on every conceivable realm of phenomena of interest to the Greek mind. In his discussion of politics Aristotle did not seek, as Plato had done, to lay foundations for a moral reconstruction of human community existence; instead, he sought to understand the distinctive form of Greek community life, the *polis*. The result of his work was the establishment of a classic body of normative political concepts capable of being applied by later generations of Western political analysts.

Characteristic of Aristotle's organismic perspective on the whole spectrum of phenomena is his concept of the city-state as a natural entity developing in response to inherent needs and drives in man. Man has a natural place in a hierarchy of life wherein each genus and species creature has its own distinctive inherent possibilities of development and modes of formal self-realization. At his own level in this hierarchy man not only enjoys and participates in the plant and animal forms of development and realization, but as a creature uniquely endowed with reason, he builds upon the foundation of these lower life-activities a distinctively human mode of development and formal perfection.

Because he has the power of reason, man is able not only to experience pain and pleasure like the lower animals, but also to discriminate between good and evil, justice and injustice, and to share with others of his kind a community of values. For this reason man, more than any other animal, fulfills himself naturally in forms of shared existence. The forms of community are themselves derived from a natural complementarity of the differing natures of human persons participating in a community. At the most primitive level, the household reaps the advantages of association of man and woman for procreation and of ruler and ruled for mutual security. In the man suited by nature for rule the power of reason is sufficiently developed to discern what is advantageous for the common welfare, while in the man who is by nature a servant resides the physical power to effect such policy and sufficient reason to recognize the advantage of obedience to his wiser master.

Beyond the primitive community of the household is the village, a community of households established in order to secure on a more permanent

343

basis the advantages of shared existence. And beyond the village-community stands the natural form of fully realized community life, the association of villages, or *polis*. While the *polis* comes into existence in order to sustain human life in a fully self-sufficient form, the *polis* continues to exist, according to Aristotle, in order to achieve the optimal perfection of human existence.

It should be noted that in designating the *polis* as the natural form of fully realized human community, Aristotle was thinking not of the large nation-state or of the industrial state of other historical times and places, but specifically of the relatively small Greek city-state, whose members could be reasonably familiar with one another. Once this is realized, the meaning of Aristotle's dictum, "Man is by nature a *polis*-animal," can be appreciated in its uniquely Greek and Aristotelian context.

Polis-communities may differ widely from one another, but the factor determining the distinctive form of each is its *politeia,* or constitution, which defines who are the citizens of the *polis* and in what category of citizens the primary authority for judicial and policy decisions resides. The citizen in the proper sense, according to Aristotle, is he who participates in dispensing justice and determining policy. While a constitution may confer supreme authority upon one man, upon a few, or upon all freeborn members of the *polis,* Aristotle viewed as a legitimate constitution one wherein the authoritative body in the *polis* dispenses justice and formulates policy with a view to the well-being of all freeborn citizens, and not the well-

being of the authoritative body itself alone. In the latter case, the constitution would not be a legitimate form but a perversion. On this basis Aristotle distinguished between three legitimate forms, which he termed monarchy, aristocracy, and *politeia* in a distinctive sense which we might translate as "republic" or "constitutional democracy," and three corresponding perversions, which he called tyranny, oligarchy, and *demokratia* which we might perhaps best translate as "rule of the proletariat."

A survey of the functions necessary to a fully self-sufficient *polis* that maximizes the potentials of human well-being and of Aristotle's distribution of status among those who perform these functions makes fully clear to a modern mind that Aristotle's political theory was not so much a universally applicable conceptual scheme as it was a distillation of distinctively Greek aristocratic notions of what constituted optimal human well-being in a *polis*-community. These necessary functions were : (1) food production, (2) provision of essential goods and services, (3) maintenance of order within and defense against enemies, (4) accumulation of surplus wealth to sustain private expenditures and security forces, (5) cultic functions of *polis*-religion, and (6) policy-making and dispensation of justice. In Aristotle's view, those performing the first two of these functions, farmers and laborers, while essential to the self-sufficiency and well-being of the *polis,* could not be citizens. Lacking the requisite leisure to develop the higher uses of reason into the citizen-virtues of participation in judicial and policy-making decisions, they were servants sustaining the plant and animal functions of a corporate body, of which only the true citizens could achieve full realization of the well-being possible to man. The last three functions were performed by the true citizens at the ages at which they were best suited by nature to discharge them, and surplus wealth would also be in the possession of the citizens proper.

Pertinent Literature

Voegelin, Eric. *Order and History.* Volume Three: *Plato and Aristotle.* Baton Rouge: Louisiana State University Press, 1957.

The stated theme of Eric Voegelin's ambitious six-volume study, *Order and History,* is "the principal types of order of human existence in society and history as well as the corresponding symbolic forms." The motivating impulse of the study is a sense of our own era as one of crisis over legitimate forms of order, crisis with deep historical roots extending back to the era of Mesopotamian civilization. The continuing thread of his work is a concept of successive epochs in major approaches to the solution of one central problem: how can man in history relate his social existence to a transcendent source of order? Aristotle's approach to this problem in the *Nicomachean Ethics* and in the *Politics* forms the focus of the second half of Voegelin's third volume.

Voegelin sees both the shortcomings and the positive achievements of Aristotle's investigation of political order as a consequence of his overall tendency to look for form as immanent in empirical phenomena. With regard to social and political order, therefore, he shifts attention away from a Platonic conception of a transcendent source of order (the Good) which validates human virtues and legitimate forms of political community, toward those forms of moral be-

havior and political order recognizable as immanent in the empirical *polis.* At the same time Aristotle cannot surrender his conviction, his heritage from Socrates and Plato, that human nature can be fulfilled completely only in a social order naturally corresponding to the fullest development of the innate potentiality of man's soul. While Aristotle thus formulates a conception of a "natural" human political community that maximizes the possibilities of human well-being and communal self-sufficiency, when he turns to analysis of the empirical forms of *polis*-communities in his own era, he is compelled to recognize, as the essential form of the *polis,* the constitution which designates the locus of judicial and policy-making power within the citizenry according to distinctive subspecies. And although his empirical analysis of the spectrum of monarchic, oligarchic, and democratic constitutions in Books IV-VI of the *Politics* is rich and of immeasurable historical value, Aristotle must confess that in not one of the numerous empirical *polis*-communities does his initial concept of the nature of a *polis* find its realization.

Aristotle's *Politics* is thus cleft, in Voegelin's view, into inquiries that aim at altogether different objectives.

The reason for this lies in the philosopher's "consciousness of epoch," his sense that the *polis*-community as a viable focus of a fully satisfying human existence has in fact disintegrated to the point where the most creative mind cannot find personal fulfillment in active participation in *polis*-life but only in a withdrawn private existence of philosophic speculation and scientific inquiry. In the *Nicomachean Ethics* Aristotle formulates a conception of human happiness as the full exercise of rationality on a lower level of moral self-regulation and on a higher level of contemplation. In the *Politics* he sets out initially to demonstrate that a *polis*, if it is really to be a *polis*, should actualize the possibilities of human happiness thus defined for as many persons as are naturally endowed to achieve it. But the *polis* of that sort

which Aristotle outlines in Books VII and VIII is an ideal construction not to be found in empirical reality, while the investigations of empirical *polis*-communities in Books IV-VI aim rather at determination of factors responsible for securing maximal social and political stability in the diverse subspecies of *polis*-constitutions in the contemporary Greek world.

Voegelin appears to take the view that Aristotle ought logically to have advanced speculatively beyond the historically moribund *polis*-form of community, but he could not have done so because he was still bound within the characteristic Greek conception of a cosmic and cyclical natural order, and so was inhibited from uncovering the radically new Jewish-Christian concept of an order of history.

Barker, Ernest. *The Politics of Aristotle: Translated, with An Introduction, Notes and Appendixes.* Oxford: The Clarendon Press, 1946.

The scholarship of Ernest Barker on the political thought of Aristotle must be accorded a commanding, authoritative rank. Greek political thought was the labor of his life, and one of the finest fruits of that painstaking labor is this volume comprising a translation into contemporary idiomatic English not only of the *Politics* but also of portions of other works of Aristotle bearing on his political thought, a running commentary and numerous excursuses on particular topics, and a copious introduction summarizing half a century's study of the *Politics*.

One of Barker's major insights into the nature of the Greek *polis*-community, especially as it was understood

by Aristotle, is that this community is not at all a "state" in the modern sense of an institution standing over against a society of private citizens. Rather it has the character of a church, inasmuch as it is "an integrated system of social ethics, which realizes to the full the capacity of its members, and therefore claims their full allegiance." From Aristotle's conception of the *polis* as a natural entity fulfilling an innate human impulse toward moral perfection it follows that in the fully developed *polis* the end of the moral perfection is the measure of all things. For this reason the *polis* legitimately sets standards for every aspect of human existence, many of which from a modern perspective are not legitimate concerns of the "state" but rather self-regulating activities of families, churches, or voluntary associations in the "private" sphere of human life. Economics, for instance, is a part of politics, from the Aristotelian perspective, because wealth is a means to the moral end of the best possible human existence. Similarly, the *polis* is an educational institution, and the legitimate function of the lawmaker in the *polis* is to set moral standards and to train the young as well as to uphold in the mature proper standards of moral behavior; and Aristotle did not consider righteous behavior any less moral because it is prescribed by law rather than voluntarily performed through the citizen's good will. Education is thus the business of the authorities of the *polis,* and it is directed at the molding of character.

In his discussion of the impact of Aristotelian political theory upon later history, Barker notes that Aristotle, standing at the end but still spiritually within the *polis*-epoch of ancient history, believed that the distinction between an urbanized life-style of the Greek world and a rural life-style of the barbarian or non-Greek world was a natural one that should be maintained. With more foresight and perhaps because he came from the fringe of the Greek world, his pupil Alexander disregarded Aristotle's advice and ushered in an era of the *cosmopolis,* a concept of the equality and fraternity of all men sharing a common culture and a common law which dominated the Hellenistic, Roman, and medieval European understanding of the nature of human society. In the doctrine of Thomas Aquinas, however, the most substantial legacy of Aristotelian political thought, "constitutionalism," or the sovereignty of law over the executors of political authority, gained a dominant position of influence which Barker feels can be traced from Aquinas through Hooker to Locke and Burke, and so to the heart of Western European political assumptions. — *C.W.C.*

Additional Recommended Reading

Barker, Ernest. *The Political Thought of Plato and Aristotle.* London: Methuen & Co., Ltd., 1906. Barker's earlier detailed analysis of the *Politics,* including a valuable discussion of its later influence.

Jaeger, Werner. *Aristotle: Fundamentals of the History of His Development.* Oxford: The University Press, 1932. A provocative and influential work which interprets Aristotle as gradually relinquishing his early Platonic influences in favor of a studied empirical approach to philosophy.

Randall, John Herman, Jr. *Aristotle.* New York and London: Columbia University Press, 1960. Perhaps the most readable exposition of Aristotle's fundamental approach to philosophic questions, with a clear account of the relation of his political thought to his overall methodology and concepts.

Ross, Sir David. *Aristotle.* 5th ed., revised. London: Methuen & Co. Ltd., 1949. A full exposition of all Aristotle's major philosophic works, including the *Politics,* which follows closely the order of Aristotle's original text.

FORMULATION OF LOGIC

Type of event: Intellectual: development of new rules of thinking
Time: 335-323 B.C.
Locale: Athens

Principal personages:
ARISTOTLE (384-322), founder and head of the Lyceum
THEOPHRASTUS (c.370-c.287), successor to Aristotle and editor of his works on logic

Summary of Event

Aristotle's lecture notes on reasoning and demonstration were collected by his pupils and given the title *Organon,* meaning "instrument" or, in this case, "tool" for correct thinking. It is presumed that Theophrastus was in charge of this editing since he succeeded Aristotle as head of the Lyceum. The actual term "logic" as we understand it today was not used until five hundred years later by Alexander of Aphrodisias, a commentator on the works of Aristotle.

Six treatises make up the *Organon:* (1) *The Categories,* which is Aristotle's classification of terms as predicates; (2) *Topics,* a discussion on dialectical reasoning, or reasoning that proceeds from premises that are "generally accepted opinions"; (3) *Sophistical Refutations,* an appendix to the *Topics* and Aristotle's classification of common fallacies; (4) *On Interpretation,* a treatise dealing with the various relationships of propositions; (5) *Prior Analytics,* an analysis of the forms of argumentation and the development of the syllogism; and (6) *Posterior Analytics,* a section dealing with the content rather than the form of reasoning, and hence an analysis of the kinds of demonstration that will yield true conclusions.

Aristotle's work in logic has its most mature moment in the theory of the syllogism developed in the *Prior Analytics.* Basically, the syllogism is a construction of word relations, or premises, from which a necessary conclusion is deduced. In the earlier *Topics,* the term "syllogism" was used in a general way to signify any conclusive argument drawn from several premises. In the *Prior Analytics,* however, Aristotle specifically defines the syllogism as "a formulation of words in which from certain assumptions laid down, something other than what is assumed necessarily follows."

Aristotle then gives a detailed analysis of the various forms that the terms and premises must have in order to yield a valid conclusion. Symbols are used to represent any terms in the syllogism. For example, Aristotle states, "If A is predicated of all B, and B is predicated of all C, then A must necessarily be predicated of all C." If we substitute ordinary expressions for the letters, we can construct a syllogism as it is commonly understood. Let A represent "rational," B represent "men," and C stand for "Athenian citizens." Then we have: "All men are rational. Athenian citi-

348

zens are men. Therefore, Athenian citizens are rational."

Aristotle's subsequent analysis of the syllogism discloses its important components. In the syllogism constructed above, the term "men" appears in both premises, but not in the conclusion. Aristotle labels this the "middle term" since it mediates the necessary relationship between the other two terms. The term "rational" stands in the predicate position in the conclusion and is called the "major term." It also appears in one of the premises, now called the "major premise." The term "Athenian citizens" stands in the subject position of the conclusion, and is labeled the "minor term." It appears in the other premise, called the "minor premise." So the basic Aristotelian syllogism has three terms, each used twice; the major, the minor, and the middle terms. These terms are structured into three propositions; the major and minor premises, and the conclusion.

Concerning the propositions of the syllogism, Aristotle distinguishes their quantity from their quality. By the quantity of a proposition he means how many members of a class are to be included in the predication. For example, "A belongs to all B" is a universal proposition, while "A belongs to some B" is a particular proposition. The quality of a proposition is determined by whether the predicate is affirmed or denied of the subject. Combining quality with quantity, we have a four-fold classification of possible propositions that can be used in a syllogism: (1) universal affirmative (A belongs to all B); (2) universal negative (A belongs to no B);

(3) particular affirmative (A belongs to some B); and (4) particular negative (A does not belong to some B). The specific quantity and quality of each proposition in a syllogism determines the mood of that syllogism, and Aristotle works out in great detail which moods are valid and which are invalid.

A last important element of the syllogism is the figure, or *schema;* that is, the possible positions that the major and minor terms may have in relation to the middle term. He lists three possible figures depending upon the position of the middle term; why he does not give a fourth figure is a point of controversy. If A stands for the minor term, B for the middle term, and C for the major term, then possible figures are as follows: in the first, if C is predicated of B and B is predicated of A, then C is predicated of A; in the second, if B is predicated of C and B is predicated of A, then C is predicated of A; and in the third, if C is predicated of B and A is predicated of B, then C is predicated of A. Aristotle then constructs and tests logical forms according to their possible moods and figures.

While the syllogism is perhaps the greatest achievement of Aristotle's logic, it is only a portion of his legacy. His work includes an investigation of the conditions of valid argumentation, the use of categories which permit the development of a purely formal logic, and a systematic treatment of the rules of inference and implication. His was pioneering work as he himself attests, though he does not mean that no one had ever adduced cogent arguments before him. Rather the meaning is that no one predating Aristotle ever made

349

a systematic study of forms for argument, or scientifically analyzed such forms in the light of their structure and rules.

Much controversy has centered around the validity of Aristotle's claim to complete originality. Some have claimed that Aristotle owes the formulation of the syllogism to the methods of argumentation in the dialogues of Plato. Aristotle himself calls Plato's method of division a kind of "weak syllogism." He is quick to point out, however, that arriving at a conclusion through a process of dividing terms is really begging the question, since each division presupposes some knowledge prior to the division.

Aristotle's own formulation of logic was far from being complete, but it represents a monumental moment in the history of human thought. Very few areas of logical study do not trace back to Aristotle's system for points of comparison or contrast. It is difficult to measure the debt that centuries of study in logic owe to the analytical mind of Aristotle.

Pertinent Literature

Rose, Lynn C. *Aristotle's Syllogistic*. Springfield, Illinois: Charles C. Thomas, Publisher, 1968.

Aristotle's development of logic has engendered as many points of discussion as there are books on his monumental work. The *Organon* and the bulk of commentaries provided a frame of reference for most speculative thinking during the Middle Ages, a period when scholars generally interpreted Aristotle's logic as being bound to metaphysics. They believed that for every logical category of the mind there was a corresponding reality. The logic of the philosopher, therefore, was used to discover the necessary relations of things.

Post-Renaissance interpretation tended toward a more formal, or conceptual, interpretation which led to the development of new theories of logic. Contemporary logicians are almost unanimous in divorcing Aristotle's logic from any metaphysical commitments.

A perennial problem surrounding the *Organon* is the question of how much Aristotle's logic owes to Plato's method of definition and division.

Lynn C. Rose considers this problem in the first chapters of his book and claims that Aristotle's syllogistic was developed from Plato's method of division.

Rose points out a progression of methodology in Plato from the middle dialogues to the later ones which indicates the advancement of logical sophistication. Plato's method of division, Rose claims, is a form of demonstration or proof, not in the sense of a strict deductive demonstration, but in the sense of a "showing or revealing," which is precisely the kind of demonstration that Plato's doctrine of recollection demands. If learning is a recollection, then dealing with division of terms should gradually reveal the essential form that was once known but later forgotten. Aristotle's "begging the question" charge seems to lose its force in the light of this interpretation. Rose advances two reasons to show that the method of division leads directly to the formulation of the syllogism: first, Plato's method of division fits the perfect form of an Aristotelian syllogism; and second, Aristotle's terminology used in constructing the syllogism reflects the method of division.

Rose illustrates the first reason by giving an example of Platonic division: Divide the general idea of "plants" into things that are "trees" and "not trees"; next divide the idea of "trees" into "maples" and "not maples." If we now discard the non-applicable negations, we are left with three concepts: plants, trees, and maples. These concepts can be related according to the perfect syllogism of Aristotle; that is, a syllogism of the first figure whose premises are both universal affirmatives. Thus, if trees are plants and maples are trees, then it follows that maples are plants.

In the second reason, Rose claims

that the terminology of the perfect Aristotelian syllogism is reminiscent of Platonic division. For example, the "plants-trees-maples" relationship is called a "chain" or "series" and is essential to the division method of Plato. The expressions "major" and "minor" which Aristotle uses are merely the common terms "greater" and "smaller" that Plato also used. Other Aristotelian terms have a basis in mathematics which played an important role in Platonic thought.

Rose admits that Plato's dialectic does not contain a formal deductive system of logic. However, because of the similarities between Platonic division and the Aristotelian syllogistic, he infers that Aristotle was able to effect an easy transition from the former to the latter.

Solmsen, Friedrich. "Dialectic Without the Forms," in *Aristotle on Dialectic.* Pp. 49-68. Edited by G. E. L. Owen. London: Oxford University Press, 1968.

While Rose's interpretation stresses the similarities of the two thinkers, Friedrich Solmsen sees sharp differences because of Aristotle's abandonment of a Platonic ontology of Forms. First Solmsen concedes a similarity. Both Plato and Aristotle are concerned with producing proper definitions, which for both involves the right relationship of Ideas. In the case of Plato, it is the proper combining and separating of Forms. For Aristotle it is the discovery of the proper *genera* and differentiating qualities that specify the objects as members of the *genera*. In other words, Plato's approach to definition involves the Forms; Aristotle's approach involves the right *genus* and specific difference.

Solmsen points out that since the

Forms are involved in Plato's notion of definition, Plato commits his method to an ontology. For Plato, the Forms are truly Beings, so that his method of division is "designed to chart roads through the Cosmos of realities." Plato's practitioner of dialectic is one who discovers the truth of reality through reason.

According to Solmsen, Aristotle makes no such ontological commitment in formulating definitions through his dialectical syllogism. His terminology indicates that he ignores the ontological status of Forms, and is concerned with definition independent of any analogous structure of reality. If such be the case, then Aristotle would seem to be preparing the groundwork of a formal logic; that

351

is, a logic of the pure forms of thought with no reference to real things.

Solmsen claims that in abandoning the Platonic ontology of Forms (Being), and in submitting definitions to a more formal, conceptual structure, Aristotle departs from several important features of Plato's method of division: (1) Aristotle drops Plato's method of a "complete division" that begins at the point of the highest genus and continues down; (2) he "quietly shelves" Plato's organic division which was essential for a correct Platonic dieresis; (3) Aristotle is noncommittal concerning Plato's dichotomous division which seemed crucial for the important Platonic Forms of Sameness and Difference; (4) Aristotle's strict, logical distinction between genus and species "has no precedent in Plato," and in fact, Solmsen believes that the distinction would be at odds with Plato's notion of relations; (5) Pla-

to's method of division is fluid and elastic so that the search after the Forms is a trial and error method, and in abandoning the Forms, Aristotle creates hardened concept-relations because "rigid principles of logic take over," leaving little room for the flexibility that characterized Plato's method; and (6) for Aristotle, the model of scientific knowledge, *episteme,* is mathematics; therefore, dialectic is inferior to mathematics, which is a demonstrative science. For Plato, however, the reverse is true. Mathematics is inferior to dialectic since the mathematician does not have the "direct and genuine contact with Being" that the dialectician has.

Solmsen seems to have stronger arguments for the "differences" than Rose has for "similarities," but both interpretations raise interesting questions concerning the effect of Plato's dialectic on Aristotle's logic. — *J.J.R.*

Additional Recommended Reading

Kneale, William, and Martha Kneale. *The Development of Logic.* Oxford: The University Press, 1962. A detailed historical analysis which devotes an eighty-nine-page chapter to Aristotle's logic.

Lukasiewicz, Jan. *Aristotle's Syllogistic from the Standpoint of Modern Formal Logic.* Oxford: The University Press, 1957. A claim that Aristotle's syllogism is the source of modern symbolic logic, and that traditional interpretations have misrepresented Aristotelian logic.

Lloyd, G. E. R. *Aristotle: The Growth and Structure of His Thought.* Ch. 6 Cambridge: The University Press, 1968. An interesting nontechnical account of Aristotle's logic.

Patzig, Gunther. *Aristotle's Theory of The Syllogism.* New York: Humanities Press, 1968. An attempt to show that Aristotle's logic is better understood if divorced from ontology.

Ross, David. *Aristotle.* Ch. 2. New York: Barnes & Noble, Inc., 1966. A classical interpretation of Aristotle's logic.

FOUNDING OF ALEXANDRIA

Type of event: Political: the building of a new city
Time: January 20 (?), 331 B.C.
Locale: The Nile delta

Principal personages:
ALEXANDER THE GREAT, King of Macedonia 336-323,
who founded the city of Alexandria
DINOCRATES OF MACEDONIA, architect who planned the
city
PTOLEMY I, King of Egypt 306-283/2
PTOLEMY II, King of Egypt 283/2-246
SOSTRATUS OF CNIDUS, architect of the lighthouse at
Alexandria

Summary of Event

When Alexander the Great took Egypt from the Persians in 332 B.C., he had no intention of restoring the country as an independent kingdom. He meant to make it a province of his own, and he believed that a new Hellenic city would make a more suitable capital than one of the old Egyptian towns. This capital was to be named Alexandria in honor of himself as its founder. The site chosen was on the coast, on the western edge of the Nile delta, where the city would have easy communications with the interior by river and with the outside world by sea. Labor was conscripted from adjacent villages of Egyptian peasants and fishermen, and in 331 B.C. work began with impressive religious ceremonies. Greek seers prophesied that the city would become "large and prosperous, a source of nourishment to many lands." Construction of the metropolis took years to complete and was still proceeding in the time of Alexander's successors, Ptolemy I and Ptolemy II.

The original plan of the city was prepared by the architect Dinocrates, who had it laid out on the grid-pattern developed in the fifth century. It was divided into four large quarters by two broad avenues. Canopus Street, a processional boulevard one hundred feet wide, ran east and west along the long axis; a lesser street running north and south bisected it. At this intersection was the civic center containing the Court of Justice; the Gymnasium, a handsome, colonnaded building two hundred yards along its front; a series of sacred groves; and, most remarkable of all, an artificial hill dedicated to the god Pan. Its summit could easily be reached by a spiral path, and, from this point, visitors—and we know there were many—could survey the entire metropolis.

The most striking characteristic of Alexandria was its size. By the third century B.C. its population had already reached perhaps half a million. By the beginning of the Christian era it stood at nearly a million, rivaling even the capital of the Roman Empire. One quarter of the city was in-

353

habited mostly by Egyptians and half-caste Greeks, who had no civic rights and performed the menial labor of the city. Another quarter was the residence of the Jews, who came to Egypt in considerable numbers during the reign of Ptolemy I. They enjoyed a certain autonomy under their own ethnarch and council and constituted one of the most important Jewish settlements in all the ancient world.

The Greco-Macedonian quarter seems to have been near the sea breezes of the waterfront. It is probable that these Europeans were organized into *demes* and tribes, with an autonomous council and assembly. From east to west along the waterfront stretched warehouses and harbors which received merchantmen from up-river, from Mediterranean ports, and even, via a canal connecting the Nile River with the Red Sea, from the Orient. By the second century B.C. there was contact with India, and the streets of the port felt the gentle tread of Buddhist missionaries. Here, too, were the efficient dockyards of the Ptolemaic Navy.

The Royal Quarter was the most imposing of all. It was ornamented with the palaces of the Ptolemies and the nearby monumental tomb of the great Alexander. Here also was the great Serapeum, a magnificent temple dedicated to the dynasty's new god. The palace complex contained the famous Library and Museum, where the first two Ptolemies gathered the most distinguished minds of the third century for the furtherance of science and scholarship.

Dominating the skyline and even overshadowing the palace itself, rose the great stone lighthouse designed by Sostratus of Cnidus. It stood on the island of Pharos, which was connected to the mainland by a man-made mole nearly three-quarters of a mile long, pierced by two bridged channels for ships. The tower was over four hundred feet high, and was provided with a windlass so that firewood could be drawn to the top. Here fires blazed by night in front of a reflector of polished bronze.

In the third century the culture of this brilliant city eclipsed even that of Athens. The scholarship of Aristophanes of Byzantium, the astronomy of Aristarchus, the poetry of Callimachus, and the medical studies of Erasistratus all were the gifts of Alexandria to the world. The city was also an important bridge between the cultures of Greeks and Jews. The Septuagint, the Greek translation of the Old Testament, was begun here in the third century, and here the famous Philo worked later.

Alexandria was a forceful expression of both the good and evil qualities of Hellenistic culture. While the city was the birthplace of much that was good, it was also infected with hideous urban ills. Mobs of the poor sometimes rioted against the government and perpetrated scenes of frightful massacre. The city's pleasure domes housed the most sophisticated debauchery; its slums, the most sordid depravity. There was conflict between ethnic groups for the usual reasons. Egyptians swelled the ranks of the proletariat. The Greeks were the perfumed rich. Egyptians were prevented by law from marrying Greeks. Many Egyptians, therefore, could not regard the metropolis as a beneficent "source of nourishment," but hoped instead, as one oracle put it, that it could be made a dank place where fishermen dried their nets, as it had been before the coming of Alexander.

Pertinent Literature

Jones, A. H. M. *The Greek City from Alexander to Justinian.* Oxford: The Clarendon, Press, 1940.

Greek emigration overseas began about 750 B.C. and did not cease until around 200 B.C. One of the great folk-migrations of history, it carried the civilization of the Hellenes into almost every corner of the Mediterranean. The last wave followed the triumphant campaign of Alexander into Asia Minor, Syria, and Egypt, and built magnificent new cities such as Alexandria.

The city was the institution through which Hellenism expressed itself. Jones carries out his exposition on the nature and importance of the Greek city under five broad subject headings: (1) the diffusion of cities in the Orient, (2) their degree of dependence upon the suzerain when there was one, (3) their political organization, (4) the services they provided, and (5) their economic and cultural achievements. Each topic is discussed chronologically from the Hellenistic period through Roman Imperial times to the Byzantine age.

In the Hellenistic era a city was not only a physical collection of buildings; it was also a formal political institution with some degree of chartered autonomy. There was a council, or *Boule,* and usually an assembly, or *Ecclesia,* which had charge of local affairs. Civic instititutions included gymnasia, which were formally organized clubs for practicing Greek athletics and also for propagating the more important forms of Greek culture such as musical competitions, public reading of great literary works of past and present, and philosophical discussions. These functions were so important that civic magistrates called *gymansiarchs* were responsible for controlling and encouraging their memberships. Cities were also equipped with theaters where plays and mimes educated or diverted the citizens. Repertory companies of actors organized as Worshippers of Dionysos traveled from city to city under international guarantee of safe passage to perform the admired dramas of the classical period. A few metropolitan centers, such as Alexandria, Pergamum, and Antioch, accumulated huge libraries to preserve and promote Greek knowledge and wisdom. Some cities paid for the education of their citizens, although public schools did not strike deep roots. Doctors, however, were maintained at public cost fairly widely. Sewers protected public health. Fire brigades were equipped with mobile water pumps. A few places boasted street lighting.

The achievement of these cities in bringing Hellenism to the East was significant. Not only was Hellenism extended, but another great cultural innovation came out of the Greek cities and the Hellenized Oriental towns of the East; Christianity was the city-bred child of Hellenism and Judaism. Jones reminds us, however, that the depth of the impact of Hellenism may be exaggerated. While the Greek language was supreme in both the institutions of high culture and in the chambers of government, it did not really penetrate to the peasantry except in western Asia Minor. The strength of Hellenism grew less inland from the coastal regions because the Greek immigrants were, after all, too few to impress their civilization deeply on the much more numerous and sometimes hostile Oriental populations.

Sandys, Sir John Edwin. *A History of Classical Scholarship*. Volume I: *From the Sixth Century B.C. to the End of the Middle Ages*. Cambridge: The University Press, 1903. Reprinted, New York: Hafner Publishing Co., 1964.

Scholarship is defined very specifically by Sir John Sandys as studying literature to establish the exact text of an author and also to elucidate his meaning. The Greeks of the Alexandrian Library were the first to develop rules of scholarship similar to those in use today. The reason they felt compelled to do so was to help Greek education, for literary instruction was as important a part of Hellenistic schooling as it is of our own. The most important books of Greek literature were the *Iliad* and *Odyssey*, attributed to Homer. These epics were deeply revered for their poetic portraits of the gods and their vivid pictures of the human condition, at once heroic and tragic; they are now believed to have taken formal shape about 700 B.C., although alterations of the original texts were constantly taking place. Some changes occurred in copying one manuscript from another, while others were consciously made by the *rhapsodes* reciting them in public, and by forgers. The texts of the plays of the Athenian dramatists, as useful for education as Shakespeare, were subject to interpolation or omission of lines by actors, who played an important part in transmitting versions from one generation to another.

Aristotle was perhaps the first Greek to concern himself seriously with these textual problems. He was the first Greek we know of who collected a large library of manuscripts from which to deduce facts on the dates plays were written, statements of authorship, and similar data to help with literary studies. The first important research library, however, was the one established at Alexandria by Ptolemy I with the assistance of the philosopher Demetrius of Phalerum in Attica, a student trained in Aristotle's school. The library was much enlarged by Ptolemy II. Eventually it held a large number of papyrus rolls, though sources for this information give numbers varying from 400,000 to 700,000. The first librarian was Zenodotus of Ephesus who was appointed in 284 and whose work must have consisted mainly of searching for old manuscripts. Callimachus of Cyrene, who died about 240 B.C., published a descriptive catalogue of the library which itself took up 120 rolls classified by subject: drama, epic and lyric poetry, law, philosophy, history, oratory, rhetoric, and miscellaneous. Zenodotus found time to publish a new text of the *Iliad* and the *Odyssey* in which he sought to remove spurious verses.

Aristophanes of Byzantium, who died about 180 B.C., followed him as librarian and produced a superior text of Homer. The resources of the library permitted him to understand Greek dialects, including the Ionic-Aeolic in which the two epics were originally written. He excised or corrected verses which appeared in other dialects, or rejected some after carefully comparing old manuscripts. He used accents and punctuation to aid interpretation, and he also published corrected editions of the dramas of Aristophanes and Euripides.

The greatest Alexandrian scholar was Aristarchus of Samothrace, who died about 145 B.C. He was a sober, judicious, and, above all, a cautious critic. By collating different versions of Homer from places as widely separated as Athens and Chios, the published recensions of the *Iliad* and the *Odyssey* along with learned commentaries explaining words and phrases when the meaning was not clear. He also issued new texts of the plays of Sophocles and Aristophanes.

What were the results of so much activity? Very little. The scholars of the Alexandrian Library had no great influence over the texts of Homer in daily use, and the versions which have come down to us are those of the *rhapsodes. — S.K.E.*

Additional Recommended Reading

Downey, Glanville. *A History of Antioch in Syria*. Princeton: Princeton University Press, 1961. A detailed study of the capital city of the Seleucids.

Cadoux, C. J. *Ancient Smyrna. A History from the Earliest Times to 324 A.D.* Oxford: Basil Blackwell, 1938. A history of another major Greek city.

Davis, Simon. *Race Relations in Ancient Egypt*. London: Methuen & Co. Ltd., 1951. An interesting discussion of racial conflicts in Egypt and Alexandria and the various cultural backgrounds.

Parsons, Edward A. *The Alexandrian Library*. New York: Elsevier Press, 1952. Many strange details of the library are included in this curious volume.

Marrou, Henri I. *A History of Education in Antiquity*. Translated from the French by G. Lamb. New York: Sheed and Ward, 1956. An exhaustive and definitive account of the curricula and methods of ancient education.

Kenyon, Frederic G. *Books and Readers in Ancient Greece and Rome*. 2nd ed. Oxford: The Clarendon Press, 1951. A treatise on the making of ancient books or papyrus rolls, and the invention of the codex or modern leaved book, with some remarks on the book trade and literary tastes in ancient times.

ALEXANDER'S VICTORY AT GAUGAMELA

Type of event: Military: execution of a decisive battle
Time: October 1, 331 B.C.
Locale: Mesopotamia

Principal personages:
ALEXANDER THE GREAT, King of Macedon 336-323
PARMENION, Macedonian general
DARIUS III, King of the Kings of the Persian Empire
336-330
BESSUS, Persian Satrap of Bactria, who after the death of
Darius ruled as Artaxerxes IV 330

Summary of Event

After King Philip II of Macedon had defeated the Greek states in the Battle of Chaeronea, he made plans to invade the Persian Empire. His assassination in 336 B.C., however, cut short the operation of this scheme until his son Alexander had made his succession to the throne secure. In 334, Alexander invaded Asia Minor and quickly defeated the Persians on the Granicus River. He advanced eastward and in 333 at Issus, in northern Syria, defeated King Darius III himself. In 332, he took the wealthy province of Egypt.

By 331, Alexander was ready for a second and deciding battle with Darius for the supremacy of Asia. The Persian King had been collecting a large army, and he came westward as far as the plains near the village of Gaugamela (Tel Gomel in modern Iraq), where he waited to be attacked. His army consisted mainly of cavalry posted in long lines on level ground. The left wing was made up of his good Iranian horsemen, the Persians, some heavily mailed Saca, and the Bactrians, all commanded by Bessus, the Satrap of Bactria. Syrian, Mesopo-

tamian, and Median cavalry took stations on the right. Behind the cavalry was infantry, mostly troops of little fighting value who had been levied recently. Behind the center of the two fighting lines was Darius with his personal bodyguard and fifteen elephants. The Persian forces numbered over fifty thousand men.

In the autumn Alexander arrived at Gaugamela, and on October 1, led his army out of camp. He had forty thousand infantry and seven thousand horsemen, both Greek and Macedonian. His army was also in long lines, with the infantry placed in the center and half the cavalry on either flank. Parmenion commanded on the left while Alexander himself took charge of the right with his best squadrons of Macedonian heavy cavalry. Alexander's chief virtues as a general were his understanding of how to use cavalry and infantry together, and his gift for inspiring his men, either in battle or in the relentless, disciplined pursuit of a disorganized and fleeing foe. He now slowly advanced to his right while studying the enemy's array until the Hypaspists, a brigade of crack

358

Macedonian infantry, were facing some scythed chariots in front of the Persian center. He turned to face the enemy. Now Bessus sent the Saca charging at the extreme right of Alexander's cavalry. Alexander countered by bringing forward squadrons deployed behind them. There was a sharp fight with losses on both sides until Bessus' cavalry drew off to regroup. Meanwhile, the scythed chariots bounded forward against the Macedonian center, but here Alexander had posted troops armed with missiles, and these men shot down most of the chariot horses with their arrows and javelins before they reached the phalanx. The chariots, which did little damage to the Macedonians, were routed.

The cavalry action on Alexander's front had opened a gap between Bessus and the center of the long line of Persian horsemen. As soon as Alexander had his own horsemen under control, he charged into this gap, the infantry phalanx following him on the run. This blow was irresistible, and the Persians' lines began to crumple and stream towards the rear. Darius for the second time turned to flee. His personal guard of two thousand Greek mercenaries stood their ground and lost five hundred men, killed to win time for Darius to escape. As Alexander was reforming to pursue the Persian monarch, he received distress messages from Parmenion that the Persian right was pressing him hard,

and Alexander rushed across the field with his own cavalry to help. His timely arrival sent the Persian right reeling back, and the battle became a general rout. Alexander then drove his horsemen rapidly after the remnants of the Persian army, dispersing large numbers of fugitives, until he reached the city of Arbela after nightfall. But he did not succeed in catching up with Darius.

The Battle of Arbela (Gaugamela) was decisive. The Persians' forces were so scattered that they could not be reorganized. The Persian nobles believed that Darius was responsible for the debacle, and they accordingly deposed and killed him. Bessus, whose troops were the only ones to withdraw in fairly good order, became king as Artaxerxes IV. He, however, could not collect enough men to oppose Alexander's swift and inexorable advance. The Persians quickly lost their wealthiest provinces. The rich plains of Babylonia surrendered without resistance. Persis, the heartland of the empire, fell, and Persepolis, its religious capital, was also taken, along with some fourteen years' worth of accumulated tribute. Alexander eventually caught Artaxerxes and had him executed, alleging the murder of Darius III as an excuse. He also burned the magnificent royal buildings at Persepolis. This act signaled the fall of the Persian Empire, the beginning of Alexander's own, and the subjugation of the East to Macedonian imperialism.

Tarn, W. W. *Hellenistic Military and Naval Developments*. Cambridge: The University Press, 1930.

Alexander's conduct of his battles was a shining example to his junior officers, and they imitated so many features of his strategy that the Alexandrian military technique became the tactics of generals for the next century. The old-fashioned, straightforward melee of Classical Greece was finally obsolete. W. W. Tarn's small and readable book is an explanation of the new forms of warfare in Hellenistic times.

One important new feature, actually a development from the time of Alexander's father, was professionalism. Philip spent so many years campaigning that his troops acquired the experience of a standing army. This quality was maintained through the military institutions of the Hellenistic monarchies, which granted land to military settlers, who seem to have been required to spend two years on active service before passing to a kind of reserve as civilians. Technical problems raised by the increasing use of machines, the building of giant warships, and the complex new tactics ended the day of the gentleman amateur in war, such as Themistocles or Pericles had been. Generals and admirals now had to be professional students of war and tactics. Instead of charging at the head of their men, generals kept out of at least the early stages of a battle to be better able to control all their forces. For example, on the plain of Gaugamela Alexander had fed in his cavalry against Bessus without involving himself personally until the decisive charge was made at the gap in the Persian line.

Battles on land became increasingly complex, since the combined use of different kinds of troops was vital. Cavalry, which had not been important in classical times, now became a decisive arm, capable of attacking and riding down infantry. It was still impossible for horsemen to charge formed infantry frontally, but masses of cavalry could now be hurled at the flanks of a phalanx or into a gap opened in its line, as was done at Gaugamela. Infantry became more and more diversified. The heavily armored hoplite remained the basic foot soldier, but he found a complement in the *peltast,* a man equipped with lighter arms and armor for greater speed and mobility. There were also javelin men, archers, and slingers. Arrow-fire was the best counterstroke to a charge of horse, as Alexander's strategy against Darius showed. In turn, slingers were used against archers; leaden sling-bullets had a greater effective range than ancient bows and arrows.

The third century B.C. was the age of the war elephant. Contrary to some commonly held opinions, elephants were seldom used as mobile battering-rams to charge fortified places; on the few occasions when such an attack was made, the animals were repulsed. Against troops unfamiliar with elephants, especially against cavalry whose horses were unused to them, a charge of the great beasts could easily be decisive.

The technique of the siege became increasingly complicated. Covered battering-rams were used to attack walls; high, movable towers ("city-takers") were rolled forward against walls until bridges could be let down upon the top of the enemy's fortifications, whereupon assaulting infantry charged across the walls. Torsion engines of various sizes threw arrows, spears, or carefully rounded stones accurately up to an effective range of two hundred yards. A mis-

360

sile called a flame-carrier was invented; it was a cylinder filled with inflammable liquid for attack on wooden roofs or wooden siege engines. Iron armor was the main defense against it.

Navies were equipped with giant ships. The trireme was displaced by the quinquereme, a vessel with one bank of long, heavy oars, each pulled by five men. Flagships called "fifteens" were known, apparently gigantic triremes with three banks of rowers and five men on each oar.

Such craft were large enough to carry torsion artillery for attack on seaports.

The Hellenistic period was thus a time of great inventiveness and growing sophistication in the art of war. The expense of organizing properly equipped armies and navies and the need to build massive defensive works of stone added to the financial burdens of the Hellenistic states, and made the development of new sources of revenue a necessity. — *S.K.E.*

Pertinent Literature

Tarn, W. W. *Alexander the Great.* Cambridge: The University Press, 1948. 2 vols.

The personality of Alexander, like that of many great men of antiquity, remains something of an enigma. We know much about what Alexander did, but less about why he did it. What led him to attack the Persian Empire? What were his intentions in 334? Sir William Tarn attempts to answer these questions and to give as detailed a biography of Alexander as the ancient sources allow. Volume I is a well-written narrative of Alexander's career. Volume II contains a series of complicated essays explaining in detail how the author reached the more important conclusions of Volume I.

Alexander attacked the Persian Empire in 334 because he inherited the war from his father Philip. No doubt Alexander was influenced by Panhellenic idealism, that is, a desire to liberate the Greek territory in Asia Minor which had been taken over by the Persians. Tarn holds that Alexander did not intend more than the conquest of Asia Minor. The rapid

collapse of Persian resistance there possibly fired his adventurous imagination and led him on eastward, first into Syria and then on to Babylonia, Persis, and even India.

As a man, Alexander was an imperialist and conqueror. He had moments of cruel, dark passion when he was murderous towards even his friends. None of these facts can be denied. But he was at the same time much more. As an adolescent he had had no less a teacher than the great Aristotle, and if the philosopher taught him to despise non-Greeks as barbarians, a belief which Alexander outgrew as king, he also deeply influenced him to respect learning. Alexander's army escorted the first consciously organized scientific expedition of which we have record, made up of botanists, zoölogists, geographers, historians, and philosophers whose task was to record important phenomena observed in the course of the King's march. The in-

361

formation collected was sent back to Aristotle, and it came to form a significant part of the corpus of data used by the remarkable Greek scholars of the third century B.C.

Towards the end of his life Alexander devised an idealistic policy of ethnic fusion as one important facet of his plan for ruling the enormous territory he had overrun. In such a policy he ran counter to the racial narrow-mindedness of Plato and Aristotle. He persuaded eighty reluctant Macedonian officers to marry Persian and Iranian aristocratic ladies, and it was unfortunate that after his death seventy-nine divorces ensued. It may have been the experience of crossing most of the then known world that broadened his outlook and led him to enunciate the idea that "all men are sons of one Father," that is, that they are all brothers. The exact meaning and orig-inality of this notion are still argued, but some such idea was put forward by Alexander as the basis for the mixed Greco-Macedonian-Oriental government he began to shape for his polyglot empire.

Alexander passed his short life of thirty-three years in a world that he, more than any other man of antiquity, drastically changed. His stupendous march of conquest left an indelible impression on peoples everywhere. The world of the Greek was suddenly enlarged, and Greeks flocked after Alexander's standards into a new continent thrown open to them. The world of the Orient was plunged into subjection. Astonishingly enough, Alexander the imperialist became a folk hero in many Eastern lands. He became not only a Christian saint in the Abyssinian Church, but even a conquering hero of the Iranians whose empire he had pulled down.

Additional Recommended Reading

Wilcken, Ulrich. *Alexander the Great*. Translated from the German by G. C. Richards. London: Chatto and Windus, 1932. A treatment of Alexander's life by an authoritative German scholar.

Fuller, Major General J. F. C. *The Generalship of Alexander the Great*. New Brunswick: Rutgers University Press, 1960. This study of Alexander's campaigns by one of Britain's greatest professional strategists is a useful supplement to the biographies of the professional historians.

Brunt, P. A. "Persian Accounts of Alexander's Campaigns," in *Classical Quarterly*. Vol. XII (New Series, 1962), pp. 141-155. A study which shows that in our ancient Greek versions of Alexander's battles there is information derived from a source written from the Persian side.

ARISTOTLE'S ISOLATION OF
SCIENCE AS A DISCIPLINE

Type of event: Intellectual: development of an academic discipline
Time: 325-323 B.C.
Locale: Athens

Principal personage:
ARISTOTLE (384-322), founder and head of the Lyceum

Summary of Event

Aristotle came to Athens when he was seventeen years old and studied at Plato's Academy for twenty years. When Plato died in 347 B.C., Aristotle left the Academy and traveled for twelve years, visiting various centers of learning in Asia Minor and Macedonia. During this period of travel he developed his interest in the natural sciences, to which he applied his method of inquiry. He returned to Athens in 335 and established the Lyceum, a school which became a center of learning.

The range of topics discussed and developed by Aristotle at the Lyceum is overwhelming: Natural philosophy with its considerations of space, time, and motion; the heavenly bodies; life and psychic activities; ethical and political problems; animals and biological matters; and rhetoric and poetics.

Perhaps the most significant aspect of Aristotle's work is his development of a "scientific" approach to these studies. This "scientific" approach recognizes the existence of independent disciplines each employing its own principles and hypotheses. Such an approach also works out a methodology or procedure for each field of study, aiming at true and certain knowledge.

The Greek term that Aristotle uses for "scientific knowledge" is *episteme* which can best be translated as "true knowledge," or the "most certain knowledge." Medieval scholars translated the Greek *episteme* as the Latin *scientia* which came into English as "science."

In recognizing independent fields of study, Aristotle showed a significant departure from Plato's philosophy. Plato had envisioned one single science. For him true knowledge was the contemplation of the Forms: Virtue, Justice, Beauty, and Goodness. All other disciplines were subordinate to knowledge of the Forms. Aristotle, on the other hand, did not advocate a hierarchical structure of knowledge. Each study locates its own particular subject matter and defines its principles from which conclusions are to be drawn. Almost all his treatises begin with the same format: "Our task here concerns demonstrative science," that is, logic; or "Human conduct belongs to political science."

Aristotle's insistence upon the division of sciences, each using special principles, is indicative of his rejection of any absolute master plan of knowledge. He does, however, recognize "common principles," or principles

363

shared by more than one science. For example, the "equals from equals" principle of mathematics can be used in geometry to deduce a conclusion about a line. Aristotle warns the geometrician, however, that this can be done "if he assumes the truth not universally, but only of magnitudes." Aristotle never intends the same common principles to be universally applied in exactly the same way throughout all the sciences. If this were the case, there would not be "sciences," but rather "Science."

The second important feature of Aristotle's scientific approach concerns methodology. In the *Posterior Analytics,* he develops the general technique which the particular disciplines are to employ in order to achieve scientific knowledge. First, an investigation must always begin with what is "better known" to us. We must begin with observable data and facts, and not construct wild hypotheses. Second, we must proceed to a knowledge of the cause of the facts; mere observation is not enough. Observing something tells us only that something is the case; it does not tell us why it is the case. Learning the cause tells us why, and this involves a logical demonstration. Third, the cause or reason of the fact must be of "that fact and no other." This criterion is the basis for a scientific law since it demands a universal connection between the subject and its attributes.

The second and third criteria listed above require a deductive system of demonstration which is expressed in the form of the syllogism that Aristotle

developed in the *Prior Analytics.* There is also what might be called an "inductive" approach to his method of science. Aristotle raises the question of how we know the universal principles from which demonstration is to proceed. He answers that our knowledge of such principles begins with many sense perceptions of similar events. Our memory unifies these perceptions into a single experience. Our intellect or mind then understands the universal import of the experience. From many similar experiences we recognize a universal pattern.

Aristotle's method of science combines the theoretical and the practical. The theoretical aspect includes logical demonstrations and universal principles. The practical includes the necessary role of sense perception as it relates to particular objects. In the *Metaphysics* he warns that physicians do not cure men-in-general in a universal sense; rather they cure Socrates or Callias, a particular man. He adds that one who knows medical theory dealing with universals without experience with particulars will fail to effect a cure.

For Aristotle, therefore, scientific knowledge includes the observation of concrete data, the formulation of universal principles, and the construction of logical proofs. Greek "science" prior to Aristotle, largely a mélange of philosophical and quasi-mythological assumptions, blossomed, after the Stagirite's investigations, into the specialized work of a Theophrastus in botany, a Hierophilus in medicine, and an Aristarchus in astronomy.

Aristotle's Isolation of Science as a Discipline

Pertinent Literature

Randall, John Herman. *Aristotle.* New York: Columbia University Press, 1960.

In the third chapter of this book, John Herman Randall claims that it was Aristotle who invented the idea of a "science." Aristotle's *Prior Analytics* and *Posterior Analytics,* according to Randall, combine to produce all the needed ingredients of science: the syllogistic demonstration, the method of inquiry, and the subsequent division of the sciences. Concerning the method of inquiry, Randall notes that Aristotelian science comprises three factors: (1) that about which some conclusion is drawn; (2) what is concluded about the subject matter; and (3) the principles from which the conclusions are drawn. The first factor leads to the division of the sciences, since an investigation reveals that different subjects are treated with different principles. The second factor involves the deductive method of Aristotle's syllogistic demonstration.

Randall views Aristotle's method of demonstration as the scientific model employed by the "great scientific pioneers of the seventeenth century." What Aristotle did was to fit observable facts neatly into an orderly system of proofs. This, Randall says, is precisely what the great Isaac Newton did in synthesizing the work of his predecessors Copernicus, Kepler, and Galileo. In fact, Einstein uses a similar Aristotelian model in showing that Newton's prinicples were not ultimate principles of the universe, but only derived. It would seem that modern science owes a great debt to Aristotle, who showed us the "how" of a productive method of inquiry; that is,

he formulated intelligible schemata from what is commonly observed.

Randall believes that we have been mislead by "theorists of an empirical method" who have discredited Aristotle's notion of science. Men such as Francis Bacon, David Hume, and John Stuart Mill viewed Aristotle's method as sterile, and claimed that true science was born much later with the advent of the empirical method of investigation.

Randall counters this charge by labeling Aristotle's brand of empiricism correct. In this view, experience plays a necessary, but not a sufficient, role for scientific knowledge. All knowledge begins with empirical encounters, that is, with sense perceptions. However, seeing, hearing, and touching things is not the same as knowing the causal laws of things. "Experience can only 'illustrate' the law, it cannot 'prove' its truth." Scientific knowledge demands a conceptual expression. Aristotle formulated such expressions, and every scientist since has used a similar model. Galileo and Newton are excellent examples because they constructed their science in mathematical terms. Aristotle's demonstrative science was fashioned after a mathematical model.

Randall lists five steps of Aristotle's method of scientific inquiry as it is used in actual practice. (1) The object of the investigation is carefully determined. (2) All opinions and hypotheses of previous thinkers are examined. Randall believes that this step is indicative of the scientific

365

sense of "continuity" in Aristotle whereby knowledge advances by degrees with each thinker adding to the discipline. (3) A dialectical study of the previous opinions is made to see what difficulties and problems surround the subject matter. (4) The relevant facts are investigated. No arbitrary hypotheses are constructed; rather, reality is empirically searched for facts. (5) The facts are explained according to an intelligible structure. These explanations are what Aristotle calls the "causes" or "principles" of things. They are what we ultimately seek in a scientific study.

Randall concludes his interpretation by anticipating an objection: If Aristotle had such a good method, then why was he wrong about so many things? For example, Aristotle denied that light has a velocity, or that the earth moves. Randall answers that Aristotle was too much of an empiricist. He trusted his observations of nature, and had no instruments with which to observe more closely. While Aristotle may have erred in many of his observations, Randall feels that he was correct in his logical formulation of a scientific method which paved the way for modern science.

Dewey, John. *Reconstruction in Philosophy.* New York: Henry Holt, 1920.

Whereas Randall interprets Aristotle as a forerunner of modern science, John Dewey sees him as delaying the advancement of scientific knowledge for centuries. Dewey's general criticism of Aristotle's method of investigation centers on the latter's view of nature. The man of Aristotelian science is a passive observer of nature. Nature is never "worked on" and changed for the better. The centuries that followed Aristotle saw his conceptual frame of reference accepted, and the world eternalized so that new concepts of the universe were unthinkable. The true method of science, according to Dewey, began not with Aristotle, but with Francis Bacon, who published the *New Organon* in 1620.

Specifically, Dewey sharply criticizes both aspects of Aristotle's scientific method, namely, the syllogistic demonstration, and the empirical "induction" of particular events. Basing his challenge on Bacon's work, Dewey charges that the demonstrative syllogism aims at conquering the mind rather than nature. It is a "self-revolving manipulation" of what was already known. Bacon had likened the syllogism of Aristotle to the web of a spider: an orderly, elaborate structure, but in the end only a trap. The syllogistic reasoning process is a trap made to catch the universal truths that were known all along. Aristotle's empirical aspects of his science also fairs poorly under Dewey's scrutiny. Aristotle had maintained that knowledge began with sense perceptions of particular objects. This accumulation of perceptions "led up to" (induction) the universal principles of knowledge. Dewey complains, however, that once these universal concepts are grasped experience and nature are left behind, untouched and unchanged. The only way to discover new facts about nature is to conduct "active experiments" on nature. This is not found in Aristotle's science. In fact, Aristotle's "empiricism" is nothing but a "passive accumulation" of

366

gross observations. Bacon compared Aristotle's "inductive" method with that of an ant which busily gathers up heaps of raw material, but never transforms them. Dewey disputes the claim that Aristotle pioneered inductive science. The true "father of induction," he states, is Bacon, whose logical method explores the unknown aspects of nature rather than merely spinning a logical repetition of what is already known.

Dewey also discredits the important Aristotelian principle of potentiality. Dewey states that in modern science "potentiality" implies "invention," "novelty," or the possibility of a new emergence. Aristotle's notion of "potentiality," simply means the repetition with which a particular thing completes its cycle. For example, the acorn is said to have the "potentiality" for becoming an oak tree. Each thing's "potentiality," therefore, guarantees the eternal cycle of its species. According to this interpretation, there would be no room for a theory of evolution.

Dewey rejects Aristotle's notion of science from the point of view of the method of that science, and what can be gained from that method. He asserts that real scientific progress began when Aristotelian "science" was abandoned. — *J.J.R.*

Additional Recommended Reading

Anton, John P. *Aristotle's Theory of Contrariety*. London: Routledge and Kegan Paul, 1959. An appreciation of Aristotle's principles as the "beginnings" of scientific inquiry.

Jaeger, Werner. *Aristotle, Fundamentals of the History of His Development*. Oxford: The University Press, 1934. A scholarly work that represents Aristotle's thought as a continual development away from Platonism and toward an empiricism.

Smith, Vincent Edward. *Science and Philosophy*. Milwaukee: The Bruce Publishing Company, 1965. The author is sympathetic toward Aristotelian science, and although only the first chapter is devoted to Aristotle, the terminology throughout is Aristotelian.

Solmsen, Friedrich. *Aristotle's System of the Physical World*. New York: Cornell University Press, 1960. A claim that Aristotle contradicts all the "scientific" queries into nature by ultimately appealing to a cause outside of nature, namely, The Unmoved Mover.

Woodbridge, Frederick. *Aristotle's Vision of Nature*. New York: Columbia University Press, 1965. Aristotle's thought is presented as a relevant naturalism concerned with dynamic categories of life and reality.

CREATION OF THE NEW COMEDY

Type of event: Cultural: development of a new form of drama
Time: c.320 B.C.
Locale: Athens

Principal personages:
MENANDER (342/341-291/290), judged by posterity to be the greatest playwright of New Comedy
DIPHILUS (before 340 - after 289), another New Comedy playwright
PHILEMON (c.361-262), judged by his contemporaries to be the greatest playwright of New Comedy

Summary of Event

Greek New Comedy, developed in and for Athens, and representing a final phase in the brilliant development of Greek dramatic art, may be regarded as the last flowering of Attic literature, the last expression of Athens' cultural domination of the Greek world. The new form was created during the period that saw the conquests of Alexander the Great reshaped into the great Hellenistic kingdoms which became new centers of culture and produced a literature that was Hellenistic rather than Attic. But the new comedy held a place of honor in the Greek culture that spread throughout the Hellenistic world. Its popularity and its influence on subsequent literary developments were such that it may be regarded also as the first flowering of Hellenistic literature.

Old Comedy, represented for us by the surviving plays of Aristophanes (c.448-c.385 B.C.), was bawdy and hilarious, peopled by grotesques with one foot in "never-never land" and the other firmly planted in contemporary Athens. Plots were loosely strung together and consisted of a series of ad-

ventures that allowed characters, from their out-of-this-world vantage point, to exhibit and attack the follies of contemporary society. Great names were bandied about with freedom, and men of power, such as Pericles, were not immune to lampooning, nor were cultural giants such as Socrates and Euripides.

Philemon, Diphilus, and Menander are the great names of New Comedy. Their plays, despite great popularity in the ancient world, were lost during the Middle Ages, and of the two first mentioned, only fragments remain. The sands of Egypt have yielded ancient copies of Menander, however, and of the more than one hundred plays he is known to have written, we possess one in entirety, the *Dyscolus,* and extensive fragments of several others. New Comedy, as judged from these remnants and from imitations written by the Latin playwrights Plautus and Terence, owed more to Greek tragedy than to Old Comedy. Plots are carefully constructed, with complications leading to a marked reversal and resolution; the characters are drawn neither from myth nor from fantasy,

368

but from everyday city life, and they are endowed with traits of personality that motivate their actions and the plot in general. Their concerns are domestic, centering on family and property; political and religious concerns, if present, are peripheral. The plays of this new genre are comic in the Aristotelian sense of having happy endings. They do not inspire the savage laughter associated with Old Comedy; their humor is muted, indulgent, and takes note of the nobility which is mixed with the folly of man.

The difference between the works of New Comedy and the dramatic literature that preceded it is partly the result of change in the political climate of Athens, which with the rest of Greece had come under foreign domination. After Philip of Macedon defeated the largely Athenian forces at the Battle of Chaeronea in 338 B.C., Athens was governed by one foreign prince after another. After a few abortive attempts to throw off the yoke, her people gave up their former interest in matters of state. The Hellenistic Age produced no epic or drama in the old, grand style. Audience and writer alike were too little involved in political decision-making to take an interest in such literature; princes and generals, whose interest in matters of state was lively, were too powerful to be criticized or even examined.

As a result, the drama of the age was in a sense diminished, contracting its scope so as to encompass, not the life of the social or political body, but the life of the individual in the context of his immediate family. Much was lost in this change, but something was gained as well. In concerning itself with matters of everyday life, New Comedy addressed itself to broader classes of men and more universal problems than had the aristocratic drama of the preceding periods. Hellenistic literature in general followed the lead of New Comedy in concerning itself chiefly with the life and experience of the individual.

Modern critics often find New Comedy a disappointing contrast to the great dramatic literature of Athens' golden age. But the ancient world prized Menander as a poet-teacher comparable to Homer and the tragedians, and the influence of New Comedy on later dramatic literature can hardly be overestimated. New Comedy was among the models for the first works of Latin literature, which came into being only fifty years after Menander's death. Though Menander's comedies, and those of his competitors, were lost during the Middle Ages, the works of their Latin imitators survived to exercise a profound influence on Western drama in the Italian *commedia dell'arte,* in Molière, in Shakespeare, and afterwards.

Pertinent Literature

Post, L. A. *From Homer to Menander.* Berkeley and Los Angeles: University of California Press, 1951.

In an age when students read poetry little and late, it is difficult to imagine that in ancient Greece the poets were the teachers of heritage, the repository of culture, and the first object of study. In taking note of this difference Post recognizes that poetic fiction was powerful in shaping human consciousness, and he devotes his book to examination of the poets most highly valued by the Greeks: Homer; the tragedians Aeschylus, Sophocles, and Euripides; and Menander. He is particularly attentive to the moral attitudes which they embody and convey.

In Post's view, Homer's *Iliad* expressed and established the tragic view of life in presenting Achilles' choice between a long, obscure life and a short, glorious one, and in portraying, at the same time, all that men do and suffer in the face of powers they cannot control and limitations they cannot overcome. The bulk of Post's book is spent considering the writers of Greek tragedy, whom he regards as exploring and elaborating this heroic tradition, and particularly the incongruity between glory and death, or between morality and mortality.

The relationship between Greek epic and Greek tragedy is generally recognized; Post's special contribution in this book is his elucidation of the relationship between the early epic and the later comedy or New Comedy specifically, for he dismisses Old Comedy as having failed to give serious consideration to the consequences of human decision, action, and suffering.

Post proposes that the *Odyssey* provided a starting point for Greek New Comedy just as the *Iliad* had done for Greek tragedy. The *Odyssey* glorified domestic happiness. The reunion of husband and wife, or of father and son, is the goal achieved after the surmounting of great ob-

stacles on the part of all the principals. This success story, as Post designates it, represents an essentially comic point of view. The obstacles that block a character's way to welfare and happiness are not viewed as insurmountable; the tension between desire and destiny is not irreconcilable. Dangers and reversals further the cause of happiness by causing characters to develop new resources and insights in the course of overcoming them.

Like the *Odyssey* before them, Menander's plays were called "a mirror of life"; his interest in the relationship between the sexes and between the generations, and his use of scenes of recognition and reconciliation as expressions of intellectual and moral growth, reveal Menander clearly as the heir of the poet of the *Odyssey*. His writings are ethical in every sense of the word: in depicting current custom, in stressing the moral qualities of his characters, in rewarding virtue with a happy ending, and in exerting an uplifting effect upon his audience.

No account of the development of New Comedy can ignore its relationship to the dramatic literature of the preceding era, and Post makes it clear that New Comedy was as much the descendant of Greek tragedy as of Homer's *Odyssey*. Greek tragedy had developed from a preoccupation with the nature of divinity to a preoccupation with the nature of man; of the latest tragedian, Euripides, it was said that he showed men as they are rather than as they ought to be, and Post finds the immediate antecedent of New Comedy in such domestic drama as Euripides' *Alcestis*.

The plots of the new comedy depend in large part on the problems of human understanding. Misunderstanding leads to confusion and often to unkindness or even violence. Enlightenment, often represented by the famous scenes of "recognition" involving long-lost relatives, leads to repentance, forgiveness, and reconciliation. This emphasis on repentance and forgiveness, a kind of moral growth through ordeal, is largely absent from earlier Greek literature, and represents, in Post's opinion, Menander's special contribution to the Greek view of morals and the human condition.

Webster, T. B. L. *Art and Literature in Fourth Century Athens*. London: The Athlone Press, 1956.

As Post describes the place of Menander in terms of the development of classical literature over centuries of time, so Webster illumines the relationship between Menander and the philosophical and literary developments of his own time.

Webster describes the intellectual history of fourth century Athens in terms of the three philosophers who dominated that century, organizing the bulk of his book into three sections: art and literature in the time of Plato, in the time of Aristotle, and in the time of Theophrastus. He associates with the early fourth century a mode of thought familiar in the works of Plato: that of seeing the world in terms of contrasts. Plato describes a world of Forms that contrasts with and yet illuminates our world of sense-perception. Writers and artists of his time exhibit the same attitude, often referring to a higher plane of myth in order to illuminate, by way of comparison and contrast, the world about them.

The middle fourth century saw the revolution in thought that separates the Hellenic from the Hellenistic world. Aristotle's interest in, and his grasp of, biology shaped his attitudes toward society and toward art. All that exists must be shaped into systems and accounted for in terms of purposeful organic composition. Division and contrasts are minimized; artists and writers concentrate on the relationship of all parts in any system to the whole. It is the whole, however defined, that is important.

New Comedy is a development of the late fourth century, when Theophrastus succeeded Aristotle as head of the Peripatetic school. Theophrastus was a scientist and researcher of great energy, and though we possess little of his writing, we see that he developed Aristotle's thought in directions that gave new emphasis to the concepts of individuality. Where Aristotle had emphasized broad categories and the links between parts in a whole, Theophrastus emphasized minute subdivisions, and the particularity of different things.

So Menander, Theophrastus' friend and pupil, reflects intellectual developments of his own time as he brings to drama a new concern for the interplay of character and environment in everyday life. His characters fall into familiar categories, but are nicely distinguished from one another by their motives and their circumstances. Their shortcomings elicit sympathy as well as laughter, and the inevitable happy ending constitutes a statement of faith that each different individual is capable of finding his own proper good.

Each of Webster's three main sections opens with an account of the political situation in Athens during the period concerned. The period of Theophrastus' prominence, including the whole working life of Menander, was marked by political events of considerable import and interest, and it is astonishing that the literature of the period reflects so little of this. The personal lives of men of letters, including Theophrastus and Menander, were greatly affected by political changes involving restriction of citizen rights and a succession of princely rulers representing foreign domination. But events of this sort were regarded as imposed from outside, rather than as arising out of the life of Athens itself. The ordinary citizen had to learn, not how to control his political and social environment, but only how to live with it. Webster does not dwell on this point, but from his own presentation it appears that the philosophical and literary concern with everyday life represented by Theophrastus and by New Comedy was as much a response to political conditions as a natural outgrowth of Aristotelian thought. — *Z.M.P.*

Additional Recommended Reading

Bieber, Margarete. *The History of the Greek and Roman Theater.* Princeton: Princeton University Press, 1961. Full use of artistic and architectural remains helps to place the different types of ancient drama in their living context.

Norwood, Gilbert. *Greek Comedy.* London: Methuen & Co., Ltd., 1931. A history of comedy from its origins through Menander.

Lever, Katherine. *The Art of Greek Comedy.* London: Methuen & Co., Ltd., 1956. A newer and briefer history of ancient comedy.

Webster, T. B. L. *Studies in Menander.* Manchester: Manchester University Press, 1950. A thorough and readable study of Manander's work as it was known before the publication of the *Dyscolus*.

Blake, Warren E. *Menander's Dyscolus.* New York: The American Philological Association, 1966. Text and translation of the only New Comedy play we possess complete.

BUILDING OF THE APPIAN WAY

Type of event: Military: construction of a major Roman highway
Time: 312-264 B.C.
Locale: Latium and Campania, south of Rome

Principal personages:
APPIUS CLAUDIUS CRASSUS, surnamed CAECUS ("the Blind," fl.c.300 B.C.), Roman consul, censor in 312 B.C.
MARCUS ULPIUS TRAIANUS AUGUSTUS, Roman Emperor A.D. 98-117

Summary of Event

During the first centuries of the gradual conquest of Italy by the Roman Republic, there were no major roads to connect the growing city on the Tiber River with other areas. Whereas the Persians had created a partially paved road system through their wide domain, Italian travel was limited before 300 B.C. In the early fourth century short gravel or dirt trackways reached out from Rome to Alba Longa twelve miles to the south, and east to the saltbeds in the mountains. The official called *censor* was charged among other duties with maintaining such roads.

The earliest paved highway of any length in Italy was begun in the year 312 B.C. when the censor Appius Claudius Crassus surnamed Caecus, "the Blind," took the initiative in projecting a military highway south from Rome. Appius was a vigorous patrician also credited with constructing Rome's first aqueduct and with enrolling plebeians in the senate; he was consul twice. The road he began, however, which was named the Via Appia, was his chief monument.

Surveyors laid out the first fifty miles on a straight southwest line paralleling the seacoast, about a doz-

en miles inland. Rapid military access to the coast may have been one purpose for the highway. Its chief original objective, however, was the key city of Capua, in the heart of the fertile Campanian plain, which had recently been captured by Roman armies. Roman military colonies had been founded in strategic sites near Capua.

Less than twelve miles of the new road was paved immediately. Here laborers dug a trench fifteen feet wide and three feet deep. Lining this with layers of loose gravel and small rock, they carefully fitted into place as a surface large slabs of polygonal stone. This segment of the road climbed to a ridge, from which it provided panoramic views of flat lands toward the sea as well as the Alban Hills to the east. An old village, Bovillae, was the first post-station and the end of paving in 292 B.C.

Climbing and descending more steeply, travelers reached the village of Ariccia where many, including the poet Horace, spent the first night out of Rome. At such points the road was intersected by a crossroad, used by farmers to bring produce to a village market. Beyond Ariccia were the broad Pomptine Marshes, where it

373

was necessary to drive in wooden pilings to raise a causeway six feet above the swamp land. At a trade center called Forum Appii, the road ended temporarily; travelers could take boats twenty miles to Terracina or choose a long detour inland.

South of Terracina were mountains, forcing a zig-zag route until in Imperial times a sea-level road was cut into the cliffs. A four-arch brick bridge crossed the Liri River, and at Sinuessa the road turned sharply eastward along the Volturno River until it crossed on another massive bridge into Capua, 132 miles from the Roman Forum.

Too blind to see the finished project, the old censor whose name the road bears was said to have walked barefoot on it to feel that the stones were well placed. Later the highway was stretched out to Venusia, a colony settled by twenty thousand inhabitants, and by 264 B.C. the road reached the sea at the ports of Tarentum and Brundisium, a total of 366 miles from Rome.

Other highways later shared the traffic, but the Via Appia remained into Imperial times the chief route south of Rome. About 250 B.C. milestones were placed at intervals of five thousand Roman feet. Trees planted by the roadside shaded travelers. In ancient and medieval periods rich Italians built tombs along the road, which became lined also with markets, towns, temples, monasteries, and such churches as the one where by legend Saint Peter, while fleeing from Rome, met his Lord and turned back.

Finally paved to Brundisium by the Emperor Trajan in A.D. 114, the Appian Way was called the "Queen of Roads" by the poet Statius. By that time a complex web of roadways, built to the same pattern, crisscrossed the Empire. Built to last, on deep-set roadbeds resistant to flood or frost, these roads bound together Rome's conquests. Although originally military passageways, they served many other purposes, as Romans such as Cicero and provincials such as the Apostle Paul traveled on them.

In paving their fifty-three thousand miles of roads, the Romans used many local stones, but the most common type in Italy was the hard green-black volcanic basalt used along much of the Appian Way. While in many places floods or cultivation have obliterated the old road, long stretches are still usable, paralleling more modern highways.

Pertinent Literature

Ashby, Thomas. *The Roman Campagna in Classical Times.* New York: The Macmillan Company, 1927.

Although there is no monograph in English on the Appian Way, Thomas Ashby's painstaking study of the territory around Rome supplies a clear picture of the area south of the city through which Appius Claudius Caecus first pushed his road. Ashby devotes a detailed chapter to the Via Appia in ancient and modern times. Based on a review of classical and modern writings, on maps and topographical studies by many investigators as well as on his own exhaustive exploration of the plain around Rome called the Campagna as well as of the entire length of the Via Appia, this book describes all the roads leading out of Rome and their main tributaries, with particular attention to what remained in 1927 along such routes: city gates, tombs, towers, walls, villas, inscriptions, milestones, bridges, and towns.

Ashby himself owned valuable drawings made along the Via Appia in 1777 by an Italian artist, and he located many other sources of information not available outside Italy. Apparently he intended to publish a more extensive study of the Via Appia and its remains, but he never completed the project.

After explaining the geology and geography of central Italy, the author traces the early history of the Campagna, arguing that the Via Latina, the Via Salaria, and some other roads are older than the Via Appia. Since there is inadequate evidence for the precise dating of most early Roman roads, and since they were paved piecemeal over long periods, Ashby recognizes that it is difficult to designate the precise contribution of any single roadbuilder. Nevertheless, he provides a rich potpourri of history, correlating Roman conquests with road construction and the names of Roman officials recorded in ancient writings and on milestones as connected with sections of the highways.

In a review of the upkeep of Republican roads, the author critically analyzes references in classical authors to the construction and character of highways and bridges. Then, using the chief roadways as an organizing outline, he studies in order the eastern, southeastern, coastal, and northern routes radiating from the city. Forty-eight photographs, six of which especially concern the Via Appia, are given.

Although this book is a scholarly work and unfortunately lacks maps, which are badly needed to illuminate the text, Ashby's work is invaluable for any student desiring to investigate the early Roman road system. It offers fascinating word glimpses of scenes from historic events, ancient and modern, as the author narrates incidents and mentions notable personalities related to the old buildings, tombs, and other remains along the roads. A sentence from the chapter on the Via Appia will illustrate: "Here or hereabouts, too, Gavin Hamilton found the Discobolus preparing for the throw, a copy of a work of the sculptor Naucydes in 1792; it is now in the Vatican."

Ashby shows the significance of side roads by which the Via Appia and other thoroughfares open up Latium and the flatlands of Campagna to commerce and travel. By grouping together the roads leading to the Alban Hills and the southeast, and by full descriptions of the Via Latina, the Via Ardeatina, and other roads parallel to or crossing the Via Appia, he explains their interdependence.

Building of the Appian Way

Von Hagen, Victor W. *The Roads That Led to Rome.* Cleveland: World Publishing Company, 1967.

Von Hagen, Victor W. *Roman Roads.* Cleveland and New York: World Publishing Company, 1966.

These twin publications supplement each other. The author is an American ethnographer and archaeological historian who spent eight years studying Incan, Aztec, and Mayan highways in Central and South America, followed by five years heading a Roman Road Expedition which has recently and systematically explored the widespread network of Roman roads in thirty-four European, African, and Near Eastern countries. The 1967 book is a handsome publication with hundreds of color photographs showing remains of roads, bridges, tunnels, gateways, and other objects pertaining to the famous system of Roman highways. Although it is designed for the general reader and is well within the grasp of students, the book summarizes a vast amount of detailed information. Being focused more particularly on roads than Ashby's study and based on far wider exploration, Von Hagen's 1967 work offers more graphic insight into the engineering and general significance of these old arteries of transportation. It vastly enlarges the scope of study, attempting to comprehend the entire Empire, whereas Ashby concentrated on central Italy. Understandably, Von Hagen neglects some areas such as Mesopotamia, but he traces roads around the Mediterranean and north through Europe to England.

Good but not complete bibliographic information is included on ancient, medieval, and modern efforts to describe and map Roman roads.

Surprisingly lacking, however, are any detailed maps; only one vague overall view of the Roman road system is included, and this is difficult to correlate with the written text, since few towns or road names are indicated. The kaleidoscopic treatment, while vivid in some respects, is disappointingly vague on such topics as the Via Appia and the other main highways in Italy, which are given no consecutive description either geographically or historically.

In one section of his 1967 work Von Hagen begins to give a summary of the development of the Via Appia, tracing it north from Brundisium to Beneventum, a south Italian junction for six significant highways. Then he follows other roads toward Rome before returning south via Naples, illogically, to go north again on some minor coastal roads to Ostia. His literary device of following from all directions the "roads that led to Rome" seems confusing compared to the technique of Ashby, who begins the account of each major road at Rome and follows them out, with logically related attention to their side roads.

Von Hagen's earlier work, *Roman Roads*, is identical with his 1967 book in only a few features, such as a "Chronological Table of Roman Road Building" which outlines the known dates for construction and repairs of various roads. The 1966 publication is far less ambitious in scope but is better organized, beginning logically with the Via Appia's

376

construction and a review of that road's significance in Roman history. Chapters follow on the extension of roadbuilding during the Carthaginian Wars, on African roads, on Asiatic routes and their trade significance, and then on highway construction in Italy, Gaul, Spain, the Balkans, and Britain. A clear account of Rome's conquests is correlated with a fairly consecutive narrative about road construction and its significance in wars, economic development, and political evolution. Short summary chapters are included on bridges, milestones, and inns.

While the 1966 book has fewer photographs and none in color, they are well-chosen and placed to illustrate adjacent text. Younger students will find it easier to read than Von Hagen's 1967 publication, for *Roman Roads* assumes less background knowledge and tells a consecutive story in a manner interesting even to scholars. — *R.B.M.*

Additional Recommended Reading

Mooney, William M. *Travel Among the Ancient Romans.* Boston: Gorham Press, 1920. A brief description of routes and methods of travel, inns, and travel problems

DeCamp, L. Sprague. *Ancient Engineers.* Pp. 164-259, New York: Doubleday & Company, Inc., 1963. Includes a lengthy section on Roman engineering, including techniques used in building roads.

Rose, A. C. "Via Appia in the Days When All Roads Led to Rome," in *Annual Report of Board of Regents.* Washington: Smithsonian Institution, 1935. A short but valuable summary of the road and its history.

Forbes, R. J., and R. G. Goodchild. "Roads and Land Travel," in *A History of Technology.* Edited by Charles Singer. Vol. II, pp. 493-536. Oxford: The Clarendon Press, 1954-1958. A brief description of ancient and medieval roads, with excellent cross-section diagrams of Roman roadbed construction.

Adcock, F. E. "The Conquest of Central Italy," in *The Cambridge Ancient History.* Vol. VII, pp. 582-616. Cambridge: The University Press, 1928. This detailed account of Roman history in the period of Appius Claudius Caecus has an excellently detailed map of central Italy.

THE TEACHING OF EUHEMERUS

Type of event: Intellectual: propagation of a theology
Time: c.300 B.C.
Locale: Greco-Roman world

Principal personages:
EUHEMERUS (fl.c.315), Sicilian writer
HECATAEUS OF TEOS (fl. fourth century), contemporary of Euhemerus who held similar views
ENNIUS (239-170), Latin poet who translated Euhemerus' *Sacred History*

Summary of Event

Little is known about Euhemerus— apparently a native of Messana in Sicily—except that he served at the court of Cassander of Macedon c.300 B.C. and wrote a so-called *Sacred History* about the same time. However the influence of his teachings, called "euhemerism," was considerable in the Roman world and has come down to modern times. Stated briefly, euhemerism regards myths, but especially deities, as mere transformations or sublimations of actual historial events and personages. While it is, then, a specific way of interpreting myths and religions, euhemerism often is generalized to mean any rationalistic explanation of the supernatural.

Euhemerus reached manhood during the Hellenistic period, an age when the Greek world was transformed. Alexander the Great had not only broken the viability of the Greek city-states by creating an international and cosmopolitan empire, but he had also provided the opportunity for the cross-fertilization of Near Eastern and Greek traditions. That the fragmentation of the Alexandrian Empire following the founder's death in 323 did not halt the trend of disillusionment with the old beliefs and religions is obvious in the questioning attitude of the philosophic schools that arose following the Socratic revolution, especially the individualized interpretations of the Skeptic, Cynic, Stoic, and Epicurean.

The Olympian deities and the gods of other nations came under progressively closer scrutiny. An earlier contemporary of Euhemerus, and one who doubtless influenced him greatly, was Hecataeus of Teos, who explained the gods of Egypt as mere deified benefactors of mankind, and who argued that the Greek gods themselves had come from Egypt.

Euhemerus' *Sacred History* is a romantic tale of an imaginary journey from Arabia to the island of Panchaea in the Indian Ocean. In a temple there, the narrator found a golden column on which was inscribed the history of Ouranos, Kronos, and Zeus, described as outstanding men. Because of their great contributions to the happiness of mankind they were gratefully deified. Zeus began to be worshiped in the island of Crete, where Greeks came to know him. It is interesting to speculate on the question whether

378

Euhemerus was motivated by a desire to explain the origin of gods or whether, on the contrary, he was in some way preparing to justify the apotheosis of great men, a practice which after the deification of Lysander and Alexander the Great started to become increasingly fashionable in the Greek world. In any case the influence of Euhemerus and his followers was significant. Among his immediate followers were Leon of Pella and, especially, Dionysios Skytobrachion, who later claimed that such a god as Dionysus was merely an ancient king who had been granted divine honors for his service to civilization. In addition to rationalizing the origin of gods, euhemerism led to the romanticization of classic themes and the anthropomorphizing of deities in such novels as the third century *Trojan Histories* of Hegesianax and the second century work called the *Campaign of Dionysos and Athena.*

Euhemerism was introduced into Rome early in the second century B.C. when the poet Ennius provided a Latin translation, now lost, of the *Sacred History.* It is probably from this source that Diodorus Siculus and Cicero knew of euhemerist interpretations. The introduction of euhemerism to the Romans by Ennius is often interpreted as a sign of the degeneracy, skepticism, and acceptance of fashionable Hellenistic disbelief which flooded the Roman world after the Second Punic War. Cicero, in his *On the Nature of the Gods,* was one who protested that the euhemeristic view with its anthropomorphisms was essentially atheistic.

Christian apologists, on the other hand, were glad to find in pagan literature a critical treatment of the pagan deities which relegated them to the status of glorified men. In the *City of God* and elsewhere Augustine still thought it opportune to ridicule the mortality of the pagan gods. Already Firmicus Maternus, in his *On the Errors of the Pagan Religions,* had done much the same, as had Lactantius before him.

Later manifestations of euhermerism are found as recently as the eighteenth and nineteenth centuries. During the Enlightenment such writers as David Hume approached all religion in a rationalistic fashion. In his *Natural History of Religion,* published in 1755, he maintained that "Most of the divinities of the ancient world are supposed to have once been men," apotheosized by the devotion of their followers. In several works Herbert Spencer argued that all personalistic nonhuman powers or intelligences were products of a euhemerist apotheosis of mortals. Sir Alfred C. Lyall, the eminent student of Indian religions, also used euhemerism, within the framework of late nineteenth century evolutionary thinking, to explain the development of Asiatic religions, particularly Hinduism.

Not all the results of the euhemerist interpretation of myths and beliefs have been negative; indeed, selective application of euhemerist principles produced some startling results. Only when man's thinking had been freed by euhemerism was it possible to see more in the saga of Troy than mere mystery and more in the legends of ancient Crete than simple fiction. The view that a historical kernel lies beneath the myths of the past has encouraged the development of archaeology and philology.

379

The Teaching of Euhemerus

Pertinent Literature

Von Hügel, Friedrich. *The Reality of God and Religion and Agnosticism.* Edited by Edmund G. Gardner. New York: E. P. Dutton Co., 1931.

Because little has been written in English on the subject of euhemerism, it is fortunate that the literary remains of Baron Friedrich von Hügel have been published. While this book gives an unusually helpful history of the application of euhemerism throughout the ages, its most interesting part deals with the interpretation given to euhemerism by the Baron himself, a fortuitous synthesis of the opposite opinions of two leading German scholars.

The chief source for Euhemerus is in a section of the *Universal History* of Diodorus as preserved by Eusebius in his *Praeparatio Evangelica.* This fragment tells of the *Sacred History* which relates the curious journey to the island of Panchaea where Euhemerus first learned that Ouranos, Kronos, and Zeus were originally men. About 1900, two German scholars, Erwin Rohde and Otto Gruppe, each interpreted this incident and Euhemerus' intentions differently. Rohde so wanted to take Euhemerus at his word that he tried to speculate on the identity of Panchaea, suggesting that it might be the island of Rhenaea near Delos, or Ceylon, or Socotra, southeast of the Gulf of Aden. While he found his results inconclusive he maintained, nonetheless, that Euhemerus' descriptions of the Panchaneans was so sober and unadorned in an age addicted to florid writing as to invite credence in his association of the island with the proximity of India and its culture. He believed that Euhemerus' message was straightforward and that he had no other pur-

pose in mind than pragmatically to dissolve "the legends of gods into the history of human kings and adventurers." Probably the chief reason impelling Rohde to a literal acceptance of Euhemerus was the German scholar's awareness that Euhemerus' ideas were not entirely original; he was merely extending an explanation to the whole of Greek mythology which previously had been directed to single myths.

Gruppe, on the other hand, saw the *Sacred History* as having a more subtle purpose than the mere enunciation of a philosophy. It may have been a pious apology for belief in the apotheosis of Hellenistic rulers, but it is far more likely that the opposite was intended. It should be regarded as a satire reflecting the influence of the new imaginative novels and romances, and intending to poke fun at the deification of Alexander and his successors. According to Gruppe, Euhemerus was a Lucian attacking the credulous faith of the masses. Gruppe suggested that Euhemerus' account of Zeus leaving Greece, traveling to barbarian lands, permitting himself to be recognized as a god, and allowing himself to be buried in the Far East was a clear reference to Alexander. To this interpretation Rohde retorted that, far from reading any such meaning into Euhemerus, the ancient and indeed the modern world correctly found a simple, straightforward meaning in his account and based the philosophical system euhemerism on it.

Von Hügel ingeniously combines

both Rohde's and Gruppe's views in his own interpretation. He believes that Gruppe is correct in assuming that the historical apotheoses of the times made Euhemerus react, but that Rohde is correct in assuming a literal interpretation of Euhemerus' message. Considering the superstitious flavor of the times there is, says von Hügel, "no difficulty in holding him [Euhemerus] to be just simply one more of the unbelieving *litterati* of that corrupt age and to have meant to explain away the gods, one and all." Euhemerus discovered his beliefs, and his proofs for them, not as a traveler in India or the Far East but in Europe or in the Hellenistic Near East.

Drachmann, A. B. *Atheism in Pagan Antiquity*. London: Glydendal, 1922.

This study makes it abundantly clear that atheism in ancient times is difficult enough to define without trying to classify the controversial Euhemerus. Scholars, however, usually think of Euhemerus, along with Epicurus, as a true atheist even though the ancient Greeks themselves did not consider him an original thinker. His reputation was only assured by Ennius, Christian apologists such as Lactantius, and modern atheists since the Renaissance.

In one sense, euhemerism is best seen as a rationalization of polytheism so much in line with the spirit of the Hellenistic age that it was employed by many thinkers including Herennius Philo of Byblos, who "euhemerized" even Phoenician deities. Since no great personage came to the forefront to bring about a radical transformation of ancient religion, it tended to grow into unwieldy accretion aided by changing economic and social conditions, increased intercommunication between peoples, and imaginative art. Xenophanes of Colophon, according to Drachmann, is probably the first critic of Greek religion who "reached a standpoint which . . . with some truth may be designated as atheism."

The fact that men such as Herakles and Asclepius had become gods in popular lore, and that Greek deities were never conceived of as existing from eternity, naturally encouraged ideas such as euhemerism in an age when Hellenistic rulers were busy making themselves into gods. To categorize Euhemerus as an atheist, however, is too simple. On the one hand he says that gods are merely deified men, yet on the other, he believes that the heavenly bodies are real and eternal divinities. While implying, as a true atheist, that these deified men ceased to exist after their death, he makes concessions at the same time to vulgar belief by admitting that gods once did exist. This rationalizing process was common enough. Since ancient religion had no dogma to safeguard it, it came more and more under attack in a society of free expression. Yet such a great edifice of thought could scarcely be regarded as a total fiction by its contemporaries. Plato reveals his awareness of the dilemma, Aristotle compromises by making the heavenly bodies divine and Xenocrates offers demons to explain the situation. It is in this context that Euhemerus introduces the early benefactors of mankind as gods. Euhemerus is seen in a gentler light as a person apparently safeguarding popular religion by rationalizing it rather than denying it, while assuming that the gods of polytheism do not exist eternally. Drachmann paradoxically believes that Euhemerus put forward "the last serious attempt in the old pagan world to give an explanation of the popular faith which may be called genuine atheism."

When Romans, Christian apologists, and modern thinkers discovered "euhemerism" and lifted it to prominence, it was employed, paradoxically again, both by atheists to bolster their position and also, often unwittingly, by those who would safeguard Judaism and Christianity by discrediting ancient mythology and polytheism. The Jews of ancient times resorted to euhemerism by insisting that the pagan gods were merely images representing dead men. Christian apologists suggested that demons had "assumed the mask" of dead heroes in order to be worshiped and enjoy the savor of sacrifice. Even seventeenth century Hebraism tried to derive polytheism from Judaism by claiming that the gods emerged from the Moses figure, and that goddesses developed from deifications of his sister Miriam. As knowledge of these two persons spread among ancient people they were embroidered with fable upon fable to become gods. One of the more interesting sidelights to this theory is that a true understanding of Greek mythology had to wait until after the Renaissance before demonology, allegory, Hebraism, and euhemerism could be eliminated and so allow the idea of the gods to emerge correctly as the product of nature symbols. — *R.J.W.*

Additional Recommended Reading

Hastings, James, ed. "Euhemerism," in *Encyclopedia of Religion and Ethics*. New York: Charles Scribner's Sons, 1908. A short but helpful account which argues that Euhemerus has been overrated as a philosopher when he was really a mere product of his own time.

Chase, Richard. *Quest for Myth*. Baton Rouge: Louisiana State University Press, 1949. A discussion of the impact of Euhemerism on the study of myth and its influence on the views developed during the Enlightenment concerning the skeptical approach to religion.

Moore, Clifford H. *The Religious Thought of the Greeks*. 2nd ed. Cambridge: Harvard University Press, 1925. A helpful survey in lecture form.

Murray, Gilbert. *Five Stages of Greek Religion*. Garden City, New York: Doubleday & Co., Inc., 1955. The last two parts of this learned interpretation of Greek religion are especially relevant.

Rose, Herbert J. *Ancient Greek Religion*. London: Hutchinson's University Library, 1946. A brief but helpful treatment of Greek religion.

FORMALIZATION OF GEOMETRY

Type of event: Scientific: development of mathematics
Time: c.300 B.C.
Locale: Alexandria

Principal personages:
THALES OF MILETUS (624-547), postulator of elementary geometrical results
PYTHAGORAS (572-c.500), pioneer in efforts to systematize geometry
HIPPOCRATES OF CHIOS (c.450-430), author of a book of *Elements*
PLATO (c.429-347), philosopher interested in the theoretical character of mathematics
EUDOXUS (c.408-355), scientist first attempting a mathematical theory of astronomy
EUCLID (fl.c.300 B.C.), author of the *Elements* which made geometry a deductive science
PROCLUS (c. A.D. 410-485), writer recording the history of Greek mathematics in his *Commentary on Euclid*

Summary of Event

From the beginning of history, man has been confronted with geometrical problems in measuring his land and building his home. For a long period each practical problem was solved individually without the use of general laws of computation, but as time passed it became obvious that certain general principles and relations were common to various practical problems. With this observation man's practical, particular geometry gradually became a universal geometry, that is to say, a science. Practical problems that could be solved by a general procedure gave rise to a geometrical law or rule. The time lapse from concrete geometry to scientific geometry is unknown, but it is generally agreed that scientific geometry first appeared in the Nile Valley of ancient Egypt. It was born of practical necessity as a science to assist the engineering and agricultural problems along the Nile. Similar phenomena happened along other river valleys, including the Tigris and Euphrates of Mesopotamia, the Indus and Ganges of south central Asia, and the Hwang Ho and the Yangtze of eastern Asia.

Although the pyramids of El Gîze, erected about 2900 B.C., required solutions to some practical geometry, our chief sources of information about Egyptian geometry are in the Moscow and Rhind papyri, dating from about 1850 B.C. and 1640 B.C. Twenty-six of the one hundred and ten problems of the two papyri are geometrical in nature. In all this pre-Hellenistic mathematics there is no instance of solving a problem by logical demonstration. Each solution is a step-by-step handling of a particular problem,

383

a workable empiricism.

It is difficult to estimate the debt Greek geometry owes to ancient Oriental geometry. But whatever it is, the Greeks took the empirical geometry of the Egyptians and Babylonians and transformed it into something basically different. The Greeks insisted that geometry must be based not on empirical procedures but on deductive reasoning; logical demonstration must replace trial-and-error experimentation. This placing of geometry on a logical and deductive foundation instead of on an empirical basis is the great contribution of the Greeks to mathematics, and hence to all science.

There are no primary sources for the study of the early geometry of the Greeks. All sources date from several hundred years after the occurrence of the event. The main source of information on early Greek geometry is embodied in the *Eudemian Summary* of Proclus. Proclus, who lived in the fifth century of the Christian era, in his *Commentary of Euclid,* Book I, gives a brief outline of the history of Greek geometry from earliest times to Euclid. Greek geometry seems to have begun in a serious way with the work of Thales of Miletus in the first half of the sixth century B.C. To Thales are attributed a number of elementary geometrical results whose value must not be judged by their content but by their employment of a certain amount of logical reasoning, replacing experiment and guessing.

The next outstanding Greek mathematician was Pythagoras, born on the island of Samos in about 572 B.C. He continued the systematic study of geometry begun by Thales. The students of Pythagoras, who founded a school in Croton in southern Italy, expanded the work of Pythagoras by inaugurating the properties of parallel lines. The *Eudemian Summary* claims that Hippocrates was the first to present geometry through a logical chain of propositions based on initial definitions and assumptions. Further and better attempts were made by Leon, Theudius, and others.

About 300 B.C. Euclid produced his famous *Elements,* a work of 465 propositions neatly proved by logical deductions. The work immediately received great respect and commands it even today. The effect it had on the future development of geometry and mathematics is immense. With the exception of the Bible it has been more widely used, published, and studied than any other single work. For more than two thousand years it has been the standard work on geometry.

Euclid's work is largely a collection of the works and conclusions of his predecessors. He makes no claim that its contents are his own work alone. Its chief merits lie in the manner in which Euclid defines terms, and selects and rearranges the results of his predecessors into propositions that form a logical sequence from a minimal number of assumptions. The fact that there are some imperfections does not detract from the work; some limitations are to be expected in one who charters a course for the first time. Even with its flaws it is the first great landmark in the history of mathematics.

The distinctive features of the *Elements* are that all geometrical laws are general statements postulated absolutely and not as approximations. Not only are the laws stated but they are also proved, deductively and not inductively; not once is the reader asked to measure a particular line or angle. All conclusions are established with the rigor of logical necessity and every term is precisely defined in order to eliminate any ambiguity of meaning.

The procedure of starting with postulates, axioms, and definitions before undertaking the work of proving mathematical statements is here initiated, a procedure rigorously imitated today.

Pertinent Literature

Heath, Sir Thomas L. *A History of Greek Mathematics.* Vol. 1. Oxford: The Clarendon Press, 1960.

The author is an authority on Greek mathematics, particularly on the works of Euclid. The mathematics of the Greeks from Thales to Euclid is traced in this volume.

Greek geometry begins with Thales (624-547) who went first to Egypt and then introduced his ideas into Greece. Many of the propositions he himself discovered, and he subsequently taught his successors the principles underlying their solutions. Some of his solutions were scientific, some were empirical, and some were solutions by simple inspection. Thales made geometry into a deductive science: he stated that a circle is bisected by its diameter. The theorems in Euclid I, 5; I, 15; and I, 26 are attributed to Thales.

Geometry is indebted to the Pythagorean school for the properties of parallel lines, which were used to prove that the sum of the measures of the interior angles of a triangle equals two right angles. To the Pythagoreans is due the original idea of the transformation of an area of one form into one of a different form; in short, they originated most of Euclid Book I, theorems 35-48, and the whole of Book II. They had a fully developed theory of proportion and knew the

properties of similar figures. They knew of the existence of five regular solids. The irrationality of the square root of two was proved by them, and they could approximate its value as closely as desired.

By the time of Plato, most of the *Elements* was recognized. Plato was not a researcher in mathematics but he kept up to date in things mathematical and his enthusiasm for the subject exerted great influence for years after his death.

Since one of Plato's pupils, Heraclides of Pontus (c.388-310 B.C.), had postulated that the earth was the center of the universe and rotates while the heaven is at rest, the world was ready for a mathematical theory of astronomy. Such was the chief contribution of Eudoxus (c.408-355 B.C.) whose theory of concentric spheres attempted to account for the movement of all heavenly bodies. The general theory of proportion which can be applied to geometry, arithmetic, music, and mathematics generally is contained in Book V of the *Elements,* but it was the discovery of Eudoxus. In Euclid, Book V, definition 5, equal ratios are defined in exactly the same way as Dedekind's theory of irrationals and Weierstrass' definition of equal numbers. Aristotle (384-322 B.C.), a lover of mathematics, probably taught his pupils from the *Elements* of Theudius, Euclid's predecessor; in his *Posterior Analytics* Aristotle makes clear distinctions between axioms, definitions, hypotheses, and postulates.

For a clear picture of the mathematical world before Euclid, this volume is highly recommended.

Heath, Sir Thomas L. *The Thirteen Books of Euclid's Elements.* New York: Dover Publications, Inc., 1956. 3 vols.

Using the techniques of modern research Sir Thomas Heath has given mathematicians the complete *Elements* of Euclid in these three volumes. The initial nine chapters form background material. Details are given of Euclid's works other than the *Elements,* his commentators including Proclus, and the place of Euclid in the mathematics of the Arabs. Tracing the work from the original copy to the copies of the present day is a saga in itself.

Especially interesting is the history of external criticism of the *Elements.* Since no copy of the *Elements* dating from Euclid's time has been found our texts derive either from Greek revisions or from Greek-Arabic-Latin translations. The first Latin author to mention Euclid is Cicero. With the exception of a fragment in the fourth century Verona palimpsest of some propositions of Books XII and XIII, there is no copy of the Latin text of the *Elements* earlier than that of Boethius (c.A.D. 480-524), who is mentioned by both Magnus Aurelius Cassiodorus and Theodoric as the author of a translation of Euclid. The translation that has come down to us, however, is by no means an exact translation of the *Elements.*

Until a century ago Greek texts of the work were based on manuscripts containing Theon of Alexandria's revisions made almost seven hundred years after Euclid. Between 1814 and 1818, Peyrard discovered in the Vatican Library Ms. Gk. 190 which represents a text more ancient than Theon's, and in 1888 Heiberg brought out a new and definitive Greek text based on the findings of Peyrard and the best of the Theonine manuscripts.

The earliest extant Latin translation was made from the Arabic. By the eighth century the Arabs had a copy of the *Elements,* for the Caliph al-Mansūr received a copy of Euclid from the Byzantine Emperor. The Caliph al-Ma'mun (813-833) also received some manuscripts of Euclid from the Byzantines. In general the Arabic copies of Euclid are inferior to the Greek copies. The first Latin translation was made by Athelhard of Bath, an Englishman, in 1120. Evidence of an earlier translation occurs in an Old English verse which suggests that at least fragments of the *Elements* were in England as early as 924-940.

The famous Gherard of Cremona (1114-1187) is said to have translated the fifteen books of the *Elements* from the Arabic. Another translation was made from the Arabic by Johannes Campanus about one hundred and fifty years after Athelhard. Campanus' work was the first printed translation and was published in Venice by Erhard Ratdolt in 1482. A num-

386

ber of editions followed in the next few years.

In Venice in 1505, Bartolomeo Zamberti, using a Greek text, published a translation of the complete books of the *Elements*. Commandinus (1509-1575) in 1572 furnished a most important Latin translation, since he followed the Greek text more closely and added some scholia as well as some notes of his own. Until the time of Peyrard this was the basic translation.

Leonard of Pisa (Fibonacci) in 1220 collected into his *Practica Geometriae* all that he had been taught by Euclid's *Elements* and Archimedes' books on *Measurement of a Circle* and *On the Sphere and Cylinder*.

The first printed editions of Euclid sparked a new interest in the study of the man and his work. Many separate editions and commentaries appeared in the sixteenth century. In 1570, Sir Henry Billingsley furnished the first complete English translation in folio size of 928 pages. Barrow at Cambridge had great influence in the study of Euclid by publishing a Latin edition in 1655 and an English edition in 1660. Through the influence of Barrow, Euclid's *Elements* as a textbook became universal, a position it held until recent times. — *J.F.D.*

Additional Recommended Reading

Barker, Stephen F. *Philosophy of Mathematics.* Englewood Cliffs, New Jersey: Prentice-Hall, Inc., 1964. A study contrasting Euclidean and non-Euclidean Geometry.

Cajori, Florian. *A History of Mathematics.* New York: The Macmillan Company, 1922. A masterpiece in the field of the history of mathematics.

Smith, David Eugene. *History of Mathematics.* New York: Dover Publications, Inc., 1953. 2 vols. A recent work already a classic.

Scott, J. F. *A History of Mathematics.* Ch. II. London: Taylor and Francis Ltd., 1960. A work containing proofs by the early Greeks.

STOIC CONCEPTION OF NATURAL LAW

Type of event: Philosophical: postulation of a moral concept
Time: c.300 B.C.
Locale: Athens

Principal personages:
ZENO OF CITIUM (335-263), founder of the Stoic school
of philosophy
CLEANTHES OF ASSOS (331-232), successor to Zeno as
scholarch of the Stoa
CHRYSIPPUS OF SOLOI (280-207), third scholarch of the
Stoa who was chiefly responsible for the systematic
formulation of the doctrines of the Old Stoa

Summary of Event

The formulation of the Stoic concept of natural law was the logical culmination of trends in cosmological thought and political development in the Greek world after the time of Hesiod. Implicit in Hesiod's *Theogony* is an understanding of the world-order as political in nature and of physical nature as obedient to the orderly processes of thought in the human mind. Early Ionian philosophy, especially that of Anaximander, had given explicit formulation to these implications of Hesiod's poem in the concepts of a cosmic justice governing all natural phenomena; the logos of Heraclitus expressed an active rational principle permeating all nature and directing its phenomena. Nevertheless, although these cosmological ideas were themselves derived from the political framework of the polis, there seems to have been no reapplication of them to the political and moral relationships of men within different political and ethnic communities of the world until the mid-fifth century B.C. At that time the Sophists called attention to the rel-ativity of current moral and political standards, or *nomos,* in different communities and then pointed to a common human nature, or *physis,* with laws of its own which might well conflict with the laws of human communities. As the institutions of the Greek polis were losing their power to command the loyalties of individuals, the Athenian Socrates postulated an objective and rational standard of moral human behavior based on the nature of the individual man as a rational and social being. Fourth century philosophy failed to realize the universalist implications of these ideas, probably because the polis remained the only obviously self-validating type of human community; but the conquests of Alexander demolished such claims for the polis and created in fact a universal human cultural community throughout the civilized areas of the eastern Mediterranean world. *Koine* Greek became a common language of international commerce and culture, and through this medium the cultural heritages of Greeks and "barbarians" cross-fertilized each other.

The explicit recognition of the community of mankind seems to have been more a negative statement of the individual's rejection of ties to the local polis community than a positive affirmation of human brotherhood. The Cynic Diogenes of Sinope (413-327) is said to have been the first to call himself a "citizen of the world" by way of denying any personal obligation to the polis. Far from being a political idealist, Diogenes held that all men and beasts are brothers inasmuch as man is essentially a beast. All culture is artificial; a man keenly aware of what nature requires of him will find contentment without heeding the conventions of the community in which he happens to reside.

The Stoic school of philosophy established by Zeno of Citium about 300 B.C. developed out of Cynicism and evolved more systematically the Cynic school's conception of "the life according to nature." While the Cynics, however, had set a low estimate on man's rational capacity, the Stoic conception of man and his place in nature laid a supreme value on this rational capacity. Taking the cosmology of Heraclitus as a physical foundation for his system, Zeno postulated a cosmic monism of a pantheistic nature where logos, or "active reason," pervades all nature and determines all events. God is present in all nature, yet God, or logos, has consciousness only in the soul of man and in the totality of the universe. Since God and men as conscious participants in the events of nature and of history are thus distinguished from plants, animals, and inorganic nature, God and all men are bound together in a natural community of all rational beings, the cosmopolis.

The Stoic ethic comprises two complementary levels of the rational life according to nature. One is the inner level of assent by the logos within to the pattern of events determined by the universal logos, a recognition of the necessity and rationality of all which does in fact occur, contentment with fate, or in Stoic diction *apatheia,* imperturbability. Yet on the external level of practical moral response to critical choices confronting the individual, reason guides choice to the fulfillment of duty. Duty is that portion of the responsibility for fulfilling the rational operation of nature and history which confronts the individual moral agent. Duty is not limited by geographic, ethnic, political, or even social boundaries. It is laid upon the individual not by the state or ancestral mores but by the rational principle which governs the universe, and therefore it extends to all human beings who, since they are endowed with reason, are members of the world community, the cosmopolis.

Although the early Stoic concepts of cosmopolis and natural law defining the duties of all rational beings are stated in positive form, yet in the period of the Old Stoa these ideals are essentially nonpolitical; they do not lead to any positive vision of the political unity of mankind. Citizenship is not man's highest obligation, and while it is asserted that the laws of a state ought to reflect the natural laws and ought to be disobeyed if they contradict them, Stoic idealism in the early period could not envision a universal state over which a single code

389

of law reigned supreme. Nevertheless, the concepts of cosmopolis and natural law were ultimately influential in the formulation of the Roman

imperial *ius gentium* and in the systematic formulation of the moral philosophy of the Christian Church.

Pertinent Literature

Baldry, H. C. *The Unity of Mankind in Greek Thought.* Cambridge: The University Press, 1965.

The concept of natural law is closely related to the concept of the organic unity of nature. When applied to the human community, the concept of natural law ought also to imply the unity of mankind. Baldry's book performs the service of tracing the history of this idea of the unity of mankind through antiquity from Homer to Cicero. Oft-cited generalizations are thus put to careful test and shown in many cases to be inadequate. Baldry's thesis with regard to the period of Stocism's emergence is that the universalizing tendencies of post-Socratic philosophy and of Alexander's conquests were offset by factors creating a new gulf between a majority of commoners throughout the Mediterranean world and a minority of the enlightened.

Socrates is seen by Baldry as the founder of an ideal of humanity attainable only for the few and separating them from the rest of mankind. While Socrates did not support older notions of aristocratic superiority, he certainly criticised democratic theories of the political competence of all citizens and insisted that on any question whatsoever the opinion of the wise man alone is to be regarded. Whatever Socrates' intentions with regard to social order may have been, the impact of this exaltation of the wise man on fourth century philoso-

phy was overwhelming, and its logical corollary, contempt for the unwise, tended to vitiate such theories of a common humanity as did develop in the fourth and third centuries B.C.

In discussing the Cynic school of philosophy, Baldry notes a positive tendency to disregard the older categories of social distinction in Greek society—of sex, race, and class— so that "barbarians" and slaves were attracted to the school; yet the Cynic was essentially an isolated individual, and in calling himself a world-citizen, the Cynic meant not that he was at home in any city but that he was indifferent to all cities. Thus, even though the Cynic might speak of the friendship and kinship of the wise, he felt no bond of kinship or duty to the contemptible mass of humanity which he considered to consist of fools.

In a chapter on Alexander and his influence, Baldry sets himself sharply against the assertion of the influential historian Sir William Tarn that Alexander personally championed the notion of human brotherhood and that his policies were aimed at development of a genuine world community wherein racial distinctions would be ignored. Baldry notes how short-lived was the political unity of lands conquered by Alexander, and emphasizes the ceaseless military and political struggle of the Hellenistic era. As

390

for racial barriers, they were extended throughout the world as Greeks flowed out from the mainland and became commercial, political, and cultural leaders in hitherto barbarian communities. A common Greek culture was thus shared by an upper crust dwelling in widely-scattered cities, and natives might adopt the Greek way of life and be considered "Greeks," but in each city a sharp cleavage existed between the Hellenized minority and the majority who continued to live by ancestral traditions.

Baldry regards Zeno's *Politeia* not as a description of present possibilities for a utopian world-society nor of future possibilities for a golden age when all men should be rational, but as a formulation of "how things would be if people were wise." The book was probably an early work of Zeno, written while he was still strongly under Cynic influence, and of course it was conditioned by recognition that most men are not wise. Chrysippus laid more stress on a natural law binding all things human and divine into unity, but he too stressed the gulf between the minority of wise men and the majority of fools; and therefore the real ties of kinship, affection, and duty were among the wise alone. Not until the period of Roman domination, says Baldry, did the notion of a common humanity really find meaningful expression.

Edelstein, Ludwig. *The Meaning of Stoicism.* Cambridge: Harvard University Press, 1966.

In his Martin lectures, originally delivered at Oberlin College in 1956, Ludwig Edelstein essays an interpretation of the Stoic way of life that does justice to the vitality of the school over several centuries, emphasizes its continuity as well as its capacity for self-criticism, and, while indicating some inadequacies in Stoic attitudes, explains the appeal and reasonability of the system.

Edelstein argues for the primacy of Stoic physics over ethics and thus seeks to refute the commonly held notion that Stoicism is a moral philosophy only secondarily grounded on a theory of nature. That a rational principle of organization constitutes the unity of nature is the foundation of the whole system, and man's rational identity and moral nature are conditioned by an understanding of the world which the Sto-

ics considered fully scientific.

While other philosophical schools contemporary with the Stoa aimed at the self-perfection of the individual, the Stoa focused on man in community and saw man's duties as contained within four successively larger concentric circles of self, family, occupation, and state. Within the family circle the Stoa saw the first natural unity beyond the self. It is a man's duty to marry; and husband and wife as equal partners have responsibilities to each other. The father's rights are limited by those of the son, and the household slaves, as human beings, must also be treated with respect. In a man's economic function, the Stoa saw both an aspect of self-fulfillment and an area of moral duty: work as an expression of moral character has value in itself, contrary to the older Greek aristocratic view. The businessman, as a member of a community, has a responsibility to the buyer. The man of wealth must view himself as a trustee of his wealth rather than a proprietor, and so must practice the virtue of generosity. Within the circle of the state, the primary virtue is justice, and here the Stoa emphasized the need for equity in application of the universal law to particular cases. In one respect, the Stoa emphasized the moral priority of the individual over the state, for in holding the moral law recognized by the individual as higher than the positive law of the state, the school imposed the duty of civic disobedience in cases of conflict. Edelstein emphasizes that the natural law did not recognize inalienable rights of all men so much as it imposed duties on all rational men. These duties limited the political ambitions of individuals as well as those of states: war, the Stoa held, should not lead to destruction of an enemy.

While Edelstein does not discuss the distinction between wise men and fools, which Baldry says vitiated the concept of moral duty to all mankind, he does implicitly recognize that the Stoic saw and performed his recog-

nized duties primarily in his own area of human contacts. Nevertheless the humanizing effect of the Stoic concept of natural duty upon family and economic life, its tendency to see others within the human community—wives, children, slaves, fellow-citizens, buyers—as persons to whom one is morally obligated, is an obvious advance over earlier aristocratic conceptions of masculine superiority and individualism, and even over Aristotle's conception of "natural" slavery.

From the standpoint of the historical development of Stoic ethical principles, it is perhaps unfortunate that Edelstein considers as a whole the doctrines of the school which developed over several centuries. He draws most of his documentation from the works of later Stoics, especially Epictetus, but this is, of course, a consequence of his intention in the lectures. At the conclusion of his discussion, he does note some fundamental limitations of the Stoic way of life: its imposition of the total moral responsibility on individuals, its failure to see the necessary role of institutions, and its failure to recognize "the moral ambivalence of practical reason." — *C.W.C.*

Additional Recommended Reading

Bevan, Edwyn. *Stoics and Sceptics.* Oxford: The Clarendon Press, 1913. Reprinted, Cambridge: W. Heffer and Sons, Ltd., 1959. Three of the four lectures published in this work deal with Stoicism, with the third concentrating on the eclectic middle Stoic Posidonius.

Hicks, Robert Drew. *Stoic and Epicurean.* New York: Charles Scribner's Sons, 1910. The first four chapters present a systematic account of Stoic doctrines.

Oates, Whitney J., ed. *The Stoic and Epicurean Philosophers.* New York: Random House, 1940. A translation of the complete works of the later Stoics Epictetus and Marcus Aurelius together with the Epicureans Epicurus and Lucretius.

Wenley, Robert Mark. *Stoicism and Its Influence.* Boston: Marshall Jones Company, 1924. A brief presentation of Stoic doctrines but with extensive discussion of historical sequels.

ISSUANCE OF THE *LEX HORTENSIA*

Type of event: Legal: enactment of constitutional legislation
Time: 287 B.C.
Locale: Rome

Principal personage:
QUINTUS HORTENSIUS (d.287), plebeian dictator in 287

Summary of Event

In the persistent class conflict which raged throughout the fifth and fourth centuries B.C. between the privileged patrician class and the plebeians over the distribution of political rights and powers, the plebeians managed to win increasing degrees of equality with the aristocrats. Through various laws they had gained recognition of intermarriage with patricians and the right of election to all major political offices. The patricians had also recognized the plebeians as a distinct political body within the state by granting to them the power of electing their own officials, the tribunes of the people. Most of these gains (essentially tactical concessions to the new economic and military power of the plebeians) were won only grudgingly from the patricians, who retained ultimate and decisive control over the state through control of the legislative process, among other things.

In the early Roman constitution a measure became law after it had been proposed to and ratified by a validly convened assembly, or *comitia*, of the community. Such assemblies had to be convoked by a consul or a praetor, could meet only on specified days after the performance of stipulated religious rituals, and could only vote "yes" or "no" to properly submitted proposals. Even after a proposal had been af-

firmed, it still required formal ratification by the patrician senators before it became valid. To ensure further patrician control over the legislative process, the main assembly in the early period was the *comitia centuriata,* in which the voting groups were unequal and a minority of wealthy patrician citizens could influence greatly the final ballot. Once a proposal had navigated this complex process, it became law and was binding on all members of the community regardless of class affiliation; but the restrictions on the autonomy of the legislative body allowed the predominantly patrician senate (which did not itself have the power to enact laws) to subordinate legislation to senatorial interests and programs.

From the earliest days of the Republic the plebeians had apparently formed their own assembly (the *Concilium Plebis*) which contained only plebeian members and attended to their interests alone. Although convened by its own legitimate authority, one of the tribunes, it was not considered to be a *comitia* since it was limited to the enactment of proposals which were validly binding only on the plebeians themselves. Such enactments were termed plebiscites and were rigidly distinguished from laws, which obligated everyone.

The first attempt to change this situation was contained in one of the provisions of the Valerio-Horatian laws of 449 B.C., which stipulated that validly enacted plebiscites were to enjoy the same standing as laws and bind the entire citizen populace. The ineffectiveness of this law required a similar enactment by Publilius Philo in 339 B.C., which again attempted to convert plebiscites into laws. Some historians have seen both these laws as fictitious anticipations of the later Hortensian Law of 287 B.C., while others have argued that both laws were real enough but contained some qualifying condition, such as the necessity of senatorial ratification, before plebiscites became legally binding on everyone. It is likely, however, that both laws were passed without any qualification but were simply disregarded by the patricians as invalid since they had been passed without their approval.

This situation developed into a crisis in 287 B.C., when the plebeians, who had contributed greatly to the recent victory over the Samnites, imposed a general strike by withdrawing as a group from the city to force the patricians to meet their demands. In this emergency the extreme measure was taken of appointing as dictator the plebeian and otherwise undistinguished Quintus Hortensius. Hortensius put through a law, called the *Lex Hortensia,* again making plebescites equal to laws and enforceable on the entire community. The plebeians returned to the city after the acceptance of this constitutional reform by the patricians, and thereafter there was no further opposition to this particular issue by the patricians. Roman legal theorists treat subsequent plebiscites and laws as equivalent legislative enactments differing only in their point of origin. Armed with the power of making laws, the plebs became an influential part of Roman political life; the tribunate, as the initiator of plebiscites grew into a more powerful office; and the democratic aspects of the Roman constitution became more evident and effective.

Pertinent Literature

Von Fritz, Kurt. "The Reorganization of the Roman Government in 366 B.C. and the So-called Licinio-Sextian Laws," in *Historia.* I (1951), 1-44.

Since the *Lex Hortensia* ended the struggle between the patricians and plebeians, it finds a central place in von Fritz's attempt to estimate the traditional constitutional reforms of 287 B.C. In dealing with this earlier period von Fritz demonstrates that the historical accounts of the struggle between the orders derive mainly from the time of the Gracchi, and that aspects and characteristics of the Gracchian turmoil have been projected back into the accounts of the earlier period. Since Livy used this tradition, his account is also flavored with energetic tribunes and tribunate intercessions, devices which probably became crucial only when used by the Gracchi. Von Fritz is also doubtful about many parts of the Licinio-Sextian rogations and says that one point needing elucidation is what form the rogations took. Were they laws? This raises the issue of the *plebiscitum,* since according to Livy these rogations were first approved by the plebeians.

It is quite clear that because of the Hortensian Law, a plebiscite and a law were almost exact equivalents after 287 B.C. The two earlier laws that had raised plebiscites to the level of law have either been rejected as outright historical fabrication or more commonly been accepted as genuine but containing some restrictive provision. This latter view was especially championed by the great German historian Mommsen, who relied heavily on a poorly documented part of Sulla's constitutional reforms during the last century of the Republic, which purportedly revived the earlier practice of a tribune's being unable to propose any measure for consideration by the plebeian assembly unless the senate had first given its permission. Mommsen argued that this earlier practice was the one constantly in effect until the Hortensian Law. Von Fritz thinks this obscure reference is heavily suspect, that Sulla's weakening of the tribunate was to forestall its future exploitation by reformers such as the Gracchi, and that even if Sulla did restrict the legislative capacity of the tribune, to describe such a restriction as the revival of an earlier practice may have been nothing more than propaganda to disguise the illegality of his proposal.

Von Fritz stresses instead the circumstances of the earlier plebiscites. The major ones of 494, 444, and even 287 B.C., are all associated with secessions of the plebeians in which they removed themselves bodily from Rome and imposed in effect a political strike on the state. Although there have been some recent efforts to deny any historical validity to these plebeian secessions, von Fritz points to the intriguing fact that no withdrawal is ever mentioned after 287 B.C., so that it was clearly not a later condition that historians could read back into the early period. Von Fritz goes on to accept the uniqueness of the Hortensian Law and sees two important conclusions arising from it. Plebescites were extremely important even before 287 B.C., though before that date they did not have the force of laws; they were simply an expression of the will of the plebeians and were probably first used to announce the inviolability of the person of the plebeian tribune. Since this edict required only passive observance by the patricians, it did not raise any constitutional problems. The situation was different when the plebeians expressed their will on more concrete problems such as intermarriage or reduction of the interest on debts. Although the plebeian tribune had the power to assemble the plebeians and ascertain their will, there was no legal standing for this activity. The patricians were free to disregard it and obviously did so on numerous occasions. In this case, the only remaining response of the plebeians was to withdraw from communal life in order to force the patricians to accept the plebiscite as binding upon them. This procedure of plebiscite followed by secession resulted in a form of legalized revolution which only the Roman genius for compromise prevented from becoming bloody clashes. This potentially violent situation was completely eliminated by the Hortensian Law, which by raising plebiscites to full legal standing provided a constitutional outlet to forces which before the passage of the law were only partly regulated and often unruly. The beneficial effects of the law can be gauged from the total disappearance of plebeian secessions from Roman political life once the plebeians

had gained a legal instrument for the execution of their aims.

Abbott, Frank Frost. *A History and Description of Roman Political Institutions.* Boston: Ginn & Co., 1910.

The age of this book has not diminished its usefulness as a descriptive guide through the maze of Roman constitutional developments and procedures. Because of its descriptive character, the book tends to accept as certainties many problematic aspects of Roman political history. The traditional accounts of the early period by the later Roman historians are generally accepted to permit concentration on the precise workings of the actual procedures in force. Thus, in the case of the lawmaking power of the plebeian assembly, Abbott, though skeptical that such power was given to it as early as 449 B.C. by the Valerio-Horatian laws, does accept the premise that the similar enactments of 339 and 287 B.C. reaffirmed a principle that had in some unspecified way already been established. This principle itself, however, requires the usual explanation for the historicity of the three laws; namely, that until 287 B.C. there were definite restrictions in the form of senatorial approval on the legislative capacity of the plebeian assembly. From 449 B.C. to 339 B.C., this approval was required after the plebeian assembly had acted favorably upon a legislative proposal. From 339 B.C. to 287 B.C., the approval of the patrician element of the senate was a prerequisite merely for the introduction of a measure before the plebeian assembly. The effect of the *Lex Hortensia* was to eliminate entirely all outside interference on the plebeian assembly.

From its start in 471 B.C., the plebeian assembly was open, of course, only to plebeians. As in the other assemblies, voting was conducted on a group basis by tribes. The original twenty-one tribes of the fifth century had expanded to thirty-five by 241 B.C., and remained at that number. Abbott believes that membership in the tribe was a privilege enjoyed only by the landed plebeians, and that poorer plebeians were only permitted entrance in the last decade of the fourth century. It now seems clear that all plebeians were enrolled in the various tribes from the beginning but that the plebeian inhabitants of Rome were confined to the four urban tribes. This still meant a disparity in the voting power since a vote in one of the urban tribes, with their much larger constituencies, would count for far less than a vote in the rustic tribes. An attempt was made in 307 B.C. to allow plebeians to register in any tribe they might choose, but this reform was rejected in 304 B.C. and the entire question of the precise distribution of new citizens into the tribes continued to be a matter of dispute until the end of the Republic.

Nor was this the only limitation on the legislative capacity of the plebeian assembly. Since only plebeian tribunes could propose a measure for consideration by the assembly, there was little likelihood of any radical enactments by the assembly as long as the senate was able to rely upon tribunes docile to its interests; we hear of none until the era of the Gracchi. A further imbalance resulted from the fact that the assembly had to meet within the confines of the city. This made meeting attendance more difficult for citizens who lived remote from Rome than for members of the urban populace. In addition, the size of the assembly, potentially between 250,000 and 300,000, made it unwieldy for taking a very decisive role in political matters, a condition that left the senate dominant. For these reasons, Abbott's conclusion is that the *Lex Hortensia* introduced only a modified form of democracy within Rome and left unimpaired the oligarchic character of the Roman constitution. Although this machinery was more than adequate in responding to the foreign dangers throughout the third century and the first half of the second, it was slow to adjust to the new conditions and problems of Rome itself. When decisive action was imperative, it originated in the office of the tribunes through their explosive courting of the plebeian assembly, and especially of its urban members. This development exposed Rome to an almost continuous period of violence and bloodshed. —*G.M.P.*

Additional Recommended Reading

Botsford, George W. *The Roman Assemblies*. New York: The Macmillan Company, 1909. An extremely detailed and scholarly account of the various Roman assemblies, with special attention to the ancient sources.

Jones, H. Stuart, and Hugh Last. "The Making of a United State," in *Cambridge Ancient History*. Vol. VII, Chapter XVI. Cambridge: The University Press, 1954. A reliable account of the *Lex Hortensia* emphasizing earlier developments.

Staverly, E. S. "Tribal Assemblies Before the Lex Hortensia," in *Athenaeum*. XXXIII (1955), 3 ff. An examination of the origin and early history of the tribal assemblies.

ADVANCES IN HELLENISTIC ASTRONOMY

Type of event: Scientific: interpretations of observed phenomena
Time: c.275 B.C.
Locale: Alexandria

Principal personages:
ARISTARCHUS OF SAMOS (c.310-230), Alexandrian astronomer and mathematician
ERATOSTHENES OF CYRENE (c.275-194), Alexandrian astronomer, geographer, and mathematician
HIPPARCHUS OF NICAEA (c.190-c.120), Greek astronomer and mathematician

Summary of Event

That the earth was spherical was known to learned Greeks of the fourth century B.C. by the shape of its shadow on the moon during a lunar eclipse. The accepted view of the universe, however, was that the earth remained unmoving at its center while around it in concentric circles moved the seven planets of the ancient world: the moon, Mercury, Venus, the sun, Mars, Jupiter, and Saturn. About 340 B.C. at Athens, Heraclides of Pontus postulated that the earth rotated on its axis and that Mercury and Venus revolved about the sun, which with the other four planets revolved around the earth. His book *On Things in the Heavens* is lost, so that we do not know how he arrived at these conclusions.

This theory was the most advanced position taken by Greek astronomers by the time of Alexander's conquest of Persia, which opened up a new world to scientists. At Babylon, Uruk, and Sippar, in Mesopotamia, fairly accurate observations of the movements of the heavenly bodies had been recorded and kept for centuries. Part of this mass of new knowledge became known to Greek scientists in the third century B.C. The Greeks also had their own means of acquiring data, for among the wonders of the new museum established in Alexandria as a sort of university was an observatory, a simple tower whose only instrument was a device without lenses for measuring the azimuth and angle of height of a star or planet.

From these small beginnings Greek astronomers reached astonishing conclusions. Aristarchus of Samos, invited to Alexandria, showed by the use of observations and of plane geometry that the sun was some three hundred times larger than the earth. This estimate was a considerable improvement over the fifth century guess that the sun was about the size of the Peloponnesus. Aristarchus "proved" his findings in his extant treatise *On the Sizes and Distances of the Sun and Moon.* Having established this fact to his own satisfaction, Aristarchus went on to deduce that the sun, apparently because it was so much larger than the earth, must itself be the unmoving center of the cosmos, with the earth and planets revolving about it, the moon about the earth, and the earth

398

rotating on its axis. The unmoving fixed stars were at an infinite distance. The book in which he explained his reasons for holding these bold hypotheses is lost.

Unfortunately for succeeding ages, during the next century Hipparchus of Nicaea, the best astronomer in antiquity, disproved Aristarchus's inadequately defended theses. He proposed the theory that the planets moved in epicycles around imaginary points. The points were also supposed to move in circular orbits about the earth, but their centers were not the earth itself. The complex scheme actually explained the imprecisely observed movements of the planets over short periods of time. Hipparchus said that he acted "to save the phenomena," so he was wrong for good reasons. He measured the length of the solar year to within six minutes, fourteen and three-tenths seconds, discovered the precession of the equinoxes, and catalogued more than 850 fixed stars together with their magnitudes. He estimated the mass of the sun as 1,880 times that of the earth and its distance as 1,245 earth diameters, estimates which were considerable improvements on those of Aristarchus.

At Alexandria and Syene Eratosthenes of Cyrene conducted an imaginative experiment during which he measured the circumference of the earth to within less than two percent.

He noticed that at Syene on the Nile River (modern Aswan) at noon on the summer solstice the sun was exactly overhead. His proof was that a vertical pole cast no shadow and the bottom of a deep well with vertical sides was completely illuminated. He arranged for an assistant at Alexandria to measure the angle cast by a vertical pole there at the same time on the same day. This angle measured one-fiftieth of a complete turn (7° 12'), so the distance between Syene and Alexandria was about one-fiftieth of the circumference of the earth. Determining this land distance, Eratosthenes then calculated the circumference of the earth as 250,000 stadia or 24,662 miles, an error of only about 250 miles. He later changed his estimate to 252,000 stadia, though it is not known on what basis.

Eratosthenes actually made two mistakes: he wrongly assumed that Alexandria and Syene were on the same great circle, and his measurement of the distance between the two cities was inaccurate. Fortunately the two errors tended to cancel each other, and his method was sound. Because he also knew that the distance from Gibraltar to India was only some 69,000 stadia, he made the remarkable prediction that another continental system would be found at the Antipodes by sailing west into the Atlantic Ocean or east into the Indian Ocean, an opinion held later by Columbus.

Pertinent Literature

Heath, Sir Thomas. *Aristarchus of Samos: The Ancient Copernicus.* Oxford: The Clarendon Press, 1913.

Sir Thomas Heath sets out to disprove the contention of the Italian scholar and astronomer Schiaparelli that Heraclides of Pontus anticipated Aristarchus and was actually the first to propose the heliocentric hypothesis. Heath's counterthesis is that Heraclides theorized no further than to suggest that Mercury and Venus revolved about the sun while the sun continued to circle about the earth. Heath's knowledge of astronomy and ancient Greek enables him to master the controversy from a scrupulous examination of the testimony of ancient writers.

He includes the Greek text of the sole surviving book written by Aristarchus, *On the Sizes and Distances of the Sun and Moon,* with facing English translation and explanatory footnotes. He also gives a long and detailed account of the development of Greek astronomy from the age of Homer to the period when Aristarchus lived, and concludes with a chapter on the demise of the heliocentric theory. It is unfortunate that Heath has not continued his analysis through the late Hellenistic and Roman Imperial periods to include review of the work of Hipparchus of Nicaea, Posidonius of Rhodes, and Claudius Ptolemy of Alexandria, the last great astronomer of antiquity whose refinements of the Hipparchian system dominated European astronomy until the sixteenth century A.D.

Heath shows that the scientifically minded Hellenistic astronomers based their conclusions on direct observations of the sun, moon, and stars, and that in the third century they greatly improved the accuracy of their measurements. Aristarchus himself, early in his career, believed that the angular diameter of the moon was two degrees, which is more than it really is. He later determined, as he could have done only by further observation, that the moon's angular diameter is actually only half a degree, which is more

accurate. Aristarchus is credited with the invention of a bowl-like, hemispherical sundial with an upright pointer set in the center of its pole. The pointer cast shadows on the inside surfaces of the hemisphere upon which lines were incised in such a way that the direction and height of the sun could be read easily. Unfortunately, we are told nothing more about Aristarchus' instruments, except that Hipparchus improved upon them.

Heath believes that the heliocentric hypothesis of Aristarchus was rejected for two reasons. First, there was general prejudice against it based upon centuries of belief that the earth lay at the center of the cosmos. Second, there was the simplest series of observable facts: the sun rose in the East and set in the West, while the earth made no apparent motion at all. The sun, therefore, to any reasonable man must follow a circular path around a spherical, stationary earth. Hipparchus was trying to save the observed facts, the basis of science. The strength of the geocentric idea was based not only on these facts but also on strong conceptions of a religious and philosophical nature. Cleanthes of Assos, a Stoic philosopher contemporary with Aristarchus, was incensed at the publication of the astronomer's theory, and he wrote a tract *Against Aristarchus* in which he complained that Aristarchus had "put in motion the hearth of the universe," that is, the terrestrial globe upon which the moving sun had been made to shine by a divine and providential Reason. The astronomer, he insisted, should be tried for blasphemy.

400

Advances in Hellenistic Astronomy

Sarton, George. *A History of Science.* Vol. II: *Hellenistic Science and Culture in the Last Three Centuries B.C.* Cambridge: Harvard University Press, 1959.

George Sarton conceives of science in the widest possible sense, and, although his main interest is in exact sciences such as astronomy and mathematics, he includes in his book sections on intellectual disciplines such as philosophy and philology, and remarks on poetry and the fine arts in order to give some idea of the intellectual temper of particular centuries or generations. In his preface he says that he was moved to write the book by "the love of science, or call it the love of rationality." Rationality is the touchstone which enables him to identify his heroes, the men who searched for truth in the face of ignorance, error, and superstition.

Three of the greatest scientists in his opinion were Aristarchus, Eratosthenes, and Hipparchus. Of the first he writes that his conclusions concerning the sizes and distances of moon and sun were wrong because his observations and measurements, or at least his early ones, were inexact. Aristarchus thought that when the moon was half-full, the angle made by lines drawn from the moon to the earth and from the sun to the earth was 87°, whereas in fact is is 89°50', a difference which is very important. His original measurement of the angular diameter of the moon, two degrees, was an error of four hundred percent, and it led to more errors in his calculations. Sarton's verdict on Aristarchus is that his intellectual method was good and his geometrical proofs clear and rigorous. As the first man to conceive of an attempt to measure scientifically the great distances in the solar system, his boldness deserves respect. On the

survival of the heliocentric theory Sarton makes an interesting judgment. A contemporary of Aristarchus was Aratus of Soli, who wrote a didactic poem on the heavens, a work full of folklore and mythological allusions to the constellations. It was, says Sarton, therefore very popular, and he implies that it drove the work of the serious scientist into oblivion.

Concerning Hipparchus, Sarton has nothing but praise, despite his geocentrism. His more precise observations, his anticipation of trigonometry (unknown to Aristarchus), and his devotion to ascertainable truth made him great. In 134 B.C. he discovered a new star, probably a nova, which he duly recorded. This discovery apparently led him to compile a catalogue of stars so that posterity could know if other new stars appeared or if old ones vanished. His concern for such long-term observations must have arisen from his own use of them, for his discovery of the precession of the equinoxes was based on observations made by himself, by Aristarchus, and by Babylonian astronomers of an even more remote time.

In *Hellenistic Civilization,* W. W. Tarn gave his opinion that, if the heliocentric theory of Aristarchus had prevailed, it would have killed astrology, which, coming out of Egypt and Babylonia, rapidly gained credence among Greeks in the second century B.C. Sarton sharply rejects this view, although he gives few reasons for doing so. He does mention that Hipparchus lived in an age of astral religion and divination in which he himself believed. It is hard to decide whether

401

Tarn is right or wrong. If others had accepted the hypothesis of Aristarchus, they would perhaps have realized that the mind of man had reached across the myriad stadia between earth, moon, and sun in order to learn the truth of their apparent and real motions. To have recognized so great a human achievement might have made it difficult for the majority of men to believe that human lives could really be influenced by the dull masses of those distant spheres. — *S.K.E.*

Additional Recommended Reading

Heath, Sir Thomas L. *Greek Astronomy*. New York: E. P. Dutton and Company, 1932. A collection in English translation of Greek astronomical texts from Thales to Plutarch.

Neugebauer, O. *The Exact Sciences in Antiquity*. 2nd ed. Providence: Brown University Press, 1957. A technical treatise concerning the use made by the Greeks of Babylonian and Egyptian astronomical discoveries.

Farrington, Benjamin. *Greek Science: Its Meaning for Us*. Baltimore: Penguin Books, 1961. A useful survey of Greek astronomy and other sciences by a veteran scholar.

Farrington, Benjamin. *Science and Politics in the Ancient World*. London: Oxford University Press, 1940. This interesting book asks why science declined in the ancient world, and it concludes that many governments considered truth to be dangerous.

Cumont, F. *Astrology and Religion Among the Greeks and Romans*. New York: G. P. Putnam's Sons, 1912. A standard work on the rise and importance of astral religion in the classical world.

Dodds, E. R. *The Greeks and the Irrational*. Boston: Beacon Press, 1957. In this fascinating book, the last chapter entitled "The Fear of Freedom" discusses the psychological danger of achieving freedom from inherited tradition, with cogent comments on the work of Aristarchus and Cleanthes.

DEIFICATION OF PTOLEMY PHILADELPHUS

Type of event: Politico-religious: establishment of a political religion
Time: c.272 B.C.
Locale: Alexandria

Principal personages:
ALEXANDER THE GREAT, King of Macedonia 336-323;
    son of Zeus 324/323
PTOLEMY I (SAVIOR), King of Egypt 305-283/2
PTOLEMY II (LOVER-OF-HIS-SISTER), King of Egypt
    283/2-246
EUHEMERUS (fl.c.310), Greek intellectual
ZENO OF CITIUM (335-263), founder of the Stoic school
    of philosophy

Summary of Event

The idea of divine kingship among Greeks began when Ptolemy II, about 272 B.C., proclaimed that he was both king and god, and organized a cult of himself. This act seems so strange to the modern American that some explanation of its origin should be given.

In the past Greek kings had played an important role in government and also in religion. Even when monarchies died away in the eighth century, the functions of kingship did not. In democratic Athens the king archon still performed the religious duties of the vanished dynasty. In the fourth century the failure of democratic states such as Athens and Thebes to end the horror of continual interstate warfare led some men to doubt the usefulness of democracy. And when the victory of King Philip II at Chaeronea established at once the power of a king and a condition of peace among the Greek cities, the prestige of the monarchical idea grew.

There is some question about how this idea came to be associated with divinity. Greeks did not differentiate as sharply between the human and divine as we do. Remarkable men were worshiped for marvelous achievement, as the dramatist Sophocles received the reverence due a hero and the philosopher Plato the worship accorded a son of Apollo. But political power fascinates more than the creation of literature, and rulers became the chief recipients of divine honors because kings could mete out justice, bring relief in time of dearth, and wage war as the victorious champions of peace. In 324 B.C., Alexander the Great, having destroyed the menace of Persia and having made an empire of his own, asked the Greek states to recognize him as a son of Zeus. His demand was not so remarkable. In the old days the founders of Greek colonies had been worshiped as heroes after death. It was, therefore, natural to explain Alexander's breath-taking achievement as inspired by a god; surely one might say that he was a son of Zeus. There is no evidence, however, that Alexander demanded actual worship of himself anywhere in his

403

lifetime.

The period 340-250 B.C. was a time of change and decay. Aristotle declared that a man of extraordinary excellent, *arete,* could not be equated with ordinary men, but should be regarded as a god among them. Euhemerus, a Sicilian Greek who flourished about 310 B.C., asserted that the classical gods had once really been human beings who, by conferring some great boon on mankind such as the invention of agriculture, had been deified out of gratitude. Mount Olympus was thus brought closer to men. Zeno, founder of the Stoic school of philosophy, taught that men, being endowed with reason, shared the divinity of that all-pervading, providential Reason that ruled the universe and which men equated with Zeus. This reasoning exalted man. In those decades belief in the power and philanthropy of the classical gods was beginning to fade. An Athenian might well wonder why Athena Polias, guardian of the state, had so many times let in plague or famine or allowed human foes to overthrow the city's walls. About 290 B.C. the people of Athens, saved from starvation, honored King Demetrius with a hymn. The other gods, they sang, were far away or deaf to supplication; the present, dear god Demetrius had saved them from death. Such veneration of the mighty and the good was entirely sincere. Interpretations of the philosophers fused with the popular desire for some great, charismatic leader and produced a new religious and political concept of divine kingship.

In the atmosphere of the Hellenistic East, where Persian kings had been reverenced as the human representatives of Ahura Mazdah and where Egyptian pharaohs had been worshiped as outright gods, the Greek conception of divine kingship rapidly took root. In 305 Alexander was formally deified and provided with priests and cult by Ptolemy I. He in turn was deified after death by his son Ptolemy II, who subsequently took the ultimate step of deifying himself and his sister-wife Arsinoë about 272. The Seleucid Antiochus II acted similarly some time later. Thereafter, divine kingship became common. All the Ptolemies were god-kings; most Seleucids were content to be earthly representatives of the gods. Only in Macedonia did the dynasty totally reject deification. The kings took such titles as *savior* or *benefactor* to show that they were continually concerned with the welfare of their subjects.

The institution of divine kingship enjoyed a long run. The Roman emperors were readily accorded worship by Greeks for the advent of the *Pax Romana,* and Augustus in turn authorized the establishment of cults of Roma and himself. There was slight opposition from Greek patriots or agnostically minded philosophers, and rather more from monotheistic Jews and Christians, who thought divine monarchy an abomination. But the hold that the idea had on the imagination of ancient men even survived, to some extent, the railing of the theologians, for, when the ancient world was won for Christ, and the Christian emperors surrendered divinity, they continued to claim particularly close relationship with the Deity as heads of the Church, shapers of doctrine and belief, workers of miracles, "most holy" because of their high dignity.

Pertinent Literature

Ferguson, W. S. "The Leading Ideas of the New Period," in *The Cambridge Ancient History*. Vol. 7, pp. 1-40. Cambridge: The University Press, 1927.

Professor Ferguson writes of the fresh intellectual currents which flowed through the first decades of the Hellenistic period, when the attitudes of Greeks were being altered by the decline of their city-states and the opening of the new world in the East. This period between the accession of Alexander in 336 and the death of Ptolemy II in 246 was a time of transition and creative experiment in many spheres of life. The Persian Empire was swept away and new states were formed. The Persians themselves, once the imperious lords of the East, became a local people in a remote corner of the Seleucid Empire. There was large-scale immigration of Greeks from Old Hellas and from Asia Minor into Egypt and Syria, where the native aristocracies were brusquely shouldered aside by the avid newcomers.

Some of the most important changes affected the Greek gods. The classical high gods receded in popularity; Asclepius, a minor hero in the fifth century, became a major deity, as the great healer in the fourth. Syncretism in religion, the semi-conscious adoption of the attributes and personality of one god by another, was widespread. The Greeks in Egypt equated their Zeus with the Amen-Ra of the Egyptians. Conscious synthesis of gods was practiced. Ptolemy I caused Manetho, an Egyptian priest, and Timotheus, an Athenian exegete of the mysteries of Demeter, to preside over the birth of the new god Serapis, fashioning him from both Greek and Egyptian

forebears. To many contemporaries of this hectic time divine Chance seemed to rule this world, and in many places altars were in fact reared to Chance, *Tyche*. All this gives an idea of the fluid reasoning from which the notion of divine monarchy emerged.

Monarchy itself was an idea that now appealed to Greek thinking, and kingship became the principle form of government in Europe, excluding brief periods of republicanism in Italy, from the end of the fourth century B.C. until the end of the World War I in 1918, when simultaneously the Hohenzollern, Hapsburg, and Romanoff dynasties ended. The new Hellenistic kingdoms were vast in extent when compared with the old city-states the Greeks had known. Given the technical abilities of the day, a form of government, whether democratic or republican, based on discussion was not to be thought of, for discussion could not be carried on by millions over hundreds of miles. The largest democratic state had been Athens, with a total area of slightly more than one thousand square miles. She was minuscule alongside Egypt, with Syene five hundred miles distant from Alexandria; Athens counted as nothing in comparison with the territories of the Seleucids, which stretched from Pakistan to western Turkey. Monarchy, then, making policy at some capital and ordering compliance in the provinces was the only form the government of vast territories might well take. Monarchy could, of course, be benevolent and listen to

405

advice from its people.

Deification, according to Ferguson, was essentially a political affair. To grant divine honors to, say, Antiochus I, who drove back the barbarian Gallic invaders of Asia Minor, was an act of political justice, returning gratitude to him for the relief he brought the frightened Greek cities. And deification was also a matter of political convenience, for it established a legal basis for the control of the Greek cities, a condition upon which Antiochus insisted. Kings had no legal right, in old-fashioned Greek thinking, to interfere in the affairs of a free city; the gods, on the other hand, had every right to do so, and deification of a king amounted to no more than the legalization of his absolutism. Some political thinkers of the age justified royal rule of cities with the explanation that a king was Law-incarnate, an idea which long enjoyed favor with intellectuals.

Bevan, Edwyn. *A History of Egypt under the Ptolemaic Dynasty.* London: Methuen & Co. Ltd., 1927.

This history of the Ptolemaic dynasty covers the period between the first Ptolemy's entry into Egypt as an officer in Alexander's army and the death of the famous Cleopatra VII in 30 B.C., after the country had been occupied by the Romans. The book is now admittedly out-of-date, but it remains the best synthesis in English of Ptolemaic history, embracing politics, social and economic life, and the religious policies of the dynasty.

Bevan says that Alexander's visit to the oracle of Amon at Siwah in Egypt's western desert in 331 was a decisive event in the evolution of the practice of divine kingship. There the priests hailed him: "Son of Amon," the traditional Egyptian formula for their king, and Alexander's romantic nature began to expand with the idea. His demand in 324 that the Greek cities recognize him as son of Zeus was the precedent for later deifications. Ptolemy I was aware that even in death Alexander remained an awesome figure, so he conveyed his body into his own satrapy of Egypt. Here it was interred in a magnificent golden sarcophagus, and, when the new capital of Alexandria had been sufficiently prepared, it was transferred to a tomb specially built there, and provided with a priesthood and an official cult. The deification of Ptolemy I, founder of the new dynasty in Egypt, followed upon his death.

Even though the first Greek ruler cults were instituted in Egypt, the concept was essentially Greek, and Bevan cites considerable evidence to prove it. Many Greeks, he shows, were willing to accord Alexander and the Ptolemies divine honors. Even educated men saw in the official cult no more than an expression of dynastic loyalty, because in the context of Euhemerus' idea it was easy to call a man a god without meaning very much by it. There were four kinds of king-worship in Egypt: (1) the traditional Egyptian cult of the Pharaoh, now celebrated by Egyptian priests in the name of Ptolemy; (2) an uncertain amount of private worship, expressed personally by Greeks, though no sure evidence exists of prayers addressed to the Ptolemies despite the fact that oaths of binding force could be sworn in the king's name; (3) city cults of Alexandria and Ptolemais, places that owed hero-ization to Alexander and Ptolemy I as their Founders; and (4) the official royal cult. We know some details of its practice, which show that the cult of divine monarchs more closely re-sembled the ceremonies of the Ameri-can Fourth of July than the celebra-tion of a Mass. Ptolemy I and his wife Berenike were worshiped as the *Theoi Soteres,* "the savior gods," a title Ptol-emy had taken for the help he brought to the Rhodians when they were un-der attack. The salvation brought by Hellenistic kings was always of this material kind and had nothing to do with redemption from sin. Rites were performed by a priest and a priestess. The cult called *Basileia,* "royal rites," had celebrations every year, presum-ably on the anniversary of Ptolemy's assumption of the royal title in 305. Incense was burnt and bulls were sac-rificed. The *Ptolemeia* were held every four years at Alexandria, a festival which included athletic contests simi-lar to the Olympic Games held to honor Zeus and which attracted com-petitors from all over the Greek world. — *S.K.E.*

Additional Recommended Reading

Bevan, Edwyn. *The House of Seleucus.* London: E. Arnold, 1902. 2 vols. Out-of-date, but the most recent comprehensive account in English of Seleucid his-tory and institutions.

Hansen, E. V. *The Attalids of Pergamum.* Ithaca: Cornell University Press, 1947. A full history of this important Hellenistic dynasty.

Goodenough, Erwin R. "The Political Philosophy of Hellenistic Kingship," in *Yale Classical Studies.* Vol. I (1928), 55-102. An outline of the political phi-losophy which justified absolute monarchy, including the concept of kings as Law-incarnate.

Nock, A. D. "Notes on Ruler-Cult, I-IV," in *Journal of Hellenic Studies.* Vol. 48 (1928), 21-43. An interesting series of remarks on Alexander's sonship of Zeus and subsequent developments.

Tarn, W. W. "The Hellenistic Ruler-Cult and the Daemon," in *Journal of Hellenic Studies.* Vol. 48 (1928), 206-219. Tarn argues that ruler-cult was the worship of the ruler himself, not of his daemon or inner spirit.

McEwan, C. W. *The Oriental Origin of Hellenistic Kingship.* Chicago: University of Chicago Press, 1934. A study arguing that Oriental precedents played an important part in the Greeks' development of the idea of divine kingship.

DECLARATION OF THE FIRST PUNIC WAR

Type of event: Political: use of military force
Time: 264 B.C.
Locale: Italy (especially Sicily) and Africa

Principal personages:

HIERO, King of Syracuse 265-215

APPIUS CLAUDIUS CAUDEX, consul in 264 and leader of the prowar faction in Rome, who led the first campaign into Sicily

MARCUS ATILUS REGULUS, consul in 267 and 256, another leader of the war party who led the Roman invasion of Africa

HAMILCAR BARCA (c.270-229), Carthaginian general in Sicily at the end of the war, and father of Hannibal the Great

Summary of Event

The first Punic War was a milestone in Roman history. Entry into this conflict committed Rome to a policy of expansion on an altogether new scale; prosecution of the war marked the emergence of Rome as a world power; disposition of conquered territories reshaped its political condition domestically as well as in foreign affairs.

The Mediterranean world in the early third century B.C. consisted in the east of large territorial empires in areas conquered by Alexander the Great. In the west was Carthage, dominating the coasts of Africa and Spain, while Rome ruled a network of allied cities in central Italy. In the center was Sicily, the only portion of the Greek world where the imperial ideal had failed to replace the older system of numerous independent city-states. Sicily was an anachronism, certain to attract efforts on the part of the Hellenistic monarchies to attach it to one or another of the eastern Empires. Carthage and Rome were equally certain to resist the establishment of Hellenistic powers in the western Mediterranean. When Pyrrhus, King of Epirus, led his armies into Italy and Sicily, he first met the resistance of Rome, then of Carthage. The failure of his Sicilian campaign between 280 and 275 B.C., left a power vacuum little different from that which existed before, and it was only a matter of time before Rome and Carthage could be expected to come into conflict there.

The occasion of Roman involvement in Sicily, and the beginning of the First Punic War, may have seemed of relatively slight importance. The Mamertines, once mercenary soldiers of Syracuse who had seized the city of Messana and used it as a base of operations in northeast Sicily, found themselves threatened by the growing power of Hiero, King of Syracuse. They called on the Carthaginians for aid, but then, fearing domination by these traditional rivals,

408

requested aid from Rome in order to expel the Carthaginian garrison. Rome was a land power with no navy. The Roman senate, fearing overseas campaigns against a naval power, refused to accept the Mamertines' overtures. But the Roman people, perhaps foreseeing the prosperity they might gain from involvement in the rich territories of Sicily, perhaps merely failing to foresee the extent of the military operations they were initiating, voted to aid the Mamertines. Appius Claudius Caudex, a leader in the prowar faction, was elected consul for the year 264 B.C. and led an expedition to Sicily.

In the first phase of the war, the Roman forces aided Messana, while Carthage supported Syracuse. But this phase, and with it the original pretext for the war, was soon over. Hiero of Syracuse had no interest in matching his power against Rome's, nor in being dominated by his erstwhile allies. In 263 B.C., Hiero made peace with Rome on terms that left him extensive territories as well as his independence. Messana was saved. But Carthage and Rome now were in a struggle that neither cared to give up.

Between 262 and 256, Rome pressed hard, driving the Carthaginians into a limited number of military strongholds, and mounting her first fleet, which met with surprising success against the experienced Carthaginian navy. In 256, under the consul Marcus Atilius Regulus, Rome transported an army into North Africa; it had initial successes, but the Carthaginians, directed by the Greek mercenary Xanthippus, succeeded the next year in destroying the forces of Rome.

Back in Sicily, the fortunes of war took many turns. On land, Rome controlled extensive territories but Carthage held her strongholds. At sea, the Roman navy was often victorious even though the loss ·of one fleet in battle and of others in storms weakened her position. By 247, both powers were fatigued. Peace negotiations stalled, but military efforts were at a minimum for some years.

In 244, the Roman government, too exhausted to build a new fleet, allowed a number of private individuals to mount one with the understanding that they should be repaid if the war were brought to a successful conclusion. In 242 this fleet arrived in Sicily. When a convoy of transports bringing supplies to Carthage's troops was captured, Carthage came to terms. The Carthaginians agreed to evacuate Sicily and pay an enormous indemnity over a long period of time.

Sicily, or many of the territories in it, became Rome's first province. Her annexation of it as a subject, tribute-paying territory marked the start of developments that gained in importance through the remaining history of the Roman Republic. By annexing a Hellenic territory Rome became, in a sense, a Hellenistic state, a fact that had a profound effect upon Roman cultural life as well as upon foreign relations. Rome's development of naval capacity made possible commercial and military involvement with all the Mediterranean world. Its need to govern conquered territory caused it to modify city-state institutions and begin constitutional developments that would in the end undo the republican form of government in Rome.

Pertinent Literature

Frank, Tenney. "Rome and Carthage: The First Punic War," in *Cambridge Ancient History*. Vol. VII, ch. 21. New York: The Macmillan Company, 1928.

Frank's treatment of this subject includes, besides a chronological account of the military campaigns, a discussion of the causes and effects of the war with respect to political and military conditions at Rome. In describing the debate and hesitation that preceded Rome's decision to send an expedition to Sicily, the author points out that the question at hand was not one of war against Carthage, but one of alliance with Messana. Messana was at this time a leading power in Sicily, third, perhaps, after Syracuse and Carthage. Its domination of water routes, particularly of the straits between Italy and Sicily, made friendship worth cultivating. Messana was in danger of domination by Carthage whose help it had enlisted in order to resist the might of Syracuse; if Rome allowed Carthage to gain control of one Sicilian seaport after another, it could expect the Carthaginian policy of *mare clausum,* or "closed sea," to keep out non-Carthaginian ships and block Rome and hard-won Roman allies in south Italy from commerce with the rich nations of the Greek world.

The nobles who dominated the Roman senate, however, were, for the most part, landholders interested in a strong military security on land and not at all concerned about extension of trade and foreign commerce. These men hesitated to commit themselves to military operations against a naval power; they feared, too, loss of privilege to the new classes that might gain power if Rome became a seafaring nation. The conservative party prevailed in the senate, which refused to pass a resolution which would have meant sending an army to Sicily. But the Roman people, partly under the influence of the merchants and partly enticed by the prospect of booty from campaigns in the rich territories of Sicily, enacted the alliance with Messana.

The most important result of the First Punic War, in Frank's opinion, was the conversion of Rome to an imperial nation. As Rome conquered territories already accustomed to foreign rule, it gave up its eighty-year-old policy of basing its power upon alliances with federated states, and adopted the Hellenistic forms of territorial control already in effect in most of the Mediterranean world. The results of the adoption of this foreign idea of territorial sovereignty, involving the creation of provincial administration, the use of standing armies, and the collection of tithes, were to have far-reaching effects upon political conditions in Rome itself.

Frank draws attention to two other ways in which the First Punic War affected conditions in Rome. A new nobility of men rose to prominence during the war. As families such as the Manilii, the Aurelii, and the Lutatii gained senatorial status during this period, a change was effected in the make-up of the Roman senate, and therefore in the directions of Roman policy. Furthermore, the cultural life of Rome was stimulated by the

410

experiences of vast numbers of Romans serving extended tours of duty in the Greek territories of Sicily; Roman literature had its start in the years following the war, developing Hellenic forms, chiefly dramatic and epic, in the Latin tongue. The other arts were similarly affected.

Picard, Gilbert Charles, and Collete Picard. *The Life and Death of Carthage.* Translated by Dominique Collon. London: Sidgwick & Jackson, 1968.

The difficulty in writing a history of Carthage is that Carthaginian accounts are nonexistent. The Picards have taken the trouble to collect the epigraphical and archaeological materials from Carthage and her territories and to compare these carefully with Greek and Latin sources relating to Carthaginian affairs. The Picards' account of the Punic Wars, relating these events to conditions in Carthage itself, forms a useful supplement to the traditional histories that take the Roman viewpoint throughout.

The authors review the history of Carthaginian activities in Sicily under the early kings, and again under the oligarchic regime that governed Carthage after the early fourth century. Although Carthage was a major power in Sicily in the early third century, taking, for instance, a leading role in the repulsing of the invasion by Pyrrhus in 280 B.C., its position at the start of the First Punic War was not substantially different from what it had been for some time past. The Picards ascribe the opening of hostilities, and indeed the prosecution of the war throughout, to the initiative of the Romans.

A review of Roman politics before and during the First Punic War, shows that the prowar faction was led by noble families of Campania admitted to the Roman senate during the Samnite wars, and by some few native Roman nobles who had con-

nections or landed interests in the south of Italy. The antiwar faction was led by those whose interests lay to the north. The degree of vigor with which the war was prosecuted varied from time to time as political developments in Rome favored one family or another.

The Second Punic War, in contrast to the First, was chiefly prosecuted by the Carthaginians on their own initiative, and much of the interest of the Picards' book lies in their account of how the First Punic War affected conditions in Carthage in such a way as to lead to a resumption of hostilities with Rome after a period of some twenty years.

The young general Hamilcar Barca had been left to conclude the war in Sicily after the oligarchic government in Carthage had largely lost interest in it. During the Mercenary War of 241/40, when a revolt broke out among Carthaginian troops as they returned home to be paid off and disbanded, Hamilcar was called up by the popular party to replace the oligarchs' generals and pacify the troops. He was successful in this endeavor, winning many of the mercenary troops to a personal loyalty to himself. The popular party that had called on him was able to break the power of the oligarchs in Carthage so that the civil government there, henceforth headed by popularly elected magistrates, remained on friendly terms with Hamil-

411

car and allowed him the generalship of large armies for extended periods of time.

Hamilcar used his troops to pacify large territories in Spain. His purpose in so doing was partly to gain control of Spanish mines as a means of enabling Carthage to pay the enormous war indemnities imposed upon her by the Romans. But he also wanted to create a strong military and naval base from which to resist further Roman advances, and his control of the Spanish territories was so personal as to make of them almost an independent kingdom. Killed in battle in 229 B.C., Hamilcar was succeeded as general of the Spanish armies by his son-in-law Hasdrubal, who devoted his administrative talents to consolidating Hamilcar's military gains. Hasdrubal, assassinated in 222, was succeeded by Hamilcar Barca's son, Hannibal the Great, to whom Spain was not so much a kingdom to rule as a base of military operations against the hereditary enemy, Rome. — *Z.M.P.*

Additional Recommended Reading

Grant, Michael. *The Ancient Mediterranean.* New York: Charles Scribner's Sons, 1969. A general history of the Mediterranean world from prehistoric times through the achievement of Roman domination.

Grimal, Pierre, Hermann Bengtson, *et al. Hellenism and the Rise of Rome.* Translated by A. M. Sheridan Smith and Carla Wartenburg. London: Weidenfeld and Nicolson, 1968. A survey of the Mediterranean world in the third century B.C.

Heitland, W. E. *The Roman Republic.* Cambridge: The University Press, 1923. A thorough, three-volume study of the political and military history of the Roman Republic.

Toynbee, Arnold J. *Hannibal's Legacy.* Oxford: The University Press, 1965. A two-volume account of the struggles between Rome and Carthage, and their effects on Italy and Rome.

Warmington, Brian Herbert. *Carthage.* New York: Praeger, 1960. A description and history of Carthage.

412

REVENUE LAWS OF PTOLEMY PHILADELPHUS

Type of event: Economic: publication of regulations for a state economy
Time: 259 B.C.
Locale: Alexandria

Principal personages:
PTOLEMY II (PHILADELPHUS), King of Egypt 283/2-246
APOLLONIUS, his Minister of Finance

Summary of Event

The Ptolemies, who controlled Egypt after the end of the fourth century B.C., inherited a well-articulated system for managing the economy of the country. The Pharoahs had treated the land as their personal property and had organized a bureaucracy to oversee it. It is uncertain to what extent the Ptolemies altered this system or what changes were made by which Ptolemy. Ptolemy I, however, seems to have been preoccupied with building up his army and navy, while his son Ptolemy II certainly refined the economic institutions which supported them. It is likely that the Macedonians' modifications were in the direction of a stricter and more sophisticated system. They created a corps of supervisors, clerks, and counter-checkers to keep highly detailed records of economic activity of all sorts. They put the country for the first time on a money economy, caused iron tools to be used far more extensively than before, and brought about technical improvements such as the introduction of better machines for irrigation.

The economic life of Egypt was directed from Alexandria to bring in as much money in taxes as possible. Part of a copy of the impressively compli-

cated *Revenue Laws of Ptolemy Philadelphus* of May/June, 259 B.C., has been found. They were issued by the Ministry of Finance, headed by a certain Apollonius, whose responsibility it was to formulate and carry out the state's economic policies. The best preserved sections are regulations for the government's monopoly on oil-bearing plants. Sesame oil was an edible cooking oil, and castor oil was used for lighting. The laws laid down that the amount of land to be sown annually with oleoginous plants would be determined in advance at Alexandria by the *dioecetes*, or finance ministers. Out in the villages peasants formally contracted with the state to grow a stipulated crop. These cultivators could sell their harvest in the presence of a clerk only to men whom the state licensed to trade. The growers were paid a price fixed by the government, and the king took a quarter of the crop as tax. The licensed buyers processed the remainder at a registered, state-owned oil press, and then sold the finished oil at a price also determined by the Finance Ministry. The laws provided a comprehensive schedule of fines for persons who interfered in any way with the exercise of this royal monopoly, from the lowly

Egyptian peasant up to the Greek district supervisor. We can put together enough scattered pieces of evidence to show that detailed regulations also applied to other sectors of the economy including manufacturing, fishing, and trade.

To organize the state economy, Egypt was divided into provinces called *nomes*, each governed by a *strategos,* or general, who maintained law and order, with economic affairs being administered by an *oeconomos.* Most *nomes* were divided into *topoi,* or "places," supervised by *toparchs,* and the *topoi* were subdivided into the basic *comae,* or "villages," presided over by a *comarch. Comarchs* were usually bilingual Egyptian clerks, but the higher officials were almost always monolingual Greeks. The *comarchs* kept registers of the land around their villages and classified it according to quality, also maintaining lists of cattle and other animals of value. Copies of these registers were sent to the *toparchs* who in turn compiled registers of their districts and sent copies to the *oeconomoi.* Registers for each *nome* went to the *dioecetes* in Alexandria, where from the master register the annual planting plan was prepared for wheat, barley, sesame, castor, and other crops; orders for carrying out the master plan were then dispatched down the chain of command.

The greater part of the labor force was made up of Egyptian peasants called "royal farmers." Though not serfs, they were not free men either, as they were required to remain in their villages during the growing season. Some land was used by temples of the great Egyptian high gods with most of the income going to maintaining the cults and buildings, but the priests were also subject to the master planting plan, and had to turn over any surplus to the state. Cleruchic land was granted to Greeks and Macedonians who served in the armed forces or departments of state; it was farmed by Egyptians while the Europeans performed military or administrative functions.

In western Asia the Seleucid dynasty controlled a kingdom much larger and more heterogeneous than the Ptolemaic. While they had economic policies of their own, what little we know of them shows that the Seleucid Empire was less centralized and less strict than the Egyptian. In western Asia Minor, the kingdom of the Attalids of Pergamum seems to have been consciously modeled on Ptolemaic practice, and control of peasants and workmen was as strict as it was in Egypt.

Pertinent Literature

Rostovtzeff, M. I. *The Social and Economic History of the Hellenistic World.* Oxford: The Clarendon Press, 1941. 3 vols.

Professor Rostovtzeff was a man of many linguistic skills, enormous learning, and prodigious power of research. His books have contributed enormously to our understanding of the social and economic history of the Hellenistic period and the age of the Roman Empire immediately following.

Rostovtzeff believed that the principal reason the Ptolemies treated Egypt as a money-making machine was to secure the means of importing the timber and metals which Egypt lacked, and of hiring mercenaries in time of war without which Egypt could not have competed with other well-organized Hellenistic states. He held that the Macedonian modification of the Pharaonic system was begun by Ptolemy I, and was greatly elaborated and rationalized by Ptolemy II. He regarded the organization as "marvelous in its logic and clearness of conception," although he was well aware of the ethnic injustice it caused. He argued that the Ptolemies were obliged to develop a state dominated by Europeans. The army had to be Greco-Macedonian because only Greeks and Macedonians understood the military technique invented by Philip and Alexander, whose campaigns had proved that it was greatly superior to Egyptian or Persian methods. Furthermore, the loyalty of Egyptian soldiers could scarcely be trusted. The same was true in the economic sphere. In Greece during the fourth century there had been a steady evolution of methods of state financial management. Once the Macedonians had learned how the Pharaonic system operated, they combined selected Egyptian customs with such elements of Greek practice which seemed best suited to produce the most efficient exploitation of the agricultural, mineral, and human resources of the country. While some Egyptians became Hellenized and entered into the life of the state on nearly the same terms as Greeks, the overwhelming mass of the Egyptians did not, and society was divided into a fairly small number of Macedonians and Greeks with the best jobs, a class of Greeks and mixed Greco-Egyptians who had inferior or even bad jobs, and the Egyptian masses, who tended almost always to be diggers of ditches and keepers of pigs.

Rostovtzeff admired the rational organization of the state, and paid a warm tribute to the men who worked in the creative atmosphere of Alexandria. The clever schemes of drainage and land reclamation put into effect made an area of wasteland over into a whole new *nome*. Crop rotation was enforced. Seed grains of various kinds were imported, acclimatized, and planted to increase yields. Better strains of animals were introduced and crossbreeding was practiced.

Our knowledge of some districts in Egypt is so minutely detailed that we can hazard, by extension, rough estimates of the population and income of the country as a whole. Rostovtzeff suggested that the population of Egypt at the beginning of the Christian era was about seven and a half million, not counting Alexandria whose people numbered close to one million. All these agents, soldiers, and workers toiled to support themselves and enrich the state. Rostovtzeff accepted the statement of Jerome that the annual income of Ptolemy II from Egypt alone was 14,800 talents in money. This figure does not include income in kind or taxes from overseas possessions, which were large. This figure may be compared with that for Athens in 431 B.C., when she was at the height of her power: 350,000 Athenians enjoyed a state income of one thousand talents in money from both foreign and domestic

415

sources. The difference between Athens and Egypt shows how drastically the power of the old city-states had shrunk by the third century B.C.

Bell, Sir H. Idris. *Egypt from Alexander the Great to the Arab Conquest.* Oxford: The Clarendon Press, 1948.

Bell's small book is a masterly presentation of the history of Egypt with emphasis on the early diffusion and subsequent decay of Hellenism throughout the country. The Ptolemies, he says, organized their system of planned economy to realize a maximum income for a minimum of expenditure. Under the first three Ptolemies, vigorous and energetic men, the system worked well; but under Ptolemy IV, a weaker leader, the system began to break down. Without a strong hand on the controls, the bureaucracy grew more and more incompetent and corrupt. The Egyptian peasants, treated as inferiors by Greek officials who all too often acted like *Herrenvolk,* began under the leadership of the native priesthood, to revolt against the foreign regime. Patriotic uprisings continued sporadically throughout the second and first centuries B.C. and sapped the strength of the state, which, in 30 B.C., was taken by Rome.

The Romans reorganized their new province only slightly. A prefect was appointed to take the place of Ptolemy. Tight supervision of the Egyptian temples was begun. The Romans moved to protect Hellenism in Egypt, and a Greco-Macedonian elite continued to monopolize most of the high offices. The bureaucracy was purged of incompetents and more honest men took their places, but the government and the economic system kept essentially the same form that the Ptolemies had given it. Bell thinks that the very efficiency infused into the system by the new men appointed by the Romans was one cause of fresh troubles with the Egyptian peasants. A second reason was that, although the Ptolemies had exploited the country, much of their profit was reinvested in it. The Romans now efficiently exploited Egypt's resources themselves but as absentee landlords, and they exported the country's wealth to feed their eastern armies and the Roman mob, or to embellish the palaces of the rich in Italy. By A.D. 20 many peasants fled to avoid work. Such a course was the only one left an Egyptian when the courts failed to protect him against oppression.

Enough persons fled their places in the first century A.D. for the Romans to resort to a regime of compulsory state service, including providing warships, collecting taxes, and cultivating land where lessees had decamped. From the reign of Vespasian through that of Antoninus Pius, A.D. 69-161, compulsion seems to have been applied locally and temporarily, but from the accession of Marcus Aurelius on it was more and more frequently resorted to on a broad scale. Under the military emperors of the third century it became common and provoked outbursts of anti-Hellenism and anti-Romanism. Egyptians prophesied the destruction of the hated capital Alexandria. A collection of martyrologies advertised the selfless patriotism of Greek citizens of Alexandria standing up to the cruel Latin emperors. Flight of Greek officials and Egyptian peasants alike became common, in turn bringing more compulsion, force, and repression. Rebellions broke out.

At the end of the third century A.D. the Roman Empire as a whole faced a series of political and economic crises, and the Emperors Diocletian, A.D. 284-305, and Constantine, A.D. 308-337, well aware of the bureaucratic system organized in Egypt, decided to enforce some of its institutions on the Empire as a whole. As had been the case in Ptolemaic Egypt, Diocletian decreed the separation of military and civil power in the provincial organization; the estimation of necessary state income in advance; a severe rationalization of the taxing system; the rating of land for taxation according to quality; and the fixing of prices, as the old Finance Ministry of Apollonius had done. Constantine attempted to enforce a system of serfdom throughout the Empire by compelling agricultural labor to remain on the land in perpetuity. The reforms of Diocletian and Constantine largely failed, and in the fourth century, native passions rose in Egypt, expressing themselves through the creation of Egyptian Coptic literature, and the strongly anti-Hellenic mobs of riotous Christian monks. — *S.K.E.*

Additional Recommended Reading

Grenfell, B. P., and J. P. Mahaffy. *The Revenue Laws of Ptolemy Philadelphus.* Oxford: The Clarendon Press, 1968. A study containing the Greek text, English translation, notes, and commentary.

Rostovtzeff, M. I. *A Large Estate in Egypt in the Third Century B.C.* Madison: University of Wisconsin Press, 1922. A description of the management of Apollonius' holdings.

Westermann, W. L. "The Ptolemies and the Welfare of Their Subjects," in *American Historical Review.* Vol. 43 (1938), 270-287. Argues that the Ptolemies sincerely attempted to remove the oppression caused by their corrupt or brutal agents.

Kraemer, C. J. "Bureaucracy and Petty Graft in Ancient Egypt," in *Classical Weekly.* Vol. 20 (1927), 163-168. A sketch of administrative malpractice in Greco-Roman Egypt.

Musurillo, Herbert A. *Acta Alexandrinorum. The Acts of the Pagan Martyrs.* Oxford: The Clarendon Press, 1954. An excellent book containing all that is known of the anti-Roman and anti-Semitic patriots of Greek Alexandria.

Marcus, Ralph. "Antisemitism in the Hellenistic World," in *Essays on Antisemitism.* Edited by K. S. Pinson. 2nd ed. New York: Conference on Jewish Relations, 1946. A brief outline of anti-Semitism in the ethnic struggles in Alexandria.

417

"COMMISSIONING" OF THE SEPTUAGINT

Type of event: Religious: translation of the Old Testament into Greek
Time: 250-130 B.C.
Locale: Alexandria

Principal personages:
PTOLEMY II PHILADELPHUS, ruler of Egypt 285-246 B.C.
AQUILA (c.A.D. 140), translator of the Bible
THEODOTION (c.A.D. 140), translator of the Bible
ORIGEN (A.D. 185-254), early great Christian Bible scholar

Summary of Event

While there has always been resistance among Jews to reading the Holy Scriptures in any language other than Hebrew, considered by some Jewish scholars to be the holy tongue if not the original one, conditions made translations essential. The first translation of the Bible into vernacular, or *koine,* Greek was to serve nearly one million Jews living in Egypt, primarily in Alexandria, who could no longer read Hebrew. In the two thousand years since this Greek edition, the holy book has been translated into literally hundreds of languages and dialects.

The Septuagint became so venerated that its origin was glamorized with romance. The pseudepigraphic Letter of Aristeas (c. 150 B.C.) relates that Ptolemy II Philadelphus arranged to have seventy-two Jews translate the Pentateuch into Greek for his royal library, hence the term *Septuagint,* Greek for "seventy" and the cryptic designation "LXX." The scholars, supposedly housed on the island of Pharos, completed their work according to legend in seventy-two days. A later story pictured them working in pairs in separate cells to produce thirty-six copies of the whole Old Testament, all finishing at the same moment without a single variant in their Greek texts.

As a matter of fact the translations went on piecemeal between 250 and 130 B.C. by many scholars in various synagogues whenever and wherever portions of the Old Testament were needed in the vernacular. The work was complete before the Hebrew canon as a whole had been finally set.

The Septuagint was received differently in different quarters. Greek-speaking Jews such as Philo found it indispensable. To Hebrew-speaking Jews the work had little relevance except as an occasional textual corrective for Samuel, and to some extent for Exodus, Deuteronomy, and Jeremiah. Generally renounced by Judaism because of its Christian adoption, the Septuagint was replaced by three new Greek translations in the second century A.D. Aquila, a Christian who later became a Jew, made a conservative and literal translation using the name Yahweh in the text but in Greek transliteration to replace the Septuagint's earlier substitution of

Kurios, or Lord. Theodotion, probably a Jew, also revised the Septuagint in the second century, while Symmachus a little later rendered a free translation which put more of a premium on style than on verbal accuracy.

The Septuagint differs considerably from the Hebrew text both in the order of the books and also in textual differences within them, especially in Job, I Samuel, and Jeremiah. Moreover, the Septuagint includes the so-called Apocrypha: Wisdom, Ecclesiasticus, Judith, Tobit, and Baruch. In general the Greek translation tends to tone down the anthropomorphisms of the Hebrew: the "hand of God" becomes "the power of God," and "his robe" becomes "his glory."

Christians relied exclusively on the LXX until the fourth century. New Testament writers quote from it, and it served as the foundation for the Old Latin version of the Scriptures used in the early Church. Origen, in his work the *Hexapla* (c. A.D. 235), was the first Christian to take an interest in checking the Septuagint text by comparing it with the Hebrew and the other three Greek versions of the second century. When Jerome, at the urging of Pope Damasus, restudied the Hebrew to reëstablish the text of the later official Vulgate, Augustine was disturbed. He, like most Christians, assumed that the Septuagint was divinely inspired and its variants with the Hebrew were, in his mind, divinely contrived as part of a new revelation. Finally, the Septuagint was largely responsible for the acceptance of the Apocrypha as canonical by the Western Church.

Pertinent Literature

Swete, H. B. *An Introduction to the Old Testament in Greek.* Cambridge: The University Press, 1900.

Although the Septuagint was used primarily by Jews and Christians, Swete reminds his readers that it was utilized also by many others in the classical world. Indeed, one of the purposes for translating the Old Testament into Greek seems to have been an apologetic, propagandistic one, to convince the world that Jews possessed a literature rivaling the wisdom of the Greeks.

The popularity of the Septuagint, however, was chiefly among Christians. A careful examination of New Testament citations of Old Testament verses leads Swete to confirm the fact that, statistically, at least, the Septuagint was used more by early Christians than any other Hebrew versions. Direct quotations, word usage, phraseology, and even similarity of literary form make it evident that the New Testament is the child of the Septuagint. As mistrust of the Septuagint arose among the Jews, Christian writers and teachers adhered to it all the more ardently. The many commentaries written upon it by the early Church Fathers attest to its continued Christian popularity up to the time of Jerome, and to its reputation as a book of equal or even greater inspiration than the original Hebrew. The Septuagint served the early Church well during the great crises in her early history, particularly in the struggles with Judaism, Marcionism, and the various schools of

Gnosticism and Arianism. Even after Jerome's Vulgate appeared, the Septuagint remained important for textual criticism as the oldest translation of the Old Testament. Even the Vulgate, which was purposely based on the Hebrew text, perpetuates many of the characteristics of the Septuagint.

Swete thinks the fact that the Septuagint was used by Jews, not only in Palestine and Egypt but throughout West Asia and Europe as well, was important to Christianity. This usage created, as it were, an official language of religion other than Hebrew, which Christianity as a Gentile movement could readily use to lend dignity to its New Testament. Furthermore, translation of the Old Testament into Greek set a precedent for all further translations so that as Christianity spread, the Septuagint lent itself readily to translation into Latin, Coptic, Gothic, Armenian, Slavic, Georgian, Ethiopian, and Arabic.

During the Renaissance and Reformation the rebirth of interest in Greek studies caused the Septuagint to become popular again. This renewed interest was motivated by the desire of critical language study to rediscover the original archetype behind the Massoretic text and other versions of the Bible.

Swete includes in his study a description in great detail of the other early Greek versions of the Old Testament and of the process which led to the ordering of the Christian canon.

Ottley, R. R. *A Handbook to the Septuagint.* London: Methuen & Co., Ltd., 1920.

Ottley is especially interested in the textual accuracy of the Septuagint. He accepts the usual dating of the translation with the exception of a few passages which he would place between A.D. 350 and 500. While the Septuagint preserves a fairly pure text of the Hebrew canon, there are differences in the ordering of some passages as well as some additions and omissions. Thus the LXX of Job is much shorter than the Hebrew and there are serious omissions in I Samuel and Jeremiah; also the order of chapters differs in Jeremiah and Ezekiel. On the whole the Pentateuch is regarded as the most reliable translation and probably the oldest; the Prophets and Writings were rendered more loosely. The translation inclined toward literal paraphrasing, it seems, only when the translators were uncertain of the exact meaning of the Hebrew. While some differences in the Hebrew and Greek versions are thus attributable to lack of linguistic skill on the part of the translators, others may be due to the fact that the modern Hebrew text and the Septuagint stem in part out of different Hebrew manuscripts. If, indeed, the Hebrew canon did not circulate as a single volume nor in one version, the Septuagint would naturally vary in many respects from the Massoretic or any other ancient text. On the whole, Ottley prefers the Massoretic text believing that in a majority of cases it provides equal if not superior renderings to that of the Septuagint. The latter remains the best way to approach the original Scriptures only if one does not directly study the Hebrew text itself. The Septuagint, however, remains the master translation. While the Vulgate replaced it to a great extent among early Christians, Jerome's product owed a great debt to the Greek version both directly and indirectly. The Vulgate not only employed many of the forms and usages of the Septuagint but was itself stimulated by it. — *J.R.R.*

Additional Recommended Reading

Kennedy, H. A. A. *Sources of New Testament Greek.* Edinburgh: T. and T. Clark, 1895. A discussion of the role of Septuagint in the New Testament.

Katz, Peter. *Philo's Bible.* Cambridge: The University Press, 1950. A study on the use of the Septuagint by the outstanding Jewish philosopher of Alexandria.

Tcherikover, Avigdor. *Hellenistic Civilization and the Jews.* Philadelphia, Pennsylvania: Jewish Publication Society, 1959. An excellent account of cultural background leading to the development of the Septuagint.

Thackeray, Henry St. John. *The Septuagint and the Jewish Worship.* London: Oxford University Press, 1923. A discourse on the origins of the Septuagint and its special role in Jewish worship.

Thackeray, Henry St. John, *Some Aspects of the Greek Old Testament.* London: Geo. Allen & Unwin, 1927. A treatise on the Septuagint and its development.

Swete, H. B. *The Old Testament in Greek.* Cambridge: The University Press, 1901-1905. The text of the Septuagint with detailed critical notes.

DISCOVERIES OF ARCHIMEDES

Type of event: Technological: inventions and theoretical innovations
Time: c.250 B.C.
Locale: Syracuse, Sicily

Principal personages:
ARCHIMEDES (c.287-212), Syracusan mathematician and inventor
EUCLID (fl.323-285), Greek mathematician and pioneer geometrician
CONON OF SAMOS (died c.235), astronomer friend of Archimedes at Alexandria
HIERO II OF SYRACUSE (c.309-216), king for whom Archimedes provided inventions and discoveries
MARCUS CLAUDIUS MARCELLUS (c.265-208), Roman general who led the successful siege of Syracuse 213-211
APOLLONIUS OF PERGA (265-190), younger contemporary of Archimedes

Summary of Event

By far the best known scientist of the third century B.C. was Archimedes of Syracuse, a man revered in his own age for his skill as an inventor and since recognized as one of the greatest Greek mathematicians, ranking with Pythagoras and Euclid.

Although tradition has assigned him Syracusan birth, virtually nothing is known of Archimedes' early life. He may well have been of aristocratic descent, for the young Archimedes spent several years in study at Alexandria, where he was introduced to the best mathematical and mechanical researches. While there he seems to have become such a close associate and admirer of the astronomers Conon of Samos and the great Eratosthenes that in later years he deferred to their judgment on the publication of his mathematical treatises. Following his stay in Egypt, Archimedes spent most of his remaining life in Syracuse, whose king, Hiero II, was his patron. It is around this monarch that many of the legendary episodes of Archimedes' life cluster, especially his development of a system of pulleys for drawing newly constructed ships into the water, his construction of military machinery, and his discovery of the fraudulent alloy in Hiero's crown.

Contemporaries and later generations of ancient writers praised Archimedes more for his colorful technical ingenuity than for his significant mathematical formulations. His discovery of the "law" of hydrostatics, or water displacement, and his application of this theory to determine the actual gold content of Heiro's crown may be true, but the exact methodology, if indeed he pursued any, is not at all clear in the ancient accounts. Similar vagueness surrounds the development of the *cochlias,* or Archimedian screw, a device by which water could be raised from a lower level to a higher level by means of a rotating screw inside a tube. Supposedly, Archimedes developed this invention in Egypt, but he may well have taken an existing mechanism and improved it. Other pieces of apparatus he either invented or constructed include a water organ and a model planetarium, the latter being the sole item of booty that the conqueror of Syracuse, Marcus Claudius Marcellus, took back to Rome. The great historians of the Roman Republican period, Polybius, Livy, and Plutarch, give accounts of Archimedes' genius in inventing military weapons. In this sphere, Archimedes seems to have put to use all the laws of physics at his disposal. His knowledge of levers and pulleys was applied to the construction of ballistic weapons, cranes, grappling hooks, and other devices, so that the Roman siege of Syracuse was stalemated for two years, from 213 to 211 B.C. Even the improbable use of large mirrors for directing sharply focused rays of sunlight in order to ignite the Roman fleet is credited to the Syracusan scientist. Doubtlessly Archimedes' was the mind behind the Syracusan defense, and the Romans respected his ability. Although Marcellus wished to capture Archimedes alive, the latter was killed by a Roman legionnaire when the city fell.

Archimedes preferred to be remembered for his theoretical achievements rather than his discoveries in mechanics. In the third century B.C. Greek mathematical thought had advanced as far as it could in terms of geometric methods of reasoning without algebraic notation, and the mathematical work of Archimedes appears as the culmination of Hellenistic mathematics. His work on plane curves represented an extension of Euclid's geometry, and it predicted integral calculus. His studies included conic sections, the ratio of the volume of a cylinder to its inscribed sphere, and some understanding of pure numbers as opposed to the then prevalent notion of infinity. Through his sand-reckoner, Archimedes supposedly could express any integer up to 80,000,000,000,000,000. His work has led some modern scholars to consider Archimedes to be the greatest mathematician of antiquity.

Pertinent Literature

Dijksterhuis, E. J. *Archimedes*. Translated from the Dutch by C. Dikshoorn, in *Acta Historica Scientiarum Naturalium et Medicinalium . . .*, vol. 12. Copenhagen: Ejnar Munksgaard. 1956.

Scholarship on Archimedes and his work has been extensive, ranging from the most general recognition of his contributions to highly technical investigations of his theories in mechanics and mathematics.

The Dutch scholar E. J. Dijksterhuis has composed a clear narrative about Archimedes' life and work. He quotes from and expounds such mathematical works of his subject as *The Method, On the Sphere, On the Cylinder, The Measurement of the Circle*, in addition to considering the miscellaneous problems which the Syracusan undertook.

He acknowledges his debt to Sir Thomas Heath's *The Works of Archi-*

medes (Cambridge, 1897) and P. Ver Eecke's *Les Oeuvres Completes d'Archimede* (Liege, 2nd ed., 1960), but he presents for the modern reader a clearer understanding of Archimedes than they do. While retaining as much of the original notation and procedures of proof as possible, he succeeds in avoiding an exposition which is too literal and hence too far removed from modern mathematics.

No one thought of writing a biography of Archimedes in his era, and posterity has to depend on legend, Roman historial accounts, and the inventor's own works. Roman writers helped to create the legend of Archimedes' genius, while Plutarch, in his *Life of Marcellus*, emphasized his dramatic role in the defense of Syracuse. Vitruvius (in *Architecture, Books IX and X*), Livy (in *History, Book XXIV, chapter 34*), and Polybius (in *History, Book VIII*) contributed to the aura surrounding the Syracusan scientist and his canonization as a martyr to science.

The more scholarly interpretation of Archimedes rests on extant literature attributed to Archimedes himself, most of which is mathematical in nature. In his own lifetime his works were forwarded to Alexandria, where they were studied and dispersed. Probably no coherent understanding of his mathematics emerged. The compilation of his works into major collections, and efforts to analyze them, began only in the sixth century, when the mathematicians Isidore and Anthemius used Archimedian materials as part of their instruction at Constantinople. It is significant that these two men were commissioned by Justinian in 532 for the reconstruction of the Hagia Sophia.

The most important Greek corpus of Archimedes' work emerged in ninth century Constantinople, largely through the efforts of the encyclopedist Leon of Thessalonica. The German editor Heiberg has shown that two major Greek collections of Archimedes' works made by the mathematical schools of Constantinople were passed on to Sicily and Italy, and then to northern Europe, where they were translated into Latin and widely published after the sixth century. However, since none of the Greek collections is complete, Arabic collections and associated commentaries are indispensable in tabulating the works attributed to Archimedes. The introductory texts by Archimedes himself indicate clearly the confidence with which this scientist approached the problems of his day, varying from consideration of infinitely large numbers to the number of spotted cattle in Sicily.

Heath, Sir Thomas. *Archimedes*. (Pioneers of Progress: Men of Science). New York: The Macmillan Company, 1920.

This short work by the great British authority on Archimedes consists of résumés of his introductory material for *The Works of Archimedes* (Cambridge, 1912) and his discussion of Hellenistic science and mathematics in Volume VII of the *Cambridge Ancient History*, (Cambridge, 1954). As a historian of Greek mathematics, Heath places Archimedes in the framework of major developments in geometry among the

Greeks, from Thales of Miletus (c.636-546 B.C.) to Apollonius of Perga (265-190 B.C.). This perspective dispels any immature notion of Archimedes as an isolated genius.

The Greeks credited Egypt with the origin of geometry, even though the Egyptians were less interested in developing theorems than in applying geometrical methods to the solution of practical problems such as land surveying and pyramid building. Thales, among the Greeks, first made use of the applied knowledge of the Egyptians in developing the theoretical basis of geometry, and four of his propositions appear in the first book of Euclid.

The original contributions of Pythagoras to geometry are not evident, since it is difficult to distinguish his work from that of his followers. Along with the Pythagorean theory of numbers and the famous theorem on right-angle triangles, the school of Pythagoras provided the geometrical foundations for much of Books I, II, IV, and VI of Euclid.

Eudoxus of Cnidus (c.408-355 B.C.) was perhaps the greatest of Archimedes' predecessors, and his discovery of the method of exhaustion served as an important means of determining the areas of curves and the volumes of solids. Eudoxus also developed the famous theory of proportion, which when used within the method of exhaustion, could result in the measurement of previously unknown factors.

Heath gives little attention in this book to the importance of Euclid but he has elsewhere stated that the *Elements* was most valuable in providing a sound selection and arrange-ment of the basic geometrical definitions, postulates, and axioms which had been provided by those noted above as well as many others.

The achievement in geometry in the third century B.C. was centered around the work of the two great successors of Euclid, Archimedes and his younger contemporary Apollonius of Perga. While Apollonius was concerned with the geometry of forms and situations, Archimedes continued in the tradition of Eudoxus of Cnidus and Euclid, working on the geometry of measurement. Archimedes pressed the method of exhaustion to its easiest and most workable level in order to solve a given problem of area. For example, were Archimedes to determine the area of a figure inscribed within a circle, he would proceed by reducing the area of the circle to that point in which it coincided in area with the inscribed figure. This process of deduction, when analytical equivalents are defined, resembles a process used in calculus, although Archimedes never approaches a curved surface of a figure as a measurable limiting form of that figure. In short, he calculates the quantity of curved surfaces approximately, suggesting, but not truly attaining the idea of a limit as later perfected by Leibniz and Newton.

Certainly Archimedes' facility in mechanics and hydrostatics was remarkable and indicates his great powers in experimentation and observation. As in his method of geometrical explanation, he did not stop with mere mechanical proofs for his hypotheses in these technical areas. Archimedes was the first to set

425

down mathematical explanations for the properties of levers and the relationship of fluid displacement to the weight of solids. The desire of Archimedes to be remembered for his contributions to mathematics rather than for his mechanical efforts, has been met to some extent by this concise treatment by Sir Thomas Heath. — *R.J.W.*

Additional Recommended Reading

Clagett, Marshall. *Archimedes in the Middle Ages.* Madison: University of Wisconsin Press, 1964. Introductory chapters record the transmission of the works of Archimedes from antiquity through the Middle Ages.

Clagett, Marshall. *Greek Science in Antiquity.* New York: Abelard-Schuman, Inc., 1955. A short but comprehensive treatment of Greek science in all its phases.

Farrington, Benjamin. *Greek Science.* Baltimore, Maryland: Penguin Books, Inc., 1961. A good study of the scope of the Greek scientific achievement, both practical and theoretical, from the Ionian period to the Roman conquest.

Heath, Sir Thomas, *et al.* "Hellenistic Science and Mathematics," in *Cambridge Ancient History.* Vol. VII, pp. 290-311. Cambridge: The University Press, 2nd printing, 1954. A summary of Greek endeavors in these fields during the third and second centuries B.C.

Heath, Sir Thomas. *A History of Greek Mathematics.* Vol. II. Oxford: The Clarendon Press, revised 1960. A comprehensive treatment of Archimedes' mathematical works, with modern notation, is found in Chapter XIII.

Heath, Sir Thomas. *A Manual of Greek Mathematics.* New York: Dover Publications, Inc., revised 1963. A compact presentation of material found in *A History of Greek Mathematics,* but directed to the more general reader.

RISE OF PARTHIA

Type of event: Political: establishment of a feudal monarchy
Time: c.250-140 B.C.
Locale: Parthia in northwestern Iran

Principal personages:

ANDRAGORAS, Seleucid Satrap of Parthia c.245
ANTIOCHUS III (the Great), Seleucid King 223-187
ARSACES, founder of the Parthian dynasty c.250-c.248
TIRIDATES, King of Parthia c.248-211
MITHRIDATES I, King of Parthia c.171-c.138/137

Summary of Event

Out of the historical mists surrounding the regions northeast of the Caspian Sea rode the vanguards of barbarian invaders of Iran in the first half of the third century B.C. They were the Parni. Toward the middle of the century, Diodotus, King of the Greco-Bactrian state, attacked and drove them westward into the Seleucid provinces of Hyrcania and Parthia. At that time these districts were sparsely populated by nomadic Iranian shepherds, a few agriculturalists, and occasional brigands. Here, about 245 B.C., the Parni met the Seleucid Satrap Andragoras and defeated him. The fact that such men, scarcely civilized themselves, could overcome the mighty Seleucid forces and kill their leader, was no doubt due in large measure to contemporary Seleucid involvement in the Third Syrian War (246-241) against Ptolemaic Egypt.

Their victory gave the Parni a permanent home in Parthia, and the province gave them the name by which they are known in history. Their first known king was Arsaces, who ruled about the middle of the third century B.C. and apparently died while fighting. He was succeeded by Tiridates who must have been the real founder of the kingdom. Few details of early Parthian history are known. After the death of Tiridates, Seleucid control of Parthia was reasserted by the indefatigable campaigner Antiochus the Great, who was intent on restoring to his kingdom the territory it had possessed in the days of its founder, Seleucus I. His defeat by Rome in 189 was followed by his own death at the hands of rebels in Elymais in 187, and the Arsacids seized the opportunity to throw off Seleucid suzerainty. Thereafter, Parthia grew stronger, and by 140, Mithridates I had overrun Media and Persis, and had taken most of Babylonia from the Seleucids. These rich conquests transformed Parthia, until then a third-rate power, into an important state.

Parthia was a loosely organized monarchy with its capital sometimes at Ecbatana in Iran and sometimes at Ctesiphon in Babylonia. Its kings ruled over a feudal aristocracy of Parthians dwelling mostly in Iran. The noble families were half-independent princely clans who lived in fortified castles and held sway over Iranian serfs who toiled in the valleys below. In this eastern, Iranian, half of the state, the old institutions, customs, and culture of the Orient continued, and the Arsacids pretended to be descendants of Artaxerxes I (the Achaemenid King of Persia from 464 to 425) and worshipers of the traditional gods of Iran. In the western, Babylonian, half of the state, a different set of values obtained. There the Parthians carefully fostered good relations with the Greek cities founded by Alexander, Seleucus, and Antiochus. The cities continued, as they had under Seleucid rule, to be autonomous states governing their own territory, speaking Greek and maintaining Greek institutions. To these cities the Arsacids, Mithridates I especially, advertised themselves as Philhellenes. Many Greeks readily accepted this new order, since the military strength of the Parthians protected them from participating in the miserable wars which had begun between rival branches of the Seleucid dynasty. Some Greeks, of course, did not take kindly to the Parthians, and made gibes about their kings, said so to love their horses that they would not dismount from them even to hold a trial. The Arsacids did develop a sincere admiration for Hellenistic culture; King Orodes II was interrupted once while enjoying a performance of Euripides' *Bacchae*.

After the death of Mithridates I, Parthian power continued slowly to expand until it reached the Euphrates in northwestern Mesopotamia, where, in the middle of the first century B.C.,

it met the rapidly growing empire of the Romans. There then ensued between these two powers a series of wars which caused the periodic expenditure of the resources of both to the advantage of neither. In 53 B.C. the great noble Surenas defeated the Roman plunderer Crassus in the bloody Battle of Carrhae by wearing down the sturdy Roman infantry under a hail of arrows shot by horse-archers. His men replenished their supply of missiles from a mobile ammunition column of camels. Mark Antony sought to avenge this disaster by invading the Parthian Empire in 36 B.C., but his campaign ended in a second Roman defeat. The Parthians thus appeared as the champions of eastern Greek and of Oriental alike against the rapacity of Rome. Some Hellenic historians highly approved of them in this role, and a Jewish prophet forecast that the Messiah would be nigh when a Parthian tied his horse to a tree outside Jerusalem. But that dream ended when Augustus consolidated the Roman Empire on a new and more formidable basis, and negotiated a settlement with the Arsacids. Thereafter, the Parthians were not a serious menace to Rome. Nero's great general Corbulo inflicted severe defeats on them; the Emperor Trajan actually overran all Babylonia; and Marcus Aurelius and Septimius Severus repeated Trajan's feat. The last invasion seriously weakened Parthia, and about A.D. 229, the last Parthian king was killed by the Ardishir of Persis, who founded the powerful Sassanian dynasty as the standard-bearer of revived Zoroastrianism and Iranian nationalism.

Rise of Parthia

Pertinent Literature

Debevoise, Neilson C. *A Political History of Parthia*. Chicago: University of Chicago Press, 1938.

This is a lean narrative of Parthian history from its beginning in the third century B.C. to the deaths of Artabanus V in A.D. 227 and of his son Artavasdes in 228/229, when Parthian history ends. Debevoise treats the Parthians for what they really were: a small feudal, military aristocracy settled in parts of Iran, lording it over the Iranian peasants, intermingling Greek and Oriental civilization, extracting a derivative art from them, creating nothing original, and interested in commerce only because it could be taxed. It is a commentary on the Parthian contribution to the stock of human culture that their history is known to us almost entirely from Greek and Latin sources and not from Parthian literature at all, except for a small number of official administrative documents. In general, the kings of Parthia were taxgatherers, raiders, and collectors of booty, remembered only for their military accomplishments. Debevoise's narrative of the Battle of Carrhae is an account of their most famous victory. The Parthian army was commanded by Surenas, one of the great nobles; it had a strength of eleven thousand fighting men, ten thousand horse-archers and one thousand cataphracts. A cataphract was a horseman who wore a suit of chain mail and was armed with a lance. They prevented the weak Roman cavalry from interfering with the horse-archers. In the decisive fighting the mobile Parthian horsemen evaded the dangerous but slow-moving attacks of the numerically superior Roman infantry. The horse-archers poured in endless volleys of fire from their powerful compound bows, and filled their emptied quivers from the camel train as necessary. Surenas' use of this mobile supply column was the thinking of a military genius, and it is curious that we never hear of the Parthians using it again. Surenas himself, incidentally, was executed by Orodes II, since the Parthian Empire was too small for two heroes. Crassus himself was killed, too, and his head was taken to Orodes, who was sitting watching the *Bacchae* when it arrived in time to be used as a stage-prop.

Debevoise's book is a catalogue of wars. There were Corbulo's extended campaigns from A.D. 58 to 63, which arose out of a quarrel as to whether Parthia or Rome would make Armenia its sphere of influence. Trajan made war on Parthia, using Armenia as a pretext, from 114 to 117, invading Babylonia and sacking Ctesiphon. Marcus Aurelius also invaded Babylonia from 162 to 166, again ravaging the country and taking the capital. While this was a Roman military success, it became a human disaster, for the army became infected with plague and brought it home with catastrophic results. From 195 to 199 Septimius Severus conducted the last great offensive against the Arsacids, overrunning Babylonia for the third time in less than a century, and sacking Ctesiphon. All these Roman victories were hard on

Mesopotamia, that cradle of civilization, and the level of human existence there, as shown by excavations at Dura-Europus and Seleucia-on-Tigris, was reduced by these heavy-handed campaigns.

Frye, Richard N. *The Heritage of Persia*. London: Weidenfeld and Nicolson, 1962.

Frye's book concerns itself with the history of all Persia, or, more accurately, of all Iran from the ninth century B.C., the time when the Medes and Persians invaded from the north, to the Arab conquest in the seventh century A.D. In the course of his description of this long and significant historical epoch, he includes a chapter, "The Adaptable Arsacids," which in compact fashion describes the rise and development of the Parthian Empire.

Concerning the first appearance of the Parthians in history, the author notes that the vagueness of the historical tradition which the Greeks preserved does not permit us to be precise about the details of the beginning of the Parthian Empire. We can only say that the Parni settled in Parthia, adopted the language and some of the civilization of the inhabitants, and then spread this new blend of culture into much of the rest of Iran. Their empire was really a patchwork of many elements. In the northeast of Iran was Parthia proper. In western Iran was Media, with its special traditions and strong cities. In the southwest was Persis, Persia proper, with its jealously guarded memory of Persian imperialism, its local dynasts biding their time until the Arsacids should fall. Babylonia was a mosaic of the territories of the Greek cities there and of old Seleucid royal domains which the Arsacids had inherited.

The author is inclined to defend the reputation of the Parthians against attacks by certain scholars. They were not, he thinks, entirely without virtue. First, Parthian art and architecture, far from being merely degenerate Greek, were interesting blends of Greek and Iranian ideas. Second, the Arsacids defended Iranian culture against the Greeks. In the third century B.C. Hellenism penetrated readily into Iran under the protection of the Seleucids. At that time the population was under the spell of Alexander's victories, which had so easily toppled the seemingly invincible power of the Achaemenids. The Parthians, however, by first checking and then repelling the Seleucids, served to diminish Greek influence in Iran and to afford a breathing space for the Orient. As the power of the Seleucid Empire slowly ebbed, not least because of the military blows dealt it by Mithridates I, there was something of a revival of native Iranian culture and tradition. To this the Parthians adapted themselves, and may even have supported it, although the lack of sufficient evidence does not allow a definitive judgment on this point. The Parthians, moreover, were tolerant of all religions, and their increasing interest, shown during the Christian era, in the Iranian half of their state led them to protect Zoroastrianism, which now slowly developed a more definite theology and detailed forms of organization than it had had in the Achaemenid period.

For all this, they deserve better remembrance. But their worst detractors were actually their native Persian successors. The Sassanids regarded the Parthian era as an age of darkness which fell between the glory of the Achaemenids of Persis and the period of grandeur inaugurated by themselves. There is evidence of Sassanid tampering with the tradition of Parthian history; they certainly shortened the length of time allotted Arsacid rule in Iran, possibly, as Frye believes, to make the expected reappearance of Zoroaster at the end of earthly time a more remote event. — *S.K.E.*

Additional Recommended Reading

Ghirshman, R. *Iran, from the Earliest Times to the Islamic Conquest.* Baltimore, Maryland: Penguin Books, Inc., 1954. A survey of Iranian history rather like Frye.

Tarn, W. W. *The Greeks in Bactria and India.* 2nd ed. Cambridge: The University Press, 1951. An important contribution by a leading historian to our knowledge of the Greco-Bactrian kingdom located in modern Pakistan and its relationship to the Parthians.

Lepper, F. A. *Trajan's Parthian War.* Oxford: The Clarendon Press, 1948. A detailed study of one of the many conflicts between Rome and Parthia.

CYBELE'S INTRODUCTION INTO ROME

Type of event: Religious: adoption of an Oriental deity by Rome
Time: 205-204 B.C.
Locale: Rome

Principal personages:
MARCUS VALERIUS LAEVINIUS, consul in 210
MARCUS CAECILIUS METELLUS, plebeian aedile in 208
PUBLIUS CORNELIUS SCIPIO NASICA, consul in 191
ATTALUS I (SOTER, 269-197), ruler of Pergamum 241-197

Summary of Event

During the first centuries of the Republic, Roman authorities frequently had recourse to the Sibylline Books to find some means of averting an evil omen or remedying a public disaster such as famine or pestilence. The response on such occasions usually took the form of an oracle suggesting that official recognition be given to some new deity at Rome with appropriate rites. Almost until the end of the third century B.C. these suggestions concerned Greek gods or goddesses (as, for example, the introduction of Asculapius from Epidarus), which was scarcely surprising since the Sibylline Books themselves were of Greek origin. In 205 B.C., however, an oracle was received which advised introducing an Oriental deity into the state cult at Rome, perhaps because Hannibal had been ravaging the Italian peninsula for thirteen years with little apparent dissuasion from the old Roman *numina* or the newer Greek imports. Those in charge of the books may have suggested the worship of a new and exotic deity in a somewhat desperate attempt to secure supernatural aid. Whatever may have been the reason for the oracle, the decision to follow its advice proved to be of the utmost importance for the future development of the Roman religion.

According to Livy, the event happened almost by chance. During the year 205, repeated showers of stones created considerable superstitious fear in Rome. While the Sibylline Books were being consulted, an oracle was discovered which stated that a foreign foe could be defeated and driven out of Italy if the Idaean Mother, Cybele, were brought from Asia Minor to Rome. This goddess was believed to dwell in or be symbolized by or actually be a small black meteorite which could be carried in the hand. The senate decided to send an embassy of five prominent citizens to the friendly court of Attalus of Pergamum to ask for the goddess.

On the journey they were assured by the oracle at Delphi that they would obtain their request. At Pergamum they were courteously received by Attalus who, according to Livy, actually escorted the Romans to Pessimus in Phrygia and there gave them the sacred stone.

One of the ambassadors, Marcus

Valerius Falto, returned to Rome before the others to report the coming of the goddess. The senate decided upon Publius Cornelius Scipio Nasica as the best man to receive her. Cybele was in due course welcomed into her new home with appropriate pomp and ceremony, though reports on her reception disagree. According to Livy, when news reached Rome that Cybele was nearing the city, the senate ordered Scipio and the matrons of Rome to go down to the harbor to meet her. When the ship reached the mouth of the Tiber River, Scipio sailed out to it, received the goddess from her priests, carried her to land, and there gave her to the waiting women. Through crowds of spectators and streets lined with incense-burning censers, matrons passed the sacred stone from hand to hand until it was temporarily deposited on April 12, 204, in the Temple of Victory on the Palatine until a special temple could be erected, which was done in 191. The immediate choice of the Temple of Victory was a fairly obvious indication of what the Romans expected from the newly arrived goddess.

A more elaborate account of Cybele's reception is given by Ovid. The ship carrying the goddess grounded but was miraculously refloated. A priest clad in a purple robe washed the image amid shouts from the populace accompanied by the playing of flutes and the beating of drums. The goddess was then placed in a wagon and driven into the city through the Porta Capena.

Cybele's power was witnessed by the Romans in the flight of Hannibal from Italy and the fruitful harvest which followed hard upon her arrival. At the same time, the Romans were appalled by the eunuch priests who had come with her and who prescribed wild and orgiastic rites as part of her ritual. Livy's account appears to be a deliberate attempt to suppress details of the strange and repulsive worship so eloquently described by Lucretius. Ovid and most later Roman authors emphasize the miraculous circumstances that were supposed to have coincided with her arrival and the ecstatic character of rites associated with her.

The advent of Cybele into Rome heralded the arrival of numerous other Oriental cults which eventually challenged the older Roman beliefs and rituals. Attempts to Romanize the worship of *Magna Mater* proved to be futile, and her cult became so extensive by the third and fourth centuries of the Christian era that it presented some threat to the spread of Christianity.

Pertinent Literature

Bailey, Cyril. *Phases in the Religion of Ancient Rome.* Berkeley: University of California Press, 1932.

This tenth volume in the highly respected series published by the University of California Press as the Sather Classical Lectures, is one of the best introductory books to the history of Roman religion available in English. Bailey discusses the primitive backgrounds of Roman beliefs, the yielding of animism to polytheism, the growth of the state religion, the adoption of foreign cults, the relations between ancient philosophy and religion, and finally the tendency to a syncretistic merging of cults. The sixth chapter entitled "Emotion and Mysticism; the Oriental Cults" and dealing with the introduction of Cybele to Rome is particularly helpful in showing how this foreign religion was regarded by pagan opinion during Republican times.

In order to escape from the formalism of the state religion, many Romans turned to the more emotional ceremonies of the Greeks and the peoples of Egypt and Asia Minor. The secret worship of Bacchus, was declared an aberration by the senate and was sternly repressed in 186 B.C. In contrast to this official suppression of a popular outburst of religious enthusiasm, Bailey describes the official welcome of the worship of the "Great Mother" of Phrygia some twenty years earlier. After giving a brief account of the coming of the goddess to Rome, he quotes a passage from Lucretius describing her exotic ritual: how the holy mother was borne in her wagon by a yoke of lions, how she was followed by a band of her mutilated priests or *galli,* and by armed bands who in bobbing headcrests and merry with blood jousted publicly in religious frenzy whipped up by thundering drums, clashing cymbals, and hoarse-throated horns. Money and roses were scattered in her path as her retinue passed through the streets.

The Phrygian excesses offended the staid attitude of respectable Romans. Particularly objectionable to

Roman sensitivity was the fact that Cybele's priests had as young men in a fit of madness castrated themselves to be more like the goddess's youthful lover Attis. If the worship of Cybele was to be continued at Rome as it had been in her native Anatolia, it would undoubtedly give rise to similar cruel and debasing orgies. To forestall such unfortunate events, Roman authorities did all they could to change the character of her worship. Greco-Roman rites were ordained for her. She was presented with gifts; a *lectisternium* was held in her honor, that is, a banquet was prepared for her; and games, *ludi,* were staged. Ten years later these games took the form of plays, and after the opening of her temple on the Palatine, the *ludi Megalenses* was given a regular place in the calendar.

These measures and others like them were hardly sufficient to check the harm that might come from her worship by the ordinary citizen. Regulations were therefore passed to the effect that no Roman should become a *gallus,* hold a priesthood of the Great Mother, or take part in her processions. The ritual was, as a consequence, only performed by priests brought from the goddess's native home. During the two remaining centuries of the Republic the worship of the Great Mother remained a foreign rite and was never fully absorbed into the state religion. Bailey contends that the worship of the goddess merely provided excitement and spectacle for the Romans and that her ceremonies always remained vicarious. He concludes that the "euthusiastic" cult of Cybele, along with that of Bacchus, fed by a degrading intoxication of wine and blood, had no ethical value, ideal significance, or redeeming mysticism. All was irrational frenzy, unbridled emotion, and divine obsession.

Cumont, Franz. *The Oriental Religions in Roman Paganism.* Chicago: Open Court Publishing Co., 1911.

If Bailey sees the mystery cults as something suspect and forbidding to Roman sensitivities in Republican days, Cumont views them in an entirely different light in the time of the Empire. Any earlier conflict of conscience involved in a choice between the extravagant worship of the Great Mother and the calm reserve which ancestral custom dictated in the respectful worship of the gods, was being resolved progressively, in his opinion, by the time of the Caesars. Despite various restrictions on the rites of Cybele, her cult prospered especially among slaves, freedmen, and merchants coming to Rome from the East. Even the official attitude toward it and other Oriental cults changed as the early Empire lifted restrictions, accepted Roman citizens in the role of *archgalli,* and formalized at least by the time of the Antonines Cybele's rustic worship by setting aside a celebration from March 24 to 27 characterized by much solemn pomp and ceremony.

Many considerations combine to explain the change of attitude. Imperial concerns forced more and more the recognition of gods honored by conquered Eastern peoples. The worship of the Egyptian Isis was, for instance, approved of by Caligula. Vergilian popularization of the Trojan origins of Rome, no doubt, helped to glamorize the gods of Asia Minor, and even family traditions may have encouraged interest in Cybele in the case of the Emperor Claudius, since a member of his gens had played a part in the original introduction of the Great Mother to Rome. Interest in fertility gods continued to mount as the mystery religions came to be viewed as new and rewarding ways to approach divinity, regeneration, and immortality. The later popularity of the cult of Mithra clearly reveals this unsatisfied hunger for religious security.

According to Cumont, the Oriental cults, far from being devoid of any merit, tended to give new vigor to Roman religion and to modify it as atrophied parts of old classical cults fell away with time. As antiquarian savants, most of the Christian Fathers, he believes, tended to overemphasize the old classical mythology even though the gods were dead. Hence they spoke as though no evolution had taken place in Roman religion since early times. They consequently underestimated the impact that Oriental cults were making on the contemporary religious scene of which early Christianity was a part. Cumont holds that the once rival mystery cults combined, as it were, their worship of the four constituent elements traditional in classical cosmology. The Egyptian Isis was intimately concerned with water under the guise of the Nile, the Phrygian Cybele was the Earth Mother, the Syrian-Carthaginian cults tended to worship the upper air in connection with the sun,

435

and Persian cults held fire sacred. All these cults tended to consider themselves virtual divisions or congregations of the same universal "church." The Oriental gods became an expression of the cosmic energies whose providential action controlled the "harmonious system" of the universe. The cosmology of the day had taken religious form under a final unique eternal and almighty God directing these subordinate Oriental deities. Through the worship of individual mystery cult gods, God himself was honored. Eventually, the once coarse Oriental mysteries came, through this combination or convergence, to produce an "ethereal spiritualism," a system of metaphysics and an eschatology. Their liturgy became ethically saturated and promised purity, holiness, and immortality to those who availed themselves of their sacred ceremonies. Christianity itself, Cumont reminds his readers, moved in this same "intellectual and moral sphere" along with the mystery cults, so that an ordinary devotee could pass from one religion to another with ease. The "religious and mystical spirit of the Orient" by slowly overpowering the entire social organism, in Cumont's opinion, "had prepared all nations to unite in the bosom of a universal church." — *M.J.C.*

Additional Recommended Reading

Carter, Jesse Benedict. *The Religion of Numa and Other Essays on the Religion of Ancient Rome.* New York: The Macmillan Company, 1906. A dissertation associating the coming of Cybele to Rome with a decline of orthodox Roman religion.

Farnell, Lewis Richard. *The Cults of the Greek States.* Vols. II and III. Oxford: The Clarendon Press, 1907. An old but comprehensive work, particularly useful for understanding the worship of Cybele in Greece and Asia Minor.

Fowler, W. Warde. *The Religious Experience of the Roman People.* New York: The Macmillan Company, 1911. A study regarding the advent of the Magna Mater to Italy as a brilliant idea, "something entirely new and strange, a fresh and hopeful prescription for an exhausted patient."

Halliday, W. A. *Lectures on the History of Roman Religion.* Liverpool: The University Press of Liverpool, Ltd., 1923. A brief but adequate background for the various religious developments of the Roman Republic.

James. E. O. *The Cult of the Mother-Goddess.* New York: Frederick A. Praeger, Inc., 1959. A useful treatise tracing the various manifestations of the worship of the fertility goddess.

BATTLE OF ZAMA

Type of event: Military: engagement between Roman and Carthaginian armies
Time: 202 B.C.
Locale: About sixty miles southwest of Carthage in what is now Tunisia

Principal personages:
HANNIBAL (248-182), Carthaginian general
HASDRUBAL BARCA (d.207), younger brother of Hannibal
PUBLIUS CORNELIUS SCIPIO (236-184), Roman consul and general
MASSINISSA (c.240-148), King of eastern Numidia, and an ally of Rome
GAIUS LAELIUS, consul 190, and Roman commander under Scipio

Summary of Event

After Hannibal had finally been trapped in southern Italy by the "Fabian tactics" of Rome, the tide of the Second Punic War turned against him. Scipio's victories in Spain from 208 to 206, and the frustration of the efforts by Hasdrubal, Hannibal's younger brother, to reinforce Hannibal in 207, prepared the way for an invasion of Africa by Scipio in 204. It was then Rome's turn to ravish the enemy countryside as Hannibal had done for fifteen years in Italy. With a large and well-disciplined army, mostly volunteers, Scipio outwitted two defense forces collected by Carthage, captured the rural areas around the city, and damaged its economy. The Carthaginians offered a truce to gain time in order to effect Hannibal's return from Italy; he succeeded in getting away with a force of more than ten thousand veterans.

Hannibal spent the winter of 203-202 collecting and training an army for the decisive meeting with Scipio. Since both Roman and Car-

thaginian cavalry was limited, the rival generals each sent out appeals for aid to various African chieftains. Scipio turned to an old companion in arms, the wily desert sheik Massinissa, who had fought with the Romans in Spain. In 204-203 Scipio had helped Massinissa defeat a rival for control of a kingdom in Numidia, west of Carthage. But in 202 Massinissa was slower to respond to Scipio than were other African princes who brought cavalry and elephants to aid Hannibal. So Scipio moved his army inland and westward to avoid a major battle until he had secured more cavalry.

Hannibal marched his army in pursuit of the Romans, hoping to force a confrontation before Scipio was ready. When the Carthaginian army came near the village of Zama, about five days' march southwest of Carthage, he sent scouts to search out Scipio's position. These spies were captured, but after being shown through the Roman camp they were released. Scipio by this device hoped that their reports would discourage an immediate Carthaginian attack. Polybius, the Greek historian who lived in the first half of the first century B.C., reports that before the battle the two generals actually had a dramatic face-to-face meeting, alone on a plain between two opposing hills where their armies were encamped. However, Hannibal's peace proposals were rejected by Scipio, who had recently been encouraged by the arrival of Massinissa with four thousand cavalrymen and other reinforcements.

On the following day the two armies were drawn up for battle. They were probably about equal in size, although some scholars estimate that Hannibal's force was as large as fifty thousand men while Scipio's was as small as twenty-three thousand. Certainly the Roman cavalry was stronger. Hannibal placed his eighty elephants in front of his first-line troops, who were experienced mercenaries from Europe and Africa. Scipio's front line was divided into separate fighting units with gaps between them to allow the elephants to pass through without disarranging the line.

When the battle began, bugles stampeded the elephants, which turned sideways on to Hannibal's own cavalry stationed on the wings. The Roman cavalry under Laelius and Massinissa took advantage of the confusion to drive the Carthaginian cavalry off the battlefield.

During the infantry battle which ensued, the disciplined front rank of Roman legionaires, closely supported by their second-rank comrades, managed to penetrate Hannibal's line in places. The second-line troops of Carthage, apparently not as well coördinated, allowed both Punic lines to be driven back with heavy casualties. Hannibal had kept in reserve a strong third line of veterans, intending to attack with this fresh force when the Romans were exhausted, but he allowed a fatal pause during which Scipio regrouped his detachments. The final stage of the battle raged indecisively until the cavalry of Laelius and Massinissa returned to the field to attack the Carthaginians in the rear and destroy most of those encircled by this maneuver. Polybius reports twenty thousand Carthaginian casualties compared to only fifteen hundred Romans killed.

Hannibal escaped, but Carthage was exhausted and surrendered without a siege, accepting peace terms which took away all Carthaginian possessions outside Africa, imposed a heavy indemnity, and guaranteed the autonomy of Massinissa's kingdom. Scipio returned in triumph to Rome where he was awarded the title "Africanus." Remarkably undaunted by defeat, Hannibal led Carthage within a few years to economic recovery; later he was forced by Rome into exile, and he fled eastward to aid adversaries of Rome in further wars.

By their victory at Zama, the Romans gained supremacy in the western Mediterranean and launched an imperialistic program which eventually made them dominant throughout most of Europe and the Near East, repressing eastern leadership until the rise of Moslem power.

Pertinent Literature

Scullard, H. H. *Scipio Africanus: Soldier and Politician.* Ithaca: Cornell University Press, 1970.

This new work is likely to be the definitive biography of Scipio for some time. While the author has great respect for Africanus, he finds it unprofitable to speculate on his rank among the world's great generals as did Liddell Hart in his commendable study, *A Greater than Napoleon: Scipio Africanus.* This later British soldier and military analyst devotes some sixty pages to Scipio's African campaign which ended at Zama, and gives only begrudging acknowledgment to Hannibal's skill.

Scullard agrees with Liddell Hart that Scipio was a great man. His basic claim to distinction, according to Scullard, was his realization that Rome could no longer depend upon her traditional citizen levies, commanded each year by a different general, to defeat Hannibal. A professional army was required. Scipio realized that establishment of such an army involved attacking "Republican formalities"; to pit the individual against the *mos maiorum* and the corporate body was an appalling effrontery to his fellow noble traditionalists. Consequently if Hannibal had to fight a short-sighted government, Scipio had to overcome the Roman establishment. Fortunately he made no constitutional threats against his foes in the senate, and instead of becoming a demagogue he retired voluntarily after his victory into exile. In his role as an exceptional commander, however, he foreshadowed the later military dictators of Rome.

Scipio moreover understood that the Roman army had to be more mobile so that it could not be outflanked as it was at Cannae. He preferred to arrange his forces in independent units in a decentralized organization which put a premium on the self-reliance of individual lieutenants for quick action.

Scullard would like to see in Scipio a precocious, idealistic imperialist. As such Scipio supposedly saw that Fabius' guerrilla tactics could solve nothing. Hannibal and later Antiochus had to be defeated in the open field on their own ground to make the world safe for Rome; Carthage had to be eliminated in order to lay the foundation for the later Empire. Scullard attributes to Scipio's far-sighted imperial outlook his policy of withdrawing troops and treating conquered countries mildly to foster in them the devotion to Rome which would make them loyal provinces in the future. Unlike Hannibal, Scipio came not to destroy but to offer culture and civilization without threats or fear to those who would profit by such treatment. Scipio's settlement of veterans close to the pillars of Hercules instead of near Rome reveals his confidence in Rome's mission as a future imperial power. It is interesting to note that he called his settlement "Italica" rather than naming it after himself in the manner of Hellenistic rulers.

Scipio's greatness rests in his encouragement of a new culture blending together the best of Greece and Rome. His interest in literature was a new departure among his noble colleagues in politics; his daughter Cornelia was provided with an exceptionally good education. Scullard admits that Scipio's part in the Hellenization of Rome is difficult to assess and document. He asks whether Scipio was a Grecophile in philosophy, or sincere in claiming divine guidance. Was he a Greek skeptic or atheist exploiting the religious aura surrounding him by fostering a false belief in his divine mission? Or was he a bona fide mystic trusting in divine communication? Scullard is inclined to believe in Scipio's own inner integrity. Polybius apparently judged him to be an extreme rationalist, projecting his own personal judgments rather than those of contemporary Romans who were at that time basically religious.

Scipio was in time compared to Alexander. Dante saw the hand of God in his victory at Zama which made possible the future glory of Rome. The Renaissance saw him as a bridge between the classical world and the Christian, a man having a fine sense of morality serving in Roman times the ends of Divine Providence. Petrarch was much influenced by Cicero's *Scipio's Dream* and he glorified Scipio in his *Africa* as an inspiration in the dream of Humanism to rediscover the ancient world.

Dodge, T. A. *Hannibal*. Boston: Houghton Mifflin Co., 1891. 2 vols.

This fascinating old study of Hannibal is self-opinionated and undocumented, but it remains interesting as a eulogy of the great Carthaginian general who was defeated at the Battle of Zama. In nearly seven hundred pages Dodge admires Hannibal in great detail, and while it is unfair to isolate his strong generalizations from their context, some of his conclusions follow.

Dodge's position regarding Scipio is equivocal. He recognizes the merits of the man as a great general and politician, but he regards him as inferior to Hannibal in generalship. The author reminds his readers that history has eulogistic Roman historians such as Livy to thank for Scipio's unearned reputation. Dodge moreover believes that Scipio was exceptionally fortunate in having about him able lieutenants such as Laelius and Silvanus in Spain for whose work he reaped the credit. Scipio enjoyed "marked good fortune" throughout his career which caused his ultimate success as much as his "fine abilities." Dodge regards Scipio as a brilliant but not a great general.

Scipio's reputation derives in part from his popularity despite his "many and serious errors." He entered history dramatically by saving his father's life at Trebia and by heroically presenting himself as the only volunteer to lead the dangerous assignment in Spain. He was admittedly handsome, manly, enthusiastic courageous, intelligent, self-confident, honorable, considerate, generous, educated, and refined. But he was born under a lucky star. "When he failed from the result of his own errors, Fortune always came to his rescue." Fortune was indeed as good to him as to Alexander, although the latter did far more to deserve such favors. Because he was a great, almost obnoxious, believer in his own destiny, he was haughty and considered himself to be above criticism. It is fortunate that he was never called upon to account for his high-handedness. Livy records how he blatantly threatened to bypass the senate and appeal to the people in order to gain acceptance for his resolution to take the war to Africa. He openly defied the senate and Fabius Maximus when he was asked to submit, saying that he would prefer to consult the "interests of the state" himself. Dodge suggests that such action shows he was more of a politician than a good military man dedicated to the service of the civil state. He was forced to collect his own supplies at first, and only later was he able to persuade the senate to allow him to draft some troops from Sicily.

It was not the superiority of Scipio over Hannibal which brought him victory at Zama. History shows that the best general does not always win. Scipio should be thankful that before Zama he had not faced an equal opponent except perhaps Hasdrubal, or else Fortune could not have saved him for Zama when Hannibal's forces and chances were already wrecked. Had Scipio met the great Carthaginian general earlier, he would surely have been defeated. At Zama, Carthage was almost defenseless with scarcely enough men to man her walls compared to the thirty-seven thousand enthusiastic troops under Scipio. His feeble attempts against Carthage earlier and his waste of time collecting and shipping booty to Rome should go a long way toward placing Scipio "where he fairly belongs in the ranks of generals." At Zama the Roman army won because its cavalry was superior; the victory was not the result of Scipio's brilliant generalship. Hannibal was superior in logistics and strategy, but he was handicapped by inferior forces and the stubbornness, stupidity, and short-sightedness of the Carthaginian senate. Rome had to win, not because it outgeneraled Carthage but because of the "strength of its organization and the soundness of its body politic" against the military corruption of Carthage. Had Rome not been victorious at Zama, it would have succeeded somewhere else. In fact Zama should be downgraded in importance along with Scipio, for Carthage lost long before the battle took place. When Hannibal was ordered back from Italy, the die was already cast. It was only Hannibal's genius which prolonged the struggle and made Zama possible at all. — *A.B.C.*

Additional Recommended Reading

Liddell Hart, B. H. *A Greater than Napoleon: Scipio Africanus.* Edinburgh: William Blackwood and Sons, 1926. A semipopular but solid account lauding Scipio as greater than Caesar, Alexander, and Frederick the Great.

Hallward, B. L. "Scipio and Victory," in *The Cambridge Ancient History.* Vol. 8, ch. 4. Cambridge: The University Press, 1928. In discussing the Battle of Zama, this account eulogizes Hannibal as the "consummate strategist" and statesman.

Russell, Francis H. "The Battlefield of Zama," in *Archaeology.* Vol. 23, No. 2

(April, 1970), 120-129. A beautifully illustrated study of the Battle of Zama.

Warmington, B. H. *Carthage*. London: Robert Hale Ltd., 1960. A history including a brief description of the Battle of Zama and its consequences for history.

Baker, G. P. *Hannibal*. New York: Dodd, Mead & Company, 1929. A clear account of Zama with three maps to show different stages of the battle.

Cottrell, Leonard. *Hannibal, Enemy of Rome*. New York: Holt, Rinehart, and Winston, 1960, 1961. An interesting biography which provides clear battle diagrams.

De Beer, Gavin. *Hannibal*. New York: Viking Press, 1969. This handsomely illustrated biography gives only a brief account of the Battle of Zama.

APPEARANCE OF THE INTERTESTAMENTAL JEWISH APOCRYPHA

Type of event: Religious: collection of non-Biblical Jewish literature
Time: c.200 B.C.
Locale: Palestine and Egypt

Principal personage:
JESUS (fl.180 B.C.), son of Sirach, teacher and poet

Summary of Event

Between 200 B.C. and A.D. 100, many Jewish religious writings appeared in Palestine which were destined not only to remain outside the canon but also to be completely ignored by normative Judaism by the end of the first century after Christ. When the Synod of Jamnia closed the canon, Jewish religious thought preferred to find expression in the development of oral tradition and in Rabbinical literature, rather than in the expansion of Scripture *per se.* To a Judaism already demoralized by the fall of Jerusalem, a closed canon precluded any adulteration of the word of God by contemporary books of dubious message and provenance, especially those of Christian origin clamoring for recognition. The decision that "no one should read" in more than the twenty-four recognized books led, it appears, to the deliberate destruction of the Aramaic and Hebrew manuscripts of extracanonical writings.

These noncanonical compositions have been conventionally divided into two categories: the Apocrypha and Pseudepigrapha. The former, so-called "outside books," always enjoyed a privileged position. While they failed to achieve canonicity among Palestinian Jews, they were accepted by the Greek-speaking Jews of Alexandria. The long-term preservation of these Greek manuscripts, however, is due basically to Christians who found in the apocryphal literature, without need of any adulterating interpolations on their part, a ready-made bridge between the Old and New Testaments. These writings provided in Christian eyes the evidence for continuity of doctrinal development in the intertestamental period, making the transition to Christianity gradual and logical.

The Apocrypha is made up of: Tobit, Judith, parts of Esther, the Wisdom of Solomon, Ecclesiasticus (Sirach), I Baruch, the Epistle of Jeremiah, three additions to Daniel (the prayer of Azariah and the Song of the three children; Susanna; and Bel and the Dragon), I and II Maccabees, I and II Esdras, and the Prayer of Manasses. It represents a variety of literary composition: history, poetry, apocalyptic writing, wisdom literature, and simple narrative.

There seems to be allusions to the apocryphal literature by authors of the New Testament: by Paul to the Wisdom of Solomon and possibly by James to the proverbs or Sirach

443

and the Wisdom of Solomon. But these books as a group came to be recognized by the Church in the West only gradually. The Muratorian Canon of Rome (c.180), for instance, accepts the Wisdom of Solomon as canonical. Early synods, such as those of Hippo (393) and Carthage (397), and Athanasius' Festal Letter (365), held the Apocrypha as a privileged set of books, but Augustine, who considered the Greek Alexandrian canon a divine improvement over the Hebrew list of books and, therefore, quoted the Apocrypha probably more than any other Church Father, practically guaranteed its incorporation in the Vulgate. When the Council of Trent (1546), confirmed by Vatican I (1870), declared the Apocrypha canonical (with the exception of I and II Esdras and the Prayer of Manasses), it attempted to determine the canon finally in the face of Reformation criticism. Probably the most important book for the Roman Church was II Maccabees with its strong note of angelology, prayers for the dead, intercession of saints, resurrection of the bodies of the righteous, and justification of the miraculous in general.

The second set of extracanonical writings is the corpus of the so-called Pseudepigrapha, books whose authorship was deliberately but falsely ascribed to ancient authorities. Once the idea of the inspired Law came to dominate the religious scene in post-Exilic Judaism, it was no longer necessary for a prophet or a representative of God to appear, except possibly as an occasional judge choosing between different factions. Writers who preferred to avoid repeating old shibboleths, or who hoped to challenge orthodoxy by suggesting new ideas or by advancing the mystic at the expense of the legal, or who wished to offer hope to oppressed Jews with new stirring apocalypses, chose to write anonymously after 200 B.C. and to ascribe their messages to great patriarchs of the past.

Among the many books of the so-called Pseudepigrapha, a few deserve mention because of their importance for Christianity. The Book of Jubilees, while reflecting a strong note of legalism, emphasizes the immediate advent of the Messianic kingdom from Judea heralded by a great ethical and physical transformation when men will live for a thousand years and find eventual immortality in the spiritual world. The famous Book of Enoch, a composite work in time and authorship, by airing conflicting views of the Messiah, the Kingdom, sin, final judgment, resurrection, future life, and angelology faithfully records the ferment of Jewish thought on these matters in the intertestamental period. Both Jude and II Peter seem to know Enoch well. The Testament of the Twelve Patriarchs exercised a great influence on the writers of the New Testament in the area of ethics. The Assumption of Moses, which Origen says the author of Jude used, was contemporaneous with Jesus; it stressed opposition to any alliance of religion and politics. The Apocalypse of Baruch (II) finds many parallels in the New Testament, concerned as it is with the relationship of the fall and free will, works and justification, the Messianic kingdom, and resurrection of the dead. There are still others, (the Jewish Sybilline Oracles, the Psalms of Solomon, IV Maccabees, and the Apocalypse of Elijah), which I Corinthians especially seems to use.

Without knowledge of these extra-canonical books the transition from Judaism to Christianity is largely unintelligible.

Pertinent Literature

Goodspeed, J. *The Story of the Apocrypha.* Chicago: University of Chicago Press, 1939.

Goodspeed is interested in the story of how the books of the Apocrypha came to be omitted from the modern Bible. In the early Church these books had had a checkered career; some Fathers accepted them only as fit for private pious reading and therefore not acceptable for church usage as a source of doctrine. Jerome called them "secret or hidden books" as a result of his exegesis of the passage in Second Esdras where the Apocrypha is spoken of as books "to be hidden from all except the wise." After Augustine in the *Doctrina Christiana* more or less assured the acceptance of canonical status for these books, they rested secure until the fourteenth century, when the Latin canon was again compared to the shorter old Hebrew Bible.

Luther's studies led him to isolate the Apocrypha at the end of the Bible; it was to be read by those interested in a "knowledge of history" and in instruction in godly manners but not for the purpose of eliciting any systematic theology.

While all the Reformers again put these books on a secondary list as generally superfluous, Luther considered a few of them to be superior to some regularly accepted sections of the Latin Bible as, for example, the Epistle of James. His grouping was accepted into the English Bible of 1535 and in succeeding revisions including the King James Version of 1611. However, when opposition to these books even as a secondary corpus began to mount in England, thanks to the Puritans, the Archbishop of Canterbury felt obliged to impose a one-year prison sentence on any publisher who printed the Bible without the Apocrypha. While an edition did appear without the addition in 1629, opposition increased after the turn of the century, the result in large part of the work of the famous English scholar John Lightfoot, (1602-1675), who helped Walton produce the Polyglot Bible in 1657.

The Puritans brought their objections to America, and by 1827 both British and American Bible societies, dependent on funds supplied by churches and individuals hostile to the Apocrypha, stopped including the corpus in their editions. The reputation of the disputed books declined still further until Goodspeed and others finally rescued the Apocrypha in the 1930's from neglect by issuing excellent translations and interpretations.

Metzger, B. M. *An Introduction to the Apocrypha.* New York: Oxford University Press, 1957.

Metzger includes himself with other modern Bible scholars anxious to rehabilitate the Apocrypha in Protestant circles. He takes a middle road between the Catholic assertion that the Apocrypha is of canonical authority and the Puritan extreme of ignoring these writings and denying them any importance or value. He prefers to discover elements of real moral and religious excellence in the corpus in addition to discovering in it a vivid reconstruction of the changing environment faced by Palestinian Jews and those of the Diaspora, the setting from which early Christianity ultimately emerged. Yet Metzger would, of course, relegate the Apocrypha to a position secondary to the canonical books of the Old Testament.

The controversy over the books of the Apocrypha interests Metzger because he can discover no definite criteria in the process of selection or rejection of books as "inspired". He questions why the Song of Songs should be accepted over the Wisdom of Solomon. The position of the Greek Orthodox Church was never made clear by any authoritative decision although it tends to follow Athanasius and the Council of Trent. Roman Catholics accept twelve of the fifteen books, while Jews and Protestants reject them all. Contrary to the generally accepted position, Metzger argues that among the Jews and early Christians there was no Alexandrian canon which included the Apocrypha, and that the use of these debatable books by New Testament writers does not imply that they were acknowledged as Scripture in the early Church.

Metzger is impressed not only with the religious importance of the Apocrypha but also with its long and pervasive influence on literature and art. He notes that Christopher Columbus was encouraged to undertake his voyage by a passage in II Esdras, that John Bunyan found new life through a passage in Ecclesiasticus, that Samuel Pepys was inspired by Tobit, and that such great men as Chaucer, Shakespeare, Milton, Longfellow, and Handel were seriously influenced by the apocryphal writings. Yet the author at the same time professes to see a profound difference of value and insight between the "outside books" and those of the present canon. — *J.R.R.*

Additional Recommended Reading

Pfeiffer, R. H. *History of New Testament Times with an Introduction to the Apocrypha.* New York: Harper & Row Publishers Incorporated. 1949. An excellent and detailed account of the environment which produced the Apocrypha, emphasizing its Christian aspect.

Oesterley, W. O. E. *An Introduction to the Books of the Apocrypha.* London: Society for Promoting Christian Knowledge, 1935. A useful description of the Apocrypha and its contents.

Torrey, C. C. *The Apocryphal Literature.* New Haven: Yale University Press,

1945. A concise and readable critical reëxamination of the Apocrypha with a rewarding introduction.

Schürer, E. *A History of the Jewish People in the Time of Jesus Christ.* New York: Schocken Books, 1961. An excellent account of the milieu from which the Apocrypha arose.

Charles, R. H., ed. *The Apocrypha and Pseudepigrapha.* London: Oxford University Press, 1913. 2 vols. The most critical study in English of the Apocrypha as a group of writings.

Malden, R. H. *The Apocrypha.* Oxford: The University Press, 1936. An attempt to relate the Apocrypha to other religious literature of the period.

ESTABLISHMENT OF THE *CURSUS HONORUM*

Type of event: Constitutional: postulation of regulations governing officeholders
Time: 180 B.C.
Locale: Rome

Principal personages:
PUBLIUS CORNELIUS SCIPIO AFRICANUS, consul in 205 B.C.
MARCUS PROCIUS CATO, a *novus homo* who achieved the consulship in 195 B.C. and the censorship in 184 B.C.
LUCIUS VILLIUS, plebeian tribune in 180 B.C.

Summary of Event

The growth of Rome from an insignificant river city to the administrative center of a far-flung empire brought with it numerous changes in the machinery of its government. Many of these changes were made gradually but some were concessions forced by new political situations. A significant stage in this process was marked by the law passed in 180 B.C., the *Lex Villia Annalis*. Understanding of its full significance, however, requires a historical description of the Roman magisterial offices.

Before the establishment of the Republic, all final political power in Rome resided in the person of the king, while the executive officers of the state acted solely as his personal representatives. With the overthrow of the monarchy, these officials, called magistrates by the Romans, became effective representatives of the entire community; their powers, duties, and privileges were thought to be derived from the senate and people conjointly, even though in the early period the people were limited solely to ratifying the election of patrician candidates. At that time the most powerful officials were the two consuls, elected for terms of one year. Only patricians were eligible for this office until the Licinian laws of 367 B.C. threw it open to the plebeians. So strong was the aristocratic domination of Roman political life, however, that only in 172 B.C. were both consuls plebeians. The duties of the consuls were diverse; they were charged with conducting the affairs of the senate, maintaining public order throughout Italy, and leading the army in time of war.

The second most powerful office was the praetorship. It seems probable that the first praetor was elected in 360 B.C., although there are some indications that the office may have formed part of the original constitution of the Republic. Plebeians first became eligible for it in 337 B.C. The praetor was above all the supreme civil judge. In 242 B.C. the number of annually elected praetors was raised to two, so that one could be placed in charge of lawsuits between Roman citizens and aliens. As Rome's overseas dominions increased, the number of praetors was raised to four in 227 B.C. allowing two praetors to serve as governors of the newly-formed provinces of Sicily and Sardinia, and in 197 B.C. the number was raised to six, the additional two officers being assigned to administer the two provinces of Spain.

An office not constitutionally essential for election to higher offices, but extremely influential in itself, was the aedileship. At the beginning of the Republic two aediles were appointed to supervise the temples and religious practices of the plebeians. Ultimately they were given control over public buildings, street maintenance, the distribution of the corn supply, and, above all, production of the public games. This capacity enabled ambitious politicians to stage lavish and spectacular games in an attempt to gain popularity with the urban electorate.

The lowest political office was the quaestorship. The office was probably created at the beginning of the Republic, with the number of annually elected quaestors raised to four in 421 B.C. At the same time plebeians were also made eligible for the office. Ultimately the number of quaestors was fixed at twenty. Two of the quaestors had charge of the state treasury and official archives. The others were attached as aides either to generals on campaign or to provincial governors. Their duties were diverse: financial, judicial, and military.

These four offices formed the so-called *cursus honorum,* the order in which political offices had to be held, although strictly speaking the aedileship was not a prerequisite for election to any other office. The *cursus honorum* did not exist before 180 B.C., since until that time there were no age qualifications assigned to any of these offices, nor was the holding of any one office a necessary condition for election to another higher office. Thus Scipio Africanus, the conqueror of Hannibal, was elected consul for 205 B.C. at the age of thirty-one and Flaminius, the victor at Cynoscephalae in 197 B.C., was elected consul in 198 B.C. at a similarly early age. This situation was drastically altered by the law carried in 180 B.C. by the tribune Lucius Villius,which set fixed age qualifications for the various offices. The probable age limits established were forty for the praetor and forty-three for the consul. Although no minimum age was placed on the quaestors it was generally understood that candidates who stood for this office would have already completed their ten-year military obligation and thus be approximately twenty-eight. Through these strictures, a regular and restrained order was placed over the advancement of all political careers.

Pertinent Literature

Scullard, H. H. *Roman Politics 220-150 B.C.* Oxford: The Clarendon Press, 1951.

This work relies extensively on a method of investigating Roman history that was developed in Germany during the first quarter of the twentieth century. Called "prosopography," it involves an accurate and all-inclusive determination of the definite relationships existing among prominent Romans during periods where such information is retrievable. These relationships were brought about either by birth, marriage, or intimate friendship. Once the relationships have been worked out, there emerges distinct groupings of individuals into purportedly political alliances and associations with their own programs and strategies.

Scullard has applied this methodology of historical research to the period between the opening of the Second Punic War and the middle of the first century, when Roman domination had been extended to practically every shore of the Mediterranean. Scullard's book provides a detailed catalogue of political maneuvers and feuds against which the urgency and impact of the *Lex Annalis* clearly stand out.

Marriage patterns and verifiable friendship disclose three prime groups vying for political eminence in this period: (1) a traditional, conservative right, headed by Valerius Flaccus, best embodied and articulated by the energetic newcomer Marcus Porcius Cato; (2) a philhellenic, expansionist group led by the illustrious hero of the Punic War, Cornelius Scipio Africanus; and (3) a middle-of-the-road faction centered around the families of the Claudii and the Fulvii.

There is general agreement that it is anachronistic to describe these alliances as traditional political parties. Their membership was susceptible to desertion as a result of divorce or personal animosity; nor did the separate groups devise firm ideologies or advance concrete political and economic programs. What they held in common was a membership drawn almost exclusively from the *nobilitas,* the recently formed oligarchic circle that had exercised political dominance at Rome since the middle of the third century. No longer split into plebeian and patrician factions, the nobles identified themselves as the descendants of ancestors who had attained consular offices. Considering that this pedigree made them the only qualified and competent candidates for political authority, the nobles contested among themselves for political prominence, manipulating matrimonial and personal relationships to ensure their own advancement. They were united in their desire to exclude from successful political careers men whose family trees did not include previous holders of the consulship, the so-called "new men" or *novi homines.* Their solidarity against such upstarts sometimes weakened in the face of their even greater fear of the too-rapid success of any member of their own class. Thus the Valerii backed the career of the new man Cato to offset the sudden ascendancy of Scipio Africanus.

This was the general background for the passage of the *Lex Annalis* in 180 B.C. Scullard considers that the law specified the minimum age requirements for each office, set up a mandatory sequence of offices, and ordered a minimal two-year interval between offices. Since this law prevented precipitous political advancement by ambitious young nobles, and in effect subordinated the individual noble to the code of his class, Scullard sees its main intent as tightening the oligarchs' control of the state by reducing friction among them. He points out, however, that both this law and other measures designed to check the increasing electoral corruption through bribery were passed during a period when plebeian "new men", such as Cato were prominent in office. From this standpoint, the law, presumably facilitating the gradual rise of a *novus homo,* appears as a deliberate antidote to the nobles' monopoly of political office. This reform quite possibly contributed to the general internal stability of the following fifty years but the careers of the brothers Gracchi eventually exposed the weaknesses of Roman political life which were far too basic for solely electoral reforms to eradicate.

Greenidge, A.H.E. *Roman Political Life.* London: Macmillan & Company, 1901.

The overthrow of the Republic can be ascribed in large part to the failure of the Roman constitution to provide an adequate system of government for the expanded Empire. Although the constitution underwent numerous reforms and renovations as in the case of the *Lex Annalis,* some of its features, especially its structure of magisterial offices, were never modified sufficiently to ensure the political health of the Empire. The *Lex Annalis* corrected certain defects of the *cursus honorum* by establishing an orderly sequence of office, but its limited aims prevented it from clearing up other more important and inherent shortcomings of the magisterial system. These shortcomings are readily apparent in the admirably detailed examination of the Roman magistracies available in Greenidge.

Roman politicians and theorists took pride in the mixed form of their constitution; supposedly, senate, people, and magistrates were all equipped with enough influence to prevent a usurpation of power by any one of the three. The pattern of checks and balances responsible for this internal equilibrium also characterized every Roman magistracy through the principle of collegiality of officers. Every Roman magistrate shared his executive authority with at least one other equally powerful partner. In the case of the quaestors with their circumscribed powers and extensive duties, the collegial system made possible an efficient division of labor. The provision for two consuls, however, with their untrammeled authority, was potentially anarchic and able to bring all governmental activity to a complete standstill. This difficulty could be avoided as long as the two consuls accepted the same political persuasions. Once rival political factions arose around the *optimates* and the *populares,* however, the consulship became one of the prime arenas of their violent opposition. Preferring time-honored, practical compromises rather than radical reforms, the Romans ludicrously decided that during military campaigns, the consuls should take daily turns as commanders of the expedition, to prevent their absolute veto power over one another from endangering the welfare of the army. This makeshift arrangement was alleviated somewhat by Sulla's reform which entrusted military power and responsibility to the proconsuls. In the end this reform only introduced a far more serious problem, as the career of Julius Caesar indicates.

Perhaps the most blatant weakness of the magisterial system was the office of plebeian tribune. Although the tribunate was not a requisite part of the *cursus honorum* since it was open

451

only to plebeians, it nonetheless became a focal point of political strife because of its leverage over the other magistracies. This leverage was also due to the frantic desire of the Romans to maintain equilibrium among all the sources of political power. In the case of the tribunate, however, through the personal inviolability of its holder and his extensive veto power over the activities of all the other magistrates, the Romans had in effect sanctioned legalized civil war within the state. Although the resources of the office were not fully exploited until the careers of the Gracchi, the nature of the resulting crisis can be gauged by the senatorial response which amounted to a practical declaration of war against the holders of the tribunate.

These repeated failures to adjust the constitution to changed conditions can only be grasped through an understanding of the Roman concept of *imperium*. Originally this term expressed the fullness of power that was possessed by the early kings. During the Republic, it was exercised by specially appointed dictators in grave emergencies. Under normal conditions, it was held by the consuls, but only after its scope had been significantly curtailed by the one-year term of office and the equal veto power. Behind these limitations was the fear of the return of the unlimited and arbitrary power of the kings. Although Roman statesmen made the return of monarchy unlikely, they restricted themselves in other respects, especially when the constitution was stretched to govern the expanded Empire. In this situation they failed to create a nonpartisan civil service; instead, they resorted to the *Lex Annalis* to ensure some diverse continuity to users of political power. This piecemeal and temporizing treatment of basic weaknesses in executive organization eventually led to the establishment of a dreaded unbounded *imperium* in the person of the emperor. — *G.M.P.*

Additional Recommended Reading

Astin, A. E. *The Lex Annalis Before Sulla.* Brussels: Collection Latomus XXXII. 1958. The most recent survey of the *Lex Annalis* and its problems.

Frank, Tenney. "Rome," in *Cambridge Ancient History.* Vol. VIII, ch. XII, pp. 357-387. Cambridge: The University Press, 1930. A detailed account of the historical background of the *Lex Annalis.*

Abbott, Frank Frost. *A History and Description of Roman Political Institutions.* Boston: Ginn & Co., 1901. A useful account of Roman executive offices, their powers and limitations.

Adcock, F. E. *Roman Political Ideas and Practice.* Ann Arbor: University of Michigan Press, 1959. A treatment of the theory and realities of Roman politics.

FORMATION OF THE SCIPIONIC CIRCLE

Type of event: Cultural: syncretism of values
Time: c.175 B.C.
Locale: Rome

Principal personages:

PUBLIUS CORNELIUS SCIPIO AFRICANUS MAIOR (236-184), Roman general and statesman victor over Hannibal in the Second Punic War

QUINTUS ENNIUS (239-169), Roman epic and dramatic poet

PUBLIUS CORNELIUS SCIPIO AEMILIANUS (185-129), Roman general and statesman, conqueror of Carthage in the Third Punic War

PUBLIUS TERENTIUS AFER ("TERENCE," 195-159), Roman comic poet

POLYBIUS (c.203-c.120), Greek historian, friend of Scipio Aemilianus

PANAETIUS OF RHODES (c.185-109), Stoic philosopher, friend of Scipio Aemilianus

Summary of Event

During the course of the second century B.C., it became increasingly evident both to the Romans themselves and to most of the peoples of the Mediterranean world that the military superiority of Rome was destined to bring unity and some common imperial administration of the affairs of all peoples of that world. The successful conclusion of the Second Punic War left Rome in undisputed control of the western Mediterranean, and struggles with Macedonia and Syria in the course of the century proceeded steadily in Rome's favor, so that by 133, Attalus III of Pergamum, recognizing the irreversible trend, bequeathed his kingdom to Rome on his death. Control of the government in Rome throughout the century was firmly in the hands of a senatorial military aristocracy dom-

inated in the early portion by the hero of Zama, Scipio Africanus, and in the middle years by his adopted son, Scipio Aemilianus. It was in the course of this century that Romans became conscious of their national identity and imperial destiny, and it is clear that in this process Greek culture and individual Greeks played an important role.

Roman character and moral fiber seems largely to have been molded by the institutions of the family and the army. In the tightly knit family, the authority of the father was absolute, and the disobedience of children was punishable by death at the father's discretion. The structure of the state mirrored that of the family in that the formulation of policy, legislation, and decisions of war and peace were in the hands of the *patres,* the heads

453

of the dominant families of the state. From an early period also the major citizen-assembly of Rome, the *Comitia centuriata,* was the citizen-army in march formation, and the two heads of state, the *consules,* were essentially military commanders entrusted with *imperium,* the power of command. The effect of these basic institutions was to stress obedience to constituted authority and paternal responsibility of authorities to those subject to them. There was a weakness, however, in the religious basis for this morality of authority and obedience; Roman religion, a scrupulous formal ritualism, consisted at the state level in the taking of auspices to determine the favor of the gods on particular critical occasions. It provided for the individual no conscious orientation to the powers controlling nature or human history, and no satisfying rationalization for the duty of obedience and the responsible exercise of authority.

After the end of the First Punic War, Greek literary culture was consciously and deliberately naturalized in Rome. The *Odyssey* of Homer was translated into Latin and probably became a tool of instruction for the sons of the nobility. Latin versions of Greek New Comedy were produced for public entertainment at regular festal celebrations. By the end of the first quarter of the second century B.C., Quintus Ennius, a Greek-educated Calabrian who had been brought to Rome by Cato the Elder and patronized by M. Fulvius Nobilior and Scipio Africanus, had produced a Roman epic, the *Annales.* The poem was composed in the Homeric hexameter, adapted to Latin

by Ennius, and it traced the destiny of Rome from legendary Trojan origins to the end of the Third Macedonian War. By the middle of the century there was a group of major political leaders of Rome gathering together Philhellenic aristocrats: the poets Terence and Lucilius; and two Greeks, the historian Polybius and the philosopher Panaetius of Rhodes. A century later Cicero idealized this group and its leader as the creative source of the political and literary ideals which he expounded in his own writings and attempted to realize as a statesman.

It may be that Cicero's idealized picture of the common pursuits and genuine creativity of the "Scipionic Circle" is overdrawn, but it seems likely that the conceptions of *humanitas,* of Rome's historical destiny, and of a world united and at peace under one political administration and subject to one law, did indeed originate in the second century B.C., although these ideas found explicit formulation only later in the works of Cicero and Vergil. The plays of Terence are marked by a new sophisticated and controlled Latin style and by a humanitarian spirit that seems to reflect Stoic notions of man's universal moral obligation to his fellow man. The historical work of Polybius is inspired by a sense of the unity of the Mediterranean world and of Rome's military and political fitness for leadership of that world. The philosopher Panaetius reëxpressed the ideals of the Old Stoa in terms more attractive to the Roman ruling class by modifying the older ideal of apathy, by identifying the good with the useful, and by recognizing a

454

positive political content in the Stoic concept of the unity of mankind, the cosmopolis. Through the mediating influence of Panaetius, the Stoic concept of natural law and universal moral obligations ultimately found expression in the extension of Roman citizenship to all subjects of the empire and the codification of a humane universal law code, although this development reached its culmination only after several centuries.

The total impact of Greek culture on Roman life and character during this transitional period from the end of the Second Punic War to the establishment of the Principate by Octavian is considerably more complex than what has been discussed here; there were disintegrating as well as integrating aspects of this Greek influence. Nevertheless, it may safely be stated that the Roman mind was aided by Greek literature and philosophy in its effort to understand its own national identity and its historical role in the Mediterranean world.

Pertinent Literature

Baldry, H. C. *The Unity of Mankind in Greek Thought.* Cambridge: The University Press, 1965.

Baldry's thesis is that the gulf separating a few wise men from a vast majority of fools vitiated all theoretical formulations of a conception of the unity of mankind in the fourth and third centuries B.C. In his final chapter, "The Impact of Rome," Baldry argues that it was only the impact of Roman expansion, beginning in the third century B.C., which led to expression of a meaningful concept of human unity. Baldry notes, moreover, that it was no idea of the unity of the cosmos that laid the ground for this concept, but rather the notion of mankind as an aggregate of human beings spread out over the inhabited world. Geography, which played no serious role in fourth century thought, became influential in that of the third. Eratosthenes, roughly contemporaneous with Chrysippus, mapped the inhabited world as a whole and criticized the distinction between Greeks and barbarians, asserting that there were several other civilized peoples beside the Greeks and that the only meaningful distinction among men was that between the morally good and evil.

Baldry's discussion focuses on Polybius and Panaetius, the most significant creative minds in the Scipionic Circle. By the second century B.C. the antithesis between Greek and barbarian had fully ceased to be meaningful, and only the uncivilized savage was considered outside the limits of humanity. Noting that Terence's celebrated line, "I am a man; nothing of human concern do I consider alien to myself," is probably from a Greek original of the previous century, Baldry nevertheless argues that for Terence's patrons the line had a much fuller meaning.

It is the geographical unity of mankind that underlies Polybius' conception of history's unity, a fact which he asserts first became definite and clear with the Second Punic War. This concept governed even the structure of Polybius' history, since after the battle of Cannae in 216 B.C., he departed from a scheme of narrating events in different parts of the world separately and began an annalistic description of events occurring throughout the world during the same year.

Philosophy in the second century B.C., says Baldry, gained no fresh concepts from Rome, but it developed new attitudes, shifting toward a more practical realism and moving toward synthesis of concepts from the different schools. The new realism and practical emphasis found expression in the thought of Panaetius of Rhodes, the founder of the Middle Stoa, to whom Baldry does not hesitate to attribute the views expressed by Cicero in the first two books of *De Officiis*. Panaetius stressed the older Stoic conception of the universal possession of reason by all men and deëmphasized the concept of the Sage, whose wisdom, according to the older view, was the sole basis of coöperation among men. The new

realism finds expression in Panaetius' insistence that not only an abstract ideal of man is worthy of the philosopher's concern, but also the character of individual men, and not only the best, but others as well. Justice is closely related to kindly feeling for one's fellow man, and the whole concept of appreciation for the achievements of civilized men everywhere and of moral responsibility extending from one's own immediate kinsman and neighbor to the fringes of the civilized world finds its fullest expression in the Ciceronian word *humanitas*. Thus, while not attempting to indicate any immediate impact of Polybius and Panaetius on second century Roman thought or action, Baldry makes clear his view that Rome's military and political unification of the world alone made possible the emergence of an explicit conception of the unity of mankind that became part of the heritage of first century Roman thought.

Astin, A. E. *Scipio Aemilianus.* Oxford: The Clarendon Press, 1967.

Since the middle of the nineteenth century, when the notion was first promulgated by German historians and philologists, it has been commonly held that the center of dissemination of Greek culture in Rome in the second century B.C. was a circle of men of varying political, literary, and philosophical, and other interests gathered around Scipio Aemilianus. In a study published in 1934, Ruth Martin Brown already found it necessary to expand the definition of this circle to include three generations of Roman Philhellenes loosely affiliated with one another all through the

second century and originally centering around Scipio Africanus, the hero of the Second Punic War. In one of several appendices to his new biography of Scipio Aemilianus, A. E. Astin subjects the theory to a critical review of the known facts and reaches essentially skeptical conclusions.

Philhellenism in Rome, says Astin, was by no means restricted to the friends of Scipio Aemilianus, and the uniqueness of the common cultural and intellectual interests of this circle has been greatly exaggerated. Astin names several prominent Philhellenes of the period who were either not associated with or openly hostile to Scipio, and he notes that, although Terence and Lucilius were associated with him, another dramatic writer of the period, Accius, had D. Junius Brutus Callaicus for a patron.

As for a relationship between Scipio Aemilianus and Panaetius, Astin shows the unlikelihood of any closeness of the two before 146, when Scipio returned to Rome from a long absence in Spain and Africa. The association between the two was probably philosophical, Astin admits, and they must have discussed ethics and constitutional history together, but there is no evidence of any influence of Panaetius' views on the conduct of Scipio as a statesman. Indeed, argues Astin, Scipio must have considered his relationship with Panaetius as that of a patron with a client and must surely have had a strong sense of his own superior status. Nor is there any indication that Scipio ever was a Stoic or was considered one in antiquity.

Regarding the possible influence of Panaetius on the idea of the moral justification of Roman imperialism, Astin points out that there is no clear evidence of Panaetius' espousal of the doctrine that a greater nation has the duty to rule lesser ones and to promote their material and moral welfare. Cicero's source for this idea may well be Poseidonius. The idea, moreover, is reflected already in the *Lex de rebus repetundis* (149 B.C.),

regulating misgovernment by Roman provincial governors, and thus cannot spring from an affiliation of Scipio and Panaetius which was nonexistent at that time.

There is insufficient literary evidence, says Astin, for tracing the Ciceronian concept of *humanitas* back to the middle of the second century B.C. *Humanitas* clearly embraced humanitarianism as well as culture, and Terence does use the adjectives *humanus* and *inhumanus* on occasion to mean "kind" and "cruel"; but Cicero's assertion to the contrary notwithstanding, there is no evidence that this humanitarian spirit was exhibited by Scipio and his friends, and "there are some indications of a harshness which is not easily reconciled with such an outlook."

Astin may well be going too far in his skepticism about the derivation of Cicero's ideas from the Scipionic Circle in the second century B.C. Surely the imperial ideal set forth by Cicero and by Vergil in the *Aeneid* is the culmination of a longer process of cross-fertilization of Greek culture and the Roman ethic of responsibility and obedience. A safer assertion about the impact of Greek ideals on Roman thought may be that the work of Polybius and Panaetius is indicative of a wider process of cross-fertilization rather than the primary source of dissemination of Greek influence. — *C.W.C.*

Additional Recommended Reading

Brown, Ruth Martin. *A Study of the Scipionic Circle*. Iowa Studies in Classical Philology: No. 1, 1934. A study of the development, personnel, and cultural interests of the Scipionic Circle.

Fowler, W. Warde. "Greek Philosophy and Roman Religion," in *The Religious*

Experience of the Roman People. (The Gifford Lectures for 1909-10). Lect. XVI. London: Macmillan & Company, 1911. An evaluation, among other things, of the impact of Stoicism on Roman religion and thought.

Grenier, Albert. *The Roman Spirit in Religion, Thought, and Art.* Pt. II, chs. II, IV, and V. London: Kegan Paul, Trench, Trubner & Co., Ltd., 1926. A well-known study discussing the effect which Greek ideals had on Roman thought in the second century B.C.

Toynbee, Arnold J. "The Creation of a Literature in Latin on the Pattern of Literature in Greek," in *Hannibal's Legacy: The Hannibalic War's Effects on Roman Life.* Vol. II, ch. XIII. London: Oxford University Press, 1965. In part, a discussion of the impact of Greek culture on Roman literature in the context of the impact of the Second Punic War.

REVOLT OF THE MACCABEES

Type of event: Politico-religious: outbreak of Jewish rebellion
Time: 166 B.C.
Locale: Judea

Principal personages:
ANTIOCHUS IV (EPIPHANES or "God Manifest"), Seleucid
 King 175-164
ONIAS III, Jewish High Priest to 174
JESUS (or "JASON"), Jewish notable, brother of Onias III,
 High Priest 174-172
ONIAS (or "MENELAUS"), Jewish notable, High Priest
 172-163/162
MATTATHIAS (?-c.166), Jewish notable of priestly rank
JUDAS MACCABAEUS (?-160), son of Mattathias, soldier and
 patriot
ELIACHIM (or "ALCIMUS"), High Priest 163/162-160
JONATHAN, younger brother of Judas Maccabaeus, High
 Priest 152-143

Summary of Event

The Seleucid King Antiochus III (223-187) took Judea from the Ptolemies of Egypt in the Fifth Syrian War (201-200) and made it part of his Asian empire. He lowered taxes, and guaranteed freedom to Jews to practice their religion and follow their ancestral laws. But the Jews hated the Seleucids anyway, regarding them as godless promoters of foreign customs, greedy taxers of widows and orphans, and, above all, protectors of the idols which the pagans worshiped. They failed to propagate the true worship of the Lord Yahweh. Some Jews even hoped for the return of the Ptolemies so that they might recover the lucrative official posts they had once held. On the whole, however, Seleucid rule provoked much less hostility than the Ptolemaic dynasty had caused. More Jews collaborated than had

done so under the Ptolemies because the Seleucids were milder and because the important cultural currents which had been flowing over Judea since the beginning of the Greek period now began to bring forth fruit. Hellenism at its best was an attractive way of life, with its sensible humanism and its personal freedoms; it made Jewish dietary restrictions and the painful practice of circumcision appear as barbaric superstitions. Conversions to Hellenism occurred, so that about 180 B.C. Jesus ben Sirach, the author of Ecclesiasticus, had to admonish the younger generation to have greater respect for the traditional Jewish Law.

Judaea was caught up in great international events during the reign of the Seleucid Antiochus IV (175-164), a remarkable man: efficient, brilliant, and erratic. His father Antiochus III had been badly beaten in a war with Rome, and in the aftermath of that debacle the Seleucids lost their easternmost provinces. To strengthen the weakened state, Antiochus decided to encourage the partially Hellenized towns of his empire to adopt the Greek civic institutions of gymnasia, Hellenized religious cults, and autonomous assemblies. In this way he hoped to increase the stock of Hellenized manpower available for the defense of his empire against Rome and for the recovery of his lost eastern territory.

In 174 B.C. a Hellenically-minded Jewish notable named Jesus, whose name was altered to the Greek form "Jason," proposed to make Jerusalem a Greek city if Antiochus would depose the High Priest Onias III and install Jason in his place. Antiochus accepted this offer and granted a charter to the newly organized Jerusalem. A gymnasium was built, and Jewish youths exercised in the nude, to the dismay of conservatives. A citizen body was enrolled and debated affairs in a *gerousia,* or "council," to the degradation of the Jewish Law. In 172 B.C., Jason was outbid for his office by a man called Onias, who offered to increase the taxes paid by Judea to Antiochus. The King straightway deposed Jason, who withdrew into sullen exile, and invested Onias as High Priest under the Greek name Menelaus. Jews loyal to their Law were rightly outraged at this cavalier treatment of their most sacred office, and Jews friendly to the Seleucids were disturbed to see Antiochus' sudden cancellation of his father's promise of lowered taxes. Simultaneously, Ptolemy VI was

preparing a war to recover Palestine. Antiochus, however, attacked him first, and, in the Sixth Syrian War (170-168), he defeated the Egyptian forces, captured Ptolemy, and made himself King of Egypt. At this point Rome intervened, fearful that Antiochus was growing too strong and ordered him out of Egypt on pain of instant war. Antiochus prepared to obey. His diplomatic defeat inspired a rumor reporting his death, and Jesus (Jason) decided to drive his rival Menelaus out of Jerusalem (Antioch) at this favorable moment. Antiochus, returning to Syria, came upon the city in revolt against his lawful High Priest. He suppressed the revolt by force, fined the Jews heavily, and, later in 167, decided to assist his loyal Hellenizers by forbidding the practice of the Jewish religion in Judea. In the Temple the worship of the Syrian god Baal Shamim was substituted for that of Yahweh. This provoked armed resistance. In 166 Mattathias, a landed magnate of priestly rank, revolted. From 166 until 164, while Antiochus was campaigning in the East against Parthia with first-line Seleucid troops, Mattathias' son Judas, surnamed Maccabaeus, or "The Hammer," warred against Seleucid mercenaries. and Hellenized Jewish militia alike, successfully establishing himself in the countryside. Even so, he had to accept a truce with the Seleucid government in the spring of 164. During this war, about 165 B.C., the Old Testament book of Daniel was made public in its present form. It was an important part of Jewish propaganda, looking forward to the death of Antiochus ("a mouth speaking great things"), the end of the Hellenistic age, and the dawn of a divine Fifth Monarchy, presided over by a Messianic figure. Late in 164, Antiochus unexpectedly died, and Judas took advantage of this to break the truce. He entered Jerusalem and seized the Temple, which in December was ritually cleansed and rededicated to Yahweh.

With Antiochus dead, the Seleucid dynasty soon suffered the disaster of the emergence of two rival lines of kings at war with each other. With the central government distracted, the courageous, skillful, and ruthless Maccabees made headway in Judea until, in 152, both Seleucid factions recognized Jonathan, a younger brother of Judas (who had been killed in the fighting), as High Priest. His family eventually became both Kings and High Priests of Judea, governing an independent kingdom until Rome conquered Palestine in 63 B.C. This century of Jewish independence was a time of great national, cultural, and religious revival, and of growing strife between differing schools of religious thought and belief.

Pertinent Literature

Tcherikover, Victor. *Hellenistic Civilization and the Jews.* Translated from the Hebrew by S. Applebaum. Philadelphia: The Jewish Publication Society of America, 1959.

This book, by a leading Jewish scholar, is a lengthy, detailed examination of the contacts between Greeks and Jews in Hellenistic times. Part I deals with events in Palestine from the beginning of Greek penetration under the Ptolemies at the end of the fourth century, when the towns of Palestine watched the arrival of Greek merchants, administrators, and soldiers, to the end of the Maccabean period in 63 B.C., when Pompey added Judea to the Roman province of Syria. The main emphasis is on the struggle during the second century B.C. in and around Jerusalem between the agents of Hellenization and the proponents of traditional Judaism.

Tcherikover is able to show that the main impulse towards Hellenization came not from the Seleucid dynasty of Antiochus IV but from among the Jews themselves. The Hellenizing party in Jerusalem tended to be drawn from the wealthy class, men committed to commerce, farming, and local administration. The Tobiads, (Tobias himself, his son Joseph, and his grandson Hyrcanus), were probably the most enthusiastic cultural converts. These men were anxious to copy the way of life of the Macedonian kings because they found such power attractive. Hellenization could also be good business because the Ptolemies and Seleucids controlled and regulated commerce. Antiochus did not take the initiative in reorganizing Jerusalem in 174; this change was suggested by Jason. Antiochus may have been influenced in favor of his proposal because Onias III, as Tcherikover believes, longed for the return of the Ptolemies. Jason's Hellenism was real but conservative. Menelaus, on the other hand, was a more zealous

461

Hellenist, a man who seems to have been the Tobiads' candidate.

Antiochus' proscription of Judaism, which Tcherikover calls a "persecution," was caused by the rebellion of Jason against Menelaus and not by narrow-mindedness towards religion on the King's part. The revolt of the Maccabees stemmed from several causes. By 167, patriotic Jews had already been deeply offended by the conduct of the Hellenizers. The faithful hated these converts' preference for an alien way of life, their contemptuous attitude toward the Temple and its long stored-up treasures, their consorting with pagan foreigners, their decisions made in the *Gerousia* without reference to the Law, and their Syrian mercenary troops, who expressed in Jerusalem itself a preference for the worship of Baal Shamim, Dushara, and the sexually offensive goddess Astarte. There was also sharp antagonism between the Hellenizers, mostly well-to-do city people, and the rural poor, who tended to be conservative and orthodox. When, in this atmosphere,

Antiochus was led by his "irate temper" to forbid Judaism, the Maccabees easily found a following for a war of national liberation. Tcherikover is careful to point out, however, that while Judas' rebellion began as a defense of the national religion, after his capture of the Temple in 164 it became a religious offensive against paganism and against the pagan population of those parts of non-Jewish Palestine which the Old Testament plainly proved had once been parts of the old Jewish monarchy. The Maccabees supplemented that peaceful expansion of the Jews into Philistia, Galilee, and Transjordan which had actually been in progress since about 300 B.C.

Part II of Tcherikover's book is a discussion of Jewish culture in the Diaspora, those parts of the ancient world outside Palestine, such as Alexandria in Egypt, where considerable numbers of Jews were settled. The contributions of the Diaspora to Jewish life and thought were of first importance.

Eddy, Samuel K. *The King Is Dead. Studies in the Near Eastern Resistance to Hellenism, 334-31 B.C.* Lincoln: University of Nebraska Press, 1961.

It is unfortunate for historical studies that our main sources of information for the revolt of the Maccabees are canonical or semicanonical books—Daniel in the Old Testament, and 1 and 2 Maccabees in the Apocrypha—because they have influenced some modern writers to treat the rebellion with the respect and reverence generally given to a religious event. Antiochus has been reviled as an evil, godless troublemaker; Judas has been praised as the

righteous defender of the principle of religious freedom; and the whole struggle of pagan Seleucid and Jewish Maccabee has been interpreted as a kind of preliminary to the clash between the Roman City of Men and the Christian City of God.

This approach may be good for the faith but it is bad for history. Motives other than religious ones inspired the Maccabees. There is undoubted evidence from the Ptolemaic period that an important facet of Jewish history was the rivalry of the great families for the High Priesthood, a rivalry that was sometimes carried on even within the families. One of the High Priests of the third century was a certain Onias. His powerful brother Tobias had a son, Joseph, who challenged his uncle either to give up the High Priesthood or his duties as Ptolemaic taxgatherer; Onias retained his fiscal responsibilities. This factionalism continued into the Maccabean age. The High Priest Onias III was supplanted by his brother Jesus, and the latter was ousted by a man of another noble family, Onias (Menelaus). The Maccabees themselves took part in the competition for rank, and by the second century were still seeking a higher place in the hierarchy. In the fifth century their ancestors did not even have priestly status; in the third they had risen to seventh place among the twenty-four courses of the priesthood. The Maccabees were doubtless patriotic men with religious convictions, but there is also little doubt that they took advantage of the passions aroused by Antiochus' hasty proscription of Judaism and used these strong feelings for their own ends. When Judas began the struggle against Menelaus' Hellenizers, he freely employed Gentile soldiers from the idol-worshiping city of Jamnia. It is also true that Judas made war against Jews who were not of his faction, and that not all of these Jews were Hellenizers. In 163/162, the worship of Yahweh was officially recognized by the Seleucids, and they appointed as High Priest—to re-place Menelaus—Eliachim, who traced his descent from no less a personage than Aaron and could have no better credentials; but Judas nevertheless fought on against him. This action shows that personal ambition was a strong motive in the Maccabean family and accounts for the strong possibility that the author of Daniel had a low opinion of the religiosity of their faction. The history of the family as Kings and High Priests of Judea includes a most unfortunate record of brutality towards the Pharisees, who had emerged from the years of the revolt as a national, patriotic group.

This book also covers the revolts of other non-Greek peoples against the Macedonian monarchies set up by Alexander and his successors, from the earliest Persian oracles prophesying the overthrow of Alexander himself to the last anti-Ptolemaic rebellions in Egypt. Anti-Hellenism was directed against the foreign dynasties as invaders and not against Hellenism itself as a culture. In its mildest form, anti-Hellenism was a revival of native civilization and tradition. Since kingship was the master institution of the ancient Near East, to which culture, law, and religion were all closely linked, stronger anti-Hellenists prophesied the coming of heaven-sent kings, or messiahs, who would rescue their peoples from the Hellenic yoke. These oracles helped to prepare the way for organized revolts in Persia, Judea, and Egypt against the Seleucid and Ptolemaic dynasties. — *S.K.E.*

Additional Recommended Reading

Bickermann, Elias. *The Maccabees*. New York: Schocken Books, 1947. A short but highly competent survey by an outstanding scholar.

Baron, Salo W. *A Social and Religious History of the Jews*. Volume 1: *Ancient Times, Part I*. 2nd ed. New York: Columbia University Press, 1952. A complete historical interpretation of Jewish life, including political changes, social conditions, economic aspects, and religious developments.

Farmer, W. R. *Maccabees, Zealots, and Josephus: An Inquiry into Jewish Nationalism in the Greco-Roman Period*. New York: Columbia University Press, 1956. Analyzes the growth of Jewish nationalism, which owed much to the example of the Maccabees' struggle against the Seleucids.

Goldstein, N. W. "Cultivated Pagans and Ancient Antisemitism," in *Journal of Religion*. Vol. 19 (1939), 346-364. An examination of anti-Semitism, whose roots go back to the time of the Maccabees' revolt.

Dancy, J. C. *A Commentary on I Maccabees*. Oxford: Basil Blackwell, 1954. A useful book explaining the purposes of the unknown author of I Maccabees (the most important single source of Maccabean history), with valuable notes on selected passages.

CATO WRITES THE *DE AGRI CULTURA*

Type of event: Literary: writing of a handbook on farming
Time: c.160 B.C.
Locale: Rome

Principal personage:
MARCUS PORCIUS CATO ("THE CENSOR," 234-149), Roman senator and author

Summary of Event

In the period following the Second Punic War in which Rome decisively defeated Carthage and established Roman hegemony in the Mediterranean, two schools of thought regarding Greece took shape in Roman intellectual and political circles. Greek states had fought on both sides of the conflict between Rome and Carthage, and after the war, the Roman state took punitive action against those Greek states which had refused to become her allies. Along with this policy, and partly as an attempt to rationalize it, there developed a nationalist party which was vigorously anti-Greek and anti-Carthaginian. The leader of this party was Marcus Porcius Cato, author of the *De Agri Cultura,* a didactic work with political overtones. The opponents of Cato's view were represented by the so-called "Scipionic Circle," a nebulous group of intellectuals who made a conscious attempt to assimilate the best elements of Greek culture into the Roman way of life.

Cato was born in 234 B.C. at Tusculum, about ten miles from Rome. As a prosperous farmer he knew agriculture at firsthand. He also had direct experience of the Roman military life, having fought in the Second Punic War and later in Thrace, Greece, and Spain. His political career followed the regular Roman pattern, the *cursus honorum.* He was quaestor in Sicily and Africa in 204, aedile in 199, praetor in Sardinia in 198, consul in 195, and censor in 184. In his later years he remained an active senator, and from 157 to 149, the year of his death, he established himself as a legend through his warnings against a resurgence of Carthaginian power. Cato is probably best remembered for the words which are said to have closed every speech which he made no matter what the topic: *"Carthago delenda est,"* ("Carthage must be destroyed"). According to the biographies of Cato sketched by Nepos and Plutarch, accounts which admittedly are more characteristic than factual, the Censor was a crotchety, puritanical superpatriot, a conservative old soldier with the bias of a landed aristocrat.

Though he followed an active public career, Cato was at the same time a prolific writer, and several of his works stand in the history of Latin literature as earliest examples of different genres including oratory, the didactic treatise, and history. Though there may have been earlier writings in these fields, it is

465

only from Cato that there remain sizable fragments and references in the works of later authors.

Cato's didactic works included treatments of agriculture, health, religion, military affairs, morals, and probably law. Collectively they have earned Cato the title, "Father of the encyclopedic method." The *De Agri Cultura* was written near the end of his life, apparently as a handbook for his son; it is his only work to have survived intact.

Although the treatise has no literary merit, it is significant as a witness to the pragmatic working of the Roman mind. The manual begins with a statement of the advantages of farming, commerce, and banking, and continues with haphazard advice on such topics as the duties of a bailiff, ways to exploit slaves, methods of raising and feeding livestock, the use of the winepress and care for olive stores, directions for planting and fertilizing, recipes, and diseases of plants, animals, and human beings, together with suggested cures. The work also includes information on religious practices, attitudes, and social customs.

The style, terse and unadorned, carefully avoids anything which might look like Greek influence. Cato boasted almost to the end of his life that he was ignorant of Greek, but the *De Agri Cultura* and other works of his indicate that he, or at least his secretaries, had some acquaintance with Greek works on topics which interested him.

While Cato's literary style had no particular attraction for later classical writers, his views did exert considerable influence. Cicero, for instance, made him the principal speaker in his dialogue essay *De Senectute* or *Cato Major*. The subject matter of the *De Agri Cultura* had a direct impact upon Vergil, who used Cato's treatise for his own poetic work on agriculture, the *Georgics*. The *Georgics*, in turn, remained to a great extent the accepted work on the care of soil and the keeping of bees until virtually the seventeenth century. Furthermore, Cato did a great deal not only to establish agriculture as a topic sufficiently sophisticated for literary treatment, but also to set the traditional image of the gentleman-farmer common to all succeeding ages. Since the landed senatorial class permitted a law to pass prohibiting them from engaging in commerce outside Italy, and since they generally disdained banking and contracting, Cato's concept of the aristocratic farmer became the ideal of the Roman nobility until the time of Pliny the Younger. Finally, the *De Agri Cultura* constituted a venerable endorsement of the Roman *latifundia,* or plantation, system which developed greatly during Cato's lifetime through the exploitation of slave labor. More and more this style of farming became the dominant type of Italian agriculture leading not only to the steady entrenchment of the landed aristocracy but also the growth of slavery and the consequent impoverishment of the small farmer and free laborer.

Although by modern standards many *latifundia* were relatively small, running in size from about sixty to 160 acres, they were directed toward serving a capitalistic market rather than filling domestic needs. Consequently, they encouraged the cultivation of vineyards, olive orchards, and, especially in southern Italy, grazing lands, at the expense of cereal crops which were easily imported from Roman provinces overseas. The heavy importation of slaves already begun during Cato's lifetime as Rome began to extend her control over the Mediterranean world, served to provide manpower for these growing estates. Cato himself estimated that an orchard of some seventy acres would require sixteen slaves to work it and that supplementary labor would be required at the time of the olive harvest. This slave economy in Italian agriculture worked its own drastic results not only on the Roman economy but on Roman society as well; about fifteen years after Cato wrote his treatise on agriculture, the first Sicilian slave war broke out, in which about seventy thousand slaves staged a rebellion which was not quelled for three years.

Pertinent Literature

Hooper, William Davis, translator. *Marcus Porcius Cato, On Agriculture; Marcus Terentius Varro, On Agriculture.* Revised by Harrison Boyd Ash. Cambridge: Harvard University Press, 1934.

This edition and translation of Cato's treatise on farming is a volume of the Loeb Classical Library which presents works of Greek and Latin authors in the original with English translation on facing pages. Each volume has an introductory essay which gives biographical material on the author, and an account of the manuscripts and important editions. In this edition of the *De Agri Cultura* there is also a full account of references to Cato in later Latin authors, including Quintilian, Cicero, Pliny, and Columella.

The translator's brief treatment of Cato's life calls attention to Cicero's version of Cato's life and character in the philosophical essay *De Senectute.* Also noted is Plutarch's explanation that the name "Cato" means "the shrewd," and replaced Cato's earlier name of Priscus, an indication of Cato's reputation for astute management.

Of the *De Agri Cultura* itself, the editor suggests that Cato may not have been responsible for the haphazard arrangement of the material, but that a later compiler of agricultural precepts contained in various of Cato's works may have edited the *De Agri Cultura* as we have it today. The later *Res Rusticae* of Marcus Terentius Varro (116-27 B.C.) is a much more finished work, though it in turn is inferior to the treatise *De Re Rustica* of Columella, a Spaniard who wrote in the first century A.D.

The chief value of Cato's work is in the picture it provides of Roman attitudes and customs. Four examples drawn from the text itself will serve to illustrate Cato's estimate of farming as an honorable occupation, his directions for the treatment of slaves, his advice on remedies for various illnesses, and his approach to religious beliefs and practices.

Cato insists at the outset that the bravest men and the sturdiest soldiers come from the farming class and that the livelihood of farmers is most secure and regarded with least hostility. Moreover, those engaged in agricultural pursuits are least inclined to be disaffected. He claims that the best kind of farm is one of about sixty-five acres containing a variety of soils supporting a vineyard, a garden, orchards, meadows, grainland, and woodland. It is evident that Cato does not expect the ideal farm to be isolated, for he advises his reader to be a good neighbor, reasoning that if one is popular in the neighborhood, it will be easier to sell produce and secure extra hands when needed. "If you build, the neighbors will help you with their work, their teams, and their materials; if trouble comes upon you, which God forbid, they will be glad to stand by you."

Cato refers to the chain gang when speaking of slaves, reminding us that the lowest class of field laborers were chained together and kept at night in a kind of prison. He specifies the bread ration for the slaves, advising an increase during time of heavier labor and a decrease in slack seasons. It is inescapable that for Cato a slave is a commodity and nothing more. In another place, where Cato is teaching economy, he advises the sale of worn-out oxen, blemished cattle and sheep, wool, hides, an old wagon, old tools, an old sickly slave, and whatever else is superfluous. "The master should have the selling habit, not the buying habit."

A significant portion of Cato's treatise has to do with diseases and their cures. Cabbage, "which surpasses all other vegetables," used medicinally, is undoubtedly the most versatile remedy, good for anything from indigestion to cancer. However, Cato knows other cures; for example, a charm for any kind of dislocation consists of what sounds to the modern mind like nonsense jingles to be chanted daily while a split reed is applied to the injured part.

There are also several descriptions of rituals, sacrifices, and prayers to Ceres, Janus, Jupiter, Mars, and other gods. One example will serve to give an accurate impression of this type of old-fashioned Roman piety. In chapter 139, Cato suggests the proper formula to be followed when thinning a grove; one must sacrifice a pig and recite a prayer invoking the proper deity of the grove. In return for the sacrifice, the god or goddess is expected to be gracious and merciful to the donor and his household.

Duff, J. Wight. *A Literary History of Rome from the Origins to the Close of the Golden Age.* Edited by A.M. Duff. 3rd ed. New York: Barnes & Noble, Inc. 1963.

This work, originally published in 1909, remains a classic in its field. Duff set out to give a connected account of Latin literature from its origins through the Age of Augustus, and subsequently continued the story through the next several centuries in *A Literary History of Rome in the Silver Age from Tiberius to Hadrian.* There is probably no single noteworthy figure of classical Latin literature overlooked in these works, and the major figures of the Ciceronian and Augustan periods are given the attention they deserve.

While Duff in no way neglects

468

Cato's writings on agriculture, he is interested in the author primarily as an exponent of the early, terse, unadorned Latin style. Duff sees in this style an accurate reflection of Roman life when the Republic was in the flush of prosperity and not yet caught in the web of domestic and foreign problems which led to the downfall of the republican form of government. He notes Cato's denunciation of poetry, in a fragment in which the old Roman links the versifier with the man given to riotous living, "a harbinger of François Villon." This detail is instructive for Duff, who sees in it a good example of the gulf separating the Greek and Roman life-styles during the period covered by Cato's life and extending far beyond. Roman prejudice against poetry, as expressed by Cato, extended also to singing, dancing and acting, a view corroborated by later Latin authors. The struggle between Cato's puritanism in the guise of patriotism and the liberal attitude represented by the so-called "Scipionic circle," which actively promoted an assimilation of Greek culture, is of great significance in a study of Roman social and cultural history.

Turning to the *De Agri Cultura* itself, Duff finds in it the expression of a businesslike disposition in the Romans, a trait which survived all subsequent political and social changes, even during the later periods of greatest affluence and conspicuous consumption. He calls attention to many details of the *De Agri Cultura* in which Cato teaches methods of thrift: saving time in bad weather, mending tools, economizing in the care and feeding of slaves, and avoiding unnecessary travel and too-liberal hospitality. All this, says Duff, "betrays part of the mean and unlovely side of the Roman character."

In his discussion of the growing influence of Hellenism, Duff calls attention to the foremost nineteenth century historian of Rome, Theodor Mommsen, who compares Cato's didactic writings with those of Varro a century later. The comparison illustrates the great progress in education and general cultural advance by Varro's time. For Cato, the topics worth writing about are: oratory, agriculture, law, war, and medicine. Varro, in turn, considers as worthy of study: grammar, dialectic, rhetoric, geometry, arithmetic, astronomy, music, medicine, and architecture. The practical application of the subjects in Cato's list is obvious while Varro's enumeration of worth-while activities anticipates headings of the medieval trivium and quadrivium. In Varro's day this meant the victory of Greek as an essential element in Roman education. Cato's conservative cause was irrevocably lost.

A further comparison of Cato and Varro shows, besides Varro's wider outlook and wider learning, his much greater humanity, as in his advocacy of consideration for day laborers and slaves. Gone, too, from Varro is the parsimoniousness which makes Cato so unattractive a figure.

Duff notes some slight influence of Cato on the Roman historian Sallust (86-35 B.C.), and a greater influence on Vergil (70-19 B.C.). Vergil used Cato's *De Agri Cultura* as a source for his four books of didactic poetry on agriculture, the *Georgics*, but Duff fails to provide any specific examples of Vergil's dependence on the earlier work.

This work gives as adequate attention to Cato as any history of Latin literature in English. However, the remarks are scattered throughout the book and must be carefully assembled by the reader desiring to understand the author's estimate of "the father of Latin prose" and his place in the development of Roman life and letters. — *M.E.J.*

Additional Recommended Reading

Bieler, Ludwig. *History of Roman Literature*. London: Macmillan & Company, 1966. A survey of Roman literature to 133 B.C. including a useful account of Cato.

Brehaut, Ernest, translator. *Cato the Censor on Farming*. New York: Columbia University Press, 1933. Accompanying the text, there is a commentary, analysis, and a bibliography.

Brehaut, Ernest. "Occupational Development of Roman Society About the Time of the Elder Cato," in *Essays in Intellectual History Dedicated to James Harvey Robinson*. New York: Harper and Row Publishers Incorporated, 1929. A discussion of economic aspects of Cato's world, showing the relationship between capitalist farming and Roman militarism.

Hadas, Moses. *A History of Latin Literature*. New York: Columbia University Press, 1952. A general work affording only brief accounts of Cato and other pre-Ciceronian prose writers.

SKEPTICISM OF THE MIDDLE ACADEMY

Type of event: Philosophical: attack on Stoicism
Time: 155 B.C.
Locale: Athens and Rome

Principal personages:
ARCESILAUS (c.315-241),
PYRRHO OF ELIS (c.360-c.270), and
CARNEADES (214-129), Greek philosophers

Summary of Event

In 155 B.C., Athens sent a special delegation of prominent men to Rome for political discussions. Among the members was the philosopher Carneades, who was originally from the Greek city of Cyrene in North Africa. During his stay in Rome, he gave public lectures. On one day he advanced apparently conclusive arguments for the existence and advantages of justice; on the next he returned to demolish his arguments of the previous day and to establish convincingly the mere conventionality of justice. This display of philosophical versatility so appalled Roman traditionalists such as the conservative Cato that he demanded the banishment of such amoral voices from the city. With this stormy beginning, the philosophy of skepticism left the confines of the schoolroom and entered the philosophic trends of the West.

As a philosophical position, skepticism is chiefly an outgrowth of the Academy founded by Plato. With his death in 347 B.C., his nephew Speusippus assumed control of the school, and under his management and that of his immediate successors the Academy continued its original interest in mathematical and astronomical studies. A decisive change in the school took place under the direction of Arcesilaus who appears to have become head after the death of Crates in 285 B.C. Although there was already a skeptical movement, it was Arcesilaus who surrounded it with the prestige of Plato's Academy. The original Skeptic, Pyrrho of Elis, had subordinated his own skepticism to his moral teachings. For Pyrrho, the only good was virtue, since it enabled man to achieve his end, the enjoyment of undisturbed tranquility of spirit. Since only virtue secured this state, everything else was indifferent and even suspect for its possible ruffling of tranquility. Thus the quest for truth was considered unimportant and superfluous, since its difficulty might shatter the tranquility of the seeker. Each man was encouraged to take a neutral attitude toward reality and its manifold aspects in order to preserve his own inner peace.

In the hands of Arcesilaus, this attitude becomes a systematic approach to the world. Truth is not only indifferent but undiscoverable. Nothing can be known for certain since every issue always can claim two equally valid sides. Arcesilaus adopted this inflexible posture to combat the Stoic position that the absolute certitude of sense-perception made the acquisi-

471

tion of truth possible. Arcesilaus replied that erroneous perceptions also appeared certain and irrefutable. A straight piece of wood submerged in water appears bent. Convinced that he had demolished the Stoic criterion of truth, he proceeded to the total denial of the possibility of any knowledge. This outlook dominated the Academy after his death and received its most thorough sophistication and exploitation at the hands of Carneades.

Carneades became head of the Academy sometime during the first half of the second century. Compared to Arcesilaus his skepticism was more wide-ranging and methodical. The so-called "division of Carneades" was his chief method of attack. This involved not only the familiar presentation of arguments for both sides of every question but also Carneades' conviction that no idea was so true that it could not be countered with a false idea that was yet indistinguishable from the true one. Carneades expressed this method in his remark that man was no more able to distinguish the true from the false than to distinguish one egg from another. With this methodological basis for his skepticism, Carneades launched a complete assault on the main doctrines of Stoicism. Against the Stoic concept of reliable sense impressions, he repeated the arguments of Arcesilaus. For the other tenets of Stoicism, he attempted to devise such cogent rejoinders as might render them flimsy and indefensible. Against the Stoic view of a divinely ordered and harmonious universe, he held that the supposed harmony was in conflict with the manifest defects of the universe, that rationality only made man's brutishness more

devious, and that purely natural forces could more easily account for the presence and origin of such a universe. Nor could the Stoic God claim to exist since the very concept of God required contradictory terms for its description. For man can only describe God in terms of human qualities which contradict the infinite nature of God. The impact of this argument can be seen in the theory of the later Neoplatonists which held God to be ineffable, beyond human thought and language.

Carneades also attacked the Stoic concept of an ideal justice founded on natural law. There is no one common law in nature, since different nations have different laws. Nor is man just by nature, for the very existence of large empires like that of Rome requires that ambitious nations exploit the peoples and resources of smaller ones. Furthermore, the notion of justice is antithetical to human happiness since what is understood by justice often demands that a man act contrary to his own immediate self-interest. Through these and other arguments, Carneades sought to undermine Stoic dogmatism. Although he may have been successful within the debating halls of the schools of philosophy, he did not destroy Stoicism as a creed or as the quasi-official philosophy of Roman political leaders. His success, however, is apparent in other ways. For while Stoicism succumbed with the collapse of the pagan world, the method and approach of Carneades survived under different guises in the medieval *Sic et Non* of Abélard and in the primary importance attached to the problem of epistemological certitude in modern philosophy.

Pertinent Literature

Bevan, Edwyn. *Stoics and Sceptics*. Oxford: The Clarendon Press, 1913.

Although this small book has already celebrated its golden anniversary, it still remains an admirable treatment of the skeptical movement in antiquity because it offers more than a mere handbook résumé of the various philosophers and their arguments. Bevan analyzes skepticism within the context of the historical development of Greek philosophy and with specific reference to its main *raison d'être,* Stoicism.

For Bevan there were two phases of skepticism which were chronologically distinct and representative of different influences and attitudes. The first stage reached its peak with the theories of Pyrrho, who is to be seen as the fullest manifestation of an attitude apparent in Greek philosophy from its very beginning, that the truth was extremely difficult to ascertain. Democritus (c.460-c.370 B.C.) contributed to this tendency with his attacks on the validity of sense impressions. But the chief cause for this first skeptical position was the ordinary man's confusion in the face of the increasing number of philosophical schools. Confronted with a multitude of systems, all claiming to have solved the major problems of existence and yet couching these claims often in dense, metaphysical language, the ordinary man found it easier to disregard the entire problem than to evaluate the contending theories and choose the most satisfying. This natural tendency was seized upon by the early Skeptics, who offered theoretical support for the general unconcern with philosophical problems. This support

was the simple principle that while one could know phenomena as sense impressions, still the supposed reality that lay behind the phenomena, the world of God and the soul and other philosophical topics, remained totally unknowable.

The second phase of skepticism occurred in the Academy under Arcesilaus and especially under Carneades, who popularized the skeptical position. Although skepticism used the same approach, it now had a more defined opposition, the philosophy of the Stoics. The dogmatic views of the Stoics forced the Skeptics to tighten their own arguments so that reality was not only merely unknowable but even its very unknowability became doubtful. The Skeptics felt it necessary to shed every trace of certitude in the face of the absolute dogmatism of the Stoics. In this assault on Stoicism, no one was more devastating or enthusiastic than Carneades, who displayed not so much an original approach as a rhetorical technique which converted his arguments into commonplaces for even the unphilosophical to utilize and exploit.

His success was due in part to the inevitable vulnerability of the Stoics. For their philosophy was not only a search for the truth, but a gospel of the proper conduct of human life. To support their ethical teaching, they were forced to answer metaphysical and cosmological problems. Since their philosophy was primarily a way of life, they endowed their answers with the assurance of dogmatic certainty so that the follower of Stoicism could devote his full energies to the pursuit of the virtuous life and not to philosophical inquiry. This weakness in the logical basis of Stoicism invited Carneades' critique. But Stoicism also had an existential side; it advised men how to conduct their lives. To refute this aspect, Carneades also had to offer practical advice. This he attempted through his idea of the probable. For example, he advises a man to embark on a sea voyage if there is a strong probability that he will reach his destination safely. But he left unanswered the question why the man should take the voyage in the first place. One of his disciples admitted that while Carneades had classified all the possible answers to the question asking what is the purpose of life, he had himself never disclosed his own choice. He only urged men to abide by the customs and traditions of their own environment and to choose always the more probable course of action. This is basically merely a calculus which quantifies life. His failure to devise a more satisfactory alternative to the inhuman dogmatism of the Stoics represents the final tragedy of the ancient world which had outworn all its own creeds and was disposed toward internal collapse and reformation under a new creed.

Brehier, Emile. *The History of Philosophy: The Hellenistic and Roman Age.* Chicago: University of Chicago Press, 1931, reprinted 1965.

This book presents a survey of the history of the post-Aristotelian schools of philosophy. Since skepticism was partially determined by the nature of the philosophies it criticised, Brehier's interpretation of skepticism is clarified and given greater focus by his treatment of Stoicism and Epicureanism. Brehier pays special attention to the changes incorporated into Stoicism as a result of the persistent criticism of the Skeptics. This makes possible an accurate evaluation of the historical influence of the skeptical movement.

For Brehier, formal skepticism is primarily an extension of an intellectual attitude that emerged in Greek philosophy as a reaction against the organized schools and their emphasis on physics. It is important to keep in mind that the term "physics" had a very wide meaning for the ancients. Physics was understood as a comprehensive conception of the entire universe as something that could be accepted as it appeared, and be investigated to provide support for ethical theories. This approach was rejected by all the diverse kinds of Skeptics. They substituted a humanistic approach that rejected external phenomena as inaccessible to man and concentrated on the human conditions of intellectual and ethical activity.

In Pyrrho, this humanistic outlook is all but submerged in his doctrine of quiet resignation. Nor is he to be credited with any of the technical arguments advanced by later Skeptics against the dogmatic certitude of the schools. They are the product of the Academy, of Carneades and his followers. Pyrrho began his own investigations with three simple questions: (1) What is the nature of things? (2) What attitude of mind should a man adopt with reference to things? and (3) What effect will this attitude have upon him? His answers were equally uncomplicated: all things are equal and without any real differences; they are all unstable and imperceptible; man's attitude toward them should be that nothing either is or is not. The result of such an attitude is complete tranquility of mind, since there is no chance of error where there is no opinion. From this it is clear that Pyrrho's chief concern was the perplexing nature of the existential world, which claimed among its other effects the impossibility of certain and sure knowledge. Furthermore, Pyrrho's championing of indifference was the result not of dialectic reasoning but of meditation and practice. This espousal of the quiet, reclusive life may be a result of his contact with Hindu mystics, since there is reliable evidence that he accompanied Alexander the Great on his campaign to India.

Once skepticism, however, had become the official philosophy of the Academy, it abandoned its support of the withdrawn life and began a vigorous assault on the established schools. Arcesilaus turned their own hypotheses against the schools and used dialectic reasoning against the certitude of knowledge. His success as a critic of philosophy was not continued when he attempted to answer the primary problem that confronted all the Skeptics; that is, how to justify human activity. A more developed if no happier solution to the same problem is Carneades' theory of the probable as the sole criterion of action. For Carneades every situation involved three participants: the subject, the perception, and the object. Nothing at all can be said about the object; it remains completely unknowable. The criterion applies only to the relationship between the subject and the perception. Certain perceptions appear true, others false. The criterion determines the circumstances under which some will appear true. Thus while it brings man no closer to the reality hidden behind the perceptions, it does give man a guide to practical living and a way of talking about things. Brehier considers this aspect one of the major achievements of the Skeptics. He holds that ultimately their talk was not merely logical critiques of the dogmas of the Stoics, but suggestions that the universe is more profound and complex than the Stoics realized with their rationalizations, and that its central complexity was man himself. — *G.M.P.*

Additional Recommended Reading

Zeller, Edward. *The Stoics, Epicureans, and Sceptics.* London: Longman's, Green and Co., 1892. Despite its age, this book remains the standard reference work for the history of the post-Aristotelian schools of philosophy.

De Faye, A. "The Influence of Greek Scepticism on Greek and Christian Thought in the First and Second Centuries," in *Hibbert Journal.* XXII (1924), 702-721. A thesis which argues that the nature and method of the early Christian philosophers such as Clement of Alexandria were heavily influenced by the criticism of the Skeptics.

Patrick, Mary Mills. *The Greek Sceptics.* New York: Columbia University Press, 1929. The most complete treatment in English of the history of the skeptical school in antiquity.

De Lacy, Phillip. "On Mallon and the Antecedents of Ancient Scepticism," in *Phronesis*. III (1958), 67-71. An argument that skepticism attacked only dogmatic philosophies and never intended to hinder the practical demands of everyday life.

RISE OF THE PHARISEES

Type of event: Religious: growth of a sect
Time: c.135 B.C.
Locale: Palestine

Principal personages:
JOHN HYRCANUS, King of Palestine 135-104 B.C.
HILLEL (c.30 B.C.-A.D. 30), noted Pharisaic teacher
SHAMMAI, Pharisaic leader, contemporary of Hillel
ZADOK, Pharisee who joined the Zealots in A.D. 6
JOHN THE BAPTIST (c.10 B.C.-A.D. 29), possible Pharisee
JESUS (4 B.C.-A.D. 29), independent critic of Pharisaic
   background, founder of Christianity

Summary of Event

While many older scholars associate the beginning of the Pharisees with Ezra (c.425 B.C.), current scholarship more accurately places their advent in the reign of the Hasmonaean John Hyrcanus (135-104 B.C.). After securing independence from Syria, Hyrcanus had himself designated High Priest in addition to the title of King. A group of pietists were hostile to the innovation of uniting in the person of the monarch both sacerdotal and secular functions. His control over religion was particularly objectionable since he was neither of a priestly family nor of the House of David.

The objectors called themselves Pharisees, derived from the Hebrew equivalent of "separatists." Those in official religious positions who allied themselves with the government and the *status quo* were chiefly priests who served in the Temple, members of the family of Zadok. They were called Sadducees. The Pharisees, on the positive side, sought a creative adjustment to the changes brought to Palestine by the impact of Hellenistic

civilization following the conquest of Alexander the Great. The Pharisees, in short, were rebelling against the old order which had prevailed in Palestine from the time of Nehemiah and the canonization of the Pentateuch, around 400, to the Maccabean rebellion in 168 B.C.

The Pharisees sought to recognize second century developments both in doctrine and practice by supplementing the Scriptures or the written Law with an oral law as developed by qualified teachers and rabbis. In this way the Bible would remain a flexible book allowing its legal structure and ideological message to adapt to the changing intellectual, social, and economic needs of the times.

The Pharisees stressed newer concepts of God, the individual, and life after death. God was universalized as Lord of all peoples and all lands, an idea welcome to the many Jews outside Palestine and conducive to the conversion of Gentiles. The Pharisees placed greater emphasis on the individual and his needs by encouraging the spread of synagogue-worship

477

where study and personal involvement supplanted the sacrifices and the impersonality of the Temple. A more direct emphasis was laid on the individual through the consolatory doctrine of immortality and resurrection of the dead.

As time passed, divisions appeared within the ranks of the Pharisees. An early cleavage developed between conservatives and liberals. While both factions agreed that piety was expressed through strict observance of both the written Law and oral tradition, Shammai stood for extreme rigor while Hillel was more lenient and adaptable to changing conditions. Their attitudes were formalized by their students into schools which generally split on important issues.

Tightening of Roman control over Palestine about the beginning of the Christian era brought more diverse reactions among Pharisees. Around A.D. 6 the Pharisee Zadok joined a Galilean militant, Judah, to organize a body of intransigent patriots called Zealots, who were determined to end Roman domination by direct action.

Josephus and the Dead Sea Scrolls reveal still another kind of Pharisaism, that of the Essenes, an extreme pietistic group which lived in monastic communities. After surviving a rigorous novitiate, members practiced celibacy, held property in common, and lived in seclusion from the troubled times of the Hasmonaeans and the Roman occupation.

Reacting differently to the unsettled times were the "apocalyptists," such as John the Baptist, who believed that a new world order was imminent. The Baptist, seeing himself the forerunner of the Messiah, summoned the people to repentance and purification by immersion in the River Jordan. His most famous initiate was the Galilean Jesus, reputedly the son of a Nazareth carpenter. His claim of Messiahship and his criticism of the Pharisees as hypocritical in observing vain legalism and ritualism brought him into a fatal clash with the faction.

The Pharisaic development of Judaism through the oral tradition established a new sensitivity to change on the part of the ancient religion. From this movement emerged the main stream of Jewish life as it developed in the Mishnah and the Talmud. The approach of the Sadducees was buried forever.

Pertinent Literature

Finkelstein, Louis. *The Pharisees*. 3rd ed. Philadelphia, Pennsylvania: Jewish Publication Society, 1962. 2 vols.

Louis Finkelstein presents one of the most complete analyses available dealing with the Pharisees and their historical role. Examining the religion of ancient Judaism and the Pharisaic movement from the sociological point of view in order to discover the true nature of Pharisaism, he places great emphasis on the rural-urban conflict which eventually appeared in the Jewish world as in all advanced civilizations. Consequently, he believes that the differences between the Sadducees and the Pharisees regarding the oral tradition, resurrection, angelology, and providence arose not from academic and theological conflicts but from social and economic factors.

He sees these differences as conflicts between patricians and plebeians and traces them back to the time of Samuel. Samuel represented the plebeians, while Saul, betraying the rural classes to which he belonged, joined the patricians. The opposed aspirations of the patricians and the plebeians eventually crystallized into the parties of the Sadducees and the Pharisees. After analyzing the messages of the prophets, Finkelstein declares that they were representatives of peasants' rights which were being exploited by the patricians of Jerusalem. The Pharisees continued this prophetic strain especially in Jeremiah and Second Isaiah but now directed it toward the urban plebeians. Proclaiming freedom to all in the cities, they were asserting, as certain prophets had asserted, equality for all social classes.

Finkelstein believes that the Pharisees were unique as a religious group because they achieved great influence without sacrificing their individuality or compromising their principles. While the Pharisees themselves limited their concerns to Israel alone, they were, in Finkelstein's view, destined to be mentors to all mankind, a determinative force in the formation of Christianity and Islam. The ideas which Paul and his fellow apostles carried to the world came from Pharisaism.

The Pharisaic influence on Islam is seen as even more important. Despite the low ebb of Judaism in the seventh century, there was sufficient energy left in ancient Pharisaism to kindle the spirit of the Arab Mohammed, and so transform ignorant idolators into ardent monotheists.

Finkelstein states that Pharisaism was successful not because of its promise but because of its fulfillment of redemption from urban enslavement. Pharisaism was prophecy in action. The author sees the sect as an anomaly of religious history, nationalistic and ritualistic in origin yet universal and philosophic in development.

Herford, R. Travers. *The Pharisees*. Boston: Beacon Press, 1962.

Because of the hostility directed against the Pharisees in the New Testament, their reputation has suffered unjustly. R. Travers Herford, the English scholar and churchman, hopes through the restudy of original Pharisaic documents to provide a sound interpretation of their relationship to Jesus and Christianity. He would avoid the polemical attitude of early Christian writers, the pro-Roman slant of Josephus, and the attitude of modern scholars who stress the ritualistic and legal aspects of Pharisaic religious thought at the expense of its piety, loving concern, and humaneness. Herford's goal is to reconstruct the faith of the Pharisees, their attempt to understand God's will, their ideas on revelation, divine justice and mercy, their prayers, ethics, and devotion to the study of Scriptures.

For Herford the key to understanding the Pharisees is their theory of Torah as given in the Pentateuch. They correctly understood it not as a static, legalistic corpus tailored to a given situation, but rather as a deposit of faith which would deepen spiritual life and impart a strong sense of personal responsibility in a current process.

Herford interprets the Pharisees as challenging the monopoly of the priests in behalf of a universal and democratic priesthood of the people; the synagogue's prayer and study were to be open to all in preference to the Temple's sacrificial and priestly system which centered about a faithful few.

Herford disagrees with the usual description of Judaism, which grew out of Pharisaism, as particularistic and of Christianity as universalistic. The conflict between the Pharisees and Jesus stems from two fundamentally different concepts of religion. For Jesus the key factor was the immediate intuition of God in the individual soul and conscience, while for the Pharisees it was the supreme authority of the Torah. Although the conflict between the Pharisees and the followers of Jesus developed gradually, it could not be reconciled. The Jewish concept that the fatherhood of God could be realized only through entry into the community of Israel was in fact paralleled by the Christian teaching that only through faith in Jesus could men become sons of God. Thus one limitation was replaced by another. An unqualified universalism still lay in the future, when all would be envisaged as God's children with or without Torah, with or without Christ. — *J.R.R.*

Additional Recommended Reading

Oesterley, W. O. E. *The Jews and Judaism During the Greek Period.* New York: The Macmillan Company, 1941. An excellent general background account of the time of the Pharisees.

Lauterback, J. Z. *The Pharisees and Their Teachings.* New York: Bloch, 1930. One of the earliest accounts noting the nature of the social and political differences between the Sadducees and the Pharisees.

Baeck, Leo. *The Pharisees and Other Essays.* New York: Schocken Books, 1947. A view of the Pharisees in which their separateness is related to the concept of the "Chosen People."

Abrahams, Israel. *Studies in Pharisaism and the Gospels.* Cambridge: The University Press, 1917. A study of the important ties between Pharisaism and Christianity.

Finkel, Asher. *The Pharisees and the Teacher of Nazareth.* Leiden: Brill, 1964. A detailed account of the relationship of Jesus to the Pharisees.

TRIBUNATE OF TIBERIUS SEMPRONIUS GRACCHUS

Type of event: Socio-political: attempt at government reform
Time: 133 B.C.
Locale: Rome

Principal personages:

TIBERIUS SEMPRONIUS GRACCHUS (163-133), Roman tribune

MARCUS OCTAVIUS, Roman tribune, 133, opponent of Tiberius

SCIPIO NASICA, Roman senator, chief opponent of Tiberius, consul 138

Summary of Event

By the 130's B.C., conditions in Roman Italy were changing for the worse. The acquisition of empire made necessary the posting of garrisons in distant provinces and a long-drawn-out war of pacification in Spain. Soldiers were conscripted for these duties from the citizens, and the long periods of time some of them had to spend overseas made it difficult or impossible for the less well-to-do to keep their farms going at home. The property of some of these soldiers was sold to creditors, and the land was then usually added to the wide plantations of the rich, who worked the land with non-Italian slaves taken in vast numbers during the provincial wars. For these reasons a few Roman military units had been on the verge of mutiny. Landless citizens swelled the growing numbers of the demoralized urban proletariat, who, without property, were no longer subject to military service with the Roman field armies. This tendency towards the pauperization of the small holders, who made up the bulk of the soldiers of the Roman army, was dangerous for the state. The few attempts which had been made to repair the situation had been stopped by the conservative Roman senate.

In December, 134 B.C., Tiberius Gracchus took office as one of the Tribunes of the People, and he proposed passage of the Sempronian Agrarian Law which had to do with public land, that is, land belonging to the state itself. The land was occupied, but not owned, by farmers and ranchers, many of whom were far from being poor. The bill stipulated that the amount of public land being used by any one man should not exceed three hundred acres. A man might work an additional one hundred and fifty acres for each of his first two sons. Areas above three hundred to six hundred acres the state would repossess, paying compensation for improvements made by the occupier, and this excess would be divided into allotments of about eighteen acres which the state would rent to landless citizens. Thus, the urban mob would be reduced and the numbers of men liable for overseas military service would be increased.

This statesmanlike plan was presented to the Assembly of the People, the *Consilium Plebis,* which voted it

481

into law. At this point, however, another of the ten Tribunes, a certain Marcus Octavius, who was said to have enormous tracts of public land, vetoed the Assembly's act, as it was his legal right to do.

Tiberius, resolved to counterattack with a legal innovation, provoked a constitutional crisis of the first order. He argued that a Tribune of the People should not hold office if he acted against the interests of the people. Whether he did act against them should be decided by the people themselves, namely, the *Consilium Plebis*. Conservatives strongly opposed Tiberius' proposal, pointing out that tribunes were inviolable, and, by extension, not subject to recall; additionally, there was no precedent for the deposition of a tribune. Nonetheless, Tiberius presented his proposal to the *Consilium Plebis,* which voted overwhelmingly to recall Octavius. With that obstacle out of its way, the Assembly then voted the Agrarian Bill into law, and a commission, including Tiberius, his brother Gaius, and another relative, was set up to survey the public land and proceed with its reallotment.

To function, the commission required money, and the senate now proved to be a second stumbling block for Tiberius. By custom and precedent it controlled the state's finances, and it refused to grant sufficient funds for the commission to act. At this point the astonishing news arrived that Pergamum, one of the Hellenistic monarchies, had been willed to Rome by its recently deceased king, Attalus III. Tiberius, apparently with the approval of the *Consilium Plebis,* laid hands on part of the financial reserve of Pergamum and used it to finance the commission's work. This action, while necessary to give effect to the land law, was, to conservative Romans, an outrageous breach of constitutional practice and a serious challenge to the traditional authority of the senate, whose political experience and prestige had guided Rome for more than a century. The senate determined to resist.

By now the time for the election of magistrates for the year 132 was approaching. Tiberius feared that his opponents would make a great effort to elect men friendly to their own views, and that they would try to repeal the Agrarian Law. To prevent this he presented himself for reelection. This action was also without precedent. Conservatives emotionally charged that Tiberius was collecting more and more power into his own hands to wield year after year and finally make himself king.

On polling day a crowd of senators and their clients gathered. When it became apparent that Tiberius was going to be returned to office, these men, led by Scipio Nasica, armed with staves and knives, stormed into the crowded voting areas, seized Tiberius, and clubbed him to death. Three hundred of his supporters shared his fate, and their bodies were flung like carrion into the Tiber.

Tiberius, in attempting to reform Roman society, had had to resort to extraconstitutional measures, which turned the senate sharply against him. It, however, instead of attempting some form of legal redress, resorted to the drastic expedient of murder. Thus was inaugurated an era of violence, gradually swelling until it turned into full-scale civil war.

Pertinent Literature

Last, Hugh. "Tiberius Gracchus," in *The Cambridge Ancient History*. Vol. 9. Cambridge: The University Press, 1932.

Last begins this chapter with a survey of the military and social problems which confronted Rome in 134 B.C., and then proceeds with an exposition of the measures which Tiberius undertook to meet them. His main object was to reduce the number of poor who were filling the slums of the capital and other cities of Italy. The population of Rome at this time is unknown, but it is certain that it was growing rapidly and that the city was showing then most of the signs of urban sprawl and blight with which we are familiar today. Reconstructions of the appearance of the city in history books show the Rome of another age, the Rome of the Caesars, when the city had been rebuilt and ornamented with marble. The Agrarian Law was designed to reduce the size of the mob, increase the numbers from which the army was drawn, and correct grave social injustices. It would also, perhaps, reduce the number of foreign slaves on the large estates of Italy. Tiberius' motives which were both practical and moral, were good.

Resistance to Tiberius came largely from wealthy senators who were in possession of considerable areas of public land. Octavius himself was accused of vetoing the bill because his own extensive holdings of public land were threatened by it. His opposition and that of the senate forced Tiberius to face the alternatives of abandoning his program, which he felt the good of Rome demanded, or of raising the issue of constitutional

reform. He chose the latter. Last says that the method Tiberius used shows him to have been a young man carried away by enthusiasm. His proposals amounted to the launching of a doctrine of popular sovereignty, under which the *Consilium Plebis* was to become the supreme authority in the state. This was contrary to Roman legal tradition, which had laid down a regulation that legislation was to be agreed upon by an assembly summoned by a magistrate with the consent of the senate. Tiberius' acts not only made tribunes subject to recall by this assembly, but also overrode the authority of the senate. This solution had a streak of Hellenism in it; in democratic Greek cities, affairs were managed by a sovereign assembly of citizens which might elect or depose its leaders at will. A leader might hold office for many consecutive terms if the electors assented. Roman practice, on the other hand, insisted upon an interval of years, usually two, between the time a man might hold different offices in the *cursus honorum*, or regulation for office holding, and one of ten years between his holding of the same office twice. Roman practice also insisted upon the principle of collegiality, holding that the power of a magistracy was to be shared between the equal holders of that office, which was a principle Tiberius attacked by carrying out the deposition of Octavius. Tiberius was certainly influenced by two Greek friends, the famous rhetorician Diophanes of Mytilene (later condemned to death for complicity in the Gracchan program), and the Cynic philosopher Blossius of Cumae (who was condemned to exile for the same reason).

Last believes that Tiberius' doctrine of popular sovereignty was dangerous for a state which was not really a democracy but more like an aristo-cratic republic. It was bound to cause opposition. But Tiberius, he maintains, employed argument and reason to gain the assent of one of the great assemblies of the Roman people for his actions. The senatorial opposition abandoned argument and persuasion for lynch law, thereby setting the stage for the most brutal period in the history of the Republic.

Smith, R. E. *The Failure of the Roman Republic*. Cambridge: The University Press, 1955.

This short and interesting book is not for everyone. It contains a minimum of detailed, factual presentation of Roman history, and a maximum of interpretive argument which assumes prior knowledge of Roman political and economic history on the part of the reader. Smith discusses the causes of the collapse of the republican form of government at Rome and its replacement by the monarchy of Caesar and Augustus, and he regards the actions of Tiberius Gracchus as one of the significant causes.

The Roman state in the early 130's was dominated by the senate, which, in turn, was controlled by a small number of rich and noble families. Between 234 and 134, half the consuls came from only ten families. On the whole, the senate's governing of Italy was responsible and able. The senators' point of view was broadly shared by a society that was very conservative in religion, temperament, and outlook. Religion, especially, was an important force holding Roman society together, an important part of that conglomerate of precedent, law, and tradition which the Romans called the *mos maiorum,* "the custom of the ancestors." The most important political issue the Romans had to solve in the 130's, was the problem of governing their growing empire. That sense of Roman superiority which had grown so strong by the middle of the century often expressed itself in a coarse contempt for foreigners; and the administration of provincial affairs was often corrupt, cynical, and cruel. This feeling of superiority created dangerous resentment and hatred for Rome; serious slave uprisings and provincial rebellions were imminent.

At this point Tiberius came on the scene. Smith holds that he wished to increase the number of small farmers liable to military service in order to solve problems connected with conscription. His answer, the Agrarian Law, Smith says, was the concept of a philosopher rather than the solution of a statesman. When the senators frustrated the application of the law, Tiberius impatiently challenged their authority by taking control of the Pergamene treasure, thereby infringing upon senatorial management of financial and foreign affairs. The senate had no obvious means of protecting its preëminent position, for there were no written laws defining its rights, only custom and precedent. Tiberius thus raised the question of who was to govern Rome, which was irrelevant to the main problem of finding more humane and sensible methods of governing the Empire. Therefore, while a secondary issue was being fought out in Italy during succeeding decades, the Romans failed to realize that Rome had become a world power with the moral obligation for providing good administration for the provinces.

Tiberius Gracchus was an innovator in Roman politics. He was an individualist, impatient of tradition, and strongly influenced by Hellenism. The *mos maiorum* stressed *disciplina,* "obedience," and loyalty to the Roman way of life. The arrival of Greek ideas in Rome set up a rival schedule of intellectual and moral values. The Greek philosophers, in their quest for the Good, questioned Roman standards of right and wrong, and challenged the usefulness not only of unthinking *disciplina,* but also belief in traditional Roman religion. The result was a spiritual crisis. Tiberius Gracchus had to choose between either Roman precedent and the withdrawal of his vetoed bill, or the introduction of Greek values and the government of an urban mob. He chose the latter. To put it another way, the senate, upholder of the traditions of Rome, was challenged by new ideas flooding from the Greek world into Rome, a city inhabited by a demoralized proletariat uninhibited by moral or religious restraints. The schemes Tiberius favored undermined the traditional authority of the chief organ of the state itself, and nothing could take its place, ultimately, but armed force. Tiberius thus began the process which led in time to the outright collapse of Roman religion, morals, and decency which was the first cause of that long and sordid record of civil war and rebellion in Roman Italy. — *S.K.E.*

Additional Recommended Reading

Astin, A. E. *Scipio Aemilianus.* Oxford: The Clarendon Press, 1967. A biography of the life of this great contemporary of Tiberius Gracchus and of his role in the critical 130's B.C.
Greenidge, A. H. J. *A History of Rome During the Later Republic and Early Principate.* Vol. 1. London: Methuen & Co. Ltd., 1904. This book, now outmoded on details, nonetheless contains penetrating insights into the course of Roman history from 134 to 104 B.C.
Marsh, Frank B. *A History of the Roman World from 146 to 30 B.C.* London: Methuen & Co. Ltd. 1935. A competent survey of Roman history, including a sketch of conditions in the 130's and the results of Tiberius' abortive reforms.
Oman, Sir Charles. *Seven Roman Statesmen of the Later Republic.* London: Edward Arnold, 1914. Biographies of important Romans, including Tiberius Gracchus and his younger brother Gaius.
Boren, Henry C. "Numismatic Light on the Gracchan Crisis," in *American Journal of Philology.* Vol. 79 (1958), 140-55. This article argues from an analysis of surviving coins that the brothers Gracchus were concerned with the plight of the urban poor.

TRANSFERENCE OF PERGAMUM TO ROME

Type of event: Political: expansion of Roman imperialism
Time: 133 B.C.
Locale: Pergamum, in northwestern Asia Minor

Principal personages:
ATTALUS I (269-197), first "king" of Pergamum 241-197
EUMENES II, King of Pergamum 197-160
ATTALUS II, King of Pergamum 160-138
ATTALUS III, last King of Pergamum 138-133
ARISTONICUS, illegitimate claimant to Pergamene throne
TIBERIUS GRACCHUS, plebeian tribune in 133
MANLIUS AQUILLIUS, Roman consul in 129

Summary of Event

The kingdom of Pergamum in the northwest of Asia Minor was originally part of the Seleucid state carved out of Alexander's empire. When one of Seleucus' satraps detached the area, he founded, through his successors, what came to be known as the Attalid dynasty. In any study of the politics of the area it must be remembered that Pergamum, along with all successor states in the East, was ruled by a Greek minority that domineered the original Oriental population.

In time, Pergamum came to adopt a pro-Roman policy since it became increasingly clear that Rome could be counted upon to favor Greek culture and its supporters over that of the native Easterners. Attalid involvement with Rome became active during the reign of Attalus I who early discovered that it was advantageous to favor Roman fortunes in the involved Macedonian-Seleucid conflicts of the period. It was mainly under Eumenes II, however, that the fortunes of Pergamum were cast. He first fomented a war between Rome and the Seleucid Antiochus III, and then supported the former. For his trouble he learned that Rome could be generous. It gave him for his aid Galatia, long a sought-for prize, which had been conquered by the Romans during the war. It seems to have crossed Eumenes' mind that Roman legions could be used again to advantage in suppressing any unrest fomented against the dominant Greek aristocracy by the native population, a threat which had become increasingly more realistic after 200.

By this time the city of Pergamum was a desirable prize. Adorned with majestic architecture and sculpture it became more and more the home of artists and scholars. Its library rivaled that of Alexandria, and the famous Altar of Zeus further attests to its artistic greatness. From Pergamum was obtained the fabled black stone of the Mother of the Gods, Cybele, a dubious gift at best. Rich in industry and agriculture, Pergamum became the trade outlet for much of the economic transactions in northern Asia Minor, Moreover, around it centered

486

much of the balance of power in the East.

Eumenes II pursued a policy that apparently was an attempt to create a solidarity of the Greeks against the Orientals. However, he did at times panic and pursue a tortuous diplomacy which eventually cost him Roman favor, especially when he changed his mind and belatedly helped Perseus of Macedon in his war against Rome. The temporary defection cost Pergamum the loss of Galatia. Under Attalus II, his brother, friendship with Rome was restored, so that in 146 the Roman Lucius Mummius was heavily supported by the Pergamene navy at Corinth. Scipio Africanus made a state visit to Pergamum in 140.

Little is known about the last Attalid king, Attalus III. Strabo without substantiation charges that he was insane. At his death the kingdom of Pergamum was given to the Roman Republic by his will. The reasons are not clear. It is obvious that he was faced with several problems. Among them was the matter of doubtful succession and the certainty of civil war resulting from it. The only living Attalid claimant to the throne was Aristonicus, an illegitimate son of Eumenes II and a slave. Probably sharing his father's conviction about Greek and Roman coöperation in maintaining Greek culture in the Orient, he was interested in providing a peaceful future for his people. Such an explanation seems particularly attractive when one sees Aristonicus appointing himself leader of the submerged Oriental elements in revolt. Recruiting his followers from

natives, he called them "Citizens of the Sun," an appeal to Mithraic sentiments calculated to unite and inspire the local population. Romans finally sent troops to their new territory in 131, and after some initial defeats by Aristonicus, they annexed it in 129 as the province of Asia. A ten-member senatorial commission under the consul Manlius Aquillius arrived to organize the new addition. Outlying portions of the kingdom were given to Pontus, Bithynia, and Cappadocia.

Unfortunately, the great age of Pergamum had already passed. Its wealth became fair game for ambitious Roman speculators, as well as idealistic reformers. For example, Tiberius Gracchus, probably with good intentions, proposed that the Attalid treasury be used to stock new farms for the Roman poor of Italy. Only his assassination in 132 stopped the plan. Tax farming, however, began to work Pergamum's economic ruin.

The annexation of Pergamum was a major step in the development of the new Roman imperialism which became rampant after 150, as evidenced by the annexation of Greece and Africa. The gift of Pergamum encouraged the Roman eagle to soar in the East. Nicomedes III of Bithynia, also a Greek king, bequeathed his kingdom to Rome at his death in 74; Pompey soon added the rest of Asia Minor, mostly as client kingdoms, as well as Syria and Palestine. Addition of the latter had incalculable results on Judaism and Christianity, and indeed on the entire intellectual history of the West.

Pertinent Literature

Hansen, Esther V. *The Attalids of Pergamon.* (Cornell Studies in Classical Philology, Vol. 29). Ithaca: Cornell University Press, 1947.

The history of Pergamum is of great interest to modern scholars, though the kingdom was virtually ignored by contemporary ancient writers, even those who enjoyed the patronage of the Attalid dynasty. Consequently, any re-creation of Pergamene history requires a skillful weaving of the scattered accounts of several minor ancient authors and fragmentary treatments in more noted writers such as Strabo and Polybius, with inscriptional data and archaeological evidence. Hansen has carefully considered all this material while including the results of modern scholarship, which largely dates from German interest in Pergamum since the 1870's.

In the first five chapters the author treats the political history of the Attalid dynasty from its opportunistic beginnings under Philetaerus in 282 until its transfer to Roman rule by the will of Attalus III in 133 B.C. The dynasty's skillful use of money in diplomacy and in military defense is here depicted as a major factor in the kingdom's survival and prosperity in the face of much wealthier and more powerful empires such as those of the Ptolemies, the Seleucids, and the Antigonids. In this nearly one-hundred-and-fifty-year period, the six rulers of Pergamum established themselves as the arbiters of Asia Minor and the epitome of efficiency compared with the other Hellenistic states.

The last five chapters probably more closely reflect the author's interest. Here Hansen treats the organization of the Pergamene kingdom: its dealings with the other Greek cities of western Asia Minor; its methods of raising mercenary forces, levying revenues, and promoting industries; and its way of developing its position as a cultural and artistic center of the eastern Mediterranean. Pergamum had started out rich under Philetaerus, since he had absconded with a treasury of some nine thousand talents from the Alexandrian successor Lysimachus. However, the Pergamene economy expanded, partly from the tribute and taxes levied on subject cities and peoples, and partly from such important industries as the mining of iron, copper, gold, and silver from the northwest and interior of Asia Minor; the raising of large numbers of horses, cattle, and sheep; the production of woolens, tapestries, leather and parchment; and the manufacture of fine ceramic products, bricks, tiles, and pottery.

The significance of Pergamum as a center of Hellenistic culture was assured in part by the open-handed patronage of the Attalid dynasty. A renowned school of sculpture emerged in the late third century B.C., so that Pergamene sculptures graced the many religious centers founded by the Attalids in western Asia Minor and in the Aegean islands. Best known are those sculptures which commemorated the victories over the Gauls or Galatians of central Asia Minor, the most significant being the "Dying Gaul." Not only were the plastic arts supported and encouraged; Pergamum was a center of scholarship and letters as well. Although Hansen does not develop the point, the library of Pergamum was considered to rival that of the Ptolemies at Alexandria. It is estimated to have had two hundred thousand volumes. At this library and at the Attalid court were gathered some of the finest thinkers of the Hellenistic world.

Hansen's work represents the definitive study on Pergamum available in English. Included is a good though dated bibliography, particularly helpful for providing keys to ancient literary sources.

McShane, Roger B. *The Foreign Policy of the Attalids of Pergamum.* (Illinois Studies in the Social Sciences, Vol. 53). Urbana: University of Illinois Press, 1964.

This diplomatic history of the Attalids is a partial revision of McShane's doctoral dissertation. It attempts to put in clearer focus the distinctive policies of Pergamum in providing leadership for an enlarged Greek alliance following the death of Alexander the Great and the conflict of his successors. Taking the fragmentary treatment of Pergamum found in the ancient writers, as well as a vast body of inscriptions, McShane has reconstructed events to show that while the Ptolemies, the Antigonids, and the Seleucids warred against one another between 281 and 241 B.C., Pergamum pursued a generally neutral course and encouraged the neighboring Greek cities of western Asia Minor to follow her lead. With these cities she coöperated through generous gifts and general patronage of Greek writers, artists, and religious cults; at the same time it provided them with security by maintaining an effective defense against the invading Gauls. In the process, Pergamum became recognized as the benefactor and protector of the Greeks of northwestern Asia Minor, and from this advantage, provided leadership in the formation of alliances, or symmachies to resist Macedonian and Seleucid intervention in the area. The allied cities also looked to the Attalids for diplomatic and military leadership which would stabilize their social order, protect them from invaders, and promote their political and economic autonomy.

The author sees the conflicts caused in the Greek world by the aggressive policies of Philip V of Macedonia and Antiochus III of Syria, effectively countered by Attalid leadership of the smaller powers not only of Asia Minor but on the Greek mainland as well. Pergamum, especially with help from Rhodes, led an extensive Panhellenic movement of freedom against the Macedonians and Seleucids. The Roman role in the ultimate defeats of Philip and Antiochus is minimized, particularly in view of the delay and indecision which preceded Roman intervention in Greek affairs.

Roman entrance into the affairs of the Greek world complicated the issue of independence for the Hellenistic states. After the defeat of Macedonia, Rome felt increasingly obligated to arbitrate Greek affairs. The traditionally petty jealousies among the Greek states, which erupted more and more as each tried to gain

Roman patronage, did not help the Pergamene position in the eyes of Rome, particularly when the Attalid rulers were villified before the senate by representatives of Rhodes and Bithynia. The skillful diplomacy of Eumenes II and Attalus II reinstated the Roman-Pergamene friendship. Indeed, McShane interprets the will of Attalus III as the means by which that ruler sought to insure the continuance of the Pergamene protection of the Greeks in Asia against the rising tide of Oriental unrest, and the maintenance of Greek cultural supremacy in the Near East.

While McShane may overstate his case for Pergamum's significance and goals in the Aegean world between 282 and 133 B.C., this work does provide a good study of the complexities of diplomacy in the classical world. There is an extensive bibliography. — *R.J.W.*

Additional Recommended Reading

Benecke, P. V. M. "Rome and the Hellenistic States," in *The Cambridge Ancient History*. 3rd imp. Vol. VIII, pp 279-291. Cambridge: The University Press, 1965. A survey of Roman diplomacy with the Hellenistic states.

Magie, David. "Rome and the City-States of Western Asia Minor from 200 to 133 B.C.," in *Anatolian Studies Presented to William H. Buckler*. Pp. 161-185. Edited by W. M. Calder and J. Keil. Aberdeen: Aberdeen University Press, 1939. An examination of Roman involvement in Asia Minor.

Magie, David. *Roman Rule in Asia Minor to the End of the Third Century After Christ*. Princeton: Princeton University Press, 1950. The best detailed study of the whole area.

Rostovtzeff, Mikhail. "Notes on the Economic Policy of the Pergamene Kings," in *Anatolian Studies Presented to Sir William Ramsay*. Pp. 359-390. Manchester: Manchester University Press, 1923. A good investigation into the basic industries of the kingdom.

Rostovtzeff, Mikhail. "Pergamum," in *The Cambridge Ancient History*. 3rd imp. Vol. VIII, pp. 590-618. Cambridge: The University Press, 1958. A short tract on Pergamum's history and civilization.

Rostovtzeff, Mikhail. *Social and Economic History of the Hellenistic World*. 2nd ed. Oxford: The University Press, 1952. The basic secondary treatment of this period.

INSTITUTION OF THE FORMULARY SYSTEM

Type of event: Legal: creation of judicial reform
Time: c.125 B.C.
Locale: Rome

Summary of Event

There is a recognized claim that the most impressive and important monument of Roman civilization was its system of law. In its final codification under Justinian it was transmitted to the West and exercised considerable influence upon the legal systems of many European countries and upon the Canon Law of the Church. Countless jurists contributed to this finished product, and serious alterations were required in the traditional bases of Roman Law for the creation of such a vast system as Justinian's code. One significant alteration was marked by the passage of a single law, the *Lex Aebutia,* about 125 B.C.

Historical development of Roman Law begins with the publication of the Twelve Tables in 450 B.C., the earliest collation of the original principles of Roman legal procedures. The radical change in this system brought about by the *Lex Aebutia* can only be comprehended in the light of this earlier stage. The primary characteristic of the original legal system was its rigid formalism both in legal proceedings and in private transactions. Without the impeccable use of solemn and inflexible oral forms by the parties involved, no legal effect was considered to have occurred. This rigidity meant that the intentions of the litigants had no legal standing unless they were expressed in a prescribed, stipulated form.

Similar rigidity is also evident in the procedure of the civil trial with its carefully regulated stages. The first stage took place before a public magistrate who submitted for acceptance by the litigants a formal agreement that contained a precise formulation of the principal points at issue. A third party was selected to act as judge and was empowered to investigate and decide the case. His decision was strictly limited to the formal, verbal expression of the disputed point.

The trial proper, the *legis actio,* was conducted as a formalistic procedure in which both plaintiff and defendant were required to assert their positions in the oral forms prescribed by law and custom. The slightest divergence from the traditional wording invalidated the entire proceedings. Thus, there is mention of a case in which a plaintiff was refused a suit, even though he was attempting to bring to trial a defendant who had purportedly cut down his vines. His suit was not granted since it accused the defendant of cutting down "vines," whereas the law that covered such actions allowed suits against only those who cut down "trees." This entire legal system with its subtle pitfalls was termed the *jus civile,* since it protected only the citizens of the republic. Foreigners were not treated as legal persons and were excluded from the operation of the *jus civile*.

Such a narrow legal code was adequately suited to the early conditions of Roman society with its predominantly agrarian population and its limited economic interests. Its deficiencies, however, became apparent with Rome's gradual domination of the Mediterranean. The resultant increase in foreign trade inevitably caused disputes between Roman merchants and foreigners, who came henceforth to the city to find redress for legal complaints. For the sake of commercial stability and international peace it became imperative to devise a legal process to handle disputes between citizens and foreigners. In 242 B.C., the court of the peregrine praetor was established to administer the law for foreigners, the *jus gentium*. This praetor was empowered to regulate disputes between Roman citizens and foreigners, and was free to invoke whatever rules he desired to define the judicial rights of noncitizens. Since Roman citizens had to contest claims against foreigners in the peregrine court, the praetor of this court probably applied as far as he was able the principles of the *jus civile*. Nonetheless, he was also able to adapt the *jus civile* to the unique requirements of each case. This adaptation produced in time a sizable amount of new legal principles which were grafted upon the existing body of traditional laws and legal procedures. The most important contribution was the introduction of the so-called "formulary system."

The procedure contained in the traditional *legis actio* was not binding on the praetor of the peregrine court. Instead of adhering to rigid, verbal technicalities, he was able to handle disputes at his own discretion. This was most evident in his determination of the contents of the formula, which was a writen document stating in brief and precise language the exact nature of the dispute. The formula was presented to a judge who expected to find in it a clear delineation of the issue he was called upon to adjudicate and of the points which the evidence presented should illuminate. Each praetor at the beginning of his term of office published an edict that announced the circumstances under which a formula would be granted. This edict expressed general principles of law rather than narrow definitions. The advantage of this system was that it did not tie down the praetor to previous legal authority; he simply announced that under given conditions he would allow a suit or a defense.

The obvious superiority of the peregrine court over the urban court. which adhered to the rules of the *jus civile* made change inevitable. About 125 B.C. the *Lex Aebutia* was enacted, allowing litigants in the urban court their choice of either a *legis actio* proceeding or the formulary system. Once this choice was extended to all citizens, the *legis actio* gradually fell into almost total disuse; eventually it was declared inappropriate except for a few select legal disputes, and the formulary system became the exclusive process for the operation of Roman private law. Its dominance meant greater equity for all members of the Empire, and the demise of legal ritualism and archaic formalism.

492

Pertinent Literature

Jolowicz, H. F. *Historical Introduction to the Study of Roman Law*. Cambridge: The University Press, 1952.

A layman interested in Roman law needs a guide skilled in both jurisprudence and Roman history; Jolowicz meets these requirements admirably. His treatment stresses the sources of Roman Law and the development of the Roman constitution as well as the general judicial structure and its procedures. Although he covers the history of legal evolution until Imperial times, he has valuable sections on various aspects of the formulary system with particular emphasis on its role as a creative source of new law.

Jolowicz finds three stages in the development of Roman Law: the early period of the *legis actio,* the succeeding period of the formulary system, and the final stage of the legal system of the Empire. Between the first two periods, the difference is marked. In the first period, a legal action resulted from an agreement by the contending parties to speak the appropriate language, in the second from an agreement as to the terms of the formula. The second arrangement confined the judicial process much more within the powers of the presiding magistrate. For although the contending parties with the assistance of their legal advisers agreed among themselves on the terms of the formula, they were primarily guided by the published edict of the officiating magistrate. In addition, the magistrate had the power to agree to a formula which itself had no basis in the *jus civile* and even to refuse one which attempted to enforce

a claim guaranteed by the *jus civile.* One of the most significant powers enjoyed by the magistrate in this context was his prerogative of granting an *exceptio.* This addition was a clause appended to the formula that instructed the judge not to condemn the defendant, even if the charge of the plaintiff was verifiable, if at the same time the judge found a further set of facts to be in evidence. The case of contracts will provide an illustration of this process.

Traditionally a contract was understood as a binding promise which was to be interpreted strictly according to its wording, and a person who had made such a promise was held obligated to it even if he had been fraudulently induced to make the promise. In the preformulary period, the only decisive question was whether or not the defendant had made the alleged promise. Under the formulary process, the magistrate could grant an *exceptio* clause whereby the defendant was to be adjudged not liable to the contract if he could show that he had been induced to enter into it either by fraud or by misrepresentation on the part of the plaintiff.

Even though the *exceptio* clause had no basis in the *jus civile* and was simply the magistrate's judgment that under certain conditions the *jus civile* was inadequate, it formed part of the *jus honorarium,* the law as expounded by the magistrates and ultimately combined with the *jus civile* into a harmonious legal structure. This harmony resulted partially from the customary practice of each praetor's taking over and republishing at the beginning of his term of office the edicts of his predecessors along with his own additions. This practice, along with the various applications of *exceptio,* gradually produced a sizable volume of law that enjoyed the continuity of time and came to stand as the chief repository of legal procedure.

Jolowicz also considers it important to determine whether the use of the formulary systems in trials involving only Roman citizens was first made possible by the *Lex Aebutia,* or if its use did not predate passage of the law. Since the formulary system is so integral to the operation of the *jus honorarium,* its late introduction into cases involving the *jus civile* about 125 B.C. would necessitate a much

slower evolution of Roman law. He also argues for the operation of the formulary system in trials involving the *jus civile* prior to 125 B.C. by maintaining that if the system were not already familiar to the people, the sudden bestowal of so much legal autonomy upon the magistrates in their interpretation of the law would have been too radical an innovation for immediate and unchallenged acceptance. This complex problem Jolowicz tries to resolve by holding that, until the passage of the *Lex Aebutia,* the formulary system was only employed in cases not covered by a *legis actio* procedure. This solution is a striking example of his methodology, the joining of jurisprudence and historical research to provide an elegant and probable solution.

Turner, J. W. Cecil. *Introduction to the Study of Roman Law.* Cambridge: The University Press, 1953.

This book is much less historically oriented than the preceding one. For Turner, the critical importance of the formulary system lies in its effect on the philosophical foundations of Roman Law. His central thesis is that certain aspects of the formulary system made possible a confused identification of the philosophical concept of the natural law with the so-called *jus gentium,* the law of nations. This identification is primarily a result of the diverse meanings of the term *jus gentium.*

The *jus gentium* was an outgrowth of the unique response by the Romans to the problem of providing a judicial system for the various nations of the Empire. The simple solution of extending Roman civil law to all per-

sons of the Empire was precluded by Rome's refusal to share the fruits of citizenship. No attempt was made to devise a completely new formulation of private, international law. Instead the Romans worked out piecemeal a system of rules and procedures to govern all free men regardless of their citizenship. This system was essentially Roman in its origins, but it was stripped of the technical and archaic formalism that characterized early Roman civil law. This process was accomplished mainly by the magistrates who presided over cases between Roman citizens and aliens. The delineation of the formula by the magistrate and especially his capacity to append *exceptio* clauses, as in the case of contractual disputes, was of historic importance since the extension of the formulary system to cases covered by the *jus civile* also carried with it this active source of new rules and legal interpretations. The rules and interpretations that were common to both sorts of cases gradually became known as the *jus gentium,* the part of the law that applied to Romans and noncitizens alike. The confusion began when the phrase *jus gentium* became equated with the theory of the natural law within Greek philosophy.

The notion of a natural law found its greatest exponents at Rome among the Stoic philosophers. The Stoics identified as the dominant entity in the universe reason, which was immanent in all the operations of nature through the manifest laws that regulated the harmonious activity of nature. Since man was also a part of the universe, his activity in turn betrayed the immanence of a universal law that was common to all members of mankind regardless of their citizenship. It is not surprising that Roman legal theorists saw their system of the *jus gentium* as the visible and functioning expression of the theoretical natural law, since their courtroom law did provide an actual code of law for the behavior of men in diverse nations. Such an identification made it possible for a Roman jurist to appeal to the structure of the natural law to support his own specific legal interpretations. As a result, the *jus gentium* acquired the respectability of having its own philosophical basis. Eventually this led to an inevitable interpretation of the actual working law that required its harmonization with the philosophical principles of the natural law. However gradual this process may have been, Turner finds its initial impetus in the greater flexibility imparted to Roman law by the adoption of the formulary system. — *G.M.P.*

Additional Recommended Reading

Buckland, W. W. *Textbook of Roman Law from Augustus to Justinian.* Cambridge: The University Press, 1921. The standard reference work in English for practically all aspects of Roman Law.

Buckland, W. W. *A Manual of Roman Private Law.* Cambridge: The University Press, 1953. An outstanding guidebook for the layman.

Schulz, Feitz. *Classical Roman Law.* Oxford: The Clarendon Press, 1951. Schulz, an expert on Roman law, is more radical than Buckland in many of his interpretations.

Nicholas, Barry. *An Introduction to Roman Law.* Oxford: The University Press, 1962. An admirable introductory book which takes in recent scholarship and emphasizes fundamental differences between Roman Law and modern common law.

Crook, John. *Law and Life of Rome.* Ithaca: Cornell University Press, 1966. A survey showing how Roman Law related to the social and economic conditions of Roman life.

MARIUS' CREATION OF THE PRIVATE ARMY

Type of event: Military: innovation in recruitment and organization of the Roman army
Time: 107-101 B.C.
Locale: Rome, North Africa, and North Italy

Principal personages:
> GAIUS MARIUS (157-86), commoner who gained high civilian status through military achievements
> JUGURTHA (d.104), one of three princes who inherited the kingdom of Numidia in 118

Summary of Event

Marius' reforms of the Roman army were the culmination of developments arising out of Rome's emergence as an imperial power. They were the beginning of developments that were to lead to the civil wars of the late first century and the end of the Roman Republic.

From the earliest known period, the Roman army was recruited on an *ad hoc* basis for specific campaigns. Levies were held in each year in which military operations were proposed; recruits were conscripted from freeborn citizens whose properties enabled them to provide their own arms. Although the property qualifications for military service were often extended downward, and although the extended campaigns required from the time of the First Punic War brought about the institution of military pay for soldiers, the armies of Rome were still thought of, and in large part were still treated as, a citizen militia rather than a professional force. Possession of property, regarded as a pledge of good faith and commitment to the nation, remained a requirement for eligibility to serve.

During the third and second centuries B.C., the traditional system of recruitment was subjected to increasing strain. The requirements of empire created a need for larger numbers of troops recruited for longer periods of time. Small landholders, who made up the bulk of the army, found it increasingly difficult to maintain their farms while fulfilling their military responsibilities. The importation of cheap grain from conquered territories created additional difficulties for small farmers, and small holdings fell more and more into the hands of large landowners, who operated their tracts with the help of slaves and tenants who were disqualified, by lack of property, from army service. In short, the need for troops was increasing while the class of citizens who supplied that need was diminishing.

The reforms of Tiberius and Gaius Gracchus, designed to reëstablish the small farmer class, failed in their effect while creating a climate of mutual suspicion and hostility between the ruling senatorial order and the rest of the Roman population. When Gaius Marius, an experienced soldier unconnected with the senatorial order, offered to remove the conduct of the Jugurthine War from the hands of the senate-appointed generals, he was elected to office by a large popular majority. Moreover, over the objections of the senate, he was entrusted with the African campaign. Marius, seeing the difficulties of raising an army in the traditional way, and less bound by tradition than generals of higher birth, refused to order a conscription; instead, he called for volunteers, accepting all who appeared to be physically fit, with no consideration of property qualifications.

Marius' action, superb in its simplicity, solved once and for all the problems of recruiting military forces. While the Roman countryside had been depleted of small farmers, the urban proletariat, the propertyless masses of the city, had grown large. From these, and from the rural proletariat who were chiefly tenant farmers, came an army of volunteers who regarded military service not as a civic obligation but as a means of earning a living.

The change from a citizen militia to a professional army, however, created difficulties of a new kind. Thereafter, the Roman army was not a force raised by the state, but one that had attached itself to a particular commander. Soldiers fought not to protect their possessions, but to earn a living. Their advantage lay not in a quick resolution of a specific campaign, but in the continuation of military action. The commander of such forces had to guarantee their pay and their booty; he also had to ensure them some form of pension, usually a small landholding, at the end of their service. To offer such guarantees, he had to maintain a high degree of control over Roman policies, both foreign and domestic. So Rome came under the twin threats of civil war and military dictatorship, a situation which was not resolved until the collapse of the Roman Republic, when military and civil government were combined under the emperors.

With the creation of a truly professional army came extensive reorganizations in tactics and equipment. The Roman legion, regarded as a standing force, was given an identity symbolized by a permanent name and a legionary standard. Armor and pack were improved and standardized; training and discipline received greater attention. The maniple, a tactical unit of some one hundred and twenty men of proven maneuverability against the larger and tighter Greek phalanx, was replaced by the cohort. This tactical unit of six hundred men proved itself more effective against the non-Greek forces that had become more common as opponents. Whatever its unfortunate effects upon the republican form of government, the professional army created by Marius served the Empire well for centuries of conquest, occupation, and defense.

Pertinent Literature

Perowne, Stewart. *Death of the Roman Republic.* Garden City, New York: Doubleday & Company, Inc., 1968.

The subtitle of Perowne's book is "From 146 B.C. to the Birth of the Roman Empire," but he begins with the beginnings of Rome. In five chapters he describes the rise of Rome, up to the end of the Third Punic War and the sack of Corinth. A sixth chapter, "The Fatal Flaw," assesses the weaknesses that were to lead to the decline of the Roman Republic. The rest of the book tells the story of that decline, beginning with the period of the Gracchi. It is an eminently readable account, made dramatic by the author's humane sympathy with the fortunes of institutions, societies, and, above all, individuals.

The social and military circumstances leading to Marius' rise play a large role in Perowne's story. The ruling nobles of the senate and the wealthy class of *equites,* the so-called "knights," had been estranged during the political strife of the period of the Gracchi, and this split had widened with the opening of the Jugurthine War. Originally a war of succession among three princes of an independent kingdom of North Africa, the conflict was supported by the *equites,* whose commercial interests were threatened by the conquests of Jugurtha. The senate, forced to manage a war in which its members had little interest, made slow work of it.

Gaius Marius, then a man in his middle years, was a commoner by origin. He had attracted the attention of Roman nobles by his long and capable service in the army, and he had gained admittance to the senate by being elected to the lower magistracies. Marius joined the Roman armies in Africa as second-in-command to the general Quintus Caecilius Metellus. Recognizing the alienation between nobles and commoners in the matter of the war, Marius returned to Rome against his commander's wishes,

and entered into competition for the consulship, promising a vigorous prosecution of the war.

Marius was elected, and the popular assembly, overriding the decision of the senate to the contrary, authorized him to replace Metellus in command of the African campaign. It was under these circumstances that Marius enrolled his volunteer army, creating a force attached not to the senatorial government but to himself.

Marius' subsequent commands, and much of the tactical reorganization of the army, were held in the face of a different military threat. Hordes of barbarians from the north were pressing into Italy. Marius was reëlected to the consulate in the years following the conclusion of the Jugurthine War. His newly professionalized troops succeeded in outmaneuvering and outfighting the German hordes in two dazzling victories, and he himself was regarded as savior of the state.

Perowne correctly places Marius' position in the course of Roman history between the Gracchi and Sulla. As the Gracchi had prepared the way for Marius by attempting and failing to revitalize the class of independent peasants that had previously furnished the armies of Rome, so Marius prepared the way for the military dictatorship of Sulla by his creation of a professional army permanently attached to an individual commander. The title of the chapter Perowne devotes to Marius is "Inter Arma Silent Leges," that is, "When the fighting starts, the laws are silent," a remark attributed to Marius himself. It is ironic that Marius so failed to see the implications of his own military reforms that he never attempted to use

498

his troops to gain control of Rome. Instead, he resigned his armies at the end of his campaigns, and entered politics in a more traditional manner, failing to make any lasting achievement in that sphere, and contributing to the disorder that precipitated the military dictatorship of Sulla.

Smith, R. E. *The Failure of the Roman Republic.* Cambridge: The University Press, 1955.

Smith's book is more of an interpretive essay than a straightforward history; his thesis is that the decline of the Roman Republic was due to a spiritual crisis precipitated by the Gracchi and elaborated in a vicious circle during the civil disturbances of the years between 133 and 31 B.C.

Smith begins with an account of the political, social, and cultural unity that prevailed in Rome during the first half of the second century B.C. The senate governed unchallenged with the consent of the people, whose right it was to confirm or reject proposals submitted to them in the voting assembly. Though the senate was dominated by, and the magistracies reserved to, the members of a limited number of great families, the common people were not disaffected. The client-patron relationship, whereby commoners were attached to great families in a condition of greater or less dependency, created such bonds between these classes that they found large areas of common interest. A rising class of wealthy merchants and entrepreneurs, largely independent of nobles and commoners alike, represented interests sometimes opposed to the senate's, but the three classes of society were able each to identify its interests with that of the state, and Smith finds second century Rome an uncommonly close-knit social and political body.

The destruction of Carthage in 146 B.C., removing the last supposed threat to her security, left Rome temporarily without a sense of national purpose. Domestic problems, by no means so severe that they could not have been dealt with by traditional means, came to occupy men's thoughts. The Gracchi, in attempting to deal with these domestic problems, resorted to methods that undermined the authority of the senate, disrupted the continuity of governmental policy, drove the nobles into a defensive and reactionary position, and created in the wealthy equestrians a political force specifically designed to oppose the senate. From this time forward, each social class in Rome regarded the aspirations of all other classes as hostile to its own. The harmony of the Roman state was shattered, and men identified themselves not as members of the Roman state but as members of this or that narrower group.

The Jugurthine War and the rise to power of Marius were natural results of this social disintegration. Entry into the war was forced by the wealthy *equites*, who saw in its prosecution prospects for wider and more profitable commercial activities. Senatorial opposition was overriden, and extraordinary methods were used in order to place Marius, the general commissioned by the *equites*, in charge of the African campaign. Marius' army reforms were undertaken, despite their far-reaching implications for

Roman government and for Roman society, on his own authority without consultation with the senate.

The creation of a professional army is usually viewed as the cause of the civil disorders and military dictatorships that succeeded each other for the remaining years of the Roman Republic. Smith points out, however, that such an army, whose loyalties lay with its commander rather than with its government, could not have been created except in a state whose social structure had already disintegrated. "No man marches against his ideals; if a Roman army was prepared to march on Rome, it was because Rome stood for nothing that won their loyalty." The Roman soldier, as any other Roman, gave his loyalty to his group, not to his nation. His case was no different from that of the self-seeking noble, equestrian, or commoner. Marius' reforms did not cause the disintegration of Roman society. They merely reflected it, creating yet another group, the army, to compete with the others already exploiting Roman society for their own special interests. — *Z.M.P.*

Additional Recommended Reading

Cook, S. A., F. E. Adcock, and M. P. Charlesworth, eds. *The Cambridge Ancient History.* Volume IX: *The Roman Republic, 133-44 B.C.* Cambridge: The University Press. The third chapter, by Hugh Last, provides an authoritative account of "The Wars of Marius."

Parker, H. M. D. *The Roman Legions.* Oxford: The Clarendon Press, 1928. A straightforward account of the development of the Roman army from Marius through the second century A.D.

Adcock, F. E. *The Roman Art of War Under the Republic.* Cambridge: Harvard University Press, 1940. A description of the Roman military forces on land and at sea.

Andreski, Stanislav. *Military Organization and Society.* London: Routledge & Kegan Paul, Ltd., 1954. A sociological treatise describing the relationship between the social structure of society and military organization, with examples from many ages including ancient Rome.

EXPLOITATION OF THE ARCH

Type of event: Technological: development of an artistic architectural device
Time: c.100 B.C.
Locale: The Roman Empire

Summary of Event

The arch is customarily thought of as a structural device bridging or spanning a relatively wide space with relatively small units of brick or stone. The so-called "true" arch is constructed of wedge-shaped voussoirs, the joints between which radiate from the center of the arch's curvature; or it may be constructed of rectangular bricks that are separated by wedge-shaped mortar joints. In the "corbeled" arch all joints are vertical and horizontal, and the space is spanned by having each successively higher course of masonry project further into the opening in the pattern of inverted steps until the two sides meet.

The invention of the arch as a structural device is of immense antiquity. It was used in well-constructed vaults as early as about 3500 B.C. at Dendera and at Abydos in Egypt and soon after in Mesopotamia. The corbeled arch, which can be built without supportive centering and with a minimum of lateral buttressing, was apparently developed first. But for the Egyptians and the later Greeks arcuated construction never constituted a "system of architecture." What they both were avoiding, it would seem, was not the arch as a structural device but the arch in its second and far more important aspect: that of being a shaped aperture.

The Greeks disliked the arch, we may suppose, because it gives distinctive form to a hole. It was character-istic of Greek thought to conceive of form or shape as that which determines the reality of what truly exists and to think of space or emptiness as the prime symbol of nonbeing. The shadowy spaces between the columns of the Parthenon are as completely neutral as the black background behind the light-colored figures on an Attic red-figured vase.

The first architects to accord the arcuated aperture a positive role, the first therefore to "discover" the arch, were in all likelihood Roman. This "discovery" coincided more or less in time, it appears, with the introduction of landscape painting and of those perspective devices which the Roman painter used to shape and reproduce the spatial context of nature. The arch was used both by the Etruscans and the Romans of the Republic to construct city gates, and before the end of the second century B.C. it was being employed by the Romans in arcuated bridges. Not until the building of the Tabularium around 80 B.C. was it used, so far as we know, for the creation of a "monumental" façade.

We find employed here what was to become a favorite compositional device of Roman architects: superposed arcades in the "arch order." This term designates an arch that is framed by engaged columns carrying an entablature appropriate to the order of the columns. In the arch order the formerly negative interstices between the columns are given a shape that is more distinctive than that of the masonry supports themselves.

The Romans used the arch in a variety of ways, ranging from the strictly utilitarian Cloaca Maxima and the Pont du Gard to the purely commemorative or monumental arches of triumph, between which extremes there may well seem to be no connection other than a technical one. It can be argued, however, that for the Romans the arch had a general significance which is more clearly manifested in the Pont du Gard, perhaps, than in the Tabularium.

Periclean Athens and Imperial Rome were put together differently. To the Athenians the fundamental political problem was that of grouping citizens in an appropriate number of classes of manageable size where each citizen was regarded as an equal and equally responsible voter in the popular assembly. Such a concept was in good part symbolized in the ordering of the Parthenon, a strikingly unified structure made up of many parts each of which has a standard shape, position, and name. Rome, on the other hand, was governed in Republican times by a landholding senatorial oligarchy that worked closely with the military establishment so that power came to be operated by a smaller and smaller number of hands. The populace was governed not by perfected systems of classification but by the regulation of their highly diversified and widely scattered activities.

It was as "Pontifex Maximus" or "bridge builder" that the ruler could best visibly assert his authority by binding the Empire together with roads and bridges. The massive triumphal arch bridging a principal thoroughfare most clearly expressed the essential sense of Roman arcuation. The oldest of the arches of triumph, so far as we know, was deliberately built by Augustus at Rimini in 27 B.C. to celebrate the restoration of the highway system in northern Italy. Thus the arch became the symbol of control over the passageway which both gives access as well as directs and limits it. Arches of triumph, then, along with city gate arches and the massive arcades of public buildings such as the Tabularium and the Basilica Julia, bore witness to the ability of the state to regulate and control the citizen's movements; while the arcuation of theaters and amphitheaters and the vaulting of the great public baths made manifest the beneficence of the state in providing noble spaces within which the citizen might enjoy both comfortable security and freedom of movement in lieu of political rights.

Pertinent Literature

Longfellow, W. P. P. *The Column and The Arch*. London: Sampson Low, Marston & Co., 1899.

In a forty-page section discussing Greco-Roman architecture, this study treats the arch as a flexible instrument modifying the traditional Greek "order" so that Greek and Roman architecture, rather than being two distinct styles, represent mere stages in the evolution of one architecture. The author praises the Romans as bold innovators in this development; if they were ostentatious and lacking in artistic talent, they were at the same time progressive and free from restrictive dictates of religion and piety or of sentiment and reverence. The Greeks, on the other hand, adhered religiously to their "order" which basically changed little in the two hundred and fifty years separating the early temples of Selinus from the Parthenon.

The Romans inherited the Greek "order" featuring a simple post and lintel construction of column and entablature which produced a structure of beams, horizontal and upright, made of stone, and featuring the colonnade designed to suppress the wall. At the same time, the Romans inherited the Etruscan arch which Longfellow believes was originally the child of the Oriental bricklayer who had no other way to bridge an opening.

The genius of the Roman architect entered when he set out to wed his own device, the arch, with the Greek "order"; the earliest example, according to the author, was in the Tabularium erected in 78 B.C. at the base of the Capitoline hill. To combine the arch and the Greek "order," the Roman simply, as it were, built the wall, pierced it with arches and set the Greek style of colonnades against it so as always to show an arch between two columns which still appeared to carry the entablature above. To fully ally the two elements, a "sort of capital, the impost moulding, was put about the pier to receive the arch"; the parts were further pulled together at the foot by base mouldings and "the band about the arch echoed the architrave." Finally a keystone in the crown of the arch was carried up until it bore against the architrave. The keystone was intended solely as an inventive aesthetic detail to bind the arch and the Greek "order" at its most critical point. Later architects wrongly glorified the keystone as an essential feature of the arch itself; it has no more structural value than any other stone in an arch. As a result, "all the honor due to the arch has been heaped upon it in language and literature."

The element, then, in the Greek "order" suited for combination with the arch was the column. While its reasonable place was under the arch, the classical Roman kept it married to the entablature in the traditional noble style of the Greeks by substituting the pier under the arch itself. The first time that arches were set directly on capitals of columns with no architrave was in the late palace of Diocletian. Subsequent development of the vault also forced the column eventually to stand below, since the vault at no place could be set between columns. Since the arch, reflecting the Roman character to some extent, was ambitious and domineering, it was difficult to put it and the "order" together without permitting the arch to attract the main attention because of its flexible character. It tended eventually to overbear the "order" and in the case of the vault and dome to be set above the "order."

The arch to the Roman was a matter of necessity to assure taller and more variegated buildings. Trying always to keep the arch a servant to the Greek "order," Romans piled "order on order, arcade over arcade" to throw their theaters and buildings high into the sky. The arch, and the resultant vault and dome, added great new resources of flexibility, power, dignity, and grace, helping to span wide openings and spaces with magnificence and habituating the world to a new order of curved lines and surfaces.

Curtis, D. "Roman Monumental Arches," in *Supplementary Papers* of the American School of Classical Studies in Rome. Vol. II, 1908.

One of the more perplexing forms that the arch assumed is that of the "monumental" arch, represented by more than four hundred and fifty known specimens scattered around the Roman Empire from the days of the kings until about A.D. 600.

Despite the fact that the author promises to discuss "the origin of the so-called 'triumphal arch,' " it appears that neither he nor any other later writer has dealt definitely or even imaginatively with the subject. He has been more successful in attacking the term "triumphal" as applied to these structures than in illuminating their beginnings. The term "triumphal," he points out, is misleading as anachronous, since it occurs only once in Roman literature and then only at the end of the fourth century. Four inscriptions using the designation are also late.

Most authors, Curtis avers, assume that the free-standing arch derived its origin from early temporary wood structures erected over roads to bear wreaths and trophies after a triumph. Eventually these primitive and temporary structures would become stylized and constructed of durable materials. This thesis the author discredits on the basis of archaeological evidence as well as the testimony of Pliny. Archaeologically, it appears, only one of the six or seven small Republican arches dating, according to Livy, from as early as 196 B.C. clearly bore any honorary statues presumably as permanent commemorative evi-dence of a triumph. Pliny makes it clear that although the custom of placing honorary statues on columns and in other places was an old one, arches were not used for the purpose until the end of the Republic.

The author asserts correctly that it is too naïve to assume that because triumphal processions passed beneath arches over roads that these structures were intended originally as triumphal monuments. Romans in their literature seem to be aware of no such connection; physically any procession simply had to pass beneath arches placed over a pathway or road.

The origin of the monumental arch seems, according to the author, in no way illuminated by reference to occasional Greek usage of arches at city gates and over streets. The examples of employment of the true arch by Greeks are too few and nebulous for postulating generalities. Moreover, inscriptions are equally uninformative. Only slightly more than half of the arches studied by the author bore any inscriptions at all. This fact seems strange since, according to Curtis, arches were architecturally constructed so as to provide a façade, however varied or profusely decorated, which readily could "resolve itself in most cases into something like a framed picture." Such a space would appear to be an ideal locus for inscriptions. Those arch inscriptions that are available are useful only in determining the date of the monument and scarcely illuminate the origin of the species. Since inscriptions are not informative in regard to the provenance of the monumental arch, the author views as unconvincing the thesis advanced by some scholars that these arches are monuments of civil liberty because a few of them are dedicated to the local diety, or the genius of the city.

Since inscriptions and other literary evidence thus give the term "triumphal arch" little support, Curtis concludes that these monumental edifices were not originally erected to commemorate military events. He therefore sees no need to investigate their origin as possible stylized psychological monuments suggested by the early custom of making an enemy pass under the yoke. Rather, since his archaeological and literary evidence reveals that arches did not hold statues until Imperial times, Curtis is forced to conclude that the "monumental arch," wrongly called the "triumphal arch," is really an Imperial invention intended simply as a free-standing and totally honorary structure to bear inscriptions, bas-reliefs, or statues of emperors and other important persons. As such they are not essentially different from other simple bases formerly used for the purpose and occasionally employed later, as the columns of Trajan and Antoninus Pius attest. — *N.K.S.*

Additional Recommended Reading

Brown, Frank E. *Roman Architecture*. New York: George Braziller, 1971. A fundamental, illustrated account integrating the arch into the development of Roman architecture.

Frothingham, Arthur L. "Memorial Arch," in *A Dictionary of Architecture and Building*. Vol. II, pp. 854-864. New York: The Macmillan Company, 1902. A classification and description of the various commemorative arches of the Roman Empire.

Richmond, I. A. "Commemorative Arches and City Gates in the Augustan Age," in *The Journal of Roman Studies*. Vol. XXIII, pp. 147-174. A descriptive survey suggesting the origin of memorial arches as reproductions of city gates which had been decorated for triumphant occasions.

ENACTMENT OF THE JULIAN LAW

Type of event: Legal: social reform
Time: 90 B.C.
Locale: Rome

Principal personages:
MARCUS LIVIUS DRUSUS, tribune in 91 B.C.
LUCIUS JULIUS CAESAR, consul 90 B.C.
SILO POMPAEDIUS, leader of the Italic allies
GNAEUS POMPEIUS STRABO, Roman military commander,
consul 89 B.C.

Summary of Event

In political practice, the enjoyment of Roman citizenship conferred three distinct effects: the possession of duties, privileges, and rights. The foremost duties were the payment of various taxes and compulsory service in the military; the chief privilege was eligibility for elective public office. The rights of citizenship covered a wider area: *conubium,* the right to contract a valid marriage, *commercium,* the right to own private property and to enter into contracts that were enforceable in court, the right of appeal in the face of cruel and arbitrary punishment by a public official, and the right to vote on proposed legislation and on candidates for elective office. The internal history of the early Republic is dominated by the struggle between two opposite factions for an equitable distribution of the fruits of citizenship. In the later Republic an analogous struggle prevailed between Rome and certain cities of Italy.

By the end of the First Punic War, Rome had gained complete mastery over the peoples and cities of Italy, which had thereby lost their status as independent city-states. This development compelled Rome to devise a new political arrangement that recognized its altered relationship with the cities of Italy. As most peoples of antiquity, the Romans considered citizenship solely as a fact of birth. A child was restricted to the citizenship of his parents. To be a Roman citizen required descent from Roman parents on both sides. This traditional viewpoint prevented Rome from incorporating the conquered communities completely within the Roman state as full members endowed with all the effects of citizenship. Also prohibiting this simple solution was Rome's desire to maintain its own exclusive city-state status. Instead, a complex scheme was worked out so that the separate cities of Italy were treated in different ways.

In some cases, Rome broke with its own traditions and bestowed full citizenship outright on a few individual cities. This was a selective and limited process. Other cities were granted partial citizenship, enjoying *commercium* and *conubium* but not voting rights. Although such cities gradually came to receive voting rights as well, by the end of the second century their number remained small. Another

506

common arrangement was the bestowal of the so-called "right of the Latin Name," which conferred on certain cities, generally racially and geographically close to Rome, *commercium* and *conubium* together with limited voting rights in Rome. An added feature was the granting of full citizenship to those who held local political office. This ingenius and not altogether disinterested provision ensured each city a small ruling class, primarily loyal to Rome. The remaining cities of Italy were treated as allies, *socii*, who were bound to Rome by formal treaties that specified their obligations and rights. Such cities retained their local autonomy except in matters of foreign policy, where they had to follow the will of Rome. Although they were exempt from the payment of tribute and taxes, they had to provide troops at Rome's request even for wars which did not affect their own security directly. Furthermore they were under the vague and general obligation to respect Rome's dignity and to preserve its power.

This complex system with its fine gradations functioned smoothly in the beginning. Hannibal's efforts at fomenting insurrection among Rome's allies in the Second Punic War had insignificant results. In the course of the second century, however, the situation gradually worsened. The attitude of several Roman officials toward the allies was especially severe, and there are cases during this period of cruel and arbitrary treatment of allied citizens. Their repeated demands for the protection of full citizenship were rejected by the conservative senate and the jealous urban proletariat. In 125 B.C., when the tiny town of Fregellae revolted, Rome's response was the total destruction of the city and the resettlement of its inhabitants. Similar reprisals increased the grievances of the allies and rendered war more probable.

In B.C. 91, the tribune Marcus Livius Drusus undertook among his other reforms the enactment of legislation to extend citizenship to the allies. He was opposed on all sides, his program was rebuffed, and he himself was murdered. This failure made war inevitable. Under the leadership of a Marsian, Silo Pompaedius, the allies revolted and established their own confederation of *Italia* with its capital seat at Corfinium. They began issuing their own coinage and put a hundred-thousand-man army in the field. After initial military successes, the massive might of Rome began to wear them down. With the capture of the city of Asculum, a center of the revolt, by Pompeius Strabo (the father of Pompey the Great), and the defeat and death of Silo Pompaedius in 88 B.C., the war ceased gradually, hastened by political concessions on the part of the Romans. In 90 B.C., the consul Lucius Julius Caesar, the uncle of the more famous Gaius Julius Caesar, carried the *Lex Julia: De Civitate Latinis et Sociis Danda,* which granted full Roman citizenship to any community that had not joined in the revolt or which ceased its insurrection. Another law passed the following year, the *Lex Palutia-Papiria,* carried the same process even farther. The net effect was to make all inhabitants of Italy south of the river Po potential citizens of Rome. The internecine war was brought to a close, and the concept of citizenship was extended considerably beyond the geographic confines of the city of Rome, the first real step of an upward climb that ended in A.D. 212 with the bestowal of citizenship generally throughout the Empire.

Pertinent Literature

Sherwin-White, A. N. *The Roman Citizenship.* Oxford: The University Press, 1939.

This erudite study of all aspects of Roman citizenship devotes two chapters to the problem of Rome's relationship with other parts of Italy. The author emphasizes that it was above all a relationship between separate political states; the Romans did not consider or deal with the Italians as a single bloc of equal individuals, but only as members of distinct cities and municipalities. This outlook had the effect of casting the Italians in a dual role, on the one hand as citizens of their own municipalities with their own traditions and political structure, and on the other as partial Romans, depending on the degree of enfranchisement granted them. This degree of enfranchisement was heavily influenced by geographic, racial, and cultural considerations on the part of the Romans. While the various grades of citizenship extended to the Latins and other favored neighbors tended to overlap in certain key aspects, the treatment of allies remained a source of discontent and eventual insurrection.

The allies were those Italians that for all practical purposes the Romans regarded as foreigners. Rome established the same relationship with them as she employed towards the barbarian tribes which had been subdued. This sentiment was expressed in a treaty that contained the mutual obligations of the contracting parties without allowing room for an exchange of rights and genuine loyalties. In the case of the allies, such treaties were specific with regard to the inferior and disadvantaged position of the allies *vis-a-vis* Rome. In return for Rome's military protection, the allies renounced any independent foreign policy, agreed to assist in Rome's wars, and swore to preserve the power and dignity of Rome. These conditions were not onerous when both Rome and the allies faced the common danger of Hannibal and foreign domination. The second century, however, saw the virtual disappearance of such threats. Henceforth, the allies were called upon to support Rome's external and offensive campaigns in the East and in Spain.

This support, instrumental in the success of Roman imperialism, did not bring with it for the allies a share in the fruits of that success. It is in this context that the author sees the basis and aim of the allies' demands on Rome. They did not seek Roman citizenship outright, but social and political equality of treatment and opportunity in the new world they had materially helped Rome to win. Above all they sought relief from the oppressive superiority of the Romans, which was so conspicuous in the annihilation of Fregellae. A more ordinary manifestation of this oppression was continually at hand in the arbitrary and cruel punishment inflicted on the allies by Roman magistrates. The tragedy of the Social War is that this grievance could have been eliminated merely by extending to the allies the right of appeal which would have protected them from physical abuse. Rome refused even this minor concession because it endangered her status as an independent city-state, distinct from and dominant over the remainder of Italy. The war, however, forced Rome to adjust its concept of citizenship to the ideas that the allies had formed about it as a result of the unsuccessful reforms of Drusus.

Rome's response turned out to be a renewal of the earlier practice which she had employed towards her immediate neighbors and had allowed to slip into disuse. The effect was to introduce real unity throughout Italy, so that Rome ceased to be a traditional city-state, distinct from the other municipalities of Italy. This loss was offset by the emergence of the idea of Rome. Although the Italians took over the governing of Italy, Rome became and remained the symbol of their unity and the formal, if not physical, birthplace of all Italians.

Hammond, Mason. *City-State and World State.* Cambridge: Harvard University Press, 1951.

This book provides a good balance to the work of Sherwin-White, whose chief concern is with the theoretical and technical effects of the *Lex Julia* on the status and concept of Roman citizenship. Hammond examines the larger topic of the Social War within the context of the decline of the Roman Republic. His concern is to isolate the general tendencies of Roman political life that led to the outbreak of the war. This makes easier an analysis of the different effects of the war, both those whose impact was immediately felt and those which ultimately changed the tenor of life in Italy.

The generic causes of the war are to be found in the destructive tendencies that permeated Roman political behavior as a result of her recent conquests. The dominant aristocracy that had directed this successful expansion degenerated into an exclusive oligarchy, jealous of its new-found wealth and power, and suspicious of anyone who might upset its supremacy. Ambitious individuals who were cut off from political advancement by the oligarchic monopoly sought new avenues of power; they curried favor with the lower classes and secured independent military commands so that the victorious army owed allegiance not to the state but to its successful commander. The short-sighted exclusivity of the oligarchs and the unrestrained ambition of the generals encouraged a disregard for the interests of the average citizen and especially of the Italian allies, who found their vague treaty rights increasingly violated. When proposals for reform encountered continual senatorial opposition, the frustrated allies abandoned the expectation of the orderly redress of their grievances, and turned to rebellion and war.

The *Lex Julia* and the war itself brought significant changes for the future of Italy. Rome was compelled to renounce its preferred position and to admit all loyal Italian communities to equality of citizenship, which meant almost the total elimination of the manifold cultures which had persisted among the Italian towns that had shared only tenuous ties with Rome. While some local traditions and dialects maintained their independence, a gradual homogenization of culture spread throughout the peninsula. The "Romanization" of Italy bore fruit in a common language, law, and citizenship.

These effects, however, required time to become beneficial. A more immediate result was intensification of the already critical condition of Roman society. Although the extension of citizenship throughout Italy theoretically implied the end of Rome's status as a city-state, it produced little change in the actual mechanics of government, since the election of the chief magistrates and the ratification of legislation were still conducted exclusively in Rome. To exercise his rights and obligations, a Roman citizen had to come to Rome. Since the citizenship had been extended well beyond the limits of easy and convenient access to the capital, the conduct of affairs remained as before in the votes of the urban populace, which could still be either cajoled or intimidated by ambitious politicians. In this respect, the war only magnified the incapability of the city to provide the Empire with efficient and peaceful government.

Furthermore, the opposing political factions found in the unsettled conditions of the war new opportunities to achieve dominance. The military necessities of the war required the conscription of whole new armies, and trained commanders to lead them. The veteran general Marius was again called into service, but his troops fought not only the allies but also the senatorial forces under the command of Sulla. This internecine strife came to an end with Sulla's victory at the Colline Gates in 82 B.C., a battle which also signaled the end of the last resistance among the few remaining allies still opposed to Rome. Less than forty years later, this truce dissolved into an even more catastrophic civil war. The allies had won the equality of citizenship, but they had to wait until the principate of Augustus for real peace and the enjoyment of their gains. — *G.M.P.*

Additional Recommended Reading

Last, Hugh, and R. Gardiner. "The Enfranchisement of Italy," in *Cambridge Ancient History*, Vol. IX, ch. V. Cambridge: The University Press, 1932. The most authoritative account of the events of the Social War.

Badian, E. *Foreign Clientelae*. Oxford: The Clarendon Press, 1958. A valuable analysis of the interaction between the demand of the Italians for citizenship and the struggles of the political factions of Rome.

Gruen, Erich. "Political Prosecutions in the 90's B.C.," in *Historia*. XV (1966), 32-65. A study tracing the internal political problems of Rome which brought into the open issues that exploded into the Social War.

Smith, R. E. *The Failure of the Roman Republic*. Cambridge: The University Press, 1955. An attempt to diagnose the Social War as symptomatic of the diseased condition of the Roman Republic caused by the proposed reforms and careers of the Gracchi.

LUCRETIUS WRITES THE *DE RERUM NATURA*

Type of event: Literary: composition of a didactic poem
Time: c.58 B.C.
Locale: Rome or the Italian countryside

Principal personages:
TITUS LUCRETIUS CARUS (94-55), Epicurean poet
EPICURUS (342/1-271/0), Athenian philosopher who founded the system expounded by Lucretius
GAIUS MEMMIUS (before 85-after 49), statesman and patron of poets to whom the *De Rerum Natura* is dedicated

Summary of Event

The dates of Lucretius' life are recorded in a later chronicle which adds that the poet was driven mad by a love potion, wrote the *De Rerum Natura* during lucid interludes, and died by his own hand. The dates are generally accepted as plausible; the love potion is rejected as implausible; and the madness and suicide are regarded with suspicion as being, like the love potion, too easily derived from an unsympathetic reading of the poem itself. We have no other information about the poet's life. His work is dedicated to a leading statesman, his name is that of a noble family, and he was clearly well educated. We may suppose that he was wellborn, but it seems clear that he took no part in public life.

Lucretius' poem *De Rerum Natura* (On the Nature of Things) consists of six books, some 7500 lines in all, of hexameter verse. Two books contain an exposition of physics, two describe the nature and function of the soul, and two describe the origin and present condition of the known universe. The philosophical system is that of Epicurus. The first book, beginning with the propositions that nothing comes from nothing, nor is reduced to nothing, argues that the known world is composed of combinations of atoms and void. The second book describes the behavior of these atoms as they combine and separate in an endless cycle of creation and destruction. The third book describes the atomic composition of the soul, arguing that, like everything else in the universe, this part of us is both born and subject to death. The first half of the *De Rerum Natura* ends in a solemn celebration of assent to, as the poet calls it, immortal death.

Book Four describes the operation of the living soul in terms of sense perception and physiological process. Book Five describes the history of the world we know, beginning with the creation of the universe, and ending with the development of human society. Book Six completes the account of this world by explaining the operations of phenomena that puzzled ancient man. Lucretius accounts for everything from thunderbolts to magnets, from earthquakes to plagues. It is with plague, specifically with a description of the Athenian plague of

430 B.C., that the poem ends.

For all its orderly treatment of topics, this poem is not a mere descriptive text, but an eloquent summons to belief. The poet's purpose, put before us at the outset and maintained throughout, is to relieve man of the anxiety that haunts his life by dispelling the fear of death, on the one hand, and, on the other, the fear of the gods. Fully persuaded that true knowledge rests on the twin foundations of experience and reason, the information provided by the senses being subjected to the analysis of the mind, the poet requires hard thinking in those who mean to follow his argument. His persuasiveness, however, resides chiefly in the vivid summoning of the faculties of observation and experience that are universal to mankind. The combination of experience and reason causes the poem to emerge as a microcosm of the universe it describes, with a wealth of particular events and observations ordered by the regular laws of argument and verse. And the intended effect upon the reader is to enable him to govern his life by the same combination of sensual and rational considerations that govern the universe and the poem. However, even Lucretius seems to recoil from his stark materialism by allowing the atoms of the mind to "swerve" in an unpredictable manner.

The *De Rerum Natura* is the earliest surviving work of Latin hexameter poetry. Like that of his contemporary Catullus, Lucretius' verse prepared the way for and was soon superseded by the technical mastery of the poets of the following generation. And like Catullus, Lucretius conveys an uncommon intensity of personal feeling; the devotion of the two poets to their private passions, different though they were, is often seen as a response to the violence and confusion of public life at the end of the Republic.

Public life was restored to order, however, with the establishment of the principate under Rome's first emperor, Augustus. The poets and thinkers of the age of Augustus grant Lucretius' poetry high praise both of compliment and imitation, but those who had come of age during the late Republic and had felt the attractions of Epicurean philosophy saw the age of their maturity as requiring the expression of different ideals. Lucretius' denial of providence, traditional religion, and political and economic competition was not in the spirit of the Roman Empire, and his thought was increasingly neglected even while his poetry continued to be held in high esteem. The advent of Christianity brought even stronger disapproval of Lucretius' materialistic philosophy, and during the Middle Ages the *De Rerum Natura* all but ceased to be read. It remained for the modern world, having rediscovered the beauty of Lucretius' poetry during the Renaissance, to discover also, with the development of modern natural and social sciences, the value of his philosophy.

Lucretius Writes *the* De Rerum Natura

Pertinent Literature

Farrington, Benjamin. *Science and Politics in the Ancient World*. London: George Allen & Unwin Ltd., 1946.

The aim of this book is to contribute to an understanding of the ultimate failure in the ancient world of the scientific outlook so vigorously promoted in the work of Lucretius. In his first chapters, the author compares the thought and writings of pre-Socratic scientists with those of writers in late antiquity, comparing the vigor, self-reliance, and promise of the former with the passive and unproductive reliance upon authority of the latter. He then proceeds to review the history of Greek and Roman philosophy in terms of the competition between free scientific inquiry and authoritarian reaction.

Pre-Socratic science, best illustrated by the development of the atomic theory and of Hippocratic medicine, described a new relationship of man to his environment: confident, rational, and free from restraints of tradition and authority. The spread of this attitude, however, was soon felt to threaten the fabric of the Greek city-state, which depended in large measure on the subordination of large classes to tradition and authority. The political philosophy of Plato, going so far as to endorse the "noble lie," or the propagation of fiction for political purposes, is seen as a conservative reaction against the dissemination of the scientific spirit. Epicurus and his followers, working more freely as the power of the city-state declined, rescued the best traditions of pre-Socratic science, and, recognizing its social implications, set out to free mankind, including even women and slaves in their society, from the trammels of religion and politics. Power structures resisted bitterly. Epicureans practiced a refined devotion aimed at the achievement of psychological rather than material benefit, and were denounced as irreligious. They lived simply, and were called voluptuaries. They attempted to shape a society that promoted the welfare of its members, instead of demanding the sacrifice of personal well-being to political interests, and were called antisocial. Their numbers and influence grew rapidly, and soon reached Rome.

In Rome, as in Athens before her, philosophy was at first resisted, and then subordinated, by the state. Epicureanism, though it enjoyed considerable popularity near the end of the Republican period, could not be made to serve the interests of the state; though it found a supremely persuasive spokesman in Lucretius, it was rejected by the majority of contemporary writers and thinkers such as Cicero and Varro, who identified their interests with those of the state. With the establishment of a monolithic central government under Augustus, Epicureanism was doomed. Roman Stoicism, with a belief in divine providence that could be turned to the support of earthly powers, became the popular creed.

Farrington was brought to this study by his interest in Lucretius, whose passionate attack upon religious superstition has generally been misunderstood. Following the lead of Cicero, who remarks that Epicureans spend an inappropriate amount of energy denouncing superstitions so primitive that no one believes in them anyway, modern scholars find nothing in the popular religion of contemporary Rome to justify Lucretius' passion. Consequently, they attribute it to an unbalanced mind. Farrington's contribution consists in placing Lucretius within the framework of a social and political struggle that determined the shape of ancient civilization. It was not popular superstition but official state religion that Lucretius felt bound to resist with such vigor. The first issue at stake was the survival of the spirit of free scientific inquiry; the second was the nature and governance of human society. That Lucretius' passion in this struggle was justified is amply demonstrated by the outcome of it. Much was at stake, and all was lost.

Hadzsits, George Depue. *Lucretius and His Influence.* New York: Longmans, Green and Co., 1935.

In an introductory review of Lucretius' philosophical antecedents, Hadzsits finds much in Epicurus and his school that is sympathetic, but nothing that is so admirable as the work of Lucretius himself. Epicureanism was a philosophy of escape; Lucretius was a poet of reform. The appeal of Epicureanism lay in an easy amiability and a society of friends; the power of Lucretius consisted of an evangelical summons to national regeneration. Epicureanism was the symptom of a Greek civilization in decline; Lucretius was the product of a Roman nation on the rise.

It is not, however, the question of Lucretius' relation to earlier philosophical or social movements that chiefly occupies Hadzsits in this book, but an examination, first, of the poet's life and work, and, second, of his effect upon subsequent generations of poets, philosophers, and scientists. Hadzsits explores our sources for the life of Lucretius, dramatizing their inadequacy by comparison with the more extensive information available concerning other poets and philosophers of his time. He describes Lucretius' poem in three chapters on the atomic theory; a fourth chapter treats his ethics, a subject woven into the fabric of the *De Rerum Natura* throughout.

Brief notices by prose writers, and widespread imitation on the part of poets during the end of the Republican and the beginning of the Imperial period confirm that Lucretius' poem soon took its rightful place as a literary masterpiece. But the recognition accorded his poetry gained his philosophy no hearing in an empire whose official creed was compounded of traditional Roman religion, Greek mythology, and Stoic speculation. During the remaining centuries of the Roman Empire, Lucretius was admired or studied by poets and critics, but ignored or rejected by philosophers and scientists. Christian apologists revived Lucretius' thought to the extent of using his arguments against pagan religion; with his own materialistic philosophy, of course, they could have no sympathy. As Christianity occupied itself less with combating paganism and more with its own development, Lucretius and his thought were violently rejected. From the triumph of Christianity, we have less and less indication of the influence, or even the knowledge, of the *De Rerum Natura.* The Middle Ages were, for this poem, a time of almost total eclipse.

With the Renaissance came the rediscovery of the *De Rerum Natura,* and, once again, the poetry was extravagantly admired, while the philosophy, once again, was extravagantly condemned. But with the progress of the physical sciences since the seventeenth century, with the humanistic liberalism of the eighteenth, and with the progress of the biological sciences since the nineteenth century, has come ever new appreciation of Lucretius' exposition of the atomic theory, of his religious unorthodoxy and humane ethics, and of his grasp of natural history.

It would be too much to argue that modern thought in science and philosophy has been profoundly influenced by Lucretius; it is not too much to assert that the *De Rerum Natura* has proved, in modern times, a source of hope and courage for many a thinker led by conscience and conviction to scientific and philosophical positions as unorthodox in their time as Lucretius'. To Aristotle's dictum that science is not the proper stuff of poetry, and to the puzzlement of modern scholars over Lucretius' choice of the poetic medium for the exposition of his system, Hadzsits' book provides a practical, if not a theoretical, reply: the sheer force of Lucretius' poetry gained him hearing through centuries so in contempt of his thought that a bare exposition of it in textbook prose would have been consigned to oblivion. As Lucretius himself recognized, the message depends upon the medium. — *Z.M.P.*

Additional Recommended Reading

Bailey, Cyril, ed. *Titi Lucreti Cari De Rerum Natura Libri Sex.* Oxford: The Clarendon Press, 1947. 3 vols. The standard English-language text and translation: introduction, Latin text, and translation in Volume One, with notes in Volumes Two and Three.

Masson, John. *Lucretius, Epicurean and Poet.* London: John Murray, 1907. A full and useful study of the poet and his work.

Winspear, Alban. *Lucretius and Scientific Thought.* Montreal: Harvest House, 1963. A newer study of Lucretius' scientific and philosophical thought, and its place in the ancient world.

West, David. *The Imagery and Poetry of Lucretius.* Chicago: Aldine Publishing and Edinburgh University Press, 1969. A recent investigation of poetic device in the *De Rerum Natura.*

Minadeo, Richard. *The Lyre of Science: Form and Meaning in Lucretius'* De Rerum Natura. Detroit: Wayne State University Press, 1969. Describes and interprets the cyclical theme in Lucretius.

Lucretius. *The Nature of the Universe.* Translated from the Latin by R. E. Latham. Harmondsworth, England: Penguin Books, Inc., 1951. A very good translation for the layman.

CAESAR'S CONQUEST OF GAUL

Type of event: Military: annexation of territory to Rome
Time: 58-51 B.C.
Locale: Modern central and northern France, Belgium, Britain, and the German Rhineland

Principal personages:

GAIUS JULIUS CAESAR (100-44), Roman politician and general

GNAEUS POMPEIUS MAGNUS (POMPEY, 106-48), Roman politician and general, originally an ally but subsequently a rival of Caesar for power

MARCUS LICINIUS CRASSUS, "DIVES" (c.115-53), wealthy Roman consul, triumvir with Caesar and Pompey, who was killed in an invasion of Parthia

VERCINGETORIX (died c.46), Gallic king chosen in 52 to lead the Gauls against Caesar

AMBIORIX (fl. mid-first century), Gallic chieftain whose troops slaughtered a Roman legion and who was never captured by the Romans

Summary of Event

Supported by Pompey and Crassus in the political coalition called the "First Triumvirate," Julius Caesar as consul in 59 B.C. secured the right to recruit an army of three legions along with proconsular authority for five years to govern northern Italy and "the Province," a strip of territory containing Massilia or modern Marseilles along what is now the French Riviera, which Rome had controlled for sixty years. North of "the Province" lay most of Gaul, a diverse but fertile area between the River Rhine and the Pyrenees and inhabited mostly by Celts. Divided into more than one hundred tribes, the Gauls were unstable politically, with a feuding nobility and rival factions even within tribes.

In the spring of 58 B.C. the Helvetii, a group of tribes in western Switzerland, were migrating in search of richer lands. They requested the right to pass through the Roman "Province" in southern Gaul. Perceiving an opportunity to use his newly formed legions and gain military renown, Caesar rushed from Rome to Geneva to block the Helvetii at the Rhone River. Those he did not annihilate he forced to return to their Alpine homes. Later that year, under the pretext of defending Gallic allies, Caesar boldly marched northward to drive back across the Rhine a Germanic chieftain whose aggressions were threatening central Gaul.

Recruiting additional legions in the winter and gaining more Gallic allies, Caesar in 57 B.C. ravaged Belgic territory in northern Gaul, overwhelming one tribe after another. When one town resisted a siege, he sold over fifty

516

thousand of the Belgae into slavery. The following year, building a fleet, Caesar crushed the Venetii who lived along the Atlantic coast. Thus by the end of 56 B.C. he had ruthlessly asserted Roman dominance in most of Gaul.

Back at Rome, Caesar's political enemies charged that he had far exceeded his authority. However, in 56 B.C. the triumvirs renewed their coalition and the extension of Caesar's proconsulship for another five years encouraged him to press on toward permanent occupation of northern Gaul.

In 55 B.C. two German tribes had crossed the Rhine seeking land. When their leaders came to Caesar to negotiate, he detained them and by a surprise attack massacred the Germans, his cavalry hunting down even their women and children. Caesar's enemy Cato demanded in the Senate at Rome that Caesar be handed over to the Germans to atone for his butchery. Bridging the Rhine, Caesar's forces briefly invaded Germany, to forestall further Germanic inroads. That same summer he led two legions in a reconnaissance of Britain, and the following year, 54 B.C., he led a large-scale invasion army across the English Channel, receiving the nominal submission of a British king north of the Thames. Although he gained no lasting control in Britain or Germany, these expeditions were impressive features in Caesar's reports to Rome.

Many Gallic tribes refused to accept Roman rule, and in the years 54-52 B.C. Caesar faced a series of dangerous rebellions. One crafty chieftain, Ambiorix, wiped out a Roman legion; Roman merchants as well as Roman supply trains were butchered by Gauls. Enlarging his army to ten legions or about sixty thousand men, Caesar vowed vengeance. But a new Gallic leader, Vercingetorix, unified a rebel coalition. His "scorched-earth" policy forced the Romans to besiege Gallic hill forts. Frustrated, Caesar's men massacred the inhabitants of several towns. His siege of a stronghold at Gergovia, however, failed miserably, encouraging further desertions by Gauls who had been supporting Rome. Only by employing German mercenary cavalry and by dogged discipline and shrewd strategy did Caesar finally outmaneuver and corner Vercingetorix. After a bitter and bloody siege the Gallic hero surrendered.

By clemency to some larger enemy tribes, Caesar won their allegiance and pacified an exhausted Gaul. The country was devastated, with over half of its men of military age slaughtered or enslaved. Its agriculture and towns were badly damaged.

For Caesar this eight-year campaign brought wealth and glory. His reports to Rome cleverly justified his actions, and his veteran army, intensely loyal to him, enabled him to return to Italy to seize sole power after a civil war. Even more significant to Rome in the long run was the conquest of a populous new territory. Economically and culturally Gaul became the heart of the western Roman Empire, its virile people fully adopting Roman culture and playing a vital role in transmitting that culture to the modern world. In a sense, too, the conquest pointed Rome, hitherto a strictly Mediterranean society, geographically toward a European locus.

Pertinent Literature

Holmes, Thomas Rice. *Caesar's Conquest of Gaul*. London: Oxford University Press, 1911.

This masterly work of British scholarship is the fullest study in English of Caesar's campaigns in Gaul. It is reprinted almost verbatim in the second volume of Holmes's *The Roman Republic* and supplemented by the same author's *Ancient Britain and the Invasions of Julius Caesar*. An eminent classicist, Holmes skillfully interweaves the ancient historical evidence with well-reasoned commentary. His elaborate critical notes on debated questions are a rich mine for continuing study, as he analyzes the opinions of literally hundreds of previous writers on a wide variety of topics such as topography and battle strategies.

Accepting Caesar's own reports as a highly trustworthy record, in spite of minor errors of fact, Holmes seems less able to evaluate Caesar himself objectively than have more recent scholars. He considers him to be "the greatest man in the world" and "the greatest man of action who ever lived." Not seriously disturbed over Caesar's bloody extermination of Gauls by the hundreds of thousands, Holmes at several points defends the military necessity for Caesar's trickery and ruthlessness in much the same way that Victorian Englishmen were accustomed to view the military necessities of the British Empire. Caesar conquered Gaul with the aid of Gauls, he noted, just as the British conquered India with the help of Indians.

His admiration of Caesar's military skills is also considered by some recent historians to be excessive. He describes Caesar's secret service as "perfectly organized" even though he admits that Caesar was frequently surprised and often badly informed. Where raw Roman recruits were lured into ambush, Holmes following Caesar's *Commentaries* blames the error on subordinate officers. Caesar's moderation and generosity always loom large, in Holmes' account.

For full factual detail, with maps, illustration, and scrupulous documentation, none of the numerous English studies of Caesar's campaigns compare with the technical precision of this remarkable and definitive study by Holmes, one whose outlook is doubtless reflecting the fascination of conquest inspired by the imperialism of the late nineteenth century continuing into the early twentieth.

Fuller, John F. C. *Julius Caesar, Man, Soldier, and Tyrant*. New Brunswick: Rutgers University Press, 1965.

This general review of the life of Julius Caesar includes two lengthy chapters on his expedition into Gaul. Without undertaking to discuss many of the questions already debated by Holmes and other writers, Fuller attempts a different portrait of Caesar as an "amoral" politician and a far less brilliant strategist than most historians have pictured. Fuller argues that the apotheosis of Caesar as a superman is not based on ancient sources; it arrived at full form only in the Renaissance and subsequently be-

518

came a myth distorting Shakespeare's drama and many modern historical accounts.

There is much truth in Fuller's statement that Caesar's stature developed in later history. In the period of nation building during the nineteenth century, German scholars tended to take a sharp view of both Cicero and Caesar. After the disillusionment of 1848, Cicero, the hero of the Renaissance, was judged in the light of the hopeless speeches, debates, and assemblies which failed to bring unity to Germany. He became a voluble, empty talker, out of touch with reality and unable to bring order to government in his own day. Caesar, by contrast, became the symbol of the man-of-the-hour, the real politician, the Bismarck who could proceed by blood and iron. Much of this reputation as a great civil leader seems to have been transferred to his military career.

In his narrative of the Gallic campaigns Fuller stresses the brutality and treachery of Caesar, as well as his frequent mistakes in strategy and the defeats suffered by the Romans. After citing Plutarch's charge that Caesar killed one million men in Gaul and took captive another million,

Fuller judges that "the atrocities he perpetrated on unfortunate Gauls have seldom been exceeded by civilized soldiers."

After concluding his account of the career and death of Caesar, Fuller adds a chapter evaluating the famous Roman, chiefly reviewing his Gallic campaigns. Admitting that Caesar had notable abilities "as a demagogue" and "genius as a soldier," Fuller tries to point out serious deficiencies in Caesar's judgment, partly as a result of "an Olympian sense of superiority." He sees Caesar as "a supreme Machiavellian," whose invasions of Britain were "amateurish" through lack of careful organization. His Gallic conquests were based on a strategy of annihilation, Fuller believes, and only through experiences in Gaul did Caesar learn the value of moderation.

Those interested in military history will find Fuller's analysis of Caesar's generalship more critical than that of most other writers; he concludes that Caesar was a "strategical Jekyll and Hyde." This lively and opinionated study of Caesar led Fuller to a somewhat startling theory: "that, at times, Caesar was not responsible for his actions and toward the end of his life not altogether sane." — *R.B.M.*

Additional Recommended Reading

Fowler, W. W. *Julius Caesar*. New York and London: G. P. Putnam's Sons, 1891, 1908. More than one hundred pages and fifteen illustrations and maps are devoted to the Gallic Wars.

Dodge, Thomas A. *Caesar: A History of the Art of War Among the Romans*. Vol. 1, Boston: Houghton Mifflin Co., 1892. A work giving details, with one hundred and fifty maps, charts, and illustrations, of the Gallic conquest.

Walter, Gerard. *Caesar: A Biography*. Translated by Emma Crawford. New York: Charles Scribner's Sons, 1952. A large section, with good documentation, deals with the conquest of Gaul.

Gelzer, Matthias. *Caesar: Politician and Statesman*. Translated by P. Needham.

Cambridge: Harvard University Press, 1968. A careful popular account, viewing Caesar in heroic proportions.

Grant, Michael. *Julius Caesar.* New York: McGraw-Hill Book Company, 1969. This well-illustrated study is critical of Caesar's "atrocities."

Balsdon, J. P. V. D. *Julius Caesar.* New York: Athenaeum, 1967. A short biography with a clear summary of the Gallic conquest defending Caesar against criticism.

CICERO WRITES THE *DE ORATORE*

Type of event: Literary: publication of treatise on oratory
Time: 55 B.C.
Locale: Rome

Principal personages:

MARCUS TULLIUS CICERO (106-43 B.C.), Roman statesman, orator, and author

LUCIUS LICINIUS CRASSUS (140-91 B.C.), Roman orator whom Cicero makes a participant in his literary dialogue

MARCUS ANTONIUS (143-87 B.C.), Roman praetor, censor, and consul, also depicted as a participant in Cicero's dialogue on oratory

Summary of Event

After a quarter of a century of practical experience as an orator, Marcus Tullius Cicero wrote *De Oratore,* a major treatise on public speaking which he considered to be one of his best works. Certainly it has commanded the attention of students of Western literature from Cicero's day to our own, and has been a formative factor in the Western rhetorical tradition.

The *De Oratore* was the first product of Cicero's voluntary retirement in 55 B.C. Three years earlier, in 58 B.C., he had been exiled for a year because of his involvement in the allegedly illegal executions of some of the Catilinarian conspirators four years before. When soon after his return to Rome in 57 he heard the triumvirs, Julius Caesar, Crassus, and Pompey, proclaim a five-year extension of their joint *imperium,* Cicero withdrew from public life of his own accord in 55 B.C. and turned to what he claimed was his first love, the art of letters.

Cicero shows a characteristically Roman practical approach to litera-ture in attempting a treatise on oratory because he saw oratory basically as an indispensable tool to anyone choosing a public career, a career which set one well above other men and even made him godlike. *De Oratore* should be seen in relation to three of the author's other works on the same general topic. When he was only twenty-two, Cicero had written a treatise on rhetoric, *De Inventione,* a dull and unimaginative exercise which he later regretted. Nine years after *De Oratore,* he added the *Brutus* and the *Orator* to his works on the subject of public speaking. In the *Brutus,* Cicero sketches the history of Roman oratory from early times to his own day. The work, like many of his other essays, is in dialogue form, the principal speakers besides Cicero being his friends Brutus and Atticus. In the *Orator,* Cicero is chiefly concerned with style, and specifically with the structure of the sentence.

Whereas the *Brutus* is chiefly historical and the *Orator* mainly technical, *De Oratore* is a more comprehensive work concerned with the ideal orator, his qualifications and training. The treatise, divided into three books, is in the familiar Ciceronian conversational style. The conversation, supposedly taking place at a Tusculan villa in September, 91 B.C., involves as chief participants Lucius Licinius Crassus, renowned as an orator before Cicero, Marcus Antonius, Cicero's own tutor in rhetoric and an eminent Roman praetor and censor later to be murdered by followers of Marius, and two younger men named P. Sulpicius Rufus and C. Aurelius Cotta. Throughout, Cicero puts his own views in the mouth of Crassus.

In Book I, Crassus speaks of the prerequisites of an oratorical vocation, of the nature and range of oratory, and of its social uses. Since Cicero considered that all literature is intended for reading aloud, he sees no fundamental distinction between oratory and other forms of prose. Hence the *De Oratore* has a practical quality which partly accounts for its popularity and lasting influence. Cicero sets down such requirements for an oratorical career as talent, training, technique, knowledge of the law, and common sense. The orator cannot succeed if he is a narrow specialist; he must have a knowledge that is wide-ranging and deep, together with a command of language. He must understand human psychology and be gifted with insight, wit, and humor. A good memory is also essential. Obviously, what Cicero here describes is a humanistic ideal of education.

In Book II, Antonius explains rhetoric in a narrower sense, attempting to describe its rules with particular attention to the construction of an argument. The third book deals with style and delivery—matters which are further developed in the *Orator*—and it includes a long digression by Crassus on the philosophical training needed by an orator, in which Cicero explores the relationship of form, or style, and the subject matter of oratory.

Some idea of the influence of *De Oratore* can be seen from its subsequent history. In the fifteenth century, at the height of the humanistic Renaissance, the work saw four Italian editions between 1465 and 1480. The earliest edition containing a commentary in English is that of A. S. Wilkins, published in Oxford in 1892.

Pertinent Literature

Sutton, E. W., and H. Rackham, eds. *Cicero, De Oratore.* Translated by the editors. Rev. ed. Cambridge: Harvard University Press, 1948.

This translation, part of the Loeb Classical Library, has the format of other works in the series; the original and an English translation are presented on facing pages for easy comparison, and the English version is accompanied by a summary in the margin. The text is preceded by an introductory essay including a brief analysis of the work, an account of the manuscript history and printed editions, and an explanation of the political and social context in which *De Oratore* was written.

Of particular interest in the introductory essay is the discussion of the relationship of Cicero to Aristotle and of the difference between the Platonic and Ciceronian dialogue as literary forms. In one of his informal letters, Cicero said he wrote the *De Oratore* "in the Aristotelian manner," in a way that implies Aristotle used the dialogue form for some of his works. None of Aristotle's extant works corroborates this impression, though there is evidence from other sources that Aristotle did write dialogues as a means of popularizing his teachings. In any case, Cicero believed he was imitating the great Greek philosopher. Of the difference between Plato's and Cicero's use of the dialogue, much more can be said. In Plato's works the dialogue reflects a corporate probing into metaphysical questions. The reader feels himself drawn into the dialogue as a participant, and leaves satisfied that he has been helped to ask some of the right questions and that he possesses at least approaches to adequate answers. In Cicero's dialogues the impression is that Cicero has all the answers, and the dialogue is simply a literary device for stating Cicero's dogmatic conclusions. In *De Oratore,* Cicero puts his views on the lips of Romans of an earlier generation; later, he was to present his major ideas under his own name while still using the dialogue or conversational form. As a literary device the Ciceronian dialogue prevents what would otherwise be an unbearable tedium, inasmuch as Cicero seldom offers an original idea.

Early in Book I, Cicero insists on the importance of a broad liberal education for the orator, lest public speaking be "but an empty and ridiculous swirl of verbiage." In a later passage he attempts to limit somewhat the range of subjects the orator can reasonably be expected to know, and he concludes that the orator may safely ignore the "mysteries of nature" and the "subtleties of dialectic," and concentrate on the problems of human life and conduct. Cicero finds an affinity between the poet and the orator, both of whom are expected to express human experience in heightened language.

Shortly after the opening of Book II there is a digression on the nature and function of leisure. Crassus, through whom Cicero expresses his own ideas, argues strongly in favor of a Greek view which sees physical exercise as a fitting recreation following strenuous intellectual labor, a practice supported by the "best people," the members of the Roman elite enlightened with Greek culture. Crassus goes further and claims that a full life cannot be bound completely by utilitarian goals, insisting, "For to my mind he is no free man, who is not sometimes doing nothing."

In Books II and III there are passages dealing with Greek philosophers, particularly Aristotle and the Stoics. The passages are noteworthy not for any profound understanding of the Greeks whose ideas they attempt to echo, but rather for the apologetic way in which they are introduced. Cicero is evidently writing for an audience which still includes members who look with suspicion on the subtleties of Greek philosophy. While Cicero is sensitive to such an attitude, he clearly does not share it.

In the discussion of wit and humor, there is a good example of the elaborate system of classification which became a feature of the European rhetorical tradition precisely through such works as *De Oratore.* Wit is divided into "irony" and "raillery," and examples are given, along with rules for judging witticisms. Not content with illustration and definition, Cicero follows with a discussion of laughter, again subdividing the topic into five matters for consideration: the nature of laughter, its source, its questionable desirability, the limits of license, and finally, the classification of things laughable. After giving this outline, Cicero backs away from the first problem, the nature of laughter, remarking that he would leave the question to Democritus, the fifth-century Greek physicist known as "the laughing philosopher," for, after all, the present conversation was not really concerned with the matter. Even if it were, Cicero felt he need not be ashamed of something which even its professed expositors and apologists did not understand. The passage on laughter is an apt illustration of the pragmatic and often wearisome quality of Cicero's treatise on oratory. Cicero was clearly more effective at delivering orations than in writing about the art.

Duff, J. Wight. *A Literary History of Rome from the Origins to the Close of the Golden Age.* Edited by A. M. Duff, 3rd ed. New York: Barnes and Noble, 1963.

Besides frequent references to Cicero and his writings throughout the book, one well-annotated chapter, "Cicero and Oratory," devotes itself exclusively to all aspects of the versatile Roman's career and writings.

The great value of Duff's treatment of Cicero is that he makes the man come alive and provides a graphic picture of the milieu in which Cicero worked. The *De Oratore* is a heavy, formal, pompous work, yet Duff says there is not another of Cicero's works which is written in more richly polished Latin. To know Cicero only through his orations and his writings about oratory would be to know less than half the man. Duff's account eliminates the possibility of such an error by giving equal attention to the letters and philosophical essays, and even sympathetic treatment to Cicero's early attempts at poetry.

The *De Oratore,* the *Brutus,* and the *Orator* are treated together as the major triad of Cicero's writings on oratory and rhetoric. Duff calls attention to the earlier works, not only to *De Inventione,* but also to several others of negligible importance. The *De Oratore* is clearly superior to the *Brutus* and the *Orator* in Duff's estimation. He explains that Cicero's aim was to construct a system of oratory for his brother Quintus, in order to correct the inadequacies of the earlier *De Inventione.* Cicero himself thought he succeeded in this attempt, and history has in the main agreed with him.

Duff gives additional information about the chief interlocutors of the dialogue, Lucius Licinius Crassus and Marcus Antonius, claiming that Cicero's portrayal of the two is inexact, particularly in the case of Crassus, whom Cicero draws in his own image. The reader who wants to test the theory of oratory with Cicero's own practice will also find a useful guide in Duff, who recognizes Cicero's fifty-seven extant speeches and fragments of many more, explaining these in relation to other writings and major events in Cicero's career.

Duff makes it clear that to know Cicero is to know the history of the

524

era, for "Cicero is the supreme index to his age." But to know Cicero through his works, as Duff does, is a formidable task, and one that the author has accomplished with outstanding success, largely because he has made such judicious use of Cicero's correspondence with personal friends and associates. He knows him as high-strung, vain, and "too morbidly sensitive in the face of criticism to maintain a strong line of independence." Such faults do not affect his stature as a creator of Latin prose, a field in which he was master. His genius and infinite pains raised Latin prose to a level of universality. In Duff's view, the *De Oratore* plays a significant role in fitting out Latin as the "vehicle of thought for centuries and the basis of expression over a wide area of modern Europe." — *M.E.J.*

Additional Recommended Reading

Bieler, Ludwig. *History of Roman Literature.* London: Macmillan & Company, 1966. A careful survey of Cicero's works, though without detail.

Frank, Tenney. *Life and Literature in the Roman Republic.* Berkeley: University of California Press, 1930. An emphasis on Cicero's contributions to the development of Roman Law.

Haskell, H. J. *This Was Cicero: Modern Politics in a Roman Toga.* New York: Alfred A. Knopf, Inc., 1942. A vivid account of Cicero the politician.

Marsh, Frank Burr. *A History of the Roman World from 146 to 30 B.C.* Revised by H. H. Scullard. 3rd ed. London: Methuen & Co. Ltd., 1963. A predominantly political history, particularly valuable for references to recent studies.

Syme, Ronald. *The Roman Revolution.* Oxford: The University Press, 1939. A scholarly account of Cicero's career, particularly his political activities.

CICERO WRITES THE *DE REPUBLICA*

Type of event: Literary: publication of a political philosophy
Time: 52 B.C.
Locale: Rome

Principal personage:
MARCUS TULLIUS CICERO (106-43), Roman orator and statesman, consul in 63 B.C.

Summary of Event

Although we do not possess the full text of Cicero's *De Republica,* or *On the Republic,* it is sufficiently intact to reveal its main argumentation and to justify an assessment of its contribution to political theory.

It is fairly certain that Cicero had completed the writing of the *De Republica* before his term as a provincial governor in Asia Minor in 51 B.C. This date is decisive for proper appraisal of the work. Cicero's political career had reached its crest immediately after his successful exposé of the Catilinarian conspiracy during his consulship in 63 B.C. In the succeeding years, however, his opposition to the first triumvirate gradually weakened his influence and culminated in his exile in 58 B.C. Although he was recalled to Rome the next year, his political initiative was henceforth curtailed severely. During this period, as he himself says, he turned to philosophy, especially to Plato, for consolation. The result was the *De Republica,* to which was added later a companion piece on the nature of law, the *De Legibus.*

Cicero's efforts are not to be seen as translations of Plato. Both works have a Roman setting and famous Romans as the interlocutors of the dialogue. In the *De Republica* the chief speaker is Scipio Africanus, the conqueror of Carthage in 149 B.C., while Cicero himself leads the discussion in the *De Legibus.* Nor are the two works merely Roman replicas of Greek originals. In both works Cicero is more dependent on Platonic form than content. He draws upon the teaching of many other philosophical schools, especially Stoic philosophy, and on the Greek historian Polybius, to form his own conception of the ideal state and of the nature of law.

The *De Republica* is composed of six books. Unlike Plato's *Republic,* its theme is not the nature of justice reflected in the workings of the perfect state, but the state itself reflected in its constitution and government. In Book I Scipio examines the three types of government: monarchy, aristocracy, and democracy. He shows that the best state is formed from a mixture of elements drawn from the three separate types. In Book II he shows how the Roman state, itself a mixed form of government, achieved in the course of history this composite form. Book III discusses the nature of justice and its relation to the state. Book IV treats of education, while Book V and Book VI portray the ideal statesman. The work ends with an almost mystic vision of the rewards to be enjoyed in the afterlife by those who have administered the state properly.

Two aspects of the *De Republica* have been especially influential among later thinkers: the theory of the mixed constitution, and the relation of justice to the state. Cicero was not the originator of either idea, but he is primarily responsible for transmitting them to later ages.

The virtue of the mixed constitution is that it is immune to the defects inherent in the three types of government. In ancient political theory there was an inevitable cycle in which monarchy degenerated into tyranny, aristocracy into oligarchy, and democracy into anarchic mob rule. Yet if the three types are combined into a single system of government, their differences interact upon one another and form a series of checks and balances to prevent the dominance and subsequent degeneration of any one type. The influence of this theory is readily apparent in the structure of the American Constitution.

Cicero's treatment of the role of justice within the state is equally relevant. The initial argument is that justice is inimical to the efficient operation of the state since it is opposed to self-interest. Since each state has diverse laws and customs, there is no universal concept of justice which all states can follow. Among states as among men the accepted principle is

that the stronger dominate and exploit the weaker to ensure their own security and self-interest. If a state attempts to observe justice, it will only expose itself to mediocrity and external control. Against this view it is argued that justice forms the very fabric of the state, without which the state cannot even exist since by definition the state is the union of persons who are joined by a common agreement about law and rights and by a desire to share mutual advantages. But justice is concerned precisely with the due observance of law and rights. Without justice the members of the state have nothing to share in and can only become a band of mutual exploiters. Cicero thus placed as the bedrock of his republic the inextricable bond of justice and law, and he transmitted to the West the concept that the very existence of the state depends on its being just; indeed, the unjust state has no right to continue.

The philosophers of the Enlightenment found the *De Republica* invigorating. Plato's *Republic* appealed to them more as an allegory than as a practical treatise for real politicians. Cicero's *De Republica* and his *De Officiis,* however, typified a Roman tough-mindedness urging upon men a role of action as statesmen. To the philosophers Cicero remained the ideal of the active man, a thinker in action.

Pertinent Literature

Sabine, George Holland and Stanley B. Smith. *One the Commonwealth of Marcus Tullius Cicero.* Translated with Notes and Introduction. Columbus: Ohio State University Press, 1929.

This work, besides providing a generally reliable translation of the *De Republica,* contains a copious commentary that explains many of the characteristics of Roman political and constitutional institutions. This knowledge, not generally available to the layman, is fundamental for a clear understanding of Cicero's ideas. The authors also describe in some detail the political climate of Rome during the composition of the *De Republica*. The political struggles at Rome in the late fifties B.C. between the opposing factions dictated to Cicero the expediency and necessity of balance and compromise within the state that the mixed type of constitution afforded. The authors believe that Cicero aimed not to publish merely a theoretical treatise but to write a practical work persuading men to engage in politics, the highest profession and the summit of human achievement. He hoped to furnish them a model on which to reconstruct the battered Roman Republic.

The authors also tend to stress Cicero's lack of original political theory. They are assiduous in ascertaining not only his actual sources but also the ideas of Greek political theory which had become accepted political presuppositions and appear as almost unconscious assumptions on the part of Cicero. Included in these ideas are his concepts of law and justice which were certainly derived from the Stoics. The Stoic identification of nature and God had led to the conclusion that since nature exhibits a reasonable order, God must exist as pure reason or mind. Since man possesses reason in part, he also shares in the divine and in the natural law that permeates and directs nature. Endowed with reason, men are in a position to agree about the law that ought to direct their society, since their common reason discloses the natural law to all men. This agreement about law is imperative, since the state must have one common factor to affect all men in the same way in order to ensure their solidarity. Because of the obvious physical and material discrepancies among men this common factor can only be common equality before the law.

Cicero's emphasis on the primacy of law within the state leads, however, to the most noticeable limitation of his theory. Since reason is common to all men and since it further likens them to the divine, it follows that all men are in the most fundamental respect equal. While Cicero's espousal of the natural equality among mankind distinguishes him from previous thinkers such as Aristotle, who found men fundamentally unequal, he is not prepared for the full implications of his own idea. Part of the argument against justice in the third book derives from the enslavement of man by man. Cicero's lame reply is that slavery is only an apparent violation of justice, since it is in accord with the natural order for the inferior to be ruled by the superior. The contradiction between this idea and the concept of natural equality based on reason is readily apparent.

For Sabine and Smith this does not in any way vitiate the significance of the *De Republica*. Although they firmly deny that Cicero anticipates the eventually widespread notion of the divine right of kingship, they find in him a tremendous advance over previous theorists in his insistence that it is the common duty of all men to serve their country, in his espousal of the principles of justice and law, and in his recognition of the universal society of mankind founded on reason. Although Cicero did not grasp the political institutions through which such a society could be realized, he prepared the way for the eventual extension of citizenship throughout the Roman Empire.

How, W. W. "Cicero's Ideal in His *De Republica*," in *Journal of Roman Studies.* XX (1930), 24-42.

How sees two main difficulties confronting any interpretation of Cicero's *De Republica:* the mutilated nature of much of the text, especially at certain critical passages, and the assumption that Cicero's work is essentially a transcript of previous Greek political theory. The first difficulty can be overcome only by the unlikely retrieval of the original text, but the second can be challenged and made to shed significant light on the originality and meaning of the *De Republica.*

The fact that Cicero worked on the *De Republica* for three years is ample indication that he was engaged in more than a collation of Greek thought. Furthermore Cicero considered himself to be in a unique position to make a significant contribution to political thought. Whereas previous writers were chiefly theorists, Cicero claimed a certain authority from his experience as an active political statesman. It is of course true that Cicero drew upon previous thinkers, but he selected his authors carefully and judiciously, combining their thoughts to form his own synthesis. He added his own understanding of Roman history and the lessons it provided for political theory.

How makes it clear that not only did Cicero avoid transcribing his Greek predecessors obsequiously, but that he also diverged from them significantly in many instances. Whereas Plato's similarly titled work repre-

sents a utopian ideal, Cicero presents a real and historical model of the ideal state in a purified vision of the old Roman constitution. While Cicero borrowed greatly from the Stoic Panaetius, he did not consider his work a Stoic handbook, since he expected it to find acceptance among all the major philosophic schools. In the case of the historian Polybius, probably the most decisive influence on Cicero, How argues that this influence did not take the form of uncritical adherence on Cicero's part, but his conviction that Polybius confirmed Cicero's philosophy of history and his political experience.

There is an additional significant difference between Polybius and Cicero. Although both saw the supremacy of Rome residing in its mixed form of constitution, Polybius finds political equilibrium in the careful system of checks and balances between magistrates, senate, and people. Cicero, however, made the senate the true center of gravity in the Roman constitution. His senate was not to be an exclusive oligarchic circle, but a continuous advisory body composed of the best members of Italian society, freely chosen by the entire populace on merit.

This divergence from Polybius also indicates the thrust of Cicero's ideal. The basis of constitutional stability was to be a union of all the more respectable elements in Italy. There can be no doubt that Cicero saw this fusion as the only solution to the constant crises at Rome. Nonetheless the impracticality of his scheme is amply demonstrated by How. There was little chance that the Roman nobles who controlled the existing senate would extend their concern toward the whole of Italy. The difficulty of journeying to Rome for political elections and the limited local interests of the diverse Italian municipalities would prevent their active participation in the running of the state. Furthermore, How argues that Cicero's panacea neglected the main problem, the relation of the central government at Rome to the powerful and ambitious military commanders in the provinces. The Ciceronian notion of the moderator of the state did not deal with this problem, since the so-called moderator would use only wisdom and his own personal example to guide the state and its chief men. This would rule out any anticipation by Cicero of the principate idea of Augustus. Instead, Cicero's ideal was that of the pristine Roman Republic, infused with a new and greater unity and guided by the influence of virtue and education. — *G.M.P.*

Additional Recommended Reading

Cowell, F. R. *Cicero and the Roman Republic*. London: Pitman Press, 1948. A useful guide into the political and social background of the Ciceronian age.

Sinclair, T. E. *A History of Greek Political Theory*. London: Routledge & Paul, 1952. A reliable history of Greek political thought.

Von Fritz, Kurt. *The Theory of the Mixed Constitution in Antiquity*. New York: Columbia University Press, 1954. An extremely detailed and critical appraisal of the idea of the mixed constitution in its Greek origins and Roman adaptation.

Anderson, W. *Man's Quest for Political Knowledge. The Study and Teaching of Politics in Ancient Times*. Minneapolis: University of Minneapolis Press, 1964. An examination of ancient political theory by a professional political scientist.

Smith, R. E. *Cicero the Statesman*. Cambridge: The University Press, 1966. A favorable and yet well-balanced assessment of Cicero's political career, both in his theory and in his policies.

REFINEMENT OF LATIN PROSE

Type of event: Cultural: the perfection of classical Latin
Time: c.50 B.C.
Locale: Rome and centers of Roman culture

Principal personages:
CATO THE ELDER (234-149 B.C.)
SCIPIO AEMILIANUS (185-129 B.C.)
CICERO (106-43 B.C.)
JULIUS CAESAR (102-44 B.C.)
LIVY (59 B.C.-A.D. 17)
SENECA THE YOUNGER (4 B.C.-A.D. 65)
QUINTILIAN (A.D. 39-95)
TACITUS (A.D. 55-120)

Summary of Event

Latin prose as a consciously organized mode of expression had its origins in public oratory, priestly records, and the formulas of Roman law. From the first it generally sought clarity and conciseness, standards which probably originated in the written documents and were later applied to speeches. Appius Claudius Caecus, the first Roman prose writer, was famous in later times for his speech against peace with Pyrrhus (about 280 B.C.) and over a century later Marcus Porcius Cato, the Elder, established a straightforward prose style in his history of Rome entitled *Origines* and in a handbook for farmers. His basic principle was that if the writer kept to his point, the words would follow.

With the great victory at Zama in 202 B.C., Rome won the Second Punic War and thereby gained control of the western Mediterranean. During the following decades, however, she was drawn into the eastern Mediterranean in the search for political solutions to the wars among the kingdoms carved from the legacy of Alexander the Great. In the process the Romans became exposed to the great literary and artistic achievements of Classical Greece, and the more perceptive among them quickly saw the necessity of adopting and adapting Greek standards to their native language and traditions. In fact, the first historians at Rome, Q. Fabius Pictor and L. Cincius Alimentua, wrote in Greek, not Latin. Cato opposed this introduction of the Greek language and culture, but it was vigorously advocated by the Scipionic Circle, headed by Scipio Aemilianus and including the orator Gaius Laelius, the satirist Lucilius, the comic dramatist Terence, and Greeks such as the historian Polybius and the philosopher Panaetius. The influence of the Scipionic Circle in its own time was not widely felt, but in the liberalizing of Roman culture its humanistic ideals found full expression in the following century.

More than any other Roman, M. Tullius Cicero in his career and writings embodied the ideals of both the native traditions and the Greek stan-

531

dards advocated by the Scipionic Circle. It is significant that Cicero paid his respects to both sources in some of his most famous works. In his *De Republica*, the imagined participants in a discussion on the best form of government are the leading members of the Scipionic Circle, and in the *Cato Maior de Senectute* the idealized figure of the old Cato discusses the consolations and compensations of old age with his young friends Scipio Aemilianus and Gaius Laelius. In his own youth Cicero had known some of the surviving members of the Circle, such as the Scaevolas, the one the *augur* and the other the *pontifex maximus,* and in preparing himself for a public career his attention to rhetorical theory and practice was matched by his study of the various philosophical views of the Stoics, Epicureans, and Academics. He could also observe the techniques of the ranking orators of the period, M. Antonius (died 87 B.C.) and L. Licinius Crassus (died 91 B.C.), the former of whom was famed for his wit and ability to improvise, while the latter stressed careful diction, seriousness, and a knowledge of the law.

Following the Greeks' loss of political liberty at the end of the fourth century B.C., rhetoric deteriorated into a scholastic discipline, the handbooks advocating the so-called Asianist style, florid in presentation, emotional in manner, and melodramatic in theme. Near the middle of the second century, a reaction known as the Atticist movement began calling for a return to the literary standards of the great Classical stylists, and models such as the canon of the ten Attic orators, as well as Plato, Thucydides, and

Xenophon, were recommended for study. But Demosthenes was presented as the paragon of literary excellence, to be studied carefully for his argumentation, psychological insight, and mastery of language. When Cicero began his career, his speeches favored the Asianist style, and such a preference is understandable in a young barrister seeking to attract public notice. However, from about the time of his praetorship in 66 B.C., he achieved a stylistic balance both in his speeches and in his philosophic works which avoided the excesses of Asianism as well as the severity of a too simple presentation. In fact, he so developed the Latin periodic sentence, with its organization of subordinate clauses around the central theme of the main clause, that his achievement in later ages became the model for the full and symmetrical sentence in which grammatical form and essential meaning are completed only at its termination. Cicero did revert to a more orotund and emotional style after the outbreak of the civil war between the forces of Caesar and Pompey in 49 B.C., and his series of speeches known as the *Philippics,* delivered against Mark Antony in 44-43 B.C., are good examples of this change. But the orator was then desperately fighting for the survival of the Republic against the unscrupulous Antony, and thus his change in rhetorical style is understandable. It so happened, however, that the Republic was already moribund and Cicero lost his life in 43 B.C. to the vengeance of Antony.

Other ranking prose stylists include Julius Caesar, whose seven books *Commentarii de Bello Gallico* are a straightforward, unimpassioned description of his campaigns in Gaul. Purity of expression is gained by eschewing all novelty in vocabulary and construction, and detachment by Caesar's always referring to himself in the third person. Livy, the great historian of the Roman Republic, fashioned a symphonic prose of unrivaled fullness in order to treat eight centuries in 142 books. In the first century of the Empire a reaction set in against Ciceronian standards, with the result that novel, epigrammatic, and poetic modes of expression found their way into prose. Quintilian upheld the style and literary principles of the great orator in his *Institutio Oratoria,* but Tacitus, greatest of all the Roman historians, brilliantly used a perfected form characterized by brevity, irony, intensity, and psychological perception to describe the Empire and its rulers in the first century of our era.

Pertinent Literature

Duff, J. Wight. Edited by A. M. Duff. *A Literary History of Rome, from the Origins to the Close of the Golden Age.* 3rd ed. London: Ernest Benn, 1953.

Duff, J. Wight. Edited by A. M. Duff. *A Literary History of Rome in the Silver Age from Tiberius to Hadrian.* 2nd ed. London: Ernest Benn, 1960.

This two-volume study of Latin literature, which has recently been reëdited by the son of the late author, is the fullest treatment of the subject in English. One of its advantages for the general reader is that lengthy translations of passages from the various authors appear in the text, and the original Latin is relegated to a footnote. The first volume begins with a full introduction to the peoples and geography of Italy, the history and qualities of the Latin language, and the Roman character and religion. The book is then divided into three parts: first, the earlier literature of the Republic from the origins to 70 B.C.; second, the Ciceronian Period, 70-43 B.C., including Lucretius, Catullus, Varro, Cicero, Caesar, and Sallust; and third, the Augustan Period, 43 B.C.-A.D.14, including Vergil, Horace, Tibullus, Propertius, Ovid, and Livy. The volume ends with an epilogue, a useful supplementary bibliography, and an index. In the second volume, after a prologue and a discussion on Roman education under the Empire, the work is divided according to the reigns of emperors from Tiberius to Hadrian, A.D.14-138. Major literary figures treated in these parts are the Elder Seneca; Petronius, Seneca the Younger, and Lucan; the Elder Pliny, Quintilian, and Martial; Pliny the Younger, Tacitus, and Juvenal; and Suetonius. The volume concludes with an epilogue, a bibliography, and an index.

This brief analysis reveals that classical Latin prose had two periods of great brilliance: 70 B.C.-A.D.14, when Cicero, Caesar, and Livy flourished; and A.D. 54-138, when Petronius, Seneca the Younger, Quintilian, Pliny the Younger, Tacitus, and Suetonius published their works. Yet if writers of the first rank be named there are only four in both periods: Cicero, Caesar, Livy, and Tacitus. It is remarkable that each differed radically from the others in his approach to the problems of language and style. In fact, a careful study of the prose techniques of these four offers the student a full range of stylistics in metaphors, rhetorical figures, and syntactical patterns.

In recognizing Cicero as Rome's greatest orator and the master of an ample yet moderate style, Duff does not neglect his faults. To modern tastes these seem excessive and serious: prolixity, self-conceit, unrelenting invective or excessive praise, puns, and similar shortcomings. For example, in the relatively short *Pro Lege Manilia* there is too much praise of Pompey, but in the four *Catilinarians,* too much vituperation of the conspirators. Yet the failings are surface ones often expected in such situations, and it is by his virtues that Cicero must be judged: his command of moods and language, and his mastery of the techniques of organization and prose rhythms. On the attack, for example, his indictment of the corrupt governor of Sicily in the *In Verrem* orations (70 B.C.) often follows the course of a straightforward and unadorned description of the rapacity and injustice which most effectively condemns the defendant. Yet in quite different circumstances the orator can skirt the legal situation of his client Archias, a Greek poet threatened with loss of citizenship (62 B.C.), and deftly identify the writer with the satisfactions and benefits to be found in the study of literature. In a single sentence from this speech, famous for its rhetorical balance and psychological impact, Cicero makes his point:

"These studies [of literature] nurture youth and give joy to older age; they enhance our achievements in good times and offer a refuge and consolation in bad; in private life they give delight and in public they are no hindrance; they are with us in the hours of the night, in our travels away from home, and in our time in the countryside."

Hadas, Moses. *A History of Latin Literature.* New York: Columbia University Press, 1952.

This work is especially useful for the novice in the study of Latin literature, and since almost all quotations from texts are given in English translation, a knowledge of Latin is not necessary for an appreciation of the subject. The first chapter, entitled "The Nature of Latin Literature," offers a balanced judgment of the achievement and rank of this great body of prose and poetry. In originality, imagination, scope, and taste, Latin literature is not equal to Greek. On the other hand, the Romans, unlike the Greeks, never placed literature at the center of their value system, for civic and social considerations directed the Roman genius to the practical problems of civilization and government. These concerns are reflected in Latin literature, which borrowed yet transformed genres, themes, and techniques from the Greek, and also shaped the concepts of community, duty, decency, integrity, and loyalty to give literature a civilizing function. As a result this body of writing, expressive of the achievements and aspirations of Rome, became a primary factor in the formation of European and Western culture. The language is sonorous but efficient, precise but economical, formal but polished. It was a perfect instrument for legal formulas, executive decrees, and epigraphs on both public and private monuments, while in the hands of its greatest prose writers it also demonstrated its capacity for argumentation, analysis, narration, rhetoric, and oratory.

As modern criticism has made clear, actions and reactions take place just as frequently in literary style as in other aspects of life. The varied elegance of Ciceronian Latin, with its periodic structure and prose rhythms and cadence, is not necessarily the model by which all later Latin should be judged, but for a variety of reasons later ages came to consider Cicero's style as a model of perfection. Quintilian in the first century after Christ established this view, the Church Fathers later lent their authority to it, and the scholars of the Renaissance from the time of Petrarch onward canonized it. In English two major writers who especially reflect the Ciceronian prose style are Samuel Johnson and Edward Gibbon. But in the century and a half after Cicero's death there was a definite turning away from his style toward a pointed epigrammatic style in which antitheses, paradoxes, and polished phrases a-bound, and Seneca the Younger is the best illustration of this later style. Such *sententiae* as "Fire makes trial of gold, misfortune of brave men," and "If you put a high value on liberty, you must put a low value on all else" are representative of Senecan style, and the historian Tacitus pushed the trend to its limits in his mature writing. In his descriptions of the early emperors and the members of their courts, Tacitus so delineates character, so penetrates into thoughts and motives, that Tiberius, Germanicus, Nero, Agrippina, and the others come alive in vivid and dramatic fashion. In pursuit of his aims the writer used a new arsenal of techniques: asyndeton, grammatical ellipses, unbalanced clauses and phrases, new words, and the free use of poetic diction and devices. By these means Tacitus takes the reader beyond the capacity of conventional prose and forces him to note and reflect on the implications of a sentence. Two such examples will suffice here, the first criticizing Roman military policy, and the second stating the psychological defenses needed by a guilty party: "They make a wasteland, but they call it peace," and "It is in the character of men to hate the very person they have injured." — *K.H.*

Additional Recommended Reading

Leeman, A. D. *Orationis Ratio. The Stylistic Theories and Practice of the Roman Orators, Historians, and Philosophers.* Amsterdam: Adolf M. Hakkert, 1963. 2 vols. A complete and scholarly study of Latin prose style with extensive quotations requiring knowledge of Latin.

Atkins, J. W. H. *Literary Criticism in Antiquity.* Cambridge: The University Press, 1934. This work includes Greek literary theories and practice as well as Latin.

Bieler, Ludwig. *History of Roman Literature.* New York: St. Martin's Press, 1966. A short but incisive treatment of classical Latin literature.

ESTABLISHMENT OF THE JULIAN CALENDAR

Type of event: Cultural: change in system of recording time
Time: 46 B.C.
Locale: Rome

Principal personages:
JULIUS CAESAR (100-44), Roman general and statesman
SOSIGENES (fl.first century B.C.), Alexandrian astronomer

Summary of Event

In the period preceding Julius Caesar's rise to power the Romans had used a calendar based on the Greek system with each year ordinarily comprised of twelve lunar months. Four of these, March, May, July, and October, had thirty-one days each; February had twenty-eight, and the remaining seven had twenty-nine days each. Hence a combination of the twelve months accounted for three hundred and fifty-five days, or ten and one fourth less than the number of days in the solar year. The Romans were well aware of this discrepancy and had charged the *pontifices* with the responsibility of taking care of it by inserting intercalary months from time to time in order to keep the calendar in tune with the seasons. For special reasons of their own, however, the *pontifices* often failed to insert intercalary months when they were needed, with the result that months that were supposed to be winter months eventually fell in some other season. In the year 46 B.C., because of the earlier failure of Julius Caesar himself to declare intercalary months in his capacity as *Pontifex Maximus,* the calendar was found to be sixty-seven days behind the true date as indicated by the position of the sun.

Caesar, with the help and advice of the Alexandrian astronomer Sosigenes, set out to rectify this situation. In addition to proclaiming a regular intercalary month for 46 B.C., he inserted two additional months between the last of November and the first of December, thereby adding sixty-seven more days to that year. Consequently, January 1 of the following year, 45 B.C., corresponded to the solar January 1, or kalends of January as the Romans named the day.

To remove the need for inserting intercalary months in the future, Caesar lengthened some of the months by one or two days. January, August, and December were given two additional days each, being changed from twenty-nine to their present thirty-one. April, June, September, and November each acquired one additional day, being changed from twenty-nine to the present thirty. These two sets of changes accounted for the addition of ten days. February retained its former quota of twenty-eight days, but the one-fourth day left over was accommodated by the inclusion of an extra day in February every fourth year in anticipation of our present leap-year arrangement.

This new Julian calendar was so nearly accurate in its measurement of the solar year that only one minor revision was required in the interval between antiquity and modern times to bring it up to date. The year is actually a little less than three hundred and sixty-five and one fourth days in length. To rectify this minor error Pope Gregory XIII in 1582 introduced a plan of ignoring leap-year once every four hundred years.

Caesar retained for the time being the system which had prevailed in earlier periods whereby days of the month were designated as falling on or a certain number of days before the *kalends, ides,* or *nones* of a given month. The kalends are in all cases the first of the month, but in the case of March, May, July, and October the nones fall on the seventh and the ides on the fifteenth, while in the other months the nones fall on the fifth and the ides on the thirteenth. January 12 is ordinarily designated as the day before the ides of January, but January 11, because of the inclusive system of counting used by the Romans, is designated as the third day before the ides of January. The names of the months as used by the Romans are actually adjectives which modify the forms of the words *kalendae, nonae,* and *idus* used in the formulae. In most cases the Latin names of the months can readily be recognized from their similarity to the English names which are borrowed from them. It should be noted, however, that July was originally called *quinctilis* and August *sextilis,* the fifth and sixth months in a system in which the year began with March rather than with January. At a later date the names July and August were established in honor of Julius Caesar and Augustus Caesar respectively.

In converting Roman dates listed as preceding the nones or ides of a given month, one uses the same rules for both the pre-Julian and Julian calendars. Since a date preceding the kalends, however, falls in the preceding month, it is necessary to take into account the number of days in that month in making the conversion. This procedure in turn means that in such cases a careful distinction must be made between the pre-Julian and Julian calendars, since the number of days for several months differs in the two cases.

Pertinent Literature

Nilsson, Martin P. *Primitive Time-Reckoning.* London: Humphrey Milford. 1920.

This book, dealing as it does with the development of systems of measuring time employed in numerous primitive and modern societies, provides excellent background materials for the student of various phases of the Roman calendar, including the Julian calendar. Nilsson devotes much more attention to the Greek methods of measuring time than to those employed by the Romans, but since the Roman calendar, like so many other features of Roman civilization, is based ultimately on the Greek, the information provided by this author is of great value to the student seeking to learn more about the origins of the Roman calendar.

Nilsson devotes special attention to the development among various primitive peoples of various units for the measurement of time. In this connection he has special chapters on the day, the seasons, the year, and the month, Chapters I, II, III, and V respectively.

The unit of measurement which is most widely employed among peoples of different backgrounds is the day, but the term is defined differently in different parts of the world. The concept of "day" as a period of twenty-four hours including both periods of light and of darkness is a concept which developed only at a comparatively late date, as is indicated by the fact that many languages are without a special word for "day" in this sense. English, for instance, has no such word, but on the *pars pro toto* principle uses the word day which originally designated the portion of the twenty-four-hour period when the sun was shining. Some languages on an extension of this principle use the word for "sun" to designate the day, as in the sentence, "He worked for three suns." Most of the early Indo-European languages, however, count time by nights rather than by days, as seen in the English expression "fortnight" for fourteen nights. The reasons for this practice, which is also prevalent among the Polynesians and some North American Indians, are hard to determine. Some think the custom is determined by the role of the moon in the measurement of time, since the various phases of the moon are for the most part visible only at night. Other believe that periods of sleep, which usually fall in night hours, have something to do with the custom of measuring time by nights.

In his chapter on the seasons Nilsson points out that a number of different systems prevail in different parts of the world, with a vast number of different criteria employed for separating the seasons. The most primitive system seems to be one which recognizes a distinction between heat and cold or summer and winter. This dual system was later expanded to include transitional periods, but in the early Indo-European system apparently only three seasons were recognized: winter, spring, and summer. The inclusion of the harvest season was a much later development.

In his discussions of the month and the year as units for measuring time, the author emphasizes that the attempt to compromise between a lunar year of twelve lunar months and a solar year of greater length is one that has been made by many different nations in various parts of the world. The method used to bring about this compromise in almost all cases is that of intercalation, or the insertion of additional months in certain years to take care of discrepancies. In some cases the addition of intercalary months was provided for by well-fixed rules; in other instances, as in early Roman history, the matter was left to the decision of the official priests, and in numerous instances the confusion which prevailed, as at Rome, became common. The importance of the Julian reform was that it removed the need for the addition of intercalary months and thus removed control of the calendar from the whims of political leaders.

538

Michels, A. K. *The Calendar of the Roman Republic.* Princeton: Princeton University Press, 1967.

A calendar is an indispensable device to measure time so that men may regulate their activities. Societies have sought from earliest times to erect a system of time based on the alternation of day and night, the rising and setting of the sun, phases of the moon, and even upon the change in position of stellar constellations. Greek astronomers after the fifth century tried constantly to calculate the solar year more accurately. Caesar's fame in respect to the calendar rests not only on the fact that he availed himself of the latest Hellenistic knowledge to adjust the year but also on the fact that he had his system adopted as the official calendar of Rome.

Since much Roman work on the calendar has been lost, Ovid's *Fasti* and certain inscriptions are invaluable. Intricacies, uncertainties, and contradictions abound in the study. It is clear enough that Rome started out with a lunar reckoning and changed to a lunisolar calendar which kept the lunar months as basic units for the year but adjusted the year to sun time by inserting intercalary months. This calendar, which the author refers to as the "pre-Julian," was adopted, she thinks, by the Decemviri probably in 451 B.C. in connection with the Twelve Tables. In a cycle of four years, each with 355 days, or 1420 days in all, twenty-two or twenty-three days were added to the second and fourth year. This arrangement closely approximated the solar year. The pontiffs, charged with the task of intercalation, often manipulated these additions to benefit or injure politicians and contractors.

If most calendars have religious implications so that it takes a caesar or a pope, or a French or Russian revolution, to change them, the Roman calendar was by its very nature religious. Aware that there is no distinction between the civic and the religious in Roman thought, the author rightly assumes the religious character of the Roman calendar throughout without belaboring the point. If without the approval of the gods no law could be passed, it was to be expected that all activities of the state must be carried out when the gods approve. Consequently it was natural that the colleges of priests as official bureaus charged with divining the will of the gods should control the calendar. It has to be accepted that everything which the Roman calendar tried to regulate, whether actions at law, meetings of the assembly, market days, or festal days, was associated with religion. All days of the calendar were religiously designated to mark their distinct character. Certain days were clearly listed as *dies nefasti* when actions at law or civil and legislative functions could not be conducted without risking divine displeasure. Some days were *nefasti* in the morning apparently when the sacrifice was being immolated, and in the evening when the final offering of the victim was made. The period in-between was *fastus.*

Of the three hundred and fifty-five days of the Republican year, the character of only forty-eight is uncertain. *Dies fasti,* when action at law was permitted, seem to have occurred regularly on the same dates each month.

Only forty-two are listed for the year, obviously less than the demand for justice would require. Clearly other days were used for legal affairs. Since only that legal action in which the praetor played a part was forbidden on *dies nefasti,* action probably went on almost any other day in individual courts to which he referred cases. The largest group of days designated in the calendar allowed the *comitia,* the assembly of the people, to meet, although these days might be changed to a nonbusiness status if priests or magistrates announced special times to expiate prodigies or to engage in thanksgiving or supplication. The rules by which the character of comitial days could be altered were naturally used to the advantage of politicians.

Probably the *dies feriati* show best the basic religious nature of the Roman calendar. In the late Republic, these days having lost much of the original meaning, purpose, and activity became simply optional holidays of rest when courts were shut down and certain agricultural work was restricted. The fact that *dies feriati* could

show a cheerful or a serious mood points to a religious origin; apparently they were days believed to be defiled by work. Since the basic pattern of the Roman calendar was no doubt dictated by rites connected with seasonal activities dealing with crops and flocks, plowing and sowing, ferial days were of agricultural origin. Since weather is important in this context *dies feriati* were movable. As the state grew more urban and citizenship became wider, the *feriae* took on a vague religious character for the whole state and were given fixed dates. In time they came to be connected with legendary or historical events so that in 45 B.C. the senate honored Julius Caesar by establishing *feriae* on the anniversary of his victories.

Caesar changed little. The division of the months into ides, nones, and kalends is of lunar origin. Moreover the civic-religious designation of each day was retained even though much of the meaning had been lost. The author believes that the old designations were kept to make it easier to remember the calendar. — *C.E.F.*

Additional Recommended Reading

Philip, A. *The Calendar.* Cambridge: The University Press, 1921. An uncomplicated study of the history, structure, and improvement of the calendar.

Minor, A. C. "The Roman Calendar." M. A. thesis, Washington University, St. Louis, 1933. A study based largely on inscriptions.

Sandys, J. E. *A Companion to Latin Studies.* Chap. III, part I. Cambridge: The University Press, 1910. An old study which is out-of-date to some extent but worth perusing.

CICERO WRITES THE *DE OFFICIIS*

Type of event: Literary: composition of an ethical treatise
Time: 44 B.C.
Locale: Rome

Principal personages:
MARCUS TULLIUS CICERO (106-43 B.C.) author of the treatise
MARCUS TULLIUS CICERO (65-c.25 B.C.), only son of the author, to whom the treatise was addressed
PANAETIUS (c.185-109 B.C.), Stoic philosopher
GAIUS JULIUS CAESAR (100-44 B.C.), dictator of Rome, in whose shadow Cicero composed the bulk of his philosophical writings
MARCUS ANTONIUS (MARK ANTONY, c.83-30 B.C.), usurper of power after Caesar was assassinated, and whose misdemeanor drew Cicero out of retirement and into his last political struggle after the completion of *De Officiis*

Summary of Event

The series of philosophical treatises to which the *De Officiis* (On Duties) belongs was the penultimate product of Cicero's literary career. It was written in the years 45 and 44 B.C. when the author's personal and political fortunes were at a low ebb; the death of his beloved daughter had saddened his life, and the political ascendancy first of Caesar and then of Mark Antony was eclipsing his career. These treatises, some thirteen in number, cover the range of philosophical topics from theology to physics, but they begin and end in examination of ethics, of the principles of right conduct. The *De Officiis,* written at the end of the series, was completed only shortly before Cicero emerged from retirement to plunge into his final political struggle when he attacked Antony in the series of speeches called *Philippics,* destined to be his final literary production. Cicero's last campaign was politically unsuccessful and personally disastrous, ending in his own proscription and assassination, but the *De Officiis* and the *Philippics* have survived the ages as the last manifesto of a noble cause: the *De Officiis* describes the ideal of right conduct in individuals and society, while the *Philippics* is an indictment of the individual and the society that betrayed that ideal.

The *De Officiis* is divided into three books: one on virtue, another on expediency, and a third on the relationship between them. The first book treats the cardinal virtues: wisdom, the true knowledge that guides action; justice, the proper consideration of fellow men; courage, the will to right action; and moderation, the self-control that permits one to govern one's own actions. A comparative assessment of these virtues reveals that social considerations, a proper regard for one's fellow man, take precedence over all others.

In the second book Cicero shows that social considerations, such as the favor and esteem of one's fellow men, are also the basis of expediency, the pursuit of the individual's self-interest. Advantageous social position is to be gained by affection; by glory, which depends on honorable achievement; and by generosity, not only in material contributions but especially in personal services to individuals and society. In the third book of the *De Officiis,* Cicero examines the time-honored contest between virtue and expediency, and finds it to be unreal. Personal gain, sought at the expense of the common good, cannot secure the respect and goodwill upon which true advantage depends. Action that violates wisdom, justice, courage, or moderation is by definition foolish and odious, and cannot be expected to benefit society or the individual.

Part of Cicero's purpose in his philosophical writings was to incorporate the fruit of Greek philosophy into Latin letters, thus making this material available to a larger class of Roman society than had been able to study it before. In other works Cicero writes in dialogue form, allowing for a full expression of different opinions drawn from different Greek sources. In the *De Officiis,* however, his final study of ethics, Cicero writes in essay form, drawing on a single source, and altering it in form and content in accordance with his own final judgment on the subject. The source was Panaetius' essay *On Duty.* As a Stoic, Panaetius represented a school of thought that Cicero especially admired; he was, moreover, the most Roman of the Greek philosophers, having spent much of his life at Rome and among the group of that Scipionic Circle whose members Cicero had represented in many of his writings as the finest embodiments of the traditional Roman virtues. Cicero's departures from Panaetius' text were generally such as to further modify the originally rigid and remote Stoic ethic along the lines of the greater liberality and practicality of the other school he particularly admired, the Academic

If it was Cicero's aim in the *De Officiis* to create out of the stuff of Greek philosophy a pattern of conduct for Romans in a Republican society, he met with little success. At the time of Cicero's death, Rome was well on its way to an imperial mode of government, allowing only a strictly subordinated form of civilian participation; moralists of the succeeding period, such as Seneca, withdrew into the privacy of the intensely personal Stoic ethic. But the reconciliation of private interest with the public good is of continuing concern in human society, and the *De Officiis* was cherished in later antiquity, incorporated into early Christian thought, preserved and respected through the Middle Ages, and brought to the pinnacle of its reputation in the Renaissance and succeeding periods of humanistic and republican thought. Its lasting significance is testified by the multitude of manuscripts surviving from as early as the tenth century, and of editions from the fifteenth; by the loving and close imitation of such writers as Ambrose in the fourth century, and William of Conche in the twelfth; and by the constant consideration of statesmen and philosophers in modern times.

542

Pertinent Literature

Hunt, H. A. K. *The Humanism of Cicero.* Melbourne: Melbourne University Press. 1954.

Cicero's philosophical writings, frankly derivative and intended more as an intelligent critical survey in Latin of the issues current in Greek philosophy than as original enquiry, are often studied by modern scholars for their contribution to our knowledge of the lost writings of the post-Aristotelian Greek philosophers. But it was as independent essays, rather than as source-books, that these texts survived the ages, and the merit of Hunt's book is that it aims at an understanding of Cicero's philosophical works themselves, singly and in relation to one another.

In Hunt's view, the philosophical treatises produced by Cicero in the years 45 and 44 B.C. form not merely a comprehensive group examining the major issues of contemporary philosophy, but also a coherent corpus, orderly and purposeful, tending to express Cicero's own judgment of the relative merits of the doctrines examined. The first work in the series was the *Hortensius,* now lost; we have in Augustine of Hippo and others explicit testimony as to its eloquence and effectiveness as a call to the study of philosophy. The *Academica* followed, with its study of problems of perception and knowledge; then the *De Finibus* and the *Tusculanae Disputationes,* with their argument of ethics; the *De Natura Deorum, De Divinatione,* and *De Fato,* on religion and cosmology; finally, the *De Officiis,* a concluding essay on ethics. Hunt leaves aside the *Consolatio, De Senectute, De Amicitia,* and *De Gloria* as being outside the main outline of the series; to the other surviving works he gives thorough study of their contents in the central chapters of his book.

A mere perusal of Hunt's outline makes clear to what extent Cicero's chief interest, not surprisingly in a man whose life was spent in political and governmental activity, lay in the realm of ethics. Epistemological investigations are regarded as introductory to the study of ethics; the cosmological investigations form the basis of the final judgment, expressed in the *De Officiis,* on questions of ethics already raised in the *De Finibus* and *Tusculanae Disputationes.*

The ethical systems of chief interest in Cicero's time were those of the Stoics and the Epicureans. Cicero found Epicurean ethics unsympathetic, based as they are on physical science and aiming at a rather pastoral disengagement from the preoccupations of urban society. Since as such they could hardly appeal to the statesman, and since Cicero had already described them at some length in earlier essays, he left them out of account in the *De Officiis.* The Stoic ethic of sure knowledge and pure virtue unaffected by the vicissitudes of earthly existence, while admired by Cicero, seemed to be too private and remote in tendency, taking too little account of the powerful bonds of human society. Hence, while basing the *De Officiis* upon a Stoic text, Cicero modifies it with the relatively humane Academic doctrine of imperfection of human knowledge and circumstance. Above all, he attempts to establish that practical action is not merely consistent with, but actually necessary to, the accomplishment of true virtue.

Hunt stresses that the *De Officiis* was primarily philosophical and literary in intention, the necessary completion of Cicero's philosophical writings, and not to be referred to his immediate political or familial problems. Still it is clear that this call to the re-

alization of personal virtue in social action is not without reference to, and in fact may serve as *apologia* for, the life of the statesman who wrote it. The dedication to his son may be read as a dedication to posterity; the whole as a commitment to the relative permanence of literature of ideals that Cicero attempted to realize in the perishable world of political action.

Nelson, N. E. "Cicero's *de Officiis* in Christian Thought: 300-1300," in *University of Michigan Essays and Studies in English and Comparative Literature.* X, 1933, pp. 59-160.

The system of ethics expounded in Cicero's *De Officiis,* where not only self-interest but also virtue is constantly referred to the social interests of stable communities, seems chiefly relevant to highly developed urban society. It is no surprise that the *De Officiis* was preserved and admired in the Roman Empire, and again during the Renaissance and in succeeding centuries; what is cause for surprise is that the *De Officiis* survived the Middle Ages, with the collapse of city and Empire, mass migrations and social upheavals, the development of chivalric society and otherworldly religion. Nelson's study reveals that the *De Officiis* not only survived, but was in fact incorporated into the thought of, and so helped to shape, the medieval period in the Western world.

Nelson's approach is chronological: he traces the influence of the *De Officiis* in Western literature of the fourth through the thirteenth centuries. For the bulk of the period, though the *De Officiis* was known, he finds scant indication of such influence. Neoplatonism was the more potent

classical influence upon the thought of the period, and of the Latin moralists Seneca was the most influential.

At the beginning of this period, however, in the fourth century, and again at the end, in the twelfth, Nelson finds strong evidence of the incorporation into Christian tradition of not only the substance, but even the structure, of the *De Officiis.* The great writers of the fourth century, such as Augustine, Jerome, and Lactantius Firmianus, give evidence of the effect upon them of Cicero's thought, as well as of his style. It was Ambrose, however, who, seeking to provide practical guidance to the servants of the Church, found in the *De Officiis* material of immediate relevance. Ambrose's *De Officiis Ministrorum* is Cicero's treatise lightly Christianised. With God as the source both of virtue and self-interest, the Bible to provide historical example, and the Church as the social and political unit, Ambrose is able to incorporate virtually the whole of Cicero's ethics.

In the twelfth century, the treatise *Moralis Philosophia de Honesto et Utili,* attributed to William of Conches, presents once again the very structure, and much of the matter, of Cicero's *De Officiis.* The treatise differs from Cicero's and from Ambrose's in being intended for the guidance, not of republican or ecclesiastical government, but of a medieval kingdom. The same century sees extensive use of Cicero's *De Officiis* in John of Salisbury's *Policraticus.*

Nelson surveys ethical writings of the thirteenth century in three categories: ecclesiastical, royal, and republican treatises. In ecclesiastical writings, Thomas Aquinas and the scholastics established Aristotelian ethics as the standard; Ciceronian influence, however, so well incorporated since the time of Ambrose, was not so much discarded as subordinated. Treatises on royal government, most notably Giraldus Cambrensis' *Liber de Instructione Principis,* follow the example of the *Moralis Philosophia* in adapting Cicero's ethics to the requirements of kingly administration. The republican tractates produced by Italian laymen, as might be expected, rely in no small part, and with no very great need of special adaptation, on Cicero in general and on the *De Officiis* in particular.

Nelson's study of the *De Officiis* contributes much to the understanding of the Middle Ages and the role of classical wisdom in it. Not so wholly martial as heroic and chivalric literature would suggest, nor so otherworldly as the literature of the cloister, the Middle Ages found in Cicero a guide for the practical administration of the Church and the state, both preserving the *De Officiis* itself, and contributing to the evolution of the new world in which that treatise would be found even more relevant. — Z.M.P.

Additional Recommended Reading

Higginbotham, John. *Cicero on Moral Obligation.* London: Faber and Faber Ltd., 1967. A recent and highly readable translation of the *De Officiis,* with an excellent brief introduction.

Boissier, Gaston. *Cicero and His Friends.* New York: G. P. Putnam's Sons, 1925. A classic among the many modern biographies of Cicero.

Rolfe, John C. *Cicero and His Influence.* Boston, Massachusetts: Marshall Jones Company, 1923. A survey of Cicero's life and writings, and especially of their later influence.

Dorey, T. A., ed. *Cicero.* London: Routledge & Kegan Paul, 1965. An excellent collection of essays on Cicero's life and writings.

Douglas, A. E. *Cicero.* Oxford: The Clarendon Press, 1968. A scholarly and humane assessment of Cicero's personal and literary accomplishments.

PROSCRIPTIONS OF THE SECOND TRIUMVIRATE

Type of event: Political: purge of enemies and wealthy citizens
Time: 43 B.C.
Locale: Rome

Principal personages:

GAIUS JULIUS CAESAR OCTAVIANUS (AUGUSTUS), heir of Julius Caesar, first Roman Emperor 63 B.C.- A.D. 14

MARCUS ANTONIUS (MARK ANTONY, c. 83 B.C.-A.D. 30), colleague and later rival of Octavian

MARCUS AEMILIUS LEPIDUS (d. 13 B.C.), member of the Second Triumvirate who was ultimately deposed

MARCUS TULLIUS CICERO (106-43 B.C.), statesman, orator, and philosopher who was a victim of the proscriptions

Summary of Event

The Roman Republic came more and more to experience a time of troubles after 135 B.C. The inadequacy of its city-state constitution for a growing empire, the stranglehold of great families on its offices, the rise of the equites and the consequent class struggle, and the twisting of its constitution initiated already by the Gracchi between 130 and 120 and by Marius and Sulla between 100 and 80, all contributed to the Republic's travail. Especially significant were the great rivals born in the decade between 110 and 100, men such as Pompey, Crassus, Caesar, Cicero, Catiline, and Sertorius, who were ready to fulfill their ambitions between 70 and 60. Most of them proved to be too big for the constitution to contain. The rise of private armies, extraordinary commands, absentee governorships, extended tenures of office, bribery, demagogery, political manipulation, and outright violence became more and more commonplace. Marius and Sulla even dared to liquidate each other's adherents by outright proscriptions, or purges, a precedent set for the leaders who were to emerge as the Second Triumvirate. Their proscriptions, in turn, by decimating the old patrician stock and silencing Republican sentiments, brought an end to the civil wars by enabling Octavian in the long run to become the first Emperor of Rome.

The formation of the Second Triumvirate by Octavian, Antony, and Lepidus in 43 B.C. was a pragmatic arrangement of three leaders who were united only because of their common enemies: a faction under the leadership of Brutus and Cassius and another under the leadership of Sextus Pompey, the son of Pompey the Great. Unlike the First Triumvirate, this three-man dictatorship was given legal sanction. The three leaders met on a small island in a river near Bologna, and formulated a joint policy. Although in effect they established a three-man dictatorship, of necessity they avoided the term, since Antony, when consul, had abolished the office of dictator for all time. They formed themselves into an executive committee which was to hold absolute power for five years in order to rebuild the Roman state. The triumvirs planned to unite their armies for a war against the Republican forces in the East. The West, already under their control, was divided among themselves, Lepidus keeping his provinces in Spain and Transalpine Gaul, Antony taking the newly conquered parts of Gaul together with the Cisalpine province, and the junior member, Octavian, being assigned North Africa, Sardinia, Corsica, and Sicily, territories largely held by Pompeian adherents. Italy itself was to be under their combined rule.

At the same meeting the triumvirs determined to insure the success of their rule by declaring a proscription against their Republican enemies. In this purge, hundreds of senators and about two thousand wealthy equites were marked for destruction. Livy gives one hundred and twenty as the number of senators proscribed; Appian gives three hundred; and Plutarch gives two hundred to three hundred. The names of almost one hundred of the proscribed have been recorded. Not all were killed; a few obtained pardon and many successfully escaped from Italy. In most cases the victims suffered only the confiscation of their properties.

In the official proclamation of the proscription, the triumvirs emphasized the injustices suffered at the hands of the enemies of the state and pointed out the necessity of removing a threat to peace at home while they were away fighting against the Republican armies. To justify their position and gain for it some semblance of respectability, they pointed out that when Julius Caesar had adopted a policy of clemency towards his enemies, he had paid for that policy by forfeiting his life.

While personal vengeance and political pragmatism played a part in the proscriptions, there is no doubt that the unadmitted reasons were largely economic. Octavian, Antony, and Lepidus had bought the support of their troops with lavish promises, and it was imperative that they pay them with more than words. Altogether, the triumvirs commanded forty-three legions, and they needed their support in the impending campaign against Brutus and Cassius.

In drawing up the lists, each of the three triumvirs had to give up some of his friends to satisfy the vengeance of one or the other of his colleagues. So it was that the most famous of the victims, Cicero, was found on the list of the condemned. Octavian would have spared the famous orator, but Antony insisted on his death. While many of the proscribed acted quickly and escaped, Cicero dallied, uncertain of the best course to take, and died as a result. The historian Livy has given a full account of his death.

Pertinent Literature

Syme, R. *The Roman Revolution*. Oxford: The University Press, 1939.

Syme's book treats the critical period of the fall of the Roman Republic and the first years of the Principate which succeeded it. Spanning the seventy-five years between 60 B.C. and A.D. 14, it centers on the career of Augustus and the establishment of his rule. The book has a clear thesis, namely, that there never could have been a restoration of the Republic, that Augustus, expert in *Realpolitik,* was ruthless as the leader of a faction in winning his power at the expense of the aristocracy and basing it ultimately on a wide basis of support: the people and the army. In accord with this thesis, the proscriptions appear to be perfectly logical.

Logical or not, they were undoubtedly a traumatic experience of horror, as Appian and Suetonius attest through Syme's pages. The effect on Rome was terrifying. The early proscriptions of Sulla could still be remembered by many who could only fear that the new one would be more ruthless than ever. If the total number of victims has been exaggerated, Roman feelings were shocked when the triumvirs sacrificed, as a pledge of solidarity to terrorize their enemies, their own friends such as Cicero, and their own relatives such as Lepidus' brother and Antony's uncle. Following Appian, Syme notes, too, the terror tactic of the triumvirs in beginning the proscriptions by the sacrilegious arrest and execution of a tribune of the Roman people. There were, fortunately, compensating instances of bravery and devotion. In Cales the citizens manned the walls and refused to surrender a certain Sittius who had patronized the town, and slaves were known even to substitute willingly for their condemned masters.

The proscriptions were pitiless and calculated. The abolition of the private rights of citizenship by the triumvirs seemed to them "no disportionate revenge" for having been declared public enemies. Of the three members of the Second Triumvirate, Octavian was, if not the most ruthless, certainly not the puppet of Antony. In Syme's view he was "a chill and mature terrorist" who had good reason to try later to exonerate himself. His success was the work of fraud, bloodshed, rapacity, and ambition, a monument to his cleverness and skill in using opportunities and methods introduced by others, and eventually in employing effective subalterns to compensate for his inadequacies.

In keeping with the prevailing view of historians that the motive for the proscriptions was the need for money, that they were essentially a levy on capital rather than desire for revenge, Syme tells of a number of the proscribed whose only crime was their affluence. "The triumvirs declared a regular vendetta against the rich, whether dim, inactive Senators or pacific knights, anxiously abstaining from Roman politics." Retirement proved no defense, as for instance in the case of the old, innocuous Pompeian Varro. Moreover, lesser rivals took occasion, by feigning coöperation with the triumvirs, to settle private scores and to liquidate wealthy enemies, all serving to greatly expand the extent of the proscription.

Because the confiscated lands did not bring in the anticipated returns on the open market, the purge was followed by a number of novel taxes, a portent at the beginning of the Principate of a situation which was to be a major factor in Rome's eventual decline. Another effect of the proscription was the depeletion of the senate and its replenishment with minions of the triumvirs, men with little or no ability for government. Syme concludes his chapter on the proscriptions with the statement that the Republic had been permanently abolished. "Despotism ruled, supported by violence and confiscation. The best men were dead or proscribed." To him the proscriptions are a watershed in the history of Roman civilization.

Buchan, J. *Augustus*. Boston: Houghton Mifflin Co., 1937.

This widely acclaimed biography of Octavian Augustus is less interested in the political and economic causes of the proscriptions than in the personal role Octavian played in them. In trying to assess his motives from evidence of his character and personality, the book is remarkable for the level of its analysis, especially since it was written before the trend toward psychohistorical studies had developed very far. Besides the penetrating study of Octavian's role in the proscriptions there is also a finely nuanced estimate of Cicero, the triumvirs' most famous victim. For his views Buchan draws data not only from secondary studies but from the Latin sources he knows so well and uses with discrimination: Seneca, Suetonius, and Macrobius.

Some writers have suggested that Octavian had a split personality; Seneca claimed that Octavian's later moderation could be attributed to sheer satiety with evil. Buchan develops a more complex explanation. Octavian, he claims, was a man who matured unevenly. His emotional development was exceptionally slow, and his capacity for affection was highly restricted. In his early years he regarded most men with suspicion, and under the circumstances, this attitude is not surprising. However, it was neither callousness nor careless politics which made Octavian so ready a party to the purge of 43 B.C. Rather, the proscriptions were a logical outcome of Octavian's feeling that it was his destiny to reconstruct the state. He was motivated by three principles: the need to avenge the death of Julius Caesar, a determination to bring order out of political chaos, and finally, the conviction that no sacrifice was too great to carry out his mission. Octavian was ready to give up happiness, friendship, ease, and common morality; Buchan says that he acted on the premise that only violence could curb violence. "To this task he brought both the stony-heartedness of self-absorbed youth, and the moral opportunism of the fanatic. His view was that of Horace Walpole: 'No great country was ever saved by good men, because good men will not go to the lengths that may be necessary.'"

Buchan goes on to explain the reasonableness—if moral scruples are disregarded—of Octavian's action by noting that Octavian's archenemies would have done the same to him had they been granted the opportunity, and furthermore, that a policy of mercy would have been equivalent to the surrender of all the hopes which Octavian had cultivated since boyhood.

Moreover, contemporary historical circumstances must be considered: Brutus and Cassius were still in the East, senatorial and Republican enemies were everywhere, and assassins lurked in all corners. Considering, too, the bloody backlog of civil wars, shocking assassinations, and a series of political murders from the Gracchi to Julius as well as earlier proscriptions, Octavian can scarcely be judged by modern standards. Even in his relationship with Cicero, it must be remembered that they were never really friends, that Cicero was the brains of those who would restore the Republic, that he was ungrateful to Julius and so exulted over the Ides of March that he made gods of the assassins, and finally, that he, too, wanted to use Octavian as a tool.

Buchan does not explain away the proscriptions, which remain "the darkest stain upon Octavian's record." Instead, he attempts to interpret them in terms of Roman culture, not according to modern standards. He succeeds in his task, and for this reason he contributes to a better understanding of a particularly black page in the annals of Roman history. — *M.E.J.*

Additional Recommended Reading

Cary, M. *A History of Rome.* 2nd ed. London: Macmillan & Company, 1954. A lively narrative of events leading to the proscriptions, with special attention being given to Cicero.

Cowell, F. R. *The Revolutions of Ancient Rome.* London: Thames & Hudson Ltd., 1962. A tendentious account of the Second Triumvirate as the outcome of a bargain between "thieves and murderers."

Weigall, A. *The Life and Times of Marc Antony.* London: Thornton Butterworth Limited, 1931. A work interpreting the proscriptions as a means of placating the antiaristocratic sentiments of the Roman mob.

Rostovtzeff, M. *Rome.* Translated from the Russian by I. D. Duff. New York: Oxford University Press, 1928, reissued 1960. A classic study of Rome which has little to say specifically about the proscriptions but which supplies details about conditions which existed at the time.

Scullard, H. H. *From the Gracchi to Nero: A History of Rome from 133 B.C. to A.D. 68.* 2nd ed. London: Methuen and Co., 1964. A standard work placing the proscriptions in a fully developed context.

BATTLE OF ACTIUM

Type of event: Military: naval engagement
Time: September 2, 31 B.C.
Locale: The Ambracian Gulf, on the west coast of northern Greece

Principal personages:
MARCUS ANTONIUS (MARK ANTONY, c.83-30 B.C.), Roman general, member of the Second Triumvirate
GAIUS JULIUS CAESAR OCTAVIANUS (OCTAVIAN, 63 B.C.-A.D. 14), grandnephew of Julius Caesar, later called Augustus
CLEOPATRA VII (69-30 B.C.), Queen of Egypt, consort of Mark Antony
MARCUS VIPSANIUS AGRIPPA (63 B.C.-A.D. 12), general and admiral serving Octavian

Summary of Event

In the decade following the assassination of Julius Caesar in 44 B.C., a political struggle developed between Mark Antony and Octavian. Alternately rivals for power and reluctant allies, they became bitter enemies after Antony in 34 B.C. openly attached himself to Cleopatra, thus repudiating his legal wife who was Octavian's sister. In Italy Octavian's supporters excoriated Antony's liaison with the Oriental enchantress and published a purported will of Antony deposited with the Vestal Virgins by which Antony donated eastern territories to Cleopatra and her children. In 32 B.C. the two consuls and three hundred senators went east to join Antony, thus terminating negotiations between him and Octavian.

Antony had recruited a heterogeneous army, variously estimated from forty thousand to a hundred thousand men, while Octavian raised an Italian force almost as large. Battle strategy eventually depended on navies, with Octavian's admiral Agrippa the most experienced commander at sea. Antony's fleet, perhaps at first slightly greater in size, was composed of larger, slower ships, some of his "sea castles" having eight or ten banks of oars.

In 31 B.C. Octavian with his army and navy crossed to Epirus, just north of Greece. Meanwhile Antony had stationed his forces so as to block the eastward passage of his adversary, most of his navy occupying the Gulf of Arta and his army fortifying the nearby sandy promontory of Actium, one of two peninsulas which pointed toward each other across the mouth of the gulf. After several months of skirmishing and entrenching, Octavian's army held the northernmost peninsula and his navy seized crucial bases to the south, thus cutting off Antony's supply routes. The morale of Antony's troops was lowered by hunger and malaria, and he suffered significant desertions.

In a council held in Antony's camp on September 1, 31 B.C., his officers

551

were divided over strategy. A Roman faction advocated retreat by land; Cleopatra with some supporters favored a naval attack or an escape to Egypt. While Antony's enigmatic aims and actions are variously reported by later historians, it seems less likely that Antony wanted a showdown by naval action than that he hoped to break out of the blockade in order to fight later in a more favorable situation. Any ships he may have burned were probably unusable. All records agree that he left some of his troops ashore to retreat by an inland route, and that he kept aboard his ships the masts and sails, which were ordinarily jettisoned before action, in order to allow his fleet either to escape if the battle went against it or else pursue its defeated enemy.

The following day's battle was a chaotic imbroglio, shrouded from our view in conflicting accounts. Antony's ships advanced through the narrow exit from the gulf, aligned so as to take advantage of an expected shift in the wind at midday. The Caesarian fleet blocked their passage. One squadron of sixty ships under Cleopatra was placed in the rear, carrying the treasure chest which undoubtedly belonged to her more than to Antony. After several hours of tense inactivity one wing of Antony's fleet was drawn into conflict, forcing Antony to commit the remainder of his forces. His soldiers aboard the large ships hurled missiles and shot arrows into Octavian's smaller vessels, which attempted to ram or surround and capture their clumsy opponents. Except for the use of oars, the battle vaguely resembled the one fought later between the sixteenth century Spanish Armada and the small English ships of Francis Drake.

Suddenly, at the height of the conflict, when a breeze rose from the northwest, Cleopatra's reserve squadron hoisted purple sails and moved through the battle line, in evident flight southward. Although Antony's flagship was entrapped, he transferred to a smaller ship and with a small portion of his fleet followed Cleopatra. Plutarch vividly portrays the gloom of defeat on the escaping ships.

Abandoned by their leader, the remnants of Antony's fleet backed into the gulf. Over five thousand men had been killed or drowned. Octavian and Agrippa made little attempt to pursue Antony; instead, they kept their ships at sea to bottle up the enemy and thus prevented further escape. Within about a week the ships and soldiers left behind by Antony surrendered. Octavian claimed to have captured three hundred vessels.

Antony and Cleopatra returned to Egypt, where some final desperate expedients were contemplated but not effectively carried out. The next year Octavian came to Egypt where he met little resistance and precipitated the romanticized suicides of both Antony and Cleopatra. The civil wars and the Republic were at an end, for Octavian was now the undisputed ruler of the Mediterranean world.

Pertinent Literature

Tarn, W. W. "The Battle of Actium," in *The Journal of Roman Studies.* 21 (1931), 173-199.

This highly respected British scholar proposes an explanation of the tantalizing Battle of Actium which differs sharply from theories previously accepted. In particular he considers that treachery in Antony's fleet was the primary reason for the victory of Octavian. Reviewing carefully the numerous ancient authors who describe the battle, among them Velleius Paterculus, Plutarch, and Dio Cassius, and also examining the works of modern authors on the subject, Tarn concludes that Antony intended to wage a hard and decisive battle and that escape was contemplated only as a last resort and not as a primary objective.

Ingeniously reconstructing the fragments of evidence, Tarn argues that the fleets were roughly equal in size and that Antony employed all usable ships, without burning any significant part of his fleet before the battle, as Plutarch reported. Tarn rejects Plutarch's account as a confusion arising from the later burning of ships by Octavian. Antony's strategy, in Tarn's view, was to wait for the wind to veer from west to northwest about noon, then to turn Octavian's left, thus gaining the momentum of the wind in order to drive Octavian's fleet south away from his army and camp. This plan required sails, and so Antony took sails aboard. After a period of inaction, Tarn believes that the battle became a race between Octavian's left wing under Agrippa and Antony's right wing, to see which could gain position windward of the

other. Therefore, Antony himself commanded the three squadrons of the right wing in this endeavor, which proved indecisive when Agrippa's left wing countered the attempt and grappled with Antony's ships.

Concerning this critical stage in the battle, at the point when other historians believe that Cleopatra's retreat decided the issue, Tarn theorizes that the three central squadrons composing Antony's center and left wings, not yet actively engaged, now backed into the gulf, unwilling to fight. Tarn bases this reconstruction of the turning point of the battle on two lines of Horace's poem about Actium which referred to retreat by some of Antony's ships. He argues that it was only because of this mass desertion by most of their fleet that Antony and Cleopatra carried out their alternate plan, to escape to Egypt.

Thus Cleopatra really deserved little blame for the defeat; indeed, she had been left in reserve because Antony trusted her loyalty; her squadron was to move into the breach in the line left by Antony's windward movement. When such a gap did open, Cleopatra moved forward, not intending flight but rather action. However, seeing the desertion of a major section of their fleet, Cleopatra continued southward with the wind, followed by Antony.

Tarn argues that Antony's decision to keep sails aboard his ships may have unsettled his officers, who doubted his determination to fight a decisive battle and were suspicious that they were fighting for Cleopatra and Egypt rather than for Antony and Rome. Since such a conflict involved personal ambition rather than patriotic principle, and since Roman soldiers were usually reluctant to slaughter other Romans, Tarn does offer an appealing solution to the puzzle of Actium.

According to Tarn, Octavian and later historians concealed the mutiny of Antony's fleet in order to make the Caesarian victory more glorious, and because it served Octavian's purposes to portray Cleopatra in a bad light as a traitress and coward.

Unfortunately Tarn's scholarly article is difficult for most readers to follow. He includes no charts of his reconstruction of the battle, and his argument turns on such obscure fragments of evidence that what he presents, although influencing subsequent popular narratives of this pivotal and dramatic event, leaves most historians dissatisfied with his conclusions.

Richardson, G. W. "Actium," in *The Journal of Roman Studies.* Vol. 27 (1937), 153-164.

Almost directly contradicting Tarn's theory of the Battle of Actium, which was given wide circulation in the 1934 edition of Volume X of *The Cambridge Ancient History,* Professor Richardson prefers to accept the more traditional reconstruction of the evidence by giving weight to "secondary" ancient accounts by Plutarch, Dio Cassius, Florus, and Orosius, writers largely rejected by Tarn. Richardson believes that Antony never intended to make a hard-fought battle at Actium; that Antony's fleet had not been fully concentrated at Actium but was partly dispersed elsewhere; and that, since his fleet was already inferior in size to Octavian's, Antony did indeed burn many of his slower ships the night before the battle, accepting the advice of Cleopatra to attempt to escape with a major part of his fleet but without the stigma of defeat.

Rejecting entirely Tarn's theory about treachery or desertion by a major part of Antony's fleet in the midst of the battle, Richardson argues that Antony, expecting a more aggressive attack by Octavian's fleet, was surprised when Octavian's ships refused to engage and blocked his exit from the gulf, thereby forcing him to advance into the open sea where Octavian's larger fleet and more mobile ships had the advantage. Richardson agrees with Tarn's view that Cleopatra was neither cowardly nor overly hasty in retreat; he believes that once Octavian had drawn Antony's fleet into action, the skill and speed of Agrippa's ships allowed them almost to surround Antony's smaller fleet.

Thus, Richardson claims, the battle did not develop along lines of a strategic plan by Antony, as Tarn had theorized, but rather as a frustrated struggle by Antony to elude the Caesarian fleet and get his own fleet away in order to fight another day. If sections of Antony's fleet did retreat in the midst of the battle, Richardson considers that it was not desertion but an effort to regroup or to seek safety in the gulf. He supposes that Octavian and Agrippa, in blocking Antony's escape, turned their formation so as to leave a gap in their line. At this point, Richardson believes, Antony in desperation signaled Cleopatra and she responded by hoisting sail and moving forward through the gap to escape southward, followed by a few ships accompanying Antony.

Later reports that Actium was a hard-fought battle could not have been mere inventions or exaggerations by Octavian and his propagandists, in Richardson's reasoning. When hundreds of senators and thousands of soldiers knew the truth, why would Caesarian eulogists not have accepted and indeed publicized the unwillingness of Antony's forces to support him, if this were the truth? If such betrayals on a large scale had really taken place, Richardson argues, it would not have been necessary to create an imaginary battle but only to report what actually happened.

Richardson's article supports several non-English scholars who have replied to Tarn, and his viewpoint is the most widely accepted interpretation of the Battle of Actium. Yet since it involves a complex synthesis of scraps of evidence and leaves numerous questions unanswered, it has no definitely settled the issues. — *R.B.M.*

Additional Recommended Reading

Holmes, T. Rice. *The Architect of the Roman Empire*. Pp. 136-168 and 246-260. Oxford: The Clarendon Press, 1928. This careful scholar narrates in detail the struggle between Antony and Octavian.

Tarn, W. W. and M. P. Charlesworth. "The War of the East Against the West," in *The Cambridge Ancient History*. Vol. X, ch.3, pp. 66-111. Cambridge: The University Press. 1934. An account of the period from 37 B.C. to the death of Antony and Cleopatra which incorporates Tarn's theories about Cleopatra's aims and the battle strategy at Actium.

Weigall, Arthur, E. P. B. *The Life and Times of Cleopatra, Queen of Egypt*. New York and London: G. P. Putnam's Sons, 1924. The traditional interpretation with some imaginative details.

VERGIL WRITES THE *AENEID*

Type of event: Literary: creation of Latin epic
Time: 30-19 B.C.
Locale: Rome, Naples, Siciliy

Principal personages:

PUBLIUS VERGILIUS MARO (VERGIL, 70-19 B.C.), Roman poet

GAIUS JULIUS CAESAR OCTAVIANUS (AUGUSTUS, 63 B.C.-A.D. 14), first Roman Emperor, sponsor of the *Aeneid*

GAIUS MAECENAS (died 8 B.C.), influential confidant of Augustus, literary patron of Vergil

PLOTIUS TUCCA, friend of Vergil, member of literary circle of Maecenas, coeditor of the *Aeneid*

VARIUS RUFUS, elegiac, epic, and tragic poet of the circle of Maecenas, friend of Vergil and coeditor with Plotius Tucca of the *Aeneid*

Summary of Event

The unfinished *Aeneid,* saved by order of Augustus from the fire to which Vergil wished it consigned at his untimely death in 19 B.C., was edited and published by his friends Plotius Tucca and Varius Rufus. Sponsored by the *princeps* himself to play a role in the national moral and cultural revival of the Augustan era, the poem celebrates Rome's glorious Imperial destiny; yet it is at the same time a probing examination of the tragic human cost which that Imperial idea demanded. Although deliberately modeled on the characters' mythological frame of reference, and the same plot structure as Homer's *Iliad* and *Odyssey,* the poem is original in its exploitation of rhythm and symbol and in its insight into the human condition. While its hero is a Trojan in doubtful quest of a destined home in a strange land, and its moral code is distinctly Stoic and Roman, the poem nevertheless communicates a sense of the spiritual growth of a civilized man, thus transcending Roman nationalism and ancient patterns of thought.

The epic begins with Juno's rousing of a sea tempest which wrecks and scatters the fleet of Aeneas, forcing him from the vicinity of Sicily toward the coast of north Africa near the city of Carthage, a city newly founded by its queen Dido, herself an exile from Phoenician Sidon. Graciously received by Dido in her palace and feasted at a nocturnal banquet, Aeneas narrates the tale of the Greek sack of Troy and his subsequent wanderings in search of a new fatherland dimly envisioned as the home of a people destined to rule the world at some later date. Dido, who doubtless reminded Roman readers of Cleopatra, so tempts Aeneas with her city and herself that for one winter he forgets his mission and succumbs to an amorous adventure with the Queen.

When destiny summons the hero to leave Carthage and renew his quest for a home for the Trojan exiles, the forsaken Queen immolates herself and pronounces a curse that forebodes the long historical death-duel between Rome and Carthage. Aeneas proceeds to Italy where, in the region of Cumae, he enters the underworld, buries his past and is reborn in a vision of the destined future of Rome. Setting sail once more, Aeneas finally reaches Latium at the mouth of the Tiber River, where he is received by the aged King Latinus and eventually betrothed to the King's daughter, Lavinia. However, the Rutulian prince Turnus, once a suitor for Lavinia but rejected by Latinus at the bidding of oracles, rouses the native peoples against the Trojan newcomers. Aeneas visits the site of Rome, where the Arcadian Evander offers troops and his own son Pallas to assist Aeneas. In the furious battles which follow, Pallas is slain by Turnus, and Turnus himself is finally killed by Aeneas in single combat at the somewhat abrupt close of the poem.

The poem depicts the inner struggle of Aeneas to gain *pietas,* the Roman virtue of loving acceptance of duty to family, fatherland, and the will of the gods. Not the natural endowment of man, *pietas* is a goal laboriously achieved. For Aeneas it entails a long course of adversity. First, he suffers the tragic loss of his original home, wife, and country, and he rebels with passionate violence; then he is forced to endure seemingly endless and aimless wanderings in quest of an elusive goal that is only gradually revealed to him in repeated attempts to settle his exiled family in one land after another; next he experiences the death of his father, his last link with the past and for long his sole source of moral direction toward the future. A trying temptation of romantic love and a merely personal happiness is next inflicted upon Aeneas, as well as a vision of the future glory of his race ambiguously clouded by numerous scenes of personal suffering of his unborn descendants. Finally, he sees an agonizing war on Italian soil entailing untold loss of human life and waste of zeal in blind fury that mocks heroic ideals. The Stoic morality of endurance in the face of harsh fortune, of the mastery of mind over the passions, and of trust in the providential purposes of a Supreme Mind guiding the destiny of the world and its real though unseen moral order enter into the *pietas* of Vergil's hero. Yet the hero rarely loses his mere humanity, evil does not cease to be tragically real and ruinous, and the *pietas* of neither Aeneas himself nor of countless other human characters in the poem wins any tangible reward of happiness. Aeneas as a paradigm of ideal humanity is comparable to the Greek Heracles, perhaps even more so to the Suffering Servant of Second Isaiah. Vergil's gods, like his men, are expressions of a world order that is at the core moral and purposive, yet partly at war within itself: Jove is the calm and righteous helmsman of destiny, whose will is wrought in history more through respect for his *auctoritas* than through fear of his thunderbolt; Juno is the raging, elemental fury at work in nature and in history to thwart what is destined, yet bent at last to yield to the masculine authority of Jove; Venus is in part the patroness

557

of her son Aeneas, as Athena is protectress of Odysseus in the *Odyssey,* and almost symbolizes the dimension of vision of divine will in Aeneas, yet at Carthage she is the amoral erotic impulse that sports tragically with the human agents in the drama of destiny.

The impact of the publication of the *Aeneid* in Rome was immediate and powerful. The language and metrical art of Vergil became classic for the hexameter, and even prose was henceforth colored by Vergilian poetic diction. The Imperial ideal and the paradigm of national character stood defined, however rarely they may have been attained thereafter. Defined also for future generations of humanity was an ideal of responsible, civilized manhood open to the promise of a dimly envisioned future and ready to undertake the moral burdens of leadership.

Pertinent Literature

Pöschl, Viktor. *The Art of Vergil: Image and Symbol in the Aeneid.* Ann Arbor: University of Michigan Press, 1962

The past decade has witnessed a veritable renaissance in literary and historical appreciation of the poetry of Vergil as embodying a fundamental unity of development and perspective through the three genres of pastoral idyl, didactic narrative, and epic. A conscious break with an age-old tradition of scholarly focus on the content of the poems has yielded fresh and sensitive studies of Vergilian form. Viktor Pöschl's book, first published in German in 1950, is a rich exposition of the symbolic structure of key scenes of the *Aeneid,* of the formal motifs associated with the three principal characters, Aeneas, Dido, and Turnus, and of the principles of symbolism employed in every portion of Vergilian narrative.

Perhaps the most successful and enlightening portion of Pöschl's book is his analysis of the first sequence of scenes in Book I, lines 8-296, as a symbolic anticipation of themes of the whole epic. This section is framed by two passages revealing the divine context within which the epic narrative and the history to which it points is to be understood. In the first passage Juno's bitter wrath against Troy and its survivors and her cherished yearning for the world-dominion of Carthage lead her to conspire with the storm-king Aeolus to drive the fleet of Aeneas in a furious tempest to the coast of Africa near Carthage. In the second passage, Jove consoles the goddess-mother of Aeneas, Venus, with assurance that it is the destiny of Rome to be founded at last by Aeneas after long wanderings, and ultimately to pacify and govern the world. Juno and Jove are symbols of opposing forces ever active in the cosmos, in nature, and in human history. Juno is demonic violence, passion, furious resistance to the rational purpose motivating the course of all that happens in the world; Jove is serenity, and calm, authoritative, reasoned guidance of thought, word, and deed. Platonic dualism and the Platonic conception of an ultimately monistic world order binding Cosmos and Politeia into a unity find expression here, mediated by the Ciceronian idea of "the unity of world order and true *res Romana.*" This theme finds expression throughout the opening sequence of scenes: in the description of Aeolus in the cave of winds holding the raging powers of nature in check and restraining their destructive potential with a political type of authority; in the description of Neptune calming the storm at sea, an act deliberately characterized as political in a simile comparing Neptune to a statesman calming a seditious mob through the sheer authority of his august presence; and finally, in the historical event foretold by Jove in prophecy, the closing of the gates of war by Augustus and the chaining of *furor impius* within to mark the pacification of the world.

Pöschl's discussion of the character of Aeneas concentrates on similes and symbolic aspects of his gestures and utterances in moments of crisis. Although Aeneas is clearly a hero of duty, Pöschl argues against any simple Stoic interpretation of duty as "a response to the dictates of reason";

rather duty is "a response to love, and is without the harsh associations evoked by the word." It is not Stoic imperturbability that Aeneas strives for, but strength of character "to deny sorrow's influence on action." Particularly revealing is the simile of the stout oak tree on the mountain top, battered by winds, a simile of Aeneas' resolve to be victorious over intense anguish in the crisis with Dido in Book IV. Like the oak, the hero is "lashed on one side and on the other by the ceaseless entreaties, and senses anguish deep within his heart; his resolve stands unshaken, in vain his tears roll down his face." Any interpretation of Aeneas that fails to balance against each other the traits of Stoic heroism and sensitivity to human suffering must be false. Aeneas, says Pöschl, is a symbol of "a mood existing between chaos and salvation." This mood has its roots in the historical era between the Roman civil wars and the Augustan peace, but its relevance and appeal to humanity are timeless.

Otis, Brooks. *Virgil, A Study in Civilized Poetry*. Oxford: The Clarendon Press, 1963.

The recognition that the *Aeneid* is an adaptation of Homeric motifs to Roman themes has been the point of departure for the literary criticism of the epic since antiquity. Only recently, however, has attention been focused upon the essential unity of Vergil's poetic achievement in three different genres and thereby on the positive complex of ideals governing Vergil's use of the Homeric motifs. Brooks Otis' book is a carefully detailed analysis of common symbolic and structural principles in the *Eclogues,* the *Georgics,* and the *Aeneid* and an ef-

fort to characterize what is uniquely Vergilian thought and art in works patently modeled on traditional forms.

In the narrative structure of the Aeneid, says Otis, three elements have been fused: (1) psychologically continuous narrative, (2) the symbol-complex of *fatum, furor,* and *pietas,* and (3) Homeric motifs. The first two of these elements are already evident in the *Eclogues* and the *Georgics*. Individual idyls of the *Eclogues* and the Orpheus episode of Book 4 of the *Georgics* are dramatic narrative portrayals of an inner psychological development. Dominant also in both works is a moral antithesis between *furor,* the expense of energy on unworthy goals of endeavor characterized by violent emotion both in the individual and in society at large, on the one hand, and, on the other, *pietas,* the rational direction of energies in accordance with a clearly envisioned moral order of nature and of history, *fatum,* again both in the individual and in society at large. A process of conversion of man and society from the one condition to the other is embodied in symbols of death and resurrection: Caesar-Octavian in *Eclogue 5* and the bee-society in *Georgics 4.*

In the *Aeneid* these elements are combined and given a more readily comprehensible form in the narration of the destiny of a man who undergoes an experience of death and resurrection, of transformation into a semidivine character. The process of death and resurrection is indeed symbolic, but it is portrayed with psychological realism in the continuous narrative of a man's struggle to liberate himself from a tragic past, to resist the temptation of commitment to goals that are unworthy and inconsistent with the moral order of destiny and his role in it, and to prevail over forces of nature and society that are but external representatives of the same *furor* against which his internal struggle is directed. The death and resurrection of Aeneas, begun in the descent to the underworld in Book VI, is completed at the end of Book VIII, when Aeneas lifts upon his shoulders "the burden and the grandeur of his family-to-be."

This theme governs the structure of the *Aeneid* and the use by Vergil of the Homeric motifs. The first six books, culminating in the descent to the underworld, comprise the "Odyssean *Aeneid.*" Here is depicted the inner struggle of Aeneas for *pietas* in a series of adventures rich in subjective, internal, and psychological dimensions. Yet the Homeric motif of homecoming is inverted: Aeneas journeys ever further away from home and comfort. The Homeric Calypso entangelement is not simply an erotic adventure, but a test of the capacity of the hero to master his passions and submit to a greater love revealed by conscience and divine will. The last six books are the "Iliadic *Aeneid*" depicting the triumph of mature *pietas* over the social *furor* of what is really a civil war in Italy conducted by misguided persons who fail to see their common destiny with the Trojan exiles. Here there are many scenes of Homeric heroism, but they serve to emphasize the antithesis in Aeneas of a non-Homeric and non-Greek civilized attitude toward war. War is no source of satisfaction, no proving ground of heroic *arete*; it is an ugly, tragic necessity, the price of pacification. The proud aggressors must be humbled, the conquered treated with compassion so that ultimately the "habit of peace" may be imposed upon Italy and the world. This goal is ultimately the sole justification for Rome's military *imperium.* — *C.W.C.*

Additional Recommended Reading

Commager, Steele, ed., *Virgil, A Collection of Critical Essays.* Englewood Cliffs, New Jersey: Prentice-Hall, Inc., 1966. Essays on Vergil, mostly concerned with the *Aeneid,* by several noted contemporary scholars.

Knight, W. F. Jackson. *Roman Vergil.* 2nd ed. London: Faber & Faber, 1944. A study of Vergil's work as a whole, with emphasis on language and style.

Prescott, H. W. *The Development of Virgil's Art.* Chicago: University of Chicago Press, 1927. A concentrated analysis of Vergil's adaptation of Homeric and Hellenistic epic motifs in the *Aeneid.*

Putnam, M. C. J. *The Poetry of the Aeneid.* Cambridge: Harvard University Press, 1965. Detailed studies of four books of the *Aeneid.*

COMPLETION OF THE AUGUSTAN SETTLEMENT

Type of event: Constitutional: political reform
Time: 27-23 B.C.
Locale: Rome

Principal personage:
GAIUS OCTAVIUS (63 B.C.-A.D. 14), known as Gaius Julius Caesar Octavianus after his recognition as Caesar's adopted son in 43 B.C., and as Augustus after this title was conferred upon him by the senate in 27 B.C.

Summary of Event

The last century of the Roman Republic was marked by almost continuous turmoil. There were foreign and civil wars: in Gaul with the Cimbri and Teutones, in the East with Mithridates, in North Africa with Jugurtha, in Italy with the Italian allies, and in Rome itself between the followers of Marius and Sulla. There was a constant struggle for political power between the *optimates,* who were satisfied with the *status quo* and wished to retain the privileges of the Roman nobility, and the *populares,* who favored the lower classes and were pressing for social and economic reforms that would lead to a better distribution of public lands, the founding of new colonies, and the betterment of the urban poor. Bribery at elections, struggles for control of the courts by the *senatores,* the senatorial party, and by the *equites,* the Roman knights or businessmen, the armed clashes of such politicians as Clodius and Milo as well as a corrupt system of provincial administration, all pointed up the inability of the old Republican constitution to cope with the problems of the times. There was an obvious need for reform. The senate, however, had enjoyed its privileges for so long that it would not voluntarily relinquish them; true representative government was something that had as yet not been tried; and monarchy was so repugnant to the Republican mentality that it offered little promise. Although Julius Caesar rejected the title of *rex,* or "king," he was assassinated for his assumption of extraordinary power and acceptance of minor symbols of royalty. Even the staunch republican Cicero saw that a strong man was needed to guide the affairs of state who would be willing, nonetheless, to be subjected to traditional constitutional restraints.

Caesar's heir, Gaius Julius Caesar Octavianus, seems to have made an admirable compromise to achieve a balance of power. He outwardly maintained that he had "restored liberty to the Republic" and that in 28 and 27 B.C., after the civil war, he transferred the absolute power over the Republic which had been conferred on him by universal consent, from his own control to the will of the senate and the Roman people.

His settlement was the piecemeal result of protracted developments stemming out of his adoption by Julius Caesar. After defeating Antony and Cleopatra at Actium in 31, occupying Egypt in 30 and celebrating a triple triumph in 29 at Rome, he was free as the *princeps senatus,* or "first man in the Senate," to effect his settlement. On January 13, 27, he went before this body and renounced all extraordinary powers given him during the period of the triumvirate. Though he ostensibly "restored the Republic," he retained his consulship and control over Spain, Gaul, and Syria for ten years, together with his dominion over Egypt as a kind of private possession. As a reward for his generosity, the senate conferred upon him a number of singular honors, the most important of which was the title "Augustus," which surrounded him with an aura of sanctity and placed him in intimate connection with Romulus, the founder of the city. The name of the month Sextilis was changed to Augustus in his honor. By general consent he was given the title of *princeps,* a Republican honor conferred on those citizens who enjoyed a certain primacy in the state because of their reputation, power, and influence and which allowed him to speak first in the senate.

On July 1, 23, Augustus made another, and what may be considered final, settlement with the senate. He resigned his consulship and received in return a proconsular *imperium* that surpassed that of any provincial governor. This act enabled him to intervene and correct abuses in provinces where he allowed the senate to govern as well as in those generally younger and less peaceful ones which he ruled through his own legates. He also received the *tribunicia potestas* for life, which gave him the all-important right to initiate or veto measures in the senate, and made him a protector and champion of the ordinary people. It seems somewhat ironic that the tribunate, once a weak, negative plebeian office, should eventually be the chief source of imperial power. After the death of Lepidus he was elected *pontifex maximus* in 12 B.C., thus reuniting in his person the supreme authority in both sacral and secular affairs that had been the prerogative of the early kings. In 2 B.C. he was hailed as *pater patriae,* "Father of his Country."

Cautious and conservative by nature, Augustus was careful to retain during his rule a Republican façade. As he himself declared in his *Res Gestae,* he took precedence over the other magistrates not because of personal power but because of conferred authority. This view perhaps best explains the Augustan settlement. Each of the offices and priesthoods held by Augustus was Republican in character and duly conferred by the senate and the people, but their agglomeration in a single individual, the *princeps,* endowed him with such prestige and authority that the result was the creation of a new system of rule and, consequently, of a new constitution. Such was to be, more or less, the settlement under which the famous emperors of Rome operated until the time of Domitian.

Pertinent Literature

Hammond, Mason. *The Augustan Principate in Theory and Practice During the Julio-Claudian Period.* Cambridge: Harvard University Press, 1933.

Mason Hammond introduces his thoughtful, well-documented study of the Augustan principate by indicating the challenge which Augustus's character presents to historians: "Like Janus at the parting of the ways, he is two-faced in more than one sense." As a youth he sacrified Cicero to his own advancement, yet later as a venerable old man he lived to receive the titles of "Father of his Country" and "Savior," together with the esteem and affection of the civilized world. The gossip recorded by Suetonius with respect to his personal life, whether true or false, is not at all in keeping with his established reputation as a devoted husband, stern parent, and censorial prince. Because of these personal ambiguities, it is not easy to determine how sincerely Augustus wished to restore the Republic, or, how cleverly he manipulated events to become the "Autocrat of the Empire," or, whether he assumed "the monarchical mantle of his uncle, the Deified Julius, or wished merely to be the servant extraordinary of the Senate and the Roman People."

The interpretation of Augustus's role in the founding of the Empire is further complicated, as Hammond notes, by the fact that the Romans had no fixed or written constitution. Like Great Britain, Rome was ruled in accordance with precedent and separate legislative enactments. Because its growth and development were not restricted by prescribed formulas, it resembled a living organism, subject to continual change. Despite Augustus's claims to the contrary, his constitution was not identical with that of the Republic of Cicero. And his system of rule was in turn modified by his successors. For a number of reasons it is not always easy to determine Augustus's intentions and achievements within this changing political structure. One reason is the character of our sources; for example, the author considers that Tacitus was biased in his portrayal of Augustus as a diplomatic hypocrite. Another reason is the wide variety of interpretations which have been made of the Augustan reform. Hammond takes particular exception to the interpretation proposed by Theodor Mommsen, that under Augustus the Roman state was a dyarchy with two heads of government: the emperor, who derived his authority from the army and represented the subjects as a whole, and the senate, which stood for the Roman state, the old legal fiction of *Senatus Populusque Romanus* (SPQR) under which Rome had prospered.

In opposition to this interpretation, Hammond maintains that the Romans with their strong insistence upon a unity of authority would never have subscribed to such an abstract and unstable form of government. He therefore argues against Mommsen's position, insisting that in the Augustan Principate "there was a single final authority" and that it was not vested in the Emperor but in the *Senatus Populusque Romanus;* in short, Augustus "was sincere in his claim that he had restored the Republic."

To support this contention, Hammond discusses twenty-three different aspects of the principate in as many chapters. From his inquiry into such topics as the proconsular *imperium,* the *tribunicia potestas,* the Augustan titulary, and the *consilium,* he concludes that Augustus "conceived himself to be the agent of the Senate, the permanent representative of the state." Rejecting the absolutism of his adoptive father, Julius Caesar, Augustus returned to the ideals of Cicero and Pompey. If he was eventually driven towards autocracy, it was not through personal ambition but because of the failure of the Republican institutions. The senate and the people were to blame if "the restored Republic with its extraordinary prince" turned into the military autocracy described by Dio in the speech of Maecenas, because they were either unable or unwilling to cope with the problems of empire. Whatever the verdict on the sincerity of Augustus, he represents to history the apogee of Roman emperorship.

Syme, Ronald. *The Roman Revolution.* New York: Oxford University Press, 1939.

Though objections can be raised against Ronald Syme's main thesis and its ramifications, there can be no doubt that his book, which describes Augustus's rise to power, is one of the most significant contributions to Roman history of this century. He starts with the assumption that the Roman constitution as generally understood "was a screen and a sham." Throughout the centuries Rome was not ruled by individuals or by the will of the people so much as by a party, a syndicate, a political minority, or a dominant class. During any age of the Republic a monopoly of power was held by twenty or thirty men from a dozen dominant families. According to Syme, the central epoch of Roman history, that is, the transformation of state and society between 60 B.C. and A.D. 14, is no exception to this general rule. He therefore directs his inquiries toward discovering how Augustus, a revolutionary leader, "arose in civil strife, usurped power for himself and his faction," and established "a stable and enduring government."

Though he acknowledges the material benefits that were conferred by the revolution, Syme is not inclined to praise the political success of its instigators. The career of Pompey "opened in fraud and violence"; Caesar was assassinated for attempting to escape from "the shackles of party to supreme and personal rule." Antony, however, "was distinctly superior to what Rome had learned to expect of the politician in power." Syme is deliberately critical of Augustus and feels that his subject compels him to adopt "a pessimistic and truculent tone." As Caesar's heir Augustus sought to seize "the power and the glory along with the name of Caesar"; from the beginning he showed that "his sense for realities was unerring, his ambition implacable."

Though the rhetoric of the ancients and the constitutional theories of modern scholars have obscured the true nature and real sources of political power at Rome, they were apparent to Octavianus and his contemporaries. In making use of "extra-consti-

tutional resources, bribery, intrigue, and even violence," Octavianus proved himself to be no different from earlier Roman dynasts. His supremacy was eventually established through extraordinary concessions on the part of the senate, particularly through his reception of the *imperium proconsulare* and the *tribunicia potestas,* but even more effectively through the weight of his accumulated *auctoritas,* and through the respect which he had earned for his person. He had been the object of a personal oath of allegiance in 32 B.C.; he was the son of the divinized Caesar, the *Divi filius;* the Roman plebeians were his inherited *clientela;* he was in control of the armies in fact if not in law; he was by far the wealthiest person in the Empire; and, "above all, he stood at the head of a large and well organized political party as the source and fount of patronage and advancement." Contrary to what has been frequently maintained, Augustus did not intend that the Republican constitution should continue to function. Rather, he ruled after the manner of the earlier dynasts, but with greater effectiveness. Augustus merely successfully converted "a party into a government." Sacrificing anything for power he reached the height of his ambition, an ambition through which he "saved and regenerated the Roman People."
— *M.J.C.*

Additional Recommended Reading

Holmes, T. R. *The Architect of the Roman Empire.* Oxford: The University Press, 1931. 2 vols. A standard classic on the subject, favorable to Augustus.

Buchan, John. *Augustus.* Boston: Houghton Mufflin Company, 1937. In this study, Augustan settlement is seen as "a practical solution" not to be regarded too strictly in the light of constitutional theory.

Grant, Michael. *From* Imperium *to* Auctoritas: *A Historical Study of* Aes *Coinage in the Roman Empire 49 B.C.-A.D. 14.* Cambridge: The University Press, 1946. This work purports to reconstruct the political dispensation from a study of the *aes* coinage of the Augustan age.

Greenidge, A. H. J. *Roman Public Life.* London: Macmillan & Company, 1901. An old but clear and useful work by an authority on Roman law and constitutional theory.

Jones, A H. M. *Studies in Roman Government and Law.* New York: Barnes and Noble, Inc., 1960, reprinted 1968. Professor Jones considers the Republic in three phases, the last of which was its restoration "in a less obtrusive form."

Jones, Henry Stuart. "The *Princeps,*" in *The Cambridge Ancient History.* Vol 10, pp. 127-158. New York: The Macmillan Company, 1934. An interpretation suggesting that Augustus's statements with respect to his restoration of the Republic should not be taken at their face value.

Rowell, Henry Thompson. *Rome in the Augustan Age.* Norman: University of Oklahoma Press, 1962. A clear and interesting account of the "new order."

BIRTH OF JESUS

Type of event: Religious: appearance of the leader of a new faith
Time: c.4 B.C.
Locale: Bethlehem, Judea

Principal personages:
JESUS THE CHRIST (c.4 B.C.-A.D. 29), the religious leader
   crucified under Pontius Pilate
MARY, mother of Jesus

Summary of Event

The birth of Jesus is unique among all events of which we have historical evidence. In the case of other eminent historical personages birth is important with the significance of beginnings, as marking the starting point of a great career. By hindsight, the historian notes a birth to satisfy his sense of order, and to provide him with clues to the future growth and development of his subject, clues derived from the subject's background and the conditions surrounding his birth. The birth of Jesus is significant in its own right, and has been seen this way from the early days of the Christian community, where the story was included in the traditional oral accounts recorded by Luke and Matthew. From the beginning, the birth of Jesus was perceived as the entrance into the human situation of someone who, while true man, was uniquely other and more than man. To express this perception, the tradition was handed down colored by mythopoeic elements which suggested its deeper meanings.

Jesus was born in Bethlehem, in the southern part of Palestine near Jerusalem. Mary and Joseph came from Nazareth in Galilee, a northern province of Palestine. Christian influence on the development of the calendar has made the birth of Jesus the dividing line in occidental history, giving us our expression B.C., before Christ, and A.D., from the Latin *anno Domini,* "in the year of the Lord." The history of Jesus cannot be found in Jewish or Roman documents and annals; nevertheless, non-Christian written sources help to corroborate the Gospel accounts that the birth occurred before the death of Herod the Great in 4 B.C. Since there is also strong evidence that Jesus died in full manhood during the reign of Augustus' immediate successor Tiberius, who died in A.D. 38, his birth must have occurred early in Augustus' reign. The weight of scholarly opinion favors a year between 8 and 4 B.C. as the time of Jesus' birth.

Little is known about Mary and Joseph. Luke gives a picture of his mother, Mary, a young woman engaged to a local carpenter, Joseph. Luke gives an account of the miraculous conception announced by an angel, Mary's puzzlement at the news, and her act of trusting faith and willing coöperation with God's act. Matthew records Jesus' parentage from the standpoint of Joseph. The simplicity of the two accounts reveals the conviction of the early Christians who held a solid tradition of a single historical person who was really born; that is, Jesus is not a myth. At the same time, the Gospel accounts make clear a tradition of a community holding fast to an experience of a transcendent reality which cannot be carried adequately by human language. The best way to catch these levels of meaning is to consider the Gospel accounts themselves:

"In the sixth month the angel Gabriel was sent from God to a city of Galilee named Nazareth, to a virgin betrothed to a man whose name was Joseph, of the house of David; and the virgin's name was Mary. And he came to her and said, 'Hail, O favored one, the Lord is with you!' But she was greatly troubled at the saying, and considered in her mind what sort of greeting this might be. And the angel said to her, 'Do not be afraid, Mary, for you have found favor with God. And behold, you will conceive in your womb and bear a son, and you shall call his name Jesus. He will be great and will be called the Son of the Most High; and the Lord God will give to him the throne of his father David, and he will reign over the house of Jacob for ever; and of his kingdom there will be no end.' And Mary said to the angel, 'How can this be, since I have no husband?' And the angel said to her, 'The Holy Spirit will come upon you, and the power of the Most High will overshadow you; therefore the child to be born will be called holy, the Son of God. And behold your kinswoman Elizabeth in her old age has also conceived a son; and this is the sixth month with her who was called barren. For with God nothing will be impossible.' And Mary said, 'Behold, I am the handmaid of the Lord; let it be to me according to your word.' And the angel departed from her.

In those days Mary arose and went with haste into the hill country, to a city of Judah, and she entered the house of Zechariah and greeted Elizabeth. And when Elizabeth heard the greeting of Mary, the babe leaped in her womb; and Elizabeth was filled with the Holy Spirit and she exclaimed with a loud cry, 'Blessed are you among women, and blessed is the fruit of your womb! And why is this granted me, that the mother of my Lord should come to me? For behold when the voice of your greeting came to my ears, the babe in my womb leaped for joy. And blessed is she who believed that there would be a fulfillment of what was spoken to her from the Lord."

(Luke 1:26-45)

"Now the birth of Jesus Christ took place in this way. When his mother Mary had been betrothed to Joseph, before they came together she was found to be with child of the Holy Spirit; and her husband Joseph, being a just man and unwilling to put her to shame, resolved to divorce her quietly. But as he considered this, behold, an angel of the Lord appeared to him in a dream, saying, 'Joseph, son of David, do not fear to take Mary your wife, for that which is conceived in her is of the Holy Spirit; she will bear a son, and you shall call his name Jesus, for he will save his people from their sins.' All this took place to fulfil what the Lord had spoken by the prophet: 'Behold, a virgin shall conceive and bear a son, and his name shall be called Emmanuel' (which means, God with us). When Joseph woke from sleep, he did as the angel of the Lord commanded him; he took his wife, but knew her not until she had borne a son; and he called his name Jesus."

(Matthew 1:18-25)

The circumstances surrounding the birth of Jesus in Bethlehem as recorded by Matthew and Luke also bear witness to the early Christian community's understanding of the meaning of the event. Jesus was a man for others whose destiny was bound up with that of every man without respect to social condition. In Luke's account there is the manifestation of the child to the poor shepherds, while in Matthew there is the account of the visit of the wise men from the East, in which Scripture scholars see a midrashic element, that is, a story used to carry a religious or moral truth. Other details such as the fact that there was no room at the inn and that Mary for this reason cradled the child in a manger, carry a hint of mystery which lies too deep for words but which has fascinated the imagination and captured the hearts of men as no other event of history, except those other great events surrounding Jesus, his death and Resurrection. The evangelists alone convey at once the simplicity and the mysterious depths of the birth of Jesus

Pertinent Literature

McKenzie, John L. "The Gospel According to Matthew," and Stuhlmueller, Carroll, C. P. "The Gospel according to Luke," in *The Jerome Biblical Commentary.* Chs. 43 & 44. Edited by Raymond E. Brown, S. S., Joseph A. Fitzmeyer, S. J., and Roland E. Murphy, O.Carm. Englewood Cliffs, New Jersey: Prentice-Hall, Inc., 1968.

In this major work of Biblical criticism, John McKenzie's article on Matthew begins with a treatment of the literary character of the Gospel, its theology, and the relationship of Matthew to Mark, Luke, and John. Authorship and date and place of composition are given adequate coverage. In discussing the Matthean account of the birth of Jesus, McKenzie notes the differences between it and Luke. Matthew presents the birth of Jesus as the fulfillment of Old Testament prophecy as given in Isaiah 7:14, "Behold, a young woman shall conceive and bear a son, and shall call his name Immanuel." The theme of fulfillment is a predominant one in Matthew, whose gospel contains the formula eleven times, which is more often than the other three gospels combined. This concept of fulfillment is difficult for the modern mind to comprehend, says McKenzie. In Matthew's view, the Gospel or Good News of the New Testament gives the Old Testament a new dimension of reality. "The birth [of Jesus] initiates the Messianic age of salvation to which the whole Old Testament looks forward." Another

569

theme of Matthew is that the Jews remained for the most part indifferent to Jesus as King and Messiah. This theme is developed in the account of the worship of the Magi. The Magi, who were Gentiles, were the first to recognize Jesus in Matthew's account. Jesus is Messiah, but not the kind of King Messiah expected by the people. Matthew shows him rather as a suffering servant, a lowly Messiah who saves men by his passion and death. The theological depths of the Gospel according to Matthew, as also the riches of McKenzie's treatment, cannot be appreciated by isolating the narrative of Jesus' birth, but only by studying his entire life.

Stuhmueller's article on Luke also includes material on authorship, sources, literary style, and characteristics. For Stuhlmueller, there are three infancy gospels, including that of the Gospel according to John. John's account may be seen as an early Christian hymn, which proclaims Jesus' preëxistence as well as his becoming flesh. Matthew's account is an official statement used to hand on tradition, while Luke's narrative is a combination of three styles: hymnic, doctrinal, and meditative. Stuhl-

mueller accepts the view that the infancy narratives were not an original part of the apostolic preaching. Rather, they developed to answer a need for an ever fuller understanding of Jesus' work.

The article has an exceptionally lucid exposition of evidence pointing to the author's "tentative conclusion . . . that Luke's Infancy Narrative originated at Jerusalem within the early, post-Pentecostal days of Jewish Christianity," though he goes on to discuss arguments pointing to a second and later stage in the development of the narrative. After he has given full attention to the stylistic details, pointing out the close parallels between Luke's account and Old Testament passages which can be seen as models, he nevertheless holds that there is some historical material in the Lucan Gospel. There are also historical problems. For example, Luke's reference to Quirinius as governor of Syria at the time of Jesus' birth poses a puzzle which has yet to be solved.

The Jerome Biblical Commentary has other material pertinent to the story of the birth of Jesus in chapters on Biblical geography, archaeology, and the history of Israel.

Bruckberger, R. L. *The History of Jesus Christ.* Translated by Denver Lindley. New York: The Viking Press, 1965.

This book is not a history of Jesus, which is impossible according to modern Scripture scholarship, but a good example of a literary work in sharp contrast to the exegetical and theological commentary found in *The Jerome Biblical Commentary*.

Bruckberger's book is the result of many years of thoughtful reflection on the Gospel of Jesus, written from

the standpoint of one who accepts in faith that Jesus is the Son of God. The great value of the book derives largely from its view of Jesus as a person within the historical process, and at the same time transcending it. For Bruckberger, Jesus is highly relevant because still active in history where he works as a dynamic factor in the shaping of men's lives. How that influence works in Bruckberger's own life is subtly shown in many pages of the book. The author was a leader of the French Resistance during World War II, and this experience forms a lens through which he views the Gospel message.

The birth of Jesus is considered in a chapter entitled "Noel," in which the author writes with clarity of the power of poetic language to express realities which cannot be contained within the limits of prosaic forms. He shows the relationship of the historical event of Jesus' birth to the richly symbolic handling of it in the Christian liturgy, which sings of the mystery in words from the Apocrypha: "For when peaceful stillness compassed everything and the night in its swift course was half spent, your all-powerful Word from heaven's throne bounded." (Wisdom 18:14-15). Bruckberger notes that the context of this passage is a description of the night of the Exodus, when Yahweh led the Israelites from Egyptian captivity to freedom as his chosen people. He then shows the parallel to the Church's understanding of the coming of Jesus as the beginning of man's deliverance from the bondage of sin, not omitting the Scriptural images of war and liberation. In no way does the author suggest that this level of interpretation negates the historical "fact"; rather, it enlarges its significance. Writing of the contrast between Scripture as poetry and as law, he observes: "I firmly believe that the Holy Scriptures considered as a poem are more profoundly true and, in a very real sense, more binding, than when they are considered solely as law . . . They give us knowledge even of the universe that no science will ever be able to give. It is when the clouds conceal from the enemy the camp of Israel . . . when the whole of nature protects the friends of God and obeys them, that the Scriptures are most profoundly true. It is the miraculous that is the rule since it is the rule of God."

Not everyone will share Bruckberger's view of Jesus, nor of the Scriptures which are the written historical source for our knowledge of him. Nevertheless, the book is an apt witness to the power of the Gospel to engage men in thoughtful meditation on the fathomless depths of the meaning of man, and even of God. — *M.E.J.*

Additional Recommended Reading

Bornkamm, Gunther. *Jesus of Nazareth.* New York: Harper and Row Publishers Incorporated, 1960. A leading German New Testament scholar's effort to arrive at a historically sound picture of the sort of person Jesus was.

Filson, Floyd V. *A New Testament History: The Story of the Emerging Church.* Philadelphia: The Westminster Press, 1964. A useful account of the historical background and religious setting of the life of Jesus.

Goodspeed, Edgar J. *An Introduction to the New Testament.* Chicago: University of Chicago Press, 1937. Although in many respects outdated, the comparison of the accounts of Luke and Matthew remains valuable.

Jones, Alexander. *The Gospel According to St. Matthew.* Pt. I. New York: Sheed and Ward, 1965. A work valuable for its discussion of modern methods of interpretation of Scripture.

Metzger, Bruce Manning. *The New Testament: Its Background, Growth, and Content*. New York: Abingdon Press, 1965. The layman will find here basic information concerning the content of the New Testament and important aspects of its historical background.